THE
OBIE
WINNERS

THE OBIE WINNERS

The Best of Off-Broadway

Edited and with an Introduction by
ROSS WETZSTEON

DOUBLEDAY & COMPANY, INC.
Garden City, New York

Library of Congress Cataloging in Publication Data
Main entry under title:

The Obie winners.

CONTENTS: Wetzsteon, R. Off-Broadway, a new voice in the American theatre.—Gelber, J. The connection.—Beckett, S. Krapp's last tape. [etc.]
1. American drama—20th century. 2. Off-Broadway theater. 3. Drama—20th century. I. Wetzsteon, Ross.
PS634.02   812'.5408
ISBN: 0-385-17005-x
Library of Congress Catalog Card Number 79-6096

Copyright © 1980 by Nelson Doubleday, Inc.
All Rights Reserved
Printed in the United States of America
Design by Jeanette Portelli

CONTENTS

OFF-BROADWAY

A NEW VOICE IN THE AMERICAN THEATRE

Ross Wetzsteon

Off-Broadway began—as its name implies—in opposition: in opposition to the way Broadway had become a part of the entertainment industry, in opposition to its slick comedies and lavish musicals designed only to please the largest possible audience, in opposition to its attitude that theatre was merely a commodity. In its place, young playwrights, performers, and directors in New York's Greenwich Village sought to create a theatre where success was measured not at the box office but on the stage, a theatre where they could experience the risks and rewards of art. But although Off-Broadway began in opposition, it soon asserted a positive vision of its own. And although it began in New York City, it transformed American theatre as a whole—so that today we no longer have just two theatres, uptown commerce and downtown artistry, but many theatres, many Off-Broadways, from Los Angeles to Louisville, from Minneapolis to New Haven, from Chicago to Washington, and even on Broadway itself.

Off-Broadway's roots go back over fifty years. Such New York City groups as the Washington Square Players, the Provincetown Players, and the Neighborhood Playhouse all flourished in the 1920s; Eva Le Gallienne's Civic Repertory Theatre and the Experimental Theatre prospered in the 1930s and 1940s; but it wasn't until the 1950s that a full-scale movement emerged to challenge the commercial colossus of Broadway.

To fix the precise date of birth of Off-Broadway is as impossible as determining the genesis of an idea. Was it the Circle-in-the-Square theatre's production of Tennessee Williams' *Summer and Smoke* in 1952, or its staging of Eugene O'Neill's *The Iceman Cometh* in 1956? Julie Bovasso's 1955 production of Jean Genet's *The Maids*, or Joseph Papp's 1957 staging of Shakespeare on the back of a truck? The promulgation of Actors Equity regulations for non-Broadway productions in 1950, or the establishment of the Obie Awards for creative achievement in the Off-Broadway theatre in 1956?

During this early stage in Off-Broadway's history, most productions were revivals of unappreciated American masterpieces (both *Summer and Smoke* and *The Iceman Cometh* had failed on Broadway) and neglected European classics (for example, Ibsen and Chekhov were rarely staged outside university communities). At the time, there was little interest in producing new plays or experimenting with the nature of the medium—challenging the dominance of psychological realism in scripts, developing new performance styles, or exploring the relationship between actor and audience, all of which were to become important in the 1960s. There was simply an insistence that theatre was an art form, not a money machine. But after the astonishing success of these initial revivals proved that there was a sizable audience interested in serious theatre, more and more new plays began to join the Off-Broadway repertory.

Jack Gelber's *The Connection* (1959) and Edward Albee's *The Zoo Story* (1960) marked the emergence of Off-Broadway's second stage. Now that theatrical classics had been successfully restaged, young avant-garde playwrights felt liberated to take a further step— to test the conventions of theatre itself, to attempt to alter its vision. In the Living Theatre production of Gelber's script, the "fourth wall" separating the stage from the audience came crashing down and spectators were jolted out of the safety of their seats into the desperate ennui of the drug addicts on stage. In Albee's widely influential one-act drama about an innocent park bench encounter that leads inexorably to murder, the conventions of the "well-made" play and realistic dialogue gave way to the elliptical events and "absurd" logic of nightmares.

Off-Broadway, after only a few short but dynamic years, had split into two groups—the traditionalists and the avant-garde. Although in later years this split caused Off-Broadway to question its role (was its primary purpose to conserve or to innovate?), in the early 1960s these two kinds of theatre were mutually supportive—the traditionalists were nourished by new ideas and the avant-garde had a past to build upon. A theatre-goer in New York, for instance, could see a performance of Shakespeare in Central Park one evening, and the next night attend the Theatre of the Absurd downtown. The same performers and directors who staged O'Neill one week would produce the work of an unknown writer the next. Off-Broadway was less a place than a state-of-mind—a commitment to the idea that whatever else theatre might be, it was not a packaged product.

While adherents of Off-Broadway always believed that artistic success would bring an audience, they did not foresee that audience success would bring money—and with it many of the problems and temptations they had hoped to escape. In the early 1960s, it seemed that many of the same people who had denounced the commercialism of Broadway were adopting its hit-flop mentality themselves. It was after only a decade that Off-Broadway entered its third stage —Off-Off-Broadway, or the revolution against the revolutionaries.

Off-Off-Broadway made an even stronger break with convention than the Off-Broadway movement had done. Its productions were staged in church basements, coffeehouses, and converted lofts in Greenwich Village—most notably the Judson Poets' Theatre, the Caffe Cino, and Ellen Stewart's Cafe La Mama. In its combative anarchy and outrageous iconoclasm, in its rebellion against traditional definitions of "talent," and in its aggressive intimacy with its audience, Off-Off-Broadway made even Off-Broadway seem conventional.

Off-Off-Broadway rejected not only the theatrical formulas of Broadway but its trite story lines and irrelevant concerns as well. Boy-meets-girl was transformed into boy-meets-revolution, and subject matter too controversial for the play-it-safe money-makers became its very staple. In White America (1963) was only the first of many dramas documenting the anguish of American blacks; Viet Rock (1966) and MacBird! (1967) were only the beginning of a savage indictment of America's war machine; and Che! (1969) initiated the assault of nudity and onstage sex against Victorian repression. The farthest fringes of Off-Off-Broadway came to regard Off-Broadway itself as nothing but a cultural museum—serious in intent, but lacking the immediacy and urgency the 1960s demanded.

In the early 1960s, Off-Off-Broadway was exclusively devoted to the work of new, experimental playwrights (some theatres produced as many as fifty new scripts a year, which differed greatly in quality). But by the middle of the decade, another split began to appear, this time between text and nontext theatre. Inspired by the communal consciousness of the times, and by the distrust of language (words were regarded as the medium by which we lie to one another), new groups banded together to produce largely nonverbal theatre pieces "improvised" not by a playwright but by the ensemble itself, based on the personalities and experiences of its members. New performance styles evolved, which stressed emotional authenticity rather than professional training ("professionalism" was now a pejorative). In addition, a new relationship with the audience was established, stressing participation rather than detachment (a word that suggested complicity with evil).

Much of the work of this period seems in retrospect like cultural barbarism—self-indulgence in the name of honesty, titillation in the guise of shock—and ironically the "tyranny of the text" was frequently replaced by the tyranny of the director. But the work of such ensembles as Julian Beck and Judith Malina's Living Theatre and Joseph Chaikin's Open Theatre revealed that if—as was usually forgotten—experimentalism meant failure 99 times out of 100, the 100th time could be a success that would alter our very perception of theatre. The legacy of these groups—in particular, the relationship of movement to feeling, the emphasis on personal commitment, and the involvement of the audience—should not be underestimated merely because it cannot be easily articulated. (Unfortunately, it is impossible to anthologize such works as the Living Theatre's *Frankenstein* or the Open Theatre's *Mutation Show.* While these plays did have rudimentary texts, the words were so closely connected to the personal lives of the ensembles that created them that it was virtually impossible for any other company to do them justice.)

Throughout the middle and late 1960s, Off-Broadway found itself being pulled between Broadway (which had begun to hire away Off-Broadway "stars") and Off-Off-Broadway (which had rejected its increasing conformity). Having lost many of its most creative talents to either the Great White Way or the counterculture, Off-Broadway now seemed to have only two functions: to produce essentially Broadway shows on smaller budgets (slick comedies like *The Boys in the Band* became Off-Broadway boffo), or to serve as a cheap in-town replacement for the expensive out-of-town tryout (when meretricious musicals like *Oh! Calcutta!* began to attract audiences, they quickly moved to the larger theatres uptown).

The turning point occurred in 1967, when *Hair*, a modest hippie musical in Joseph Papp's Public Theatre on the Lower East Side of New York, was transformed into a Broadway smash hit—proving that even insurgency could be profitable. By the 1970s, Broadway producers who used to jet to London to scout new "properties" would simply take a cab to an Off-Broadway theatre. In fact, such box-office bonanzas as *A Chorus Line* and *Ain't Misbehavin'*, to give the two most prominent examples, were originally Off-Broadway projects. It seemed that Off-Broadway had become the spawning ground of Broadway, not its enemy.

Off-Broadway was now forced to question its identity. Could it recapture its status as a truly alternative theatre, or was it merely a place for apprenticeship? Was it a place where one could make one's career, or did the concept of a career mean that one eventually moved up to the big time? For every playwright or director who went off to bigger, more commercial ventures, another continued to believe that stimulating theatre could only survive and flourish in the noncommercial, nonpressured atmosphere of Off-Broadway. For every performer who felt that Off-Broadway was merely a training school from which one "graduated" to Broadway, Hollywood, or television, another continued to believe it was the only place where innovative theatre could be created.

Off-Broadway has finally learned that it can serve both functions without compromising its integrity. No one who saw the Off-Broadway performances of George C. Scott in Shakespeare's *Richard III* in Central Park, or Dustin Hoffman in *The Journey of the Fifth Horse*, or Al Pacino in *The Indian Wants the Bronx*, can make glib distinctions between stardom and artistry. And no one who has seen the work of Richard Foreman's Ontological-Hysteric Theatre or Lee Breuer's Mabou Mines can deny that Off-Broadway also remains a place whose goal is artistic achievement rather than career advancement. Even those who have "graduated" from Off-Broadway—Scott, Hoffman, and Pacino, as well as such gifted artists as Edward Albee, Jason Robards, Jr., Barbara Harris, James Earl Jones, José Quintero, Ron Leibman, Judd Hirsch, Richard Dreyfuss, Meryl Streep, Martin Sheen, Christopher Walken, and Alan Arkin, to name only a few— have two things in common: first, they have taken with them the revitalizing influence of Off-Broadway; and second, no matter where they are working now, they feel, as Colleen Dewhurst once said, that whenever they return to Off-Broadway they are returning home.

An important part of the feeling of going home is attending the annual Obie ceremonies, a kind of funky family reunion where Off-Broadway actors, playwrights, and directors have gathered every May since 1956 to honor their own. The Obie Awards—the inspiration of Jerry Tallmer, at the time the theatre critic for New York City's *Village Voice* newspaper—honor creative achievement in the Off-Broadway theatre. (The awards were expanded to include excellence in Off-Off-Broadway theatre in 1964.) The Obie judges consist of members of *The Village Voice* theatre staff, plus two guest critics selected by *The Voice*, usually from the New York daily newspapers or national weekly magazines. The voting is as informal as Off-Broadway itself—the judges meet monthly throughout the year, gradually compiling a "master list" of from seventy to one hundred names, which is painstakingly winnowed down to approximately twenty to twenty-five winners at a final meeting in early May. There are no formal nominations—any of the several hundred plays that have opened during the twelve months preceding the ceremony are eligible. In fact, over the years many of the awards have gone to productions that ran only a weekend or two in a church basement or the back room of a bar. As veteran actor Mike Kellin said in accepting his award for his performance in *American Buffalo*, "only ten people saw our show, but luckily seven of them were Obie judges." And as Edward Albee, an early Obie winner, once put it: "Unlike other awards, seven out of ten times the best play prize actually goes to the best play." The award itself—presented at ceremonies at either the Village Gate or the Bottom Line, Greenwich Village cabarets—is a simple plaque, in keeping with Off-Broadway's emphasis on the work itself.

Since the Obie is almost always the first recognition a playwright or actor or director has ever received, even people familiar with Off-

Broadway theatre often have not heard of the winners. Albee himself was an unknown when he won in 1960, and when the names Robards, Scott, Hoffman, and Pacino were announced, many in the audience had to turn to their friends and ask, "What was that name again?" And so it went with the ten playwrights in this anthology—for the Obie is not so much an acknowledgment of a successful career as an announcement that a major new talent has just emerged. The lasting achievement of Off-Broadway, then—if these ten plays were not enough—has been to provide a place for that talent to emerge, to establish an atmosphere in which creativity can flourish, not in the service of show business but in the adventure of art.

Considering the extraordinary quality and range of Off-Broadway theatre during the past twenty-five years—from traditional plays to avant-garde experiments, from full-length scripts to one-act vignettes, from socially conscious works to poetic dramas, from deeply moving tragedies to hilarious comedies—it was hardly an easy task to select ten plays to represent the best of Off-Broadway. The achievement of each play, as well as reaction to its initial production, will be discussed in brief notes preceding the texts. For now it is only necessary to say that if Off-Broadway began in opposition, defined as what it was *not*, these ten plays prove beyond doubt that it soon created a positive vision of what it *is*.

THE CONNECTION
Jack Gelber

THE CONNECTION

The Connection by Jack Gelber was not only the first Off-Broadway play to challenge the conventions of "realistic" theatre but also the first original play to become an Off-Broadway "hit." Whereas New York's powerful daily newspapers, such as the *Times,* all gave it unfavorable reviews, the critics from the weekly cultural magazines were much more flattering. Robert Brustein, in the *New Republic,* called it "the only honest and balanced work ever created by a Beat Generation writer," Donald Malcolm in *The New Yorker* described it as the "first really interesting new play to appear Off-Broadway," and Henry Hewes of *The Saturday Review* wrote that "*The Connection* emerges as the most original piece of new American playwriting in a long, long time."

Jerry Tallmer, theatre critic for New York's new weekly newspaper, *The Village Voice,* was especially enthusiastic. In issue after issue he argued that "if *The Connection* can't make it in Greenwich Village, then nothing can." Largely due to his relentless praise and insistence that his readers attend, the production finally found an audience and ran for nearly a year.

The Connection—Jack Gelber's first play, written when he was twenty-seven years old—was revolutionary in both content and form, which accounts for the excitement, even shock, that it aroused. According to Kenneth Tynan, one of the most influential critics of the time, "Gelber's play deals with a subject that the theatre (or the cinema, or television) hardly ever approaches except as a pretext for pathetic melodrama. The people . . . . are heroin addicts, from which it follows that they are almost totally passive as human beings."

This passivity was made dramatic by the intriguing use of the play-within-a-play device. A "producer" and "writer" tell the audience that they have gathered together a group of addicts to improvise an evening of theatre. As the "producer" and "writer" are gradually drawn more and more deeply into the desperate world of addiction, so is the audience. In fact, the Living Theatre's staging of the play was so realistic that many spectators believed that they were witnessing actual addicts on stage. (The effect was intensified by having the "addicts" panhandle the audience in the lobby during intermission.)

During the 1960 Obie ceremonies, *The Connection* was honored as Best New Play and as Best Production; in addition, Warren Finnerty won an Obie Award for his performance as Leach. During the next decade, the Living Theatre staged many of Off-Broadway's most controversial works, and Jack Gelber wrote several more plays for both Off-Broadway and Broadway. Although his name is not listed in the credits, one member of the original production went on to become one of our most well-known performers—the man who rises in the audience to speak briefly in the second act was a young actor named Martin Sheen.

"I don't think there is such a thing as learning a lesson," says one of the characters in *The Connection*, and Gelber certainly does not give us any simple answers to the problem of drug addiction. However, he does suggest that "the connection" the addicts seek—the man who will bring them their heroin fix—is a metaphor for the connections that all people need, not to a momentary and illusory ecstasy, but to each other.

THE CONNECTION was first performed on July 15, 1959, at The Living Theatre in New York City, with the following cast:

JIM DUNN	*Leonard Hicks*
JAYBIRD	*Ira Lewis*
LEACH	*Warren Finnerty*
SOLLY	*Jerome Raphel*
SAM	*John McCurry*
ERNIE	*Garry Goodrow*
1ST MUSICIAN	*Freddie Redd*
4TH MUSICIAN	*Michael Mattos*
FIRST PHOTOGRAPHER	*Louis McKenzie*
SECOND PHOTOGRAPHER	*Jamil Zakkai*
2ND MUSICIAN	*Jackie McLean*
3RD MUSICIAN	*Larry Ritchie*
HARRY	*Henry Proach*
SISTER SALVATION	*Barbara Winchester*
COWBOY	*Carl Lee*

The play was directed by Judith Malina; the set was designed by Julian Beck; original tunes were by Freddie Redd.

NOTE: The jazz played is in the tradition of Charlie Parker. There are approximately thirty minutes of jazz in each act.

ACT ONE

The players arrange themselves on stage a few minutes before the play begins. SOLLY is looking out of a window with binoculars. Behind him is a room full of homemade furniture. In center stage SAM is stretched out sleeping on a bed. Downstage left LEACH and ERNIE are slumped over a table. The 1ST and 4TH MUSICIANS are at extreme right dozing at a piano. A small green light bulb hangs in the center of the room. A door to the toilet is rear left. There is, perhaps, a sign on the wall, "Heaven or Hell: which road are you on?" Perhaps there is a painting or an orange crate bookcase in the room. The house lights dim. JIM DUNN and JAYBIRD stroll up the aisle. They are wearing suits. Perhaps JAYBIRD has a darker shirt. They jump or hop on stage.

JIM: Hello there! I'm Jim Dunn and I'm producing *The Connection*. This is Jaybird, the author. Hardly a day goes by without the daily papers having some item involving narcotics. Any number of recent movies, plays and books have been concerned with the peculiar problems of this anti-social habit. Unfortunately few of these have anything to do with narcotics. Sometimes it is treated as exotica and often as erotica. Jaybird has spent some months living among drug addicts. With the help of [name of director] we have selected a few addicts to improvise on Jaybird's themes. I can assure you that this play does not have a housewife who will call the police and say, "Would you please come quickly to the [name of theatre]. My husband is a junkie."
(*House lights up.*)
Please turn the house lights down.

4TH MUSICIAN: Hey, Jim, is Cowboy back?

JIM: No, man, Cowboy is not back.
(1ST MUSICIAN *plays his instrument hurriedly.*)

JIM: Stop it kids. We haven't begun yet. I'm not finished. Turn those lights down.
(*Lights down.*)
Yes. We shall hear more from the musicians. A little better than that. That's what hooked me into this thing: jazz. I mean the music they try to stuff into movies and plays can't be called jazz. Not really. Tonight will be different.
(*Loses his place*)
When you're dealing with a taboo such as narcotics and trying to use the theatre in a way that it hasn't quite been tried before, you —I am taking a big gamble. Of course we are starting small. The [name of theatre] is small. I think playgoers should have some place to . . . you know what I mean.

JAYBIRD: Jimmie, you're goofing. You've got your speeches mixed. What Jim is trying to say is that I am interested in an improvised theatre. It isn't a new idea. It just isn't being done. Remember: for one night this scene swings. But as a life it's a damn bore. When all the changes have been played, we'll all be back where we started. We end in a vacuum. I am not a moralist. However, some of you will leave this theatre with the notion that jazz and narcotics are inextricably connected. That is your connection, not—

JIM: This word magician here has invented me for the sole purpose of explaining that I and this entire evening on stage are merely a fiction. And don't be fooled by anything anyone else tells you. Except the jazz. As I've said, we do stand by the authenticity of that improvised art. But as for the rest it has no basis in naturalism. None. Not a bit. Absol—

JAYBIRD: This is getting embarrassing. We've gone through this. The improvising comes later.

JIM: What I mean to say is that we are not actually using real heroin. You don't think we'd use the real stuff? After all, narcotics are illegal.
(A knock. Everyone stiffens. LEACH opens the door. Enter 2ND and 3RD MUSICIANS.)

2ND MUSICIAN: Have we started yet?

JIM: Emphatically not! Not until I'm finished. Dig?

2ND MUSICIAN: What are you selling this time, Jim? Aren't you the cat that was trying to sell me valve oil last week?

JIM: I only asked you—oh, what's the use? Can't you do something?

JAYBIRD: Why should I? Pay no attention to them. My primitive tribe is getting restless.

2ND MUSICIAN: I have a gig for us. They're even going to pay us money.

JIM: You see, I am taking a gamble. But why are salesmen put down? I'm selling an idea. What's so immoral about that?

2ND MUSICIAN: Swing Baby. [1ST MUSICIAN's name], we have to get some tunes prepared.

JIM: Anyway, I was talking about the problem of naturalism. Did I say anything about that? Well, it's out of the question. Where could it lead? A sociologist's report on the pecking order of Bowery bums. No, out of the question. Right, Jaybird? Right.

JAYBIRD: No!
(House lights on.)

JIM: Again? What's happening backstage? Is everyone high before we start? Turn those damn lights off!

JAYBIRD: I have had enough for now. Isn't it time to leave?
(*Exits into the audience. House lights down.*)

2ND MUSICIAN: Please don't leave us! Please don't leave us!

JIM: Why don't we do the whole play in the dark? There's an idea for you, Jaybird.

JAYBIRD: I've had enough of your ideas.

JIM: Well, Jaybird did have some prepared things about unions that I thought were pretty funny, but—I shall return.
(*Exit* JIM. LEACH *stands up and unfolds a tablecloth. He snaps it and lays it out. With a large knife he starts cutting a pineapple. He has a handkerchief around a boil on his neck.*)

LEACH: I'm hungry. This is my place, why shouldn't I eat? These people never eat. Don't they know it's nutritious? Oh, this boil. Damn this boil. Dream world. Narcotics. I live comfortable. I'm not a Bowery bum. Look at my room. It's clean. Except for the people who come here and call themselves my friends. My friends? Huh! They come here with a little money and they expect me to use my hard earned connections to supply them with heroin. And when I take a little for myself they cry, they scream. The bastards. They wait here and make me nervous. Sleeping. That's all they can do. Sleep. Last night I dreamt I was on a ladder. I wish Solly were awake. You know what I mean? He'd know. There were a hundred clowns dangling on this rope ladder, laughing to someone. You know what I mean? Then it was all a painting and the name psychology was written on the bottom.
(*Rapid entrance of* JIM *with* 1ST *and* 2ND PHOTOGRAPHERS. 1ST PHOTOGRAPHER *is a Negro in a white suit, the* 2ND PHOTOGRAPHER *white in a black suit. The* 1ST *is swift and agile, the* 2ND *slow and clodlike. As the play unfolds they exchange, piece-by-piece, their clothing and personalities.*)

JIM: I hope I haven't interrupted anything, Leach? I couldn't have. In keeping with our improvisation theme, I have an announcement. Have you been introduced to the cast?

LEACH: Aw, Jimmie, I didn't want to wake anybody up.

JIM: How kind of you. First things first. This is Leach.

LEACH: (*Staring ahead and saluting*) Yessir!

JIM: This is Ernie. He's our dope-addict psychopath.
(ERNIE *blows his mouthpiece.*)

JIM: Solly? Wake up, Solly.

SOLLY: (*Raises his hand and waves*) Ad sum!

JIM: Sam is our expert in folk lore.

SAM: Don't fire until you see the whites of their eyes.

JIM: These are the musicians. I'm sure they need no introduction.
This is [names all the musicians].
(1ST, 2ND *and* 3RD MUSICIANS *stand, bow their heads, and sit. The*
4TH MUSICIAN *is asleep.* JIM *tugs at him.*)

4TH MUSICIAN: (*Reaching for his sleeve*) Cowboy here?

JIM: No, he is not. Now, friends—

1ST MUSICIAN: I can't tell the performance from the rehearsal.

JIM: Steady, boys, we have a long trip. Our other actors are off in
the real world procuring heroin.

LEACH: Actors?

JIM: All right, junkies. During our trip we will incorporate an allied
art—the motion picture.

JAYBIRD: (*From the audience*) What?

JIM: This is the ad lib part. Don't worry. Money! And, if everything goes right, you will be able to see the film version of this play. It was the only hip thing to do.

2ND MUSICIAN: You're hip, my ass!

LEACH: (*To* JIM) Will you stop this cornball stuff.

ERNIE: I knew they would pull something like this. I told you I didn't trust this cat!

JIM: Come on, Jaybird. This can't go on like this.

JAYBIRD: So far so good. Don't worry. Conflict!

JIM: It just means more money. For you and for me. Besides, we aren't going Hollywood. They're making an avant-garde movie. The photographers know something about Griffith and Eisenstein.

LEACH: You sure have to mention the right names.

SOLLY: Leave him be.

JIM: Okay, you cats ought to smoke pot instead of using junk. It would make you more agreeable.
(*Exit*)

ERNIE: (*To* 1ST PHOTOGRAPHER) How much they paying you, man?
(1ST PHOTOGRAPHER *ignores him and moves in and about the stage with a light meter, framing with his fingers different parts of the set.*)
What are you getting out of this, man?

2ND PHOTOGRAPHER: Oh, it'll pay the rent. Oh. Ah. Er. I'm visual, you see. I'm not able to express, ah, myself. Let's get the rest of the equipment. Ah.
(1ST PHOTOGRAPHER *mentally adds up on his fingers, and they exit into the audience.*)

LEACH: Do you see that lightbulb? Do you realize that light travels at 186,000 miles per second per second? Solly, wake up. I want you to hear this.

SOLLY: (*Apparently asleep*) I haven't slept since the night I met you. Two years ago. But, for once, pretend that I am asleep.

LEACH: So, I was saying that light travels at 186,000 miles per second per second. You know what I mean? We, the human race, are being bombarded constantly with the light particles. And now the question is: why aren't we dead? At 186,000 miles per second per second we should be annihilated. But we aren't. Why? I'll tell you. Man is transparent. You know what I mean? Man is transparent. Yes, transparent. That's why the light goes through him and doesn't hurt me or you. Now this is the interesting part. Are you listening, Solly?
(*Pause*)
If man is transparent, how do you account for his shadow? You know? To tell you the truth, I don't know the whole answer. You know what I mean? But I think that it has something to do with the alchemical nature of man. Got it? Some weird alchemical changes make the light's color different shades of black. Not too sure of that. Solly, what do you think of it? Does it have something to do with Indian philosophy?

SOLLY: I'm hungry. What are you cutting to death today?

LEACH: (*Places fruit on a dish*) Hey, Sam, you want some pineapple?
(*Pushes* SAM)
Don't you want to eat?

SAM: Now, man, you know I hate to be pushed. I have but one life. I'm waiting on Cowboy. What happened to Cowboy? And Leonard the Locomotive?

LEACH: They ran off and got married! How do I know? Go on, eat something.

SAM: No, I's sick. Honest, I couldn't eat a thing.

LEACH: Hey, Ernie! Wake up, boy! Time to eat. Huh? Here's some nourishment.

ERNIE: Don't be a drag, man. Where's Cowboy and Leonard the Locomotive?

LEACH: Cowboy, Cowboy. You rotten junkies. Is that all you can think about is dope? Dope? Dope?

2ND MUSICIAN: Somebody call me?

3RD MUSICIAN: (*To himself*) My wife thinks I'm insane for doing this.

LEACH: I'm offering you the fruit of the land. Cowboy is just going to kill you. I want to save you.

ERNIE: Come off it, man. You steal so much shit from us that there are rumors of you opening a drug store.

SOLLY: Sure, Leach is trying to turn on the whole world.

LEACH: That's right. I'm saving all the heroin I can so that I can put it in vitamin pills. Can't you see everyone in the whole world being hooked without them knowing it?
(*Totters and laughs*)
Besides, I only take what's coming to me, and you don't have to come up here.
(*Crosses to* 1ST MUSICIAN)
How about you, man? Pineapple?
(1ST MUSICIAN's *head slowly falls and his body lapses into a deep sleep.*)
Hey, man. Pineapple?

1ST MUSICIAN: (*Just before falling off his chair he straightens up*) What's happening? What tune are we blowing? Cowboy back?

3RD MUSICIAN: My wife thinks I'm insane.

LEACH: No, Cowboy is not back.

2ND MUSICIAN: Cowboy went to cop and got copped.

1ST MUSICIAN: Oh.
(Starts falling asleep again)

1ST PHOTOGRAPHER: *(In audience. Enthusiastically)* That's the way
it really is. That's the way it is.

SOLLY: I'm hungry, Leach.

LEACH: Okay.
(Hands him the plate)
Take the whole thing.

SOLLY: Ernie, do you see where you make your mistake? Ask and
you shall receive.

ERNIE: I'm not much for tact. I guess I'll never be.

SOLLY: Well, man, it is a very rotting black shadow that seeps
through your body.

LEACH: So you were listening? Maybe you know that you're not the
only one who thinks about these things.
(Holds his neck)
My lousy boil!

SOLLY: Put some hot water on it.

LEACH: I think I will. Maybe I'll shave.

ERNIE: *(To the audience)* Cut your throat.

LEACH: I've invited some chicks over. Jimmie thought it was a good
idea to put in a little battle of the sexes. Where does he get his

ideas? If anybody knocks you take care of it, Solly. I don't feel like being arrested today. I haven't had dinner yet. Or my fix.
(*Exits to toilet*)

ERNIE: Hey, Solly, what were you talking about morals?

SOLLY: Nothing much. I thought it would be easier if you pretended that Leach was a very good friend of yours. Let him think he's helping you.

ERNIE: Oh. I thought you wanted me to follow the ten commandments or something.

SAM: (*Reclining*) Not a bad idea. I'm sick. Oh, powerful sick and hungry. I hope Cowboy gets back soon. I didn't like the idea of Leonard the Locomotive going with him. He's a practical joker. Every day he goes out. Or I go out. Or we're both way out. Every day.
(*Sings*)
Sko-bah-dee. Skee-boh-dah. Same old stuff.
(*Laughs*)
Yeah. Where is the old Cowboy? I remember when I got out of Quentin with the Cowboy a few years ago. We were walking down Broadway.
(*Gets up and walks in place*)
We swore off of swearing anything off. That's the way it is—you know something in your mind for so long and you know that talking nonsense is just that and nothing more. Yeah, man, we were going to stay clean. Clean, man, clean. We collared the first connection we could find. I said, "What am I doing?" Just one fix won't hurt anything.
(*Starts jogging in place*)
What is this thing I'm fighting? That taste come back to your mouth. And that's what you want. That taste, that little taste. If you don't find it there you look some place else. And you're running, man. Running. It doesn't matter how or why it started. You don't think about anything and you start going back, running back. I used to think that the people who walk the streets, the people who work every day, the people who worry so much about

the next dollar, the next new coat, the chlorophyll addicts, the aspirin addicts, the vitamin addicts, those people are hooked worse than me. Worse than me. Hooked.
(*Stops jogging and falls on the bed*)

SOLLY: They are. Man, they sure are. You happen to have a vice that is illegal.

1ST PHOTOGRAPHER: (*In audience*) That's the way it is. That's the way it really is.

SAM: I guess so. What am I talking about?

SOLLY: You are fed up with everything for the moment. And like the rest of us you are a little hungry for a little hope. So you wait and worry. A fix of hope. A fix to forget. A fix to remember, to be sad, to be happy, to be, to be. So we wait for the trustworthy Cowboy to gallop in upon a white horse. Gallant white powder.

SAM: There ain't nothing gallant about heroin, baby.

ERNIE: Will you stop talking about it? You cats are a drag. It's getting on my nerves. I've got a job tonight and I've got to get straight.
(*Blows his mouthpiece*)
Why doesn't that bastard get here? He probably took all our money and burned us.
(*Knock.*)

LEACH: (*Off stage*) See who it is, Solly.

SOLLY: (*At the window*) It's Harry. He's got his suitcase.

LEACH: (*Off stage*) Let him in. I hope he doesn't want to stay here.
(SOLLY *opens the door and* HARRY *walks in and looks around. Then he goes to the light socket in center stage and plugs in the cord of the portable phonograph. He opens the phonograph and puts on a Charlie Parker record—all in silence. The record plays for two minutes. Everyone assumes an intense pose of listening.*

Afterwards there is a silence and HARRY *carefully picks up the record, closes the phonograph, unplugs the cord, and leaves. There is a long pause. One of the musicians starts playing and the others join him in cementing their feelings. They play for about one minute.*)

JAYBIRD: (*Enters from the audience*) Cut it! Cut it! You are murdering the play. What are you doing? Let's go over it again. You're to give the whole plot in the first act. So far not one of you has carried out his dramatic assignment.
(*Calms himself.* LEACH *enters.*)
I had characters, with biographies for each of them. I thought that was clear. This is improvised theatre! And what have you provided? Do you think you are doing a slice of life?

SOLLY: (*Shouting*) Stop! Stop the action! Why did you seek out dope addicts? We didn't have to go through with this. Now quit complaining. Besides you've changed into a monster. Why don't you stay on stage with us?

JAYBIRD: Never mind that now. There are to be no realistic body movements as we rehearsed. No longer is your hand your own hand. You are part of something infinitely larger. Solly, where is the philosophy I put into your mouth?

SOLLY: It went up in smoke before the show.

JAYBIRD: A monster? I'm a monster? What do you know about the theatre?
(*Pause. Softly*)
Leach, where is the plot? Give it away, expose it, say it three times. Don't be anal.

LEACH: I flushed it down the toilet.

JAYBIRD: Sam, Ernie, is this a conspiracy? Where are your confessions? Your capsule comments?

ERNIE: Where are my capsules?

SAM: Man, you've been telling us to act natural. Now we don't own our own hands.

JAYBIRD: You may know more about junk, but let me swing with this production. Okay, let's get on with it.

SOLLY: Go ahead [name of 1ST MUSICIAN], it's our stage now.
(JAYBIRD *exits into the audience to the jeers of those on stage. The musicians play for five minutes while the photographers move about the stage with their camera and glaring lights.*)

1ST PHOTOGRAPHER: Take 27-A.

2ND PHOTOGRAPHER: This is terrific stuff! I wonder how much will have to be cut out of it? Terrific! Do you think we'll get a shot of the connection?

1ST PHOTOGRAPHER: You mean Cowboy or Leonard the Locomotive?

2ND PHOTOGRAPHER: No, no. I mean the man behind them. I mean the big connection.

1ST PHOTOGRAPHER: If I were him I wouldn't want to show my face.

LEACH: So you fellows want to see the man, the man behind the man.

2ND PHOTOGRAPHER: Will he be here?

LEACH: No, kiddies, he will not. I have been on this scene for a long, long time and I have never seen him. Sit down. Sit down. I have never seen the man because there is no man.

2ND PHOTOGRAPHER: You mean there isn't any organized international setup?

LEACH: No.

ERNIE: Sure there is.

2ND PHOTOGRAPHER: Then somebody must be the head of it.

ERNIE: No, I don't think there's any head.

2ND PHOTOGRAPHER: If you have an organization, somebody must be in charge. Hey, Sam, who's in charge?

SAM: I am.

2ND PHOTOGRAPHER: You are?

SAM: Sure. I am the man as much as anyone. Listen, I am your man if you come to me. You are my man if I go to you.

2ND PHOTOGRAPHER: Well, where does it start?

SOLLY: Right here!

SAM: Or over there.

2ND PHOTOGRAPHER: I don't understand.

SOLLY: (*At the window with binoculars*) Nobody here understands that. They wouldn't be here if they were that interested. To us here it is a mystery where Cowboy goes. Anyone coming to Leach feels that he is the central actor in his own drama. An artificial and melodramatic organization. But that is the setup. Surely it starts in the ground and grows up as a poppy. After that it is a mundane game for me, that is, for me.

1ST PHOTOGRAPHER: That's the way it is. Really, that's the way it is.

SOLLY: The man is you. You are the man. You are your own connection. It starts and stops here. You come here to take pictures. And now you're getting involved at your own risk.

LEACH: You think we ought to turn them on, Solly?

SAM: I'm not donating anything.

LEACH: I'm not asking you.

SOLLY: Don't look at me. Ask them.

LEACH: Well?

2ND PHOTOGRAPHER: They say one shot and you can never stop. You're hooked.
(LEACH *laughs*)

1ST PHOTOGRAPHER: You got any pot?

LEACH: (*Laughs*) Oh, this is the end. They send two square photographers. And one of them turns out to be a pot-head.

1ST PHOTOGRAPHER: (*To* 2ND PHOTOGRAPHER) Marijuana.

LEACH: Mari-juana. No, I don't have any pot. But how quaint of you to ask.

2ND PHOTOGRAPHER: They say marijuana leads to the stronger stuff.

1ST PHOTOGRAPHER: Shut up.

LEACH: (*Pointing to the* 1ST PHOTOGRAPHER) I'd like to turn that one on. He'd be crazy. I'd like to see that.

ERNIE: No, I'd like to turn the other one on, and knock him out. Oh, he'd be helpless. At first, that is.

SAM: You are certainly a mean bunch of boys.

LEACH: Mind your own business.

SOLLY: (*Looking out of the window*) I can't see you. Yes, now you are in focus.

LEACH: Is that Cowboy and Leonard the Locomotive?

SOLLY: No, man, I'm looking for a woman.
(*Exit photographers into the audience.*)
Goodbye.

ERNIE: I'm tired of waiting. Let's do something.

SOLLY: Hello there! I'm the nineteenth century and I'm producing the twentieth. Unfortunately, the twentieth century has developed anti-social habits. There isn't a day that goes by without some item in the daily papers involving insanity. We've gone out and bribed a few natives. Actually, I'm the only white man the natives trust. If we can start a small opium war—I always wanted to start a war.

LEACH: Cool it, Solly. Those cats make our living. Oh, my neck. My boil!

SOLLY: You're right. I've always wanted an audience, but now I've got one. Imagine someone wanting to have real junkies on stage. Wow! Believe me, we're not here for the money.

ERNIE: Speak for yourself.

SOLLY: It's not that much. As you have gathered, we are, as they say in the tabloids, dope fiends. We are waiting. We have waited before. The connection is coming. He is always coming. But so is education, for example. The man who will whisper the truth in your ear. Or the one who will shout it out among the people. I can't generalize and believe it. I'm not made that way. Perhaps Jaybird has chosen this petty and miserable microcosm because of its self-annihilating aspects. This tells us something about Jaybird, but nothing about me. Hurry, hurry, hurry. The circus is here. Suicide is not uncommon among us. The seeking of death is at once fascinating and repellent. The overdose of heroin is where that frail line of life and death swings in a silent breeze of ecstatic summer. The concept of this limbo you can hold in your palsied hand. Who else can make so much out of passing out? But existence on another plane is sought, whether to alleviate the suffering from this one, or to wish for death, it doesn't matter. I hate over-simplification. Sam! Sam is simple. Sam, someone, say something. Say something to the customers.

1ST PHOTOGRAPHER: (*In audience*) Man, that's the way it really is.

SAM: Oh, man. I'm not much for this sort of thing.

SOLLY: Pay your dues. Pay your dues.

SAM: Okay. If that's the way it is. But who's to say? Who's there to squeeze the ball into his own shape and tell me this is right. You know that. What does Jaybird want? A soft shoe dance? I don't need any burnt cork, you know. Now, Solly, you know Leach. When you met him he came on with how easy it would be to exist if you two shared expenses. I remember you slept there. It was cheap. Little rent, some food here and there whenever the bastard felt like sharing what he had. Or Cowboy cooking up a storm of food that he swiped in the supermarket. But Leach, man, Leach is a queer without being queer. He thinks like a chick. You wouldn't live with that. I certainly wouldn't. Sometimes I wish he would stop fighting it and make the homosexual scene. It would be easier on all of us. Besides, he would swing more himself. Now he's undependable, like a woman. He's like everybody's mother. Cowboy treats him like a woman and everything is fine. I can't do it. I just look at him, and I can't do it. And there's Solly. Man, he's hard to figure. Educated, shit, he knows an awful lot. But then he's here waiting on the same stuff I am. And he ain't rich. He don't get high unless he's happy. I can never figure that out. Most cats get high when they're down. Not him. Mostly I sees him in my mind with dancing on the street. Yeah, dancing down through the people. Sometimes yelling, sometimes whispering to people. Always with a book. I don't remember ever seeing him on the street without a book. He watches everything. I was playing with this hoop
(*Picks up hoop*)
and he tells me about the Romans' symbols of death or some shit like that. He's always telling me what I do is got to do with the

Africans or the Navahos. He breaks me up. A stand up cat. I like
him.
(*Pause*)
Ernie?
(*Pause*)

ERNIE: What do you want? Get us all busted?

SAM: You don't want much. A little dope and your horn. I don't
trust you.

ERNIE: The same.
(*Blows his mouthpiece*)

LEACH: Your confession is next, son. Shut up. You think it's easy?

SAM: As long as Ernie is straight with me, I am with him. But I
don't like him. I hold back, you know? He has no will power
when it comes to not having anything to get high with. Hey, is
there any beer left?

2ND MUSICIAN: No.

LEACH: My neck hurts. I'm going to put more hot water on it.
(*Exits to toilet*)

SAM: They have a saying in this world: It isn't the shit that will do
you in, it's the lack of it. I can't put Ernie down too hard. I steal.
But I steal from people I don't like, and I wouldn't touch a match
stick of a friend of mine. Listen! I like telling stories best. I have
quite a rep . . . repi . . . quite a lot of stories that would tickle
the hairs on your ass. But I'm kinda sick right now. You can imagine. I mean, you've seen pictures of guys like me. It's torturous.
Well, I'm coming off this here stage in a minute or so and I'll be
in the lobby. I could use a little money.
(*Music begins softly.*)
Only till I get myself straightened out. I'm supposed to see this
guy next week about working in a book store. Solly introduced
me. Didn't you, Solly? Well, I'll be making a lot of bread then. I's

sick, good people. I'll talk to you when I come offen this silly
stage. I got some powerful stories in me when that shit flows in
my veins. Right now I'm going to lay down for a minute. Maybe
the music will help.
(*Musicians play for about five minutes.*)

ERNIE: Trust me? Man, I don't care one way or the other. Sam's
right about me in his own way—I only care to play. And . . .
(*Smile*)
. . . a little dope makes life enjoyable. I play the same—with or
without it.
(*Blows his mouthpiece here, and throughout the speech*)
That's the truth. No square bullshitter is going to change me.
That's for sure. I've had to hock my horn. Do you know what that
feels like? I take the few measly pennies to some connection and
get high. That's where my horn is now—the hock shop. I got a
job tonight and no horn. Maybe someone will borrow me theirs. I
don't know. I'm lonely! Not for you or anybody on this stage. I
know these people. I've known them a long time. Too long.
(*Walks over to* 2ND MUSICIAN)
Can I use your horn tonight, man?
(*No answer*)
Did you see? Do you? Sam isn't too bad. He could of told some
really rotten bits that people tell about me. Thanks, Sam.
(*No answer*)
They say I threw a kid out the window, after he took an overdose.
Don't believe it.
(*Photographers enter and circle around* ERNIE.)
Well, there's Leach. An orphan. Not too many people know that.
Yeah, his old man was a musician. Died when he was eight.
County authorities took him to a farm until he was seventeen.
Poor kid. Bah! Leach went to work in a book store and one day he
left with everything in the till and went to New York. He became
a cheap businessman. He's always trying to be so hip. He still is
just a petty conniving businessman. Leach has run away with the
till from more cities and people than I'll ever know. Of course,
Leach tells another story: he was cheated, he was insulted, he was
dealing with squares, he was . . . you know the story.
(*Smiles*)

So do I, for that matter. Get this straight. I admit when I've sinned. That's more than you will get from most.

VOICE: Come off it.

ERNIE: Who said that?
(*No answer*)
Money and sex. That's all I hear from you. So here it is right back. Leach, sexually speaking, can't be with a girl for more than one night. He likes the courtship. The playing up. The making out. Not it itself. You don't like hearing the truth, do you, Leach?
(*No answer*)
Leach uses junk that way. He doesn't enjoy junk, ever. I'm suspicious of people who never enjoy getting high. Oh, but he loves the excitement of getting it.

VOICE: Come off it.

ERNIE: Leonard the Locomotive? Cowboy? Hey, Solly, didn't that sound like Leonard the Locomotive?
(*No answer*)
He's crazy, that Leonard is. He must have been crazy about trains when he was a kid. He really thinks he's a locomotive at times. You photographers stop taking my picture! Where's Jim? We aren't being paid for being film actors.
(*Pause*)
Solly and Sam are very much alike. Surprise you? It's funny, in a way. They are of course very different people. Solly can read Greek and Hebrew.
(*Speaking progressively faster*)
I don't think Sam can read English. But they are the same. In this way. They swing with being high. Sam has been around junk and junkies all his life and no one is more familiar with that peculiar code that goes with it, you dig? He learned the hard way. Solly knows instinctively. I mean he was born hip. God knows why he's here. I tell everyone that he is just like that damned author who wrote this damned play. He just came around and acted like he was a junkie so that he could go home to his wife and kids and

get us on paper. No, that was a bad act and everyone knew it. Not Solly. If he's acting then I'm fooled. And yet—well.
(*Toots mouthpiece. Starts again, slowly*)
Well, Sam is going to be around junk and junkies the rest of his life. He has no choice. Really. I don't feel that way about Solly. Both of them dig music. I mean they dig it. I mean they have an emotional digging. Which brings us to Cowboy. He's a good businessman. Some cats think he is a sweetheart. I mean he's noted for his honesty. I mean I hope he gets here soon, but he is the guy who will not run out. I think it's good business. Not a kind heart. After all, cross country gossip travels at high speed in my world. And nobody cheats him. And he used to blow [name of horn] like myself. I mean I still blow [name of horn] but he used to.

VOICE: Come off it.

ERNIE: Magic. That's what Cowboy does. I mean he makes something out of nothing. I've got the horrors. Where is Cowboy? Oh, he's fast with a knife. I saw him in action. I never believed it but there it was: knowing the danger before it happened. And then the quick move.

VOICE: Come off it.

ERNIE: Stop it. Shit! Shit! I don't trust any of you. Yes, I've tied everything into nice small packages for you. You can go home and say that Ernie really knows. Boy, he really can rip things apart. Shit. Do you hear? I don't trust one son of a bitch here or in the audience. Why? Because I really don't believe any of you understand what this is about. You're stupid. Why are you here? Because you want to see someone suffer. You want to laugh at me? You don't want to know me. And these people? Sam doesn't care about me or my music when it comes right down to it. He's for number one—himself. Solly's young. Besides, he won't be a junkie all his life. He will be so far out of it he won't have to hear the rotten stories about his life being vomited up by thieves and misfits. It's Cowboy's business to screw me. And Leach? He wants to have me begging. He wants my guts out. I knew this would happen when I started talking. I knew it. I've tried. I just can't

make it. I can't explain any more to you. I tried. A little anyway. I tried. My old man made me work on his farm every day until I was seventeen and never paid me a dime. All I got was a slap across the face for thanks. Where's Cowboy? Where is he? That bastard better come back. It's no use. No use. I want my money. Where is my pay? We're supposed to be paid. Jaybird, where's my pay? I'll kill you. Do you hear?
(*Starts off stage.* SOLLY *restrains him. Photographers exit.* JAYBIRD *leaves the theatre.*)
He's leaving, Solly. That's what the confession was for, wasn't it? Solly, he's leaving. We'll never get paid. I won't sign the confession. I won't sign! We'll never get paid. They made movies and it's no use. No use.
(*Sits down. Mumbles*)
No use. No use.
(*Silence.* 2ND MUSICIAN *falls off his seat. He gets up and starts playing. The others join him for about five minutes of music.*)

ERNIE: Give me a cigarette.

2ND MUSICIAN: Let's split. No sense getting hung on a hanger. Cowboy got himself busted.

1ST MUSICIAN: He'll be here. Let's stick.

3RD MUSICIAN: My wife thinks I'm insane.
(SAM *gives him a cigarette.* ERNIE *lights it and throws the match on the floor.*)

LEACH: (*Enters and looks around. His boil still hurts*) Who threw the match on the floor? What do you think I'm running here? A hotel for slobs? I feed you and even give you my clothes. And what do you do? Look at this place! Look at it! It's a pigsty. A pigsty. I just mopped the floor, too. Oh, what else could I expect?
(*Pause*)
Where's Cowboy?
(*No answer*)
Oh, my neck! Solly, what do you think I ought to do? Solly, Sam? Ernie, take a look at this. Will you?
(*Ernie examines Leach's neck.*)

ERNIE: Looks bad, Leach. I'd see a doctor. I hope you might die. And listen: I threw the match on the floor. I want my money. I want out. Now.

LEACH: What do you mean?
(*Turns suddenly and* ERNIE *accidentally breaks the boil*)
Aaaaah!
(*Everyone except* SOLLY *runs to him.* LEACH *is on the verge of tears.* SAM *takes control of the situation and puts* LEACH *on the bed.* ERNIE, *in disgust, stands next to* SOLLY *at the window. Everyone calms down.* SAM *gets a clean cloth and wraps it around* LEACH's *neck.* LEACH *brushes everyone aside, picks up a mirror, examines his boil, and then turns to* ERNIE.)
Ernie, I'm a man of principle. I want you to pick up that match and whatever else you've thrown on the floor. Or get out.

ERNIE: (*Pause*) Man, I'm a musician. I blow my horn. I'm no goddamn housekeeper. Not for you or anyone else.

LEACH: I think you better leave.

ERNIE: I'm waiting on the Cowboy. I got my bread in his pocket. And I'm not leaving until I get my fix.

LEACH: How many times have I turned you on? For nothing! How many times did you flop here? Have I ever turned you out into the cold? Man, you're ungrateful. You're selfish. And don't forget it.

ERNIE: I'm going to vomit. Man, I can't take this. Give me back my bread and I'll get out of here.

LEACH: You didn't give me any money. Besides, I haven't got any money.

1ST PHOTOGRAPHER: (*In audience*) That's the way it is. Man, that's the way it really is.

ERNIE: You've got enough on you. You always have enough on you.

Miserly bastard. Like what happened to the dollar cap, to the three dollar bag? And that was some good shit, too.

LEACH: Man, you are living in another time. That was years ago. Don't blame me for what it costs.

ERNIE: Who else is there to blame? As far as I know you're just a screwball who is playing the small businessman.

LEACH: Get out! Get out! Why don't you stop pretending that you're a musician? Why do you carry that silly mouthpiece? Why? You're never going to use it. You can't play any more. You've got to practice, you dig?

ERNIE: What do I do now? Drop my pants and bend over? I'm waiting for Cowboy. And I'm not leaving until he gets back.
(SOLLY *picks up a chair and smashes it on the floor. Silence.*)

LEACH: What did you do that for?

SOLLY: I hate petty arguments. Besides, Cowboy's coming.

LEACH: What do you mean?

SOLLY: Cowboy's coming.

LEACH: Let me have the binoculars.
(*Pause*)
Who is that with him? It doesn't look like Leonard the Locomotive. Man, it's someone in uniform. It's the cops.

SOLLY: No. No. It isn't any cop. Take another look.
(*Laughs*)

LEACH: It's some kind of uniform. I don't like it. Who is it?

SOLLY: It's some kind of salvation sister.

LEACH: Are you sure?

SOLLY: I'm not sure of anything. I think it's beautiful. Whatever Cowboy's up to certainly is good for a laugh.

LEACH: What in the world is he doing with a salvation sister? Do you think he's going to bring her in here? He's crazy. Crazy! And what happened to Leonard the Locomotive?

JIM: (*Quick entrance with a cigarette with holder in one hand*) Hello again. Did you miss me, my charming audience? Ah, how sweet. Things are getting exciting around here. Don't you think so?
(*Photographers enter and move around him while he is thinking of what to say. He dismisses them with a movement.*)
I am told that Leach has invited some lovely ladies to our little party. We shall see what we shall see. I may even convince Jaybird to come back.

ERNIE: Where's our money?

SOLLY: Cool it.
(*To* JIM)
You'd better come through. I'm not responsible for what Ernie will do.

JIM: Huh? Good people, do not be intimidated by any of these boys during the intermission. No matter what they tell you they will be turned on by a scientifically accurate amount of heroin in the next act. And that is their payment for the performance, excluding the money made on the movie. Also, we are selling some Turkish delight [and whatever else that is sold] in the lobby. Now . . . anyone in the audience for a smoke?
(*Lights slowly fade.*)

ACT TWO

(*Music, then lights slowly up. As the music continues for about 5 minutes, the musicians take turns going into the toilet. As the last musician exits,* ERNIE *enters the toilet.* SOLLY *is sleeping at the window.* SISTER SALVATION *is looking around the room on tiptoe.* SAM, *on the center couch, begins to stir and the* SISTER *"shshes" him. The music ends.* ERNIE *enters, high, spots a chair and goes to it.* COWBOY *enters: he has a red bandana around his neck.*)

COWBOY: Sam?

SAM: Coming, right now.

SISTER: Shsh. You heard Brother Cowboy. There's a nice young woman next door that is very sick. Now please don't make any noise. One can say things in a tiny voice as well as a big one.

COWBOY: Thank you, Sister Salvation. You are a great help to all of us.

SISTER: Is there a bathroom, Brother Cowboy?

COWBOY: Yes, mam. But Sam here hasn't had a bath in a long time. I thought I'd help him wash away those sins of his. Understand?

SISTER: Surely, Brother Cowboy.
(SAM *and* COWBOY *exit.*)
(*To* ERNIE)
You look very pale, son. Is something the matter? Hungry, son?

ERNIE: Leave me alone. I'm in no mood for conversation.

SISTER: Soul. Yes, my dear child, the soul. I'm sure of it.

ERNIE: You have invited yourself to a den of vipers, Sister Salvation. I'm sure you will find enough sins crossing your path today. So leave me alone.
(COWBOY *enters.*)

COWBOY: Understand this, Brother Rat, Brother Sun and Brother Eel! Leonard the Locomotive and I met this fine woman just one mile from our home. You know where the central police station is? Not far from there, under a flag symbolizing American freedom of speech and religion, I stopped to hear the words of the Lord.

SISTER: Amen.

COWBOY: Amen. A few gentlemen we know began a conversation with me. They asked the all important questions. Where were you? What have you been doing? How was the rodeo and horse tricks? Leonard the Locomotive succeeded in attracting some attention with his famous locomotive yell, and this worker of the Lord . . .

SISTER: Amen.

COWBOY: . . . . this worker and I engaged in a most enlightening discussion. We took a quiet walk home and I invited her up for a little tea.

LEACH: Orange Pekoe.

COWBOY: Possibly she, Leonard the Locomotive, and the power of the Lord saved us all. For the moment, that is.

SISTER: Amen to that, Brother Cowboy.

COWBOY: Amen, Sister Salvation. Now excuse me please.
(*Exit*)

SOLLY: Sister Salvation, Sister Salvation, when did your record of saving souls start?

LEACH: Cool, cool water, Solly.

SOLLY: Have a little trust in the Lord, friend.

SISTER: Brother, I began in the service of the Lord fourteen years ago. But I have only been active these past seven. If you could see the hundreds of faces smile and light up when someone holds out a helping hand to show the path of salvation, it would warm your heart. You haven't known joy until you have seen the way to God.
(*Pause*)
Do you know Harry McNulty?

LEACH: We don't know anyone.
(COWBOY *enters.*)

COWBOY: Excuse me, Sister Salvation. Solly, you're next.

SISTER: There's something crazy going on.

SAM: (*Following* COWBOY) Save yourself, you sinners! Brother Cowboy has some potent medicine made from the rarest, finest witch doctor white flower that ever grew.
(*Laughs*)
Shiiiit. Oh, excuse me, Sister Salvation.

COWBOY: Leach, how about making Sister Salvation a nice cup of tca while you're waiting.

LEACH: I'm waiting to get on. Man, I'm sick.

SOLLY: (*At the toilet door*) I don't take long. Start the tea, I'll finish it.
(*Exits with* COWBOY)
(ERNIE *starts playing "There is a Fountain Filled with Blood" on his mouthpiece. Then he starts singing it. After a few lines the*

words disappear and he is scat singing. SISTER SALVATION *claps her hands in time and everyone joins her. The photographers enter from the audience.*)

SISTER: Oh, it is good, good, good to hear such young men appreciate songs like that.
(*Notices the photographers*)
Who are they? Where did they come from?

LEACH: They're all right. Friends of the family. Did Jaybird come back?

1ST PHOTOGRAPHER: Not yet.

SISTER: What's a nice Negro boy like you doing here?

SAM: I've seen the light!
(*Melodramatically*)
Yes, I've seen the light! Brethren, I used to be a sinner! A sinner!
(LEACH *and* ERNIE *laugh. Photographers exit.*)
A sinner that done bad to his fellow man. But now! Praise the Lord!

SISTER: Amen.

SAM: I am redeemed! From my eternal suffering I am redeemed! Like a pawn ticket.
(*Laughter.*)
I want to take the opportunity to thank each and every kind, gentle and good contributor in the audience. You have helped a most noble cause, and a cause that is dear to our hearts. That goodness, that goodness that flows in our veins is the evidence—is the evidence of our gratitude toward you and every one of our fellow men.

SISTER: Amen.

LEACH: I'm not on yet.

SAM: You, too, Brother Eel, will be saved by Brother Cow in just . . .
(SOLLY *enters with* COWBOY.)
Ah, you see before you with your very own eyes Brother Sol. Hello, Brother.

SOLLY: You weren't kidding, Sambo. This is powerful medicine. I'm going around and will become butter any minute.

SAM: I should wash your mouth out with soap.

SISTER: Amen. Amen. Are you through in the bathroom, Brother Cowboy?
(*Exit* LEACH.)

COWBOY: There is just Brother Leach, mam. And then our baptism will be all over.
(*Exit* COWBOY.)

SISTER: That's all right, Brother Cowboy. You just keep working.
(2ND MUSICIAN *falls to the floor and* 1ST MUSICIAN *helps him up.* SISTER SALVATION *starts over to him, but* SOLLY *interrupts her.*)

SOLLY: Praise the Lord!

SISTER: Amen.

SOLLY: Sister Salvation, I want you to see the light. I mean, man, light travels at 186,000 miles per second per second. I'd like to see that, too. Watch it closely. Faster and faster around your head. Now let your eyes cross. The light is forming an enormous circle around you. You're not helping me, baby. Help me.
(*Starts to fall.* SAM *catches him and carries him to his seat*)
Mercy on me. I falleth before the Lord. Oh, man, it is too tiring. Man, whew! Where do all those sinners get the energy to be saved? Fantastic. I couldn't make it. You have to hand it to them. Day after day, trudging and pulling, they seek out energetic sinners. Each of them is saved ten or twenty times. It's just too much.

SAM: You got to let yourself go. When you feel it inside, just let yourself go and wail.

SOLLY: Man, I feel it inside, but I can't move. I'm stoned.
(*Sits at window*)

SISTER: (*To* ERNIE) Where do you come from, son?

ERNIE: (*Almost asleep*) What?

SISTER: Are you all right, son?

ERNIE: Yeah. Sure. Of course, baby, I'm all right. Where do I come from? See, I can remember.

SISTER: Yes. Where do you come from?

ERNIE: California.

SISTER: That's marvelous.

ERNIE: What's so marvelous about it?

SISTER: It's so clean and healthy there. The trees, and everything is so green.
(*Pause*)
I thought perhaps—perhaps you know Harry McNulty. He's Irish.

ERNIE: Yes.
(*Falling asleep*)
It is. Green.
(*Falls out of the chair.* SISTER SALVATION *helps him up and* COWBOY *comes over and slaps him gently.*)
I'm all right. Man. Leave me alone. It's green. I want to sleep.

COWBOY: The poor boy hasn't slept in days.

SISTER: Oh, we better leave him alone. He looks like a good prospect to save.

COWBOY: Why don't you make yourself a nice cup of tea.
(SISTER SALVATION *exits.*)

LEACH: I'm not even high. I don't feel a thing. I don't feel a thing.

SAM: If you don't feel a thing, man, then you're higher than any of
us.

LEACH: You gave them more. How much did you give Ernie, Cowboy? He's knocked out. And I don't feel a thing.

COWBOY: Cool it. You know Ernie has been chipping. I gave him
the same as you, but you got a higher tolerance. Dig?
(*Photographers enter from the audience.*)

2ND PHOTOGRAPHER: I . . . I don't know how to say this.

COWBOY: I don't know you, man. Who are you?

2ND PHOTOGRAPHER: I'm here to do the film.

LEACH: Jim sent him. But weren't you the one that was so afraid?
Yeah. What about the other photographer?

1ST PHOTOGRAPHER: Count me out. I don't want nothing to do with
this.

LEACH: (*Laughs*) This is going to be fun. Cowboy, give him a taste.

COWBOY: Not out of mine.

LEACH: Out of mine. Go ahead, give him a little taste.

COWBOY: Are you sure you want to go through with this?

2ND PHOTOGRAPHER: (*Mumbles*) Yes.

JAYBIRD: (*Enters from the audience*) Okay. Okay. Aren't you carrying this too far? What is happening here? You aren't here to do
this sort of thing. Destroy yourself, but this wasn't in our deal.

COWBOY: Jaybird, I don't want to initiate anyone into the club. This boy is asking for it. You stop him. I'm too tired to talk.

JAYBIRD: I don't like it. It's not supposed to work this way. I've given you latitude. But this is too much.

LEACH: Hey, Jaybird, you've never made it. Why don't you find out what it's all about before you put it down.

JAYBIRD: Me? No. Not me. Never. Me?

LEACH: You're supposed to know all about it. I mean this all is a play, man. It's not really real.
(*Snicker*)
Hey, I want to watch.

COWBOY: Let's not talk here.
(*Smiling*)
You stay, Leach. Come on back.
(*Exit* COWBOY, 1ST PHOTOGRAPHER *and* JAYBIRD.)

LEACH: So Jaybird will take a little taste for himself.

SISTER: (*Enters. Walks to the window*) Where are all those people coming from? Who are they? I don't see anybody out there.
(*Uses binoculars*)
I don't see anyone out there at all. This is very confusing.
(*To* SOLLY)
Do you know Harry McNulty?

SOLLY: No. There are some questions I can't answer. That's one of them.

SISTER: [Gives a short description of actor who plays HARRY]

SOLLY: What makes you think I would know him?

SISTER: Oh, he loves jazz music. I thought perhaps . . . never mind, I'm probably wrong anyway. The Lord willing, that is.

(2ND MUSICIAN *falls off his seat.* 1ST MUSICIAN *mechanically picks him up.*)

1ST PHOTOGRAPHER: That is the way it is. Really, it is that way.

SAM: Yes, it is. As long as we are talking religion, I got one that happened not too long ago.
(*To the musicians*)
You know Abdul the drummer? Well, Abdul is from Harlem and he has taken up the Moslem faith. A religious man if I ever saw one. Is there any beer?

2ND MUSICIAN: No.

SAM: One night Abdul and Cowboy and me were looking for some small connection. No luck anywhere. Everybody is tearing their hair out. Cowboy and I decide to try to score outside the city. Abdul gave us some money and told us to meet him at his pad. We go outside the city and score and everything is crazy. It is getting light out by now and we hurry back to town and go to Abdul's pad. We knock. No answer. Knock again. No answer. Cowboy tries the door and it's open. We go in and there is Abdul in his underwear kneeling on this rug and he got his hands clasped together and eyes is tight shut. I say, "Abdul, we're back." No answer. "Abdul, baby, everything's cool. We made it." Still no answer. Cowboy tries to stop me from talking to him because Cow figures it must be important if Abdul won't even turn around. We sit down. I can't stand the silence any more. So I say, "Abdul, what the hell you doing, man? Do you know who I am? What are you doing on your knees, baby?" He turns around and stares at me. Finally, he says, "Man, I was praying that you would come back and turn me on!"

SISTER: (*Pause*) That's a wicked story! Such language!

LEACH: (*Enters*) Here's your cup of tea, Sister Salvation.

SISTER: Thank you, brother.
(COWBOY *enters with* 2ND PHOTOGRAPHER *and* JAYBIRD. JAYBIRD *has*

COWBOY's *red bandana around his neck*, 1ST PHOTOGRAPHER *exits to the audience.* 2ND PHOTOGRAPHER *takes* SISTER SALVATION's *cup and sits.*)

COWBOY: Well, what's been happening? Sister Salvation, the bathroom is yours.
(*Sister exits*)
What have you been doing to that chick? I don't want her to leave with a suspicious thought in her head.

LEACH: You shouldn't have brought her here. I think she knows what's happening. Or she doesn't know and wants to.

COWBOY: There were two narcotic bulls on my back. Leonard the Locomotive went one way, and they followed him. I left with her. Man, it was close. I was about to throw the shit away.

SAM: What happened in there?

COWBOY: What a miserable sight it was. A night for comedy. I think Jaybird is pretty sick.
(*Pointing to the* 2ND PHOTOGRAPHER)
He is.

LEACH: He's out of his skull. Look at him. Hey, man, how do you feel?

2ND PHOTOGRAPHER: Don't be a drag, man.
(*They all laugh.*)

JAYBIRD: I've got to lie down.

LEACH: Go ahead! There's a bed.

JAYBIRD: No, not here.
(*Whispers*)
There are too many people around. Wait a minute. I'm sick.
(*Exits to toilet*)

SISTER: (*Entering*) Drink!
(*Backs up* JAYBIRD. JAYBIRD *runs into toilet, holding his mouth*)
That's what you've been doing in there!

COWBOY: What do you mean, Sister Salvation?

SISTER: What do you mean, Brother Cowboy? There are at least ten bottles of wine in the bathroom. All empty. Oh, Lord, before my very own eyes I have been deceived. Wine is a mocker, strong drink is raging: and whosoever is deceived thereby is not wise.
(*The following dialogue is underscored with the bass playing with* SOLLY, *and the horn with* SISTER SALVATION.)

SOLLY: A false balance is an abomination to the Lord; but a just weight is his delight.

SAM: Swing!

SISTER: Be not among winebibbers, among riotous eaters of flesh. For the drunkard and glutton shall come to poverty. Who hath woe? Who hath sorrow? Who hath babbling? Who hath wounds without cause? Who hath redness of eyes? They that tarry long at the wine. They that go to seek mixed wine. At last it biteth like a serpent and stingeth like an adder.

SOLLY: Who invented that uniform?

SISTER: What?

SOLLY: Who invented the uniform you are wearing?

SISTER: I don't know. What has that got to do with it? It isn't what I was talking about. You can't get out of this that easily. You will pay . . .

SOLLY: Foggy day in London, London, London town. It's the War Congress. 1878. Winter. The flock is assembling. Coming back to you now, Sister Salvation? Elijah Cadmen stood up and said, (*sotto voce*) "We need a military type uniform. War to the teeth and salvation to the world."

SISTER: I thought that General Booth invented . . . I could look it up in the library. Where did you learn these things? You would like our library. It's open to the public.

SOLLY: Your bonnet was invented by the General's wife. There will be equality of the sexes, they scream. Dress shall be according to climate. 1880. International meeting. Fur caps in the Arctic. Veils in India. All embracing salvation.

SISTER: I give up. I give up. Stop.

SOLLY: Don't surrender now. Or do. It was just, just, just, just one of those things.

SISTER: What's a nice young man like you doing here?
(*Laughter by all.*)
I don't understand. Why do you . . . ?
(*Laughter by all.*)

SOLLY: No more war. You had better leave while the spirit of brotherhood prevails.

SISTER: I don't want to leave. I know I'm a burden. I went to see about my funeral. The man at Morgen's funeral parlor said it would cost three hundred dollars for opening and closing the grave. Eighty-five dollars for the head stone. I'm growing old and my eyes are going. I don't want to leave. I've been in the hospital. They put the needle in my arm, too.

SOLLY: Cowboy?
(*Nods to him*)
Go ahead, Sister Salvation, before we tell you who Harry McNulty is.

SISTER: (COWBOY *takes her to the door*) You are not alone. You are not alone.

(*Exit*)
You are not alone.

JAYBIRD: (*Enters from toilet*) Glad to have met you?
(*Laughs and sits down to sleep*)
(*The musicians play for about ten minutes. When finished there
is a pause. JIM enters, taking notes.*)

JIM: Leach? Leach? Where are the chicks? Where are the chicks?

LEACH: Oh, man, my job was to invite them. I didn't guarantee anything. They'll probably show up. Hold your pants.

COWBOY: Hey, man, are we getting any extra money for being in
this movie scheme?

JIM: You would have.
(*Pointing to* 2ND PHOTOGRAPHER)
He isn't going to make any movies so far as I can see.

COWBOY: Do I detect a note of hostility?

JIM: No. No, but it wasn't right for you to give these people dope.
Look at Jaybird. Oh, Jaybird!

COWBOY: I didn't want to give either of them anything. It's their
own responsibility. Man, they're old enough to know what they're
doing.

JIM: Okay. All right. I'm not a moralist. But we should get the
chicks here. Oh, it didn't have to be chicks. Homosexuals would
do. Some kind of chorus. I should have seen to it myself. You people are so unreliable.

JAYBIRD: (*Mumbles*) It's out of my hands! It's out of my hands!
There is this wall between you and me, Jim. So that's what it
does!

JIM: I want a good show too. Is that too much? You know it's every penny I've got. You can't go on amusing yourself! Get girls or something. I'm telling you that'll do it, man.

LEACH: Maybe you would like to turn on, too. Since you're not a moralist.

JIM: No.
(*Points to his head*)
I've got a brain. Why are you cats really here?

LEACH: It's fun.

SOLLY: The money.

ERNIE: It's something to do.

COWBOY: Because we all love you.
(JIM *exits.*)

LEACH: I'm not high, Cowboy.

COWBOY: Wait awhile, man. Don't hurry it. Enjoy it, baby.

LEACH: I didn't get a flash, Cowboy, I didn't get a flash.

COWBOY: (*Laughs*) It's been ten years since I've had a flash. Just sit down and look at a picture book.
(ERNIE *blows his mouthpiece.*)
Not while I'm around. No, no. Practice in your bathroom. Hey, Solly, what did your White Sox [or any current sports reference] do today?

SOLLY: The Yankees [or any appropriate sports reference] beat them. Again. There's the worst habit I know—the congenital losers.

COWBOY: It's only a game. How did that new shortstop do?

LEACH: You square bastards! Square daytime bastards. Baseball ain't hip.

SAM: I ain't hip. Do you call it hip spending half the time in jail?
(*Nods*)

LEACH: They haven't got me yet.

COWBOY: You better expect it. Besides, what's wrong with day jobs?
Or being square? Man, I haven't anything against them. There are
lousy hipsters and lousy squares. Personally I couldn't make the
daily work scene. I like my work hours as they are. But it doesn't
make me any better. No, man, no.

LEACH: You know what I'd do if I had a day job? Man, I'd work
about six months and then establish credit. You know what I
mean? Then I'd get every charge card there is. Food, liquor and
travel. Man, I'd go all over the world. What could they do?
Throw me in debtor's prison? Not in America. No sir, we're free
here. You know what I mean? Man . . .

COWBOY: What movies you been watching?

LEACH: Others have done it.

COWBOY: Seems like a lot of work. An awful lot of work. Could you
work six months? At what?
(*Sings*)
I'm dreaming of a white Christmas, just like the ones I used to
know.
(*Says*)
You know we live in a white society. Did you ever see black snow?

SAM: (*Wakes up*) Who said snow?

SOLLY: I've seen brown heroin from Mexico.

COWBOY: But that's Mexico.

LEACH: I'm not high, Cowboy, I'm not high.

COWBOY: Give it time. Go eat something. Read a picture book.
Man, walk outside and let life—

MAN: (*In audience*) I gave Sam five bucks and I want a story. I want a story from Sam.

COWBOY: Who said that? Stand up.

MAN: (*Stands*) I want a story.

COWBOY: Insistent bastard.
(*Takes hoop and wakes* SAM)
Here, man, roll out some kind of jive. It's that cat there. Did he give you five?

SAM: Yeah. Can't you see that someone gave me five?

COWBOY: Then tell him a story.

SAM: (*Intermittently scratching his face and body*) Three, four years ago: let's see, there was me and the Cowboy and Leach. Yeah. Leach was selling books downtown. He always walked out of that store with one under his coat. Cowboy and he had a pad down near the waterfront. Me? I was scuffling. As usual. The point is we were very hot. I don't know whose fault that was. Leach can be loud. Scream like a bitch in heat. Of course, Cowboy's and my record speak for itself. Anyway, what I last remember is how it first began. Shiiit. Is that what I wanted to say? Man, this is very nice stuff. Anyway, there was a party. Leach was bribing this hustler with good old heroin. Funny thing, Leach always seems to have a place. If he and I have the same amount of money, I wind up on the street and he always got a weird kind of joint with foolish signs all around. This party. Did I tell you about the party? Kelly was there. He had his harem, too. That was when we called Kelly "Upsidedownface!" He didn't like it. He did have that kind of head. But, he always had three or four chicks with him. And did he like them go-go pills! Man, he took thirty or forty benzedrine a day. And believe me, I was brought up to believe that it was best to have just one man and one bitch in bed at the same time. But Upsidedownface wouldn't be satisfied with less than two and usually more. Maybe that's got something to do with him hanging himself. I don't know. That night one of his chicks was taking the trouble to bring me beer and to rub up against me. Man, she was a beautiful animal. Oh! Well, she was hung up in her head like everyone else I know. She kept talking about how she always wanted to marry a Negro. She came from the South or something. She kept calling me her Black Prince. Well, I don't care what a bitch say with her mouth. It's what she say with her body that has got my eye. Upsidedownface is a generous person. If you let him announce to everyone what you can take away from him. You dig? While he was announcing the departure of the chick from his harem, the phonograph was playing and Leach was arguing with this bitch he invited. I think he was kissing her breasts or something. What made it an argument was that there were so many people around. Prostitutes sure can have prissy morals. The woman next door started complaining, knocking on the walls. Finally she came over. Leach told her off. About ten minutes later the cops knock politely on the door. They come in. What's going on here? Who rents this apartment? What's your name? and yours? Those sort of questions. We all played it cool. No searching. Nothing like that. The party went on. Not the same. The cops shake everyone. But, in a curious way, most cops and junkies are alike. Sado . . . Solly, sado what?

SOLLY: Masochist.

SAM: Anyway, we wondered if they would come back. People left, the music stopped. Leach started bitching. He felt insulted that everyone was going. The cops didn't come back. About a week later to the day we three were in the pad again. Cowboy cooked dinner that night. Ham. And peas. Yeah. We were finished eating and Leach was teaching me how to play chess. Which meant that he was playing with himself. He moved all the pieces and I would sit back and stroke my chin and say, "Yeah. Yeah." Cowboy was reading some kind of hot book. The phone rings and it is some chick that doesn't particularly knock Leach out. But he gives a story and makes a date. I suppose this was to make Cowboy and me jealous. Leach has a funny mind. He tell us that he will be back at eleven o'clock. Sure. After he leaves, Cowboy pulls out some marijuana and we get high and have a few laughs about Leach. I was going to sleep.
(Footsteps offstage, coming and going.)
On the wall that I was looking at was a painting in orange and

red, circles and lines. They began moving out of the painting and
in my head, you know what I mean? Next thing I know the door
is knocked down and these two guys with guns are over Cowboy
and me. Wham! We're thrown against the wall. Well, this is old
stuff in a way. If that sort of thing can ever be old stuff. First
there is the scare. A few whacks and threats and we are supposed
to tell all. All? Actually, Cowboy and I didn't know Leach had
hidden about a quarter of an ounce in the couch. The greedy
bastard! Then something funny happened. It seemed that they
were after Leach. They looked at our arms. They could have
thrown us in jail for those long snakes of old needle marks. Or
they could have claimed that it was our stuff that they had found.
But no. For some reason they know that Leach rented the apartment and they wanted him. Perhaps they thought he was the King
of the Junkie World. That's what the papers call every squirt that
is caught. Cowboy tells them that we are supposed to meet Leach
in a certain bar not too far. Meanwhile, it is getting very close to
eleven o'clock. They fall for it and we leave and start walking up
the block. Arm in arm, of course. Leach is walking straight towards
us. He's got this chick with him. Cowboy drops his cigarette and
bends down to get it. While the cops are watching him, I raised
my hand to my mouth. Leach got the idea, and kicks the chick
who is about to scream hello to us. They walked right by. We
didn't see Leach for two years. Heard he went to Texas, or some
place unfit for humans. Anyway, we go into this candlelighted bar
and the Cowboy looks very carefully at everyone. The cops hurry
him up. So Cowboy gets mad and picks out a rather well-tailored
looking kid. Bing! They collar him, and take him along with us to
the station. That poor kid screamed all the way down to the station and they put him in the observation room. They let us go. I
don't know if they ever let that kid go. Man, that was a long one.
I'm tired.
(*Mumbles and stretches, then sits*)

JAYBIRD: (*Stands. Scratches face and body*) You cats are actors?

COWBOY: I'm not acting. You should have thought about that when
you hired us.

JAYBIRD: I'm not angry. Just amused. All you do is talk, talk, talk. Is there no end to this babbling?
(*Calms himself*)
This part was to be blood and guts drama. It's not for me that I plead with you. Think of the audience. Jimmie thinks of the audiences. I dream about them. So far one would think this was a drawing room comedy. If you were in the audience you'd know what I'm talking about. Listen, I researched everything carefully. I lived among you. Now what are you doing? You've all changed. Man, you aren't supposed to change. Just act naturally. Is that all you know—destruction? I know better. Maybe it's the audience. It's that? They're making you nervous. They're making me nervous. Maybe we should have tried it without an audience the first few nights.
(*Starts to fall asleep*)

COWBOY: It's not the audience, Jaybird.

JAYBIRD: Don't feel inadequate. After all, I have a prison record too. We've all been in the army. We're veterans, you and I. We're veterans.
(*Laughs*)
(ERNIE *blows his mouthpiece*)

COWBOY: I feel great, don't you, man?

JAYBIRD: I don't know . . . I don't know what's happening to me.
(*Wearily*)
I do know that there isn't any hero in this play. I wrote a play with four heroes. Didn't I explain that part? You are all heroes. I mean in the theatrical sense. Cowboy, can't you act like a hero? It's the basis of Western drama, you know. Can't you make an heroic speech? You have not been upstaging it, at all. Look what you've done to the cameraman. Where's the other photographer?
(1ST PHOTOGRAPHER *enters from audience.*)
We want some angle shots of Cowboy. Our hero.
(2ND PHOTOGRAPHER *wakes up and wobbles around* COWBOY *with* 1ST PHOTOGRAPHER.)

Cowboy, you can do for the show, Cowboy. We're all together. Say something.

COWBOY: It's too much risk going out and scoring every night. I mean I'm followed every night and I have to scheme a way of getting back here. I'm tired. Man, I've been moving my whole life. You think I enjoy leaving love behind? I haven't anything to say. Is that what you wanted, Author?
(*To the photographers*)
I'm sick of the sight of you fake beboppers.
(*He takes hold of the* 1ST PHOTOGRAPHER *and pushes him to the end of the stage*)
Get out of here! I'm sick of the sight of you.
(*To the author*)
Sit down and quit worrying about your precious play. Sit down, Mother. Damn it! You can't find anything out about anything by flirting with people. What do you think we live in, a freak show? You be the hero. Relax, we won't run out on you. You're just high.

LEACH: (*Softly at first*) I'm not high. I'm not high at all. You know what I mean? I want more. Cowboy? Cowboy? You have some left. I'm not high. It's mine, Cowboy. Strictly speaking, it's mine and I want some more. Everybody's high and I'm not. You didn't give me as much as you gave them.

COWBOY: Now, baby, why should I want to cheat you?

LEACH: I want more.

COWBOY: Man, you are high. That shit is in your system.

LEACH: I want more.

COWBOY: Okay, it's your life.
(*Exit* COWBOY. *Musicians play.* COWBOY *enters and gives* LEACH *a small package.* LEACH *performs the ritual of fixing and taking the heroin. No one pays any attention to him. He falls, dropping the "works."*)

COWBOY: There goes my last spike!
(*Goes to* LEACH. *He realizes* LEACH *has taken an overdose*)
Sam!
(SAM *slowly goes to him. One by one the musicians stop playing.*
COWBOY *and* SAM *bring* LEACH *to the couch.* COWBOY *starts
artificial respiration.*)

2ND MUSICIAN: Give him a salt shot.

COWBOY: That was my last spike.

3RD MUSICIAN: Let's pack up.

4TH MUSICIAN: Let's get to that gig.
(COWBOY *and* SAM *walk* LEACH *back and forth. He doesn't respond. They lay him on the couch.* JAYBIRD *starts to* LEACH *but
stops and sits again.*)

ERNIE: I'm leaving. I don't like it. You know what I mean? I've got
a gig tonight. I've got to find a horn to use. You dig?

2ND MUSICIAN: Can we help?

SAM: No, you might as well make that gig.
(ERNIE *exits.*)
Chicken shit!
(*Musicians exit, each saying:* "We'll see you tomorrow, Cow-
boy.")
Later on, gentlemen, later on.
(*Looks at* SOLLY)
Why don't you go, too?

SOLLY: I'm not in a hurry.

SAM: (*Picks up and plays with the hoop*) I'm sorry, Solly. But that
bastard Ernie just upsets me. He always runs out. He hasn't
played that rotten horn for five years now. And him coming on
like he was the great artist of something or other. Bullshitter.
(JAYBIRD *again starts to* LEACH *but stops and sits.*)

SOLLY: How is he?

COWBOY: Not good.

SOLLY: Shall I get a doctor?

COWBOY: No, not yet. No use of all of us getting in trouble.

SAM: I remember when that bastard Ernie threw a kid who took an overdose out the window. Didn't even know whether he was dead or not.

SOLLY: We never found out for sure.

SAM: I always believed it.
(*Rolls hoop to the other side of the stage*)

LEACH: (*Mumbles*) Three eighty four. Three eighty four. My number's up. I can see it.
(*Laughs crazily*)

JAYBIRD: Is he dying?
(*Mumbles*)
Why did I start this?
(*Sits next to* SOLLY)

SOLLY: I don't blame Ernie for leaving. Listen to that madman.

SAM: Well, he's alive.

SOLLY: Which one?
(*Pause*)
I ever tell you the Chinese laundry story? It was in Chicago. I was living above this Chinese laundry and one day the owner knocked on my door and told me that my bathroom was leaking into his store. I told him he could fix it if he wanted to. And he did! Which flipped me because he was a notorious cheap skate. At that time shit was relatively scarce and I had to go out of the city to score. One afternoon I happened to be sitting on the front fire

escape and I noticed some photographers taking pictures of the building. I couldn't figure it out. Besides, I was very high and got paranoid and went inside. That afternoon the headlines were screaming about the biggest narcotics ring in America being rounded up. Where? Downstairs. Two million dollars worth of opium right under my leaking bathroom and I had to go miles to get a pittance. At least I made the front page.

SAM: That's a good five dollar story.

LEACH: (*Still in a coma*) They're coming! Hide! Hide. You can't have me!

SOLLY: Is he all right?

COWBOY: The more he talks the better I'll feel.

SOLLY: Yes, he'll probably live. Whatever that means. I don't think there is such a thing as learning a lesson. At least not with him. Somehow you get the feeling Leach will try again and again until he kills himself. Or the cops get him and he spends a few years in jail. Talking calms me. There is something perverse in me looking for meaning all the time.

LEACH: Who killed Cock Robin?
(*Insistent*)
Who killed Cock Robin?

COWBOY: I don't know what he's talking about and I don't know what you're talking about. And once more, babies, I don't care. But, both of you keep blowing. Just blow.

SOLLY: I can remember that when I was a kid the word marijuana was in the dictionary between marigold and marimba.

SAM: It probably still is.
(*Lights a book of matches, then stamps them out*)
Hey, man, how long has heroin been illegal?

SOLLY: In this country since 1928, I think.

SAM: Why? I mean, man, why did they make it illegal?

SOLLY: I really don't know. To protect people from themselves. Maybe popular opinion. Maybe the liquor lobby. I once heard it was a plot of the rich. Beats me.

SAM: I wish I knew.

COWBOY: Who cares? Man, they got a bomb, haven't they? Protect us from ourselves. Man, the Japanese cats don't feel that way. That's your theory, Solly. Just a theory. Doesn't have anything to do with us.

SOLLY: Well, Leach doesn't need any theories, if that's what you mean.

COWBOY: Everything that's illegal is illegal because it makes more money for more people that way.

SOLLY: That may be right. But, junk does take its effect.

COWBOY: We all pay our dues whatever we do.

JAYBIRD: (*Mumbles incoherently. Wakes up*) So they all left. What happened to the ending? We've lost the end. Well, well. All's well. Is he dead?

COWBOY: No.

SOLLY: You look like the Jaybird I first met.

JAYBIRD: Mmph. I'm here and you're here. Just like a couple of months ago. Something happened in between. Maybe the idea of an audience. But . . .
(*He touches* SOLLY's *shoulder*)
I'm still alone and naïve. And hooked on people. All sentiment aside, why don't you cats kick junk?

SOLLY: How many times have we heard someone swearing he was going to kick?
(*No answer*)
I look out this window and watch the crowds looking into store windows. I try to remember that they are human beings. Most of the time, it doesn't make sense. When I talk, I'm a pessimist. Yet, I want to live. I don't jump into the street against the lights and just miss killing myself a hundred times a day. That's what happens out there. And in here, too. Why are some hunted and others hunt? The tyranny of the majority. I remember once I moved out of a hotel without paying the old Italian who ran it. Two months later I was walking by the hotel and he ran out after me. He wanted to grab me by the collar and start a fight. Instead he looked at me and said, "You aren't one of the people." Now what in God's creation did he mean?
(*Pause on stage.*)

JIM: (*Enters from audience*) I'm getting panicked. I'm getting panicked. There's a rumor the fuzz are coming. The fuzz are coming. We're going to get busted. Busted. Oh, the publicity! What's wrong with you?

JAYBIRD: I'm sick. We've lost it. We've lost it.
(*Stands*)

JIM: What have we lost?

JAYBIRD: The end, you fool. The end.

JIM: (*Thinks*) We'll all die. That's a great idea for you. We just die.

SOLLY: Don't be silly. I can't. I'm out of it.

JIM: That's not the point. How do you propose to get off stage logically? Ah, you see. Shakespeare, tragedy, that sort of thing has been making it for a long time. This is a time-tested formula. What more can you ask? I'll die too. Don't think I'm not willing

to die. If it will bring in the revenue. I'll die of exhaustion of carrying you off.
(*Laughs*)
You see? Perfect plot, eh, Jaybird.

JAYBIRD: You stink!

JIM: All right, so I hired photographers. One of them had to take a shot.

JAYBIRD: I'm not blaming you. How did I ever get into this? Oh, yes . . .
(*Pacing the stage*)
. . . I wanted to do something far out. Yes, I'm guilty of trying to have a little shock value. Is there a politician in the house? Then I've failed.

JIM: It wasn't your fault. We should have had chicks. You planned it with chicks and it was my fault they didn't show up. Maybe we'll get them for the movie version. Besides I thought you'd be delighted with my photographer idea. I thought you liked Dada.

JAYBIRD: Shut up!
(*Long pause*)
It was my fault. I thought perhaps the doctors would take over. That's the message for tonight from me. Maybe I'm supposed to be the hero. But I'm not a martyr. We don't need women. We need a martyr. Let Dada doctors take control of narcotics.

COWBOY: Man, doctors wouldn't help me. I'd be out of a job. Hell, the doctors would be the big connection.

SOLLY: I don't trust them. Those are the people who mildly electrocute thousands of people every year. And how many prefrontal lobotomies are performed? Oh, no. I don't trust them as a group any more than I trust the police as a group. Or Junkies, especially the likes of Ernie and Leach.

JAYBIRD: Yes.

SAM: Why didn't you get on the H-Bomb riff? If you needed a riff. I've always liked mushrooms.

JIM: I've had a run for my money.

JAYBIRD: All right. All right. So that isn't the answer. I've lost it. But one thing I've learned about the theatre. I believe it all fits together.

SOLLY: It doesn't have to fit.

JAYBIRD: Yes. Yes, it does. We wouldn't all be on stage if it didn't fit. That's what I had in mind in the first place. I didn't learn anything. I knew it. Find a horror. Then you try to tell people it isn't a horror. And then I have the gall to be horrified. Well, if it wasn't junk, I would have been involved with something else.
(*Takes off* COWBOY's *red bandana*)

COWBOY: Well, doctor, that's very heroic.
(*Loud knocking on the door.*)

JAYBIRD: No doctors, no heroes, no martyrs, no Christs. That's a very good score. I didn't get burned. Maybe short counted, but not burned.
(*Pacing*)
It's all yours now.
(*Pause on stage.* JIM *opens the door. It is* HARRY. *He performs his record ritual. Lights slowly fade. Music ends in the dark.*)

END

KRAPP'S LAST TAPE
Samuel Beckett

KRAPP'S LAST TAPE

Krapp's Last Tape was first performed in London in 1958 and, after winning enormous acclaim there and in Paris, opened on a double bill with Edward Albee's *The Zoo Story* at New York's Provincetown Playhouse in January 1960.

As Brooks Atkinson wrote in the New York *Times,* "The whole portrait is wonderfully alive. If *Krapp's Last Tape* is a joke, the joke is not on Mr. Beckett!"

Jerry Tallmer of *The Village Voice,* who had by then established himself as Off-Broadway's most influential critic, wrote "*Krapp's Last Tape* is almost certainly the most amazing piece of 'incidental' writing of the decade. In one and the same pungent breath it is a comment on time past, passing, and to come; on the tinny mechanization of the age and the yet unquenchable wellsprings of the heart; on the anal desiccation and sterilization of all feelings or response in modern man, and his nevertheless immutable thrust toward love."

Samuel Beckett was born in Ireland in 1906 and in the late 1920s went to Paris, where he became James Joyce's secretary. During the 1930s he wrote many novels, but he turned to the theatre in the 1940s, writing in both French and English and serving as his own translator. After his play *Waiting for Godot* closed on Broadway after only a few weeks—dismissed by critics and audiences alike as little more than an avant-garde joke—Beckett's plays were produced in America exclusively Off-Broadway.

Beckett's plays seem extremely difficult to understand by those people who are unfamiliar with his work, but ironically this is the result of the plays' radical simplicity. Rather than adding layers of complexity, Beckett *eliminates* almost everything we think of as essential to theatre—realistic settings, "well-rounded" characters, conventional plot development—finding instead the drama of the unadorned human spirit. *Krapp's Last Tape*, for instance, is a one-character monologue in which virtually nothing happens except that an old man listens to a tape he recorded thirty years before, on his thirty-ninth birthday.

Beckett's plays seem despairing to those seeing or reading them for the first time—in *Krapp's Last Tape* the first sound uttered is a deep sigh, and by the end of the play Krapp seems to feel that all hope of happiness is irretrievably lost. Yet, considering that the play's theme is the passage of time and the elusiveness of identity, the work nevertheless ends in lyrical affirmation, leaving us in awe at the wonders of "memory and desire."

Krapp's Last Tape was performed on an almost totally darkened stage, with virtually no scenery—a table and chair, a lamp, a messy array of cartons—with very little movement, and with extended periods of silence. Veteran Canadian actor Donald Davis won an Obie Award for his largely mimed performance as Krapp (a role later memorably performed by Hume Cronyn).

In addition to the Obie Award for *Krapp's Last Tape*, Beckett has also won Obies for *Endgame* (1958), *Happy Days* (1962), *Play* (1964), and *Not I* (1973)—the total of five being the most won by any theatre artist to date, with the exception of American playwright Sam Shepard.

KRAPP'S LAST TAPE was first performed at the Royal Court Theatre in London on October 28, 1958. The play was directed by Donald McWhinnie.

KRAPP   *Patrick Magee*

KRAPP'S LAST TAPE was first performed in the United States at New York's Provincetown Playhouse in January 1960.

KRAPP   *Donald Davis*

A late evening in the future.

KRAPP's den.

Front centre a small table, the two drawers of which open towards audience.

Sitting at the table, facing front, i.e. across from the drawers, a wearish old man: KRAPP.

Rusty black narrow trousers too short for him. Rusty black sleeveless waistcoat, four capacious pockets. Heavy silver watch and chain. Grimy white shirt open at neck, no collar. Surprising pair of dirty white boots, size ten at least, very narrow and pointed.

White face. Purple nose. Disordered grey hair. Unshaven.

Very near-sighted (but unspectacled). Hard of hearing.

Cracked voice. Distinctive intonation.

Laborious walk.

On the table a tape-recorder with microphone and a number of card-board boxes containing reels of recorded tapes.

Table and immediately adjacent area in strong white light. Rest of stage in darkness.

KRAPP remains a moment motionless, heaves a great sigh, looks at his watch, fumbles in his pockets, takes out an envelope, puts it back, fumbles, takes out a small bunch of keys, raises it to his eyes, chooses a key, gets up and moves to front of table. He stoops, unlocks first drawer, peers into it, feels about inside it, takes out a reel of tape, peers at it, puts it back, locks drawer, unlocks second drawer, peers into it, feels about inside it, takes out a large banana, peers at it, locks drawer, puts keys back in his pocket. He turns, advances to edge of stage, halts, strokes banana, peels it, drops skin at his feet, puts end of banana in his mouth and remains motionless, staring vacuously before him. Finally he bites off the end, turns aside and begins pacing to and fro at edge of stage, in the light, i.e. not more than four or five paces either way, meditatively eating banana. He treads on skin, slips, nearly falls, recovers himself, stoops and peers at skin and finally pushes it, still stooping, with his foot over the edge of stage into pit. He resumes his pacing, finishes banana, returns to table, sits down, remains a moment motionless, heaves a great sigh, takes keys from his pockets, raises them to his eyes, chooses key, gets up and moves to front of table, unlocks second drawer, takes out a second large banana, peers at it, locks drawer, puts back keys in his pocket, turns, advances to edge of stage, halts, strokes banana, peels it, tosses skin into pit, puts end of banana in his mouth and remains motionless, staring vacuously before him. Finally he has an idea, puts banana in his waistcoat pocket, the end emerging, and goes with all the speed he can muster backstage into darkness. Ten seconds. Loud pop of cork. Fifteen seconds. He comes back into light carrying an old ledger and sits down at table. He lays ledger on table, wipes his mouth, wipes his hands on the front of his waistcoat, brings them smartly together and rubs them.

KRAPP: (*briskly*). Ah! (*He bends over ledger, turns the pages, finds the entry he wants, reads.*) Box . . . thrree . . . spool . . . five. (*He raises his head and stares front. With relish.*) Spool! (*Pause.*) Spooool! (*Happy smile. Pause. He bends over table, starts peering and poking at the boxes.*) Box . . . thrree . . . thrree . . . four . . . two . . . (*with surprise*) nine! good God! . . . seven . . . ah! the little rascal! (*He takes up box, peers at it.*) Box thrree. (*He lays it on table, opens it and peers at spools inside.*) Spool . . . (*he peers at ledger*) . . . five . . . (*he peers at spools*) . . . five . . . five . . . ah! the little scoundrel! (*He takes out a spool, peers at it.*) Spool five. (*He lays it on table, closes box three, puts it back with the others, takes up the spool.*) Box thrree, spool five. (*He bends over the machine, looks up. With relish.*) Spooool! (*Happy smile. He bends, loads spool on machine, rubs his hands.*) Ah! (*He peers at ledger, reads entry at foot of page.*) Mother at rest at last . . . Hm . . . The black ball . . . (*He raises his head, stares blankly front. Puzzled.*) Black ball? . . . (*He peers again at ledger, reads.*) The dark nurse . . .

(*He raises his head, broods, peers again at ledger, reads.*) Slight improvement in bowel condition . . . Hm . . . Memorable . . . what? (*He peers closer.*) Equinox, memorable equinox. (*He raises his head, stares blankly front. Puzzled.*) Memorable equinox? . . . (*Pause. He shrugs his shoulders, peers again at ledger, reads.*) Farewell to—(*he turns the page*)—love.

He raises his head, broods, bends over machine, switches on and assumes listening posture, i.e. leaning forward, elbows on table, hand cupping ear towards machine, face front.

TAPE: (*strong voice, rather pompous, clearly* KRAPP's *at a much earlier time.*) Thirty-nine today, sound as a—(*Settling himself more comfortably he knocks one of the boxes off the table, curses, switches off, sweeps boxes and ledger violently to the ground, winds tape back to beginning, switches on, resumes posture.*) Thirty-nine today, sound as a bell, apart from my old weakness, and intellectually I have now every reason to suspect at the . . . (*hesitates*) . . . crest of the wave—or thereabouts. Celebrated the awful occasion, as in recent years, quietly at the Winehouse. Not a soul. Sat before the fire with closed eyes, separating the grain from the husks. Jotted down a few notes, on the back of an envelope. Good to be back in my den, in my old rags. Have just eaten I regret to say three bananas and only with difficulty refrained from a fourth. Fatal things for a man with my condition. (*Vehemently.*) Cut 'em out! (*Pause.*) The new light above my table is a great improvement. With all this darkness round me I feel less alone. (*Pause.*) In a way. (*Pause.*) I love to get up and move about in it, then back here to . . . (*hesitates*) . . . me. (*Pause.*) Krapp.

Pause.

The grain, now what I wonder do I mean by that, I mean . . . (*hesitates*) . . . I suppose I mean those things worth having when all the dust has—when all *my* dust has settled. I close my eyes and try and imagine them.

Pause. KRAPP *closes his eyes briefly.*

Extraordinary silence this evening, I strain my ears and do not hear a sound. Old Miss McGlome always sings at this hour. But not tonight. Songs of her girlhood, she says. Hard to think of her as a girl. Wonderful woman though. Connaught, I fancy.

(*Pause.*) Shall I sing when I am her age, if I ever am? No. (*Pause.*) Did I sing as a boy? No. (*Pause.*) Did I ever sing? No. *Pause.*

Just been listening to an old year, passages at random. I did not check in the book, but it must be at least ten or twelve years ago. At that time I think I was still living on and off with Bianca in Kedar Street. Well out of that, Jesus yes! Hopeless business. (*Pause.*) Not much about her, apart from a tribute to her eyes. Very warm. I suddenly saw them again. (*Pause.*) Incomparable! (*Pause.*) Ah well . . . (*Pause.*) These old P.M.s are gruesome, but I often find them—(KRAPP *switches off, broods, switches on*) —a help before embarking on a new . . . (*hesitates*) . . . retrospect. Hard to believe I was ever that young whelp. The voice! Jesus! And the aspirations! (*Brief laugh in which* KRAPP *joins.*) And the resolutions! (*Brief laugh in which* KRAPP *joins.*) To drink less, in particular. (*Brief laugh of* KRAPP *alone.*) Statistics. Seventeen hundred hours, out of the preceding eight thousand odd, consumed on licensed premises alone. More than 20%, say 40% of his waking life. (*Pause.*) Plans for a less . . . (*hesitates*) . . . engrossing sexual life. Last illness of his father. Flagging pursuit of happiness. Unattainable laxation. Sneers at what he calls his youth and thanks to God that it's over. (*Pause.*) False ring there. (*Pause.*) Shadows of the opus . . . magnum. Closing with a— (*brief laugh*)—yelp to Providence. (*Prolonged laugh in which* KRAPP *joins.*) What remains of all that misery? A girl in a shabby green coat, on a railway-station platform? No? *Pause.*

When I look—

KRAPP *switches off, broods, looks at his watch, gets up, goes backstage into darkness. Ten seconds. Pop of cork. Ten seconds. Second cork. Ten seconds. Third cork. Ten seconds. Brief burst of quavering song.*

KRAPP: (*sings*).   Now the day is over,
                            Night is drawing nigh-igh,
                            Shadows—

Fit of coughing. He comes back into light, sits down, wipes his mouth, switches on, resumes his listening posture.

TAPE: —back on the year that is gone, with what I hope is perhaps a glint of the old eye to come, there is of course the house on the canal where mother lay a-dying, in the late autumn, after her long viduity (KRAPP *gives a start*), and the—(KRAPP *switches off, winds back tape a little, bends his ear closer to machine, switches on*)— a-dying, after her long viduity, and the—
KRAPP *switches off, raises his head, stares blankly before him. His lips move in the syllables of "viduity." No sound. He gets up, goes backstage into darkness, comes back with an enormous dictionary, lays it on table, sits down and looks up the word.*

KRAPP: (*reading from dictionary*). State—or condition of being—or remaining—a widow—or widower. (*Looks up. Puzzled.*) Being— or remaining? . . . (*Pause. He peers again at dictionary. Reading.*) "Deep weeds of viduity" . . . Also of an animal, especially a bird . . . the vidua or weaver-bird . . . Black plumage of male . . . (*He looks up. With relish.*) The vidua-bird!
Pause. He closes dictionary, switches on, resumes listening posture.

TAPE: —bench by the weir from where I could see her window. There I sat, in the biting wind, wishing she were gone. (*Pause.*) Hardly a soul, just a few regulars, nursemaids, infants, old men, dogs. I got to know them quite well—oh by appearance of course I mean! One dark young beauty I recollect particularly, all white and starch, incomparable bosom, with a big black hooded perambulator, most funereal thing. Whenever I looked in her direction she had her eyes on me. And yet when I was bold enough to speak to her—not having been introduced—she threatened to call a policeman. As if I had designs on her virtue! (*Laugh. Pause.*) The face she had! The eyes! Like . . . (*hesitates*) . . . chrysolite! (*Pause.*) Ah well . . . (*Pause.*) I was there when—(KRAPP *switches off, broods, switches on again*)—the blind went down, one of those dirty brown roller affairs, throwing a ball for a little white dog, as chance would have it. I happened to look up and there it was. All over and done with, at last. I sat on for a few moments with the ball in my hand and the dog yelping and pawing at me. (*Pause.*) Moments. Her moments, my moments. (*Pause.*)

The dog's moments. (*Pause.*) In the end I held it out to him and he took it in his mouth, gently, gently. A small, old, black, hard, solid rubber ball. (*Pause.*) I shall feel it, in my hand, until my dying day. (*Pause.*) I might have kept it. (*Pause.*) But I gave it to the dog.

Pause.

Ah well . . .

Pause.

Spiritually a year of profound gloom and indigence until that memorable night in March, at the end of the jetty, in the howling wind, never to be forgotten, when suddenly I saw the whole thing. The vision, at last. This I fancy is what I have chiefly to record this evening, against the day when my work will be done and perhaps no place left in my memory, warm or cold, for the miracle that . . . (*hesitates*) . . . for the fire that set it alight. What I suddenly saw then was this, that the belief I had been going on all my life, namely—(KRAPP *switches off impatiently, winds tape forward, switches on again*)—great granite rocks the foam flying up in the light of the lighthouse and the wind-gauge spinning like a propellor, clear to me at last that the dark I have always struggled to keep under is in reality my most—(KRAPP *curses, switches off, winds tape forward, switches on again*)—unshatterable association until my dissolution of storm and night with the light of the understanding and the fire—(KRAPP *curses louder, switches off, winds tape forward, switches on again*)—my face in her breasts and my hand on her. We lay there without moving. But under us all moved, and moved us, gently, up and down, and from side to side.

Pause.

Past midnight. Never knew such silence. The earth might be uninhabited.

Pause.

Here I end—

KRAPP *switches off, winds tape back, switches on again.*

—upper lake, with the punt, bathed off the bank, then pushed out into the stream and drifted. She lay stretched out on the floorboards with her hands under her head and her eyes closed. Sun blazing down, bit of a breeze, water nice and lively. I noticed a scratch on her thigh and asked her how she came by it. Picking gooseberries, she said. I said again I thought it was hopeless and no good going on, and she agreed, without opening her eyes. (*Pause.*) I asked her to look at me and after a few moments— (*pause*)—after a few moments she did, but the eyes just slits, because of the glare. I bent over her to get them in the shadow and they opened. (*Pause. Low.*) Let me in. (*Pause.*) We drifted in among the flags and stuck. The way they went down, sighing, before the stem! (*Pause.*) I lay down across her with my face in her breasts and my hand on her. We lay there without moving. But under us all moved, and moved us, gently, up and down, and from side to side.

Pause.

Past midnight. Never knew—

KRAPP *switches off, broods. Finally he fumbles in his pockets, encounters the banana, takes it out, peers at it, puts it back, fumbles, brings out the envelope, fumbles, puts back envelope, looks at his watch, gets up and goes backstage into darkness. Ten seconds. Sound of bottle against glass, then brief siphon. Ten seconds. Bottle against glass alone. Ten seconds. He comes back a little unsteadily into light, goes to front of table, takes out keys, raises them to his eyes, chooses key. Unlocks first drawer, peers into it, feels about inside, takes out reel, peers at it, locks drawer, puts keys back in his pocket, goes and sits down, takes reel off machine, lays it on dictionary, loads virgin reel on machine, takes envelope from his pocket, consults back of it, lays it on table, switches on, clears his throat and begins to record.*

KRAPP: Just been listening to that stupid bastard I took myself for thirty years ago, hard to believe I was ever as bad as that. Thank God that's all done with anyway. (*Pause.*) The eyes she had! (*Broods, realizes he is recording silence, switches off, broods. Finally.*) Everything there, everything, all the—(*Realizes this is not being recorded, switches on.*) Everything there, everything on this old muckball, all the light and dark and famine and feasting of . . . (*hesitates*) . . . the ages! (*In a shout.*) Yes! (*Pause.*) Let that go! Jesus! Take his mind off his homework! Jesus! (*Pause. Weary.*) Ah well, maybe he was right. (*Pause.*) Maybe he was right. (*Broods. Realizes. Switches off. Consults envelope.*) Pah! (*Crumples it and throws it away. Broods. Switches on.*) Nothing to say, not a squeak. What's a year now? The sour cud and the iron stool. (*Pause.*) Revelled in the word spool. (*With relish.*) Spooool! Happiest moment of the past half million. (*Pause.*) Seventeen copies sold, of which eleven at trade price to free circulating libraries beyond the seas. Getting known. (*Pause.*) One pound six and something, eight I have little doubt. (*Pause.*) Crawled out once or twice, before the summer was cold. Sat shivering in the park, drowned in dreams and burning to be gone. Not a soul. (*Pause.*) Last fancies. (*Vehemently.*) Keep 'em under. (*Pause.*) Scalded the eyes out of me reading *Effie* again, a page a day, with tears again. Effie . . . (*Pause.*) Could have been happy with her, up there on the Baltic, and the pines, and the dunes. (*Pause.*) Could I? (*Pause.*) And she? (*Pause.*) Pah! (*Pause.*) Fanny came in a couple of times. Bony old ghost of a whore. Couldn't do much, but I suppose better than a kick in the crutch. The last time wasn't so bad. How do you manage it, she said, at your age? I told her I'd been saving up for her all my life. (*Pause.*) Went to Vespers once, like when I was in short trousers. (*Pause. Sings.*)

> Now the day is over,
> Night is drawing nigh-igh,
> Shadows—(*coughing, then almost*
>   *inaudible*)—of the evening
> Steal across the sky.

(*Gasping.*) Went to sleep and fell off the pew. (*Pause.*) Sometimes wondered in the night if a last effort mightn't—(*Pause.*) Ah finish your booze now and get to your bed. Go on with this drivel in the morning. Or leave it at that. (*Pause.*) Leave it at that. (*Pause.*) Lie propped up in the dark—and wander. Be again in the dingle on a Christmas Eve, gathering holly, the red-berried. (*Pause.*) Be again on Croghan on a Sunday morning, in the haze, with the bitch, stop and listen to the bells. (*Pause.*) And so on. (*Pause.*) Be again, be again. (*Pause.*) All that old misery. (*Pause.*) Once wasn't enough for you. (*Pause.*) Lie down across her.

Long pause. He suddenly bends over machine, switches off, wrenches off tape, throws it away, puts on the other, winds it forward to the passage he wants, switches on, listens staring front.

TAPE: —gooseberries, she said. I said again I thought it was hopeless and no good going on, and she agreed, without opening her eyes. (*Pause.*) I asked her to look at me and after a few moments— (*pause*)—after a few moments she did, but the eyes just slits, because of the glare. I bent over her to get them in the shadow and they opened. (*Pause. Low.*) Let me in. (*Pause.*) We drifted in among the flags and stuck. The way they went down, sighing, before the stem! (*Pause.*) I lay down across her with my face in her breasts and my hand on her. We lay there without moving. But under us all moved, and moved us, gently, up and down, and from side to side.

Pause. KRAPP'*s lips move. No sound.*

Past midnight. Never knew such silence. The earth might be uninhabited.

Pause.

Here I end this reel. Box—(*pause*)—three, spool—(*pause*)—five. (*Pause.*) Perhaps my best years are gone. When there was a chance of happiness. But I wouldn't want them back. Not with the fire in me now. No, I wouldn't want them back.

KRAPP *motionless staring before him. The tape runs on in silence.*

CURTAIN

THE BLACKS
a clown show
Jean Genet

TRANSLATED BY BERNARD FRECHTMAN

Originally published as *Les Nègres*
by Marc Barbezat, Décines, Isère, France, 1958

THE BLACKS

"One evening an actor asked me to write a play for an all-black cast," Jean Genet wrote in the preface to the published version of *The Blacks*. "But what exactly is a black? First of all, what's his color?" From this we know at once that *The Blacks* is not going to deal straightforwardly with the subjects of race and racial injustice, as such plays had done before. Rather, *The Blacks* has many levels of action and meaning. Genet presents a play within a play, a ceremony in which black actors re-enact the murder of a white woman before a group of white judges (actually black actors wearing white masks). In the process, he shows the relationship between acting a role and being considered a member of a racial group, and how role-playing determines the ways in which people view each other. This is a play in which ritual, ceremony, and even magic illuminate the sources of man's inhumanity to man.

Howard Taubman, in the New York *Times*, wrote: "On any level that matters, Jean Genet's *The Blacks* is an event . . . Genet is like a demonic sorcerer. He pours startling phrases, images, and attitudes into his witches' brew, and the potion he offers you is strange and familiar, shocking and seductive, exhilarating to the eye and ear and provocative to the mind."

Newsweek magazine proclaimed: "Genet has strong claims to be considered the greatest living playwright."

In one of the few theatre reviews of his career, Norman Mailer wrote that "*The Blacks* gives life because it is a work of perceptions which slice like razors; it cuts at once through the cancerous smog of partial visions and dim faith."

Jean Genet, a white Frenchman, was born a foundling, raised in reformatories, and spent most of his first thirty years as a petty thief. The first of his many novels was written in prison in 1942, and seven years later a petition signed by such artists as Jean Cocteau, Pablo Picasso, and Jean-Paul Sartre secured his release. *The Balcony* was Genet's first play produced in America, and it won an Obie Award in 1959.

The Blacks, after its premiere in Paris in 1959—where it was staged by the legendary director Roger Blin—opened at the St. Mark's Playhouse in New York in May 1961. The production was staged on a series of platforms connected by a curving ramp, with sumptuous costumes and masks, and with luxuriant music and movement.

In addition to Genet's Obie Award for *The Blacks*, other Obie recipients were Godfrey Cambridge, for his performance as Diouf, and Bernard Frechtman for his translation. Other members of the cast—all of whom were at the very beginning of their careers—were such outstanding performers as James Earl Jones, Cicely Tyson, and Lou Gossett. A small role was played by Charles Gordone, who in 1969 became the first black author to win the Pulitzer Prize for Drama for his play *No Place to Be Somebody*.

THE BLACKS (*Les Nègres*) was performed for the first time on October 28, 1959 at the Théatre de Lutèce in Paris. The play was directed by Roger Blin.

The Blacks was first performed in the United States on May 4, 1961 at the St. Mark's Playhouse in New York City. The cast, in order of appearance, was as follows:

ROSCOE LEE BROWNE	*Archibald Absalom Wellington*
JAMES EARL JONES	*Deodatus Village*
CYNTHIA BELGRAVE	*Adelaide Bobo*
LOUIS GOSSETT	*Edgar Alas Newport News*
ETHEL AYLER	*Augusta Snow*
HELEN MARTIN	*Felicity Trollop Pardon*
CICELY TYSON	*Stephanie Virtue Secret-rose Diop*
GODFREY M. CAMBRIDGE	*Diouf*
LEX MONSON	*Missionary*
RAYMOND ST. JACQUES	*Judge*
JAY J. RILEY	*Governor*
MAYA ANGELOU MAKE	*Queen*
CHARLES GORDONE	*Valet*
CHARLES CAMPBELL	*Drummer*

The play was produced by Sidney Bernstein, George Edgar and André Gregory, by arrangement with Geraldine Lust, and was directed by Gene Frankel. The sets were designed by Kim E. Swados, the costumes and masks by Patricia Zipprodt, the lighting by Lee Watson, the movement by Talley Beatty, and the music supervised by Charles Gross.

One evening an actor asked me to write a play for an all-black cast. But what exactly is a black? First of all, what's his color?

This play, written by a white man, is intended for a white audience, but if, which is unlikely, it is ever performed before a black audience, then a white person, male or female, should be invited every evening. The organizer of the show should welcome him formally, dress him in ceremonial costume and lead him to his seat, preferably in the front row of the orchestra. The actors will play for him. A spotlight should be focused upon this symbolic white throughout the performance.

But what if no white person accepted? Then let white masks be distributed to the black spectators as they enter the theatre. And if the blacks refuse the masks, then let a dummy be used.

J.G.

The curtain is drawn. Not raised—drawn.

THE SET: *Black velvet curtains. Right and left, a few sets of tiers with landings of different heights. One of them, far in the background, toward the right, is higher than the others. Another, rather like a gallery, goes up to the flies and all around the stage. That is where the Court will appear. A green screen is set on a higher landing, just a trifle lower than the one mentioned above. In the middle of the stage, on the floor, a catafalque, covered with a white cloth. On the catafalque, bouquets of flowers: irises, roses, gladiolas, arum lilies. At the foot of the catafalque, a shoeshine box. The lighting: very garish neon light.*

When the curtain is drawn, four NEGROES *in evening clothes—no, one of them,* NEWPORT NEWS, *who is barefoot, is wearing a woolen sweater—and four negresses in evening gowns are dancing a kind of minuet around the catafalque to an air of Mozart which they whistle and hum. The evening clothes—white ties for the gentlemen— are accompanied by tan shoes. The ladies' costumes—heavily spangled evening gowns—suggest fake elegance, the very height of bad taste. As they dance and whistle, they pluck flowers from their bodices and lapels and lay them on the catafalque. Suddenly, on the high platform, left, enters the Court.*

THE COURT. *Each actor playing a member of the Court is a masked Negro whose mask represents the face of a white person. The mask is worn in such a way that the audience sees a wide black band all around it, and even the actor's kinky hair.*

THE QUEEN. *White, sad mask. Drooping mouth. Royal crown on her head. Sceptre in her hand. Ermine-trimmed cloak with a train. Superb gown. At her right:*

HER VALET. *A puny, mincing little fellow wearing a valet's striped waistcoat. On his arm a towel, with which he toys as if it were a scarf, but with which he will wipe Her Majesty's eyes.*

THE GOVERNOR. *Sublime uniform. Is holding a pair of field glasses.*

THE JUDGE. *Black and red robe. At* THE QUEEN'S *left.*

THE MISSIONARY. *White robe. Rings. Pectoral cross. At* THE JUDGE'S *left.*

The members of the Court, all standing on the same tier, seem interested in the spectacle of the dancing NEGROES, *who suddenly stop short, breaking off the minuet.* THE NEGROES *approach the footlights, make a ninety degree turn, and bow ceremoniously to the Court, then to the audience. One of them steps forth and speaks, addressing now the audience, now the Court:*

ARCHIBALD: Ladies and gentlemen . . . (*The Court burst into very shrill, but very well orchestrated laughter. It is not free and easy laughter. This laughter is echoed by the same but even shriller laughter of* THE NEGROES *who are standing about* ARCHIBALD. *The Court, bewildered, becomes silent.*) . . . My name is Archibald Absalom Wellington. (*He bows, then moves from one to the other, naming each in turn.*) . . . This is Mr. Deodatus Village (*he bows*) . . . Miss Adelaide Bobo (*she bows*) . . . Mr. Edgar Alas Newport News (*he bows*) . . . Mrs. Augusta Snow (*she remains upright*) . . . well . . . well . . . madam (*roaring angrily*) bow! (*she remains upright*) . . . I'm asking you, madam, to bow! (*extremely gentle, almost grieved*) I'm asking you, madam, to bow—it's a performance. (SNOW *bows*) . . . Mrs. Felicity Trollop Pardon (*she bows*) . . . and Miss Diop—Stephanie Virtue Secret-rose Diop.

DIOUF: And me.

ARCHIBALD: And he.—As you see, ladies and gentlemen, just as you have your lilies and roses, so we—in order to serve you—shall use our beautiful, shiny black make-up. It is Mr. Deodatus Village who gathers the smoke-black and Mrs. Felicity Trollop Pardon who thins it out in our saliva. These ladies help her. We embellish ourselves so as to please you. You are white. And spectators. This evening we shall perform for you . . .

THE QUEEN: (*interrupting the speaker*) Bishop! Bishop-at-large!

THE MISSIONARY: (*leaning toward her, though without changing place*) Hallelujah!

THE QUEEN: (*plaintively*) Are they going to kill her? (THE NEGROES *below burst into the same shrill and orchestrated laughter as before. But* ARCHIBALD *silences them.*)

ARCHIBALD: Be quiet. If all they have is their nostalgia, let them enjoy it.

SNOW: Grief, sir, is another of their adornments . . .

THE VALET: (*looking about him*) What's happened to my chair?

THE MISSIONARY: (*doing the same*) And to mine? Who took it?

THE VALET: (*to* THE MISSIONARY, *querulously*) If my chair hadn't disappeared too, you'd have suspected me. It was my turn to sit down, but I don't know where the hell my chair is. You can count on my good humor and devotion if I have to remain standing all through the show.

THE QUEEN: (*increasingly languid*) I repeat—are they going to kill her?

THE MISSIONARY: (*very somberly*) But Madam . . . (A *pause*) she's dead!

THE VALET: Is that all you can say to your sovereign? (*as if to himself*) This crowd could stand a good clouting.

THE MISSIONARY: The poor unfortunate has been in my prayers since this morning. In the very forefront.

THE QUEEN: (*leaning forward to call* SNOW) Is it true, young lady, that all we have left is our sadness and that it's one of our adornments?

ARCHIBALD: And we haven't finished embellishing you. This evening we've come again to round out your grief.

THE GOVERNOR: (*shaking his fist and making as if to descend*) If I let you!

THE VALET: (*holding him back*) Where are you going?

THE GOVERNOR: (*with a martial air*) To stamp out the Blacks!
(THE NEGROES *below shrug their shoulders in unison.*)

ARCHIBALD: Be quiet. (*to the audience*) This evening we shall perform for you. But, in order that you may remain comfortably settled in your seats in the presence of the drama that is already unfolding here, in order that you be assured that there is no danger of such a drama's worming its way into your precious lives, we shall even have the decency—a decency learned from you—to make communication impossible. We shall increase the distance that separates us—a distance that is basic—by our pomp, our manners, our insolence—for we are also actors. When my speech is over, everything here—(*he stamps his foot in a gesture of rage*) here!—will take place in the delicate world of reprobation. If we sever bonds, may a continent drift off and may Africa sink or fly away . . .
(*For some moments,* THE GOVERNOR, *who had taken a paper from his pocket, has been reading in a low voice.*)

THE QUEEN: May it fly away—was that a metaphor?

THE GOVERNOR: (*reading more and more loudly*) ". . . when I fall to earth, scurvily pierced by your spears, look closely, you will behold my ascension. (*in a thundering voice*) My corpse will be on the ground, but my soul and body will rise into the air . . ."

THE VALET: (*shrugging his shoulders*) Learn your role backstage. As for that last sentence, it oughtn't to be rolled off as if it were a proclamation.

THE GOVERNOR: (*turning to* THE VALET) I know what I'm doing. (*He resumes his reading.*) "You'll see them and you'll die of fright. First, you'll turn pale, and then you'll fall, and you'll be dead . . ." (*He folds the paper and puts it back into his pocket very conspicuously.*) That was a device to let them know that we know. And we know that we've come to attend our own funeral rites. They think they're compelling us, but it is owing to our good breeding that we shall descend to death. Our suicide . . .

THE QUEEN: (*touching* THE GOVERNOR *with her fan*) . . . Preparations for it have begun, but let the Negro speak. Look at that poor, gaping mouth of his, and those columns of flies streaming out of it . . . (*she looks more closely, leaning forward*) . . . or swarming into it. (*to* ARCHIBALD) Continue.

ARCHIBALD: (*after bowing to* THE QUEEN) . . . sink or fly away. (*The members of the Court protect their faces, as if a bird were flying at them.*) . . . but let it be off! (*A pause.*) When we leave this stage, we are involved in your life. I am a cook, this lady is a sewing-maid, this gentleman is a medical student, this gentleman is a curate at St. Anne's, this lady . . . skip it. Tonight, our sole concern will be to entertain you. So we have killed this white woman. There she lies. (*He points to the catafalque. The members of the Court wipe away a tear with a very theatrical gesture and heave a long sob of grief to which* THE NEGROES *respond with their very shrill and perfectly orchestrated laughter.*) . . . Only *we* could have done it the way we did it—savagely. And now, listen . . . (*he takes a step back*) . . . listen . . . oh, I was forgetting, thieves that we are, we have tried to filch your fine language. Liars that we are, the names I have mentioned to you are false. Listen . . . (*He steps back, but the other actors have stopped listening to him.* MRS. FELICITY, *an imposing sixty-year-old negress, has gone up to the top tier, right, where she sits down in an armchair, facing the Court.*)

BOBO: The flowers, the flowers! Don't touch them!

SNOW: (*taking an iris for her bodice*) Are they yours, or the murdered woman's?

BOBO: They're there for the performance. Which doesn't require that you burst into bloom. Put back the iris. Or the rose. Or the tulip.

ARCHIBALD: Bobo's right. You wanted to be more attractive—there's some blacking left.

SNOW: All right. Although . . . (*She spits out the flower after biting into it.*)

ARCHIBALD: No needless cruelty, Snow. And no garbage here.
(SNOW *picks up the flower and eats it.* ARCHIBALD *runs after* SNOW, *who hides behind the catafalque.* VILLAGE *catches her and brings her back to* ARCHIBALD, *who wants to lecture her.*)

SNOW: (*to* VILLAGE) A regular cop!

ARCHIBALD: (*to* SNOW) The rite doesn't call for your behaving like a spoiled child. (*While all the other* NEGROES *stand still and listen, he turns to* NEWPORT NEWS) And you, sir, you're superfluous. As everything is secret, you've got to get going. Clear out. Go tell them. Let them know we've started. They're to do their job just as we'll do ours. Everything will go off in the usual way. I hope so. (NEWPORT NEWS *bows and is about to leave by the left wing, but* VILLAGE *stops him.*)

VILLAGE: Not that way, you fool. You were told not to come back. You're spoiling everything.

NEWPORT NEWS: The trouble . . .

ARCHIBALD: (*interrupting him*) Later. Get going.
(*Exit* NEWPORT NEWS, *left.*)

SNOW: (*spitting out the iris*) You always start by picking on me.

BOBO: You let your moods get the better of you. You give way to your temperament, and you've no right to.

SNOW: I have so! Because of my special outlook on the whole business. If it weren't for me . . .

ARCHIBALD: You've done neither more nor less than the others.

SNOW: And my moods are special too, and so is my temperament, and they suit your purpose. And if it weren't for my jealousy where you're concerned, Village . . .

VILLAGE: (*interrupting her*) We know all about it. You've repeated it often enough. Long before her death (*pointing to the cat-afalque*) you hated her bitterly. But her death wasn't meant to signify merely that she lost her life. With tenderness we all brooded over it, and not lovingly. (*A long sob from the Court.*)

SNOW: Really? Then let me tell you now—all of you—I've been burning for so long, burning with such ardent hatred, that I'm a heap of ashes.

DIOUF: What about us? What are we?

SNOW: It's not the same thing, gentlemen. There was a touch of desire in your hatred of her, which means a touch of love. But I, and they (*pointing to the other women*), we, the negro women, we had only our wrath and rage. When she was killed, we felt no awe, no fear, but no tenderness either. We were dry, gentlemen. Dry, like the breasts of old Bambara women. (THE QUEEN *bursts out laughing.* THE MISSIONARY *motions to her to be quiet. Holding her handkerchief to her mouth,* THE QUEEN *gradually calms down.*)

ARCHIBALD: (*severely*) The tragedy will lie in the color black! It's *that* that you'll cherish, *that* that you'll attain, and deserve. It's *that* that must be earned.

SNOW: (*ecstatically*) My color! Why, you're my very self! But you,

Village, what was it you wanted in going after her? (*She points to the catafalque.*)

VILLAGE: You're starting again with your silly suspicions. Do you want a detailed description of the humiliations she made me feel? Do you? Tell me, do you?

ALL: (*with a terrible cry*) Yes!

VILLAGE: Negroes, you've yelled too soon and too loud. (*He takes a deep breath.*) This evening, there'll be something new.

ARCHIBALD: You've no right to change anything in the ceremonial, unless, of course, you hit upon some cruel detail that heightens it.

VILLAGE: In any case, I can keep you on tenterhooks waiting for the murder.

ARCHIBALD: You're to obey *me*. And the text we've prepared.

VILLAGE: (*banteringly*) But I'm still free to speed up or draw out my recital and my performance. I can move in slow motion, can't I? I can sigh more often and more deeply.

THE QUEEN: (*amused*) He's charming! Continue, young man!

THE JUDGE: Indeed, your Majesty is forgetting herself!

THE VALET: I rather like him, I must say. (*to* VILLAGE) Do sigh more often and more deeply, charming blackboy!

THE GOVERNOR: (*to* THE VALET) That'll do! Instead of that, tell us how rubber stands on the stock exchange.

THE VALET: (*saluting, and in a single breath*) Goodyear, 4,500 (*The members of the Court pull a long face.*)

THE GOVERNOR: What about gold?

THE VALET: Eastern Ubangi 1,580. Saint Johnny-get-your-gun 1,050. Macupia, 2,002. M'Zaita 20,008.
(*The Members of the Court rub their hands.*)

VILLAGE: (*continuing*) . . . can sigh more often and more deeply, can relax in the middle of a sentence or word. Besides, I'm tired. You forget that I'm already knocked out from the crime I had to finish off before you arrived, since you need a fresh corpse for every performance.

THE QUEEN: (*with a cry*) Oh!

THE JUDGE: (*fiercely*) I told you so.

THE VALET: (*very affectedly*) Don't condemn them at the very start. Listen to them. They're exquisitely spontaneous. They have a strange beauty. Their flesh is weightier . . .

THE GOVERNOR: Be quiet, you whippersnapper! You and your damned exoticism!

DIOUF: (*to* ARCHIBALD) Actually, we *could* use the same corpse a number of times. Its presence is the thing that counts.

ARCHIBALD: What about the odor, Mr. Vicar General?

BOBO: (*to* ARCHIBALD) Does the stench frighten you now? That's what rises from my African soil. I, Bobo, want to draw my train over its thick waves! May I be wafted by an odor of carrion! And carried off! (*to the Court*) And you, pale and odorless race, race without animal odors, without the pestilence of our swamps . . .

ARCHIBALD: (*to* BOBO) Let Virtue speak.

VIRTUE: (*prudently*) All the same, we ought to be careful. It gets more dangerous every day. Not only for Village, but for every hunter.

SNOW: All the better. Since we're working this evening for a Court of Justice that's been set up especially for us, we'll dedicate our follies to it.

ARCHIBALD: That'll do. (*to* VILLAGE) Tell me, Village, there wasn't any alert this evening either, was there? Everything went off smoothly, I hope. Where did you find her?

VILLAGE: I told you just before, when I arrived. Right after dinner, Mr. Herod Adventure and I were walking along the docks. The evening was rather mild. A little before the entrance to the bridge, there was an old tramp squatting—or lying—on a pile of rags. But I've told you all about it . . .

BOBO: The old tramp may consider herself fortunate. She'll have a first-class funeral.

ARCHIBALD: (*to* VILLAGE) But tell us more. Did she scream?

VILLAGE: Not at all. Hadn't time to. Mr. Herod Adventure and I went straight up to her. She was dozing. She half awoke. The blackness of the night . . .

BOBO and SNOW: (*laughing*) Oh! the blackness!

VILLAGE: In the darkness, she must have taken us for policemen. She reeked of wine, like all those they cast out on the docks. She said, "I'm not doing any harm . . ."

ARCHIBALD: And then?

VILLAGE: As usual. It was I who bent down. Mr. Herod Adventure held her hands while I strangled her. She stiffened a bit . . . then she had what's called a spasm, and that was that. Mr. Herod Adventure was slightly nauseated by the crone's ugly mug, by the smell of wine and urine, by the filth. He almost puked. But he pulled himself together. We carried her to our Cadillac and brought her here, in a crate. (*A pause.*)

SNOW: But that stench, which isn't ours . . .
      (VILLAGE *takes a cigarette from his pocket.*)

BOBO: You're right, let's smoke.
(THE NEGROES *seem not quite to understand.*)

ARCHIBALD: Let's all have a cigarette. Let's smoke her out.
(*Each* NEGRO *takes a cigarette from his pocket. They light matches for each other, bowing ceremoniously as they do, then arrange themselves in a circle and puff smoke around the catafalque. They sing the first line of "Mary had a little lamb" and hum the rest.*)
(*During the sing-song the Court grows agitated.*)

THE GOVERNOR: (*to* THE VALET) Now they're smoking her out! It's a hive, it's a nest of hornets, it's a wooden bed swarming with bedbugs, it's a burrow, it's a den of rebels . . . Our corpse! They're going to cook her and eat her! Take their matches away!
(*The entire Court kneels before* THE QUEEN; THE VALET *dries her eyes with a towel.*)

THE MISSIONARY: Let us pray, Madam. (*to the others*) All of you, on your knees before that august grief.

THE QUEEN: Ahaaha!

THE MISSIONARY: Have confidence, Majesty, God is white.

THE VALET: You seem sure of yourself . . .

THE MISSIONARY: Would he have allowed—you young milksop—would he have allowed the Miracle of Greece? For two thousand years God has been white. He eats on a white tablecloth. He wipes his white mouth with a white napkin. He picks at white meat with a white fork. (*A pause.*) He watches the snow fall.

ARCHIBALD: (*to* VILLAGE) Recite the rest to them. Any trouble on the way back?

VILLAGE: None at all. Besides, I had this. (*After working the breech noisily, he shows a revolver, which he lays on the shoeshine box, where it will remain.*)

VIRTUE: (*still very calm*) But after all, do you imagine that this kind of thing can go on much longer, these corpses that are discovered at dawn—and even in broad daylight—in disgusting places and postures? Sooner or later there'll be a big blow-up. We've also got to beware of possible betrayal.

SNOW: What do you mean?

VIRTUE: That a Negro is capable of ratting on another Negro.

SNOW: Speak for yourself, madam.

VIRTUE: It's because of what I see and what goes on in my own soul and what I call the temptation of the Whites . . .

THE GOVERNOR: (*triumphantly*) I was sure of it. Sooner or later, they come round. All you have to do is pay the price.

THE QUEEN: I'll offer my jewels! I have cellars full of chests full of pearls fished up by them from their mysterious seas, diamonds, gold, pieces of eight unearthed from their deep mines, I'll give them away, throw them away . . .

THE VALET: What about me?

THE QUEEN: You'll still have your queen, you naughty boy . . . Aged, in rags, but stately. Grand.

ARCHIBALD: (*to* THE QUEEN) Allow us to continue.

THE JUDGE: (*to* ARCHIBALD) It's you who keep stalling. You promised us a re-enactment of the crime so as to deserve your condemnation. The Queen's waiting. Hurry up.

ARCHIBALD: (*to* THE JUDGE) No one's cooperating. Except Virtue.

THE JUDGE: Well then, let Virtue lead off, or Village.

VILLAGE: (*panicky*) Negroes, it's not time yet for the part that's to be declaimed. All I have to say now is that the woman was white and that she gave our odor as an excuse for fleeing me. For fleeing me, because she didn't dare chase me away. Ah, the great days when they used to hunt the Negro and the antelope! My father once told me . . .

ARCHIBALD: (*interrupting him*) Your father? Sir, don't use that word again! There was a shade of tenderness in your voice as you uttered it.

VILLAGE: And what do you suggest I call the male who knocked up the negress who gave birth to me?

ARCHIBALD: Dammit, do the best you can. Invent—if not words, then phrases that cut you off rather than bind you. Invent, not love, but hatred, and thereby make poetry, since that's the only domain in which we're allowed to operate. For their entertainment? (*pointing to the audience*) We'll see. You referred, quite rightly, to our odor—our scent, which used to lead their hounds to us in the bush—you too were on the right track. Take a whiff and say that "she" (*pointing to the catafalque*) knew that we stink. Proceed delicately. Be clever and choose only reasons for hatred. Keep from magnifying our savageness. Be careful not to seem a wild beast. If you do, you'll tempt their desire without gaining their esteem. So you murdered her. We're going to begin . . .

VILLAGE: Just a minute. What can I substitute for the word father?

ARCHIBALD: Your circumlocution is quite satisfactory.

VILLAGE: It's rather long.

ARCHIBALD: By stretching language we'll distort it sufficiently to wrap ourselves in it and hide, whereas the masters contract it.

BOBO: Generally I'm brief.

ARCHIBALD: You're generally eager to see the others hide behind their words. But, like us, my dear Bobo, you delight the ear with morning-glories that twine round the pillars of the world. We must charm. From their toes to their ears, our pink tongues—the only part of us that suggests a flower—move artfully and silently round and about our fine, lackadaisical ladies and gentlemen. Will the phrase do?

VILLAGE: Yours?

ARCHIBALD: Yours, stupid . . . "the Negro who knocked up" and so on . . . Does everyone approve? Except Snow—still stubborn?

SNOW: (*very acrimoniously*) If I were sure that Village bumped the woman off in order to heighten the fact that he's a scarred, smelly, thick-lipped, snub-nosed Negro, an eater and guzzler of Whites and all other colors, a drooling, sweating, belching, spitting, coughing, farting goat-fucker, a licker of white boots, a good-for-nothing, sick, oozing oil and sweat, limp and submissive, if I were sure he killed her in order to merge with the night . . . But I know he loved her.

VIRTUE: He didn't.

VILLAGE: I didn't.

SNOW: (*to* VIRTUE) So you think he loves you, you, the submissive black wench?

ARCHIBALD: (*severely*) Snow!

SNOW: (*to* VIRTUE) To turn pink, to blush with emotion, with confusion—tender expressions that will never apply to us. Otherwise you'd see Virtue's cheeks turn flaming purple.

VIRTUE: Mine?

BOBO: Someone's.
(*All* THE NEGROES *are now gathered at the right. They cease to speak.* NEWPORT NEWS *enters from the wings. He moves forward quietly.*)

ARCHIBALD: (*going up to him*) Well? Has anything happened yet?

NEWPORT NEWS: He's arrived. We've brought him along, handcuffed.
(*All* THE NEGROES *cluster about* NEWPORT NEWS.)

SNOW: What are you going to do?

NEWPORT NEWS: (*bending down and picking up the revolver from the shoeshine box*) First of all, question him . . .

ARCHIBALD: (*interrupting*) Say only what you have to. We're being watched.
(*They all look up at the Court.*)

THE JUDGE: (*crying out*) Just because you're disguised as trained dogs you think you know how to talk, and you start inventing riddles . . .

VILLAGE: (*to* THE JUDGE) Some day . . .

ARCHIBALD: (*interrupting*) Cut it. If you lose your temper, you'll betray yourself and betray us. (*to* NEWPORT NEWS) Did he say anything to justify himself? Anything at all?

NEWPORT NEWS: Nothing. Shall I go?

ARCHIBALD: When the Court of Justice has been set up, come back and let us know.
(NEWPORT NEWS *moves away from the group and is about to leave.*)

DIOUF: (*timidly*) Do you really want to take that object with you?
(*pointing to the revolver in* NEWPORT NEWS' *hand*)

ARCHIBALD: (*to* DIOUF, *violently*) I repeat once again—you're wasting your time. We know your argument. You're going to urge us to be reasonable, to be conciliatory. But we're bent on being unreasonable, on being hostile. You'll speak of love. Go right ahead, since our speeches are set down in the script. (*All except* DIOUF *and* NEWPORT NEWS *let out an orchestrated laugh.*)

NEWPORT NEWS: You really ought to listen to him . . .

ARCHIBALD: (*imperiously*) Clear out! Get back into the wings. Take the revolver and go do your job.

NEWPORT NEWS: But . . .

VILLAGE: (*breaking in*) No buts about it. Obey Mr. Wellington. (*Resignedly,* NEWPORT NEWS *starts to leave, but* VILLAGE *stops him.*) Not that way, you fool! (*Exit* NEWPORT NEWS, *left.*)

BOBO: You asked for the floor, Mr. Clergyman. Speak up!

DIOUF: (*with an effort*) Everything about me seems ludicrous to you. I know it does . . .

ARCHIBALD: Bear one thing in mind: we must deserve their reprobation and get them to deliver the judgment that will condemn us. I repeat, they know about our crime . . .

DIOUF: All the same, let me try to come to an understanding with them, to propose some kind of agreement . . .

ARCHIBALD: (*irritably*) All right, you may speak, Mr. Diouf. But we'll close our eyes and seal our mouths, and our barren faces will suggest the desert. Let's all shut up . . .

DIOUF: (*panicky*) Gentlemen, gentlemen, ladies, don't leave!

ARCHIBALD: (*implacably*) Let's shut up! Let's efface ourselves. Now speak.

DIOUF: But who'll hear me? (*The Court bursts out laughing.*) You? That's not possible. (*He wants to talk to* THE NEGROES, *but they have closed their eyes and mouths and put their hands over their ears.*)
After all, gentlemen, my good friends, it's not a fresh corpse that we need. I'd like the ceremony to involve us, not in hatred . . .

THE NEGROES: (*ironically, and in a dismal voice*) . . . but in love!

DIOUF: If it's possible, ladies and gentlemen.

THE MISSIONARY: . . . to involve you, above all, in your love of us.

THE VALET: Are you speaking seriously, Monsignor?

THE JUDGE: Then we shall deign to hear you.

THE GOVERNOR: Although, after this orgy. . . .

DIOUF: (*with an appeasing gesture of his hand*) May I explain? I should indeed like the performance to re-establish in our souls a balance that our plight perpetuates, but I should like it to unfold so harmoniously that they (*pointing to the audience*) see only the beauty of it, and I would like them to recognize us in that beauty which disposes them to love.
(*A long silence.*)

BOBO: (*slowly opening her eyes*) The crossing of the desert was long and arduous. Poor Diouf, finding no oasis, you probably opened your veins to drink a little blood!

THE MISSIONARY: (*after coughing*) Tell me, my dear Vicar, what about the Host? Yes, the Host. Will you invent a black Host? And what will it be made of? Gingerbread, you say? That's brown.

DIOUF: But Monsignor, we have a thousand ingredients. We'll dye it. A gray Host . . .

THE GOVERNOR: (*breaking in*) Grant the gray Host and you're sunk. You'll see—he'll demand further concessions, more oddities.

DIOUF: (*plaintively*) White on one side, black on the other?

THE VALET: (*to* DIOUF) Would you be so kind as to inform me—for, after all, I have chosen to be understanding—where the Negro went with his revolver just before?

ARCHIBALD: Backstage. (*to* DIOUF) And stop jabbering. Good God, one would think you were trying to ridicule us.

DIOUF: (*to* ARCHIBALD) Sir, I apologize. I'd like to glorify my color, just as you do. The kindness of the whites settled upon my head, as it did upon yours. Though it rested there lightly, it was unbearable. Their intelligence descended upon my right shoulder, and a whole flock of virtues upon my left. And at times, when I opened my hands, I would find their charity nestling there. In my Negro solitude, I feel the need, just as you do, to glorify my exquisite savageness, but I'm old and I think . . .

BOBO: Who's asking you to? What we need is hatred. Our ideas will spring from hatred.

DIOUF: (*ironically*) You're a technician, Bobo, but it's not easy to cast off a guilty meekness that the heart desires. I've suffered too much shame not to want to befoul their beauteous souls, but . . .

ARCHIBALD: No buts about it, or get out! My anger isn't make-believe.

DIOUF: Please, Archy . . .

ARCHIBALD: Don't be so familiar. Not here. Politeness must be raised to such a pitch that it becomes monstrous. It must arouse fear. We're being observed by spectators. Sir, if you have any intention of presenting even the most trivial of their ideas without caricaturing it, then get out! Beat it!

BOBO: He wouldn't mind—it's his day off.

VILLAGE: Let him keep talking. The sound of his voice moves me.

SNOW: Bravo! I was expecting something like that from you. Because you, too, fear this moment. Perhaps because the action will separate you and Virtue for a while.

THE GOVERNOR: (*suddenly*) You were told what to do—start off with Village, start off with Virtue.
(THE NEGROES *are taken aback for a moment and look at each other, then resign themselves.*)

VILLAGE: (*bowing to* VIRTUE, *and sighing deeply*) Madam, I bring you nothing comparable to what is called love. What is happening within me is very mysterious and cannot be accounted for by my color. When I beheld you . . .

ARCHIBALD: Be careful, Village, don't start referring to your real life. [From this point until he says "Careful, Village," Archibald saws the air with his hands like an orchestra leader, as if he were directing Village's recital.]

VILLAGE: (*with one knee on the floor*) When I beheld you, you were walking in the rain, in high heels. You were wearing a black silk dress, black stockings, patent leather pumps and were carrying a black umbrella. Oh, if only I hadn't been born into slavery! I'd have been flooded with a strange emotion, but we—you and I— were moving along the edges of the world, out of bounds. We were the shadow, or the dark interior, of luminous creatures . . . When I beheld you, suddenly—for perhaps a second—I had the strength to reject everything that wasn't you, and to laugh at the illusion. But my shoulders are very frail. I was unable to bear the weight of the world's condemnation. And I began to hate you when everything about you would have kindled my love and when love would have made men's contempt unbearable, and their contempt would have made my love unbearable. The fact is, I hate you.
(*For some moments, the Court seems to have been growing agitated.* THE VALET *seems to be yelling silently into the cupped ear of* THE GOVERNOR.)

ARCHIBALD: (*to the Court*) Please!

THE VALET: (*yelling*) M'Zaita 2,010!

THE GOVERNOR: What about coffee?

THE VALET: (*The entire Court listens very attentively.*) Extra-Special Arabica 608–627. Robusta 327–327. Kuilu 313–317.

VILLAGE: (*who had lowered his head, raises it to resume his speech*) . . . I know not whether you are beautiful. I fear you may be. I fear your sparkling darkness. Oh darkness, stately mother of my race, shadow, sheath that swathes me from top to toe, long sleep in which the frailest of your children would love to be shrouded, I know not whether you are beautiful, but you are Africa, oh monumental night, and I hate you. I hate you for filling my black eyes with sweetness. I hate you for making me thrust you from me, for making me hate you. It would take so little for your face, your body, your movements, your heart to thrill me . . .

ARCHIBALD: Careful, Village!

VILLAGE: (to VIRTUE) But I hate you! (to the others) But let me tell her and tell you about all the pain I have to endure. If love is denied us, I want you to know . . .

BOBO: We know all about it. We're black too. But in order to refer to ourselves, we don't adorn our metaphors with stars. Or grand nocturnal images. But with soot and blacking, with coal and tar.

DIOUF: Don't make it so hard for him. If his suffering is too intense, let him use language to ease the strain.

VILLAGE: Ease the strain? I remember how I suffered to see that tall, gleaming body walking in the rain. Her feet were getting soaked . . .

BOBO: Her black feet. Black feet!

VILLAGE: In the rain. Virtue was walking in the rain, looking for White customers, as you know. No, no, there'll be no love for us . . . (he hesitates)

VIRTUE: You may speak. Every brothel has its negress.

THE GOVERNOR: (after clearing his throat) To the whorehouse, dammit! Egad, to the whorehouse! I make my troops tear off a piece every Saturday. Pox and shankers, doesn't matter a damn! Troops should end up lame and limping. To the whorehouse, dammit! (The entire Court applauds. THE GOVERNOR puffs himself up.)

VIRTUE: Then let me tell you that this evening's ceremony will affect me less than the one I perform ten times a day. I'm the only one who experiences shame to the bitter end . . .

ARCHIBALD: Don't allude to your life.

VIRTUE: (*ironically*) You've been infected by the squeamishness you've picked up from the Whites. A whore shocks you.

BOBO: She does, if she's one in real life. There's no need for us to know about your personal sufferings and dislikes. That's *your* business . . . in your room.

VILLAGE: This ceremony is painful to me.

ARCHIBALD: To us, too. They tell us that we're grown-up children. In that case, what's left for us? The theater! We'll play at being reflected in it, and we'll see ourselves—big black narcissists slowly disappearing into its waters.

VILLAGE: I don't want to disappear.

ARCHIBALD: You're no exception! Nothing will remain of you but the foam of your rage. Since they merge us with an image and drown us in it, let the image set their teeth on edge!

VILLAGE: My body wants to live.

ARCHIBALD: You're becoming a specter before their very eyes and you're going to haunt them.

VILLAGE: I love Virtue. She loves me.

ARCHIBALD: Yes, she, perhaps. She has powers that you haven't. There are times when she dominates the Whites—oh, I know, by her magic wiggle. But that's also a way of dominating them. She can therefore bring you what most resembles love: tenderness. In her arms, you'll be her child, not her lover.

VILLAGE: (*obstinately*) I love Virtue.

ARCHIBALD: You think you love her. You're a Negro and a performer. Neither of whom will know love. Now, this evening—but
this evening only—we cease to be performers, since we are
Negroes. On this stage, we're like guilty prisoners who play at
being guilty.

VILLAGE: We don't want to be guilty of anything any more. Virtue
will be my wife.

ARCHIBALD: Then get the hell out! Beat it! Go away. Take her with
you. Go join them (*pointing to the audience*) . . . if they'll have
you. If they accept you both. And if you succeed in winning their
love, come back and let me know. But first discolor yourselves.
Get the hell out. Go join them. Go down and be spectators.
We'll be saved by *that* (*pointing to the catafalque*).

THE VALET: (*in an oily tone*) Gentlemen, what if it happened to be
a man that you caught in your net one fine summer evening?
What would you do about the seduction scene? Have you ever
captured a carpenter with his plane? Or a bargeman with his
canalboats and his clothes hanging on a line?

BOBO: (*very insolently*) Yes, we have! We picked up an old down-
and-out vaudeville singer: wrapped up and cased. There (*pointing
to the catafalque*). Only too happy to dress him up for the ceremony as a governor-general, when he was killed before the eyes of
the crowd—last night's, ladies and gentlemen. We deposited him
in the attic. Where he still is. (*pointing to the corpse*) Similarly,
we did away with a decent, helpless old lady, a milkman, a post-
man, a seamstress, a government clerk . . . (*The Court shrinks in
horror.*)

THE VALET: (*persisting*) And what if there'd been nothing available
but a four-year-old lad on his way home from the grocer's with a
bottle of milk? Be careful how you answer and bear in mind the
great effort I am making to regard you as human . . .

BOBO: We know only too well what he'll become when he's drunk too much milk. And if we can't find a kid, then an old horse will do, or a dog or a doll.

VILLAGE: So it's always murder that we dream about?

ARCHIBALD: Always, and get going!

VILLAGE: (*to* VIRTUE, *though still hesitantly*) Come. Follow me. (*He starts leaving the stage, as if going down to join the audience.*)

ARCHIBALD: (*holding them back*) No, no, that's not necessary. Since we're on the stage, where everything is relative, all I need do is walk backwards in order to create the theatrical illusion of your moving away from me. Off I go. And I'm giving you rope enough to hang yourself, Mr. Wise-guy, by leaving you alone with that woman. You're on your own. The rest of us, let's go.
(ARCHIBALD, BOBO, DIOUF, SNOW *and* FELICITY *turn away and, holding their faces in their hands, move off, when suddenly nine or ten white masks appear about the Court.*)

VILLAGE: (*to* VIRTUE) I love you.

VIRTUE: Let's not rush matters, Village.

VILLAGE: I love you.

VIRTUE: That's an easy thing to say. An easy sentiment to feign, especially if it's limited to desire. You speak of love, but do you think we're alone? (*She points to the Court.*)

VILLAGE: (*alarmed*) As many as that!

VIRTUE: You insisted on being alone.

VILLAGE: (*more and more panicky*) But without them. Archibald! (*he cries out*) Archibald! Bobo! (*They all remain unmoved.*)

Snow! (*He rushes over to them, but they do not move. He comes back to* Virtue.) Virtue? They won't go away, will they?

Virtue: Don't be afraid. You wanted to love me. You spoke of leaving everything for . . .

Village: I don't know whether I'll have the strength to. Now that they're here . . .

Virtue: (*she puts her hand on his mouth*) Be still. First, let's love each other, if you have the strength to.
(*But the members of the Court seem to be getting excited, except for* The queen, *who is dozing. They stamp their feet, fidget, clap hands.*)

The governor: Damn it, they're going to gum up the works! Don't let them continue. (*to* The queen) Madam, madam, wake up!

The judge: The Queen is asleep. (*with a finger to his lips*) She's hatching. Hatching what? Celtic remains and the stained-glass windows of Chartres.

The governor: Damn it, wake her up . . . Give her a dousing, the way they do at the barracks . . .

The judge: You're out of your mind! Who'll do the hatching? You?

The governor: (*sheepishly*) I never knew how.

The valet: Neither did I. Especially standing up. For of course no one has seen my chair.

The missionary: (*annoyed*) Nor mine. And I have to remain on my feet, although I'm a bishop-at-large. Nevertheless, they've got to be prevented from continuing. Listen . . .
(*Below,* Village *and* Virtue, *who have been talking voicelessly, now continue aloud.*)

Village: Our color isn't a wine stain that blotches a face, our face isn't a jackal that devours those it looks at . . . (*shouting*) I'm handsome, you're beautiful, and we love each other! I'm strong! If anyone touches you . . .

VIRTUE: (*thrilled*) It would make me happy.
(VILLAGE *is taken aback.*)

THE GOVERNOR: (*to the Court*) Do you hear them? We've got to stop them. Right away. The Queen ought to speak. Madam, jump out of bed! (*He imitates with his mouth the bugle call of reveille.*)
(THE JUDGE, THE MISSIONARY *and* THE VALET *are bent over* THE QUEEN. *They stand up straight, looking woebegone.*)

THE MISSIONARY: There's no doubt about it, she's snoring.

THE GOVERNOR: What about that great voice of hers? I'm listening.
(*A brief silence.*)

VIRTUE: (*softly, as if in a state of somnambulism*) I am the lily-white Queen of the West. Only centuries and centuries of breeding could achieve such a miracle! Immaculate, pleasing to the eye and to the soul! . . .
(*The entire Court listens attentively.*)
Whether in excellent health, pink and gleaming, or consumed with languor, I am white. If death strikes me, I die in the color of victory. Oh noble pallor, color my temples, my fingers, my belly! Oh eye of mine, delicately shaded iris, bluish iris, iris of the glaciers, violet, hazel, gray-green, evergreen iris, English lawn, Norman lawn, through you, but what do we see . . .
(THE QUEEN, *who has finally awakened but is in a dazed state, listens to the poem and then recites along with* VIRTUE)
. . . I am white, it's milk that denotes me, it's the lily, the dove, quicklime and the clear conscience, it's Poland with its eagle and snow! Snow . . .

VILLAGE: (*suddenly lyrical*) Snow? If you like. Haunt me, lance bearer. With my long dark strides I roamed the earth. Against that moving mass of darkness the angry but respectful sun flashed its beams. They did not traverse my dusky bulk. I was naked.

VIRTUE and THE QUEEN: (*together*) It's innocence and morning.

VILLAGE: The surfaces of my body were curved mirrors in which all things were reflected: fish, buffaloes, the laughter of tigers, reeds. Naked? Or was my shoulder covered with a leaf? And my member adorned with moss . . .

VIRTUE and THE QUEEN: (*together*) . . . except that a bit of shade remained in my armpits . . .

VILLAGE: (*with rising frenzy*) . . . with moss, or seaweed? I was not singing, I was not dancing. Standing insolently—in short, royally —with hand on hip, I was pissing. Oh! Oh! Oh! I crawled through the cotton plants. The dogs sniffed me out. I bit my chains and wrists. Slavery taught me dancing and singing.

VIRTUE: (*alone*) . . . a swarthy violet, almost black, ring is spreading to my cheek. The night . . .

VILLAGE: . . . I died in the hold of the slave ship . . .
(VIRTUE *approaches him.*)

VIRTUE and THE QUEEN: I love you.

VILLAGE: I'm a long time dying.

THE QUEEN: (*suddenly wide awake*) That'll do! Silence them, they've stolen my voice! Help! . . .
(*Suddenly* FELICITY *stands up. Everyone looks at her and listens in silence.*)

FELICITY: Dahomey! . . . Dahomey! . . . Negroes from all corners of the earth, to the rescue! Come! Enter into me and only me! Swell me with your tumult! Come barging in! Penetrate where you will: my mouth, my ears—or my nostrils. Nostrils, enormous conches, glory of my race, sunless shafts, tunnels, yawning grottoes

where sniffling battalions lie at rest! Giantess with head thrown back, I await you all. Enter into me, ye multitudes, and be, for this evening only, my force and reason.
(*She sits down again. The dialogue continues.*)

THE QUEEN: (*very solemnly and almost swooning*) "The hind that would be mated by the lion must die for love."—Shakespeare.

THE VALET: Madam is dying!

THE QUEEN: Not yet! To the rescue, angel of the flaming sword, virgins of the Parthenon, stained-glass of Chartres, Lord Byron, Chopin, French cooking, the Unknown Soldier, Tyrolean songs, Aristotelian principles, heroic couplets, poppies, sunflowers, a touch of coquetry, vicarage gardens . . .

THE ENTIRE COURT: Madam, we're here.

THE QUEEN: Ah, that's a comfort. I thought I'd been abandoned! They would have harmed me!

THE JUDGE: There's nothing to worry about. Our laws still hold.

THE MISSIONARY: (*to* THE QUEEN, *and facing her*) Have patience. We've only just begun the long death struggle, which gives them such pleasure. Let's put a good face on it. It's in order to please them that we're going to die . . .

THE QUEEN: Can't they hurry and get it over with? I'm weary, and their odor is choking me. (*She pretends to be fainting.*)

THE MISSIONARY: Impossible. They've planned it down to the last detail, not in accordance with their own strength, but with our state of exhaustion.

THE QUEEN: (*in a dying voice*) And we're still too lively, aren't we? Yet all my blood's ebbing away.
(*At that moment,* ARCHIBALD, DIOUF, SNOW *and* BOBO *draw themselves up, turn about and move toward* VILLAGE.)

ARCHIBALD: Village, for the last time, I beseech you . . .

VILLAGE: For the last time? This evening? (*with sudden decision*)
All right. This evening, for the last time. But you'll have to help
me. Will you? Will you help me work myself up? Will you work
me up?

SNOW: Me first, because I'm sick and tired of your cowardice.

VILLAGE: (*pointing to the catafalque*) It was I who killed her, and
yet you accuse me.

SNOW: You had to bring yourself to do it.

VILLAGE: How do you know? You were hidden in the garden, you
were waiting for me under the locust tree. How could you have
possibly seen me hesitating? While you were munching flowers in
the twilight, I was bleeding her, without turning a hair.

SNOW: Yes, but you've been speaking about her lovingly ever since.

VILLAGE: Not about her, but about my gesture.

SNOW: You're lying!

VILLAGE: You're in love with me!
(*From this point on, the entire troupe becomes increasingly
frenzied.*)

SNOW: You're lying. When you speak of her, such a gentle expression, a look of such poignant sadness, comes over your thick lips
and sick eyes that I can see Nostalgia in person peeping out. It
wasn't your gesture that you were describing when you spoke to
me about her lifted blue dress, nor your anger when you described
her mouth and teeth, nor the resistance of the flesh to the knife
when you mentioned her weary eyelids, nor your nausea when you
told of how her body fell to the rug . . .

VILLAGE: You liar!

SNOW: . . . nor your sorrow when you thought of her pallor, nor your fear of the police when you outlined her ankles. You were talking of a great love. From far off, from Ubangi or Tanganyika, a tremendous love came here to die, to lick white ankles. Negro, you were in love. Like a sergeant in the marines. (*She drops to the floor, exhausted, but* BOBO *and* ARCHIBALD *lift her up.* BOBO *gives her a slap.*)

BOBO: (*holding up* SNOW's *head, as if she were vomiting*). Continue. Spill it all out. Spill it out! Spill it out! (VILLAGE *gets more and more irritated.*)

SNOW: (*as if trying to find more insults and vomiting them forth, with hiccoughs*) Swear! Just as others change their family or city or country or name, just as they change gods, swear that it never occurred to you to change color in order to attain her. But since you couldn't even dream of royal white, you wished for a green skin . . . You've still got it!

VILLAGE: (*as if on edge*) You misunderstand completely. In order to arouse her, to attract her, I had to dance my nupital flight. I beat my wing sheaths. When it was over, I died, completely exhausted. My body was abandoned, and perhaps she entered while I was resting from my dance—or while I was dancing, who knows?

SNOW: So you admit!

VILLAGE: Not at all! All I know is that I killed her, since there she is (*pointing to the catafalque*). All I know is that one evening, when I went out hunting in the street, hunting the White-woman, I killed the one I brought back to you.
(*But they all turn their heads away.* MRS. FELICITY *steps down from her throne very majestically. She goes to the catafalque, bends down and slips a few grains under the sheet.*)

BOBO: Already!

FELICITY: I'm not stuffing her, you know. All the same, it's better for her not to dwindle away.

DIOUF: What do you feed her? Rice?

FELICITY: Corn. (*She silently returns to her place.*)

BOBO: Well well, it's a long time since anyone's noticed Mr. Diouf. Look at how he's perked up. My word, he seems quite pleased with himself.

DIOUF: (*alarmed*) Madam . . .

BOBO: What, Madam? Madam yourself. His eyes are gleaming. Does he already see his voluptuous bosom that the Negro lusts after?

DIOUF: (*frightened*) Madam! Bobo! It was wrong of me to have come this evening. Please let me go. Village is the one you ought to be concerned with. He's the one who has to be spurred on!

ARCHIBALD: We'll attend to Village. His crime saves him. If he committed it with hatred . . .

VILLAGE: (*screaming*) But it was with hatred! How can you doubt it? Are you all out of your mind? Tell me, ladies and gentlemen, are you crazy? She was standing behind her counter.
(*A long silence. The actors seem to be hanging on his words.*)

SNOW: You said before: sitting at her sewing-machine.

VILLAGE: (*obstinately*) She was standing behind her counter.

BOBO: Well, what did she do?
(*They are all attentive.*)

VILLAGE: Negroes, I beseech you! She was standing . . .

ARCHIBALD: (*gravely*) I order you to be black to your very veins. Pump black blood through them. Let Africa circulate in them. Let Negroes negrify themselves. Let them persist to the point of madness in what they're condemned to be, in their ebony, in their odor, in their yellow eyes, in their cannibal tastes. Let them not be content with eating Whites, but let them cook each other as well. Let them invent recipes for shin-bones, knee-caps, calves, thick lips, everything. Let them invent unknown sauces. Let them invent hiccoughs, belches and farts that'll give out a deleterious jazz. Let them invent a criminal painting and dancing. Negroes, if they change toward us, let it not be out of indulgence, but terror. (*to* DIOUF) And you, Mr. Vicar General, for whom Christ died on the cross, you've got to make up your mind. (*to* VILLAGE) As for Village, let him continue his spiel. So she was standing behind her counter. And what did she do? What did she say? And you, what did you do for us?

VILLAGE: (*pointing to* ARCHIBALD) She was standing there, where you are.

ARCHIBALD: (*stepping back*) No, no, not me.

VILLAGE: (*dancing in front of the coffin*) Then who? (*No one answers.*) Well, who? Now that she's dead, do you want me to open the coffin and repeat what I did with her when she was alive? You realize I'm supposed to re-enact it. I need a straight-man. This evening, I'm going through the whole thing. This evening, I'm giving a farewell performance. Who'll help me? Who? After all, it doesn't much matter who. As everyone knows, the Whites can hardly distinguish one Negro from another.
(*They all look at* FELICITY. *She hesitates, then draws herself up and speaks.*)

FELICITY: Mr. . . . Samba Graham Diouf! You're it.

DIOUF: (*frightened*) But Madam . . .

FELICITY: This evening, you're the dead woman. Take your places.
(*Slowly and solemnly, each takes his place.* DIOUF *stands in front of the catafalque, facing the audience.*)

FELICITY: (*Sitting down again*) Bring in the implements.
(BOBO *brings from behind the right screen a console-table on which are lying a blond wig, a crude cardboard carnival mask*

representing a laughing white woman with big cheeks, a piece of pink knitting, two balls of wool, a knitting needle and white gloves.)

FELICITY: Mr. Diouf, make your declaration. You know the formula, I take it.

DIOUF: (*facing the audience*) I, Samba Graham Diouf, born in the swamps of Ubangi Chari, sadly bid you farewell. I am not afraid. Open the door and I shall enter. I shall descend to the death you are preparing for me.

FELICITY: Good. Let's get on with the farewell.
(DIOUF *remains standing in front of the catafalque, while the other actors line up toward the left and walk slowly backward, gently waving small handkerchiefs which the men have drawn from their pockets and the women from their bosoms. Standing in line, they walk backward very slowly about the catafalque, while* DIOUF, *facing the audience, keeps bowing to them in acknowledgement. In an undertone, they sing a kind of lullaby.*)

ALL: (*singing*) Whistle gentle blackbirds
Nimble pickaninnies
Swimming in the water
Like any other birdies,
Birdies of the islands.
Charming little rascals
Be careful of the sharks
There's redness in the sky
Come back again and sleep
In shadows on the lawn
My tears and sobs will comfort me.
(DIOUF *bows and thanks them.*)

DIOUF: Your song was very beautiful, and your sadness does me honor. I'm going to start life in a new world. If ever I return, I'll tell you what it's like there. Great black country, I bid thee farewell. (*He bows.*)

ARCHIBALD: And now, ready for the mask!

DIOUF: (*grumblingly*) Are you sure we couldn't do without it? Look about you—people manage to do without all kinds of things, salt, tobacco, the subway, women, and even salted peanuts for cocktails and eggs for omelettes.

ARCHIBALD: I said let's get on with it. The implements.
(*The actors ceremoniously bring the wig, mask and gloves, with which they bedeck* DIOUF. *Thus adorned, he takes the knitting. While this goes on,* VILLAGE *gets impatient.*)

ARCHIBALD: (*to* VILLAGE) Carry on.

VILLAGE: (*stepping back, as if to judge the effect*) I'd gone to have a drink after work . . .

BOBO: Stop! You're too pale.
(*She runs to the shoeshine box and comes back to blacken* VIL- LAGE's *face and hands, which she spits on and rubs.*)

BOBO: And if her teeth don't chatter now!

VILLAGE: So there she was . . . (*suddenly he stops and seems to be groping for words*) Are you sure there's any point in going straight through to the end?

SNOW: A little while ago you had no qualms about insulting me, and now you haven't strength enough to kill a white woman who's already dead.

BOBO: Snow's right. She's always right. Your hesitations throw us off. We were beginning to drool with impatience.

ARCHIBALD: (*angrily*) Take back that word, Bobo. No hysteria. This isn't a revival meeting, it's a ceremony.

BOBO: (*to the audience*) I beg your pardon, ladies. I beg your pardon, gentlemen.

VILLAGE: So there she was . . . But, Negroes, you've forgotten the insults.
(*They all look at each other.*)

ARCHIBALD: So we have. He's right. You take it, Virtue. And roll them out, high and clear.
(*Bowing to* DIOUF, VIRTUE *recites a litany the way litanies of the Blessed Virgin are recited in church, in a monotone.*)

VIRTUE: LITANY OF THE LIVID
      Livid as a t.b. death rattle,
      Livid as the droppings of a man with
      jaundice,
      Livid as the belly of a cobra,
      Livid as their convicts,
      Livid as the god they nibble in the morning,
      Livid as a knife in the night,
      Livid . . . except: the English, Germans
      and Belgians, who are red . . . livid as
      jealousy.
      Hail, the livid!
(VIRTUE *steps aside.* SNOW *takes her place and, after bowing to* DIOUF)

SNOW: I, too, greet you, Tower of Ivory, Gate of Heaven flung wide open so that the Negro can enter, majestic and smelly. But how livid you are! What malady consumes you? Will you play Camille this evening? Wondrous, indeed, the malady that makes you ever whiter and that leads you to ultimate whiteness. (*She bursts out laughing*) But what's that I see flowing down your black stockings? So it was true, Lord Jesus, that behind the mask of a cornered White is a poor trembling Negro. (*She steps back and says to* BOBO) Take it.

BOBO: Let's both take it! (*She tucks up her skirt and does an obscene dance.*)

ARCHIBALD: All right. Take it, Village.

VILLAGE: I don't know whether I'll be able . . .

ARCHIBALD: (*furiously*) What? Changing tone again? Whom are you talking to? What are you talking about? This is the theater, not the street. The theater, and drama, and crime.

VILLAGE: (*with sudden fury, he seems about to spring forward, makes a gesture as if to thrust everyone aside*) Stand aside! Here I come! (*He had stepped back, and now moves forward.*) I enter. And I fart. Lumbering along on my thighs, cast iron columns. And I breeze in. I take a look around . . .

BOBO: You're lying. Last night you entered slyly, very cautiously. You're distorting things.

VILLAGE: (*continuing*) I enter, and I approach, softly. I take a furtive peep. I look about me. To the right. To the left. "How do you, Madam?" (*He bows to DIOUF, who, with the knitting in his hand, returns the bow.*) How do you do, Madam? It's not warm. (*They all cock their ears to hear what the Mask says. He stops talking, but the actors must have heard him, for they raise their heads and laugh, with their orchestrated laugh.*) It's not warm. I've made so bold as to come in for a moment. Here at least it's nice and comfortable. Are you knitting a helmet? A pink one? The light is very soft. It suits your pretty face. Yes, I'll have a glass of rum. I'll have a nip. (*in a different tone, addressing* THE NEGROES) That the right tone?

ALL: (*breathlessly*) Yes!

VILLAGE: The moon—for it was almost night—rose artfully over a landscape inhabited by insects. It's a distant land, madam, but my whole body could sing it. Listen to the singing! Listen! (*Suddenly he breaks off and points to the Mask, who is knitting.*) But he's not wearing a skirt! What kind of masquerade is that? I'll stop my speech if you don't put a skirt on him.

ARCHIBALD: Snow, your shawl . . .

SNOW: My net shawl? He'll step on it and tear it.

ARCHIBALD: Well, doesn't anyone have something to give him?
(*They are all silent. Suddenly* FELICITY *stands up. She takes off her skirt and tosses it to* DIOUF.)

FELICITY: Slip it on. It'll hide your shoes.
(DIOUF *stops knitting. He is helped on with the skirt.*)

VILLAGE: I'll go back a little . . . "The moon . . ."

BOBO: No, you've already recited that.

VILLAGE: (*resignedly*) All right. I continue. Listen to the singing of my thighs . . . Because . . . (*a rather long pause, during which he pretends to have an important revelation to make*) . . . because my thighs fascinated her. (*fatuously*) Ask her. (THE NEGROES *go to the Mask and whisper in his ear. The Mask remains silent, but* THE NEGROES *burst out laughing.*) You see! She even has the nerve to boast of it! (*A pause.*) But that's not all, she has to raise a laugh besides! From the attic, where her bed was, I could hear her mother calling for her evening medicine. (*A brief pause; then, to* FELICITY) Well, that's your cue. Play the Mother.

FELICITY: (*imitating a plaintive patient, with her eyes to the ceiling*) Ma-a-rie! Maa-a-arie! Daughter, it's time for my sugared almonds and aspirin! And it's prayer-time.
(*The Mask seems to be moving toward the voice. He takes a few short steps in the direction of* FELICITY, *but* VILLAGE *calmly and sternly steps between them.*)

VILLAGE: (*assuming a woman's voice*) Yes, mother dear, right away. The water's heating. I'll iron another couple of sheets and then bring up your sugared almonds. (*to the Mask*) Take it easy, girlie. You don't give a damn about the old hag. Any more than I do. She's had her day. To hell with her and her sugared almonds. If you're heating water, it's for after the fun. What's the matter, what's . . .

FELICITY: Ma-a-arie! My darling little daughter. It's time for my sugared almonds. When your father was still a magistrate, he always used to bring me one at this time of day, in the gloaming. Don't leave me alone in the attic. (*A pause.*) And don't forget, the baker's wife's coming.

ARCHIBALD: (*to* BOBO, *whom he pushes toward the right wing*) Your cue. Enter.
(BOBO, *who has stepped back to the wing, enters hesitantly, as if she were in a procession.*)

BOBO: (*acting the neighbor*) Good evening, Marie. Aren't you in? Goodness me, how dark it is. As our constable would say, in that roguish way of his, it's as dark here as up a nigger's ass-hole. Oh! I beg your pardon—I mean a Negro's. One should be polite. (*A pause.*) What, you're checking the day's accounts? All right, then I'll come back tomorrow. I know what that's like. I'm a sensible person. Goodbye, Marie, and goodnight.
(*She mimes all the gestures of departure, but remains on-stage, near the wing, looking off-stage and fixed in an attitude of departure.*)

VILLAGE: (*resuming the formal tone of his recital*) So there I was, nestling in the shadow. And I whispered to her: Listen to the singing of my thighs! Listen! (*He makes his thighs bulge under his trousers.*) That sound is the mewing of panthers and tigers. When they bend, that means leopards are stretching. If I unbutton, an eagle of the Great Empire will swoop down from our snowy summits to your Pyrenees. But . . . I'm not dead set on unbuttoning. The fires are being lit. Under our dry fingers, the drums . . .
(*They all start dancing in place—even* BOBO, *who is looking into the wings, even the Court, but not the Mask—and clapping their hands very softly.*)
Then, in the glade, the dance began! (*turning to the others*) For I had to cast a spell on her, didn't I? My aim, then, was to draw her gently toward her room. The door of the shop opened out into the street, the old bitch was dying upstairs . . .

FELICITY: (*imitating the old mother*) Almonds! A-a-almonds! Prayers! Pra-a-ayers! It's time for your prayer! Don't forget!

VILLAGE: (*very annoyed*) She's going to spoil everything. (*reassuming the woman's voice*) I have one more layette to finish, mother dear, and then I'll be right up. (*resuming the formal tone of his recital*) I asked for another glass of rum. The liquor kindled my genius. I was feeling, as they say, a little high. In my eye I trotted out a big parade of our warriors, diseases, alligators, amazons, straw huts, cataracts, hunts, cotton, even leprosy and even a hundred thousand youngsters who died in the dust. Along my teeth I set adrift our pointiest canoes. With a hand in my pocket, as if I were going to dance the tango, I went up to her and said, "Kind lady, it's nasty outside." She replied:
(*As before, they all listen to the Mask, who says nothing. Then they burst out in their orchestrated laugh.*)
. . . Yes, you're quite right. We must be careful. People gossip in small towns . . .

BOBO: (*pretending to return and to want to enter the shop*) Marie, you still haven't put the light on. You'll spoil your eyes working in the dark. (*A pause.*) I hear someone whistling on the road. It's probably your husband. Good night, Marie.
(*Same pantomime as before. All this time, VILLAGE has been looking as if he were very much afraid of being discovered.*)

VILLAGE: (*tone of the recital*) Indeed, one can never be too careful: suns revolve about the earth . . .

FELICITY: (*imitating the old mother*) Ma-a-arie! A-a-almonds! Beware of the night, child. All cats are black in the dark, and one forgets to give the evening almond to one's old mother. (*A pause.*) Tell your sister Susan to come in.

VILLAGE: (*assuming the voice of a woman*) Susan! Susan! Where are you?

SNOW: (*who has run behind the catafalque, where she is hidden*) Why, I'm here. I'm in the garden.

VILLAGE: (*holding back the Mask, who seems to want to go toward the catafalque, and still imitating a woman's voice*) Are you all alone in the garden?

THE MISSIONARY: (*to* ARCHIBALD) Your cue, Archibald.
(ARCHIBALD *runs to the left wing, from which he now seems to be entering very casually, whistling as he walks. However, he merely imitates the movement of walking and actually remains where he is.*)

SNOW: I'm all alone, all by myself. I'm playing knuckle-bones.

VILLAGE: (*still in a woman's voice*) Be careful, Susan, watch out for prowlers. It hasn't been safe in these parts ever since they began recruiting aviators in Guiana.

VOICE OF SNOW: In Guiana! Aviators!

VILLAGE: (*voice of the recital*) In Guiana, you slut! . . . suns revolve about the earth, eagles swoop down on our battlefields . . . so let's close the window. She acted as if she didn't understand. Gallantly I closed the window. Snow was falling on the town.

VIRTUE: (*rushing toward him in a panic*) Stop it!

BOBO: (*still fixed in a movement of departure, but turning her head to blurt out the following*) Look at how he's carrying on. He's foaming. He's fuming. It's a mirage!

VIRTUE: Village, Village, please, I'm asking you, stop.

VILLAGE: (*looking at* VIRTUE) The limpidity of your blue eyes, that tear gleaming at the corner, your heavenly bosom . . .

VIRTUE: You're raving. Whom are you talking to?

VILLAGE: (*still looking at* VIRTUE) I love you and I can't bear it any longer.

VIRTUE: (*screaming*) Village!

SNOW: (*peeping out from behind the catafalque just long enough to say the following*) But, my dear, it has nothing to do with you, you might have realized it.

VILLAGE: (*turning slowly to the Mask, who mechanically goes on with his knitting*) Your feet, the soles of which are the color of periwinkles, your feet, which are varnished on top, walked along the pavement . . .

VIRTUE: You've already said that to me. Stop talking.

ARCHIBALD: (*breaking off his silent whistling and immobile walk and assuming an angry expression*) Negroes, I'm losing my temper. Either we continue the re-enactment or we leave.

VILLAGE: (*imperturbably, now fully facing the Mask*) The gentlest of your movements delineate you so exquisitely that when I'm on your shoulder I feel you're being borne by the wind. The rings under your eyes distress me. Madam, when you go . . . go on. (*to the audience*) For she wasn't coming, she was going. She was going to her bedroom . . .

FELICITY: (*imitating the old woman*) My almond and my prayer!

VOICE OF SNOW: Yes, yes, I'm alone in the garden, astride the jet of water.

BOBO: (*seeming to come back*) Good evening, Marie. Lock your door.

VILLAGE: (*voice of the recital*) . . . to her bedroom, where I followed her in order to strangle her. (*to the Mask*) Get going, slut. And go wash yourself. (*to the audience*) I had to work fast, the cuckold was on his way.
(*The Mask is about to start walking.*)
Stop! (*to the audience*) But first let me show you what I was able to get out of my tamed captive . . .

THE JUDGE: But what's Virtue's role in the crime?
(ARCHIBALD *and* BOBO *turn their heads.* SNOW *shows hers. They seem very much interested.*)

VILLAGE: (*after a moment's hesitation*) None. She never ceased to be present, at my side, in her immortal form. (*to the audience*) . . . my tamed captive. For she was clever and highly reputed among those of her race. Come. Stand in a circle. (*He pretends to be speaking both to the audience and to invisible* NEGROES *on the stage.*) Not too close. There. Now I'm going to make her work. (*to the Mask*) Are you ready, kid?

THE JUDGE: No, no. It's better to maintain a formal tone.

VILLAGE: Do you really want me to?

THE JUDGE: Yes, it's better. Don't be afraid to establish distance.

VILLAGE: As you like. (*to the audience*) She can play the piano. Very, very well. Would anyone like to hold her knitting for a moment?
(*He addresses the audience directly, until a spectator comes up and takes the needle from the Mask's hands.*)
(*to the spectator*) Thank you, sir (or "madam").
(*to the Mask*) Now play us a Strauss melody.
(*The Mask docilely sits down on an invisible stool and, facing the audience, plays on an invisible piano.*) Stop! (*He stops playing. The Court applauds.*)

THE QUEEN: (*simperingly*) Perfect, perfect, she was almost too perfect. Even in adversity, in disaster, our melodies will sing.

THE VALET: (*to* VILLAGE) What else can she do?

VILLAGE: As you've seen, she knits helmets for little chimney-sweeps. On Sunday she sings at the harmonium. She prays. (*to the Mask*) On your knees! (*He kneels.*) With your hands clasped. Eyes upward. Good. Pray! (*The entire Court applauds in elegant fashion.*) She's good at lots of other things. She does water-colors and rinses glasses.

FELICITY: (*voice of the old mother*) Marie! Ma-a-arie! My a-a-almond! Child, it's time for it.

VILLAGE: (*woman's voice*) Right away, mother dear. I've almost finished rinsing the glasses. (*voice of the recital*) One day she even roasted in the flames . . .

THE COURT: (*except* THE MISSIONARY) Speed it up, talk faster!

THE MISSIONARY: How dare you allude to that wicked affair.

THE VALET: (*to* THE MISSIONARY) Haven't you placed her in heaven since then?

THE QUEEN: But, what do they mean?

VILLAGE: One day they caught her as she was wheeling about on her horse amidst the banners. They put her into prison and burned her at the stake.

SNOW: (*showing her head, and, with a burst of laughter*) Then they ate the pieces.

THE QUEEN: (*with a piercing cry*) My saint! (*Exit, hiding her face and sobbing her heart out;* THE VALET *accompanies her.*)

VILLAGE: But, for the most part, she does what she can. When the time comes, she calls the midwife . . .
(*to* BOBO) Take it, Bobo.
(BOBO *approaches the Mask and speaks to him gently.*)

BOBO: You'd better lie down so that it doesn't hurt too much. (*She listens to the Mask, who makes no answer.*) Your pride? . . . All right. Remain standing. (*She kneels and puts her hand under the Mask's skirt, from where she takes out a doll about two feet long representing* THE GOVERNOR.)

THE GOVERNOR: (*to the Court*) I'm entering the world! With boots on, decorated . . .
(BOBO *keeps searching and pulls out another doll:* THE VALET.)

THE VALET: Here comes my mug!
(BOBO *searches and takes out* THE JUDGE.)

THE JUDGE: (*in amazement*) Me?

THE GOVERNOR: (*To* THE JUDGE) It's the spitting image of you!
(BOBO *pulls out* THE MISSIONARY.)

THE MISSIONARY: The ways of Providence . . .
(BOBO *takes out a doll representing* THE QUEEN.)

THE QUEEN: (*re-entering just as the doll emerges*) I'd like to see myself come out of there . . . There I come! My mother spawned
me standing up! (*Exit.*)
(THE NEGROES *have hung up the dolls on the left side of the
stage, under the Court's balcony. They gaze at them and then resume their recital.*)

SNOW: (*still fixed in an attitude of departure, as if about to enter
the right wing; turning her head*) In any event, the one who's rotting in the packing case never had such a high old time.
(*Exit* THE GOVERNOR.)

VILLAGE: Let's forget about her. (*to the spectator who is holding
the knitting*) Give her back her knitting. Thank you, sir. You may
go. (*The spectator returns to his seat.*) (*to the Mask*) And now,
let's continue. Go on, madam . . .
(*The Mask starts walking very slowly toward the right screen.*)
Walk! This evening you have the noblest gait in the realm. (*to
the audience*) As you see, the husband arrived too late. He'll find
only his wife's corpse, disemboweled but still warm. (*to the Mask,
who had stopped but who starts walking again*) It's no longer a
Negro trailing at your skirt; it's a marketful of slaves, all sticking
out their tongues. Just because you've kindly given me a drink of
rum you think . . . eh, you bitch! Pull me toward your lace . . .
(*They both move toward the screen, very slowly, the Mask in
front of* VILLAGE.) . . . Underneath you're surely wearing some
sort of black petticoat that's silkier than my gaze . . .

VIRTUE: (*falling to her knees*) Village!

VILLAGE: (*to the Mask*) Walk faster, I'm in a hurry. Follow the corridor. Turn right. Good. You know the door of your room. Open it. How gracefully you walk, oh noble and familiar rump!
(*They mount the steps and are about to go behind the screen. But before following the Mask there, VILLAGE turns to the audience.*)
Are they following me? (*to THE NEGROES*) Are you following me?
(*THE NEGROES, that is, ARCHIBALD, BOBO and SNOW—VIRTUE remains kneeling—place themselves behind him, in a procession, softly clapping their hands and stamping their feet.*)
But if I go too far, stop me.
(*Enter THE GOVERNOR.*)

THE JUDGE: What's the Queen doing?

THE GOVERNOR: She's weeping, sir. Torrents are pouring from her eyes and flowing down to the plains, which, alas, they cannot fertilize, for the water is warm and salty.

THE MISSIONARY: Does she have need of religion?

THE VALET: I'll go and console her. I know how to handle her.

ALL: (*except VIRTUE, to VILLAGE*) We'll help you. Don't be afraid. Keep walking.

VILLAGE: (*imploringly*) Tell me, Negroes, what if I couldn't stop?

ALL: (*except VIRTUE*) Keep going.

BOBO: The Valet has set an example for you. He's already with the Queen.

VILLAGE: (*falling to one knee*) Negroes, I beg of you . . .

BOBO: (*laughing*) Inside with you, you lazy lubber!

SNOW: (*kneeling*) Pour forth torrents. First, showers of sperm and then streams of her blood. (*cupping her hands*) I'll drink it, Village, I'll wash my chin with it, my belly, my shoulders.

VILLAGE: (A *white-gloved hand, that of the Mask, who is behind the screen, comes down on his shoulder and remains there.*) Friends, friends, I beg of you . . .

ALL: (*still clapping their hands and stamping their feet gently*) Go on in. She's already lying down. She's put aside her knitting. She's calling for your big ebony body. She has blown out the candle. She's darkening the room to put you at ease!

VILLAGE: Friends . . .

FELICITY: (*suddenly standing up straight*) Dahomey! Dahomey! To my rescue, Negroes, all of you! Gentlemen of Timbuctoo, come in, under your white parasols! Stand over there. Tribes covered with gold and mud, rise up from my body, emerge! Tribes of the Rain and Wind, forward! Princes of the Upper Empires, Princes of the bare feet and wooden stirrups, on your caparisoned horses, enter! Enter on horseback. Gallop in! Gallop in! Hop it! Hop it! Hop along! Negroes of the ponds, you who fish with your pointed beaks, enter! Negroes of the docks, of the factories, of the dives, Negroes of the Ford plant, Negroes of General Motors, and you, too, Negroes who braid rushes to encage crickets and roses, enter and remain standing! Conquered soldiers, enter. Conquering soldiers, enter. Crowd in. More. Lay your shields against the walls. You, too, who dig up corpses to suck the brains from skulls, enter unashamedly. You, tangled brother-sister, walking melancholy incest, come in. Barbarians, barbarians, barbarians, come along. I can't describe you all, nor even name you all, nor name your dead, your arms, your ploughs, but enter. Walk gently on your white feet. White? No, black. Black or white? Or blue? Red, green, blue, white, red, green, yellow, who knows, where am I? The colors exhaust me . . . Are you there, Africa with the bulging chest and oblong thigh? Sulking Africa, wrought of iron, in the fire, Africa of the millions of royal slaves, deported Africa, drifting continent, are you there? Slowly you vanish, you withdraw into the past, into the tales of castaways, colonial museums, the works of scholars, but I call you back this evening to attend a secret revel. (*pondering*) It's a block of darkness, compact and evil, that holds its breath, but not its odor. Are you there? Don't leave the stage unless I tell you to. Let the spectators behold you. A deep, almost invisible somnolence emanates from you, spreads all about, hypnotizes them. We shall presently go down amongst them, but before we do . . .

VILLAGE: Madam . . .

FELICITY: . . . but before we do, allow me to present the most cowardly of all Negroes. Need I name him?
(*to* VILLAGE) Well, get going!

VILLAGE: (*trembling. The white-gloved hand is still resting on his shoulder.*) Madam . . .

FELICITY: If he's still hesitating, let him take the place of the dead woman. (*She sits down, exhausted.*)

VILLAGE and VIRTUE: (*together*) No!

ARCHIBALD: (*to* VILLAGE) Go on in.

VILLAGE: (*to the melody of the "Dies Irae"*) Madam . . . Madam . . .

SNOW: (*to the "Dies Irae"*) Enter, enter . . . deliver us from evil. Hallelujah . . .

BOBO: (*all the speeches will now be sung to the same melody*) Oh descend, my cataracts!

VILLAGE: Madam . . . Madam . . .

SNOW: I still snow upon your countryside,
        I still snow upon your tombs, and I calm you . . .

VIRTUE: The north winds have been forewarned:
          Let them load it on their shoulders
          All the horses are untethered.

VILLAGE: (*still kneeling; moving backwards, as if drawn by the
          white-gloved hand, he disappears behind the screen, where the
          Mask is*) Madam . . . Madam . . .

VIRTUE: And thou, evening twilight,
          Weave the cloak that shrouds him.

SNOW: Expire, expire gently,
          Our Lady of the Pelicans,
          Pretty sea gull, politely,
          Gallantly, let yourself be tortured . . .

VIRTUE: Beshroud yourselves, tall forests,
          That he may steal in silently.
          Shod his big feet, oh white dust, with felt slippers.

THE JUDGE: (*to* THE GOVERNOR, *who is looking through his spyglass
at what is going on behind the screen*) What do you make out?

THE GOVERNOR: Nothing out of the ordinary. (*laughing*) The
woman is giving in. You can say what you like about them, but
those fellows are terrific fuckers.

THE MISSIONARY: You're forgetting yourself, my dear governor.

THE GOVERNOR: I'm sorry. I mean that the flesh is weak. It's a law of
nature.

THE JUDGE: But what is it they're doing? Describe it.

THE GOVERNOR: Now he's washing his hands . . . he's drying them
. . . those people are clean. I've always noticed that. When I was
a lieutenant, my orderly . . .

THE JUDGE: What else is he doing?

THE GOVERNOR: He's smiling . . . he's taking out his pack of Chesterfields . . . puff! He's blown out the candle.

THE JUDGE: Not really?

THE GOVERNOR: Take the spyglass, or the lantern, and have a look. (THE JUDGE *shrugs his shoulders.*)

ARCHIBALD: (*suddenly aware of the presence of* NEWPORT NEWS, *who entered very slowly while* FELICITY *was delivering her long speech*) You! I told you to come back and let us know only when everything was finished. So it's over? It's done? (*turning to the Court, all of whose members have put their hands to their faces, he screams*) Keep your masks on!

NEWPORT NEWS: Not quite. He's defending himself as best he can, but he'll certainly be executed.

ARCHIBALD: (*he has changed his voice; instead of declaiming, he speaks in his natural tone*) The shot'll make a noise. (*A pause.*) Are you sure he's guilty? And are you sure he's the one we've been looking for?

NEWPORT NEWS: (*a little ironically*) Are you suddenly getting suspicious?

ARCHIBALD: Bear in mind that it's a matter of judging and probably sentencing and executing a Negro. That's a serious affair. It's no longer a matter of staging a performance. The man we're holding and for whom we're responsible is a real man. He moves, he chews, he coughs, he trembles. In a little while, he'll be killed.

NEWPORT NEWS: That's very tough. But though we can put on an act in front of them (*pointing to the audience*), we've got to stop acting when we're among ourselves. We'll have to get used to taking responsibiity for blood—our own. And the moral weight . . .

ARCHIBALD: All the same, as I've said, it's a matter of living blood, hot, supple, reeking blood, of blood that bleeds . . .

NEWPORT NEWS: But then what about the act we put on? Was it just an entertainment, as far as you were concerned?

ARCHIBALD: (*interrupting him*) Be quiet. (*A pause.*) Is he going to be executed?

NEWPORT NEWS: He is.

ARCHIBALD: All right. Go back to them.

NEWPORT NEWS: I need to be here. In any case, it's too late. Let me go through with it. Here.

ARCHIBALD: Well . . . then stay. (*to the negresses*) And you, be quiet. Village is working for us. Help him in silence, but help him.
(*Enter* THE VALET.)

THE GOVERNOR: What about the Queen? What's she doing?

THE VALET: She's still crying. It's the warm rains of September.

THE GOVERNOR: And . . . what did she say?

THE VALET: At least save the child! And see to it that the mother is received courteously. She has gone astray, but she's a white woman.
(*A very long silence.*)

VIRTUE: (*timidly*) He hasn't come back.

BOBO: (*in an undertone*) He hasn't had time to. After all, it's far away.

VIRTUE: What do you mean far away? It's behind the screen.

BOBO: (*still in an undertone, slightly annoyed*) Of course. But at the same time they've got to go elsewhere. They have to cross the room, go through the garden, take a path lined with hazel trees, turn left, push aside the thorns, throw salt in front of them, put on boots, enter the woods . . . It's night time. Deep in the woods . . .

THE GOVERNOR: Gentlemen, we've got to start getting ready. Wake the Queen. We must go and punish them, we must try them, and the journey will be long and arduous.

THE MISSIONARY: I'll need a horse.

THE VALET: Everything has been attended to, Monsignor.

BOBO: (*resuming*) . . . deep in the woods, look for the gate of the cavern, find the key, go down the steps . . . dig the grave . . . Flee. Will the moon wait? All that takes time. You yourself, when you go upstairs with the gentleman who's on his way home from his wife's funeral . . .

VIRTUE: (*curtly*) You're right. I do a conscientious job. But Village ought to have acted it out before our eyes.

BOBO: Greek tragedy, my dear, decorum. The ultimate gesture is performed off-stage.
(ARCHIBALD, *irritated, makes a threatening gesture to them and points to* VILLAGE, *who is about to enter. A rather long silence. Then, enter* VILLAGE, *quietly. His shirt collar is awry. They all surround him.*)

ARCHIBALD: Is it over? Did you have much trouble?

VILLAGE: Same as usual.

SNOW: Nothing happened, did it?

VILLAGE: No, nothing. Or, if you prefer, it all went off as usual, and very smoothly. When Diouf entered behind the screen, he kindly offered me a seat.

SNOW: And then?

NEWPORT NEWS: Nothing else. They waited on a bench, off stage, and smiled at each other in amusement.

VILLAGE: (*catching sight of* NEWPORT NEWS) Are you back? You should still be there, with them . . .

NEWPORT NEWS: I thought that this evening, thanks to you, everything was supposed to change, and that this would be the last night.

VILLAGE: (*annoyed*) I did what I could. But what about you? What about them?

NEWPORT NEWS: What they do is no business of yours. It's for *them* to ask questions. But . . . I'm glad you performed the rite, as you do every evening. It'll be my joy to finish off the performance.

ARCHIBALD: There's nothing new, at least, in the ceremony.

NEWPORT NEWS: (*angrily*) Do you want to continue it forever and ever? To perpetuate it until the death of the race? As long as the earth revolves about the sun, which is itself carried off in a straight line to the very limits of God, in a secret chamber, Negroes will . . .

BOBO: (*screaming*) Will hate! Yessir!

THE JUDGE: (*to the Court*) I think we have no more time to waste. (*A singing is heard—a kind of solemn march, which is sung. Then,* THE QUEEN *appears, leading* DIOUF, *who is masked and wearing his trappings.*)

THE QUEEN: This is the woman whom we must go down and avenge.

SNOW: Diouf has arrived!

THE QUEEN: (*to* DIOUF) The journey must have been arduous, poor child. At last you're with your true family. From here, from on high, you'll have a better view of them.

THE MISSIONARY: When we get back, we'll try to beatify her.

THE VALET: A terrific idea! Her Majesty will adopt her. Won't she, child?

THE QUEEN: We'll have to think about that. It's a very delicate matter. After all, she *has* been defiled. Against her will, I hope, but, after all, she's liable to be a reminder of our shame. (*after a hesitation*) However, the idea is worth considering. (*to* THE JUDGE) What are they doing down there?

THE JUDGE: (*looking with* THE GOVERNOR'S *fieldglasses*) They're wild with anger, with rage, and somewhat confused.

THE QUEEN: What are they saying?

THE JUDGE: They're utterly dumbfounded.

THE QUEEN: But . . . what's going on that's so strange and rare? Is snow falling on their mangroves?

THE JUDGE: Madam . . . it may be that a crime is being committed.

THE QUEEN: No doubt.

THE JUDGE: No, another one. One that's being judged elsewhere.

THE QUEEN: But—what can we do? Prevent it? Or make use of it? (*The members of the Court all lean forward.*)

VILLAGE: (*to* ARCHIBALD) Are they going to come, sir? Are they coming to judge us, to weigh us? (VILLAGE *is trembling.*)

ARCHIBALD: (*putting his hand on* VILLAGE'S *shoulder*) Don't be afraid. It's only play-acting.

VILLAGE: (*persisting*) To weigh us? With their golden and ruby scales? And do you think, if they go off to die, that they'll let me love Virtue—or rather that Virtue will be able to love me?

NEWPORT NEWS: (*smiling, but pointedly*) Didn't you try to negrify them? To graft Bambara lips and nostrils on them? To kink their hair? To reduce them to slavery?

THE MISSIONARY: (*roaring out*) Off we go! And not another minute to waste. (*to* THE VALET) Prepare the cloak and boots, a pound of cherries and Her Majesty's horse. (*to* THE QUEEN) Madam, we must be off. It will be a long journey. (*to* THE GOVERNOR) Do you have the umbrellas?

THE GOVERNOR: (*hurt*) Ask Joseph. (*to* THE VALET) Do you have the flask?

THE VALET: On getting out of bed, the Queen knighted me and gave me a title. And don't forget it. All the same, I have the umbrellas and the quinine tablets. I also have a flask of rum—full to the brim! Because it'll be hot.

THE MISSIONARY: During the trek, I authorize drinking to beguile fatigue, and let a Palestrina Mass be sung. Everyone ready? Then, forward . . . march!
(*The entire Court disappears, leaving the platform, where* DIOUF, *still masked, remains alone. At first, he hesitates, then, timidly, approaches the handrail and looks down.*)
(*The Court remains off-stage for four or five minutes. THE* NEGROES *below have gathered together, left. In front of the group stands* NEWPORT NEWS. *They are all waiting anxiously.* BOBO *raises her head. She sees* DIOUF *leaning over the rail and looking at them.*)

BOBO: You! You, Mr. Diouf?
(THE NEGROES *all raise their heads and look at* DIOUF, *who, still masked, nods "yes."*)
Mr. Diouf, you're living a curious death. What's it like there?

DIOUF: (*slowly removing his mask*) The light there is rather queer.

BOBO: Tell us, Mr. Vicar General, what do you see there? Answer, Diouf. Seen through their eyes, what are their kings like? What do you see from the height of your blue eyes, from the height of those belvederes?

DIOUF: (*hesitating*) I see you—sorry—I see us as follows: I'm on high, and not on the ground. And I am perhaps experiencing the vision of God.

BOBO: Are you a white woman?

DIOUF: The first thing to tell you is that they lie or that they're mistaken. They're not white, but pink or yellowish.

BOBO: Then are you a pink woman?

DIOUF: I am. I move about in a light emitted by our faces which they reflect from one to another. We, that is, you, we're still suffocating in a heavy atmosphere. It all began when I had to leave your world. I was eaten with despair. But your insults and homage little by little exalted me. I was imbued with a new life. I felt Village's desire. His voice was so rough! And his gaze! Humble and triumphant. Before I knew it, I was with child by him.

BOBO: Are you proud?

DIOUF: Proud, no. Our cares and concerns no longer have meaning for me. New relationships come into being along with new things, and these things become necessary. (*pensively*) Indeed, necessity is a very curious novelty. The harmony thrills me. I had left the realm of gratuitousness where I saw you gesticulating. I could no longer see even our hatred, our hatred which rises up to them. I learned, for example, that they're able to perform true dramas and to believe in them.

NEWPORT NEWS: (*ironically*) You miss those days of the dead, don't you?

ARCHIBALD: Every actor knows that at a given time the curtain will fall. And that he almost always embodies a dead man or dead

woman: Lady Macbeth, Don Giovanni, Antigone, Camille, Dr.
Schweitzer . . .
(*A long silence.*)
(*Footsteps are heard off-stage.* DIOUF, *in a panic, puts on his
mask again. The other* NEGROES *seem frightened. All of them, in a
body, including* MRS. FELICITY, *go to the left side of the stage and
huddle under the balcony where the Court had been. The sound
of footsteps becomes more distinct. At length, from the right
wing, as if coming down a road, emerges first* THE VALET, *walking
backward. He is belching and staggering. He is obviously drunk.*)

THE VALET: (*facing the wing; belching*) Be careful with the nag!
See that he doesn't stumble. The Queen's not going (*belches*) to
arrive on a horse with broken knees. Oh, bishop-at-large, be careful that the train of the Queen's cloak and your (*belches*) white
(*belches*) purple skirt don't get caught in the cactus. Damn it,
what dust! Mouth's full of it! But you . . . (*belches*) Gives you a
certain air! Watch out . . . watch out . . . there . . . there . . .
(*He makes a gesture as if to indicate the road to take.*)
(*Finally, also walking backward, appear* THE GOVERNOR, THE MIS-
SIONARY, THE JUDGE, *and then, moving forward,* THE QUEEN. *She
seems very weary, as after a long journey. They are all drunk.*)

THE QUEEN: (*unsteady on her legs and advancing cautiously, looking
about her*) Dust! Mouth's full of it, but it gives you a certain air!
(*She belches and bursts out laughing.*) Look where it gets us, following old troopers under colonial skies. (*She takes the empty
flask and throws it away.*) And not a drop left. (*belches*) (*suddenly noble*) Thus do I set foot on my foreign possessions.
(*laughs*)

THE GOVERNOR: (*hiccoughing after each word*) Stop in your tracks.
Prudence, circumspection, mystery. All is swamp, quagmires,
arrows, felines . . .
(*Very softly at first, then more and more loudly,* THE NEGROES, *almost invisible under the balcony, utter sounds of the virgin forest:
croaking of the toad, hoot of the owl, a hissing, very gentle roars,
breaking of wood, moaning of the wind.*)
. . . here, from the skin of their bellies the snakes lay eggs from
which blinded children take wing . . . the ants riddle you with

vinegar or arrows . . . the creepers fall madly in love with you, kiss your lips and eat you . . . here the rocks float . . . the water is dry . . . the wind is a skyscraper . . . all is leprosy, sorcery, danger, madness . . .

THE QUEEN: (*wonderstruck*) And flowers!

THE JUDGE: (*hiccoughing*) Poisonous, Madam. Deadly. Sick. Drank too much rum. Leaden sky, Madam. Our pioneers tried grafts on our garden cabbage, on the Dutch peony, on rhubarb. Our plants died, madam, murdered by those of the tropics.
(THE NEGROES *laugh with their orchestrated laugh, very softly. They start making their sounds again, cracking of branches, cries, caterwauling, etc.*)

THE QUEEN: I thought as much. Even their botany is wicked. Luckily we have our preserves.

THE GOVERNOR: And reserves of energy. Always fresh troops.

THE QUEEN: (*to* THE GOVERNOR) Tell them that their sovereign is with them in her heart . . . and . . . what about the gold? . . . the emeralds . . . the copper . . . the mother-of-pearl?

THE MISSIONARY: (*with a finger to his mouth*) In safe places. They'll be shown to you. Pounds of them. Stacks of them. Avalanches.

THE QUEEN: (*still moving forward*) If it's at all possible, before the sun sets behind the mountains I'd like to go down to a mine and row on the lake. (*Suddenly she notices* THE VALET, *who is shivering.*) What's the matter? Scared?

THE VALET: Fever, Madam.

THE QUEEN: (*shaking* THE VALET) Fever? Fever or liquor? You drank more than half the supply all by yourself.

THE VALET: I did it in order to sing better, and louder. I even danced.

THE QUEEN: (*to* THE MISSIONARY) What about the dancing? Where's the dancing?

THE MISSIONARY: It takes place only at night . . .

THE QUEEN: Have the Night brought in!

THE GOVERNOR: It's coming, Madam! In quick time! One two! . . . One two!
(*The jungle sounds made by* THE NEGROES *grow louder and louder.*)

THE MISSIONARY: (*timidly*) The dances take place only at night. Each and every one of them is danced for our destruction. Go no further. This is a dread region. Every thicket hides the grave of a missionary . . . (*belches*)

THE GOVERNOR: And of a captain. (*pointing with his arm*) There the north, there the east, the west, the south. On each of these shores, at the river's edge, on the plains, our soldiers have fallen. Don't go any closer, it's swamp . . . (*He holds back* THE QUEEN.)

THE JUDGE: (*sternly*) The climate's no excuse for your laxity. I've lost none of my pride or daring. It was to punish a crime that I undertook the journey. Where are the Negroes, Mr. Governor?
(THE NEGROES *laugh as before, very softly, almost in a murmur. And the same rustling of leaves, moaning of wind, roars and other sounds that suggest the virgin forest.*)

THE QUEEN: (*falling into* THE GOVERNOR's *arms*) Did you hear? (*They all listen.*) . . . and . . . and . . . what if they were . . . if they were really Blacks? And, what if they were alive?

THE MISSIONARY: Don't be afraid, Madam. They wouldn't dare . . . You are swathed in a gentle dawn that keeps them in awe.

THE QUEEN: (*trembling*) You think so? I haven't done anything bad, have I? Obviously, my soldiers have sometimes let themselves be carried away in their enthusiasm . . .

THE GOVERNOR: Madam, I'm in command here, and it's not the moment to pass judgment on ourselves . . . You're under my protection.

THE VALET: And I'm warrant of the fact that we have their welfare at heart. I've hailed their beauty in a poem that's become famous . . .
(THE NEGROES *have moved forward very softly. The Court stops short. Then it moves back, as softly as* THE NEGROES *moved forward, so that it is at the right, at the point where it entered, opposite the side where* THE NEGROES *are, and facing them.*)

FELICITY: (*to* THE NEGROES) It's dawn! Take it, Absalom!

ARCHIBALD: (*imitating a cock*) Cock-a-doodle-doo!

FELICITY: (*still addressing* THE NEGROES) It's dawn, gentlemen. Since we've wanted to be guilty, let's be prepared. We must act and speak cautiously and with restraint.

THE GOVERNOR: (*to* THE VALET) I'm going to see whether there's a possibility of our falling back. (*Exit, right, but reappearing immediately.*) Madam, the jungle has closed behind us.

THE QUEEN: (*frightened*) But we're in our native land, aren't we?

THE GOVERNOR: Madam, all the shutters are closed, the dogs are hostile, communications are cut off, the night is bitter cold. It was a trap. We must make a stand. It's dawn! (*to* THE VALET) Take it!

THE VALET: Cock-a-doodle-doo!

THE QUEEN: (*gloomily*) Yes, it's dawn, and we're face to face with them. And they're black, just as I dreamt they were.

THE JUDGE: Let's set up the court of justice!

THE MISSIONARY: (*to* THE VALET) The throne! And stop that absurd trembling. (THE VALET *brings over* FELICITY's *gilded armchair.* THE QUEEN *sits down on it.*)

(THE NEGROES *take a step forward, then remain still.* NEWPORT NEWS *goes to the catafalque and removes the sheet, which has been stretched over two chairs.*)

THE QUEEN: My chairs!

THE VALET: They were there all the time! And I looked for them even under your skirts, Mr. Missionary!
(THE VALET *brings over the two chairs.* THE GOVERNOR *and* THE MISSIONARY *sit down in them. But first the Court bows ceremoniously to* THE NEGROES, *who, in like fashion, welcome the Court. The dolls representing the Court will remain on a kind of pedestal at the left until the curtain is drawn.*)

DIOUF: And I who saw myself shut up in the case!

THE JUDGE: The Court is now ready. (*to* THE NEGROES) Lie down. You'll approach us on your bellies.

ARCHIBALD: (*to the Court*) They're worn out, sir. If we may, we'll hear you on our haunches.

THE JUDGE: (*after exchanging glances of inquiry with the Court*) Granted.

ARCHIBALD: (*to* THE NEGROES) Squat. (THE NEGROES *squat.*) (*to* THE JUDGE) May we whimper?

THE JUDGE: If you must. (*in a booming voice*) But first, tremble! (THE NEGROES *tremble in orchestrated fashion.*) Harder! Tremble, come on, shake! Don't be afraid to bring down the coconuts that hang from your branches! Tremble, Negroes! (THE NEGROES, *all together, tremble harder and harder.*) That'll do . . . That'll do . . . We'll overlook your impertinences, which would make us more severe. We've taken stock: although we're not missing the body of either a white woman, or white man, God has intimated to us that there's an extra soul on hand. What does that mean?

ARCHIBALD: Alas, what *does* it mean?

THE MISSIONARY: (*to* THE JUDGE) Be careful. They're crafty, artful, cunning. They're fond of trials and theological discussions. They have a secret telegraph that flies over hill and dale.

THE JUDGE: (*to* ARCHIBALD) I'm not accusing *all* of Africa. That would be unjust, ungentlemanly . . .
(THE QUEEN, THE VALET, THE MISSIONARY *and* THE GOVERNOR *applaud.*)

THE QUEEN: Splendid! A fine and noble reply.

THE JUDGE: (*slyly*) No, one can't hold all of Africa responsible for the death of a white woman. Nevertheless, there's no denying the fact that one of you is guilty, and we've made the journey for the purpose of bringing him to trial. According to our statutes—naturally. He killed out of hatred. Hatred of the color white. That was tantamount to killing our entire race and killing us till doomsday. There was no one in the packing case . . . tell us why.

ARCHIBALD: (*sadly*) Alas, your Honor, there was no packing case either.

THE GOVERNOR: No packing case? No packing case either? They kill us without killing us and shut us up in no packing case either!

THE MISSIONARY: After that dodge, they won't be able to say they don't fake. They've been stringing us along. (*to* THE VALET) Don't laugh! Don't you see what they're doing with us?

THE JUDGE: (*to* THE NEGROES) According to you, there's no crime since there's no corpse, and no culprit since there's no crime. But let's get things straight: one corpse, two, a battalion, a drove of corpses, we'll pile them high if that's what we need to avenge ourselves. But no corpse at all—why that could kill us. (*to* ARCHIBALD) Do you want to be the death of us?

ARCHIBALD: We are actors and organized an evening's entertainment for you. We tried to present some aspect of our life that might interest you. Unfortunately, we haven't found very much.

THE MISSIONARY: Their dusky bodies were allowed to bear the Christian names of the Gregorian calendar. That was the first step.

THE VALET: (*insidiously*) Look at his mouth. You can see that their beauty can equal ours. Your Majesty, allow that beauty to be perpetuated . . .

THE JUDGE: For your pleasure? But my job is to seek out and judge a malefactor.

THE GOVERNOR: (*in a single breath*) And then I'll execute him: a bullet in his head and calves, spurts of saliva, bowie knives, bayonets, popguns, poisons of our Medicis . . .

THE JUDGE: He won't get out of it. I've got some tough laws, very sharp, very precise . . .

THE GOVERNOR: Puncturing of the abdomen, adrift in the eternal snows of our unconquered glaciers, Corsican blunderbuss, brass-knuckles, the guillotine, shoelaces, the itch, epilepsy . . .

THE JUDGE: Articles 280–8, 927–17, 18, 16, 5, 3, 2, 1, 0.

THE GOVERNOR: Tar and feathers, died like a rat, died like a dog, dyed in the wool, died in battle, hit the bottle, died in bed, cock-o'-the-walk. Hemlock! . . .

THE MISSIONARY: Gentlemen, be calm. The monster won't escape us again. But first, I'll christen him. For it's a matter of executing a man, not of bleeding an animal. And if Her Majesty . . .

THE QUEEN: (*gently*) As usual. I'll be godmother.

THE MISSIONARY: And then I'll give absolution for his crimes. And after that, gentlemen, it'll be your turn. When it's over, we'll pray. But first, the christening.

ARCHIBALD: You're in Africa . . .

THE QUEEN: (*ecstatically*) Overseas! Capricorn! My islands! Coral!

ARCHIBALD: (*slightly annoyed*) By being obstinate you're courting danger. Be careful. If you make one of your signs, the waters of our lakes, of our streams and rivers and cataracts, the sap of our trees and even our saliva, may boil over . . . or freeze.

THE QUEEN: In exchange for a crime, we were bringing the criminal pardon and absolution.

VILLAGE: Madam, beware. You are a great queen, and Africa is unsafe.

FELICITY: (*to* THE NEGROES) That'll do! Stand back! (*She makes a sign, and all* THE NEGROES *withdraw to the left of the stage. Then, at a sign from* THE QUEEN, *the Court withdraws to the right. The two women are face to face.*)

THE QUEEN: (*to* FELICITY) Begin.

FELICITY: You begin!

THE QUEEN: (*very courteously, as one behaves with humble folk*) I assure you, I can wait . . .

FELICITY: Admit you don't know how to begin.

THE QUEEN: I can wait. I have eternity with me.

FELICITY: (*with her hands on her hips; exploding*) Oh, really? Well, then, Dahomey! Dahomey! Negroes, come back me up! And don't let the crime be glossed over. (*to* THE QUEEN) No one could possibly deny it, it's sprouting, sprouting, my beauty, it's growing, bright and green, it's bursting into bloom, into perfume, and that lovely tree, that crime of mine, is all Africa! Birds have nested in it, and night dwells in its branches.

THE QUEEN: Every evening, and every single second, you engage, against me and mine—I know you do—in a preposterous and baleful rite. The odor of that tree's flowers spreads all the way to my country and tries to capture and destroy me.

FELICITY: (*face to face with* THE QUEEN) You're a ruin!

THE QUEEN: But what a ruin! And I haven't finished sculpting myself, haven't finished carving and jagging and fashioning myself in the form of a ruin. An eternal ruin. It's not time that corrodes me, it's not fatigue that makes me forsake myself, it's death that's shaping me and that . . .

FELICITY: If you're death itself, then why, why do you reproach me for killing you?

THE QUEEN: And if I'm dead, why do you go on and on killing me, murdering me over and over in my color? Isn't my sublime corpse —which still moves—enough for you? Do you need the corpse of a corpse?
(*Side by side, almost amicably, the two women move forward to the very front of the stage.*)

FELICITY: I shall have the corpse of your corpse's ghost. You are pale, but you're becoming transparent. Fog that drifts over my land, you will vanish utterly. My sun . . .

THE QUEEN: But if all that remained of my ghost were a breath, and only the breath of that breath, it would enter through the orifices of your bodies to haunt you . . .

FELICITY: We'd let a fart and blow you out.

THE QUEEN: (*infuriated*) Governor! General! Bishop! Judge! Valet!

ALL: (*gloomily and without moving*) Coming.

THE QUEEN: Put them to the sword!

FELICITY: If you are the light and we the shade, so long as there is night into which day must sink . . .

THE QUEEN: I'm going to have you exterminated.

FELICITY: (*ironically*) You fool, just imagine how flat you'd be without that shade to set you off in high relief.

THE QUEEN: But . . .

FELICITY: (*same tone*) For this evening, until the end of the drama, let us therefore remain alive.

THE QUEEN: (*turning to the Court*) Good God, good God, what's one to say to her . . .
(THE GOVERNOR, JUDGE, MISSIONARY *and* VALET *rush up to her and whisper encouragement.*)

THE MISSIONARY: Speak of our concern for them . . . of our schools . . .

THE GOVERNOR: Bring up the white man's burden, quote some lines from Kipling . . .

THE QUEEN: (*inspired*) All the same, my proud beauty, I was more beautiful than you! Anyone who knows me can tell you that. No one has been more lauded than I. Or more courted, or more toasted. Or adorned. Clouds of heroes, young and old, have died for me. My retinues were famous. At the Emperor's ball, an African slave bore my train. And the Southern Cross was one of my baubles. You were still in darkness.

FELICITY: Beyond that shattered darkness, which was splintered into millions of Blacks who dropped to the jungle, we were Darkness in person. Not the darkness which is absence of light, but the kindly and terrible Mother who contains light and deeds.

THE QUEEN: (*as if in a panic, to the Court*) Well? What else . . .

THE GOVERNOR: Say that we have guns to silence them . . .

THE MISSIONARY: That's idiotic. No, be friendly . . . Mention Dr. Livingstone . . .

FELICITY: Behold our gestures. Though now they're merely the mutilated arms of our ravaged rites, bogged down in weariness and time, before long you'll be stretching lopped-off stumps to heaven and to us . . .

THE QUEEN: (*to the Court*) What should I answer?

FELICITY: Look! Look, Madam. Here it comes, the darkness you were clamoring for, and her sons as well. They're her escort of crimes. To you, black was the color of priests and undertakers and orphans. But everything is changing. Whatever is gentle and kind and good and tender will be black. Milk will be black, sugar, rice, the sky, doves, hope, will be black. So will the opera to which we shall go, blacks that we are, in black Rolls Royces to hail black kings, to hear brass bands beneath chandeliers of black crystal . . .

THE QUEEN: But, after all, I haven't said my last word . . .

THE VALET: (*in her ear*) Sing a psalm!

THE MISSIONARY: Can't be helped—show your legs!

FELICITY: Twelve hours of night. Our merciful mother will keep us in her house, huddled between her walls! Twelve hours of day, so that these fragments of darkness can perform for the sun ceremonies like those of this evening . . .

THE QUEEN: (*very upset*) You fool! You see only the beauty of history. It's all well and good to come insulting us beneath our windows and to give birth every day to a hundred new heroes who put on an act . . .

FELICITY: Before long you'll see what's hidden behind our display . . . You're exhausted, all of you . . . Your journey has worn you out. You're dropping with sleep . . . You're dreaming!

THE QUEEN: (*she and* FELICITY *now talk to each other like two women exchanging recipes*) Yes, that's so. But what about you? You're going to tire yourselves too. And don't expect me to suggest tonics. Your herbs won't do the trick.

FELICITY: I don't mind being dog-tired. Others will help me.

THE QUEEN: And what about your darkies? Your slaves? Where will you get them? . . . You'll need them, you know . . .

FELICITY: (*timidly*) You might, perhaps . . . We'll be good negroes . . .

THE QUEEN: Oh no, not on your life! Governesses? Well, maybe . . .

THE MISSIONARY: If absolutely necessary, tutors for children . . . and even then . . .

FELICITY: It'll be hard, won't it?

THE QUEEN: (*leading her on*) Awful. But you'll be strong. And we, we'll be charmers. We'll be lascivious. We'll dance in order to be seductive. Just imagine what you're in for. Long labor on continents, for centuries, to carve yourself a sepulchre that may be less beautiful than mine . . . So let me manage things, won't you? No? You see how tired you are already. What is it you want? No, no, don't answer. Is it that you want your sons to be free of chains? Is that it? That's a noble wish, but listen to me . . . follow me . . . your sons—why, you don't know them yet . . . You do? Their feet are already riveted together? Your grandsons? They're unborn: so they don't exist. Therefore you can't worry about their situation. What does freedom or slavery matter since they don't exist? Really . . . smile a little! . . . Really, my argument seems false? (THE NEGROES *all look gloomy*.) Come, come, gentlemen. (*addressing her retinue*) Can I be wrong?

THE MISSIONARY: You are wisdom itself.

THE QUEEN: (*to* FELICITY) Your grandsons—who, bear in mind, do not exist—will have nothing to do. They'll serve us, no doubt, but we're not demanding. But think of the hardships for *us*. We'll have to *be*. And be radiant. (*A silence.*)

FELICITY: (*gently*) And you, think of the mosquitoes of our swamps. If they stung me, a grown Negro, fully armed, would spring from each abscess . . .

THE MISSIONARY: (*to* THE QUEEN) Madam, I told you so. They're insolent, bitter, vindictive . . .

THE QUEEN: (*weeping*) But what have I done to them? I'm kind, and sweet, and beautiful!

THE MISSIONARY: (*to* THE NEGROES) You nasty things! Look at the state into which you've dared put the kindest, sweetest and most beautiful of women!

SNOW: The most beautiful?

THE MISSIONARY: (*embarrassed*) I meant the most beautiful in our country. Display a little good will. Look at how she got all dressed up to visit you, and think of all we've done for you. We've baptized you! All of you! What about the water it took to baptize you? And the salt? The salt on your tongues. Tons of salt, painfully extracted from mines. But here I am going on and on and in a moment I'll have to allow his Excellency the Governor to speak, and he'll be followed by His Honor the Judge. Why be massacred instead of recognizing . . .

THE JUDGE: Who's the culprit? (*Silence.*) You won't answer? I'm offering you one last chance. Now listen: it doesn't matter to us which of you committed the crime. We don't care whether it's X, Y, or Z. If a man's a man, a Negro's a Negro, and all we need is two arms, two legs to break, a neck to put into the noose, and our justice is satisfied. Come, be decent about it.
(*Suddenly a firecracker explodes off-stage, followed by several more. The sparks of fireworks are seen against the black velvet of the set. Finally, everything grows quiet.* THE NEGROES, *who were squatting behind* FELICITY, *stand up.*)

NEWPORT NEWS: (*stepping forth*) I wish to inform you . . .
(*With a single movement, the members of the Court solemnly remove their masks. The audience sees the five black faces.*)

VILLAGE: (*very anxiously*) Is he dead?

NEWPORT NEWS: He has paid. We shall have to get used to the responsibility of executing our own traitors.

THE ONE WHO PLAYED THE VALET: (*sternly*) Did everything go off with all due justice?

NEWPORT NEWS: (*deferentially*) Rest assured. Not only were the forms of justice applied, but the spirit as well.

THE ONE WHO PLAYED THE MISSIONARY: What about the defense?

NEWPORT NEWS: Perfect. Very eloquent. But it was unable to sway the jury. And execution followed almost immediately upon delivery of sentence.
(*A silence.*)

THE ONE WHO PLAYED THE QUEEN: And now?

NEWPORT NEWS: Now? While a court was sentencing the one who was just executed, a congress was acclaiming another. He's on his way. He's going off to organize and continue the fight. Our aim is not only to corrode and dissolve the idea they'd like us to have of them, we must also fight them in their actual persons, in their flesh and blood. As for you, you were present only for display. Behind . . .

THE ONE WHO PLAYED THE VALET: (*curtly*) We know. Thanks to us, they've sensed nothing of what's going on elsewhere.
(*A silence.*)

THE ONE WHO PLAYED THE QUEEN: And . . . you say he has already left?

NEWPORT NEWS: That's right. Everything was planned for his departure.

THE ONE WHO PLAYED THE QUEEN: And . . . what is he like?

NEWPORT NEWS: (*smiling*) Just as you imagine him. Exactly as he must be in order to spread panic by force and cunning.

ALL: (*speaking at the same time*) Describe him! . . . Show us parts of him! . . . Let's see his knee, his calf, his toe! . . . His eye! His teeth!

NEWPORT NEWS: (*laughing*) He's on his way. Let him go. He has our confidence. Everything has been planned and prepared so that he can count on us when he's away.

THE ONE WHO PLAYED THE GOVERNOR: What about his voice? What's his voice like?

NEWPORT NEWS: It's deep. Somewhat caressing. He'll first have to fascinate and then convince. Yes, he's also a charmer.

BOBO: (*suspiciously*) But . . . at least he's black?
(*For a moment, they are all puzzled; then they burst out laughing.*)

THE ONE WHO PLAYED THE MISSIONARY: We've got to hurry . . .

VILLAGE: Are you leaving?

THE ONE WHO PLAYED THE GOVERNOR: Everything has been planned for each of us. If we want to get things done, we haven't a minute to lose.

DIOUF: I . . .

THE ONE WHO PLAYED THE MISSIONARY: (*interrupting him very brusquely*) It'll be hard for the others too—especially in the early stages—to shake off the torpor of a whole continent. Hemmed in by vapors and flies, imprisoned in pollen . . .

DIOUF: (*whimpering*) I'm old . . . I may be forgotten . . . and besides, they draped me in such a pretty dress . . .

THE ONE WHO PLAYED THE VALET: (*sternly*) Keep it. If they've turned you into the image they want to have of us, then stay with them. You'd be a burden to us.

ARCHIBALD: (*to* THE ONE WHO PLAYED THE VALET) But—is he still acting or is he speaking for himself? (*hesitating*) An Actor . . . a Negro . . . who wants to kill turns even his knife into something make-believe. (*to* DIOUF) Are you staying? (*A brief silence.* DIOUF *bows his head.*) Then stay.

SNOW: I've got to be going.

THE ONE WHO PLAYED THE VALET: Not before we finish the performance. (*to* ARCHIBALD) Resume the tone.

ARCHIBALD: (*solemnly*) As we could not allow the Whites to be present at a deliberation nor show them a drama that does not concern them, and as, in order to cover up, we have had to fabricate the only one that does concern them, we've got to finish this show and get rid of our judges . . . (*to* THE ONE WHO PLAYED THE QUEEN) as planned.

THE ONE WHO PLAYED THE QUEEN: At last they'll know the only dramatic relationships we can have with them. (*to the four* NEGROES *of the Court*) Are you willing?

THE ONE WHO PLAYED THE JUDGE: We are.

THE ONE WHO PLAYED THE QUEEN: We masked our faces in order to live the loathsome life of the Whites and at the same time to help you sink into shame, but our roles as actors are drawing to a close.

ARCHIBALD: How far are you willing to go?

THE ONE WHO PLAYED THE GOVERNOR: To the bitter end.

VILLAGE: But . . . except for the flowers, we haven't provided any-

thing . . . neither knives nor guns nor gallows nor rivers nor bayonets. Will we have to slit your throats in order to get rid of you?

THE ONE WHO PLAYED THE QUEEN: There's no need to. We're actors,
our massacre will be lyrical. (*to the four* NEGROES *of the Court*)
Gentlemen, your masks. (*One after the other, they put on their
masks again.*) (*to* ARCHIBALD) As for you, all you need to do is
give us our cues. All set?

ARCHIBALD: Begin.

THE QUEEN: You may start, Mr. Governor.

FELICITY: But, Madam, we haven't finished our oratorical contest.
Don't deprive me of the best part. There's still lots to be said
against Negroes.

THE QUEEN: I have made the journey. It was a long one. Your
warmth is inhuman, and I prefer to depart . . .

FELICITY: Nevertheless, you're going to hear what the color white
will signify from now on.

THE QUEEN: Don't waste your time. We'll be off and away before
you've even finished your speech.

FELICITY: If we let you leave.

THE QUEEN: How simple-minded! You haven't realized that we're
heading for death. We're going to it voluntarily, with a sneaking
happiness.

FELICITY: Are you committing suicide? You? (*All* THE NEGROES *and
the members of the Court, except* THE QUEEN, *burst into loud,
free laughter.*)

THE QUEEN: We chose to die so as to deprive you of pride of tri-
umph. Unless you're going to boast of having conquered a people
of shadows.

FELICITY: We'll always be able . . .

THE QUEEN: (*with great authority*) Be quiet. It's for me to speak and to give my orders. (*to* THE GOVERNOR) As I said, you may begin, Mr. Governor.

THE GOVERNOR: People usually draw lots in such circumstances . . .

THE QUEEN: No explanations. Show these barbarians that we are great because of our respect for discipline, and show the Whites who are watching that we are worthy of their tears.

ARCHIBALD: No. No, please don't die. Mr. Governor, please stay! What we enjoyed was to kill you, to slaughter you down to your white powder, to your very soapsuds . . .

THE QUEEN: Ah, ah! I've got you. (*to* THE GOVERNOR) Governor, lead off!

THE GOVERNOR: (*with resignation*) Very well! Colonially speaking, I've served my country well. (*he takes a swig of rum*) I've been given a thousand nicknames, which proved the Queen's esteem and the savage's fear. So I'm going to die, but in an apotheosis, borne aloft by ten thousand lads leaner than Plague and Leprosy exalted by anger and fury. (*At this point,* THE GOVERNOR *takes a paper from his pocket, as he did at the beginning of the play, and reads.*) When I fall to earth, scurvily pierced by your spears, look closely, you will behold my ascension. My corpse will be on the ground, but my soul and body will rise into the air. You'll see them, and you'll die of fright. It is thus that I have chosen to conquer you and rid the earth of your shadows. First, you'll turn pale, then you'll fall, and you'll be dead. And I, great. (*He puts the paper back into his pocket.*) Sublime. Terrifying. (*Silence.*) Well, you won't speak? What? You say I'm trembling? You know very well it's military gout. (*Silence.*) Well, you won't speak? Oh, you're resentful because of the ten thousand lads who were crushed by my tanks? After all, can't a warrior make growing boys bite the dust? . . . (*He trembles more and more violently*) No, I'm not trembling more and more violently, I'm sending alarm

signals to my troops . . . All the same, you're not going to kill me for good? . . . You are? . . . You're not? . . . Well, all right, take aim at this indomitable heart. I die childless . . . but I'm counting on your sense of honor to donate my bloodstained uniform to the Army Museum. Ready, aim, fire!
(VILLAGE *points a revolver and shoots, but there is no sound of a shot.* THE GOVERNOR *falls.*)

ARCHIBALD: (*indicating the middle of the stage*) No. Come and die here. (*With his heel,* ARCHIBALD *sets off a small cap, the kind children play with.* THE GOVERNOR, *who has stood up, goes to the middle of the stage and falls there.*)

THE GOVERNOR: My liver bursting, my heart bleeding.

THE NEGROES: (*bursting into laughter and, in chorus, imitating the crowing of a cock*) Cock-a-doodle-doo!

ARCHIBALD: Off to Hell. (*to* THE QUEEN) Next.
(VILLAGE *and* VIRTUE *have stepped away from the group of* NEGROES *and come to the front of the stage, left.* VIRTUE *pretends to be flirting.*)

VILLAGE: When I come back, I'll bring you perfumes . . .

VIRTUE: And what else?

VILLAGE: Wild strawberries.

VIRTUE: You're silly. And who'll pick the strawberries? You? Squatting and looking for them under the leaves . . .

VILLAGE: I'm doing it to please you, and you . . .

VIRTUE: My pride? I want you to bring me . . .
(*They continue flirting during* THE JUDGE's *speech.*)

THE JUDGE: (*standing up*) I understand. I won't use eloquence. I know all too well what that leads to. No, I've drafted a bill, the first paragraph of which reads as follows: Act of July 18th. Article 1. God being dead, the color black ceases to be a sin; it becomes a crime . . .

ARCHIBALD: You'll have your head sliced off, but sliced into slices.

THE JUDGE: You have no right . . . (*A shot is heard.*)

ARCHIBALD: Off to Hell!
(*Slowly* THE JUDGE *falls upon* THE GOVERNOR. *The moment he falls,* THE NEGROES *cry out in chorus.*)

THE NEGROES: Cock-a-doodle-doo!

ARCHIBALD: Next.

VIRTUE: (*to* VILLAGE; *both of them are now at the extreme left of the stage*) I, too, for a long time didn't dare love you . . .

VILLAGE: You love me?

VIRTUE: I would listen. I would hear you striding along. I would run to the window and from behind the curtain would watch you go by . . .

VILLAGE: (*bantering tenderly*) You were wasting your time. I strolled by like an indifferent male, without a glance . . . but at night I would come and capture a beam of light from between your shutters. I would carry it off between my shirt and skin.

VIRTUE: And I, I was already in bed, with your image. Other girls may guard the image of their beloved in their heart or eyes. Yours was between my teeth. I would bite into it . . .

VILLAGE: In the morning, I would proudly display the marks of your bites.

VIRTUE: (*putting her hand over his mouth*) Be still.

THE MISSIONARY: (*standing up*) It was I who brought you knowledge of Hell. How dare you cast me into it? Why, that's preposterous. Hell obeys me. It opens or closes at a sign from my ringed hand. I have blessed brides and grooms, christened pickaninnies, ordained battalions of black priests, and I brought you the message of One who was crucified. I understand you—for if the Church speaks all languages, she likewise understands them all— you reproach Christ for his color. Let us bear in mind that no sooner was He born than a black prince, who was a bit of a sorcerer, came to adore Him . . . (*Suddenly, he breaks off. He looks at the motionless* NEGROES. *He is visibly frightened. Panicky.*) No, no! Gentlemen, gentlemen, don't do that! (*he trembles more and more violently*) Ladies, ladies, I beg of you! It would be too awful! In the name of the Heavenly Virgin, appeal to your husbands, your brothers, your lovers! Gentlemen, gentlemen, no, no, not that! In the first place, I don't believe in it. No, I don't believe in it. Hell, which I brought to you . . . I've mistreated your sorcerers—oh, I'm sorry! Not your sorcerers, gentlemen, your miracle-workers, your priests, your clergy . . . I've made jokes, I've blasphemed, I should be punished, but not that! . . . Gentlemen, gentlemen, I beg of you . . . Don't make the gesture . . . don't utter the formula . . . No, no . . . (THE NEGROES *become more and more frozen, set, impassive. All at once,* THE MISSIONARY *becomes calm. He no longer trembles. He breathes more easily. He seems relieved, almost smiling; suddenly he blurts out*) Moo! . . . Moo! . . . (*Still mooing like a cow, he walks about on all fours, pretends to graze, and licks the feet of* THE NEGROES, *who have stepped back, as if somewhat frightened.*)

ARCHIBALD: That'll do. To the slaughterhouse.
(THE MISSIONARY *gets up and goes to fall on* THE GOVERNOR *and* JUDGE.)

THE MISSIONARY: (*screaming in a falsetto voice before falling*) Castrated! I've been castrated! I'll be canonized, high, stiff and firm.

ARCHIBALD: Next!

THE VALET: (*standing up and trembling*) Are you going to beat me? I can't stand physical pain, you know, for I was the artist. In a way, I was one of you, I too was a victim of the Governor General and the established authorities. You say that I revered them? Yes and no. I was very disrespectful. You fascinated me far more than they did. In any case, this evening I'm no longer what I was yesterday, for I also know how to betray. If you like, though without quite going over to your side . . . I can . . .

THE QUEEN: (*to* THE VALET) At least say to them that without us their revolt would be meaningless—and wouldn't even exist . . .

THE VALET: (*still trembling*) They refuse to hear anything more. (*to* THE NEGROES) I'll bring you trade secrets, plans . . . (THE NEGROES *clap their hands and stamp their feet as if to frighten him.* THE VALET *runs away and falls on the heap formed by* THE GOVERNOR, MISSIONARY *and* JUDGE. *Orchestrated laughter of* THE NEGROES.)

ARCHIBALD: Off to Hell!

THE QUEEN: (*standing up solemnly*) Well, are you satisfied—Now am I alone. (*A shot.*) And dead. Beheaded, like my illustrious cousin. I too shall descend to Hell. I shall take with me my flock of corpses that you keep killing so that they may stay alive and that you keep alive in order to kill. But, be well assured, we had become unworthy only of you. It was easy for you to transform us into an allegory, but I had to live and suffer in order to become that image . . . and I have even loved . . . loved (*suddenly she changes her tone and, turning to* ARCHIBALD) but, tell me, sir, that Negro (*she points to* DIOUF) who served you as a prop for killing a corpse, and since it's customary, once they're dead, for those corpses to rise to Heaven and judge us . . .

SNOW: (*laughing*) And hurry down to Hell again!

THE QUEEN: I grant you that, young lady, but tell me at least, before I die, what has that one become in our Court? With what title have you adorned him, with what hatred have you charged him? What image has he become, what symbol? (*They are all attentive, even the dead characters heaped on the ground raise their heads to listen.*)

THE GOVERNOR: (*lying on the ground*) Yes, who? What other prince? (THE NEGROES *seem rather puzzled.*)

DIOUF: (*very gently*) Don't mind me, Mr. Archibald. I've reached the point where I can hear anything.

ARCHIBALD: (*after a silence*) The collection would have been incomplete without the Mother. (*to* DIOUF) Tomorrow, and in the ceremonies to come, you'll represent the Worthy Mother of the heroes who died thinking they'd killed us, but who were devoured by our fury and our black ants.
(*The characters lying on the ground stand up and bow to* DIOUF, *who returns their bow. Then they lie down again in a heap, as if dead.*)

DIOUF: (*to the Dead*) Well then, I'm coming down to bury you, since that's indicated in the script. (*He leaves the balcony.*)

THE QUEEN: (*to* ARCHIBALD, *admiringly*) How well you hate! (*A pause.*) How I have loved! And now, I die—I must confess—choked by my desire for a Big Black Buck. Black nakedness, thou hast conquered me.

SNOW: (*gently*) You've got to go, Madam. You're losing all your blood, and the stairway to death is interminable. And bright as day. Pale. White. Infernal.

THE QUEEN: (*to her Court*) On your feet! (*All four stand up.*) Come with me to Hell. And mind your P's and Q's when we get there. (*She pushes them along like a flock.*)

ARCHIBALD: (*stopping her*) Just a moment. The performance is coming to an end and you're about to disappear. My friends, allow me first to thank you all. You've given an excellent performance. (*The five members of the Court remove their masks and bow.*) You've displayed a great deal of courage, but you had to. The time has not yet come for presenting dramas about noble matters. But perhaps they suspect what lies behind this architecture of emptiness and words. We are what they want us to be. We

shall therefore be it to the very end, absurdly. Put your masks on again before leaving. Have them escorted to Hell.
(*The five characters put their masks on.*)

THE QUEEN: (*turning to* THE NEGROES) Farewell, and good luck to you. Decent girl that I am, I hope all goes well for you. As for us, we've lived a long time. We're now going to rest at last. (FELICITY *makes a gesture of impatience.*) We're going, we're going, but keep in mind that we shall lie torpid in the earth like larvae or moles, and if some day . . . ten thousand years hence . . .
(*Exeunt right, while* THE NEGROES, *except* VIRTUE *and* VILLAGE, *leave quietly, left.* VILLAGE *and* VIRTUE *remain alone on the stage. They seem to be arguing.*)

VILLAGE: But if I take your hands in mine? If I put my arms around your shoulders—let me—if I hug you?

VIRTUE: All men are like you: they imitate. Can't you invent something else?

VILLAGE: For you I could invent anything: fruits, brighter words, a two-wheeled wheelbarrow, cherries without pits, a bed for three, a needle that doesn't prick. But gestures of love, that's harder . . . still, if you really want me to . . .

VIRTUE: I'll help you. At least, there's one sure thing: you won't be able to wind your fingers in my long golden hair . . .
(*The black backdrop rises. All* THE NEGROES—*including those who constituted the Court and who are without their masks—are standing about a white-draped catafalque like the one seen at the beginning of the play. Opening measures of the minuet from* Don Giovanni. *Hand in hand,* VILLAGE *and* VIRTUE *walk toward them, thus turning their backs to the audience. The curtain is drawn.*

THE END

THE INDIAN
WANTS THE BRONX

Israel Horovitz

THE INDIAN WANTS THE BRONX

Reflecting on his first season in the Off-Broadway theatre—during which four new plays premiered in the space of four months—Israel Horovitz wrote: "There has been too much emphasis on the star playwright, the star actor, the star director, the star (forgive me) producer. It's hardly a vision of genius to note these damned stars are killing us. We desperately need star *theatres*, where good actors and good directors work conscientiously on good plays until a kind of total environment springs to life." That's precisely what happened at New York's Astor Place Theatre on January 17, 1968, when *The Indian Wants the Bronx* opened to unanimous critical acclaim.

"Currently one of the most hopeful things in the New York theatre," wrote Clive Barnes in the New York *Times*, "is Israel Horovitz's shattering insight into the dark roots of fear . . . It is a beautifully observed study of the empty escalation of violence."

"Horovitz is a natural dramatist with a keen ear," wrote Edith Oliver in *The New Yorker*, adding that *The Indian Wants the Bronx* is "frightening, and the aimlessness of the utterly believable characters—their aimless cruelty and their aimless solemn fatuity— is the most frightening thing about them."

The plot of the play is extremely simple. Two ruffians confront an East Indian at a bus stop late at night. Gradually, almost playfully, they begin to taunt and harass him, and become increasingly exasperated as they discover the Indian is too helpless to respond. The power of the play lies in the fact that the cruelty of the ruffians increases in direct proportion to their futility, and their final assault has its source in frustration. In showing how his characters move with increasing menace from game-playing comedy to the final explosion of violence, Horovitz has created an extraordinary study of the psychology of terrorism.

Israel Horovitz was born in Massachusetts in 1939 and studied on a fellowship at the Royal Academy of Dramatic Art in London from 1961 to 1963. He returned to London in 1965, the first American to be chosen as playwright-in-residence with the Royal Shakespeare Company. Characteristic of the nonpressurized atmosphere of Off-Broadway, which allows a playwright time to refine and polish his work without the pressure of producer's budgets and the opening-night fanfare, *The Indian Wants the Bronx* went through four trial productions prior to its commercial opening: at The Loft Workshop in New York; the Eugene O'Neill Memorial Theatre Foundation in Connecticut; the Canoe Place Cabaret Theatre on Long Island; and The Act IV Café Theatre in Provincetown, Massachusetts. The result was ensemble acting of the highest quality.

In addition to the Obie Award which Horovitz received, a young actor named Al Pacino, making his theatrical debut, also won an Obie as the best actor of the year for his performance as Murph, and John Cazale won a supporting-actor Obie for his portrayal of Gupta. Pacino's portrayal was particularly fascinating—especially his cool, fluid, swaggering mannerisms, and the naturalness and subtlety of his growing emotional tension and final release.

The Indian Wants the Bronx was paired in its original Off-Broadway production with another Horovitz one-act play, *It's Called the Sugar Plum,* in which those who later in the evening witnessed Pacino's acting debut also saw one of the first appearances of a young actress named Marsha Mason.

THE INDIAN WANTS THE BRONX was presented by Ruth Newton Productions on January 17, 1968, at the Astor Place Theatre, New York City, with the following cast:

(In order of appearance)

GUPTA, an East Indian	*John Cazale*
MURPH	*Al Pacino*
JOEY	*Matthew Cowles*

Directed by James Hammerstein

Place: A bus stop on upper Fifth Avenue in New York City.
Time: A chilly September's night.

> There is no crime greater,
> more worthy of punishment,
> than being strange and
> frightened among the strange
> and frightened . . . except
> assimilation to the end of
> becoming strange and
> frightened, but apart from
> one's own real self.

As the curtains open the lights fade up, revealing GUPTA, an East Indian. He is standing alone, right of center stage, near a bus stop sign. An outdoor telephone booth is to his left; several city-owned litter baskets are to his right.

GUPTA is in his early fifties. Although he is swarthy in complexion, he is anything but sinister. He is, in fact, meek and visibly frightened by the city.

He is dressed in traditional East Indian garb, appropriately for mid-September.

As GUPTA strains to look for a bus on the horizon, the voices of two boys can be heard in the distance, singing. They sing a rock-'n'-roll song, flatly, trying to harmonize.

FIRST BOY:
    I walk the lonely streets at night,
    A 'lookin' for your door,
    I look and look and look and look,
    But, baby, you don't care.
    Baby, you don't care.
    Baby, no one cares.

SECOND BOY: (Interrupting) Wait a minute, Joey. I'll take the harmony. Listen. (Singing)
    But, baby, you don't care.
    Baby, you don't care.
    Baby, no one cares.
    (Confident that he has fully captured the correct harmony, boasting) See? I've got a knack for harmony. You take the low part.

BOYS: (*Singing together*)
I walk . . . the lonely, lonely street . . .
A 'listenin' for your heartbeat,
Listening for your love.
But, baby, you don't care.
Baby, you don't care.
Baby, no one cares.
   (*They appear on stage.* FIRST BOY *is* JOEY. SECOND BOY *is*
   MURPH. JOEY *is slight, baby-faced, in his early twenties.*
   MURPH *is stronger, long-haired, the same age*)

MURPH: (*Singing*)
The lonely, lonely streets, called out for lovin',
But there was no one to love . . .
'Cause, baby, you don't care . . .

JOEY: (*Joins in the singing*)
Baby, you don't care . . .

JOEY AND MURPHY: (*Singing together*)
Baby, you don't care.
Baby, you don't care.
Baby, no one cares.
Baby, no one cares.

MURPH: (*Calls out into the audience, to the back row; across to the
row of apartment houses opposite the park*) Hey, Pussyface! Can
you hear your babies singing? Pussyface. We're calling you.

JOEY: (*Joins in*) Pussyface. Your babies are serenading your loveli-
ness.
   (*They laugh*)

MURPH: Baby, no one cares.

MURPH AND JOEY: (*Singing together*)
Baby, no one cares.
Baby, no one cares.

MURPH: (*Screams*) Pussyface, you don't care, you Goddamned idiot! (*Notices* THE INDIAN) Hey. Look at the Turk.
(JOEY *stares at* THE INDIAN *for a moment, then replies*)

JOEY: Just another pretty face. Besides. That's no Turk. It's an Indian.

MURPH: (*Continues to sing*)
Baby, no one cares.
(*Dances to his song, strutting in* THE INDIAN'S *direction. He then turns back to* JOEY *during the completion of his stanza and feigns a boxing match*)
I walk the lonely, lonely streets,
A 'callin' out for loving,
But, baby, you don't give a Christ for
Nothin' . . . not for nothin'.
(*Pretends to swing a punch at* JOEY, *who backs off laughing*)
You're nuts. It's a Turk!

JOEY: Bet you a ten spot. It's an Indian.

MURPH: It's a Turk, schmuck. Look at his fancy hat. Indians don't wear fancy hats. (*Calls across the street, again*) Hey, Pussyface. Joey thinks we got an Indian. (*Back to* JOEY) Give me a cigarette.

JOEY: You owe me a pack already, Murphy.

MURPH: So I owe you a pack. Give me a cigarette.

JOEY: Say "please," maybe?

MURPH: Say "I'll bust your squash if you don't give me a cigarette!"

JOEY: One butt, one noogie.

MURPH: First the butt.

JOEY: You're a Jap, Murphy.
(*As* JOEY *extends the pack,* MURPH *grabs it*)

MURPH: You lost your chance, baby. (*To the apartment block*) Pussyface! Joey lost his chance!

JOEY: We made a deal. A deal's a deal. You're a Jap, Murphy. A rotten Jap. (*To the apartment*) Pussyface, listen to me! Murphy's a rotten Jap and just Japped my whole pack. That's unethical, Pussyface. He owes me noogies, too!

MURPH: Now I'll give you twenty noogies, so we'll be even.
    (*He raps* JOEY *on the arm.* THE INDIAN *looks up as* JOEY *squeals*)

JOEY: Hey. The Indian's watching.

MURPH: (*Raps* JOEY *sharply again on the arm*) Indian's a Turkie.

JOEY: (*Grabs* MURPH'S *arm and twists it behind his back*) Gimme my pack and it's an Indian, right?

MURPH: I'll give you your head in a minute, jerkoff.

JOEY: Indian? Indian? Say, Indian!

MURPH: Turkie? Turkie?

JOEY: Turkie. Okay. Let go.
    (MURPH *lets him up and laughs.* JOEY *jumps up and screams*) Indian! (*Runs a few steps*) Indian!

MURPH: (*Laughing*) If your old lady would have you on Thanksgiving you'd know what a turkey was, ya' jerk. (*Hits him on the arm again*) Here's another noogie, Turkie-head!
    (THE INDIAN *coughs*)

JOEY: Hey, look. He likes us. Shall I wink?

MURPH: You sexy beast, you'd wink at anything in pants.

JOEY: Come on. Do I look like a Murphy?

MURPH: (*Grabs* JOEY *and twists both of his arms*) Take that back.

JOEY: Aw! ya' bastard. I take it back.

MURPH: You're a Turkie-lover, right?

JOEY: Right.

MURPH: Say it.

JOEY: I'm a Turkie-lover.

MURPH: You're a Turkie-humper, right?

JOEY: *You're* a Turkie-humper.

MURPH: Say, *I'm* a Turkie-humper.

JOEY: That's what I said. You're a Turkie-humper. (MURPH *twists his arms a bit further*) Oww, ya' dirty bastard! All right, I'm a Turkie-humper! Now, leggo!
(JOEY *pretends to laugh*)

MURPH: You gonna hug him and kiss him and love him up like a mother?

JOEY: Whose mother?

MURPH: Your mother. She humps Turkies, right?

JOEY: Owww! All right. Yeah. She humps Turkies. Now leggo!

MURPH: (*Lets go*) You're free.

JOEY: (*Breaks. Changes the game*) Where's the bus?

MURPH: Up your mother.

JOEY: My old lady's gonna' kill me. It must be late as hell.

MURPH: So why don't you move out?

JOEY: Where to?

MURPH: Maybe we'll get our own place. Yeah. How about that, Joey?

JOEY: Yeah, sure. I move out on her and she starves. You know that.

MURPH: Let her starve, the Turkie-humper.

JOEY: (*Hits* MURPH *on the arm and laughs*) That's my mother you're desecrating, you nasty bastard.

MURPH: How do you desecrate a whore? Call her a lady?

JOEY: Why don't you ask *your* mother?

MURPH: (*Hits* JOEY *on the arm*) Big mouth, huh?

JOEY: Hey! Why don't you pick on som'body your own size, like Turkie, there.

MURPH: Leave Turkie out of this. He's got six elephants in his pocket, probably.

JOEY: (*Laughs at the possibility*) Hey, Turkie, you got six elephants in your pocket?

MURPH: Hey, shut up, Joey. (*Glances in* THE INDIAN's *direction and* THE INDIAN *glances back*) Shut up.

JOEY: Ask him for a match.

MURPH: You ask him.

JOEY: You got the butts.

MURPH: Naw.

JOEY: Chicken. Want some seeds to chew on?

MURPH: I'll give you somethin' to chew on.

JOEY: Go on, ask him. I ain't never heard an Indian talk Turkie-talk.

MURPH: He's a Turkie, I told ya'. Any jerk can see that he's a definite Turk!

JOEY: You're a definite jerk, then. 'Cause I see a definite Indian!

MURPH: I'll show you.
    (*Walks toward* THE INDIAN *slowly, taking a full minute to cross the stage. He slithers from side to side and goes through pantomime of looking for matches*)

JOEY: Hey, Murph. You comin' for dinner? We're havin' turkey tonight! Hey! Tell your Turkie to bring his elephants.

MURPH: Schmuck! How's he going to fit six elephants in a rickshaw?

JOEY: (*Flatly*) Four in front. Three in back.
    (*He reaches* THE INDIAN)

MURPH: Excuse me. May I borrow a match?

INDIAN: (*Speaking in Hindi*) Mai toom-haree bo-lee nrh-hee bol sak-tah. Mai tum-hah-ree bah-sha nah-hee sah-maj-tah.
    (*I cannot speak your language. I don't understand.*)

MURPH: (*To* JOEY, *does a terrific "take," then speaks, incredulous*) He's got to be kidding.
    (JOEY *and* MURPH *laugh*)

INDIAN: Moo-jhay mahaf kar-nah mai toom-hah-ree bah-art nah-hee sah-maj sak-tah.
    (*I'm sorry. I don't understand you.*)

MURPH: No speak English, huh? (THE INDIAN *looks at him blankly. Louder*) You can't speak English, huh?

(THE INDIAN *stares at him, confused by the increase in volume*)

JOEY: (*Flatly*) Son of a bitch. Hey, Murph. Guess what? Your Turkie only speaks Indian.

MURPH: (*Moves in closer, examining* THE INDIAN) Say something in Indian, big mouth.

JOEY: (*Holds up his hand*) How's your teepee? (THE INDIAN *stares at him. He laughs*) See.
    (THE INDIAN *welcomes* JOEY's *laugh and smiles. He takes their hands and "shakes" them*)

MURPH: (*Catches on as to why* THE INDIAN *has joined the smile and feigns a stronger smile until they all laugh aloud.* MURPH *cuts off the laughter as he shakes* THE INDIAN's *hand and says*) You're a fairy, right?

INDIAN: (*Smiles harder than before*) Mai toom-haree bah-at nah-hee sah-maj-tah. Mai ap-nay lah-kay kah gha-r dhoo-nd rah-haw hooh. Oos-nay moo-jhay mil-nah tar pahr nah-jah-nay woh cah-hah hai. Mai oos-kah mah-kan dhoo-nd rah-hah hoon. Oos-kah pah-tah yeh rah-hah k-yah.
    (*I don't understand you. I'm looking for my son's home. We were supposed to meet, but I could not find him. I'm looking for his home. This is his address. Am I headed in the correct direction?*)
    (THE INDIAN *produces a slip of paper with an address typed on it. And a photograph*)

MURPH: Gupta. In the Bronx. Big deal. (*To* THE INDIAN) Indian, right? You an Indian, Indian? (*Shakes his head up and down, smiling.* THE INDIAN *smiles, confused*) He don't know. (*Pauses, studies the picture, smiles*) This picture must be his kid. Looks like you, Joe.

JOEY: (*Looks at the picture*) Looks Irish to me. (*He hands the picture to* MURPH)

BOTH: Ohhh.

MURPH: Yeah. Why'd you rape all those innocent children? (*Pause*) I think he's the wrong kind of Indian. (*To* THE INDIAN) You work in a restaurant? (*Pauses. Speaks with a homosexual's sibilant "s"*) It's such a shame to kill these Indians. They do such superb beaded work.
    (MURPH *shakes his head up and down again, smiling*)

INDIAN: (*Follows* MURPH's *cue*) Mai-nay ap-nay lar-kay koh su-bah say nah-hee day-kha. Toom-hara shah-har bah-hoot hee barah hai.
    (*I haven't seen my son all day. Your city is so big and so busy.*)

JOEY: Ask him to show you his elephants.

MURPH: You ask. You're the one who speaks Turkie-Indian.

JOEY: White man fork with tongue. Right? (THE INDIAN *stares at him blankly*) Naw, he don't understand me. You ask. You got the right kind of accent. All you foreigners understand each other good.

MURPH: You want another noogie?

JOEY: Maybe Turkie wants a noogie or six?

MURPH: (*Shaking his head*) You want a noogie, friend?

INDIAN: (*Agrees*) Moo-jhay mahaf kar-nah. Moo-jay. Yah-han aye zyah-da sah-may na-hee hoo-ah.
    (*I'm sorry. I haven't been here long.*)

MURPH: Give him his noogie.

JOEY: Naw. He's your friend. You give it to him. That's what friends are for.

MURPH: (*Looks at the paper and photograph, gives them back*) Jesus, look at that for a face.

JOEY: Don't make it.

MURPH: Don't make it. Prem Gupta. In the Bronx. Jesus, this is terrific. The Indian wants the Bronx.

JOEY: (*Sits on a trash can*) He ain't gonna find no Bronx on this bus.

MURPH: Old Indian, pal. You ain't going to find the Bronx on this bus, unless they changed commissioners again. Now I've got a terrific idea for fun and profit.
(*Pauses*)

INDIAN: K-yah kah-ha toom-nay?
(*Excuse me?*)

MURPH: Right. Now why don't you come home and meet my mother? Or maybe you'd like to meet Pussyface, huh? (*To* JOEY) Should we bring him over to Pussyface?

JOEY: He don't even know who Pussyface is. You can't just go getting Indians blind dates without giving him a breakdown.

MURPH: Okay, Chief. Here's the breakdown on Pussyface. She's a pig. She lives right over there. See that pretty building? (*Points over the audience to the back row of seats*) That one. The fancy one. That's Pussyface's hideaway. She's our social worker.

JOEY: That's right.

MURPH: Pussyface got assigned to us when we were tykers, right, Joe?

JOEY: Just little fellers.

MURPH: Pussyface was sent to us by the city. To watch over us. And care for us. And love us like a mother. Not because she wanted to. Because we were bad boys. We stole a car.

JOEY: We stole two cars.

MURPH: We stole two cars. And we knifed a kid.

JOEY: You knifed a kid.

MURPH: (*To* JOEY) Tell it to the judge, Fella!
(*He takes a pocketknife from his pocket and shows it to* THE
INDIAN, *who pulls back in fear*)

JOEY: The Chief thinks you're going to cut him up into a totem
pole.

MURPH: Easy, Chief. I've never cut up an Indian in my life.

JOEY: You've never *seen* an Indian in your life.

MURPH: Anyway, you got a choice. My mother—who happens to
have a terrific personality. Or Pussyface, our beloved social lady.

JOEY: Where's the bus?

MURPH: It's coming.

JOEY: So's Christmas.

MURPH: Hey. Show Turkie my Christmas card for Pussyface. (*To*
THE INDIAN) Pussyface gives us fun projects. I had to make
Christmas cards last year. (*Back to* JOEY) Go on. Show the Chief
the card.
(JOEY *fishes through his wallet, finds a dog-eared photostat,
hands it to* THE INDIAN, *who accepts curiously*)

INDIAN: Yeh k-yah hai?
(*What is this?*)

MURPH: I made that with my own two cheeks. Tell him, Joe.

JOEY: Stupid, he don't speak English.

MURPH: It don't matter. He's interested, ain't he?

JOEY: You're a fink-jerk.

MURPH: Oooo. I'll give you noogies up the kazzooo. (*Takes the card away from* THE INDIAN *and explains*) This is a Christmas card. I made it! I made it! Get me? Pussyface got us Christmas jobs last year. She got me one with the city. With the war on poverty. I ran the Xerox machine.

JOEY: Jesus. You really are stupid. He don't understand one word you're saying.

MURPH: (*Mimes the entire scene, slowly*) He's interested, ain't he? That's more than I can say for most of them. (*To* THE INDIAN) Want to know how you can make your own Christmas cards with your simple Xerox 2400? It's easy. Watch. (*He mimes*) First you lock the door to the stat room, so no one can bust in. Then you turn the machine on. Then you set the dial at the number of people you want to send cards to. Thirty, forty.

JOEY: Three or four.

MURPH: Right, fella. Then you take off your pants. And your underpants that's underneath. You sit on the glass. You push the little button. The lights flash. When the picture's developed, you write "Noel" across it! (*Pauses*) That's how you make Christmas cards. (*Waits for a reaction from* THE INDIAN, *then turns back to* JOEY, *dismayed*) He's waiting for the bus.

JOEY: Me too. Jesus. Am I ever late!

MURPH: Tell her to stuff it. You're a big boy now.

JOEY: She gets frightened, that's all. She really don't care how late I come in, as long as I tell her when I'm coming. If I tell her one, and I don't get in until one-thirty, she's purple when I finally get in. (*Pauses*) She's all right. Where's the Goddamned bus, huh? (*Calls across the park*) Pussyface, did you steal the bus, you dirty old whore? Pussyface, I'm calling you! (*Pauses*) She's all right,

Murph. Christ, she's my mother. I didn't ask for her. She's all
right.

MURPH: Who's all right? That Turkie-humper? (*To* THE INDIAN)
His old lady humps Turkies, you know that? (*Smiles, but* THE
INDIAN *doesn't respond*) Hey, Turkie's blowin' his cool a little.
Least you got somebody waitin'. My old lady wouldn't know if I
was gone a year.

JOEY: What? That Turkie-humper?

MURPH: (*To* THE INDIAN) Hey! (THE INDIAN *jumps, startled.*
MURPH *laughs*) You got any little Indians runnin' around your
teepee? No? Yeah? No? Aw, ya' stupid Indian. Where is the Goddamn bus?

JOEY: Let's walk it.

MURPH: Screw that. A hundred blocks? Besides, we gotta keep this
old Turkie company, right? We couldn't let him stand all alone in
this big ole city. Some nasty boys might come along and chew
him up, right?

JOEY: We can walk it. Let the Indian starve.

MURPH: So walk it, jerk. I'm waiting with the Chief.
      (MURPH *stands next to* THE INDIAN)

JOEY: Come on, we'll grab the subway.

MURPH: Joe, the trains are running crazy now. Anyway, I'm waitin'
with my friend the Chief, here. You wanna go, go. (*Murmurs*)
Where is it, Chief? Is that it? Here it comes, huh?

JOEY: (*Considers it*) Yeah, we gotta watch out for Turkie.
      (JOEY *stands on the other side of* THE INDIAN, *who finally
      walks slowly back to the bus stop area*)

MURPH: See that, Turkie, little Joe's gonna keep us company. That's nice, huh? (THE INDIAN *looks for the bus*) You know, Joey, this Turk's a pain in my ass. He don't look at me when I talk to him.

JOEY: He oughta look at you when you talk. He oughta be polite. (*They pass the card in a game.* THE INDIAN *smiles*)

MURPH: I don't think he learned many smarts in Indiana. Any slob knows enough to look when they're being talked to. Huh?

JOEY: This ain't just any slob. This is a definite Turkie-Indian slob. (*They pass the card behind their backs*)

MURPH: He's one of them commie slobs, probably. Warmongering bastard. (*Flatly*) Pinko here rapes all the little kids.

JOEY: Terrible thing. Too bad we can't give him some smarts. Maybe he could use a couple. (*The game ends.* JOEY *has the card as in a magic act*)

MURPH: We'll give him plenty of smarts. (*Calling him upstage*) Want some smarts? Chief?

INDIAN: Bna-ee mai toom-maree bah-at nah-hee sah-maj-sak-tah. Bus yah-han kis sa-may a-tee haj. K-yah mai sa-hee BUS STOP par shoon! (*I can't understand you. Please? When is the bus due here? Am I at the right station?*)

JOEY: Hey, look. He's talking out of the side of his mouth. Sure, that's right . . . Hey, Murph. Ain't Indian broads s'posed to have sideways breezers? Sure.

MURPH: (*Grins*) You mean chinks, Joey.

JOEY: Naw. Indian broads too. All them foreign broads. Their breezers are sideways. That's why them foreign cars have the back seat facing the side, right?

MURPH: Is that right, Turkie? Your broads have horizontal snatches?

INDIAN: (*Stares at him nervously*) Mai toom-haree bah-at nah-hee sah-maj sak-tah.
(*I can't understand you.*)

MURPH: (*Repeating him in the same language*) Toom-haree bah-at nah-hee sah-maj sak-tah.

INDIAN: (*Recognizing the language finally. He speaks with incredible speed*) Toom-haree bah-sha nah-hee sah-maj-tah. Moo-jhay mah-af kar-nah par ah-bhee moo-jhay toom-ha-ray desh aye kuh-chah hee din toh Hu-yay hain. Moo-jhay toom-ha-ree bah-sha see-kh-nay kah ah-bhee sah-mai hee nah-hee milah. Mai ahp-nay lar-kay say bih-chur gah-ya hoon. Oos-say toh toom-ha-ray desh may rah-tay chai sah-al hoh gah-ye hain. Jah-b doh mah-hee-nay pah-lay oos-kee mah kah inth-kahl moo-ah toh oos-nay moo-jhay ya-han booh-lah bheh-jha or mai ah gah-hay. Woh bah-ra hon-har lar-ka hai. Moo-jhay mah-af kar-nah kee majh-nay ah-bhee toom-ha-ree bah-sha na-hee see-knee par mai see-kh loon-gha.
(*Yes, that's correct. I can't understand your language. I'm sorry, but I've only been in your country for a few days. I haven't had time to understand your language. Please forgive me. I'm separated from my son. He's been living in your country for six years. When his mother died two months ago, he sent for me. I came immediately. He's a good son to his father. I'm sorry I haven't learned your language yet, but I shall learn.*)

MURPH: (*Does a take. Flatly*) This Turkie's a real pain in the ass.

JOEY: Naw. I think he's pretty interesting. I never saw an Indian before.

MURPH: Oh. It's fascinating. It's marvelous. This city's a regular melting pot. Turkies. Kikes like you. (*Pause*) I even had me a real French lady once. (*Looks at the ground. Pauses*) I thought I saw a dime here. (*Ponders*) I knew it.
(*He picks up a dime and pockets it proudly*)

JOEY: A French lady, huh?

MURPH: Yep. A real French broad.

JOEY: (*Holds a beat*) You been at your mother again?

MURPH: (*Hits him on the arm*) Wise-ass. Just what nobody likes. A wise-ass.

JOEY: Where'd you have this French lady, huh?

MURPH: I found her in the park over there. (*Points*) Just sitting on a bench. She was great. (*Boasts*) A real *talent*.

JOEY: Yeah, sure thing. (*Calls into the park*) Hello, talent. Hello, talent! (*Pauses*) I had a French girl, too. (*Turns to avoid* MURPH's *eyes, caught in a lie*) Where the hell's that bus?

MURPH: (*Simply*) Sure you did. Like the time you had a mermaid?

JOEY: You better believe I did. She wasn't really French. She just lived there a long time. I went to first grade with her. Geraldine. She was my first girl friend. (*Talks very quickly*) Her old man was in the Army or something, 'cause they moved to France. She came back when we were in high school.

MURPH: Then what happened?

JOEY: Nothin'. She just came back, that's all.

MURPH: I thought you said you *had* her . . .

JOEY: No, she was just my girl friend.

MURPH: In high school?

JOEY: No, ya stoop. In the first grade. I just told you.

MURPH: You had her in the first grade?

JOEY: Jesus, you're stupid. She was my girl friend. That's all.

MURPH: (*Feigns excitement*) Hey . . . that's a *sweet little story.* (*Flatly*) What the hell's wrong with you?

JOEY: What do ya' mean?

MURPH: First you say you had a French girl, then you say you had a girl friend in first grade, who went to France. What the hell kind of story's that?

JOEY: It's a true one, that's all. Yours is full of crap.

MURPH: What's full of crap?

JOEY: About the French lady in the park. You never had any French lady, unless you been at your own old lady again. Or maybe you've been at Pussyface?

MURPH: Jesus, you're lookin' for it, aren't you?
    (*They pretend to fistfight*)

JOEY: I mean, if you gotta tell lies to your best buddy, you're in bad shape, that's all.

MURPH: (*Gives* JOEY *a* "*high-sign*") Best buddy? You?
    (*The sign to* THE INDIAN. *He returns the obscene gesture, thinking it a berserk American sign of welcome*)

JOEY: Is that how it is in Ceylon, sir?

MURPH: Say-lon? What the hell is say-long?

JOEY: See, ya jerk, Ceylon's part of India. That's where they grow tea.

MURPH: No kiddin'? Boy it's terrific what you can learn just standin' here with a schmuck like you. Tea, huh? (*To* THE INDIAN *he screams*) Hey! (THE INDIAN *turns around, startled*) How's your teabags? (*No response*) No? (*To* JOEY) Guess you're wrong again. He don't know teabags.

JOEY: Look at the bags under his eyes. That ain't chopped liver.
(*This is the transition scene:* MURPH *screams* "Hey!"—THE
INDIAN *smiles. They dance a war dance around him, beating a
rhythm on the trash cans, hissing and cat-calling for a full
minute.* MURPH *ends the dance with a final* "Hey!" THE
INDIAN *jumps in fear. Now that they sense his fear, the comedy has ended*)

MURPH: Turkie looks like he's getting bored.

JOEY: Poor old Indian. Maybe he wants to play a game.

MURPH: You know any poor old Indian games?

JOEY: We could burn him at the stake. (*He laughs*) That ain't such
a terrible idea, you know. Maybe make an Indian stew.

MURPH: Naw, we couldn't burn a nice fellow like Turkie. That's
nasty.

JOEY: We got to play a game. Pussyface always tells us to play
games. (*To the apartment, the back of the audience*) Ain't that
right, Pussyface? You always want us to play games.

MURPH: I know a game . . .

JOEY: Yeah?

MURPH: Yeah. (*Screams at* THE INDIAN) "Indian, Indian, Where's
the Indian?"

JOEY: That's a sweet game. I haven't played that for years.

MURPH: Wise-ass. You want to play a game, don't you?

JOEY: Indian-Indian. Where's the Indian?

MURPH: Sure. It's just like ring-a-leave-eo. Only with a spin.

JOEY: That sounds terrific.

MURPH: Look, I spin the hell out of you until you're dizzy. Then you run across the street and get Pussyface. I'll grab the Indian and hide him. Then Pussyface and you come over here and try to find us.

JOEY: We're going to spin, huh?

MURPH: Sure.

JOEY: Who's going to clean up after you? Remember the Ferris wheel, big shot? All those happy faces staring up at you?

MURPH: I ain't the spinner. You're the spinner. I'll hide the Chief. Go on. Spin.

JOEY: How about if we set the rules as we go along? (*To* THE INDIAN) How does that grab you, Chief?

INDIAN: Moo-jhay mah-af kar-nah. Mai toom-nakee bah-sha na-hee sah-maj sak-ta.
(*I'm sorry, but I can't understand your language.*)

MURPH: He's talking Indiana again. He don't understand. Go on. Spin. I'll grab the Chief while you're spinning . . . count the ten . . . hide the Chief, while you're after Pussyface. Go on. Spin.

JOEY: I ain't going to spin. I get sick.

MURPH: Ain't you going to play?

JOEY: I'll play. But I can't spin any better than you can. I get sick. You know that. How about if you spin and I hide the Chief? You can get Pussyface. She likes you better than me, anyhow.

MURPH: Pussyface ain't home. You know that. She's in New Jersey.

JOEY: Then what the hell's the point of this game, anyway?

MURPH: It's just a game. We can pretend.

JOEY: You can play marbles for all I care. I just ain't going to spin, that's all. And neither are you. So let's forget the whole game.

MURPH: (*Fiercely*) Spin! Spin!

JOEY: You spin.

MURPH: Hey. I told you to spin.
>   (MURPH *squares off against* JOEY *and slaps him menacingly.* JOEY *looks* MURPH *straight in the eye for a moment*)

JOEY: Okay. Big deal. So I'll spin. Then I get Pussyface, right? You ready to get the Chief?

MURPH: Will you stop talking and start spinning?

JOEY: All right. All right. Here I go. (JOEY *spins himself meekly, as* MURPH *goes toward* THE INDIAN *and the trash can.* JOEY *giggles as he spins ever so slowly.* MURPH *glances at* JOEY *as* JOEY *pretends.* MURPH *is confused*) There. I spun. Is that okay?

MURPH: That's a spin?

JOEY: Well, it wasn't a fox trot.

MURPH: I told you to spin! Any slob knows that ain't no spin! Now spin, God damn it! Spin!

JOEY: This is stupid. You want to play games. You want a decent spin. You spin.
>   (*He walks straight to* MURPH—*a challenge.* JOEY *slaps* MURPH. *He winces*)

MURPH: (*Squares off viciously. Raises his arms. Looks at* JOEY *cruelly. Orders*) Spin me.
>   (JOEY *brings* MURPH's *arms behind* MURPH's *back and holds* MURPH's *wrists firmly so that he is helpless.* JOEY *spins him. Slowly at first. Then faster. Faster.* JOEY's *hostility is released; he laughs*)

JOEY: You wanted to spin. Spin. Spin.
> (JOEY *spins* MURPH *frantically.* THE INDIAN *watches in total horror, not knowing what to do; he cuddles next to the bus stop sign, his island of safety*)

MURPH: (*Screaming*) Enough, you little bastard.

JOEY: (*Continues to spin him*) Now *you* get Pussyface. Go on. (*Spins* MURPH *all the faster as in a grotesque dance gone berserk*) I'll hide the Chief. This is your game! This is your game. *You* get Pussyface. I'll hide the Chief. Go on, Murphy. You want some more spin? (JOEY *has stopped the spinning now, as* MURPH *is obviously ill*) You want to spin some more?

MURPH: Stop it, Joey. I'm sick.

JOEY: (*Spins* MURPH *once more around*) You want to spin some more, or are you going to get Pussyface and come find the Chief and me?

MURPH: You little bastard.

JOEY: (*Spins* MURPH *once again, still holding* MURPH *helpless with his arms behind his back*) I'll hide the Chief. YOU get Pussyface and find us. Okay? Okay? Okay?

MURPH: Okay . . . you bastard . . . okay.

JOEY: Here's one more for good luck.
> (JOEY *spins* MURPH *three more times, fiercely, then shoves him offstage.* MURPH *can be heard retching, about to vomit, during the final spins.* JOEY *then grabs* THE INDIAN, *who pulls back in terror*)

INDIAN: Na-hee bha-yee toom ah-b k-yah kah-rogay?
> (*No, please, what are you going to do?*)

JOEY: Easy, Chief. It's just a game. Murph spun out on us. It's just a game. I've got to hide you now.

(MURPH's *final puking sounds can be heard well in the distance*)

INDIAN: Na-hee na-hee bha-yee. Mai mah-afee mah-ng-ta. Hoon. (*No. No. Please. I beg you.*)

JOEY: Easy, Chief. Look. I promise you, this ain't for real. This is only a game. A game. Get it? It's all a game! Now I got to count to ten. (*Grabs* THE INDIAN *and forces him down behind a city litter basket. He covers* THE INDIAN's *scream with his hand, as he slaps* THE INDIAN—*a horrifying sound*) One. Two. Three. Murphy? (*He laughs*) Four. Five. Murph? Come get us. Six. Seven. Pussyface is waiting. Eight. Nine. (*Pauses*) Murphy? Murph? Hey, buddy. (*Stands up. Speaks*) Ten. (*Lights are narrowing on* JOEY *and* THE INDIAN. THE INDIAN *tries to escape.* JOEY *subdues him easily.* JOEY *turns slowly back to* THE INDIAN, *who responds with open fear*) Get up. Up. (*No response*) Get up, Turkie. (*Moves to* THE INDIAN, *who recoils sharply.* JOEY *persists and pulls* THE INDIAN *to his feet.* THE INDIAN *shudders, stands and faces his captor.* THE INDIAN *shakes from fear and from a chill. There is a moment's silence as* JOEY *watches. He removes his own sweater and offers it to* THE INDIAN) Here. Here. Put it on. It's okay. (THE INDIAN *is bewildered, but* JOEY *forces the sweater into his hands*) Put it on. (THE INDIAN *stares at the sweater.* JOEY *takes it from his hands and begins to cover* THE INDIAN, *who is amazed*) I hope I didn't hurt you too much. You okay? (*No response*) You ain't sick too bad, huh? (*Pause*) Huh? (*Checks* THE INDIAN *for cuts*) You look okay. You're okay, huh? (*No response*) I didn't mean to rough you up like that, but . . . you know. Huh? (THE INDIAN *raises his eyes to meet* JOEY's. JOEY *looks down to avoid the stare*) I hope you ain't mad at me or nothin'. (*Pause*) Boy it's gettin' chilly. I mean, it's cold, right? Sure is quiet all of a sudden. Kind of spooky, huh? (*Calls*) Hey, Murphy! (*Laughs aloud*) Murph ain't a bad guy. He's my best buddy, see? I mean, he gets kinda crazy sometimes, but that's all. Everybody gets kind of crazy sometime, right? (*No response*) Jesus, you're a stupid Indian. Can't you speak any English? No? Why the hell did you come here, anyway? Especially if you can't talk any English. You ought to say something. Can't you even say "Thank you"?

(THE INDIAN *recognizes those words, finally, and mimics them slowly and painfully*)

INDIAN: (*In English, very British and clipped*) Thank you.

JOEY: I'll be Goddamned! You're welcome. (*Slowly, indicating for* THE INDIAN *to follow*) You're welcome.
(*He waits*)

INDIAN: (*In English*) You are welcome.

JOEY: That's terrific. You are welcome. (*Smiles, as though all is forgiven. In relief*) How are you?

INDIAN: You are welcome.

JOEY: No. How are ya?
(JOEY *is excited.* THE INDIAN *might be a second friend*)

INDIAN: (*In English—very "Joey"*) How are ya?

JOEY: (*Joyously*) Jesus. You'll be talking like us in no time! You're okay, huh? You ain't bleeding or anything. I didn't wanna hurt you none. But Murph gets all worked up. You know what I mean. He gets all excited. This ain't the first time, you know. No, sir!

INDIAN: (*In English*) No, sir.

JOEY: That's right. He's especially crazy around broads.

INDIAN: (*In English*) Broads.

JOEY: (*Forgetting that* THE INDIAN *is only mimicking*) That's right. Broads. (*Pauses and remembers, deeply*) What am I yakking for? Tell me about India, huh? I'd like to go to India sometime. Maybe I will. You think I'd like India? India? (*No response.* THE INDIAN *recognizes the word, but doesn't understand the question*) That's where you're from, ain't it? Jesus, what a stupid Indian. India! (*Spells the word*) I-N-D-I-A. Nothin'. Schmuck. *India!*

INDIAN: (*A stab in the dark*) Hindi?

JOEY: Yeah! Tell me about India! (*Long pause as they stand staring at each other*) No? You're not talking, huh? Well, what do you want to do? Murph oughta be back soon. (*Discovers a coin in his pocket*) You wanna flip for quarters? Flip? No? Look, a Kennedy half! (*Goes through three magic tricks with the coin:* [1] *He palms the coin, offers the obvious choice of hand, then uncovers the coin in his other hand.* THE INDIAN *raises his hand to his turban in astonishment*) Like that, huh? ([2] *Coin is slapped on his breast*) This hand right? Is it this hand, this hand? No, it's *this* hand! Back to your dumb act? Here. Here's the one you liked! (*Does* [1]. *This time* THE INDIAN *points to the correct hand instantly*) You're probably some kind of hustler. Okay. Double or nothing. (*Flips*) Heads, you live. Tails, you die. Okay? (*Uncovers the coin*) I'll be a son of a bitch. You got Indian luck. Here.
(*He hands the coin to* THE INDIAN)

INDIAN: (*Stares in question*) Na-hff?
 (*No?*)

JOEY: (*Considers cheating*) Take it. You won. No, go ahead. Keep it. I ain't no Indian giver. (*Pause. He laughs at his own joke. No response*) You ain't got no sense of humor, that's what. (*Stares upstage*) Murph's my best buddy, you know? Me and him were buddies when we were kids. Me and Murph, all the time. And Maggie. His kid sister. (*Pause*) I had Maggie once. Sort of. Well, kind of. Yeah, I had her. That's right. Murph don't know. Makes no difference now. She's dead, Maggie. (*Sings*) "The worms crawl in, the worms crawl out." (*Speaks*) What the hell difference does it make? *Right?*

INDIAN: (*In English*) No, sir.

JOEY: (*Without noticing*) That's why Murph is crazy. That's why he gets crazy, I mean. She died seventeen, that's all. Seventeen. Just like *that*. Appendix. No one around. There was no one around. His old lady? Forget it! The old man took off years ago. All there was really was just Murph and Maggie. That's why he

could take it. At home. You think my old lady's bad? She's nothing. His old lady's a pro. You know? She don't even make a living at it, either. That's the bitch of it. Not even a living. She's a dog. I mean, *I* wouldn't even pay her a nickel. Not a nickel. Not that I'd screw around with Murphy's old lady. Oh! Not that she doesn't try. She tries. Plenty. (*His fantasy begins*) That's why I don't come around to his house much. She tries it all the time. She wouldn't charge me anything, probably. But it ain't right screwing your best buddy's old lady, right? I'd feel terrible if I did. She ain't that bad, but it just ain't right. I'd bet she'd even take Murph on. She probably tries it with him, too. That's the bitch of it. She can't even make a living. His own Goddamned mother. The other one—Pussyface. You think Pussyface is a help? That's the biggest joke yet. (THE INDIAN *is by now thoroughly confused on all counts. He recognizes the name "Pussyface," and reacts slightly. Seeing* JOEY's *anxiety, he cuddles him. For a brief moment they embrace—an insane father-and-son tableau. Note: Be careful here*) Pussyface. There's a brain. You see what she gave us for Christmas? (*Fishes his knife out of his pocket*) Knives. Brilliant, huh? Murph's up on a rap for slicing a kid, and she gives us knives for Christmas. To whittle with. She's crazier than Murphy. Hah. (*Flashes his open knife at* THE INDIAN, *who misinterprets the move as spelling disaster.* THE INDIAN *waits, carefully scrutinizing* JOEY, *until* JOEY *begins to look away.* JOEY *now wanders to the spot where he pushed* MURPH *offstage*) Hey, Murph! (THE INDIAN *moves slowly to the other side of the stage.* JOEY *sees his move at once and races after him, thinking* THE INDIAN *was running away*) Hey. Where are you going? (THE INDIAN *knows he'll be hit. He tries to explain with mute gestures and attitude. It's futile. He knows at once and hits* JOEY *as best he can and races across the stage.* JOEY *recovers from the blow and starts after him, as* THE INDIAN *murmurs one continuous frightening scream.* JOEY *dives after* THE INDIAN *and tackles him on the other side of the stage.* THE INDIAN *fights more strongly than ever, but* JOEY's *trance carries him ferociously into this fight. He batters* THE INDIAN *with punches to the body.* THE INDIAN *squeals as* JOEY *sobs*) You were gonna run off. Right? Son of a bitch. You were gonna tell Murphy.
  (THE INDIAN *makes one last effort to escape and runs the length of the stage, screaming a bloodcurdling, anguished*

scream. MURPH *enters, stops, stares incredulously as* THE INDIAN *runs into his open arms.* JOEY *races to* THE INDIAN *and strikes a karate chop to the back of his neck.* JOEY *is audibly sobbing.* THE INDIAN *drops to the stage as a bull in the ring, feeling the final thrust of the sword . . .* JOEY *stands frozen above him.* MURPH *stares, first at* JOEY *and then at* THE INDIAN)

MURPH: Pussyface isn't home yet. She's still in New Jersey. Ring-a-leave-eo.

JOEY: (*Sobbing, senses his error*) Indians are dumb.

MURPH: (*Stares again at* JOEY. *Then to* THE INDIAN. *Spots* JOEY'S *sweater on* THE INDIAN. *Fondles it, then stares at* JOEY *viciously*) Pussyface isn't home. I rang her bell. She don't answer. I guess she's still on vacation. She ruined our game.

JOEY: (*Sobbing*) Oh, jumping Jesus Christ. Jesus. Jesus. Jesus. Indians are dumb.

MURPH: Pussyface ruins everything. She don't really care about our games. She ruins our games. Just like Indians. They don't know how to play our games either.

JOEY: Indians are dumb. Dumb.
  (*He sobs.* MURPH *slaps* JOEY *across the face. He straightens up and comes back to reality*)

MURPH: What the hell's going on?

JOEY: He tried to run. I hit him.

MURPH: Yeah. I saw that. You hit him, all right. (*Stares at* THE INDIAN) Is he alive?
  (THE INDIAN *groans, pulls himself to his knees*)

JOEY: He was fighting. I hit him.

MURPH: Okay, you hit him.
(THE INDIAN *groans again. Then he speaks in a plea*)

INDIAN: (*Praying*) Moo-jhay or nah sah-tao. Maih-nay toom-hara k-yah bigarah hai. Moo-jhay or nah sah-tao. Moo-jhay in-seh.
(*Please. Don't hurt me any more. What have I done? Please don't hurt me. Don't let them hurt me*)

MURPH: He's begging for something. Maybe he's begging for his life. Maybe he is. Sure, maybe he is.

JOEY: (*Embarrassed, starts to help* THE INDIAN *to his feet*) C'mon there, Chief. Get up and face the world. C'mon, Chief. Everything's going to be all right.

MURPH: What's got into you, anyway?

JOEY: C'mon, Chief. Up at the world. Everything's okay.
(THE INDIAN *ad libs words of pleading and pain*)

MURPH: Leave him be. (*But* JOEY *continues to help* THE INDIAN) Leave him be. What's with you? Hey, Joey! I said leave him be!
(MURPH *pushes* JOEY *and* THE INDIAN *pulls back with fear*)

JOEY: Okay, Murph. Enough's enough.

MURPH: Just tell me what the hell's wrong with you?

JOEY: He tried to run away, that's all. Change the subject. Change the subject. It ain't important. I hit him, that's all.

MURPH: Okay, so you hit him.

JOEY: Okay! Where were you? Sick. Were you a little bit sick? I mean, you couldn't have been visiting, 'cause there ain't no one to visit, right?

MURPH: What *do* you mean?

JOEY: Where the hell were you? (*Looks at* MURPH *and giggles*) You're a little green there, Irish.

MURPH: You're pretty funny. What the hell's so funny?

JOEY: Nothing's funny. The Chief and I were just having a little pow-wow and we got to wondering where you ran off to. Just natural for us to wonder, ain't it? (*To* THE INDIAN) Right, Chief.

MURPH: Hey, look at that. Turkie's got a woolly sweater just like yours. Ain't that a terrific coincidence. You two been playing strip poker?

JOEY: Oh, sure. Strip poker. The Chief won my sweater and I won three of his feathers and a broken arrow. (*To* THE INDIAN, *he feigns a deep authoritative voice*) You wonder who I am, don't you? Perhaps this silver bullet will help to identify me? (*Extends his hand.* THE INDIAN *peers into* JOEY's *empty palm quizzically. As he does,* MURPH *quickly taps the underside of* JOEY's *hand, forcing the hand to rise and slap* THE INDIAN's *chin sharply.* THE INDIAN *pulls back at the slap.* JOEY *turns on* MURPH, *quickly*) What the hell did you do that for, ya' jerk. The Chief didn't do nothing.

MURPH: Jesus, you and your Chief are pretty buddy-buddy, ain't you? (*Mimics* JOEY) "The Chief didn't do nothing." Jesus. You give him your sweater. Maybe you'd like to have him up for a beer . . .

JOEY: Drop it, Murph. You're giving me a pain in the ass.

MURPH: (*Retorts fiercely*) You little pisser. Who the hell do you think you're talking to?
        (*The telephone rings in the booth. They are all startled, especially* THE INDIAN, *who senses hope*)

JOEY: (*After a long wait, speaking the obvious flatly*) It's the phone.

MURPH: (*To* THE INDIAN) The kid's a whiz. He guessed that right away.
        (*The phone rings a second time*)

JOEY: Should we answer it?

MURPH: What for? Who'd be calling here? It's a wrong number.
  (*The phone rings menacingly a third time. Suddenly* THE
  INDIAN *darts into the phone booth and grabs the receiver.*
  JOEY *and* MURPH *are too startled to stop him until he has
  blurted out his hopeless plea, in his own language*)

INDIAN: Prem k-yah woh may-rah ar-kah hai. Prem (pray-em) bay-
  tah moo-jhay bachah-low. Mai fah ns ga-yah hoon yeh doh goon-
  day moo-jhay mar ra-hay hain. Mai ba-hoot ghah-bara gaya hoon.
  Pray-em.
  (*Prem? Is this my son? Prem? Please help me. I'm frightened. Please help me. Two boys are hurting me . . . I'm
  frightened. Please. Prem?*)

  (THE INDIAN *stops talking sharply and listens. He crumbles as
  the voice drones the wrong reply. He drops the receiver and
  stares with horror at the boys.* MURPH *realizes* THE INDIAN's
  horror and begins to laugh hysterically. JOEY *stares silently.*
  THE INDIAN *begins to mumble and weep. He walks from the
  phone booth. The voice is heard as a drone from the receiver.
  The action freezes*)

MURPH: (*Laughing*) What's the matter, Turkie? Don't you have a
  dime? Give Turkie a dime, Joe. Give him a dime.

JOEY: Jesus Christ. I'd hate to be an Indian.

MURPH: Hey, the paper! C'mon, Joey, get the paper from him.
  We'll call the Bronx.

JOEY: Cut it out, Murph. Enough's enough.

MURPH: Get the frigging piece of paper. What's the matter with
  you, anyway?

JOEY: I just don't think it's such a terrific idea, that's all.

MURPH: You're chicken. That's what you are.

JOEY: Suppose his son has called the police. What do you think? You think he hasn't called the police? He knows the old man don't speak any English. He called the police. Right? And they'll trace our call.

MURPH: You're nuts. They can't trace any phone calls. Anyway, we'll be gone from here. You're nuts.

JOEY: I don't want to do it.

MURPH: For Christ's sake. They can't trace nothing to nobody. Who's going to trace? Get the paper.

JOEY: Get it yourself. Go on. Get it yourself. I ain't going to get it.

MURPH: C'mon, Joey. It's not real. This is just a game. It ain't going to hurt anybody. You know that. It's just a game.

JOEY: Why don't we call somebody else? We'll call somebody else and have the Indian talk. That makes sense. Imagine if an Indian called you up and talked to you in Indian. I bet the Chief would go for that all right. Jesus, Murphy.

MURPH: Get the paper and picture.

INDIAN: Ah-b toom k-yah kah-rogay. Moo-jhay mah-af kar-doh bha-yee maih-nay soh-cha tah key woh may-rah bay-tah pray-em hai. Moo-jhay telephone kar raha. Mai-nay soh-chah thah sha-yahd woh. Pray-em hoh.
(*What are you going to do now? I'm sorry. I thought that was my son, Prem. I thought that it might be Prem calling me on the telephone. Prem. That's who I thought it was. Prem.*)

MURPH: Prem. That's the name.
(*Plays the rhyme*)

INDIAN: Pray-aim.
(*Prem?*)

MURPH: Yes, Prem. I want to call Prem. Give me the paper with his name.

INDIAN: Toom pray-aim kay ba-ray may k-yah kah ra-hay. Ho toom-nay pray-aim koh kyah key-yah. Toom oos-kay bah-ray may k-yah jan-tay ho k-yah toom jan-tay ho woh kah-han hai.
> (*What are you saying about Prem? Prem is my son. What have you done to Prem? What do you know about him? Do you know where he is?*)

MURPH: Shut up already and give me the paper.

JOEY: Jesus, Murph.

MURPH: (*Turning* THE INDIAN *around so that they face each other*) This is ridiculous. (*Searches* THE INDIAN, *who resists a bit at first, and then not at all. Finally,* MURPH *finds the slip of paper*) I got it, I got it. Terrific. "Prem Gupta." In the Bronx. In the frigging Bronx. This is terrific. (*Pushes* THE INDIAN *to* JOEY) Here. Hold him.

INDIAN: Toom k-yah kar ra-hay ho k-yah toom pray-aim k-oh boo-lah ra-hay ho.
> (*What are you doing? Are you going to call my son?*)

MURPH: Shut him up. (*Fishes for a dime*) Give me a dime, God damn it. This is terrific.

JOEY: (*Finds the coins in his pocket*) Here's two nickels. (*Hands them over*) I think this is a rotten idea, that's what I think. (*Pauses*) And don't forget to pay me back those two nickels either.

MURPH: Just shut up. (*Dials the information operator*) Hello. Yeah, I want some information . . . I want a number up in the Bronx . . . Gupta . . . G-U-P-T-A . . . an Indian kid . . . His first name's Prem . . . P-R-E-M . . . No . . . I can't read the street right . . . Wait a minute. (*Reads the paper to himself*) For Christ's sake. How many Indians are up in the Bronx? There must be only one Indian named Gupta.

JOEY: What's she saying?

MURPH: There are two Indians named Gupta. (*To the operator*) Is
the two of them Prem? (*Pauses*) Well, that's what I told you . . .
Jesus . . . wait a minute . . . okay . . . okay. Say that again . . .
Okay . . . Okay . . . Right. Okay . . . thanks. (*Hurries quickly to
return the coins to the slot.* GUPTA *mumbles.* To JOEY) Don't talk
to me. (*Dials*) Six . . . seven-four. Oh. One. Seven, seven.
(*Pauses*) It's ringing. It's ringing. (*Pauses*) Hello. (*Covers the
phone with his hand*) I got him! Hello? Is this Prem Gupta? Oh
swell. How are you? (*To* JOEY) I got the kid!

    (THE INDIAN *breaks from* JOEY's *arm and runs to the telephone
. . .* MURPH *sticks out his leg and holds* THE INDIAN *off.* THE
INDIAN *fights, but seems weaker than ever*)

INDIAN: (*Screams*) Cree-payah moo-jhay ad-nay lar-kay say bah-at
kar-nay doh.
    (*Please let me talk to my son.*)
    (MURPH *slams* THE INDIAN *aside violently.* JOEY *stands fro-
zen, watching.* THE INDIAN *wails and finally talks calmly, as in
a trance*) Cree-payah moo-jhay ahd-nay lar-kay say bah-at kar-
nay doh. Mai toom-haray hah-th jor-tah hoom mai toom-hay
joh mango-gay doon-gar bus moo-jhay oos-say bah-at kar-nay
doh.
    (*Please let me talk to my son. Oh, Prem. Please, I beg of
you. Please. I'll give you anything at all. Just tell me what
you want of me. Just let me talk with my son. Won't you,
please?*)

    (MURPH *glares at* THE INDIAN, *who no longer tries to inter-
fere, as it becomes obvious that he must listen to even the
language he cannot understand*)

MURPH: Just listen to me, will you, Gupta? I don't know where the
hell your old man is, that's why I'm calling. We found an old elephant down here in Miami and we thought it must be yours. You
can't tell for sure whose elephant is whose. You know what I
mean? (MURPH *is laughing now*) What was that? Say that
again. I can't hear you too well. All the distance between us, you
know what I mean? It's a long way down here, you follow me?

No. I ain't got no Indian. I just got an elephant. And he's eating all my peanuts. Gupta, you're talking too fast. Slow down.

INDIAN: Pray-aim bhai-yah moo-jhay ah-kay lay ja-oh moo-jhay ap-nay lar-kay say bah-at kar-nay doh moo-jhay oos-say bah-at k-yohn nah-hee kar-nay day-tay.
  (*Prem! Prem! Please come and get me. Please let me talk to my son, mister. Why don't you let me talk to my son?*)
  (JOEY *leaps on* THE INDIAN; *tackles him, lays on top of him in front of the telephone booth*)

MURPH: That was the waiter. I'm in an Indian restaurant. (*Pauses*) Whoa. Slow down, man. That was nobody. That was just a myth. Your imagination. (*Pauses. Screams into the receiver*) Shut up, damn you! And listen. Okay? Okay. Are you listening? (MURPH *tastes the moment. He silently clicks the receiver back to the hook. To* JOEY) He was very upset. (*To* THE INDIAN) He was very upset. (*Pauses*) Well, what the hell's the matter with you? I only told him we found an elephant, that's all. I thought maybe he lost his elephant.
  (THE INDIAN *whimpers*)

INDIAN: Toom-nay ai-saw k-yohn ki-yah toom-nay may-ray lar-kay koh k-yah ka-hah hai.
  (*Why have you done this? What have you said to my son?*)

MURPH: You don't have to thank me, Turkie. I only told him your elephant was okay. He was probably worried sick about your elephant. (MURPH *laughs*) This is terrific, Joey. Terrific. You should have heard the guy jabber. He was so excited he started talking in Indian just like the Chief. He said that Turkie here and him got separated today. Turkie's only been in the city one day. You're pretty stupid, Turkie. One day in the city . . . and look at the mess you've made. You're pretty stupid. He's stupid, right?

JOEY: Yeah. He's stupid.

MURPH: Hold him. We'll try again. Sure.
  (THE INDIAN *jumps on* MURPH. *He tries to strangle* MURPH)

MURPH: (*Screaming*) Get him off of me! (JOEY *pulls* THE INDIAN *down to the ground as* MURPH *pounds the booth four times, screaming hideous sounds of aggression. With this tension released he begins to call, fierce but controlled, too controlled.* MURPH *takes the dime from his pocket, shows it to* JOEY, *and recalls the number. Talking into receiver. He dials number again and waits for reply.*) Hello? Is this Gupta again? Oh, hello there . . . I'm calling back to complain about your elephant . . . hey, slow down, will you? Let me do the talking. Okay? Your elephant is a terrific pain in the balls to me, get it? Huh? Do you follow me so far? (*Pauses*) I don't know what you're saying, man . . . how about if I do the talking, all right? . . . Your elephant scares hell out of me and my pal here. We don't like to see elephants on the street. Spiders and snakes are okay, but elephants scare us. Elephants . . . yeah, that's right. Don't you get it, pal? . . . Look, we always see spiders and snakes. But we never expect to see an elephant . . . What do you mean "I'm crazy"? I don't know nothing about your old man . . . I'm talking about your elephant. Your elephant offends the hell out of me. So why don't you be a nice Indian kid and come pick him up . . . that's right . . . wait a minute . . . I'll have to check the street sign. (*Covers the receiver*) This is terrific. (*Talks again into the telephone*) Jesus, I'm sorry about that. There don't seem to be no street sign . . . that's a bitch. I guess you lose your elephant . . . well, what do you expect me to do, bring your elephant all the way up to the Bronx? Come off it, pal. You wouldn't ever bring my elephant home. I ain't no kid, you know! I've lost a couple of elephants in my day. (*Listens*) Jesus, you're boring me now . . . I don't know what the hell you're talking about. Maybe you want to talk to your elephant . . . huh? (*Turns to* THE INDIAN) Here, come talk to your "papoose."

   (*He offers the telephone.* THE INDIAN *stares in disbelief, then grabs the telephone from* MURPH's *hands and begins to chatter wildly*)

INDIAN: Pray-aim, bhai-yah Pray-aim moo-jhay ah-kay lay jah-oh k-yah? Moo-jhay nah-hee pa-tah mai kah-han hoo-n moo-jhay ah-hp-nay gha-ar lay chah-low ya-hahn do-ah bad-mash lar-kay. Jo bah-hoot kha-tar-nahk hai-don-say mai nah-hee bah-cha sak-tah ah-pa-nay koh toom aik-dam moo-jhay ah-kay.

(Prem? Oh, Prem. Please come and take me away . . . what? I don't know where I am . . . Please come and take me to your house . . . please? There are two bad people. Two young men. They are dangerous. I cannot protect myself from them. Please . . . you must come and get me.)

(MURPH takes his knife from his pocket, cuts the line. THE INDIAN almost falls flat on his face as the line from the receiver to the phone box is cut, since he has been leaning away from MURPH and JOEY during his plea)

MURPH: You've had enough, Chief.
 (MURPH laughs aloud)

INDIAN: *(Not at once realizing the line must be connected, continues to talk into the telephone in Hindi)* Pray-aim, Pray-aim, ya-hahn aa-oh sah-rak kah nah-am hai—yeh toom-nay k-yah key-yah.
 (Prem. Prem. Please come here. The street sign reads . . .)

(He now realizes he has been cut off and stares dumbly at the severed cord as MURPH waves the severed cord in his face)
Toom nay yeh k-yoh key-yah?
 (What have you done?)

MURPH: There it is, Turkie. Who you talkin' to?

INDIAN: *(To JOEY, screaming a father's fury and disgust)* Toom-nay yeh k-yohn key-yah cri-payah may-ree mah-dah-d kah-roho.
 (Why have you done this? Please. Please help me.)

(JOEY has been standing throughout the entire scene, frozen in terror and disgust. He walks slowly toward MURPH, who kicks THE INDIAN. JOEY bolts from the stage, muttering one continuous droning sob)

MURPH: *(Screaming)* Go ahead, Joey. Love him. Love him like a mother. Hey? Joey? What the hell's the matter? C'mon, buddy? *(Turns to THE INDIAN, takes his knife and cuts THE INDIAN's hand, so blood is on the knife)* Sorry, Chief. This is for my buddy, Joey. And for Pussyface. *(Calls offstage)* Joey! Buddy!

What the hell's the matter? (*Races from the stage after* JOEY)
Joey! Wait up. Joey! I killed the Indian!
(*He exits.* THE INDIAN *stares dumbly at his hand, dripping blood. He then looks to the receiver and talks into it*)

INDIAN: Pray-aim, Pray-aim, mai ah-pa-nay lar-kay key ah-wah-az k-yon nah-hee soon sak-tah Pray-aim! Toom-nay may-ray sah-ahth aih-saw k-yohn key-yaw bay-tah Pray-aim, k-yah toom ho?
(*Prem. Prem.*)

(*He walks center stage, well away from the telephone booth*)

(*Why can I not hear my son, Prem? Why have you done this to me?*)
(*Suddenly the telephone rings again. Once. Twice.* THE INDIAN *is startled. He talks into the receiver, while he holds the dead line in his bleeding hand*)
(*Prem? Is that you? Prem?*)

(*The telephone rings a third time*) Pray-aim, Pray-aim, bay-tah k-yah toom ho—
(*Prem. Prem? Is that you?*)

(*A fourth ring.* THE INDIAN *knows the telephone is dead*)
Pray-aim Pray-aim—moo-jhay bah-chald Pray-aim.
(*Prem. Prem. Help me. Prem.*)

(*As the telephone rings a fifth time, in the silence of the night, the sounds of two boys' singing is heard*)

FIRST BOY:
I walk the lonely streets at night,
A'lookin' for your door . . .

SECOND BOY:
I look and look and look and look . . .

FIRST BOY AND SECOND BOY:
But, baby, you don't care.
But, baby, no one cares.
But, baby, no one cares.

(Their song continues to build as they repeat the lyrics, so the effect is one of many, many voices. The telephone continues its unanswered ring. THE INDIAN screams a final anguished scream of fury to the boys offstage. The telephone rings a final ring as THE INDIAN screams)

INDIAN: *(Desperately, holding the telephone to the audience as an offer. He speaks in English into the telephone. The only words he remembers are those from his lesson)*

How are you? You're welcome. You're welcome. Thank you. *(To the front)* Thank you!

BLACKOUT

THE EFFECT OF GAMMA RAYS ON MAN-IN-THE-MOON MARIGOLDS

A DRAMA IN TWO ACTS

Paul Zindel

THE EFFECT OF GAMMA RAYS ON MAN-IN-THE-MOON MARIGOLDS

Award winners traditionally express gratitude to their parents, spouses, and co-workers, but Paul Zindel was probably the first artist ever to thank a rabbit. In accepting his Obie Award for *The Effect of Gamma Rays on Man-in-the-Moon Marigolds* as the Best Play of 1970, Zindel concluded by saying: "And last I'd like to thank the rabbit in our cast, for reminding us that we share this earth with all living creatures." This spirit of loving tenderness, characteristic of all his work, probably helps explain why *Marigolds* has been the most popular and the most revived of all Obie-winning plays—most recently on Broadway, with Joanne Woodward in the starring role.

When *Marigolds* opened at the Mercer-O'Casey Theatre in New York City on April 7, 1970, its thirty-four-year-old author Paul Zindel—who had also written several novels and children's books—was instantly hailed as one of our theatre's most promising young playwrights. Prior to its New York premiere, earlier versions of the play had been produced at regional theatres in Houston and Cleveland. Clearly a new trend was emerging—largely due to the influence of Off-Broadway itself—in which New York City could no longer be considered the sole focus of American theatre.

Clive Barnes, theatre critic for the New York *Times*, called *Marigolds* "one of the best (plays) of the season . . . My heart was held by it. And, unlike most of its genre, the ending is unusually satisfying . . . Sada Thompson's Beatrice, embittered, beleaguered, cynical, and yet, despite herself, supremely pitiable, is among the best things in the current New York theatre."

Critic Bernard Carragher wrote: "The theme of *Marigolds* is realistic and at times poetic and comes quite close in tone to Tennessee Williams's *The Glass Menagerie*. The lacerating family abuses that all but extinguish any love at all reminds one of Eugene O'Neill's tortured Tyrone family in *Long Day's Journey into Night*. At all times Zindel's writing in this play is first-rate."

Critic John Lahr, who was also an Obie judge that year, described *Marigolds* as "a melodrama, a play of sentiment and of people who say precisely what they mean." He went on to say that through the character of Tillie, Zindel's play "attains its nobility and haunting emotion."

The title *The Effect of Gamma Rays on Man-in-the-Moon Marigolds* is one of the oddest in theatrical history, but in reality it is an accurate description of the play. Although this appears to be a conventional domestic drama about a monstrous mother, her two frail daughters, and the failure of their dreams, the play actually assumes a deeper significance. Its theme is the way—like the flowers exposed to radiation—some people are destroyed by their environment while others survive in new and gorgeous mutations.

The cluttered, drab set of the original Off-Broadway production, with paper covering the windows and objects stuffed haphazardly throughout the room, as well as the counterpoint between the dreary and lyrical portrayals of the mother and her daughters, perfectly captured the poignancy of Zindel's script.

Marigolds was the first play to win four Obies—in addition to Zindel, awards were presented to Melvin Bernhardt for his direction, and to actresses Pamela Payton-Wright (Tillie) and Sada Thompson (Beatrice), who was selected as the best performer of the year. Zindel's play ran for over two years and was also the winner of the New York Drama Critics Circle Award as the best American play of 1970 and the 1971 Pulitzer Prize for Drama.

THE EFFECT OF GAMMA RAYS ON MAN-IN-THE-MOON MARIGOLDS was first presented in New York City on April 7, 1970, at the Mercer-O'Casey Theatre. The cast was as follows:

TILLIE	*Pamela Payton-Wright*
BEATRICE	*Sada Thompson*
RUTH	*Amy Levitt*
NANNY	*Judith Lowry*
JANICE VICKERY	*Swoosie Kurtz*

The play was produced by Orin Lehman; directed by Melvin Bernhardt; music and sound, James Reichert; scenery, Fred Voelpel; costumes, Sara Brook; lighting, Martin Aronstein; associate producer, Julie Hughes; production stage manager, Bud Coffey; press, Alan Eichler, David Powers.

THE SETTING

A room of wood which was once a vegetable store—and a point of debarkation for a horse-drawn wagon to bring its wares to a small town.

But the store is gone, and a widow of confusion has placed her touch on everything. A door to NANNY's room leads off from this main room, and in front of the door hang faded curtains which allow ventilation in the summer. There is a hallway and a telephone. A heavy wood staircase leads to a landing with a balustrade, two doors, and a short hall. BEATRICE sleeps in one room; TILLIE and RUTH share the other.

Objects which respectable people usually hide in closets are scattered about the main room: newspapers, magazines, dishes; empty bottles; clothes; suitcases; last week's sheets. Such carelessness is the type which is so perfected it must have evolved from hereditary processes; but in all fairness to the occupants, it can be pointed out that after twilight, when shadows and weak bulbs work their magic, the room becomes interesting.

On a table near the front left of the room is a small wire cage designed to hold a rabbit. Near this are several school books, notebook papers, and other weapons of high school children. A kitchen area, boasting a hot plate, has been carved near the bottom of the staircase, and the window, which was formerly the front of the vegetable store, is now mostly covered with old newspapers so that passers-by cannot see in. A bit of the clear glass remains at the top—but drab, lifeless drapes line the sides of the window.

ACT ONE

(*The lights go down slowly as music creeps in—a theme for lost children, the near misbegotten.*
From the blackness TILLIE's VOICE *speaks against the music.*)

TILLIE's VOICE: He told me to look at my hand, for a part of it came from a star that exploded too long ago to imagine. This part of me was formed from a tongue of fire that screamed through the heavens until there was our sun. And this part of me—this tiny part of me—was on the sun when it itself exploded and whirled in a great storm until the planets came to be.

(*Lights start in.*)

And this small part of me was then a whisper of the earth. When there was life, perhaps this part of me got lost in a fern that was crushed and covered until it was coal. And then it was a diamond millions of years later—it must have been a diamond as beautiful as the star from which it had first come.

TILLIE: (*Taking over from recorded voice.*) Or perhaps this part of me became lost in a terrible beast, or became part of a huge bird that flew above the primeval swamps.

And he said this thing was so small—this part of me was so small it couldn't be seen—but it was there from the beginning of the world.

And he called this bit of me an atom. And when he wrote the word, I fell in love with it.
Atom.

Atom.

What a beautiful word.

(*The phone rings.*)

BEATRICE: (*Off stage.*) Will you get that please?

(*The phone rings again before* BEATRICE *appears in her bathrobe from the kitchen.*)

No help! Never any help!

(*She answers the phone.*)

Hello? Yes it is. Who is this? . . . I hope there hasn't been any trouble at school . . . Oh, she's always been like that. She hardly says a word around here, either. I always say some people were born to speak and others born to listen . . .

You know I've been meaning to call you to thank you for that lovely rabbit you gave Matilda. She and I just adore it and it's gotten so big . . .

Well, it certainly was thoughtful. Mr. Goodman, I don't mean to change the subject but aren't you that delightful young man Tillie said hello to a couple of months back at the A&P? You were by the lobster tank and I was near the frozen foods? That delightful and handsome young man? . . . Why, I would very much indeed use the expression *handsome*. Yes, and . . .

Well, I encourage her at every opportunity at home. Did she say I didn't? Both my daughters have their own desks and I put 75-watt bulbs right near them . . . Yes . . . Yes . . . I think those tests are very much overrated, anyway, Mr. Goodman . . . Well, believe me she's nothing like that around this house . . .

Now I don't want you to think I don't appreciate what you're trying to do, Mr. Goodman, but I'm afraid it's simply useless. I've tried just everything, but she isn't a pretty girl—I mean, let's be frank about it—she's going to have her problems. Are you married, Mr. Goodman? Oh, that's too bad. I don't know what's the matter with women today letting a handsome young man like you get away . . .

Well, some days she just doesn't feel like going to school. You just said how bright she is, and I'm really afraid to put too much of a strain on her after what happened to her sister. You know, too much strain is the worst thing in this modern world, Mr. Goodman, and I can't afford to have another convulsive on my hands, now can I? But don't you worry about Matilda. There will be some place for her in this world. And, like I said, some were born to speak and others just to listen . . . and do call again, Mr. Goodman. It's been a true pleasure speaking with you. Goodbye.

(BEATRICE *hangs up the phone and advances into the main room. The lights come up.*)

Matilda, that wasn't very nice of you to tell them I was forcibly detaining you from school. Why, the way that Mr. Goodman spoke, he must think I'm running a concentration camp. Do you have any idea how embarrassing it is to be accused of running a concentration camp for your own children?

Well, it isn't embarrassing at all.

That school of yours is forty years behind the times anyway, and believe me you learn more around here than that ugly Mr. Goodman can teach you!

You know, I really feel sorry for him. I never saw a man with a more effeminate face in my life. When I saw you talking to him by the lobster tank I said to myself, "Good Lord, for a science teacher my poor girl has got herself a Hebrew hermaphrodite." Of course, he's not as bad as Miss Hanley. The idea of letting her teach girl's gym is staggering.

And you have to place me in the embarrassing position of giving them a reason to call me at eight-thirty in the morning, no less.

TILLIE: I didn't say anything.

BEATRICE: What do you tell them when they want to know why you stay home once in a while?

TILLIE: I tell them I'm sick.

BEATRICE: Oh, you're sick all right, the exact nature of the illness not fully realized, but you're sick all right. Any daughter that would turn her mother in as the administrator of a concentration camp has got to be suffering from something very peculiar.

TILLIE: Can I go in today, Mother?

BEATRICE: You'll go in, all right.

TILLIE: Mr. Goodman said he was going to do an experiment—

BEATRICE: Why, he looks like the kind that would do his experimenting after sundown.

TILLIE: On radioactivity—

BEATRICE: On radioactivity? That's all that high school needs!

TILLIE: He's going to bring in the cloud chamber—

BEATRICE: Why, what an outstanding event. If you had warned me yesterday I would've gotten all dressed to kill and gone with you today. I love seeing cloud chambers being brought in.

TILLIE: You can actually see—

BEATRICE: You're giving me a headache.

TILLIE: Please?

BEATRICE: No, my dear, the fortress of knowledge is not going to be blessed with your presence today. I have a good number of exciting duties for you to take care of, not the least of which is rabbit droppings.

TILLIE: Oh, Mother, please . . . I'll do it after school.

BEATRICE: If we wait a minute longer this house is going to ferment. I found rabbit droppings in my bedroom even.

TILLIE: I could do it after Mr. Goodman's class. I'll say I'm ill and ask for a sick pass.

BEATRICE: Do you want me to chloroform that thing right this minute?

TILLIE: No!

BEATRICE: Then shut up.

(RUTH *comes to the top of the stairs. She is dressed for school, and though her clothes are simple she gives the impression of being slightly strange. Her hair isn't quite combed, her sweater doesn't quite fit, etc.*)

RUTH: Do you have Devil's Kiss down there?

BEATRICE: It's in the bathroom cabinet.

(RUTH *comes downstairs and goes to the bathroom door, located under the stairs. She flings it open and rummages in the cabinet.*)

RUTH: There's so much junk in here it's driving me crazy.

BEATRICE: Maybe it's in my purse . . . If you don't hurry up you'll be late for school.

RUTH: Well, I couldn't very well go in without Devil's Kiss, now could I?

BEATRICE: Doesn't anyone go to school these days without that all over their lips?

RUTH: (*Finding the lipstick.*) Nobody I know, except Tillie, that is. And if she had a little lipstick on I'll bet they wouldn't have laughed at her so much yesterday.

BEATRICE: Why were they laughing?

RUTH: The assembly. Didn't she tell you about the assembly?

BEATRICE: Ruth, you didn't tell me she was in an assembly.

RUTH: Well, I just thought of it right now. How could I tell you anything until I think of it—did you ever stop to consider that? Some crummy science assembly.

BEATRICE: (To TILLIE.) What is she talking about?

RUTH: I thought she'd tell the whole world. Imagine, right in front of the assembly, with everybody laughing at her.

BEATRICE: Will you be quiet, Ruth? *Why were they laughing at you?*

TILLIE: I don't know.

RUTH: You don't know? My heavens, she was a sight. She had that old jumper on—the faded one with that low collar—and a raggy slip that showed all over and her hair looked like she was struck by lightning.

BEATRICE: You're exaggerating . . .

RUTH: She was cranking this model of something—

TILLIE: The atom.

RUTH: This model of the atom . . . you know, it had this crank and a long tower so that when you turned it these little colored balls went spinning around like crazy. And there was Tillie, cranking away, looking weird as a coot . . . that old jumper with the raggy slip and the lightning hair . . . cranking away while some boy with glasses was reading this stupid speech . . . and everybody burst into laughter until the teachers yelled at them. And all day long, the kids kept coming up to me saying, "Is that really your sister? How can you bear it?" And you know, Chris Burns says to me— "*She* looks like the one that went to the looney doctors." I could have kissed him there and then.

BEATRICE: (*Taking a backscratcher.*) Matilda, if you can't get yourself dressed properly before going to school you're never going to go again. I don't like the idea of everybody laughing at you, because when they laugh at you they're laughing at me. And I don't want you cranking any more . . . atoms.

RUTH: (*Putting the lipstick back in* BEATRICE's *bag.*) You're almost out of Devil's Kiss.

BEATRICE: If you didn't put so much on it would last longer.

RUTH: Who was that calling?

BEATRICE: Matilda turned me in to the Gestapo.

RUTH: Can I earn a cigarette this morning?

BEATRICE: Why not?

(BEATRICE *offers her the backscratcher along with a cigarette.*)

RUTH: Was it Mr. Goodman?

BEATRICE: Who?

RUTH: (*Lighting the cigarette.*) The call this morning. Was it Mr. Goodman?

BEATRICE: Yes.

RUTH: (*Using the backscratcher on* BEATRICE, *who squirms with ecstasy.*) I figured it would be.

BEATRICE: A little higher, please.

RUTH: There?

BEATRICE: Yes, *there* . . . Why did you figure it would be Mr. Goodman?

RUTH: Well, he called me out of sewing class yesterday—I remember because my blouse wasn't all buttoned—and he wanted to know why Tillie's out of school so much.

BEATRICE: Lower. A little lower . . . And what did you tell him?

RUTH: I wish you'd go back to Kools. I liked Kools better.

TILLIE: (*Gravely concerned.*) What did you tell him?

RUTH: I told him you were ill, and he wanted to know what kind, so I told him you had leprosy.

TILLIE: You didn't!

RUTH: You should have seen his face. He was so cute. And I told him you had ringworm and gangrene.

BEATRICE: What did he say?

RUTH: And I told him you had what Mother's last patient had . . . whatchamacallit?

BEATRICE: Psoriasis?

RUTH: Yeah. Something like that.

TILLIE: Tell me you didn't, Ruth!

RUTH: O.K. I didn't . . . But I really did.

BEATRICE: He knew you were joking.

RUTH: And then I told him to go look up the *history* and then he'd find out. Whenever they go look up the history then they don't bother me anymore 'cause they think I'm crazy.

BEATRICE: Ruth—

RUTH: And I told him the disease you had was fatal and that there wasn't much hope for you.

BEATRICE: What kind of *history* is it?

RUTH: Just a little folder with the story of our lives in it, that's all.

BEATRICE: How did you ever see it?

RUTH: I read the whole thing last term when Miss Hanley dragged me into the record room because I didn't want to climb the ropes in gym and I told her my skull was growing.

BEATRICE: A little *lower*, please.

RUTH: Lower! Higher! I wish you'd make up your mind. If you'd switch back to Kools it might be worth it, but ugh! these are awful. You know, I really did think my skull was growing. Either that or a tumor. So she dragged me out of gym class, and she thought I couldn't read upside down while she was sitting opposite me with the history. But I could.

BEATRICE: What does it say?

RUTH: Oh, it says you're divorced and that I went crazy . . . and my father took a heart attack at Star Lake . . . and now you're a widow—

BEATRICE: (*Referring to the backscratching.*) That's it! Hold it right there! Aaah!

RUTH: And it says that I exaggerate and tell stories and that I'm afraid of death and have nightmares . . . and all that stuff.

BEATRICE: And what else does it say?

RUTH: I can't remember everything you know. Remember this, remember that . . . remember this, that . . .

(*Go to dark. Music in.*)

Tillie's voice: Today I saw it. Behind the glass a white cloud began to form. He placed a small piece of metal in the center of the chamber and we waited until I saw the first one—a trace of smoke that came from nowhere and then disappeared. And then another . . . and another, until I knew it was coming from the metal. They looked like water-sprays from a park fountain, and they went on and on for as long as I watched.

And he told me the fountain of smoke would come forth for a long time, and if I had wanted to, I could have stayed there all my life and it would never have ended—that fountain, so close I could have touched it. In front of my eyes, one part of the world was becoming another. Atoms exploding, flinging off tiny bullets that caused the fountain, atom after atom breaking down into something new. And no one could stop the fountain. It would go on for millions of years—on and on, this fountain from eternity.

(*By the end of this speech, the lights are in to show* Tillie *preparing boxes of dirt in which to plant seeds. The rabbit is in the cage near her, and* Beatrice *is reading a newspaper on the other side of the room. She is sipping coffee from a huge coffee cup.*)

Beatrice: I thought we had everything, but leave it to you to think of the one thing we're missing . . .

(*She reads from the newspaper.*)

Twenty-two acres in Prince's Bay. Small pond. $6,000 . . . That's cheap. I'd take a look at it if I had any money . . .

What kind of seeds are they?

Tillie: Marigolds. *They've been exposed to cobalt-60.*

Beatrice: If there's one thing I've always wanted, it's been a living room planted with marigolds that have been exposed to cobalt-60. While you're at it, why don't you throw in a tomato patch in the bathroom?

Tillie: Just let me keep them here for a week or so until they get started and then I'll transplant them to the backyard.

BEATRICE: (*Reading again.*) Four-family house. Six and a half and six and a half over five and five. Eight garages. I could really do something with that. A nursing home . . .

Don't think I'm not kicking myself that I didn't finish that real estate course. I should have finished beauty school, too . . .

God, what I could do with eight garages . . .

(*There is a sound from beyond the curtained doorway.* BEATRICE *gestures in that direction.*)

You know, I'm thinking of getting rid of *that* and making this place into something.

TILLIE: Yes.

BEATRICE: I've been thinking about a tea shop. Have you noticed there aren't many of them around anymore?

TILLIE: Yes.

BEATRICE: And this is just the type of neighborhood where a good tea shop could make a go of it. We'd have a good cheesecake. You've got to have a good cheesecake . . .

(*She calculates.*)

Eight times ten—well, eight times eight, if they're falling down— that's sixty-four dollars a month from the garages alone . . . I swear money makes money.

(*There is a rustling at the curtains. Two thin and wrinkled hands push the curtains apart slowly and then the ancient face of* NANNY *appears. She negotiates her way through the curtains. She is utterly wrinkled and dried, perhaps a century old. Time has left her with a whisper of a smile—a smile from a soul half-departed. If one looked closely, great cataracts could be seen on each eye, and it is certain that all that can pierce her soundless prison are mere shadows from the outside world. She pervades the room with age.*)

(NANNY *supports herself by a four-legged tubular frame which she pushes along in front of her with a shuffling motion that re-*

minds one of a ticking clock. Inch by inch she advances into the room. TILLIE *and* BEATRICE *continue speaking, knowing that it will be minutes before she is close enough to know they are there.*)

BEATRICE: What is cobalt-60?

TILLIE: It's something that causes . . . changes in seeds. Oh, Mother —he set the cloud chamber up just for me and he told me about radioactivity and half-life and he got the seeds for me.

BEATRICE: (*Her attention still on the newspaper.*) What does half-life mean?

(NANNY *is well into the room as* TILLIE *replies.*)

TILLIE: (*Reciting from memory.*) The half-life of Polonium-210 is one hundred and forty days.

The half-life of Radium-226 is one thousand five hundred and ninety years.

The half-life of Uranium-238 is four and one-half billion years.

BEATRICE: (*Putting away her newspaper.*) Do you know you're giving me a headache?

(*Then, in a loud, horribly saccharine voice, she speaks to* NANNY *as if she were addressing a deaf year-old child.*)

LOOK WHO'S THERE! IT'S NANNY! NANNY CAME ALL THE WAY OUT HERE BY HERSELF!

I'm going to need a cigarette for this.

NANNY! YOU COME SIT DOWN AND WE'LL BE RIGHT WITH HER!

You know, sometimes I've got to laugh. I've got *this* on my hands and all you're worried about is planting marigolds.

I'VE GOT HOTSY WATER FOR YOU, NANNY. WOULD YOU LIKE SOME HOTSY WATER AND HONEY?

(NANNY *has seated herself at a table, smiling but oblivious to her environment.*)

I've never seen it to fail. Every time I decide to have a cup of coffee I see that face at the curtains. I wonder what she'd do . . .

(*She holds pot of boiling water.*)

. . . if I just poured this right over her head. I'll bet she wouldn't even notice it.

NANNY'S GOING TO GET JUST WHAT SHE NEEDS!

(*She fills a cup for her and places a honey jar near her.*)

You know if someone told me when I was young that I'd end up feeding honey to a zombie, I'd tell them they were crazy.

SOMETHING WRONG, NANNY? OH, DID I FORGET NANNY'S SPOON? MERCY! MERCY! I FORGOT NANNY'S SPOON!

(*She gets a spoon and stands behind NANNY.*)

I'll give you a spoon, Nanny, I'll give you a spoon.

(*She makes a motion behind NANNY's back as if she's going to smack her on the head with the spoon.*)

Matilda! Watch me give Nanny her spoon.

A SPOON FOR NANNY!

(*It manages to be slightly funny and TILLIE yields to a laugh, along with her mother.*)

Fifty dollars a week. Fifty dollars. I look at you, Nanny, and I wonder if it's worth it. I think I'd be better off driving a cab.

TAKE HONEY, NANNY. HONEY WITH HOTSY WATER!

You should have seen her daughter bring her here last week . . . I could have used you that day . . . She came in pretending she was Miss Career Woman of the Year. She said she was in real estate and *such a busy little woman,* such a busy little woman—she just couldn't give all the love and care and affection her little momsy needed anymore . . .

(*Then, with a great smile, she speaks right into NANNY's uncomprehending face.*)

Nanny's quite a little cross to bear, now aren't you, Nanny dear? But you're a little better than Mr. Mayo was—with the tumor on his brain—or Miss Marion Minto with her cancer, or Mr. Brougham . . . what was his first name?

TILLIE: Alexander.

BEATRICE: Mr. Alexander Brougham with the worms in his legs.

WHY, NANNY'S QUITE SOME LITTLE GIRL, AREN'T YOU, NANNY? A GIRL DRINKING HER HOTSY AND HONEY! . . .

Cobalt-60. Ha! You take me for a fool, don't you?

TILLIE: No, Mother.

BEATRICE: Science, science, science! Don't they teach our misfits anything anymore? Anything decent and meaningful and sensitive? Do you know what I'd be now if it wasn't for this mud pool I got sucked into? I'd probably be a dancer. Miss Betty Frank, The Best Dancer of the Class of 19 . . . something. One minute I'm the best dancer in school—smart as a whip—the head of the whole crowd! And the next minute . . .

One mistake. That's how it starts. Marry the wrong man and before you know it he's got you tied down with two stones around your neck for the rest of your life.

When I was in that lousy high school I was one of the most respected kids you ever saw.

I used to wonder why people always said, "Why, just yesterday . . . why, just yesterday . . . why, just yesterday . . ."

Before I knew what happened I lost my dancing legs and got varicose legs. Beautiful varicose legs. Do you know, everything I ever thought I'd be has exploded!

NANNY, YOU HURRY UP WITH THAT HONEY!

Exploded! You know, I almost forgot about everything I was supposed to be . . .

NANNY'S ALMOST FINISHED. ISN'T THAT WONDER-
FUL?

She's almost finished, all right.

NANNY'S DAUGHTER IS COMING TO SEE YOU SOON.
WILL THAT MAKE NANNY HAPPY?

The day Miss Career Woman of the Year comes to visit again I
think I'll drop dead. Nobody's too busy for anything they want to
do, don't you tell me. What kind of an idiot do people take me
for?

NANNY, YOU'RE SPILLING YOUR HOTSY! JESUS
CHRIST!

You know, I ought to kick you right out and open that tea shop
tomorrow.

Oh, it's coming. I can feel it. And the first thing I'll do is get rid
of that rabbit.

TILLIE: (*Hardly listening.*) Yes, Mother.

BEATRICE: You think I'm kidding?

TILLIE: No, I don't.

BEATRICE: You bet I'm not!

(*She rummages through some drawers in a chest.*)

I was going to do this a month ago.

(*She holds up a small bottle.*)

Here it is. Here's a new word for you.

(*She reads.*)

Trichloro . . . methane. Do you know what that is, Matilda?

Well, it's chloroform!

(*She puts the bottle away.*)

I'm saving it for that Angora manure machine of yours. Speaking of manure machines, IS NANNY READY TO GO MAKE DUTY?

(*She starts helping* NANNY *out of the chair and props her up with the tubular frame.*)

NANNY IS ALWAYS READY FOR DUTY, AREN'T YOU NANNY? BECAUSE NANNY'S A GOODY-GOODY GIRL AND GOODY-GOODY GIRLS ALWAYS GET GOODY-GOODY THINGS. GOD LOOKS OUT FOR GOODY-GOODY GIRLS AND GIVES THEM HOTSY AND HONEY —RIGHT, NANNY?

(BEATRICE *sits down in the hall and watches* NANNY *make her way toward the bathroom. There is a pause as the woman's shuffling continues.*)

(*The lights go low on* TILLIE, NANNY *becomes a silhouette, and the light remains on* BEATRICE. *She starts to read the paper again, but the shuffling gets on her nerves and she flings the paper down.*)

Half-life! If you want to know what a half-life is, just ask me. You're looking at the original half-life!

I got stuck with one daughter with half a mind; another one who's half a test tube; half a husband—a house half full of rabbit crap—and half a corpse!

That's what I call a half-life, Matilda! Me and cobalt-60! Two of the biggest half-*lifes* you ever saw!

(*The set goes to dark.*)

(*After a few seconds, the sound of someone dialing a phone can be heard. As the spot comes up on her, we see* BEATRICE *holding the phone and struggling to get a cigarette.*)

BEATRICE: (*On the phone.*) Hello—Mr. Goodman, please . . . How would I know if he's got a class? . . . Hello, Mr. Goodman? Are you Mr. Goodman? . . . Oh, I beg your pardon, Miss Torgersen . . . Yes, I'll wait . . .

(*She lights her cigarette.*)

Couldn't you find him, Miss Torgersen? . . . Oh! Excuse me, Mr. Goodman. How are you? . . . I'll bet you'll never guess who this is—it's Mrs. Hunsdorfer—remember the frozen foods?

(*She laughs.*)

You know, Ruth told me she's your new secretary and I certainly think that's a delight. You were paying so much attention to Matilda that I'll bet Ruth just got jealous. She does things like that, you know. I hope she works hard for you, although I can't imagine what kind of work Ruth could be doing in that great big science office. She's a terrible snoop . . .

(*She takes a puff.*)

Your attendance? Isn't that charming. And the *cut* cards! Imagine. You trust her with . . . why, I didn't know she could type *at all* . . . imagine. Well . . . I'll . . . Of course, *too* much work isn't good for anyone, either. No wonder she's failing everything. I mean, I never knew a girl who failed everything regardless of what they were suffering from. I suppose I should say *recovering* from . . .

Well, it's about the seeds you gave Matilda . . . Well, she's had them in the house for a week now and they're starting to grow. Now, she told me they had been subjected to radioactivity, and I hear such terrible things about radioactivity that I automatically associate radioactivity with sterility, and it positively horrifies me to have those seeds right here in my living room. Couldn't she just grow plain marigolds like everyone else?

(*She takes a puff.*)

Oh . . .

(*Another big puff, forming a mushroom cloud.*)

It does sound like an interesting project, but . . .

(*The biggest puff yet.*)

No, I must admit that at this very moment I don't know what a *mutation* is . . .

(*She laughs uncomfortably.*)

Mr. Goodman . . . Mr. Goodman! I don't want you to think I'm not interested, but please spare me definitions over the phone. I'll go to the library next week and pick me out some little book on science and then I'll know all about mutations . . . No, you didn't insult me, but I just want you to know that I'm not *stupid* . . .

I just thought prevention was better than a tragedy, Mr. Goodman. I mean, Matilda has enough problems to worry about without *sterility* . . .

Well, I was just concerned, but you've put my poor mother's heart at ease. You know, really, our schools need more exciting young men like you, I really mean that. Really. Oh, I do. Goodbye, Mr. Goodman.

(*By the end of her talk on the phone, her face is left in a spotlight, and then the stage goes black. The music theme comes in, in a minor key, softly at first, but accentuated by increasingly loud pulses which transmute into thunder crashes.*)

(*There is a scream heard from upstairs and we see the set in night shadows.*)

(TILLIE *tears open her bedroom door and rushes into* BEATRICE'S *room.* RUTH *screams again.*)

TILLIE: Mother! She's going to have one!

(RUTH *appears on the landing and releases another scream which breaks off into gasps. She starts down the stairs and stops halfway to scream again. There is another tremendous thunder crash as* BEATRICE *comes out of her room, puts on the hall light, and catches the hysterical girl on the stairs.*)

BEATRICE: (*Shouting.*) Stop it! Stop it, Ruth!

TILLIE: (*At the top of the stairs.*) She's going!

BEATRICE: Ruth! Stop it!

TILLIE: She's going to go!

BEATRICE: (*Yelling at* TILLIE.) Shut up and get back in your room!

(RUTH *screams.*)

You're not going to let yourself go, do you hear me, Ruth? You're not going to go!

RUTH: He's after me!

(*She screams, lightning and thunder crash follow.*)

BEATRICE: You were dreaming, do you hear me? Nobody's after you! Nobody!

TILLIE: I saw her eyes start to go back—

BEATRICE: (*To* TILLIE.) Get back in your room!

(*She helps* RUTH *down the rest of the stairs.*)

There, now, nobody's after you. Nice and easy. Breathe deeply . . . Did the big bad man come after my little girl?

(*She sits* RUTH *down and then puts both hands up to her own face and pulls her features into a comic mask.* RUTH *begins to laugh at her.*)

That big bad bogey man?

(*They both laugh heartily.*)

Now that wasn't so bad, was it?

RUTH: It was the dream, with Mr. Mayo again.

BEATRICE: Oh. Well, we'll just get you a little hot milk and—

(*A tremendous thunder crash throws the set into shadows.*)

Why, the electricity's gone off. Do you remember what happened to those candles?

RUTH: What candles?

BEATRICE: The little white ones from my birthday cake last year.

RUTH: Tillie melted them down for school a long time ago.

BEATRICE: (*Searching through drawers.*) She had no right doing that.

RUTH: She asked you. She used them to attach a paper straw to a milk bottle with a balloon over it, and it was supposed to tell if it was going to rain.

BEATRICE: (*Finding a flashlight.*) There! It works. I don't want her wasting anything of mine unless she's positive I won't need it. You always need candles.

(*She steers* RUTH *toward the couch as lightning flashes.*)

Why, Ruth—your skin just turned ice cold!

(*She rummages through one of the boxes and grabs a blanket.*)

This will warm you up . . . What's the matter?

RUTH: The flashlight—

BEATRICE: What's wrong with it?

RUTH: It's the same one I used to check on Mr. Mayo with.

BEATRICE: So it is. We don't need it.

RUTH: No, let me keep it.

(*Starting to laugh.*)

Do you want to know how they have it in the history?

BEATRICE: No, I don't.

RUTH: Well, they say I came out of my room . . .

(*She flashes the light on her room.*)

. . . And I started down the stairs, step by step . . . and I heard the choking and banging on the bed, and . . .

BEATRICE: I'm going back to bed.

RUTH: No!

BEATRICE: Well, talk about something nice, then.

RUTH: Oh, Mama, tell me about the wagon.

BEATRICE: You change so fast I can't keep up with you.

RUTH: Mama, *please* . . . the story about the wagon.

BEATRICE: I don't know anything about telling stories. Get those great big smart teachers of yours to do that sort of stuff.

RUTH: Tell me about the horses again, and how you stole the wagon.

BEATRICE: Don't get me started on that.

RUTH: Mama, *please* . . .

BEATRICE: (*Taking out a pack of cigarettes.*) Do you want a cigarette?

RUTH: (*Taking one.*) Leave out the part where they shoot the horses, though.

(*They both light up.*)

BEATRICE: Honey, you know the whole story—

RUTH: "Apples! Pears! Cu . . . cumbers!"

BEATRICE: No. It's "Apples! Pears! Cu*cum* . . . bers!"

(*They say it together.*)

"Apples! Pears! Cu*cum* . . . bers!"

(*And they laugh.*)

RUTH: How did you get the wagon out without him seeing you?

BEATRICE: That was easy. Every time he got home for the day he'd make us both some sandwiches—my mama had been dead for years—and he'd take a nap on the old sofa that used to be . . . there!

(*She points to a corner of the room.*)

And while he was sleeping I got the horses hitched up and went riding around the block waving to everyone.

RUTH: Oh, Mama, you didn't!

BEATRICE: Of course I did. I had more nerve than a bear when I was a kid. Let me tell you it takes nerve to sit up on that wagon every day yelling "Apples! . . .

(*Both together.*)

Pears! Cu*cum* . . . bers!"

(*They laugh again.*)

RUTH: Did he find out you took the wagon?

BEATRICE: Did he find out? He came running down the street after me and started spanking me right on top of the wagon—not hard —but it was so embarrassing—and I had one of those penny marshmallow ships in the back pocket of my overalls, and it got all squished. And you better believe I never did it again . . .

You would have loved him, Ruth, and gone out with him on the wagon . . . all over Stapleton yelling as loud as you wanted.

RUTH: "Apples! Pears! Cu . . . cumbers!"

BEATRICE: No!

RUTH: "Cu*cum* . . . bers!"

BEATRICE: My father made up for all the other men in this whole world, Ruth. If only you two could have met. He'd only be about seventy now, do you realize that? And I'll bet he'd still be selling vegetables around town. All that fun—and then I don't think I ever knew what really hit me.

RUTH: Don't tell about—

BEATRICE: Don't worry about the horses.

RUTH: What hit you?

BEATRICE: Well it was just me and Papa . . . and your father hanging around. And then Papa got sick . . . and I drove with him up to the sanatorium. And then I came home and there were the horses—

RUTH: Mother!

BEATRICE: And I had the horses . . . taken care of. And then Papa got terribly sick and he begged me to marry so that he'd be sure I'd be taken care of.

(*She laughs.*)

If he knew how I was taken care of he'd turn over in his grave.

And *nightmares!* Do you want to know the nightmare I used to have?

I never had nightmares over the fights with your father, or the divorce, or his thrombosis—he deserved it—I never had nightmares over any of that.

Let me tell you about my nightmare that used to come back and back:

Well, I'm on Papa's wagon, but it's newer and shinier, and it's being pulled by beautiful white horses, not dirty workhorses— these are like circus horses with long manes and tinsel—and the wagon is blue, shiny blue. And it's full—filled with yellow apples and grapes and green squash.

You're going to laugh when you hear this. I'm wearing a lovely gown with jewels all over it, and my hair is piled up on top of my head with a long feather in it, and the bells are ringing.

Huge bells swinging on a gold braid strung across the back of the wagon, and they're going DONG, DONG . . . DONG, DONG. And I'm yelling "APPLES! PEARS! CUCUM . . . BERS!"

RUTH: That doesn't sound like a nightmare to me.

BEATRICE: And then I turn down our street and all the noise stops. This long street, with all the doors of the houses shut and everything crowded next to each other, and there's not a soul around. And then I start getting afraid that the vegetables are going to spoil . . . and that nobody's going to buy anything, and I feel as though I shouldn't be on the wagon, and I keep trying to call out.

But there isn't a sound. Not a single sound. Then I turn my head and look at the house across the street. I see an upstairs window, and a pair of hands pull the curtains slowly apart. I see the face of my father and my heart stands still . . .

Ruth . . . take the light out of my eyes.

(A *long pause.*)

RUTH: Is Nanny going to die here?

BEATRICE: No.

RUTH: How can you be sure?

BEATRICE: I can tell.

RUTH: Are you crying?

BEATRICE: What's left for me, Ruth?

RUTH: What, Mama?

BEATRICE: What's left for me?

(The stage goes slowly to dark as the drizzling rain becomes louder and then disappears.)

(When the lights come up again NANNY *is seated at the kitchen table with a bottle of beer and a glass in front of her.* TILLIE *comes in the front door with a box of large marigold plants and sets them down where they'll be inconspicuous. She gets the rabbit out of its cage, sits down near* NANNY *and gives her a little wave.* BEATRICE *suddenly appears at the top of the stairs and drops a stack of newspapers with a loud thud. She goes back into her room and lets fly another armful of junk.)*

TILLIE: What are you doing?

BEATRICE: A little housecleaning, and you're going to help. You can start by getting rid of that rabbit or I'll suffocate the bastard.

(She takes a drink from a glass of whiskey.)

You don't think I will, do you? You wait and see. Where's Ruth? She's probably running around the schoolyard in her brassiere.

(She comes downstairs.)

TILLIE: Mother, they want me to do something at school.

BEATRICE: NANNY! DID YOU HEAR THAT? THEY WANT HER TO DO SOMETHING AT SCHOOL! ISN'T THAT MOMENTOUS, NANNY?

Well I want you to do something around here. Like get rid of that bunny. I'm being generous! I'll let you give it away. Far away. Give it to Mr. Goodman. I'd chloroform the thing myself, but that crazy sister of yours would throw convulsions for fifty years . . . and I hate a house that vibrates.

And get rid of those sterile marigolds. They stink!

HI, NANNY—HOW ARE YOU, HONEY? HOW WOULD YOU LIKE TO GO ON A LONG TRIP?

You see, everybody, I spent today taking stock of my life and I've come up with zero. I added up all the separate departments and the total reads zero . . .

zero zero zero zero zero zero zero
zero zero zero zero zero
zero zero zero
zero zero
zero

. . . And do you know how you pronounce that, with all your grammatical schoolin' and foolin'? You pronounce it o,o,o,o,O,O,O,O,O,O! o,o,o,o,O,O,O,O,O,O,O,O,O!

Right, Nanny? RIGHT, NANNY?

So, by the end of the week, you get rid of that cottontail compost heap and we'll get you a job down at the five-and-ten-cent store. And if you don't do so well with the public, we'll fix you up with some kind of machine. Wouldn't that be nice?

(RUTH *enters at a gallop, throwing her books down and babbling a mile a minute.*)

RUTH: (*Enthusiastically.*) Can you believe it? I didn't, until Chris Burns came up and told me about it in Geography, and then Mr. Goodman told me himself during the eighth period in the office when I was eavesdropping. Aren't you so happy you could bust? Tillie? I'm so proud I can't believe it, Mama. Everybody was talking about it and nobody . . . well, it was the first time they all came up screaming about her and I said, "Yes, she's my sister!" I said it, "She's my sister! My sister! My *sister!*" Give me a cigarette.

BEATRICE: Get your hands off my personal property.

RUTH: I'll scratch your back later.

BEATRICE: I don't want you to touch me!

RUTH: Did he call yet? My God, I can't believe it, I just can't!

BEATRICE: Did who call yet?

RUTH: I'm not supposed to tell you, as Mr. Goodman's private secretary, but you're going to get a call from school.

BEATRICE: (*To* TILLIE.) What is she talking about?

TILLIE: I was in the Science Fair at school.

RUTH: Didn't she tell you yet? Oh, Tillie, how could you? She's fantastic, Mama! She's a finalist in the Science Fair. There were only five of them out of hundreds and hundreds. She won with all those plants over there. They're freaks! Isn't that a scream? Dr. Berg picked her himself. The principal! And I heard Mr. Goodman say she was going to be another Madam Pasteur and he never saw a girl do anything like that before and . . . so I told everybody, "Yes, she's my sister!" Tillie, "You're my sister!" I said. And Mr. Goodman called the Advance and they're coming to take your picture. Oh, Mama, isn't it crazy? And nobody laughed at her, Mama. She beat out practically everybody and nobody laughed at her. "She's my sister," I said. "She's my sister!"

(*The telephone rings.*)

That must be him! Mama, answer it—I'm afraid.

(*Ring.*)

Answer it before he hangs up!

(*Ring.*)

Mama! He's gonna hang up!

(RUTH *grabs the phone.*)

Hello? . . . Yes . . .

(*Aside to* BEATRICE.)

It's him! . . . Just a minute, please . . .

(*Covering the mouthpiece.*)

He wants to talk to you.

BEATRICE: Who?

RUTH: The *principal!*

BEATRICE: Hang up.

RUTH: I told him you were here! Mama!

(BEATRICE *gets up and shuffles slowly to the phone.*)

BEATRICE: (*Finally, into the phone.*) Yes? . . . I know who you are, Dr. Berg . . . I see . . . Couldn't you get someone else? There's an awfully lot of work that has to be done around here, because she's not as careful with her home duties as she is with man-in-the-moon marigolds . . .

Me? What would you want with me up on the stage? . . . The other mothers can do as they please . . . I would have thought you had enough in your *history* without . . . I'll think about it . . . Goodbye, Dr. Berg . . .

(*Pause, then screaming.*)

I SAID I'D THINK ABOUT IT!

(*She hangs up the phone, turns her face slowly to* RUTH, *then to* TILLIE, *who has her face hidden in shame in the rabbit's fur.*)

RUTH: What did he say?

BEATRICE: (*Flinging her glass on the floor.*) How could you do this to me? HOW COULD YOU LET THAT MAN CALL OUR HOME!

I have no clothes, do you hear me? I'd look just like you up on the stage, ugly little you!

DO YOU WANT THEM TO LAUGH AT US? LAUGH AT THE TWO OF US?

RUTH: (*Disbelievingly.*) Mother . . . aren't you proud of her? Mother . . . it's an *honor.*

(TILLIE *breaks into tears and moves away from* BEATRICE. *It seems as though she is crushed, but then she halts and turns to face her mother.*)

TILLIE: (*Through tears.*) But . . . nobody laughed at me.

(BEATRICE's *face begins to soften as she glimpses what she's done to* TILLIE.)

BEATRICE: Oh, my God . . .

(TILLIE *starts toward her.* BEATRICE *opens her arms to receive her as music starts in and lights fade. A chord of finality punctuates the end of Act One.*)

ACT TWO

(*About two weeks later.*)

(*The room looks somewhat cheery and there is excitement in the air. It is early evening and preparations are being made for* TILLIE *to take her project to the final judging of the Science Fair.*)

(TILLIE *has been dressed by her mother in clothes which are clean but too girlish for her awkwardness. Her hair has been curled, she sports a large bow, and her dress is a starched flair.*)

(RUTH *has dressed herself up as well. She has put on too much makeup, and her lipstick has been extended beyond the natural line of her lips. She almost appears to be sinister.*)

(*A large three-panel screen stands on one of the tables.* THE EF-FECT OF GAMMA RAYS ON MAN-IN-THE-MOON MARI-GOLDS *is printed in large letters running across the top of the three panels. Below this on each panel there is a subtopic:* THE PAST; THE PRESENT; THE FUTURE. *Additional charts and data appear below the titles.*)

RUTH: The only competition you have to worry about is Janice Vickery. They say she caught it near Princess Bay Boulevard and it was still alive when she took the skin off it.

TILLIE: (*Taking some plants from* RUTH.) Let me do that, please, Ruth.

RUTH: I'm sorry I touched them, really.

TILLIE: Why don't you feed Peter?

RUTH: Because I don't feel like feeding him . . . Now I feel like feeding him.

(*She gets some lettuce from a bag.*)

I heard that it screamed for three minutes after she put it in because the water wasn't boiling yet. How much talent does it take to boil the skin off a cat and then stick the bones together again? That's what I want to know. Ugh. I had a dream about that, too. I figure she did it in less than a day and she ends up as one of the top five winners . . . and you spend months growing atomic flowers.

TILLIE: Don't you think you should finish getting ready?

RUTH: Finish? This is it!

TILLIE: Are you going to wear that sweater?

RUTH: Look, don't worry about me. I'm not getting up on any stage, and if I did I wouldn't be caught dead with a horrible bow like that.

TILLIE: Mother put it—

RUTH: They're going to laugh you off the stage again like when you cranked that atom in assembly . . . I didn't mean that . . . The one they're going to laugh at is Mama.

TILLIE: What?

RUTH: I said the one they're going to laugh at is Mama . . . Oh, let me take that bow off.

TILLIE: It's all right.

RUTH: Look, just sit still. I don't want everybody making fun of you.

TILLIE: What made you say that about Mama?

RUTH: Oh, I heard them talking in the Science Office yesterday. Mr. Goodman and Miss Hanley. She's getting $12.63 to chaperon the thing tonight.

TILLIE: What were they saying?

RUTH: Miss Hanley was telling Mr. Goodman about Mama . . . when she found out you were one of the five winners. And he wanted to know if there was something wrong with Mama because she sounded crazy over the phone. And Miss Hanley said she *was* crazy and she always has been crazy and she can't wait to see what she looks like after all these years. Miss Hanley said her nickname used to be *Betty the Loon*.

TILLIE: (*As* RUTH *combs her hair.*) Ruth, you're hurting me.

RUTH: She was just like you and everybody thought she was a big weirdo. There! You look much better!

(*She goes back to the rabbit.*)

Peter, if anybody stuck you in a pot of boiling water I'd kill them, do you know that? . . .

(*Then to* TILLIE.)

What do they call boiling the skin off a cat? I call it murder, that's what I call it. They say it was hit by a car and Janice just scooped it up and before you could say *bingo* it was screaming in a pot of boiling water . . .

Do you know what they're all waiting to see? Mama's feathers! That's what Miss Hanley said. She said Mama blabs as though she was the Queen of England and just as proper as can be, and that her idea of getting dressed up is to put on all the feathers in the world and go as a bird. Always trying to get somewhere, like a great big bird.

TILLIE: Don't tell Mama, please. It doesn't matter.

RUTH: I was up there watching her getting dressed and sure enough, she's got the feathers out.

TILLIE: You didn't tell her what Miss Hanley said?

RUTH: Are you kidding? I just told her I didn't like the feathers and I didn't think she should wear any. But I'll bet she doesn't listen to me.

TILLIE: It doesn't matter.

RUTH: It doesn't matter? Do you think I want to be laughed right out of the school tonight, with Chris Burns there, and all? Laughed right out of the school, with your electric hair and her feathers on that stage, and Miss Hanley splitting her sides?

TILLIE: Promise me you won't say anything.

RUTH: On one condition.

TILLIE: What?

RUTH: Give Peter to me.

TILLIE: (*Ignoring her.*) The taxi will be here any minute and I won't have all this stuff ready. Did you see my speech?

RUTH: I mean it. Give Peter to me.

TILLIE: He belongs to all of us.

RUTH: For me. All for me. What do you care? He doesn't mean anything to you anymore, now that you've got all those crazy plants.

TILLIE: Will you stop?

RUTH: If you don't give him to me I'm going to tell Mama that everybody's waiting to laugh at her.

TILLIE: Where are those typewritten cards?

RUTH: I MEAN IT! Give him to me!

TILLIE: Does he mean that much to you?

RUTH: Yes!

TILLIE: All right.

RUTH: (*After a burst of private laughter.*) Betty the Loon . . .

(*She laughs again.*)

That's what they used to call her, you know. Betty the Loon!

TILLIE: I don't think that's very nice.

RUTH: First they had Betty the Loon, and now they've got Tillie the Loon . . .

(*To rabbit.*)

You don't have to worry about me turning you in for any old plants . . .

How much does a taxi cost from here to the school?

TILLIE: Not much.

RUTH: I wish she'd give me the money it costs for a taxi—and for all that cardboard and paint and flowerpots and stuff. The only time she ever made a fuss over me was when she drove me nuts.

TILLIE: Tell her to hurry, please.

RUTH: By the way, I went over to see Janice Vickery's pot, that she did you know what in, and I started telling her and her mother about the worms in Mr. Alexander Brougham's legs, and I got thrown out because it was too near dinner time. That Mrs. Vickery kills me. She can't stand worms in somebody else's legs but she lets her daughter cook a cat.

TILLIE: (*Calling upstairs.*) Mother! The taxi will be here any minute.

(BEATRICE *comes to the top of the stairs. Her costume is strange, but not that strange, by any means. She is even a little attractive tonight, and though her words say she is greatly annoyed with having to attend the night's function, her tone and direction show she is very, very proud.*)

BEATRICE: You're lucky I'm coming, without all this rushing me.

TILLIE: Mama, you look beautiful.

BEATRICE: Don't put it on too thick. I said I'd go and I guess there's no way to get out of it. Do you mind telling me how I'm supposed to get up on the stage? Do they call my name or what? And where are you going to be? If you ask me, they should've sent all the parents a mimeographed sheet of instructions. If this is supposed to be such a great event, why don't they do it right?

TILLIE: You just sit on the stage with the other parents before it begins.

BEATRICE: How long is this thing going to last? And remember, I don't care even if you do win the whole damn thing, I'm not making any speech. I can hold my own anywhere, but I hated that school when I went there and I hate it now . . . and the only thing I'd have to say is, what a pack of stupid teachers and vicious children they have. Imagine someone tearing the skin off a cat.

RUTH: She didn't tear it. She boiled it off.

BEATRICE: You just told me upstairs that girl tore the skin off with an orange knife and . . . do you know, sometimes you exasperate me?

(*To* TILLIE.)

If you've got all the plants in this box, I can manage the folding thing. Do you know I've got a headache from doing those titles? And you probably don't even like them.

TILLIE: I like them very much.

BEATRICE: Look, if you don't want me to go tonight, I don't have to. You're about as enthusiastic as a dummy about this whole thing.

TILLIE: I'm sorry.

BEATRICE: And I refuse to let you get nervous. Put that bow back in your hair.

RUTH: I took it out.

BEATRICE: What did you do that for?

RUTH: (*Taking the rabbit in her arms.*) Because it made her look crazy.

BEATRICE: How would you know what's crazy or not? If that sweater of yours was any tighter it'd cut off the circulation in your chest.

(*Fussing over* TILLIE.)

The bow looks very nice in your hair. There's nothing wrong with looking proper, Matilda, and if you don't have enough money to look expensive and perfect, people like you for *trying* to look nice. You know, one day maybe you will be pretty. You'll have some nice features, when that hair revives and you do some tricks with makeup. I hope you didn't crowd the plants too close together. Did you find your speech?

TILLIE: Yes, Mother.

BEATRICE: You know, Matilda, I was wondering about something. Do you think you're really going to win? I mean, not that you won't be the best, but there's so much politics in school. Don't laugh, but if there's anyone who's an expert on that, it's me, and someday I'm going to write a book and blast that school to pieces. If you're just a little bit different in this world, they try to kill you off.

RUTH: (*Putting on her coat.*) Tillie gave Peter to me.

BEATRICE: Oh? Then you inherited the rabbit droppings I found up-stairs. What are you doing with your coat on?

RUTH: I'm going out to wait for the taxi.

BEATRICE: Oh, no you're not. You start right in on the rabbit drop-pings. Or you won't get another cigarette even if you scratch my back with an orange knife.

RUTH: I'm going down to the school with you.

BEATRICE: Oh, no you're not! You're going to keep company with that corpse in there. If she wakes up and starts gagging just slip her a shot of whiskey.

(*The taxi horn blows outside.*)

Quick! Grab the plants, Matilda—I'll get the big thing.

RUTH: I want to go! I promised Chris Burns I'd meet him.

BEATRICE: Can't you understand English?

RUTH: I've got to go!

BEATRICE: Shut up!

RUTH: (*Almost berserk.*) I don't care. I'M GOING ANYWAY!

BEATRICE: (*Shoving* RUTH *hard.*) WHAT DID YOU SAY?

TILLIE: Mother!

(*After a pause, the horn blows again.*)

BEATRICE: Hurry up with that box, Matilda, and tell him to stop blowing the horn. HURRY UP!

(TILLIE *reluctantly exits with the box of plants.*)

I don't know where you ever got the idea you were going tonight. Did you think nobody was going to hold down the fort? . . .

Now you know how I felt all those years you and everybody else was running out whenever they felt like it—because there was always me to watch over the fifty-dollar-a-week corpse. If there's one thing I demand it's respect. I don't ask for anything from you but respect.

RUTH: (*Pathetically.*) Why are you ashamed of me?

BEATRICE: I've been seen with a lot worse than you. I don't even know why I'm going tonight, do you know that? Do you think I give one goddam about the whole thing? . . .

(*She starts to fold the large three-panel screen with the titles:* THE PAST, THE PRESENT, *and* THE FUTURE.)

Do you want to know why I'm going? Do you really want to know why this once somebody else has to stick with that dried prune for a few minutes? Because this is the first time in my life I've ever felt just a little bit proud over something. Isn't that silly? Somewhere in the back of this turtle-sized brain of mine I feel just a little *proud!* Jesus Christ! And you begrudge me even that, you little bastard.

(*The taxi horn blows impatiently.*)

RUTH: (*In a hard voice.*) Hurry up. They're waiting for you . . . They're *all* waiting for you.

BEATRICE: (*Carrying the folded screen so that* THE PAST *is face out in bold black letters.*) I hope the paint is dry . . . Who's waiting for me?

RUTH: Everybody . . . including Miss Hanley. She's been telling all the teachers . . . about you . . . and they're all waiting.

BEATRICE: You're such a little liar, Ruth, do you know that? When you can't have what you want, you try to ruin it for everybody else.

(*She starts to the door.*)

RUTH: Goodnight, *Betty the Loon.*

(BEATRICE *stops as if she's been stabbed.*)

(*The taxi horn blows several times as* BEATRICE *puts down the folding screen.*)

BEATRICE: (*Helplessly.*) Take this thing.

RUTH: What for?

BEATRICE: Go with Matilda.

RUTH: I don't want to go now.

BEATRICE: (*Blasting.*) GET OUT OF HERE!

RUTH: (*After a long pause.*) Now Tillie's going to blame it on me that you're not going—and take the rabbit back.

(*The taxi beeps again, as* RUTH *puts her coat on.*)

I can't help it what people call you.

(*She picks up the screen.*)

I'll tell Tillie you'll be down later, all right? . . .

Don't answer me. What do I care!

(RUTH *exits.*)

(BEATRICE *breaks into tears that shudder her body, and the lights go down slowly on her pathetic form. Music in.*)

(*Suddenly a bolt of light strikes an area in the right stage—*JANICE VICKERY *is standing in the spotlight holding the skeleton of a cat mounted on a small platform. Her face and voice are smug.*)

JANICE: *The Past:* I got the cat from the A.S.P.C.A. immediately after it had been killed by a high-altitude pressure system. That explains why some of the rib bones are missing, because that method sucks the air out of the animal's lungs and ruptures all cavities. They say it prevents cruelty to animals but I think it's horrible.

(*She laughs.*)

Then I boiled the cat in a sodium hydroxide solution until most of the skin pulled right off, but I had to scrape some of the grizzle off the joints with a knife. You have no idea how difficult it is to get right down to the bones.

(*A little gong sounds.*)

I have to go on to *The Present*, now—but I did want to tell you how long it took me to put the thing together. I mean, as it is now, it's extremely useful for students of anatomy, even with the missing rib bones, and it can be used to show basic anatomical aspects of many, many animals that are in the same family as felines. I suppose that's about the only present uses I can think for it, but it is nice to remember as an accomplishment, and it looks good on college applications to show you did something else in school besides dating.

(*She laughs, and a second gong sounds.*)

The Future: The only future plans I have for Tabby—my little brother asked the A.S.P.C.A. what its name was when he went to pick it up and they said it was called Tabby, but I think they were kidding him—

(*She laughs again.*)

I mean as far as future plans, I'm going to donate it to the science department, of course, and next year, if there's another Science Fair perhaps I'll do the same thing with a dog.

(*A third gong sounds.*)

Thank you very much for your attention, and I hope I win!

(Janice *and her spotlight disappear as suddenly as they had arrived, and music returns as the lights come up slowly on* Beatrice.)

(*She has obviously been drinking and is going through a phone book. Finding her number, she goes to the phone and dials.*)

BEATRICE: (*Into the phone.*) I want to talk to the principal, please . . .

Well, you'll have to get him down off the stage . . .

It's none of your goddam business who I am! . . .

Oh, I see . . . Yes. I have a message for him and Mr. Goodman, and you, too . . . And this is for Miss Hanley, too . . .

Tell them Mrs. Hunsdorfer called to thank them for making her wish she was dead . . . Would you give them that message, please? . . . Thank you very much.

(*She hangs up the phone, pauses, then surveys the room. Her attention fixes on the store window covered with newspapers. The phone rings several times but she ignores it. She goes to the window and proceeds to rip the paper from it. That finished, she turns and surveys the room again. She goes to the kitchen table and rearranges its position. She spies a card table with school supplies and hurls them on the floor. Next, she goes to a bureau and rummages through drawers, finding tablecloths and napkins. She throws cloths on two or three tables and is heading toward the kitchen table when the phone rings again. The ringing triggers off something else she wants to do. She empties a cup filled with scraps of paper and finds a telephone number. She lifts the receiver off the ringing phone and hangs up immediately. She lifts the receiver again, checks to make sure there's a dial tone, and then dials the number on the scrap of paper.*)

BEATRICE: (*Into the phone.*) Hello. This is Mrs. Hunsdorfer . . . I'm sorry if I frightened you, I wouldn't want you to think Nanny had deceased or anything like that—I can imagine how terrible you'd feel if anything like that ever happened . . . Terrible tragedy that would be, Miss Career Woman of the Year . . .

Yes, I'll tell you why I'm calling. I want her out of here by tomorrow. I told you when you rolled her in here I was going to try her out for a while and if I didn't like her she was to get the hell out. Well I don't like her, so get her the hell out . . .

It's like this. I don't like the way she cheats at solitaire. Is that a good enough reason? . . . Fine. And if she's not out of here by noon I'll send her collect in an ambulance, you son of a bitch!

(*She slams down the phone and bursts into laughter. The laughter subsides somewhat as she pours herself another drink. She takes the drink to a chair and as she sits down her foot accidentally hits the rabbit cage. She gives the cage a little kick and then an idea strikes. She gets up and finds a large blue towel which she flings over her shoulder. She gets the bottle of chloroform and approaches the cage. Having reached a decision she picks up the cage and takes it upstairs.*)

(*Music in and lights fade.*)

(*From the darkness a beam of light falls on* TILLIE *in the same way* JANICE VICKERY *had been presented.*)

TILLIE: (*Deathly afraid, and referring to her cards.*) The Past: The seeds were exposed to various degrees . . . of gamma rays from radiation sources in Oak Ridge . . .

Mr. Goodman helped me pay for the seeds . . . Their growth was plotted against . . . time.

(*She loses her voice for a moment and then the first gong sounds.*)

The Present: The seeds which received little radiation have grown to plants which are normal in appearance. The seeds which received moderate radiation gave rise to mutations such as double blooms, giant stems, and variegated leaves. The seeds closest to the gamma source were killed or yielded dwarf plants.

(*The second gong rings.*)

The Future: After radiation is better understood, a day will come when the power from exploding atoms will change the whole world we know.

(*With inspiration.*)

Some of the mutations will be good ones—wonderful things beyond our dreams—and I believe, I believe this with all my heart, THE DAY WILL COME WHEN MANKIND WILL

THANK GOD FOR THE STRANGE AND BEAUTIFUL EN-
ERGY FROM THE ATOM.

(*Part of her last speech is reverberated electronically. Deep pulses of music are added as the light focuses on* TILLIE's *face.*)

(*Suddenly there is silence, except for* RUTH *picking up* TILLIE's *last words.*)

(*The lights come up on the main set, and the room is empty.* RUTH *bursts in the front door. She is carrying the three-panel card and a shopping bag of plants, both of which she drops on the floor.*)

RUTH: MAMA! MAMA! She won! Mama! Where are you? She won!

(*She runs back to the front door and yells to* TILLIE.)

Hurry up! Hurry! Oh, my God, I can't believe it!

(*Then yelling upstairs.*)

Mama! Come on down! Hurry!

(TILLIE *comes in the front door, carrying the rest of her plants, and the large trophy.*

(RUTH *takes the trophy.*)

Give me that!

(*She starts upstairs.*)

Mama! Wait till you see this!

(BEATRICE *appears at the top of the stairs. She has been drinking a great deal, and clings fast to a bunch of old cheap curtains and other material.*)

Mama! She won . . .

(BEATRICE *continues mechanically on down the stairs.*)

Didn't you hear me? Tillie won the whole thing! . . . Mama? . . . What's the matter with you? What did you rip the paper off the windows for?

(BEATRICE *commences tacking up one of the curtains.*)

TILLIE: Mama? Are you going to open a . . . shop?

RUTH: What's the matter? Can't you even answer?

BEATRICE: (*To* TILLIE.) Hand me some of those tacks.

RUTH: (*Screaming.*) I SAID SHE WON! ARE YOU DEAF?

BEATRICE: Ruth, if you don't shut up I'm going to have you put away.

RUTH: They ought to put *you* away, BETTY THE LOON!

(*There is a long pause.*)

BEATRICE: The rabbit is in your room. I want you to bury it in the morning.

RUTH: If you did anything . . . I'LL KILL YOU!

(*She runs upstairs.*)

TILLIE: Mother, you didn't kill it, did you?

BEATRICE: Nanny goes tomorrow. First thing tomorrow.

(*There is a cry from upstairs.*)

TILLIE: Ruth? Are you all right?

BEATRICE: I don't know what it's going to be. Maybe a tea shop. Maybe not.

(RUTH *appears in the doorway of her room. She is holding the dead rabbit on the blue towel. As she reaches the top of the stairs, she begins to moan deeply.*)

After school you're going to have regular hours. You'll work in the kitchen, you'll learn how to cook, and you're going to earn your keep, just like in any other business.

(TILLIE *starts slowly up the stairs toward* RUTH.)

TILLIE: (*With great fear.*) Mama . . . I think she's going to go.

(RUTH *commences to tremble.* TILLIE *speaks softly to her.*)

Don't go . . . don't go . . .

(RUTH's *eyes roll in her head, and the trembling of her body becomes pronounced throbbing. She drops the rabbit with the towel covering it.*)

Help me! Mama! Help me!

BEATRICE: Snap out of it, do you hear me? RUTH, DON'T LET YOURSELF GO!

(*To* TILLIE.)

Help me get her downstairs!

(*By the time the trio reaches the bottom of the stairs,* RUTH *is consumed by a violent convulsion.* BEATRICE *holds her down and pushes* TILLIE *out of the way.*)

BEATRICE: (*Screaming.*) Get the wooden spoon!

(TILLIE *responds as* BEATRICE *gets* RUTH *onto a sofa. The convulsion runs its course of a full minute, then finally subsides.* TILLIE *gets a blanket and covers* RUTH.)

TILLIE: Shall I call the doctor?

(*There is a long pause.*)

Shall I call the doctor?

BEATRICE: No. She'll be all right.

TILLIE: I think we should call him.

BEATRICE: I DIDN'T ASK YOU WHAT YOU THOUGHT! . . . We're going to need every penny to get this place open.

(BEATRICE *spreads a tablecloth on one of the tables and places a pile of old cloth napkins on it. She sits down and lights a cigarette.*)

TILLIE: (*Picking up the rabbit on the stairs.*) I'd better bury him in the backyard.

(*She starts out.*)

BEATRICE: Don't bury the towel.

(TILLIE *stops, sobs audibly, then gets control.*)

TILLIE: I'll do it in the morning.

(*She gently lays the rabbit near the door. She tucks* RUTH *in on the couch and sits a few minutes by her sleeping sister.*)

(*Music starts in softly as* BEATRICE *continues folding napkins with her back to the others.*

(*There is the sound of someone at the curtained doorway, and* NANNY *commences negotiating herself into the room. Slowly she advances with the tubular frame—unaware, desiccated, in some other land.*)

BEATRICE: (*Weakly.*) Matilda?

TILLIE: Yes, Mama?

BEATRICE: I hate the world. Do you know that, Matilda?

TILLIE: Yes, Mama.

BEATRICE: I hate the world.

(*The lights have started down, the music makes its presence known, and a spot clings to* TILLIE. *She moves to the staircase and the rest of the set goes to black during the following speech. As she starts up the stairs her recorded voice takes over as in the opening of the play.*)

TILLIE'S VOICE: *The Conclusion:* My experiment has shown some of the strange effects radiation can produce . . . and how dangerous it can be if not handled correctly.

Mr. Goodman said I should tell in this conclusion what my future plans are and how this experiment has helped me make them.

For one thing, the effect of gamma rays on man-in-the-moon marigolds has made me curious about the sun and the stars, for the universe itself must be like a world of great atoms—and I want to know more about it.

But most important, I suppose, my experiment has made me feel important—every atom in me, in everybody, has come from the sun—from places beyond our dreams. The atoms of our hands, the atoms of our hearts . . .

(*All sound out.*)

(TILLIE *speaks the rest live—hopeful, glowing.*)

Atom.
Atom.
What a beautiful word.

THE BASIC
TRAINING OF
PAVLO HUMMEL

David Rabe

THE BASIC TRAINING
OF PAVLO HUMMEL

The Basic Training of Pavlo Hummel, which won an Obie Award for Distinguished Playwriting in 1971, is the first of an award-winning army trilogy by David Rabe. *Sticks and Bones* received a Tony Award in 1972, and *Streamers* was selected as the Best Play of 1976 by the New York Drama Critics Circle.

In *Pavlo Hummel* David Rabe reverses the traditional character of the comically bumbling recruit and shows us instead a grimly desperate loser. Although Rabe is obviously outraged by the war in Vietnam, the character Pavlo is not a draft-card burner but an enthusiastic volunteer. Before the play's dramatic finale, Pavlo achieves a brief but touching sense of manhood. Containing some of the most frankly realistic dialogue yet heard on the American stage, *Pavlo Hummel* was presented in a fragmented, nonrealistic setting, with a kind of Greek chorus figure commenting on the action throughout the play.

According to Clive Barnes in the New York *Times,* "what interested me was the playwright's sense of what people really say and his obvious feel for the dynamics of character confrontation . . ."

Critic John Lahr, in *The Village Voice,* wrote that Rabe is "a writer with a gift for language, a speculative imagination, and a sense of the stage. He turns the formula of the protest play on its head and gets engrossing results."

David Rabe was born in Dubuque, Iowa, in 1940, and served two years in the United States Army before turning to playwriting. Taking exception to *The Basic Training of Pavlo Hummel* and *Sticks and Bones* being labelled "anti-war" plays, Rabe wrote: "An 'anti-war' play is to me a play that expects, in the very fabric of its executed conception, to have political effect. I anticipated no such consequence from my plays, nor did I conceive them in the hope that they would have any such consequence. I have written them to diagnose, as best I could, certain phenomena that went on around me. First of all, I believe that to think a play can have immediate, large-scale political effect is to vastly over-estimate the power that plays have. In addition, if there is, as I hope, more content in these plays than the thin line of political tract, then to categorize them as such is to diminish them."

The premier of *Pavlo Hummel* took place at the Public Theatre of New York's Shakespeare Festival on May 20, 1971. The masterful, fluid staging of the production by Jeff Bleckner—who also won an Obie Award for his direction—transformed the nearly barren stage into vivid, brutal glimpses of basic training, the battlefields of Vietnam, and a Saigon whorehouse.

The play was revived on Broadway in 1977, with Al Pacino starring, and received enthusiastic reviews. Performing small roles in the original cast—proving once again that many of the American theatre's leading actors begin their careers Off-Broadway—were Edward Herrmann and Garrett Morris.

THE BASIC TRAINING OF PAVLO HUMMEL was first presented by the New York Shakespeare Festival (Joseph Papp, Producer) at the Public Theatre, New York City, on May 20, 1971, with the following cast:

PAVLO HUMMEL	*William Atherton*
YEN	*Victoria Racimo*
ARDELL	*Albert Hall*
SERGEANT TOWER	*Joe Fields*
THE COMPANY	
CAPTAIN SAUNDERS	*Edward Cannan*
CORPORAL FERRARA	*Anthony R. Charnota*
PARKER	*Peter Cameron*
BURNS	*Stephen Clarke*
RYAN	*John Walter Davis*
HALL	*Bob Delegall*
GRENNEL	*Tom Harris*
HINKLE	*Edward Herrmann*
KRESS	*Earl Hindman*
PIERCE	*Robert Lehman*
HENDRIX	*D. Franklyn Lenthall*
MICKEY	*Frederick Coffin*
MRS. HUMMEL	*Sloane Shelton*
CORPORAL JONES	*Garrett Morris*
SERGEANT BRISBEY	*Lee Wallace*
MAMASAN	*Christal Kim*
SERGEANT WALL	*John Benson*
PARHAM	*Bob Delegall*
FIRST VIETCONG	*Hoshin Seki*

SECOND VIETCONG	*Victoria Racimo*
FARMER	*Hoshin Seki*

The play was directed by Jeff Bleckner. Settings by David Mitchell; costumes by Theoni V. Aldredge; lighting by Martin Aronstein. Associate producer: Bernard Gersten. Production stage manager: Dean Compton.

Place and time: The United States Army, 1965–1967

ACT ONE

The set is a space, a platform slanting upward from the downstage area. The floor is nothing more than slats that run in various directions with a military precision. It has a brownish color. The backdrop is dark with touches of green. Along the back of the set runs a ramp elevated about two feet off the floor. Stage left and a little down from the ramp stands the drill sergeant's tower. This element is stark and as realistic as possible. Farther downstage and stage left the floor opens into a pit two feet deep. There is an old furnace partly visible. Downstage and stage right are three army cots with footlockers at their base. Upstage and stage right there is a bar area: an army ammunition crate and an army oil drum set as a table and chair before a fragment of sheet-metal wall partly covered with beer-can labels. All elements of the set should have some military tone to them, some echo of basic training.

To start the play, pop American music is heard for an instant in the dark. Then lights up on the bar area: evening. A drunken GI sits slumped on the crate, leaning forward on the drum. YEN (pronounced "Ing"), a Vietnamese girl dressed in purple silk pajamas—slacks and pullover top—moves about with a beer, trying to settle PAVLO down.

PAVLO: (*dressed in fatigues, moving with the music, dealing somehow with the other two in the room as he speaks*) Did I do it to him? The triple-Hummel. Can you hear your boy? (*A sort of shudder runs through his shoulders; he punches.*) A little shuffle and then a triple boom-boom-boom. Ain't I bad, man? Gonna eat up Cleveland. Gonna piss on Chicago. (*Banging with his palms on the sides of the oil drum.*)

YEN: Creezy, creezy.

PAVLO: Dinky dow!

SOLDIER: (*disturbed by the banging, looking up, deeply drunk*) Les . . . go . . . home. . . .

YEN: Paablo creezy.

PAVLO: Dinky dow.

YEN: Paablo boocoup love. Sleep me all time . . .

PAVLO: Did I ever tell you?—thirteen months a my life ago—Joanna was her name. Sorrentino, a little bit a guinea-wop made outa all the pins and sticks all bitches are made a. And now I'm the guy who's been with the Aussies. *I had tea with 'em. It was me they called to*—"Hummel!" "MEDIC!" (*With a fairly good Australian accent*) "The dirty little blighters blew me bloody arm off." (YEN *brings a beer*.) Yeh, girl, in a little bit a time. (*And back to the air*) We had a cat, you know? So we had a kitty box, which is a place for the cat to shit.

YEN: Talk "shit." I can talk "shit." Numba-ten talk.

PAVLO: Ohhh, damn that Sorrentino, what she couldn't be taught. And that's what I'd like to do—look her up and explain a few things like, "Your face, Sorrentino, I don't like your ugly face." Did I ever tell you about the ole lady? Did I ever speak her name, me mudda.

YEN: Mudda you, huh, Paablo? Very nice.

PAVLO: To be seen by her now, oh, she would shit her jeans to see me now, up tight with this little odd-lookin' whore, feelin' good, and tall, ready to bed down. Ohhh, Jesus Mahoney. You see what she did, she wrote Joanna a letter. My mother. She called Joanna a dirty little slut, and when I found out, I cried, I wailed, baby, big tears, I screamed and threw kitty litter; I threw it in the air. I screamed over and over, "Happy Birthday, Happy Birthday," and then one day there was Joanna in the subway and she said, "Hello," and told me my favorite jacket I was wearing made me look ugly, didn't fit, made me look fat.

(*A grenade, thrown by a hand that merely flashes between the curtains, hits with a loud clump in the room, and everyone looks without moving.*)

GRENA-A-ADE!

(PAVLO *drops to his knees, seizing the grenade, and has it in his hands in his lap when the explosion comes, loud, shattering, and the lights go black, go red or blue. The girl screams. The bodies are strewn about. The radio plays. And a black soldier,* ARDELL, *now appears, his uniform strangely unreal with black ribbons and medals; he wears sunglasses, bloused boots. A body detail is also entering, two men with a stretcher to remove the dead.*)

ARDELL: (*moving to turn the radio off*) You want me, Pavlo? You callin'? Don't I hear you? Yeh, that the way it happen sometimes. Everybody hit, everybody hurtin', but the radio ain't been touched, the dog didn't feel a thing; the engine's good as new but all the people dead and the chassis a wreck, man. (*Bowing a little toward* PAVLO) Yeh, yeh, some mean motherfucker, you don't even see, blow you away. Don't I hear you callin'? (*Pivoting, moving swiftly down center stage*) Get off it. Bounce on up here.

(PAVLO *leaps to his feet, turns to join* ARDELL.)

PAVLO: PFC Pavlo Hummel, Sir. R.A. seven four, three one three, two two six.

ARDELL: We gonna get you your shit straight. No need to call me Sir.

PAVLO: Ardell!

ARDELL: Now what's your unit? Now shout it out.

PAVLO: Second of the Sixteenth, First Division, BIG RED ONE!

ARDELL: Company.

PAVLO: Bravo.

ARDELL: C.O.?

PAVLO: My Company Commander is Captain M. W. Henderson. My Battalion Commander is Lieutenant Colonel Roy J. S. Tully.

ARDELL: Platoon?

PAVLO: Third.

ARDELL: Squad.

PAVLO: Third.

ARDELL: Squad and platoon leaders.

PAVLO: My platoon leader is First Lieutenant David R. Barnes; my squad leader is Staff Sergeant Peter T. Collins.

ARDELL: You got family?

PAVLO: No.

ARDELL: You lyin', Boy.

PAVLO: One mother; one half brother.

ARDELL: All right.

PAVLO: Yes.

ARDELL: Soldier, what you think a the war?

PAVLO: It's being fought.

ARDELL: Ain't no doubt about that.

PAVLO: No.

ARDELL: You kill anybody?

PAVLO: Yes.

ARDELL: Like it?

PAVLO: Yes.

ARDELL: Have nightmares?

PAVLO: Pardon?

ARDELL: What we talkin' about, Boy?

PAVLO: No.

ARDELL: How tall you? you lyin' motherfucker.

PAVLO: Five-ten.

ARDELL: Eyes.

PAVLO: Green.

ARDELL: Hair.

PAVLO: Red.

ARDELL: Weight.

PAVLO: One-five-two.

ARDELL: What you get hit with?

PAVLO: Hand grenade. Fragmentation-type.

ARDELL: Where about it get you?

PAVLO: (*touching gently his stomach and crotch*) Here. And here. Mostly in the abdominal and groin areas.

ARDELL: Who you talkin' to? Don't you talk that shit to me, man. Abdominal and groin areas, that shit. It hit you in the stomach, man, like a ten-ton truck and it hit you in the balls, blew 'em away. Am I lyin'?

PAVLO: (*able to grin, glad to grin*) No, man.

ARDELL: Hurt you bad.

PAVLO: Killed me.

ARDELL: That right. Made you dead. You dead man; how you feel about that?

PAVLO: Well . . .

ARDELL: *Don't you know? I think you know!* I think it piss you off. I think you lyin' you say it don't. Make you wanna scream.

PAVLO: Yes.

ARDELL: You had that thing in your hand, didn't you? What was you thinkin' on, you had that thing in your hand?

PAVLO: About throwin' it. About a man I saw when I was eight years old who came through the neighborhood with a softball team called the Demons, and he could do anything with a softball underhand that most big-leaguers could do with a hardball overhand. He was fantastic.

ARDELL: That all?

PAVLO: Yes.

ARDELL: You ain't lyin'.

PAVLO: No.
(A *whistle blows loudly and figures run about behind* PAVLO *and* ARDELL, *a large group of men in fatigues without markings other*

than their name tags and U. S. Army. And on the high drill instructor's tower, which is dimly lit at the moment, stands a large Negro Sergeant. A CAPTAIN observes from the distance. A CORPORAL prowls among the gathering troopers, checking buttons, etc.)

PAVLO: *(looking about)* Who're they?

ARDELL: Man, don't you jive me. You know who they are. That Fort Gordon, man. They Echo Company, Eighth Battalion, Third Training Regiment. They basic training, baby.

PAVLO: *(removes PFC stripes and 1st Division patch)* Am I . . . really . . . dead . . . ?

ARDELL: Damn near, man; real soon. Comin' on. Eight more weeks. Got wings as big as streets. Got large, large wings.

PAVLO: It happened . . . to me. . . .

ARDELL: Whatever you say, Pavlo.

PAVLO: Sure . . . that grenade come flyin', I caught it, held it. *(Pause.)*

ARDELL: New York, huh?

PAVLO: Manhattan. Two thirty-one East Forty-fifth. I—

ARDELL: Now we know who we talkin' about. Somebody say "Pavlo Hummel," we know who they mean.

SGT. TOWER: GEN'LMEN! *(As the men standing in ranks below the tower snap to parade rest and PAVLO, startled, runs to find his place among them)* You all lookin' up here and can you see me? Can you see me well? Can you hear and comprehend my words? Can you see what is written here? Over my right tit-tee, can you read it? Tower. My name. And I am bigger than my name. And can you see what is sewn here upon the muscle of my arm? Can you see it? ANSWER!

THE MEN: (*yell*) NO.

SGT. TOWER: No, what? WHAT?

THE MEN: NO, SERGEANT.

SGT. TOWER: It is also my name. It is my first name. *Sergeant.* That who I am. I you Field First. And you gonna see a lot a me. You gonna see so much a me, let me tell you, you gonna think I you mother, father, sisters, brothers, aunts, uncles, nephews, nieces, and children—if-you-got-'em—all rolled into one big black man. Yeh, Gen'lmen. And you gonna become me. You gonna learn to stand tall and be proud and you gonna run as far and shoot as good. Or else you gonna be ashamed; I am one old man and you can't outdo no thirty-eight-year-old man, you ashamed. AM I GONNA MAKE YOU ASHAMED? WHAT DO YOU SAY?

THE MEN: Yes, Sergeant!

SGT. TOWER: NO! NO, GEN'LMEN. No, I am not gonna make you ashamed. SERGEANT, YOU ARE NOT GONNA MAKE US ASHAMED.

THE MEN: SERGEANT, YOU ARE NOT GONNA MAKE US ASHAMED.

SGT. TOWER: WE ARE GONNA DO EVERYTHING YOU CAN DO AND DO YOU ONE BETTER!

THE MEN: WE ARE GONNA DO EVERYTHING YOU CAN DO AND DO YOU ONE BETTER!

SGT. TOWER: YOU A BUNCH A LIARS. YOU A BUNCH A FOOLS! Now you listen up; you listen to me. No one does me one better. And especially no people like you. Don't you know what you are? *Trainees!* And there ain't nothin' lower on this earth except for one thing, and we all know what that is, do we not, Gen'lmen?

THE MEN: *Yes* . . . Sergeant. . . .

SGT. TOWER: And what is that? (*Pause*) And you told me you knew!
Did you lie to me? Oh, no, nooo, I can't believe that; please,
please, don't lie. Gen'lmen, did you lie?

THE MEN: (*they are sorry*) Yes, Sergeant.

SGT. TOWER: No, no, please. If there something you don't know, you
tell me. If I ask you something and you do not know the answer,
let me know. Civilians. That the answer to my question. The only
creatures in this world lower than trainees is civilians, and we
hate them all. All. (*Quick pause.*) And now . . . and finally . . .
and most important, do you see what is written here? Over my
heart; over my left tit-tee, do you see? U. S. Army. Which is
where I live. Which is where we all live. Can you, Gen'lmen, can
you tell me you first name now, do you know it? (*Quick pause as
he looks about in dismay.*) Don't you know? I think you do, yes, I
do, but you just too shy to say it. Like little girls watchin' that
thing just get bigger and bigger for the first time, you shy. And
what did I tell you to do when you don't know the answer I have
asked?

THE MEN: What is our first name?

SGT. TOWER: You! You there! (*Suddenly pointing into the ranks of
men*) You! Ugly! Yeah, you. That right. You ugly. Ain't you.
YOU TAKE ONE BIG STEP FORWARD.
(*And it is* PAVLO *stepping hesitantly forward. He does not know
what he has done or what is expected from him.*)
I think I saw you were not in harmony with the rest of these men.
I think I saw that you were looking about at the air like some
kinda fool and that malingering. Trainee, and that intol'able. So
you drop, you hear me. You drop down on your ugly little hands
and knees and lift up you butt and knees from off that beautiful
Georgia clay and you give me TEN and that's push-ups of which
I am speaking.
(PAVLO, *having obeyed the orders step by step, now begins the
push-ups.* TOWER *goes back to the men.*)

NOW YOU ARE TRAINEES, ALL YOU PEOPLE, AND YOU LISTEN UP. I ASK YOU WHAT IS YOUR FIRST NAMES, YOU TELL ME "TRAINEES"!

THE MEN: (*yell*) TRAINEE!

SGT. TOWER: TRAINEE, SERGEANT!

THE MEN: TRAINEE, SERGE—

SGT. TOWER: I CAN'T HEAR YOU!

THE MEN: *TRAINEE, SERGEANT!*

SGT. TOWER: AND WHAT IS YOUR LAST NAMES? YOU OWN LAST FUCKING NAMES?

THE MEN: (*A chorus of American names.*)

SGT. TOWER: AND YOU LIVE IN THE ARMY OF THE UNITED STATES OF AMERICA.

THE MEN: AND WE LIVE IN THE ARMY OF THE UNITED STATES OF AMERICA.

SGT. TOWER: WITH BALLS BETWEEN YOU LEGS! YOU HAVE BALLS! NO SLITS! BUT BALLS, AND YOU—
(*Having risen,* PAVLO *is getting back into ranks.*)

THE MEN: AND WE HAVE BALLS BETWEEN OUR LEGS! NO SLITS, BUT BALLS!

SGT. TOWER: (*suddenly back at* PAVLO) UGLY! Now who tole you to stand? Who you think you are, you standin', nobody tole you to stand. You drop. You drop, you hear me.
(*And* PAVLO *goes back into the push-up position.*)
What your name, Boy?

PAVLO: Yes, Sir.

JOHN WULF

*A "cameraman" comes on stage to photograph
a "drug addict" in an effort to
capture "the way it really is."*

Hume Cronyn listens over and over again to a tape he recorded thirty years ago, on his thirty-ninth birthday.

MARTHA SWO

The blacks are on trial for murdering a white woman: her body
is in the coffin in front; the all-black court,
wearing white masks, is on the platform behind.

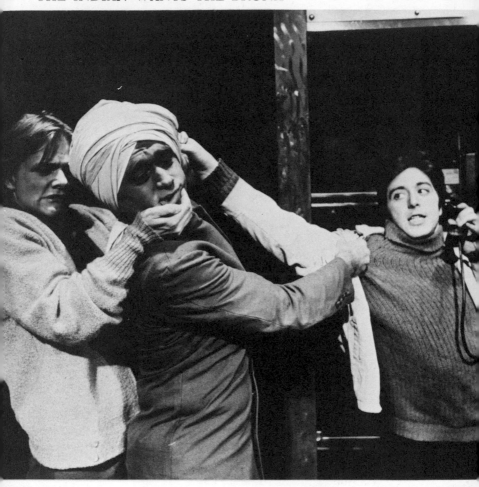

Al Pacino as Murph (right) taunts the lost East Indian by calling his son and then refusing to tell him where they are.

BERT ANDREWS

SGT. TOWER: Your name, Boy!

PAVLO: Trainee Hummel, Sir!

SGT. TOWER: Sergeant.

PAVLO: Yes, Sir.

SGT. TOWER: Sergeant. I AM A SERGEANT!

PAVLO: SERGEANT. YOU ARE A SERGEANT!

SGT. TOWER: All right. That nice; all right, only in the future, you doin' push-ups, I want you countin' and that countin' so loud it scare me so I think there some kinda terrible, terrible man comin' to get me. Am I understood?

PAVLO: Yes, Sergeant.

SGT. TOWER: I can't hear you!

PAVLO: Yes, Sergeant! Yes, Sergeant!

SGT. TOWER: All right! You get up and fall back where you was. Gen'lmen. You are gonna fall out. By platoon. Which is how you gonna be doin' most everything from now on—by platoon and by the numbers—includin' takin' a shit. Somebody say to you, "One!" you down; "two!" you doin' it; "three!" you wipin' and you ain't finished, you cuttin' it off. I CAN'T HEAR YOU!

THE MEN: YES, SERGEANT.

SGT. TOWER: I say to you "squat!" and you all hunkered down and got nothin' to say to anybody but "How much?" and "What color, Sergeant?"

THE MEN: Yes, Sergeant.

SGT. TOWER: You good people. You a good group. Now I gonna call you to attention and you gonna snap to. That's heels on a line or as near it as the conformation of your body permit; head up, chin in, knees not locked; you relaxed. Am I understood?

THE MEN: Yes—

SGT. TOWER: AM I UNDERSTOOD, GODDAMNIT, OR DO YOU WANT TO ALL DROP FOR TWENTY OR— (ARDELL, *off to the side, is drifting nearer.*)

THE MEN: YES, SERGEANT, YES, SERGEANT!

ARDELL: Pavlo, my man, you on your way!

CORPORAL: PLATOOOON! PLATOOOON!

SGT. TOWER: I GONNA DO SOME SINGIN', GEN'LMEN, I WANT IT COMIN' BACK TO ME LIKE WE IN GRAND CANYON—

CORPORAL: TEN-HUT!

ARDELL: DO IT, GET IT!

SGT. TOWER: —AND YOU MY MOTHERFUCKIN' ECHO!

SQUAD LEADERS: RIGHT FACE!

CORPORAL: FORWARD HARCH!

SGT. TOWER: (*singing*) LIFT YOUR HEAD AND LIFT IT HIGH . . .

THE MEN: LIFT YOUR HEAD AND LIFT IT HIGH . . .

SGT. TOWER: ECHO COMPANY PASSIN' BY!

THE MEN: ECHO COMPANY PASSIN' BY!
(*They start going off in groups, marching and singing.*)

ARDELL: MOTHER, MOTHER. WHAT'D I DO?

THE MEN: MOTHER, MOTHER, WHAT'D I DO?

ARDELL: THIS ARMY TREATIN' ME WORSE THAN YOU!

THE MEN: THIS ARMY TREATIN' ME WORSE THAN YOU!

SGT. TOWER: LORD HAVE MERCY I'M SO BLUE!

THE MEN: LORD HAVE MERCY I'M SO BLUE! IT EIGHT
MORE WEEKS TILL WE BE THROUGH! IT EIGHT
MORE WEEKS TILL WE BE THROUGH! IT EIGHT
MORE WEEKS TILL WE BE THROUGH!
(*And all the men have marched off in lines in different directions,
giving a sense of large numbers, a larger space, and now, out of
this movement, comes a spin-off of two men, KRESS and PARKER,
drilling down the center of the stage, yelling the last of the song,
marching stomping, then breaking and running stage left and
into the furnace room, where there is the hulk of the belly of the
furnace, the flickering of the fire. KRESS is large, muscular, with a
constant manner of small confusion as if he feels always that
something is going on that he nearly, but not quite, understands.
Yet there is something seemingly friendly about him. PARKER is
smaller; he wears glasses.*)

KRESS: I can't stand it, Parker, bein' so cold all the time and they're
all insane, Parker. Waxin' and buffin' the floor at five-thirty in
the morning is insane. And then you can't eat till you go down
the monkey bars and you gotta eat in ten minutes and can't talk
to nobody, and no place in Georgia is warm. I'm from Jersey. I
can jump up in the air, if there's a good wind, I'll land in Fort
Dix. Am I right so far? So Sam gets me. What's he do? Fort Dix?
Uh-uh. Fort Gordon, Georgia. So I can be warm right? Down
South, man. Daffodils and daisies. Year round. (*Hollering*) BUT
AM I WARM? DO YOU THINK I'M WARM? DO I LOOK
LIKE I'M WARM? JESUS H! EVEN IN THE GODDAMN
FURNACE ROOM, I'M FREEZIN' TA DEATH!

PARKER: So, what the hell is hollerin' like a stupid ape gonna do except to let 'em know where we're at?

KRESS: (*as* PAVLO *enters upstage, moving slowly in awe toward the tower, looking*) Heat up my blood!

ARDELL: (*to* PAVLO) What you doin' strollin' about like a fool, man? You gonna have people comin' down all over you, don't you know—

OFFICER: (*having just entered*) What're you doin' walkin' in this company area? Don't you know you run in this company area? Hummel, you drop, you hear me. You drop!
(PAVLO *drops and begins the push-ups.*)

ARDELL: (*over him*) Do 'em right, do 'em right!

KRESS: Why can't I be warm? I wanna be warm.

PARKER: Okay, man, you're warm.

KRESS: No; I'm not; I'm cold, Parker. Where's our goddamn fireman; don't he ever do nothin' but push-ups? Don't he ever do nothin' but trouble!

PARKER: Don't knock that ole boy, Kress; I'm tellin' you Hummel's gonna keep us laughin'!

KRESS: Yesterday I was laughin' so hard. I mean, I'm stupid, Parker, but Hummel's *stupid.* I mean, he volunteers to be fireman 'cause he thinks it means you ride in a raincoat on a big red truck and when there's nothin' to do you play cards.

PARKER: Yeah! He don't know it means you gotta baby-sit the goddamn furnace all night, every night. And end up lookin' like a stupid chimney sweep!

KRESS: Lookin' what?

PARKER: (*as* PIERCE *enters at a jog, moving across the stage toward* ARDELL *and* PAVLO) Like a goddamn chimney sweep!

PAVLO: Where you goin'?

PIERCE: (*without hesitating*) Weapons room and furnace room.

PAVLO: (*getting to his feet*) Can I come along?

PIERCE: (*still running, without looking back*) I don't give a shit.
(*He exits,* PAVLO *following, as* ARDELL *is drifting the opposite direction.*)

PAVLO: . . . great . . .

KRESS: Yeh? Yeh, Parker, that's good. Chimney sweeps!

PARKER: Yeh, they were these weird little men always crawlin' around, and they used to do this weird shit ta chimneys.
(PIERCE *and* PAVLO *enter. They have their rifles.* PIERCE *is a trainee acting as a squad leader. He has a cloth marked with corporal's stripes tied on his left sleeve.*)

PIERCE: At ease!

KRESS: Hey, the Chimney Shit. Hey, what's happenin', Chimney Shit?

PAVLO: How you doin', Kress?

KRESS: Where's your red hat, man?

PAVLO: What?

PARKER: Ain't you got no red fireman's hat?

PAVLO: I'm just with Pierce, that's all. He's my squad leader and I'm with him.

PARKER: Mr. Squad Leader.

PAVLO: Isn't that right, Pierce?

PARKER: Whose ass you kiss to get that job, anyway, Pierce?

PIERCE: At ease, Trainees.

KRESS: He's R.A., man. Regular Army. Him and Hummel. Lifer morons. Whata they gonna do to us today, anyway, Mr. Actin' Sergeant, Corporal. What's the lesson for the day: first aid or bayonet? I love this fuckin' army.

PIERCE: The schedule's posted, Kress!

KRESS: You know I don't read, man; hurts my eyes; makes 'em water.

PAVLO: When's the gas chamber, that's what I wanna know.

KRESS: For you, Chimney Shit, in about ten seconds when I fart in your face.

PAVLO: I'm all right. I do all right.

KRESS: Sure you do, except you got your head up your ass.

PAVLO: Yeh? Well maybe I'd rather have it up my ass than where you got it.
(*Slight pause: it has made no sense to* KRESS *at all.*)

KRESS: What?

PAVLO: You heard me, Kress.

KRESS: What'd he say, Parker? (*There is frenzy in this.*) I heard him, but I don't know what he said. WHAT'D YOU SAY TO ME, HUMMEL?

PAVLO: Just never you mind, Kress.

KRESS: I DON'T KNOW WHAT YOU SAID TO ME, YOU WEIRD PERSON!

PARKER: (*patting* KRESS) Easy, man, easy; be cool.

KRESS: But I don't like weird people, Parker. I don't like them. How come I gotta be around him? I don't wanna be around you, Hummel!

PAVLO: Don't you worry about it, I'm just here with Pierce. I just wanna know about the gas chamber.

KRESS: It's got gas in it! Ain't that right, Parker! It's like this goddamn giant asshole, it farts on you. THHPPBBBZZZZZZZ! (*Silence.*)

PAVLO: When is it, Pierce?

KRESS: Ohhhhh, Jesus, I'm cold.

PAVLO: This ain't cold, Kress.

KRESS: I know if I'm cold.

PAVLO: I been colder than this. This ain't cold. I been a lot colder than—

KRESS: DON'T TELL ME IT AIN'T COLD OR I'LL KILL YOU! JESUS GOD ALMIGHTY I HATE THIS MOTHER ARMY STICKIN' ME IN WITH WEIRD PEOPLE! DIE, HUMMEL! Will you please do me that favor! Oh, God, let me close my eyes and when I open them, Hummel is dead. Please. Please.
(*He squeezes his eyes shut, clenches his hands and then looks at* PAVLO, *who is grinning.*)

PAVLO: Boy, I sure do dread that gas chamber.

KRESS: He hates me, Parker. He truly hates me.

PAVLO: No, I don't.

KRESS: What'd I ever do to him, you suppose.

PARKER: I don't know, Kress.

PAVLO: I don't hate you.

PARKER: How come he's so worried about that gas chamber, that's what I wonder.

PAVLO: Well, see, I had an uncle die in San Quentin.
(KRESS *screams.*)
That's the truth, Kress.
(KRESS *screams again.*)
I don't care if you believe it. He killed four people in a fight in a bar.

PARKER: Usin' his bare hands, right?

PAVLO: You know how many people are executed every damn day in San Quentin? One hell of a lot. And every one of 'em just about is somebody's uncle and one of 'em was my Uncle Roy. He killed four people in a barroom brawl usin' broken bottles and table legs and screamin', jus' screamin'. He was mean, man. He was rotten; and my folks been scared the same thing might happen to me; all their lives, they been scared. I got that same look in my eyes like him.

PARKER: What kinda look is that?

KRESS: That really rotten look, man. He got that really rotten look. Can't you see it?

PAVLO: You ever steal a car, Kress? You know how many cars I stole?

KRESS: Shut up Hummel! You're a goddamn chimney sweep and I don't wanna talk to you because you don't talk American, you talk Hummel! Some goddamn foreign language!

PARKER: How many cars you stole?

PAVLO: Twenty-three.

KRESS: Twenty-three!
    (PARKER *whistles*.)

PAVLO: That's a lotta cars, huh?

PARKER: You damn betcha, man. How long'd it take you, for chrissake? Ten years?

PAVLO: Two.

PARKER: Workin' off and on, you mean.

PAVLO: Sure. Not every night, or they'd catch you. And not always from the same part of town. Man, sometimes I'd hit lower Manhattan, and then the next night the Bronx or Queens, and sometimes I'd even cut right on outa town. One time, in fact, I went all the way to New Haven. Boy that was some night because they almost caught me. Can you imagine that. Huh? Parker? Huh? Pierce? All the way to New Haven and cops on my tail every inch a the way, roadblocks closin' up behind me, bang, bang, and then some highway patrolman, just as I was wheelin' into New Haven, he come roarin' outa this side road. See, they must a called ahead or somethin' and he come hot on my ass. I kicked it, man, arrrrgggggghhhhh . . . ! Eighty-two per. Had a Porsche; he didn't know who he was after; that stupid fuzz, eighty-two per, straight down the gut, people jumpin' outa my way, kids and businessmen and little old ladies, all of 'em, and me kickin' ass, up to ninety-seven now, roarin' baby sirens all around me, so I cut into this alley and jump. Oh, Jesus, Christ, just lettin' the car go, I hit, roll, I'm up and runnin' down for this board fence, up and over, sirens all over now, I mean, *all over*, but I'm walkin' calm, I'm cool. Cops are goin' this way and that way. One of 'em asks me if I seen a Porsche go by real fast. Did *I* see—

KRESS: *Jesus-goddamn*—the furnace room's smellin' like the gas chamber!
(*He rises to leave*, PARKER *following.*)

PARKER: Right, Hummel. That's right. I mean I liked your story about your really rotten uncle Roy better than the one about all the cars.

KRESS: Gotta go get our weapons.

PARKER: Defend our fuckin' selves.

PAVLO: I'll see you guys later.
(*They are gone. Silence.*)
Hey Pierce, you wanna hear my General Orders; make sure I know 'em, okay? Like we're on guard mount and you're the O.D. . . . You wanna see if I'm sharp enough to be one a your boys. Okay? (*Snapping to attention*) Sir! My first general order is to take charge of this post and all government property in view, keeping always on the alert and . . .

PIERCE: Gimme your eighth, Hummel.

PAVLO: Eighth? No, no, lemme do 'em one, two, three. You'll mess me up I don't do them one, two, three.

PIERCE: That's the way it's gonna be, Hummel. The man comes up to you on guard mount he's gonna be all over you—right on top a you yellin' down your throat. You understand me? He won't be standin' back polite and pretty lettin' you run your mouth.

PAVLO: Just to practice, Pierce. I just wanna practice.

PIERCE: You don't wanna practice shit. You just wanna stand there and have me pat your goddamned head for bein' a good boy.

Don't you know we stood here laughin' at you lyin' outa your ass? Don't you have any pride, man?

PAVLO: I got pride. And anyway, they didn't know I was lyin'.

PIERCE: Shit.

PAVLO: And anyway, I wasn't lyin'; it was story telling. They was just messin' with me a little, pickin' on me. My mom used to always tell my dad not to be so hard on me, but he knew.
(*Whistle blows loudly from off.*)

PIERCE: Let's go.

PAVLO: See, he was hard on me 'cause he loved me. I'm R.A. Pierce.

PIERCE: You got an R.A. prefix, man, but you ain't Regular Army.

PAVLO: They was just jumpin' on me a little; pickin' on me.
(*Again the whistle.*)

PIERCE: That whistle means formation, man.

PAVLO: They're just gonna draw weapons and I already got mine.

PIERCE: That ain't what I said, Jerkoff!

PAVLO: Well, I ain't goin' out there to stand around doin' nothin' when I can stay right here and put the time to good use practicin' D and D.
(*Again the whistle. The men are gathering; we hear their murmuring.*)

PIERCE: You ain't no motherin' exception to that whistle!

PAVLO: You ain't any real corporal anyway, Pierce. So don't get so big with me just because you got that hunk a thing wrapped around you—

PIERCE: Don't you mess up my squad, Hummel! Don't you make me look bad or I'll get you your legs broken.

PAVLO: (*as whistle blows and* PIERCE *is running and gone*) I bet you never heard a individual initiative.
(*Whistle again as soldiers rush in to line up in formation at parade rest while* SGT. TOWER *climbs to stand atop the platform.*)

ARDELL: They don't know, do they? They don't know who they talkin' to.

PAVLO: No.

ARDELL: You gonna be so straight.

PAVLO: So clean.
(*As* SGT. TOWER, *noticing that someone is missing from formation, turns, descends, exits.*)
Port Harms!
(*And he does the move with only a slight and quickly corrected error.*)

ARDELL: Good, Pavlo. Good. (*Slight pause.*) Order Harms!
(*There is some skill in the move.*)

PAVLO: Okay . . .

ARDELL: RIGHT SHOULDER . . . HARMS!
(PAVLO's *head flinches, the rifle nicking the top of his helmet. His back is toward the group.* SGT. TOWER *enters, watches for a time.*)

PAVLO: Goddamnit. Shit.
(*Again the rifle back to order arms.*)

ARDELL: RIGHT SHOULDER . . .

PAVLO: HARMS!
(*Again it is not good.*)
You mother rifle. You stupid fucking rifle. RIGHT SHOULDER,

HARMS. (*He tries.*) Mother! Stupid mother, whatsamatter with you? I'll kill you! (*And he has it high above his head. He is looking up.*) Rifle, please. Work for me, do it for me. I know what to do, just do it.

ARDELL: Just go easy. Man . . . just easy. It don't mean that much. What's it matter?

SGT. TOWER: What you doin', Trainee?

PAVLO: (*snapping to attention*) Yes, Sir! Trainee Pavlo Hummel, Sir.

SGT. TOWER: I didn't ask you you name, Boy. I asked you what you doin' in here when you supposed to be out on that formation?

PAVLO: Yes, Sir.

SGT. TOWER: No, I don't have no bars on my collar; do you see any bars on my collar?

PAVLO: (*looking*) No . . . No . . .

SGT. TOWER: But what do you see on my sleeve at about the height a my shoulder less a little, what do you see?

PAVLO: Stripes, Sergeant. Sergeant stripes.

SGT. TOWER: So how come you call me Sir? I ain't no Sir. I don't want to be no Sir. I am a Sergeant. Now do we know one another?

PAVLO: Yes, Sergeant.

SGT. TOWER: That mean you can answer my question in the proper manner, do it not?

PAVLO: I was practicin' D and D, Sergeant, to make me a good soldier.

Sgt. tower: Ohhhhhhh! I think you tryin' to jive this ole man, that what you doin'. Or else you awful stupid, because all the good soldiers is out there in that formation like they supposed to when they hear that whistle. Now which?

Pavlo: Pardon, Sergeant?

Sgt. tower: Which is it? You jivin' on me or you awful stupid, you take your pick. And lemme tell you why you can't put no jive on the old Sarge. Because long time ago, this ole Sarge was one brand-new, baby-soft, smart-assed recruit. So I see you and I say, "What that young recruit doin' in that furnace room this whole company out there bein' talked at by the C.O.?" And the answer come to me like a blast a thunder and this voice sayin' to me in my head, "This here young recruit jerkin' off, that what he doin'," and then into my head come this picture and we ain't in no furnace room, we in that jungle catchin' hell from this one little yellow man and his automatic weapon that he chained to up on top of this hill. "Get on up that hill!" I tell my young recruit. And he tell me, "Yes, Sergeant," like he been taught, and then he start thinkin' to hisself, "What that old Sarge talkin' about, 'run on up that hill'? Ah git my ass blown clean away. I think maybe he got hit on his head, he don't know what he talkin' about no more—maybe I go on over behind that ole rock—practice me a little D and D." Ain't that some shit the way them young recruits wanna carry on? So what I think we do, you and me, long about twenty-two hundred hours we do a little D and D and PT and all them kinda alphabetical things. Make you a good soldier.

Pavlo: (thinking he wants to work with Sgt. tower) I don't think I can. That's nighttime, Sergeant, and I'm a fireman. I got to watch the furnace.

Sgt. tower: That don't make me no never mind. We jus' work it in between your shifts. You see? Ain't it a wonder how you let the old Sarge do the worryin' and figurin' and he find a way?
(Turns, starting to leave.)

Pavlo: Sergeant, I was wondering how many push-ups you can do.

How many you can do, that's how many I want to be able to do before I ever leave.

SGT. TOWER: Boy, don't you go sayin' no shit like that, you won't ever get out. You be an ole bearded blind fuckin' man pushin' up all over Georgia.
(SGT. TOWER *moves to leave, and* PAVLO, *speaking immediately and rapidly, in a single rush of breath, again stops him. Incredulously* SGT. TOWER *watches, starts to leave, watches.*)

PAVLO: And I was wondering also, Sergeant Tower, and wanted to ask you—when I was leaving home, my mother wanted to come along to the train station, but I lied to her about the time. She would have wanted to hug me right in front of everybody. She would have waved a handkerchief at the train. It would have been awful.
(SGT. TOWER *turns; now he is leaving.*)
She would have stood there waving. Was I wrong?

CORPORAL: TEN-HUT! FORWARD HARCH!
(*And the men begin to march in place, while* PAVLO, *without joining them, also marches.*)

SGT. TOWER: AIN'T NO USE IN GOIN' HOME.

THE MEN: (*beginning to exit*) AIN'T NO USE IN GOIN' HOME.

SGT. TOWER: (*at the side of the stage*) JODY GOT YOUR GAL AND GONE.

THE MEN: JODY HUMPIN' ON AND ON.

SGT. TOWER: AIN'T NO USE IN GOIN' BACK.
(*And* PAVLO, *in his own area, is marching away.*)

THE MEN: JODY GOT OUR CADILLAC.

CORPORAL: AIN'T NO MATTER WHAT WE DO.

ALL: JODY DOIN' OUR SISTER TOO.

CORPORAL: Count cadence, delayed cadence, count cadence, count!

ALL: One— two— three— four— One, two, three, four. One, two, three, four. *Hey!*
(*All are now gone except* PAVLO, *who spins out of his marching pattern to come stomping to a halt in the furnace-room area, while* ARDELL *drifts toward him.*)

ARDELL: Oh, yeh; army train you, shape you up, teach you all kinds a good stuff. Like Bayonet. It all about what you do you got no more bullets and this man after you. So you put this knife on the end a your rifle, start yellin' and carryin' on. Then there Hand to Hand. Hand to Hand cool.
(PAVLO *is watching, listening.*)
It all about hittin' and kickin'. What you do when you got no gun and no knife. Then there CBR. CBR: Chemical, Biological, and Radiological Warfare. What you do when some mean motherfucker hit you with some kinda chemical. You (ARDELL *mimes throwing a grenade at* PAVLO.) got green fuckin' killin' smoke all around you. What you gonna do? You gotta git on your protective mask. You ain't got it?

PAVLO: (*choking*) But I'm too beautiful to die. (*Rummages about in the furnace room.*)

ARDELL: (*throwing a mask to him*) But you the only one who believe that, Pavlo. You gotta be hollerin' loud as you know how, "Gas!" And then, sweet lord almighty, little bit later, you walkin' along, somebody else hit you with some kinda biological jive. But you know your shit. Mask on.
(*And* PAVLO, *having put the mask on, is waving his arms.*)

PAVLO: GAS! GAS! GAS!

ARDELL: You gettin' it, Pavlo. All right. Lookin' real good. But now you tired and you still walkin' and you come up on somebody bad —this boy mean—he hit you with radiation.
(PAVLO *goes into a tense, defensive posture.*)

PAVLO: (*realizing his helplessness*) Awww.

ARDELL: That right. You know what you do? You kinda stand there, that what you do, whimperin' and talkin' to yourself, 'cause he got you. You gotta be some kinda fool, somebody hit you with radiation, man, you put on a mask, start hollerin', "Gas." Am I lyin'? Pavlo. What do you say?

PAVLO: Aww, no. . . . No man— No, No— No, no. No, no. Oh . . .

(*There has been, toward the end of this, a gathering of a group of soldiers in the barracks area.* PAVLO, *muttering in denial of the radiation, crosses the stage hurriedly, fleeing the radiation, and runs into* PARKER, *who grabs him, spins him.*)
I did not.

KRESS: The hell you didn't.

PARKER: (*kneeling behind* PAVLO *to take a billfold from his pocket*) You been found out, Jerkoff.

PAVLO: No.

KRESS: We got people saw you. Straight honest guys.

PARKER: Get that thing (*meaning the mask*) off your face.

BURNS: The shit I didn't see you.

PARKER: You never saw a billfold before in your life, is that what you're tryin' to say? You didn't even know what it was?

KRESS: Is that what you're tryin' to say, Hummel?

PAVLO: No.

KRESS: What are you tryin' to say?

PAVLO: I'm goin' to bed. (*Moves toward his bed but is stopped by* KRESS.)

KRESS: We already had two guys lose money to some thief around here, Shitbird, and we got people sayin' they saw you with Hinkle's billfold in your pudgy little paws.

HINKLE: (*in a deep Southern drawl, as* PARKER *hands him the billfold he found on* PAVLO) Is that right, Hummel?

PAVLO: I was just testin' you, Hinkle, to see how stupid you were leavin' your billfold layin' out like that when somebody's been stealin' right in our own platoon. What kinda army is this anyway, you're supposed to trust people with your life, you can't even trust 'em not to steal your money.

PARKER: Listen to him.

PAVLO: That's the truth, Parker. I was just makin' a little test experiment to see how long it'd be before he'd notice it was gone. I don't steal.

KRESS: What about all them cars?

PAVLO: What cars?

PARKER: The New Haven Caper, Jerkoff. You know.

PAVLO: Ohhh, that was different, you guys. That was altogether different.

KRESS: Yeh, they were cars and you couldn't fit them in your pocket.

PAVLO: Those people weren't my friends.

PARKER: You don't steal from your friends. That what you're sayin'? Kress, Hummel says he don't steal from his friends.

KRESS: (*jumping up on* PAVLO's *bed, standing, walking about*) Don't that make his prospects pretty damn near unlimited.

PAVLO: Hey! Kress; what're you doin'?

KRESS: What?

PAVLO: I said, "What're you up to?" You're on my bed.

KRESS: Who is?

PAVLO: You are. You are.

KRESS: Where?

PAVLO: Right here. You're on my bed. That's my bed.

KRESS: No it isn't. It's not anybody's. It's not yours, Hummel.

PAVLO: It is too.

KRESS: Did you buy it?

PAVLO: Get off my bed, Kress!

KRESS: If you didn't buy it, then how is it yours, Ugly!

PAVLO: It was given to me.

KRESS: By who?

PAVLO: You know by who, Kress. The army gave it to me. Get off it.

KRESS: Are you going to take it with you when you leave here? If it's yours, you ought to be planning on taking it with you; are you?

PAVLO: I can't do that.

KRESS: You're taking people's billfolds; you're taking their money; why can't you take this bed?

PAVLO: Because it was just loaned to me.

KRESS: Do you have any kind of papers to prove that? Do you have papers to prove that this is your bed?

PAVLO: There's proof in the orderly room; in the orderly room, or maybe the supply room and you know it. That bed's got a number on it somewhere and that number is like its name and that name is by my name on some papers somewhere in the supply room or the orderly room.

KRESS: Go get them.

PAVLO: What do you mean?

KRESS: Go get them. Bring them here.

PAVLO: I can't.

KRESS: If they're yours, you can.

PAVLO: They're not my papers, it's my bed. Get off my bed, Kress.
(KRESS *kneels, taking a more total possession of the bed.*)
Goddamnit, Kress. GODDAMNIT!
(*Silence as* KRESS *seems in fact about to lie down.*)
All right. Okay. You sleep in my bed, I'm gonna sleep in yours.
(PAVLO *charges toward* KRESS's *bed.* KRESS *rises a little, tense, as all stand watching* PAVLO.)

KRESS: No, Hummel.

PAVLO: (*yelling*) The hell I ain't, Kress.

KRESS: No, no, I strongly advise against it. I do strongly so advise. Or something awful might happen. I might get up in the middle of the night to take a leak and stagger back to my old bed. Lord knows what I might think you are . . . laying there. Lord knows what I might do.

PAVLO: (*yelling*) Then get out of my bed.

KRESS: You don't understand at all, do you, Shitbird! I'm sleeping here. This is where I'm going to sleep. You're not going to sleep anywhere. You're going to sit up, or sleep on the floor, whatever. And in the morning, you're going to make this bed. This one. Because if you don't, it'll be unmade when Sergeant Tower comes to inspect in the morning and, as we've already discussed, there's papers somewhere in one room or another and they show whose bed this is.

PAVLO: (*rushing back, stomping, raging*) GODDAMN YOU, KRESS, GET OUT OF MY BED! GET OFF MY BED! GET OUT OF IT!
(*Whistle blows and everyone scrambles. There is the popping of many rifles firing as on the ramp across the back three or four men are in firing position; others stand behind them at port arms until* SGT. TOWER *calls,* "Cease fire!" *and the firing stops. The men who have been firing put their rifles on their shoulders to be cleared.* SGT. TOWER *walks behind them, tapping each on the head when he has seen the weapon is clear. The men leap to their feet.* SGT. TOWER *then steps out in front of them, begins to pace up and down.*)

SGT. TOWER: GEN'LMEN! IT GETTIN' TOWARD DARK NOW AND WE GOT TO GET HOME. IT A LONG LONG WAYS TO HOME AND OUR MOTHERS GOT SUPPER READY WAITIN' FOR US. WHAT CAN WE DO? WE GOT TO GET HOME FAST AS WE CAN, WHAT CAN WE DO? DO ANYBODY HAVE AN IDEA? LET ME HEAR YOU SPEAK IF YOU DO. . . . I HAVE AN IDEA. ANYBODY KNOW MY IDEA, LET ME HEAR IF YOU DO.

PAVLO: Run . . .

BURNS: Run?

SGT. TOWER: WHAT?

MORE MEN: RUN!

SGT. TOWER: I CAN'T HEAR YOU.

THE MEN: WHAT?

SGT. TOWER: RUN!

THE MEN: RUN!

SGT. TOWER and THE MEN: RUN! RUN! RUN! RUN! RUN!

SGT. TOWER: (*as the men still yell, "Run, run"*) PORT HARMS
. . . WHOOO! DOUBLE TIME . . . WHOOOOO!
(*They have been running in place. Now* SGT. TOWER *leads them
off. They exit, running, reappear, exit, and reappear, spreading out
now, though* PAVLO *is fairly close behind* SGT. TOWER, *who enters
once again to run to a point downstage, where he turns to* PAVLO
entering staggering, leading.)
FALL OUT!
(*And* PAVLO *collapses. The others struggle in, fall down.*)

PIERCE: FIVE GODDAMN MILES!
(*All are in extreme pain.*)

KRESS: MOTHER-GODDAMN-BITCH—I NEVER RAN NO
FIVE GODDAMN MILES IN MY LIFE. YOU GOTTA BE
CRAZY TO RUN FIVE GODDAMN MILES. . . .

PARKER: I hurt. I hurt all over. I hurt Kress. Oh, Christ.

PIERCE: There are guys spread from here to Range Two. You can be
proud you made it, Parker. The whole company, man—they're
gonna be comin' in for the next ten days.
(*And* PARKER *yells in pain.*)

KRESS: Pierce, what's wrong with Parker?

PARKER: SHIT TOO, YOU MOTHER!

KRESS: It'll pass, Parker. Don't worry. Just stay easy.
(*While a little separate from the others,* PAVLO *is about to begin
doing push-ups. He is very tired; it hurts him to do what he's
doing.*)
Oh, Hummel, no. Hummel, please.
(PAVLO *is doing the push-ups, breathing the count, wheezing,
gasping.*)

Hummel, you're crazy. You really are. He really is, Parker. Look at him. I hate crazy people. I hate 'em. YOU ARE REALLY CRAZY, HUMMEL. STOP IT OR I'LL KILL YOU. (As PAVLO *pivots into a sit-up position*) I mean, I wanna know how much money this platoon lost to that thief we got among us.

PIERCE: Three hundred and twelve dollars.

KRESS: What're you gonna do with all that money?

PAVLO: Spend it. Spend it.

KRESS: Something gonna be done to you! You hear me, Weird Face? You know what's wrong with you? You wouldn't know cunt if your nose was in it. You never had a piece of ass in your life. (*There is a loud blast on a whistle.*)

PAVLO: Joanna Sorrentino ga' me so much ass my mother called her a slut.

KRESS: YOU FUCKING IDIOT!
    (*Again the whistle.*)

PIERCE: Oh, Christ . . .

PAVLO: Let's go. LET'S GO. LET'S GET IT.

KRESS: Shut up.

PAVLO: (*moving*) Let's GO, GO, GO—
    (*All start to exit.*)

KRESS: SHUT YOUR MOUTH, ASSHOLE!

PAVLO: Let's—GO, GO, GO, GO, GO, GO, GO . . . (*yelling, leading, yelling, as all ran off stage*).
    (*Simultaneously, in the light on the opposite side of the stage, two soldiers—the* CORPORAL *and* HENDRIX—*are seen with pool cues*

at a pool table. There are no pool balls: the game will be panto-mime; they use a cue ball to shoot and work with.)

HENDRIX: You break.

CORPORAL: Naw, man, I shoot break on your say so, when I whip your ass, you'll come cryin'. You call.
(*He flips a coin, as* PAVLO *comes running back to get his helmet, which lies near where he was doing the push-ups.*)

HENDRIX: Heads.

CORPORAL: You got it.
(PAVLO, *scurrying off with his helmet, meets* SGT. TOWER *entering from opposite side.*)

SGT. TOWER: Trainee, go clean the dayroom. Sweep it up.

PAVLO: Pardon, Sergeant? I forgot my helmet . . .

SGT. TOWER: Go clean the dayroom, Trainee.
(PAVLO *runs off, as at the pool game* HENDRIX *shoots break.*)

CORPORAL: My . . . my . . . my. . . . Yes sir. You're gonna be tough all right. That was a pretty damn break all right. (*Moving now to position himself for his shot.*) Except you missed all the holes. Didn't nobody tell you you were supposed to knock the lit-tle balls in the little holes?

PAVLO: (*entering*) Sergeant Tower said for me to sweep up the dayroom.

HENDRIX: And that's what you do—you don't smile, laugh, or talk; you sweep.

CORPORAL: You know what "buck a ball" means, Trainee?

PAVLO: What?

CORPORAL: Trainee's rich, Hendrix. Can't go to town, got money up the ass.

PAVLO: Sure I know what "buck a ball" means.

CORPORAL: Ohh, you hustlin' trainee motherfucker. New game. Right now. Rack 'em up!
(HENDRIX *moves as if to rerack the balls.*)

PAVLO: You sayin' I can play?

CORPORAL: Hendrix, you keep an eye out for anybody who might not agree Trainee can relax a bit. You break, man.

PAVLO: I'll break.

CORPORAL: That's right.

PAVLO: You been to the war, huh? That's a First Division patch you got there, ain't it? (*Shooting first shot, missing, not too good.*)

CORPORAL: That's right.

PAVLO: Where at?

CORPORAL: How many wars we got?

PAVLO: I mean exactly where.

CORPORAL: (*lining up his shot*) Di An. Ever hear of it?

PAVLO: Sure.

CORPORAL: Not much of a place but real close to Da Nang. (*He shoots, watches, moves for the next shot.*)

PAVLO: You up there too?

CORPORAL: Where's that?

PAVLO: By Da Nang.

(*The* CORPORAL *is startled by* PAVLO *knowing this. He shoots and misses.*)

I mean, I thought Di An was more down by Saigon. D Zone. Down there. They call that D Zone, don't they?

CORPORAL: You're right, man; you know your shit. We got us a map-readin' motherfucker, Hendrix. Yeh, I was by Saigon, Hummel.

PAVLO: I thought so.

CORPORAL: Your shot.

(*He has moved off to the side where* HENDRIX *has a hip flask of whiskey.*)

PAVLO: (*moving for his shot*) Big Red One, man, I'd be proud wearin' that. (*He shoots and misses.*) Shit.

CORPORAL: (*moving again to the table*) Good outfit. Top kinda outfit. Mean bastards, all of 'em. Every place we went, man we used ta tear 'em a new asshole, you can believe me. (*Shooting, making it, he moves on.*) I'm gonna win all your damn money, man. You got your orders yet for where you go when you're finished with basic?

PAVLO: No.

CORPORAL: Maybe if you're lucky, you'll get infantry, huh? Yeh, yeh, I seen some shit, you can believe me. (*And he moves about the table, shooting, shooting, as he speaks.*) But you go over there, that's what you're goin' for. To mess with them people, because they don't know nothin'. Them slopes; man they're the stupidest bunch of people anybody ever saw. It don't matter what you do to 'em or what you say, man they just look at you. They're some kinda goddamn phenomenon, man. Can of bug spray buy you all the ass you can handle in some places. Insect repellent, man. You ready for that? You give 'em can a bug spray, you can lay their fourteen-year-old daughter. Not that any of 'em screw worth a shit. (*He thinks it all interesting.*)

You hear a lot of people talkin' Airborne, One Seventy-third, Hundred and First, Marines, but you gotta go some to beat the First Division. I had a squad leader, Sergeant Tinden. He'd been there two goddamn years when I got there, so he knew the road, man; he knew his way. So we was comin' into this village once, the whole company, and it was supposed to be secure. We was Charlie Company and Alpha'd been through already, left a guard. And we was lead platoon and lead squad, and comin' toward us on the path is this old man, he musta been a hundred, about three foot tall, and he's got this little girl by the hand and she's maybe a half-step behind him. He's wavin' at us, "Okay, okay, GI." And she's wavin', too, but she ain't sayin' nothin', but there's this funny noise you can hear, a kind of cryin' like. (*He still moves about, shooting.*) Anyway, I'm next to the Sarge and he tells this old boy to stop, but they keep comin' like they don't understand, smilin' and wavin', so the Sarge says for 'em to stop in Vietnamese and then I can see that the kid is cryin'; she's got big tears runnin' outa her eyes, and her eyes are gettin' bigger and bigger and I can see she's tuggin' at the old man's hand to run away but he holds her and he hollers at her and I'm thinkin', "Damn, ain't that a bitch, she's so scared of us." And Tinden, right then, man he dropped to his knees and let go two bursts— first the old man then the kid—cuttin' them both right across the face, man you could see the bullets walkin'. It was somethin'.

(*He sets and takes his shot. He flops the cue onto the table.*)

You owe me, man; thirteen bucks. But I'm superstitious, so we'll make it twelve.

(PAVLO *pulls out a wad of money to pay.*)

That's right. My ole daddy—the last day he saw me—he tole me good—"Don't you ever run on nobody, Boy, or if you do I hope there's somebody there got sense enough to shoot you down. Or if I hear you got away, I'll kill you myself." There's folks like that runnin' loose, Hummel. My ole man. You dig it.

(*But* PAVLO *doesn't and he stares.*)

What the fuck are you lookin' at?

PAVLO: I don't know why he shot . . . them.

CORPORAL: Satchel charges, man. The both of them, front and back. They had enough TNT on 'em to blow up this whole damn state and the kid got scared. They was wearing it under their clothes.

PAVLO: And he knew . . .

CORPORAL: That's right. Been around, so he knew. You ready, Hendrix?
(*They are moving to exit.*)

HENDRIX: Ain't that some shit, Hummel? Ain't that the way to be?
(PARKER *can be seen far across the stage in dimness. Near him,* KRESS *and three or four other soldiers crouch among the beds.*)

PARKER: Dear Mother. It was the oddest thing last night. I sat near my bunk, half awake, half asleep . . .

CORPORAL: You keep your ear to the ground, Hummel, you're gonna be all right. (*Exiting*) We'll see you around.

PAVLO: Just to see and to move; just to move.
(*He mimes with his broom the firing of a rifle, while* ARDELL *stares and lunges suddenly backwards, rapidly hauling the table off.*)

PARKER: (*loudly and flamboyantly*) Yes, yes, good Mother, I could not sleep, I don't know why. And then for further reasons that I do not know, I happened to look behind me and there . . . was a space ship, yes a space ship, green and golden, good Mother, come down to the sand of our Georgia home. A space ship . . .
(PAVLO *wanders nearer.* PARKER *glances toward* KRESS—*who is kneeling with a blanket—and the others.*)
And out of it, leaping they came, little green men no larger than pins. "Good Lord in Heaven," said I to myself, "what do they want? Sneaking among us, ever in silence, ever in stealth." Then I saw Hummel. "Hummel is coming," said I. "I will ask Hummel," said I to myself. "Hummel is coming."
(PAVLO *enters.*)
THIEF!

(*And the blanket is thrown over him. He is dragged to the floor. They beat and kick him. Call him "thief." He cries out. Squirms. A second blanket is thrown upon him, a mattress—it is his own bedding. As they beat and kick him, a whistle blows. All go running out, grabbing rifles and helmets, to form up for bayonet practice where* SGT. TOWER *awaits them.*

PAVLO *emerges from beneath the blankets and no one is there but* ARDELL.)

PAVLO: Didn't I do enough push-ups? How many do you have to do, Ardell?

ARDELL: You got to understand, Pavlo, it fun sometimes to get a man the way they got you. Come down on him, maybe pivot kick. Break his fuckin' spine. Do him, man. Do . . . him . . . good.

SGT. TOWER: (*atop his platform, bayonet in hand*) You got to know this bayonet shit, Gen'lmen, else you get recycled, you be back to learn it all again. Eight more beautiful weeks in the armpit a the nation. Else you don't get recycled, you get killed. Then you wish for maybe half a second you been recycled. Do you know the spirit of the bayonet is to kill? What is the spirit of the bayonet?

THE MEN: TO KILL!
(*While* PAVLO *stirs about,* PIERCE *enters the barracks. He is disheveled, a little drunk.*)

SGT. TOWER: You sound like pussies. You sound like slits.

THE MEN: TO KILL!

SGT. TOWER: You sound like pussies.

THE MEN: TO KILL!
(PAVLO, *sensing* PIERCE, *hurriedly opens his footlocker, digs out a book, which he tries to pretend to read.*)

PIERCE: Look at you. Ohhh, you know how much beer I hadda drink to get fucked up on three-two beer? Hummel, look at me.

You think it's neat to be a squad leader? It's not neat to be a squad leader.
(PAVLO *reads from the little book*.)
I hear you got beat up this afternoon.

PAVLO: I got a blanket party.

PIERCE: You're in my squad and other guys in my squad beat you, man; I feel like I oughta do somethin'. I'm older, see. Been to college a little; got a wife. And I'm here to tell you, even with all I seen, sometimes you are unbelievable, Hummel.

PAVLO: I don't care. I don't care.

PIERCE: I mean, I worry about you and the shit you do, man.

PAVLO: You do what you want, Pierce.

PIERCE: I mean, that's why people are after you, Hummel. That's why they fuck with you.

PAVLO: I'm trying to study my Code a Conduct, Pierce, you mind? It's just not too damn long to the proficiency test. Maybe you oughta be studyin' your Code a Conduct too, insteada sneakin' off to drink at the PX.

PIERCE: I wanna know how you got those rocks down your rifle. It's a two-mile walk out to the rifle range, and you got rocks in your barrel when we get there. That's what I'm talkin' about.

PAVLO: I don't know how that happened.

PIERCE: And every fight you get into, you do nothin' but dance, man. Round in a circle, bobbin' and weavin' and gettin' smacked in the mouth. Man, you oughta at least try and hit somebody. (*And then, suddenly, strangely, he is laughing.*) Jesus Christ, Hummel, what's wrong with you? We're in the shower and I tell you to maybe throw a punch once in a while, step with it, pivot,

so you try it right there on that wet floor and damn near kill yourself smashin' into a wall.

PAVLO: Fuck you, Pierce.

PIERCE: Fuck you, Hummel.
(*Silence.*)

PAVLO: You know somethin', Pierce. My name ain't even really
Pavlo Hummel. It's Michael Hummel. I had it legally changed. I
had my name changed.

PIERCE: You're puttin' me on.

PAVLO: No, no, and someday, see, my father's gonna say to me,
"Michael, I'm so sorry I ran out on you," and I'm gonna say, "I'm
not Michael, Asshole. I'm not Michael anymore." Pierce? You
weren't with those guys who beat up on me, were you?

PIERCE: No.
(PAVLO *begins making his bunk.*)

ARDELL: Sometimes I look at you, I don't know what I think I'm
seein', but it sooo simple. You black on the inside. In there where
you live, you that awful hurtin' black so you can't see yourself no
way. Not up or down or in or out.

SGT. TOWER: (*down from the platform, he moves among the men*)
There ain't no army in the world got a shorter bayonet than this
one we got. Maneuverability. It the only virtue. You got to get inside that big long knife that other man got. What is the spirit of
the bayonet?

THE MEN: TO KILL!

SGT. TOWER: You sound like pussies.

THE MEN: TO KILL!

SGT. TOWER: You sound like slits.

THE MEN: TO KILL!

SGT. TOWER: EN GARDE!

THE MEN: AGGGH!

SGT. TOWER: LONG THRUST, PARRY LEFT . . . WHOOO-OOO!
(And the men growl and move, one of them stumbling, falling down, clumsy, embarrassed.)
Where you think you are? You think you in the movies? This here real life, Gen'lmen. You actin' like there ain't never been a war in this world. Don't you know what I'm sayin'? You got to want to put this steel into a man. You got to want to cut him, hurt him, make him die. You got to want to feel the skin and muscle come apart with the push you give. It come to you in the wood. RECOVER AND HOLD!

THE MEN: AGGGH!
(They yell and growl with each thrust. Another falls, gets up.)

SGT. TOWER: EN GARDE

THE MEN: AGGGH!

SGT. TOWER: Lookin' good, lookin' good. Only you ain't mean.
(The men growl.)
How come you ain't mean?
(The men growl.)
HORIZONTAL BUTT-STROKE SERIES, WHOOO!
(And they move, making the thrust, recovery, upper-cutting butt stroke, horizontal butt stroke, and downward slash. The growling and yelling get louder.)
Look at you; look at you. Ohhh, but you men put into my mind one German I saw in the war. I got one bullet left, don't think I want to shoot it, and here come this goddamned big-assed German. "Agggghhhh," I yell to him and it a challenge and he ac-

cept. "Agggghhhh," he say to me and set hisself and I just shoot him. Boom! Ohhh, he got a look on his face like I never saw before in my life. He one baffled motherfucker, Jim.
(*Without command, the men begin to march.*)

ARDELL: (*singing*) ONCE A WEEK I GET TO TOWN . . .

THE MEN: THEY SEE ME COMIN', THEY ALL LAY DOWN.

ARDELL: IF I HAD A LOWER I.Q. . . .
(*All are marching, exiting.*)

THE MEN: I COULD BE A SERGEANT TOO.

SGT. TOWER: LORD HAVE MERCY, I'M SO BLUE. . . .

THE MEN: LORD HAVE MERCY, I'M SO BLUE. . . .

SGT. TOWER: IT SIX MORE WEEKS TILL I BE THROUGH. . . .

THE MEN: IT SIX MORE WEEKS TILL I BE THROUGH.

SGT. TOWER: SOUND OFF!

THE MEN: ONE—TWO.
(BURNS, PIERCE, *and another soldier enter the barracks area still singing, as others are exiting, and these three men set up a crap game on a footlocker.*)

SGT. TOWER: SOUND AGAIN!

THE MEN: THREE—FOUR.
(PAVLO, HINKLE, *and others enter.*)

SGT. TOWER: COUNT CADENCE, COUNT.

THE MEN: ONE, TWO, THREE, FOUR. ONE, TWO, THREE, FOUR. ONE, TWO, THREE, FOUR.
(*And they are all spread about the barracks, reading, sleeping.*)

PAVLO: (to HINKLE, *as the crap game goes on nearby*) Can you imagine that, Hinkle? Just knowin'. Seein' nothin' but bein' sure enough to gun down two people. They had TNT on 'em; they was stupid slopeheads. That Sergeant Tinden saved everybody's life. I get made anything but infantry, I'm gonna fight it, man. I'm gonna fight it. You wanna go infantry with me, Hinkle? You're infantry and good at it too, you're your own man. I'm gonna wear my uniform everywhere when I'm home, Hinkle. My mother's gonna be so excited when she sees me. She's just gonna yell. I get nervous when I think about if she should hug me. You gonna hug your mother when you get home?

HINKLE: My mom's a little bitty skinny woman.

PAVLO: I don't know if I should or shouldn't.

HINKLE: What's your mom like?

PIERCE: You tellin' him about your barn-house exploits, Hinkle?

HINKLE: Oh, no.

PIERCE: Hinkle says he screwed sheep. He tellin' you that, Hummel?

PARKER: How about pigs, Hinkle?

HINKLE: Oh, yeh.

KRESS: I'm tellin' you, Parker, it was too much; all that writin' and shit, and runnin' around. They ain't got no right to test you; proficiency test, proficiency test; I don't even know what a proficiency is—goddamn people—crawlin' and writin'—I'm tellin' you they ain't got no right to test you. They get you here, they mess with you—they let you go. Who says they gotta test you?

PIERCE: (*who has the dice and is laying down money*) Who's back, man? I'm shootin' five.

KRESS: I got so nervous in hand-to-hand, I threw a guy against the wall. They flunked me for bein' too rough.

PIERCE: Who's back, man?

KRESS: I'll take three.
 (*He puts down money, while* PARKER *drops a couple of ones.*)
 I get recycled, I'll kill myself, I swear it.
 (*As* PIERCE *is shaking the dice, saying over and over "Karen loves me, Karen loves me."*)
 I'll cut off my ear.

PIERCE: (*throwing the dice*) Karen says I'm *good!*

KRESS: Goddamn! Shit! How they do it again, Parker?

PARKER: Pierce, you're incredible.

KRESS: Parker!

PARKER: They add up your scores, man; your PT, plus your rifle, plus the score they got today. Then they divide by three. (*Throwing down a five*) You lettin' it ride, Pierce?

PIERCE: Karen loves me.

KRESS: (*putting in money*) Where they get the three?

PARKER: There's three events, man.

PIERCE: (*throwing the dice*) Karen says, "I know the *road!*"

KRESS: You fucking asshole.

PARKER: Goddamnit, Pierce!

PIERCE: Who wants me? Back man's got no heart. Shootin' twenty I come seven or eleven—double or nothin'. Whose twenty says I can't come for all out of the gate? . . .
 (*A soldier enters on the run.*)

SOLDIER: Tower's right behind me; he's got the scores.

(*General commotion as they hide the dice and the money, and* SGT. TOWER *strides across the stage and enters their area.*)

PIERCE: TENHUT!
(*All come to attention before their bunks.*)

SGT. TOWER: AT EASE!
(*Men to parade rest.*)
Gen'lmen. It's truth-and-consequences time. The sad tidings and (*handing a paper to* PIERCE *for him to post*) the glad tidings. You got two men in this platoon didn't make it. They Burn and Kress. They gonna have to stay here eight more weeks, and if they as dumb as it look, maybe eight more after that and eight fuckin' more. The rest a you people, maybe you ain't got no spectacular qualities been endowed upon my mind, but you goin' home when you figured. (*He turns, leaving.*)

PIERCE: TENHUT!

SGT. TOWER: Carry on.
(*They are silent.* KRESS *stands. All start talking and yelling at once.*)

PIERCE: Lemme holler . . . just one . . . time, lemme holler . . .

HINKLE: Mother, Mother, make my bed!

A SOLDIER: (*at the bulletin board*) Me! My name! Me!

PIERCE: AGGGGGGGGGHHHHHHHHHHHHHHHHHHHHAAAA!

PARKER: Lemme just pack my bags!

HENDRIX: (*entering with civilian clothes, shirt and trousers on a hanger, hat on his head*) Lookee—lookee—

HINKLE: What're them funny clothes?

PIERCE: CIVILIAN CLOTHES! CIVILIAN—

HINKLE: CI-WHO-LIAN?

PIERCE: PEOPLE OUTSIDE, MAN! THAT'S WHY THEY AIN'T ALL FUNNY AND GREEN, BECAUSE YOU'RE OUTSIDE WHEN YOU WEAR 'EM. YOU'RE BACK ON THE BLOCK, BACK IN THE WORLD!

PAVLO: (*standing on his bed*) DON'T NOBODY HEAR ME CALLIN' "KRESS!" (*He has said the name during the yelling.*) I think we oughta tell him how sorry we are he didn't make it. I'm gonna. I'm gonna tell him. I'm sorry Kress, that you're gonna be recycled and you're not goin' home. I think we're all sorry. I bet it's kinda like gettin' your head caught in a blanket, the way you feel. It's a bad feelin', I bet, and I think I understand it even if I am goin' back where there's lights and it's pretty. I feel sorry for you, Kress, I just wanna laugh, I feel so sorry—
(*And* KRESS, *leaping, pushes him.* PAVLO *staggers backward.*)
Sonofabitch, what're you—SONOFABITCH!
(*He swings a wild right hand. They flail and crash about.* KRESS *grabs* PAVLO's *wrist, drawing him forward into a hammer lock.*)

KRESS: Down. (*Then lifting*) Don't you hear me? Down, I'm sayin'. Don't you hear me? Thata boy. . . . Called crawlin'. . . .
(*And* PAVLO *is thrown to the floor,* KRESS *on top of him.*)
You got the hang of it . . . now. . . . Crawlin'. . . . Yeh. Now I'm gonna ask you something? Okay?

PAVLO: . . . okay . . .

KRESS: What I'd like to know is who is it in this platoon steals money from his buddies? Who is it don't know how to talk decent to nobody? and don't have one goddamn friend? Who is that person? You tell me, Hummel? The name a that person passed his test today by cheatin'.

PAVLO: I don't . . . know . . .

KRESS: (*working the arm*) Who?

PAVLO: No—
(*And the arm is twisted again.*)
Stop him, somebody. Pierce. You're my squad leader, Pierce.
Ohhhh . . . Pierce, please . . . Aggghhhh . . . Pierce . . .

KRESS: WHO?
(*And* PAVLO *yells.*)

PIERCE: Ease off a little. . . .

KRESS: I CAN'T HEAR YOU!

PIERCE: Kress, I—

PAVLO: HUMMEL!

KRESS: WHAT? WHAT?

PAVLO: HUMMEL! HUMMEL!

KRESS: WHAT?

PAVLO: HUMMEL! HUMMEL! He did 'em. All of those things.
All of 'em. He cheated. He cheated. HUMMEL! HUM—

PIERCE: Kress, goddamnit. GODDAMNIT! (*Leaping, he lifts* KRESS
away from PAVLO *and throws him sideways.*)

KRESS: What? What you want, Corporal? Don't mess with me,
man. (*Staring at* PIERCE, *who is between him and* PAVLO, KRESS
backs away, yet he rages.) Don't mess with Kress. Not when he's
feelin' bad. He'll kill ya, honest to God. He'll pee in your dead
mouth.
(*And* PAVLO *rushes at* KRESS, *howling.*)

PIERCE: Noooooooooo. (*Seizes* PAVLO, *pushing him back.*)

PAVLO: (*as* KRESS *storms out and the other soldiers follow in an
effort to console him*) I'm all right. I'm all right. I do all right!

PIERCE: Will you listen to me, man; you're goin' home; not Kress. You got him.

PAVLO: Fucking asshole!

PIERCE: Will you listen? (*Shoving* PAVLO, *scolding him*) You gotta learn to think, Hummel. You gotta start puttin' two and two together so they fit. You beat him; you had ole Kress beat and then you fixed it so you hadda lose. You went after him so he hadda be able to put you down.

PAVLO: I just wanted to let him know what I thought.

PIERCE: No, no!

PAVLO: He had no call to hit me like that. I was just talkin'—

PIERCE: You dared him, man.

PAVLO: You shoulda stopped him, that's the problem. You're the squad leader. That's just this whole damn army messin' with me and it ain't ever gonna end but in shit. How come you're a squad leader? Who the fuck are you? I'm not gonna get a chance at what I want. Not ever. Nothin' but shit. They're gonna mess with me—make a clerk outta me or a medic or truck driver, a goddamn moron—or a medic—a nurse—a fuckin' Wac with no tits—or a clerk, some little goddamn twerp of a guy with glasses and no guts at all. So don't gimme shit about what I done, Pierce, it's what you done and done and didn't—
(*During this whole thing*, PIERCE *has moved about straightening the bunks and footlockers, and* PAVLO, *in growing desperation, has followed him. Now* PIERCE *in disgust, starts to leave.*)
That's right; keep on walkin' away from your duties, keep—

PIERCE: You're happy as a pig in shit, I don't know why I keep thinkin' you ain't.

PAVLO: I am not.

PIERCE: Up to your eyeballs!

PAVLO: I'm gonna kill myself, Pierce! (*It bursts out of him.*)

PIERCE: If you weren't in my squad, I'd spit in your face. . . .
(*He pivots and goes off after* KRESS *and the other soldiers.*)

PAVLO: (*rocking backward, then bowing forward*) Fuck you, fuck
you.
(*He is alone and yelling after them as* ARDELL *enters.*)
I hate you goddamn people!

ARDELL: I know.

PAVLO: Ardell.
(*At his footlocker,* PAVLO *rummages.*)

ARDELL: I know. I know. All your life like a river and there's no
water all around—this emptiness—you gotta fill it. Gotta get
water. You dive, man, you dive off a stone wall (PAVLO *has a
canteen and paper bag in his hands.*) into the Hudson River
waitin' down dark under you. For a second, it's all air . . . so
free. . . . Do you know the distance you got to fall? You think
you goin' up. Don't nobody fall up, man. Nobody.

PAVLO: What is it? I want to know what it is. The thing that sergeant saw to make him know to shoot that kid and old man. I
want to have it, know it, be it.

ARDELL: I know.

PAVLO: When?

ARDELL: Soon.

PAVLO: If I could be bone, Ardell; if I could be bone. In my deepest
part or center, if I could be bone.
(*Taking a bottle from the bag, he takes pills, washes them down*

with water, and crawls under the covers of his bunk, while Sgt.
tower, *already on the platform, speaks.*)

Sgt. tower: Now I'm gonna tell you gen'lmen how you find you
way when you lost. You better listen up. What you do, you find
the North Star and the North Star show you true north accurate
all year round. You look for the Big Dipper and there are two
stars at the end a that place in the stars that look like the bowl on
the dipper and they called the pointer. They them two stars at
where the water would come out the dipper if it had some water
and out from them on a straight line you gonna see this big damn
star and that the North Star and it show you north and once you
know that, Gen'lmen, you can figure the rest. You ain't lost no
more.

The men: (*beginning to enter to position themselves for the next
scene*) YESSSS, SERGEANT!

Sgt. tower: I hope so. I do hope so. . . .
(Pierce, Parker, *and others set up a card game on a footlocker.*)

Kress: (*passing the bunk where* Pavlo *is a lump beneath his blanket*) I wonder what the fuckin', chimney-shittin' shit is doin'
now?
(Hinkle *settles curiously on the bunk next to* Pavlo.)

Parker: You gonna see me Pierce?

Pierce: And raise you.

Parker: Ten ta one, he's under there jerkin' off.

Hinkle: (*bending near to* Pavlo) No, no, he's got this paper bag
and everything smells funny. Y'all some kind of acrobat, Hummel?

Kress: He's got some chick's bicycle seat in a bag, man.

Hinkle: And the noises he's makin'.

PIERCE: Poor pathetic motherfucker.

KRESS: He ain't pathetic.

PIERCE: He is too.

PARKER: Under there pounding his pud.

KRESS: You musta not seen many pathetic people, you think he's pathetic.

PIERCE: I seen plenty.

PARKER: Call.

PIERCE: (*laying down his cards*) Full boat. Jacks and threes!

PARKER: Jesus Goddamn Christ.

HINKLE: I was wonderin' can ah look in you all's bag, Hummel? (*He reaches under the blanket.*)

PARKER: Jesus Goddamn Christ.

HINKLE: Ohhhh . . . it's . . . you been sniffin' airplane glue. . . . (*And he laughs, turns toward the others.*) Hummel's been sniffin' airplane glue.

KRESS: ATTAWAY TO GO, HUMMEL.

HINKLE: (*holding the bottle*) An' where's all the asp'rins . . . ?

PAVLO: Tumtum Pavlo.

HINKLE: You all kiddin' me.

PAVLO: No.

HINKLE: Y'all ate 'em?

PAVLO: Yeah!

HINKLE: Hey y'all. . . . (*To* PAVLO) Was it full?
(PAVLO *attempts to sit up, flops back down.*)

PAVLO: Tippy top.

HINKLE: Hummel just ate—(*examining the bottle*) one hundred asp'rins. Hummel just ate 'em.

KRESS: Attaway to go, Hummel.

PARKER: Nighty-night.

HINKLE: Won't it hurt him, Pierce?

KRESS: Kill him probably.

PARKER: Hopefully.

KRESS: Hinkle, ask him did he use chocolate syrup?

HINKLE: He's breathin' kinda funny, Pierce, don't you think?

KRESS: Hummel does everything funny.

PIERCE: (*beginning to deal*) Five cards, Gen'lmen; jacks or better.

HINKLE: Pierce.

PIERCE: Hummel, you stop worryin' that boy. Tell him no headache big enough in the world, you're gonna take a hundred asp'rins. (*Slight pause.* KRESS *begins imitating* PAVLO's *odd breathing.*) How come everybody's all the time bustin' up my good luck.

BURNS: Shit, man, he took a hundred asp'rins, he wouldn't be breathin' period.

RYAN: Sounds like a goddamn tire pump.

BURNS: Hummel, TENHUT!

PIERCE: Hummel, you just jivin' 'cause you don't know what else to do, or did you eat them pills?

BURNS: Tryin' to blow himself up like a balloon . . . drift away. Float outa the fort.
(PARKER *begins to imitate* KRESS *imitating* PAVLO's *breathing.*)

RYAN: He's fakin', man.

BURNS: How you know?

RYAN: They'd kill you like a bullet.

HINKLE: Get over here, Pierce!

KRESS: How come the army don't throw him out, Parker?

PARKER: Army likes weird people, Kress.

KRESS: I hate weird people.

PARKER: Sure you do.

KRESS: Weird chimney-shittin', friendless, gutless, cheatin' . . .
(PIERCE *is examining* PAVLO. PAVLO *makes a sound and then begins to cough.*)

PIERCE: NOOO! NOT IN MY SQUAD, YOU MOTHER. GET UP!
(*He is trying to get* PAVLO *to his feet; another soldier is helping.*)
YOU SILLY SONOFABITCH. We got to walk him.
(PAVLO *is feebly resisting.*)
Hinkle, doubletime it over the orderly room.

HINKLE: Right.

PIERCE: Tell 'em we got a guy over here took a hundred asp'rins, they should get an ambulance.

HINKLE: (*turning to head for the door*) Right.

KRESS: Hinkle!

HINKLE: (*hesitating*) Yeh!

KRESS: Pick me up a Coke on your way back.

PIERCE: Hold him steady. I think we oughta get him outside, more air.

ARDELL: (*standing over near the base of the tower*) Pavlo. You gonna have ambulances and sirens and all kinds a good shit. Ain't you somethin'? It gonna be a celebration. C'mon over here.
(*As if* ARDELL'*s voice draws them,* PIERCE *and the other soldier lug* PAVLO *toward the tower: they lay him down, remove all clothes from him but his underwear and T-shirt.*)
Pavlo! Look at you. You got people runnin' around like a bunch a fools. That what you wanted? Yeah, that what you want! They sayin' "Move him. Lift him. Take his shirt off." They walkin' you around in the air. They all thinkin' about you, anyway. But what you doin' but cryin'? You always think you signifyin' on everybody else, but all you doin' is showin' your own fool self. You don't know nothin' about showboatin', Pavlo. You hear me? Now you get on up off that floor. You don't get up, man, I blow a motherfuckin' whistle up side you head. I blow it loud. YOU THINK YOU GOT A MOTHERFUCKIN' WHISTLE IN YOUR BRAIN.
(PIERCE *and the other man have turned away. Everything* PAVLO *does is performed in the manner of a person alone: as if* ARDELL *is a voice in his head. The light perhaps suggests this.* KRESS, *all others, are frozen.*)
I'm tellin' you how to be. That right.
(PAVLO *slumps back down.*)
Ohhh, don't act so bad; you actin', man. What you expect, you go out get you head smokin' on all kinds a shit sniffin' that goddamn glue, then fallin' down all over yourself. Man, you lucky you alive, carryin' on like that.
(PAVLO *is doubled over.*)

Ain't doin' you no good you wish you dead, 'cause you ain't, man. Get on up.

(PAVLO *takes a deep breath and stands.*)

You go in the latrine now, get you a bromo, you wash off you face . . .

(PAVLO *exits, staggering.*)

Then get you ass right back out here. And you don't need no shave, man, you ain't got no beard no ways. (*Sees* PAVLO'*s uniform lying on the floor.*) What kinda shit this? Your poor ole Sarge see this, he sit down on the ground and he cry, man. Poor ole Sarge, he work himself like he crazy tryin' ta teach you so you can act like a man. An' what you do? (*Turning suddenly, yelling after* PAVLO) *Pavlo!* You diddlin' in there, you take this long. And you bring out you other uniform. We gonna shape you up.

(PAVLO *enters carrying military dress uniform, in a clothing bag, which he hangs on the tower.*)

It daytime, man, you goin' out struttin'. You goin' out standin' tall. You tear it open. Trousers first, man. Dig 'em out.

(PAVLO, *having selected the trousers, moves as if to put them on.*)

NOOOO! Damnit, ain't you got no sense at all?

(*He has rushed to* PAVLO, *lifted the trouser bottoms off the floor.*)

You drag 'em all over the floor like that, man, they gonna look like shit. Get on this footlocker.

(*Now* PIERCE *and the other soldier move in to help* PAVLO *dress. All is ease now.*)

That right, that it. Make 'em look like they got no notion at all what it like ta be dirty. Be clean, man. Yeh. Now the shirt.

(*It is a ritual now:* PAVLO *must exert no effort whatsoever as he is transformed.*)

Lemme look you brass over. Ain't too bad. It do. Lemme just touch 'em up a little. (*He brushes with his handkerchief at the brass.*) You put on you tie. Make you a big knot. Big knot make you look tall. Where you boots?

(*And, finished with the jacket,* PIERCE *and the other soldier move to the boots.*)

Where you boots? An' you got some shades? Lemme get you some shades. (*Walking backward*) And tuck that tie square. Give her little loop she come off you throat high and pretty.

(As ARDELL exits, PAVLO sits on the footlocker. PIERCE and the
other soldier kneel to put the boots onto him.)
HUT . . . HOO . . . HEE . . . HAW. . . . (Singing) IF I HAD
A LOWER I.Q.

ALL THE MEN: IF I HAD A LOWER I.Q.

ARDELL: I COULD BE A SERGEANT TOO.

THE MEN: I COULD BE A SERGEANT TOO!
(Across the back of the stage, two men march.)

ARDELL: LORD HAVE MERCY, I'M SO BLUE.
(The two men do an intricate drill-team step.)

THE MEN: IT FOUR MORE WEEKS TILL I BE THROUGH.
(The two men spin their rifles and strike the ground smartly with
the butts, as ARDELL returns, carrying a pair of sunglasses.)

ARDELL: You gonna be over, man, I finish with you.
(PAVLO stands up fully dressed.)
You gonna be the fat rat, man; you eatin' cheese.
(ARDELL moves about PAVLO, examining him, guiding him toward
the tower. As ARDELL talks, PAVLO climbs the tower and stands on
it; ARDELL joins him.)
OVER, BABY! Ardell can make you straight; you startin' ta look
good now; you finish up, you gonna be the fattest rat, man, eatin'
the finest cheese. Put you in good company, you wear that uniform. You go out walkin' on the street, people know you, they say,
"Who that?" Somebody else say, "Man, he straight. He look
good." Somebody else say, "That boy got pride." Yeh, baby,
Pavlo, you gonna be over, man. You gonna be that fat fat rat,
eatin' cheese, down on his knees, yeh, baby, doffin' his red cap,
sayin', "Yes, Massa." You lookee out there.
(Both are atop the tower. ARDELL is a little behind PAVLO and
gesturing outward. PAVLO stands. He has sunglasses on.)
Who you see in that mirror, man? Who you see? That ain't no
Pavlo Hummel. Noooo, man. That somebody else. An' he somethin' else.

(PAVLO *is looking.*)
Ohhh, you goin' out on the street, they gonna see you. Ardell tellin'
you and Ardell know. You back on the block an' you goin' out
struttin'. An' they gonna cry when they see you. You so pretty,
baby, you gonna make 'em cry. You tell me you name, you pretty
baby!

PAVLO: (*snapping to attention*) PAVLO MOTHERHUMPIN'
HUMMEL!

Blackout.

ACT TWO

Set changes: The debris of the bar wall remains upstage and stage right, though the barrel and crate are gone. Downstage and stage right there is a larger, more detailed version of the bar: metal wall, barrel used as table, two crates used as chairs, a footlocker off to the side, beer cans and bottles scattered about. The drill sergeant's tower remains. Far downstage and just a little left of center, a telephone sits on the floor near another footlocker. Stage left of the tower there is an army cot with a green but non-military bedspread.

The lights come up on the men in formation. PAVLO is still atop the tower, standing, looking out as he was. The men face upstage. Standing at the rear of the set are the CAPTAIN and SGT. TOWER. They face the men. Downstage stands MICKEY, PAVLO's half-brother. MICKEY wears slacks, T-shirt, shoes. He is standing as if looking into a mirror about to comb his hair; however he does not move. The CAPTAIN, stiffly formal, addresses the troops.

CAPTAIN: As we enter now the final weeks of your basic training, I feel a certain obligation as your company commander to speak to you of the final purpose of what we have done here. Normally this is more difficult to make clear. Pleiku, Vietnam, is the purpose of what we have done here. A few nights ago, mortar and machine-gun fire in a sneak attack in the highlands killed nine Americans and wounded a hundred and forty serving at our camp there in Pleiku. In retaliation, a bombing of the North has begun, and it will continue until the government of Hanoi, battered and reeling, goes back to the North.

SGT. TOWER: Company, fall out!

(*And the troops scatter. Music starts from* MICKEY'S *radio.* PAVLO *descends, picks up duffle bag and AWOL bag.* MICKEY *starts combing his hair.*)

PAVLO: Hey Mickey, it's me. I'm home! It's me. I'm home, I'm home.

MICKEY: Pavlo. Whata you say, huh? Hey, hey, what happened? You took so long. You took a wrong turn, huh? Missed your stop and now you come home all dressed like a conductor. What happened? You were down in that subway so long they put you to work? Huh? Man, you look good though; you look good. Where were you again?

PAVLO: Georgia.

MICKEY: Hot as a bitch, right?

PAVLO: No. Cold.

MICKEY: In Georgia?

PAVLO: Yeh, it was real cold; we used to hide out in the furnace room every damn chance we ever got.

MICKEY: Hey, you want a drink? Damn that don't make much sense does it?

PAVLO: What?

MICKEY: They send you to Georgia for the winter and it's like a witch's tit. Can you imagine that? A witch's tit? Eeeeeeggggggg. Puts ice on your tongue. That ever happened to me, man, I'd turn in my tool. Ain't you gonna ask about the ole lady? How's she doin' and all that, cause she's doin' fine. Pickin' and plantin' daisies. Doin' fine.

(*And* PAVLO *laughs, shaking his head, taking the drink* MICKEY *has made him.*)

Whatsa matter? You don't believe yo-yos can be happy? Psychotics have fun, man. You oughta know that.

PAVLO: I just bet she's climbin' some kinda wall. Some kinda wall and she's pregnant again, she thinks, or you are or me or somebody.

MICKEY: Noo, man, noo, it's everybody else now. Only nonfamily.

PAVLO: (laughing, loudly) THAT'S ME AND YOU! NONFAMILY MOTHERFUCKERS!

MICKEY: All the dogs and women of the world!

PAVLO: Yeh, yeh, all the guys in the barracks used to think I was a little weird, so I'd—

MICKEY: You are a little weird—

PAVLO: Yeh, yeh, I'd tell 'em. "You think I'm weird, you oughta see my brother, Mickey. He don't give a big rat's ass for nothin' or nobody."

MICKEY: And did you tell 'em about his brains, too. And his wit and charm. The way his dick hangs to his knees—about his eighteen thou a year? Did you tell 'em all that sweet shit?

PAVLO: They said they hoped you died of all you got.
(MICKEY has been dressing as they speak, and now he wears a shirt and tie and suit coat.)

MICKEY: How come the troops were thinkin' you weird? You doin' that weird stuff again. You say "Georgia" and "the army." For all I know you been downtown in the movies for the last three months and you bought that goddamn uniform at some junk shop.

PAVLO: I am in the army.

MICKEY: How do I know?

PAVLO: I'm tellin' you.

MICKEY: But you're a fuckin' liar; you're a fuckin' myth-maker.

PAVLO: I gotta go to Vietnam, Mickey.

MICKEY: Vietnam don't even exist.

PAVLO: I gotta go to it.

MICKEY: Arizona, man; that's where you're goin'. Wyoming.

PAVLO: Look at me! I'm different! I'm different than I was! (*This is with fury.*) I'm not the same anymore. I was an asshole. I'm not an asshole anymore. I'm not an asshole anymore! (*Silence as he stares in anguish.*) I came here to forgive you. I don't need you anymore.

MICKEY: You're a goddamn cartoon, you know that.

PAVLO: (*rapidly, in a rush of words*) I'm happier now than I ever was, I got people who respect me. Lots of 'em. There was this guy Kress in my outfit. We didn't hit it off . . . and he called me out . . . he was gonna kill me, he said. Everybody tried to stop me because this guy had hurt a lot of people already and he had this uncle who'd taught him all about fightin' and this uncle has been executed in San Quentin for killing people. We went out back of the barracks. It went on and on, hitting and kicking. It went on and on; all around the barracks. The crowd right with us. And then . . . all of a sudden . . . this look came into his eye . . . and he just stopped . . . and reached down to me and hugged me. He just hugged and hugged me. And that look was in all their eyes. All the soldiers. I don't need you anymore, Mickey. I got real brothers now.

MICKEY: You know . . . if my father hadn't died, you wouldn't even exist.

PAVLO: No big thing! We got the same mother; that's shit enough. I'm gonna shower and shave, okay? Then we can go out drinkin'.

MICKEY: All those one-night stands. You ever think of that? Ghostly pricks. I used to hear 'em humpin' the ole whore. I probably had my ear against the wall the night they got you goin'.

PAVLO: (*after a slight silence*) You seen Joanna lately?

MICKEY: Joanna?

PAVLO: Joanna. My ole girl. I thought maybe she probably killed herself and it was in the papers. You know, on account of my absence. But she probably did it in secret.

MICKEY: No doubt.

PAVLO: No doubt.

MICKEY: Ain't she the one who got married? I think the ole lady tole me Joanna got married and she was gonna write you a big letter all about it. Sure she was. Anyway, since we're speaking of old girls and pregnant people, I've got to go to this little party tonight. Got a good new sweet young thing and she thinks I'm better than her daddy. I've had a run of chicks lately you wouldn't believe, Pavlo. They give away ass like Red Cross girls dealin' out doughnuts. I don't understand how I get half a what I get. Oh, yeh, old lady comes and goes around here. She's the same old witch.

PAVLO: I'm gonna go see Joanna. I'll call her up. Use the magic fuckin' phone to call her up.

MICKEY: I'll give you a call later on.

PAVLO: I'll be out, man. I'll be out on the street.

MICKEY: (*exiting*) You make yourself at home.
(*And soldiers appear far upstage, marching forward, as* ARDELL, *off to the side, counts cadence, and other soldiers appear at various points about the stage.*)

ARDELL: HUT . . . HOO . . . HEE . . .

SGT. TOWER: (*entering as* PAVLO, *glancing at him, exits*) SAW SOME STOCKIN'S ON THE STREET . . .

THE MEN: WISHED I WAS BETWEEN THOSE FEET.

SGT. TOWER: WISHED I WAS BETWEEN THOSE FEET. HONEY, HONEY, DON'T YOU FROWN.

THE MEN: I LOVE YOU DRUNK AND LAYIN' DOWN.

SGT. TOWER: STANDIN' TALL AND LOOKIN' GOOD. WE BE-LONG IN HOLLYWOOD.
(*He is atop the tower, as the men come to a stomping halt.*)

THE MEN: WE BELONG IN HOLLYWOOD.

SGT. TOWER: Take five, Gen'lmen, but the smokin' lamp is not lit.
(PAVLO *is there, off to the side, disheveled, carrying a pint whiskey bottle. He undresses, speaking his anger, throwing his uniform down. The men are relaxing a little.*)

PAVLO: Stupid fuckin' uniform. Miserable hunk a green shit. Don't we go to good bars—why don't you work for me? And there's this really neat girl there sayin' to me how do I like bein' a robot? How do I like bein' one in a hundred million robots all marchin' in a row? Don't anybody understand about uniforms? I ain't no robot. You gotta have braid . . . ribbons and patches all about what you did. I got nothin'. What's so complicated? I look like nothin' cause I done nothin'. (*In his T-shirt and underwear, he kneels now with the bottle.*)

SGT. TOWER: Gen'lmen, you best listen up real close now, even though you restin'. Gonna tell you little bit about what you do you comin' through the woods, you find a man wounded in his chest. You gotta seal it off. That wound workin' like a valve, pullin' in air, makin' pressure to collapse that man's lung; you get him to breathe out and hold his breath. You apply the metal-foil side a the waterproof wrapping of the first-aid dressing, tie it off. Gonna hafta tie it extra; you use your poncho, his poncho, you get strips of cloth. You tear up you own damn shirt. I don't care. You let that boy have his lung. You let him breathe. AM I UNDERSTOOD?

THE MEN: YES, SERGEANT!

SGT. TOWER: FALL IN!
(*The men leap to attention.*)
DISMISSED!
(*And the troops run off, leaving* PAVLO *alone, in his underwear, near the bed.*)

PAVLO: I wanna get laid . . . Bed . . . Bottle. (*Pause.*) I wanna get laid! I wanna get laid, Phone! You goddamn stuck-up motherin' phone. Need a piece of ass, Bed. Lemme walk on over to that phone. Lemme crawl on over to that phone. Lemme get there. Gonna outflank you. Goddamn army ant. Thas right. Thas right. Hello. (*He has crawled drunkenly to the phone and is dialing now.*) This is Pavlo, Joanna. Hello. Certainly of course. I'd be glad to screw your thingy with my thingy. BSZZZZZZZ . . .

WOMAN'S VOICE: (*over the phone*) Hello?

PAVLO: BSZZZZZZZZZZZZZZZZZZZZZ . . .

WOMAN'S VOICE: Hello?

PAVLO: Little bitty creature . . . hello, hello. . . .

WOMAN'S VOICE: Who is this?

PAVLO: Hollering . . . hollering . . . poor creature . . . locked inside, can't get out, can't—

WOMAN'S VOICE: Pavlo?

PAVLO: Do you know me? Yes. Yes, it is me, Pavlo. Pavlo Hummel. . . . Joanna. . . . And I am calling to ask how can you have lived to this day away from me?

WOMAN'S VOICE: Pavlo, listen.

PAVLO: Yes. I am. I do.

WOMAN'S VOICE: This isn't Joanna.

PAVLO: What?

WOMAN'S VOICE: This is Mrs. Sorrentino, Pavlo. Joanna isn't here.

PAVLO: What?

WOMAN'S VOICE: I said "Joanna isn't here," Pavlo. This is her mother; may I have her call you?

PAVLO: What?

Woman's VOICE: I said, "May I have her call you?" Or did you just call to say hello?

PAVLO: Who is this?

WOMAN'S VOICE: Pavlo, what's wrong with you?

PAVLO: Who are you? I don't know who this is. You get off the line, goddamnit, you hear me, or I'll report you to the telephone company. I'll report you to Bell Telephone. And G.E., too. And the Coke Company and General Motors.
(*The woman hangs up the phone.*)
You'll be hurtin' baby. I report you to all those people. Now you tell me where she is. Where is she?
(*And behind him a light pops on, a table lamp. His mother, a small dark-haired woman, plump, fashionably dressed, has been there for some time, sitting in the dark, listening. She begins to speak almost at the same instant the light goes on.*)

MRS. HUMMEL: In Stratford, Connecticut, Pavlo. Pregnant more than likely. Vomiting in the morning. Yes . . . trying to . . . get . . . rid of . . . it. . . . Hello, Pavlo . . . I wrote you that. . . . I wrote you.

(*Silence*)

Hello . . . Pavlo. I wrote you she was married. Why are you calling? Why?

(*Silence.*)

Pavlo? Listen, are you finished on the phone and could we talk a minute? I don't want to interrupt. . . . I only have a few . . . few things to say. They won't take long. I've been working since you've been gone. Did you know?

(*As she continues to talk,* PAVLO *slowly hangs up the telephone and places it on the footlocker.*)

Doing quite well. Quite well indeed. In a department store. Yes. One of the smaller ones. Yes. And we had an awful, awful shock there the other day and that's what I want to tell you about. There's a woman, Sally Kelly, and Ken was her son, in the army like you now, and he went overseas last August. Well, I talked to Sally when I went in at noon and she was in the lunchroom writing a little card to Ken and she let me read it. She knew that you were in the army so she said she was sure I knew the way it was consolation to write a little note. Then about five forty-five, I was working on the shoes and I saw two army officers come up the escalator and talk to one of the other clerks. I never gave them another thought and at six o'clock Sally came through and went down the escalator and made a remark to me and laughed a little and went on down. In about fifteen more minutes, I was waiting on a lady and she said to me, "Isn't that terrible about the lady's son who works downstairs?" I said, "Who?" She said, "The lady who works at your candy department just got word her son was killed in Vietnam." Well, I was really shook when I heard that and I said, "Oh, you must be mistaken. She just went downstairs from her supper hour and I talked to her and she was fine." She said, "Well, that's what I heard on the main floor." Well, I went right to the phone and called the reception desk and they said it was true. That is what happened, this is what I want to tell you. The officers had gone to Sally's house but no one was home so they talked to the neighbors and found out Sally worked at the store. So they went up to our receptionist and asked for our manager. He wasn't in so they asked for one of the men and Tommy Bottle came and they told him they needed his help because they had to tell one of the employees that her son was killed in Vietnam. Tommy really got shook, as you can imagine, and he took the officers to Mr. Brenner's office and closed the door. While they were in there, Sally came out of the lunchroom and came downstairs. Joyce, the girl who is the receptionist, knew by this time and Sally laughed when she went by and said that she better get to work or something like that. Joyce said later on that she could hardly look at her. Anyway, Tommy called the floorman from first floor to come up and he told him what had happened and then he had to go back down to first floor and tell Sally she was wanted in Mr. Brenner's office. She said, "Oh boy, what have I done now?" By the time she got to the fourth floor, the office door was open and she saw the two army men and said, "Oh, dear God, not Kenny." (*Pause.*) A mother . . . and her children should be as a tree and her branches. . . . A mother spends . . . but she gets . . . change. You think me a fool . . . don't you. There are many who do. (*Pause.*) He joined to be a mechanic and they transferred him to Infantry so he was killed on December first. So you see . . . I know what to expect. I know . . . what you're trying to do.

PAVLO: Who . . . was . . . my father? Where is he?

MRS. HUMMEL: You know that.

PAVLO: No, I want you to tell me.

MRS. HUMMEL: I've already told you.

PAVLO: No, where is he now? What did he look like?

MRS. HUMMEL: I wrote it all in a letter. I put it all in an envelope, I sealed it, mailed it.

PAVLO: I never got it.

MRS. HUMMEL: I think you did.

PAVLO: No!

MRS. HUMMEL: No, you had many fathers, many men, movie men, filmdom's great—all of them, those grand old men of yesteryear,

they were your father. The Fighting Seventy-sixth, do you remember, oh, I remember, little Jimmy, what a tough little mite he
was, and how he leaped upon that grenade, did you see, my God
what a glory, what a glorious thing with his little tin hat.

PAVLO: My real father!

MRS. HUMMEL: He was like them, the ones I showed you in movies,
I pointed them out.

PAVLO: What was his name?

MRS. HUMMEL: I've told you.

PAVLO: No. What was his name? I don't know what it was.

MRS. HUMMEL: Is it my fault you've forgotten?

PAVLO: You never told me.

MRS. HUMMEL: I did. I whispered it in your ear. You were three. I
whispered the whole thing in your ear!

PAVLO: Lunatic!

MRS. HUMMEL: Nooooo!

PAVLO: Insane, hideous person!

MRS. HUMMEL: I've got to go to bed now. I have to get my rest.
(Her back is turned. She is walking to leave him.)

PAVLO: (yelling) I picked this girl up in this bar tonight and when I
took her home and got her to the door and kissed her, her tongue
went into my mouth. I thought that meant she was going to let
me into her apartment. "Don't get hurt," she said, "and get in
touch when you get back; I'd love to see you." She knew I was
going overseas; did you? And then the door was shut and all I
wanted to say was, "What are you doing sticking your tongue in

my mouth and then leaving me, you goddamn stuck-up motherin' bitch." But I didn't say anything.

MRS. HUMMEL: (*as she leaves*) Yes . . . well . . . I'll . . . see you in the morning.

ARDELL: (*who has been watching*) Oh, man, how come? You wanted to get laid, how come you didn't do like the ole Sarge told you steada gettin' all tore up with them walkin' blues? Take you a little money, the ole Sarge say, roll it up longways, put it in your fly, man, so it stickin' out. Then go on walkin' up and down the street, that green stickin' right outa your fly. You get laid. You got that money stickin' outa your fly, you get laid. You get your nut! How come you didn't do that?

OFFICER: (*who has been standing on the rear platform at parade rest*) And the following will depart CONUS twelve August nineteen sixty-six for the Republic of Vietnam on assignment to the Twenty-third Field Hospital. Thomas. Simpson. Horner. Hinkle. Hummel.

PAVLO: I don't wanna be no medic.
(*And the bar music starts. YEN and MAMASAN, an older Vietnamese woman, enter from one side of the stage. SGT. BRISBEY is calling from the other, and then his hospital bed on wheels is pushed on by two soldiers. Meanwhile ARDELL has hauled off the footlocker with the telephone. Now visible on the floor is a pile of clothes, PAVLO's jungle fatigues, which he immediately starts getting into. YEN is at the bar. All this happens nearly simultaneously. MAMASAN, scurrying about, exits.*)

YEN: Hey, GI cheap Charlie, you want one more beer?

JONES: (*offstage*) One Bomniba, one beer.

SGT. BRISBEY: Pavlo.

YEN: (*as JONES, in a bright-colored walking suit, enters*) EEEEEE-aaaaaa? What you talk? One Bomniba, one beer. Same-same, huh? I no stand. What you want?

JONES: (*pursuing her*) (*both are playing, yet both have real anger*) You gimme boocoup now?

YEN: Boocoup what? I don't know what you want. Crazy GI, you dinky dow.

SGT. BRISBEY: *Pavlo.*

PAVLO: (*who is still putting on the fatigues*) I'm in the can, Brisbey. I'll be there in a minute.

ARDELL: He be there, Brisbey.

JONES: You got lips as fat as mine, you know that, Ho?

YEN: Tôi không biêt.

JONES: Shit, you don't know.

YEN: Shit. I can say, too. I know. Shit.
(*And he is reaching for her.*)
No. We fini. Fini. You no talk me no more, you numba fuckin' ten.
(*She bounces away to sit on a crate and look at sheet music.*)

SGT. BRISBEY: Do you know, Pavlo? I saw the metal point of that mine sticking up from the ground just under my foot—I said, "That's a mine. I'm stepping on a mine." And my foot went right on down and I felt the pin sink and heard the first small . . . pop. I jumped . . . like a fool. And up she came right outa the ground. I hit at it with my hand as if to push it away, it came up so slow against my hand. . . . Steel . . . bits . . . of dirt . . .

PAVLO: I'm off duty now, Brisbey.

ARDELL: Ole Brisbey got himself hit by a Bouncin' Betty. That a kind of land mine; you step on it, she jump up to about right here (*indicating his waist*). . . . Then she blow you in half. That why she got that name. Little yellow man dug a hole, put it in, hoped he'd come around. He an old man, damn near; got seventeen years in the army; no legs no more, no balls, one arm. (*A small Vietnamese boy comes running by and grabs* PAVLO's *hand.*)

BOY: Hey, GI, show you numba one! (*He guides him into the whorehouse-bar and leaves him there.*)

PAVLO: (*to* JONES, *who is sitting there drinking a beer*) Hey, what's goin' on?

JONES: What's happenin', man?

MAMASAN: (*returning*) Hello, hello! You come my house, I am glad. Do you want a beer? I have. Do you want a girl? I have. Numba one girl. Numba one. You want?

PAVLO: (*pointing to* MAMASAN) You?

MAMASAN: No, no, I am Mamasan. But I have many girl. You see, maybe you like. Maybe you want short time, huh? Maybe you want long time. I don't know, you tell me. All numba one.

JONES: (*laughs*) Man, don't you believe that ole lady, you just gotta get on and ride. (*Indicating* YEN) Like her. I been. And I'm restin' to go again; an' I don't think it any kinda numba one; but I been outa the world so *damn* long. I jus' close my eyes an' jive my own self—"That ain't no dead person," I say, "that ain't no dead Ho jus' 'cause she layin' so still. I saw her walk in here." I mean, man they so screwed up over here. They got no nature. You understand me, Bro? They got no nature, these women. You—how long you been over here?

PAVLO: Not long; couple a weeks.

JONES: You new then, huh?

PAVLO: Yeh.

JONES: You wanna go? (*Reaching out toward* YEN, *who is across the room, calling to her*) Hey, Ho! C'mon over here!

YEN: You talk me?

JONES: Yeh, Baby, you. C'mon over here. You wanna go, man?

PAVLO: (*taking a seat*) What about the V.D.?

JONES: (*big laugh*) What about it?

YEN: (*approaching with a beer*) I no have. I no sick. No. No sweat, GI. You want short-time me, no sweat.

JONES: Shit, Ho, you insides rotten. You Vietnamese, ain't you? Vietnamese same-same V.D.

YEN: No! No sick! (*As* JONES *grabs her, sets her down on* PAVLO's *lap*) What you do? No.

JONES: I'm jus' tryin' ta help you get some money, Baby. I be you Sportsman. Okay. (*Holding her in place*) You just sit on down an' be nice on the man's lap, pretty soon he ain't gonna be worried 'bout no V.D. If you jus' . . . sorta shift (*he demonstrates*) every now and then. Okay. . . .
(*She is still now and he turns his attention to* PAVLO.)
Now, lemme tell you 'bout it, lemme tell you how it is. It be hot, man. I come from Georgia, and it get hot in Georgia, but it ain't ever been this kinda hot, am I lyin'? An' you gonna be here one year, and that three hundred sixty-five days, so you gonna sweat. Now do you think I'm lyin'?
(YEN *is touching* PAVLO, *rubbing under his shirt.*)

PAVLO: I ain't never sweat so much.

JONES: So that's what I'm sayin'. You gonna be here and you gonna sweat. And you gonna be here and you gonna get V.D.! You worried about sweatin'? Ahhhhh. You grinnin'. So I see I have made my meanin' clear.

(YEN *has been rubbing* PAVLO's *thigh*.)
How you feelin' now? She kinda nice, huh? She kinda soft and nice.

PAVLO: Where you work?

JONES: (*laughs*) Don't you be askin' me where I work. That ain't what you wanna know. I gotta get you straight, my man, gotta get outa here, buy myself some supplies. My ole mom all the time tellin' me, "Don't you go near that PX. You get blown away for sure. Them V.C.s gotta wanna get that PX." Ain't it a world of trouble?

PAVLO: (*to* YEN) What's your name?

YEN: Name me Yen.

PAVLO: Name me Pavlo. Pavlo.

YEN: Paaa-blo.

PAVLO: How much?

JONES: Lord, she says his name, he loves her.

YEN: You want short-time: I ask Mamasan.
(*But* MAMASAN *has been watching*.)

MAMASAN: (*approaching*) Okay. Okay. Yen numba one. I am happy. Five hundred P's.

JONES: Two hundred.

MAMASAN: She very beautiful.

JONES: Two fifty.

MAMASAN: Four hundred, can do. No sweat.

JONES: Mamasan, who you think you jivin'?

MAMASAN: Yen boocoup boy friend! She very love!

JONES: Two fifty.

MAMASAN: (*to* PAVLO) Three hundred twenty. You, huh? Three hundred twenty.

JONES: Pavlo, give her three hundred; tell her things is tough at home, she don't know.

MAMASAN: (*as* PAVLO *hands her the money*) No, no, I talk you three hundred twenty!

JONES: And I talk him three hundred, Mamasan, three hundred!

MAMASAN:(*softly, whiny, to* PAVLO) GI, you be nice; you give Mamasan ten P's more. GI? Ten P's very easy you!

PAVLO: (*to* JONES) How much *is* ten P's, man?

JONES: Eight cents, or about—

PAVLO: Eight cents! Eight cents. Over eight goddamn stupid cents I'm standin' here!

JONES: (*as* PAVLO *is giving more money to* MAMASAN) Man, no!

MAMASAN: (*patting* PAVLO *on the back*) Okay, okay. You numba one—

YEN: (*taking* PAVLO *by the hand toward the bed*) I show you.

JONES: (*as he leaves*) Oh man, deliver me from these green troops; they makin' everybody fat but me.
(*The whistle blows loudly, and the troops come roaring on and into formation, facing the tower.*)

SGT. TOWER: GEN'LMEN!
(*And his voice stops* PAVLO, *who comes to attention kneeling on the bed.* YEN *has jumped onto the bed. As* SGT. TOWER *continues*

his speech, she unbuttons PAVLO's *pants, unbuttons his shirt, takes his pants down—all this as* SGT. TOWER *gives instructions.*)
(*Holding up a rifle*) This an M-sixteen rifle, this the best you country got. Now we got to make you good enough to have it. You got to have feelin' for it, like it a good woman to you, like it you arm, like it you rib. The command is "Right shoulder . . . *harms!*" At the command "harms," raise and carry the rifle diagonally across the body, at the same time grasping it at the balance with the left hand, trigger guard in the hollow of the bone. Then carry the left hand, thumb and fingers extended, to the small of the stock, and cut away smartly, and everything about . . . you, Trainee, is at the position of attention. RIGHT SHOULDER . . . HARMS!

THE MEN: (*performing the drill as* PAVLO *also yells and performs it in pantomime with them*) ONE, TWO, THREE, FOUR.

SGT. TOWER: You got to love this rifle, Gen'lmen, like it you pecker and you love to make love. You got to care about how it is and what can it do and what can it not do, what do it want and need. ORDER HARMS!

THE MEN and PAVLO: ONE, TWO, THREE, FOUR.

SGT. TOWER: RIGHT SHOULDER . . . HARMS!

THE MEN and PAVLO: ONE, TWO, THREE, FOUR.

CORPORAL: FORWARD HARCH!
   (*And* PAVLO *pulls up his trousers and marches.*)

SGT. TOWER: AIN'T NO USE IN GOIN' HOME . . .

THE MEN: AIN'T NO USE IN GOIN' HOME . . .
   (PAVLO's *marching is joyous.*)

SGT. TOWER: JODY GOT YOUR GAL AND GONE . . .

THE MEN: JODY HUMPIN' ON AND ON.
   (*Something of* PAVLO's *making love to* YEN *is in his marching.*)

Sgt. tower: AIN'T NO USE IN GOIN' BACK . . .

The men: JODY GOT OUR CADILLAC.

Corporal: LORD HAVE MERCY, I'M SO BLUE . . .

The men: IT TWO MORE WEEKS TILL I BE THROUGH.

Corporal: Count cadence, delayed cadence, count cadence—count!
(*And the men, performing delayed cadence, exit.* Pavlo *counts with them, marching away beside the bed, around the bed, leaping upon the bed as the counting comes to its loud end.*)

Sgt. brisbey: (*who has been onstage in his bed all this while*), *calling*: Pavlo!

Pavlo: Just a second, Brisbey!

Sgt. brisbey: Pavlo!

Pavlo: (*crossing toward* Brisbey) Whatta you want, Brisbey?

Sgt. brisbey: Pavlo, can I talk to you a little?

Pavlo: Sure.

Sgt. brisbey: You're a medic, right?

Pavlo: Yeh.

Sgt. brisbey: But you're not a conscientious objector, are you? So you got a rifle.

Pavlo: Sure.
(Pavlo *is busy now with* Brisbey's *pulse and chart, straightening the bed, preparing the shot he must give.*)

Sgt. brisbey: I like the feel of 'em. I like to hold 'em.

Pavlo: I'm not gonna get my rifle for you, Brisbey.

SGT. BRISBEY: Just as a favor.

PAVLO: No.

SGT. BRISBEY: It's the only pleasure I got anymore.

PAVLO: Lemme give you a hypo; you got a visitor; you can see him
before you sleep.

SGT. BRISBEY: The egg that slept, that's what I am. You think I look
like an egg with a head?
(PAVLO *is preparing the needle. There is a figure off in the shadows.*)
Or else I'm a stump. Some guys, they get hit, they have a stump. I
am a stump.

PAVLO: What about your visitor; you wanna see him?
(*And the figure,* SGT. WALL, *steps forward. He is middle-aged, gray-
haired, chunky.*)

SGT. BRISBEY: Henry?

SGT. WALL: It's me, Brisbey, how you doin'?

SGT. BRISBEY: Henry, Henry, who was the first man round the world,
Henry? That's what I want to know. Where's the deepest pit in
the ocean? You carryin'? What do you have? Forty-five? You must
have a blade. Magellan. Threw out a rope. I ever tell you that
story? Gonna go sleepy-bye. Been tryin' to get young Pavlo Hummel to put me away, but he prefers to break needles on me. How's
the unit? You tell 'em I'll be back. You tell 'em, soon as I'm well,
I'll be back.

SGT. WALL: I'm off the line . . . now, Brisbey. No more boonies.
I'm in Supply now.

SGT. BRISBEY: Supply? What . . . do you supply? (*Slight pause, as if
bewildered. Thinking, yet with bitterness*) If I promise to tell you
the secret of life, Henry, will you slit my throat? You can do it
while I'm sleeping.

PAVLO: Don't he just go on?

SGT. BRISBEY: Young Hummel here, tell him who you love. Dean Martin. Looks at ole Dino every chance he gets. And "Combat." Vic Morrow, man. Keeps thinkin' he's gonna see himself. Dino's cool, huh. Drunk all the time.

PAVLO: That's right.

SGT. BRISBEY: You fuckin' asshole. Henry. Listen. You ever think to yourself, "Oh, if only it wasn't Brisbey. I'd give anything. My own legs. Or one, anyway. Arms. Balls. Prick." Ever . . . Henry? (*Silence.*)

SGT. WALL: No.

SGT. BRISBEY: Good. Don't. Because I have powers I never dreamed of and I'll hear you if you do, Henry, and I'll take them. I'll rip them off you. (*Silence.*)

SGT. WALL: You'll be goin' home soon. I thought . . . we could plan to get together. . . .

SGT. BRISBEY: Right. Start a softball team.

SGT. WALL: Jesus Christ, Brisbey, ain't you ever gonna change? Ain't you ever gonna be serious about no—

SGT. BRISBEY: I have changed, Motherfucker. You blind or some-thin' askin' me if I changed. You get the fuck outa here, hear me? (WALL *is leaving, having left a pint of whiskey.*) You take a tree, you cut off its limbs, whatta you got? You got a stump. A living feeling thinking stump.

PAVLO: You're not a tree, Brisbey.

SGT. BRISBEY: And what terrible cruelty is that? Do you know?

There is responsibility. I want you to get me that rifle. To save you from the sin of cruelty, Pavlo.
(As PAVLO *is moving with alcohol, cotton, to prepare the shot*)
You are cruel, Pavlo . . . you and God. The both of you.

PAVLO: Lemme do this, man.

SGT. BRISBEY: (*as* PAVLO *gives the shot*) Do you know . . . if you were to get that rifle, Pavlo, I'd shoot you first. It's how you'll end up anyway. I'd save you time. Get you home quicker. I know you, boy.

PAVLO: Shut up, man. Relax . . .

SGT. BRISBEY: You've made me hate you.

PAVLO: I'm sorry. I didn't mean that to happen.

SGT. BRISBEY: No, no, you're not sorry. You're not. You're glad it's me, you're glad it's not you. God's always glad that way because it's never him, it's always somebody else. Except that once. The only time we was ever gonna get him, he tried to con us into thinkin' we oughta let him go. Make it somebody else again. But we got through all that shit he was talkin' and hung on and got him good—fucked him up good—nailed him up good . . . just once . . . for all the billion times he got us.

PAVLO: Brisbey, sometimes I don't think you know what you're sayin'.
(A CAPTAIN *enters upstage left, carrying clipboard*.)

CAPTAIN: Grennel.

GRENNEL: (*appearing from the back, far upstage*) Yes, Sir.

CAPTAIN: Go get me Hummel. He's down with Brisbey.

SGT. BRISBEY: I keep thinkin', Pavlo, 'bout this kid got his hand blown off and he kept crawlin' round lookin' for his fingers.

Couldn't go home without 'em, he said, he'd catch hell. No fingers.

(PAVLO *shakes his head.*)

I keep thinkin' about ole Magellan, sailin' round the world. Ever hear of him, Pavlo? So one day he wants to know how far under him to the bottom of the ocean. So he drops over all the rope he's got. Two hundred feet. It hangs down into the sea that must go down and down beyond its end for miles and tons of water. He's up there in the sun. He's got this little piece of rope danglin' from his fingers. He thinks because all the rope he's got can't touch bottom, he's over the deepest part of the ocean. He doesn't know the real question. How far beyond all the rope you got is the bottom?

PAVLO: Brisbey, I'm gonna tell you somethin'. I tried to kill myself once. Honest to God. And it's no good. You understand me. I don't know what I was thinkin' about. I mean, you understand it was a long time ago and I'd never been laid yet or done hardly anything, but I have since and it's fantastic. I just about blew this girl's head off, it was fantastic, but if I'd killed myself, it'd never a happened. You see what I'm sayin', Brisbey? Somethin' fantastic might be comin' to you.

GRENNEL: (*entering*) Hummel. Man, the Captain wants to see you.

PAVLO: Captain Miller? Captain Miller!

(*He leaves.*)

SGT. BRISBEY: Pavlo!

GRENNEL: (*as he wheels* BRISBEY *off*) How you doin', Brisbey?

PAVLO: (*rushing up to the* CAPTAIN, *who stands with his clipboard*) Sir, PFC Hummel reporting as ordered.

CAPTAIN: Good afternoon, Hummel.

PAVLO: Good afternoon, Sir.

CAPTAIN: Are you smiling, Hummel?

PAVLO: Excuse me, Sir.

CAPTAIN: Your ten-forty-nine says you're not happy at all; it says you want a transfer out of this unit because you're ashamed to serve with us. I was wondering how could you be ashamed and smiling simultaneously, Hummel.

PAVLO: I don't know, Sir.

CAPTAIN: That's not a very good answer.

PAVLO: No, Sir.

CAPTAIN: Don't you think what you're doing here is important? You helped out with poor Brisbey, didn't you?

PAVLO: Yes, Sir.

CAPTAIN: That's my point, Hummel. There are people alive who would be dead if you hadn't done your job. Those invalids you care for, you feed them when they can't, you help them urinate, defecate, simple personal things they can't do for themselves but would die without. Have you asked any one of them if they think what you are doing is important or not, or if you should be ashamed?

PAVLO: Yes, Sir . . . more or less. But . . . I . . . just think I'd be better off in squad duty.
(*Distant firing and yelling are heard to which neither the* CAPTAIN *nor* PAVLO *respond. There is a quality of echo to the gunfire; then there is a clattering and* PARHAM, *a young Negro PFC, appears at the opposite side of the stage in full combat gear except for his helmet, which is missing. He has come a few steps onto the stage. He crouches.*)

PARHAM: Damn, baby, why that ole sarge gotta pick on me?

PAVLO: I'm Regular Army, Sir; I'm going to extend my tour.

CAPTAIN: You like it here, Pavlo?

PARHAM: Damn that ole sarge. I run across the field I get shot sure as hell. (*He breathes.*) Lemme count to five. Lemme do it on five.

CAPTAIN: How many days left in your tour, Hummel?

PARHAM: Lemme do it like track and field.

PAVLO: I enlisted because I wanted to be a soldier, Sir, and I'm not a soldier here. Four nights ago on perimeter guard, I tried to set up fields of fire with the other men in the bunker—do you know what I mean, Sir? Designating who would be responsible for what sector of terrain in case of an attack? And they laughed at me; they just sat on the bunker and talked all night and they didn't stay low and they didn't hide their cigarettes when they smoked or anything.

PARHAM: FIVE!
(*And he runs no more than two steps before a loud explosion hits. He goes down, bounces, and rolls onto his back, slamming his fist into the ground in outrage.*)
DAMNIT! I KNEW IT! I KNEW IT! I KNEW IT!

CAPTAIN: You want the V.C. to come here?

PAVLO: I want to feel, Sir, that I'm with a unit Victor Charlie considers valuable enough to want to get it. And I hope I don't have to kill anyone; and I hope I don't get killed.

PARHAM: (*still trying but unable to rise*) Medic? Medic? Man, where you at? C'mon out here to me! Crawl on out here to me.

PAVLO: But maybe you can't understand what I'm saying, Sir, because you're an R.O.T.C. officer and not O.C.S., Sir.

CAPTAIN: You mean I'm not Regular Army, Hummel.

PAVLO: An R.O.T.C. officer and an O.C.S. officer are not the same thing.

CAPTAIN: Is that so, Hummel?

PAVLO: I think so, Sir.

CAPTAIN: You want to get killed, don't you, Hummel?

PAVLO: No, Sir. No.

CAPTAIN: And they will kill you, Hummel, if they get the chance. Do you believe that? That you will die if shot, or hit with shrapnel, that your arm can disappear into shreds, or your leg vanish— do you believe that, Hummel? That you can and will, if hit hard enough, gag and vomit and die . . . be buried and rot—do you believe yourself capable of that? . . .

PAVLO: Yes . . . Sir. I . . . do . . .

PARHAM: Nooooooo! (*Quick pause. He looks about.*) Ohhh, shit, somebody don't help me, Charlie gonna come in here, cut me up, man. He gonna do me.

CAPTAIN: All right, Hummel.

PARHAM: Oh, Lord, you get me outa here, I be good, man. I be good, no shit, Lord, I'm tellin' it.

CAPTAIN: All right . . . you're transferred. I'll fix it.
(PAVLO *salutes. The* CAPTAIN *salutes, pivots, exits.* PAVLO *moves to change into combat gear, which he finds in a footlocker. He exits.*)

PARHAM: What's happenin'? I don't know what's happenin'!
(*And the light goes, and he is alone in the jungle, in a center of flickering silver. It is night, there are sounds.*)
Hummel, c'mon. It's me, man, Parham; and I ain't jivin', mister. I been shot. I been truly shot.
(*He pauses, breathing, raises his head to look down at himself.*)
Ohhhh, look at me; ohhh, look at my poor stomach. Ohhhh, look at me, look at me. Oh, baby, stop it, stop bleedin', stop it, stop it; you my stomach, I'm talkin' to you, I'm tellin' you what to do, YOU STOP IT!

(*His hands are pressing furiously on his stomach. And he lies for a moment in silence before shuddering and beginning again.*) SOMEBODY GET ME A DUSTOFF! Dustoff control, do you hear me? This here PFC Jay Charles Johnson Parham. I am coordinates X-ray Tango Foxtrot . . . Lima. . . . Do you hear me? I hurtin', baby . . . hear me. Don't know what to do for myself . . . can't remember . . . don't know what it is gone wrong. . . . Requesting one med-evac chopper. . . . I am one litter patient, gun shot wounds, stomach. Area secure. C'mon hear me . . . this ole nigger . . . he gonna die.

(*Two* VIETCONG, *appearing soundlessly, are suddenly upon him. One carries a rifle.*)

1ST V.C.: Hello, GI.

PARHAM: Oh, no. Oh, no. No.

1ST V.C.: (*very singsong*) Okay. Okay.

2ND V.C.: You numba one.

PARHAM: Get away from me! I talkin' to you, Charlie, you get away from me! You guys get away from me! MEDIC! ME—
(*They say, "Okay, okay," "You numba one." At a nod from the* VIETCONG *with the weapon, his partner has jumped forward into a sitting position at* PARHAM's *head, one leg pinning down each shoulder, the hands grasping under his chin, stuffing a rag into his mouth. There are only the sounds of the struggle. The other* VIETCONG *approaches and crouches over* PARHAM, *holding a knife over him.* PARHAM *stares, and his feet move slowly back and forth.*)

1ST V.C.: Numba one, you can see, GI? Airplane me . . . Vietnam. Have many bomb. Can do boom-boom, you stand! (*He moves the knife up and down.*) Same-same you, many friends me, fini. Where airplane now, GI? Where Very gun?
(*And he places the blade against* PARHAM's *chest, and* PARHAM *behind his gag begins to howl, begins to flail his pinioned arms and beat his heels furiously upon the ground.*)
Okay, okay . . . ! Ông di dâu?

(*Then the knife goes in and the* VIETCONG *get up to stand over* PARHAM, *as he turns onto his side and pulls himself into a knot as if to protect himself, knees tight to his chest, arms over his head. They unbuckle his pistol belt, take his flak vest and billfold from his pocket, and are working at removing his shirt when they both straighten at a sound. They seize his fallen rifle and run to disappear.* PAVLO *appears, moving low, accompanied by* RYAN.)

RYAN: Man, I'm tellin' you let's get outa here.

PAVLO: (*pointing*) No, no. There. (*He has a circular belt hooked over his shoulder, and he moves toward the body.*) Just look.
(RYAN *is following.*)
Hey, man . . . hey . . . (*He rolls* PARHAM *over.*) Ohhhhh . . . look at him.

RYAN: It's Parham.

PAVLO: Man, he's all cut. . . .

RYAN: Pavlo, let's get outa here! (*And he starts to move off.*) What the hell's it matter?

PAVLO: I'll carry him.

RYAN: (*as* PAVLO *hands him his rifle*) I ain't worried about who has to carry him, for chrissake, I wanna get outa here. (*On the move*) I'm gonna hustle over there to the side there.

PAVLO: Nooooooo . . .

RYAN: Give you some cover.
(*And* RYAN *is gone, leaving* PAVLO *with the body. The carrier's procedure, which* PAVLO *undertakes through the following speeches, is this: He places the circular belt under the dead man's buttocks, one length along his back, the other below and across his legs, so that two loops are formed, one on either side of the man. He then lies down with his back to the dead man and fits his arms through the two loops. He grasps the man's left arm with*

his own right hand and rolls to his right so that the man rolls with him and is on his back. He then rises to one knee, keeping the body pressed tightly to his own. As PAVLO *begins this task,* ARDELL *is there, appearing as* RYAN *departs.*)

ARDELL: How many that make?

PAVLO: What's that?

ARDELL: Whatta you think, man? Dead bodies!

PAVLO: Who the hell's countin'?

ARDELL: Looookeeeee. Gettin' ta *beeeee bad!*

PAVLO: This one's nothin'. When they been out here a couple a days, man, that's when it's interesting—you go to pick 'em up, they fall apart in your hands, man. They're mud—pink mud—like turnin' over a log, all maggots and ants. You see Ryan over there hidin' in the bushes. I ain't hidin' in no bushes. And Parham's glad about that. They're all glad. Nobody wants to think he's gonna be let lay out here.

ARDELL: Ain't you somethin'.

PAVLO: I'm diggin' it, man. Blowin' people away. Cuttin' 'em down. Got two this afternoon I saw and one I didn't even see—just heard him out there jabberin' away—(*and he makes a sound mimicking a Vietnamese speaking*). And I walked a good god-damn twenty rounds right over where it sounded like he was: he shut up his fuckin' face. It ain't no big thing.

ARDELL: Like bringin' down a deer . . . or dog.

PAVLO: Man, people's all I ever killed. Ohhhh, I feel you thinkin', "This poor boy don't know what he's doin'; don't know what he got into." But I do. I got a dead boy in my hands. In a jungle . . . the middle a the night. I got people maybe ten feet away, hidin'—they're gonna maybe cut me down the minute I move. And I'm

gonna . . . (*During all this he has struggled to load the body like a pack on his back. Now he is rising. Is on his knee.*) . . . take this dead thing back and people are gonna look at me when I do it. They're gonna think I'm crazy and be glad I'm with 'em. I'm diggin'—
(*And the* FIRST VIETCONG *comes streaking out from a hiding place.*)
Ryan, Ryan, Ryan!
(*And the* VIETCONG, *without stopping, plunges the knife into* PAVLO's *side and flees off.* PAVLO *falls, unable, because of the body on his back, to protect himself.*)
What happened?

ARDELL: The blood goin' out a hole in your guts, man; turn you into water.

PAVLO: He hit me. . . .

ARDELL: *Turn you into water!* Blood goin' in the brain makes you think; in your heart make you move; in your prick makes you hard, makes you come. *You lettin' it drop all over the ground!*

PAVLO: I won't . . . I'll . . . noooooo. . . . (*Trying to free himself of the body*) Ryan . . .

ARDELL: The knowledge comin', baby. I'm talkin' about what your kidney know, not your fuckin' fool's head. I'm talkin' about your skin and what it sayin', thin as paper. We melt; we tear and rip apart. Membrane, baby. Cellophane. Ain't that some shit.

PAVLO: I'll lift my arm. (*But he can't.*)

ARDELL: Ain't that some shit.

PAVLO: Noooooo . . .

ARDELL: A bullet like this finger bigger than all your fuckin' life. Ain't this finger some shit.

PAVLO: RYAN.

ARDELL: I'm tellin' you.

PAVLO: Nooooo.

ARDELL: RYAN!

PAVLO: RYAN!

ARDELL: (as Ryan comes running on with a second soldier) Get on in here.
(The two soldiers struggle to free PAVLO from the body, as SGT. TOWER comes striding on and mounts his platform. PAVLO, being dragged off by the soldiers, yells and yells.)

PAVLO: Ryan, we tear. We rip apart. Ryan, we tear. (He is gone.)

SGT. TOWER: You gonna see some funny shit, Gen'lmen. You gonna see livin' breathin' people disappear. Walkin' talkin' buddies. And you gonna wanna kill and say their name. When you been in so many fights and you come out, you a survivor. It what you are and do. You survive.
(As a body detail removes PARHAM.)

ARDELL: Thin and frail.

SGT. TOWER: Gen'lmen, can you hear me?

ARDELL: Yes, Sergeant.

SGT. TOWER: I saw this rifle one time get blown right outa this boy's hands and him start wailin' and carryin' on right there how he ain't ever goin' back on no line; he'll die for sure, he don't have that one rifle in all the world. You listenin' to me, Gen'lmen? I am gonna tell you now what you do when you lost and it black, black night. The North Star show you true north accurate all year round. You gonna see the Big Dipper and two stars on the end called the pointer and they where the water would come on outa that dipper if it had water in it, and straight out from there is this big damn star, and that the North Star, and once you know north you ain't lost no more!

(*And* PAVLO *has appeared, walking slowly as in a dream, looking at* SGT. TOWER.)

PAVLO: YES, SERGEANT!
(*An explosion hits, and* PAVLO, *yelling, goes down.*)

ARDELL: What you sayin'? Yes, Sergeant.

PAVLO: (*struggling to rise*) YES, SERGEANT!

ARDELL: Ask him what about that grenade come flyin'? How come if you so cool, if you such a fox, you don't know nothin' to do with no grenade but stand there holdin' it—get your abdominal and groin area blown to shit.

PAVLO: I DON'T KNOW WHAT YOU'RE TALKING ABOUT!

ARDELL: You walkin' talkin' scar, what you think you made of?

PAVLO: I got my shit together.

ARDELL: HOW MANY TIMES YOU GONNA LET 'EM HIT YOU?

PAVLO: AS MANY AS THEY WANT.

ARDELL: That man up there a fool, Jim.

PAVLO: Shut up.

ARDELL: You ever seen any North Star in your life?

PAVLO: (*on the move toward* YEN, *who is kneeling in the distance*) I seen a lot of people pointin'.

ARDELL: They a bunch a fools pointin' at the air. "Go this way, go that way."

PAVLO: I want her, man. I need her. (*He touches her.*)

ARDELL: Where you now? What you doin'?

PAVLO: I'm with her, man.

ARDELL: You . . . in . . . her . . .

PAVLO: (taking her blouse off) . . . soon . . .

ARDELL: Why you there? . . .

PAVLO: I dunno. . . . Jus' wanna . . .

ARDELL: You jus' gonna ride. . . .

PAVLO: I jus' wanna . . .

ARDELL: There was one boy walkin' . . .

PAVLO: (seizing her, embracing her) I know; don't talk no shit.

ARDELL: Walkin' . . . singin' . . . soft, some song to himself, thinkin' on mosquitoes and Coke and bug spray, until these bushes in front of him burst and his fine young legs broke in half like sticks. . . .

PAVLO: (rising, trying to get his trousers off) Leave me alone!

ARDELL: At seven his tonsils been cut out; at twelve there's appendicitis. Now he's twenty and hurtin' and screamin' at his legs, and then the gun come back. It on a fixed traversing arc to tear his yellin' fuckin' head right off.

PAVLO: Good; it's Tanner; it's Weber. It's Smith and not Pavlo. Minneti, not Pavlo. Klaus and you. You motherfucker. But not Pavlo. Not ever.

ARDELL: You get a knife wound in the ribs.

PAVLO: It misses my heart. I'm clean.

ARDELL: You get shrapnel all up and down your back.

PAVLO: It's like a dozen fifteen bee stings, all up and down my back.

ARDELL: And there's people tellin' you you can go home if you wanna. It's your second wound. They're sayin' you can go home when you been hit twice and you don't even check. You wanna go back out, you're thinkin', get you one more gook, get you one more slopehead, make him know the reason why.

PAVLO: (*whirling, scooping up a rifle*) That's right. They're killin' everybody. They're fuckin' killin' everybody! (*The rifle is aimed at* ARDELL.)

ARDELL: Like it's gonna make a difference in the world, man, what you do; and somethin' made bad's gonna be all right with this one more you're gonna kill. Poor ole Ryan gets dinged round about Tay Ninh, so two weeks later in Phu Loi you blow away this goddamn farmer. . . .
(A FARMER, *wearing Vietnamese work clothes and a conical hat, appears in the distance, waving.*)

FARMER: Okay, GI, okay.

ARDELL: And think you're addin' somethin' up.

PAVLO: I blew him to fuckin' smithereens. He's there at twenty yards, wavin'.

FARMER: Okay, GI, okay. (*He sways in the distance.*)

PAVLO: (*yelling at the farmer*) DUNG LYE. DUNG LYE. (*This is* "Stop" *in Vietnamese.*)

ARDELL: You don't know he's got satchel charges.

PAVLO: I do.

ARDELL: You don't know what he's got under his clothes.

PAVLO: I do. He's got dynamite all under his clothes. And I shoot him.

(*Gunshot, as* PAVLO *fires.*)

I fuckin' shoot him. He's under me. I'm screamin' down at him. RYAN. RYAN. And he's lookin' up at me. His eyes squinted like he knows by my face what I'm sayin' matters to me so maybe it matters to him. And then, all of a sudden, see, he starts to holler and shout like he's crazy, and he's pointin' at his foot, so I shoot it. (*He fires again.*) I shoot his foot and then he's screamin' and tossin' all over the ground, so I shoot into his head. (*Fires.*) I shot his head. And I get hit again. I'm standin' there over him and I get fuckin' hit again. They keep fuckin' hittin' me.

(*Explosion and* PAVLO *goes flying forward.*)

I don't know where I'm at. In my head . . . it's like I'm twelve . . . a kid again. Ardell, it's going to happen to meeeeeee. (*He is crawling.*)

ARDELL: What do you want me to do?

PAVLO: I don't want to get hit anymore.

ARDELL: What do you want me to do?

PAVLO: Tell mc.

ARDELL: He was shot . . . layin' down under you, what did you see?

PAVLO: What?

ARDELL: He was squirmin' down under you in that ditch, what did you see?

PAVLO: I saw the grass . . . his head . . .

ARDELL: Nooooooooooo.

PAVLO: Help me, I saw the grass, his head . . .

ARDELL: Don't you ever hear?

PAVLO: I want out, Ardell. I want out.

ARDELL: When you gonna hear me?

PAVLO: What are you tryin' to tell me? I saw blood . . . bits of brain . . .

ARDELL: Noooooooooooo!

PAVLO: The grass, the grass . . .

ARDELL: When you shot into his head, you hit into your own head, fool!

PAVLO: What? NOOOOOOOOOOOOOO!

ARDELL: IT WAS YOUR OWN.

PAVLO: NOOOOOOOOOOO!
(As ARDELL *has turned to leave*)
Don't leave me you sonofabitch, I don't know what you're saying!
(*And* ARDELL *has stopped, with his back turned, far upstage.*)
JIVE MOTHERFUCKING BULLSHIT!
(*And* ARDELL *is leaving and gone.*)
And I . . . stood . . . lookin' . . . down . . . at that black, black Hudson River. . . . There was stars in it. . . . I'm a twelve-year-old kid. . . . I remember. . . . (*He is turning toward* YEN, *who is kneeling, singing.*) I went out toward them . . . diving . . . down. . . . (*He is moving toward* YEN, *crawling.*) They'd said there was no current, but I was twisted in all that water, fighting to get up . . . all my air burning out, couldn't get no more . . . (*still moving toward* YEN) and I was going down, fighting to get down. I was all confused, you see, fighting to get down, thinking it was up. I hit sand. I pounded. I pounded the bottom. I thought the bottom was the top. Black. No air.
(*The* OFFICER *enters, striding swiftly.*)

OFFICER: Yes!
(*He carries a clipboard, on which he writes as* PAVLO *runs up to him.* YEN, *though she remains kneeling, stops singing.*)

PAVLO: SIR! I've just been released from Ward Seventeen, gunshot wound in my side, and I've been ordered back to my unit, Second of the Sixteenth, First Division, and I don't think I should have to go. This is the third time I been hit. I been hit in the ribs and leg and back. . . . I think there should be more trainin' in duckin' and dodgin', Sir. I been hit by a knife, shrapnel, and bullets.

OFFICER: Could you get to the point?

PAVLO: That is the point. I want to know about this regulation sayin' you can go home after your second wounding?

OFFICER: Pardon, Hummel?

PAVLO: I been told there's this regulation you can go home after your second wound. When you been hit twice, you can go home.

OFFICER: Hummel, wouldn't you be home if you were eligible to be home?

PAVLO: I don't know, Sir; but I wanted to stay the first two times, so I don't know and I was told I had the option the second time to go home or not, but I never checked and if I passed it by, Sir, I'd like to go back and pick it up.

OFFICER: You didn't pass it by; there's no such regulation.

PAVLO: It was a sergeant who told me.

OFFICER: These orders are valid.

PAVLO: Could you check, Sir?

OFFICER: I'm an expert on regulations, Hummel. These orders are valid. You've earned the Purple Heart. Now, go on back and do your job.
(*Raising his hand to salute, he pivots, as* PAVLO *is about to salute.*)

ARDELL: No, no.

PAVLO: I do my job.
(SGT. WALL *enters the bar, calling to* YEN. *He wears civilian clothes —slacks and a flowered, short-sleeved shirt.* YEN *moves quickly to the bar area, where she pets him and then moves to prepare a drink for him.*)

SGT. WALL: Come here, Pretty Piggy, we talk boocoup love, okay? Make plans go my home America.

YEN: Sao. (*Vietnamese for "Liar."*)

SGT. WALL: No lie.

SGT. TOWER: (*atop his platform*) (PAVLO *standing before him*) Gen'lmen. (*In a mournful rage*) Lemme tell you what you do, the enemy got you, he all around you. You the prisoner. You listenin', Gen'lmen?

ARDELL: (*all despairing sarcasm*) Yes, Sergeant.

SGT. TOWER: You got to watch out for the enemy. He gonna try to make you feel alone and you got no friends but him. He gonna make you mean and afraid; then he gonna be nice. We had a case with them North Koreans, this group a American POWs, one of 'em was wounded so he cried all night. His buddies couldn't sleep. So one night his buddies picked him up, I'm tellin' you, they carried him out the door into that North Korean winter, they set him down in the snow, they lef' him there, went on back inside. They couldn't hear him screamin' the wind was so loud. They got their sleep. You got to watch out for the enemy.
(PAVLO *pivots, turning away from* SGT. TOWER *and into the bar, where* MAMASAN *greets him.* YEN *is still with* SGT. WALL, *who is taking a big drink.*)

MAMASAN: Paaablooooo . . . how you-you. I give you beer, okay?

PAVLO: (*unmoving, rigid*) Mamasan, chow ba.

SGT. WALL: (*having finished his drink, takes up as if in mid-sentence*) ". . . so who," he says, "was the first motherfucker to sail 'round the world? Not Vasco da Gama." I don't know what he's sayin'. "Who was the first motherfucker to measure the ocean?" (*He is loud and waving his arms.*) I don't know! He wasn't even asking. MAMASAN! MAMASAN! ONE BEER! ONE BEER, ONE SAIGON TEA! (*And he reaches now to take* YEN's *hand and tug her gently around to his side of the table, drawing her near to sit on his lap.*) Come here; sit down. No sao. Fini sao. Boocoup love, Co Yen. Boocoup love. (*His hand is on her breast, as she nibbles his ear.*)

YEN: I think you maybe papasan America. Have many babysan.

SGT. WALL: No . . . no.

YEN: I think you sao.

SGT. WALL: No lie, Yen. No wife America, no have babysan. Take you, okay?

PAVLO: Sarge!
(SGT. WALL *looks up to* PAVLO.)
Listen, I don't have too much time; I got to go pretty soon. How long you gonna be talkin' shit to that poor girl? I mean, see, she's the whore I usually hit on. I'm a little anxious. I'd like to interrupt you, you gonna be at her all fuckin' night. I'll bring her back in half an hour.

SGT. WALL: Sorry about that. Sorry—

PAVLO: I didn't ask you was you sorry.

SGT. WALL: This little girl's my girl.

PAVLO: She's a whore, man—

SGT. WALL: We got a deal, see, see; and when I'm here, she stays with me.

PAVLO: You got a deal, huh?

SGT. WALL: You guessed it, PFC.

PAVLO: Well, maybe you shoulda checked with me, you shoulda
    conferred with me maybe before you figured that deal was sound.

SGT. WALL: You have been informed.

PAVLO: But you don't understand, Sarge. She's the only whore here
    who moves me.

SGT. WALL: My baby.

PAVLO: You rear-echelon asshole!

SGT. WALL: (*beginning to rise*) What's that?

PAVLO: Where you think you are, the goddamn PX? This the gar-
    bage dump, man, and you don't tell me nothin' down here, let
    alone who I can hit on, who I can't hit on, you see what I'm
    sayin' to you, Fuckface.

YEN: Paablo . . . no, no . . .

PAVLO: You like this old man?

YEN: (*moving to face* PAVLO *and explain*) Can be nice, Paablo . . .

PAVLO: Old man, Papasan. Can do fuck-fuck maybe one time one
    week. Talk, talk. Talk. No can do boom-boom. PAPASAN.
    NUMBA FUCKIN' TEN!

YEN: (*angry at his stupidity*) Shut up, Paablo. I do him. Fini him.
    Do you. Okay.

PAVLO: Shut up?

SGT. WALL: You heard her.

PAVLO: Shut up? (*His hand twisting in her hair*) I don't know who
    you think this bitch is, Sarge, but I'm gonna fuck her whoever you

think she is. I'm gonna take her in behind those curtains and I'm gonna fuck her right side up and then maybe I'm gonna turn her over, get her in the asshole, you understand me? You don't like it you best come in pull me off.

SGT. WALL: (*switchblade popping open in his hand*) I ain't gonna have to, Punk.
(PAVLO *kicks him squarely in the groin. He yells, falls.*)

PAVLO: The fuck you ain't. Hey . . . were you ready for that? Were you ready for that, ole man? (*Dragging him along the ground, shoving him*) Called crawlin', you gettin' the hang of it, you ole man. Get up, get up.
(*And* SGT. WALL *moans as* PAVLO *lifts him.*)
I want you gone, you mother, you understand? I don't wanna see you no more. You gonna disappear. You are gonna vanish.
(*And he flings* SGT. WALL *away.* WALL *staggers, falls, and* PAVLO *picks the knife off the floor, goes for a beer, as* SGT. TOWER *begins to speak.*)

SGT. TOWER: This is a grenade, Gen'lmen. M-twenty-six-A-two fragmentation, Five-point-five ounces, composition B, time fuse, thirteen feet a coiled wire inside it, like the inside a my fist a animal and I open it and that animal leap out to kill you. Do you know a hunk a paper flyin' fast enough cut you in half like a knife, and when this baby hit, fifteen meters in all directions, ONE THOUSAND HUNKS A WIRE GOIN' FAST ENOUGH!
(ARDELL *enters, joining* PAVLO, *who celebrates*)

PAVLO: Did I do it to him, Ardell? The triple Hummel? Got to be big and bad. A little shuffle. Did I ever tell you? Thirteen months a my life ago.

YEN: Paaaabloooo, boocoup love!

PAVLO: Thirteen months a my life ago.
(*And* SGT. WALL, *there in the corner, beginning to move, is pulling pin on a grenade.*)
What she did, my ole lady, she called Joanna a slut and I threw kitty litter, screamin'—cat shit—"Happy Birthday!" She called

that sweet church-goin' girl a whore. To be seen by her now, up
tight with this odd-lookin' whore, feelin' good and tall, ready to
bed down. Feelin'—
(*And the grenade, thrown by* SGT. WALL, *lands.* WALL *flees, as*
PAVLO *drops to his knees, seizing the grenade. He looks up in awe
at* ARDELL. *The grenade is in his hands in his lap.*)
Oh Christ!
(*And the explosion comes, loud; it is a storm going into darkness
and changing lights. Silence. Body detail enters, as* ARDELL, *looking
at* PAVLO *lying there, begins to speak. The body detail will wrap*
PAVLO *in a poncho, put him on a stretcher, carry him to* ARDELL.)

ARDELL: He don't die right off. Take him four days, thirty-eight
minutes. And he don't say nothin' to nobody in all that time. No
words; he just kinda lay up and look, and when he die, he bitin'
on his lower lip, I don't know why. So they take him, they put
him in a blue rubber bag, zip it up tight, and haul him off to the
morgue in the back of a quarter-ton, where he get stuck naked
into the refrigerator 'long with the other boys killed that day and
the beer and cheese and tuna and stuff the guys who work at the
morgue keep in the refrigerator except when it inspection time.
The bag get washed, hung out to dry on a line out back a the
morgue. (*Slight pause.*) Then . . . lemme see, well, finally he get
shipped home, and his mother cry a lot, and his brother get so depressed he gotta go out and lay his chippie he so damn depressed
about it all. And Joanna, she read his name in the paper, she let
out this little gasp and say to her husband across the table, "Jesus,
Jimmy, I used to go with that boy. Oh, damn that war, why can't
we have peace? I think I'll call his mother." Ain't it some kinda
world? (*And he is laughing.*) Soooooooo . . . that about it. That
about all I got to say. Am I right, Pavlo? Did I tell you true? You
got anything to say? Oh, man, I know you do, you say it out.
(*Slight pause as* ARDELL *moves to uncover* PAVLO.)
Man, you don't say it out, I don't wanna know you. Be cool as
you wanna be, Pavlo! Beee cool; lemme hear you. . . . You tell it
to me: what you think of the cause? What you think a gettin'
your ass blown clean off a freedom's frontier? What you think a
bein' R.A. Regular Army lifer?

PAVLO: (*softly, with nearly embarrassed laughter*) Sheeeeee . . .
ittttt. . . . Oh, lord . . . oh . . .

ARDELL: Ain't it what happened to you? Lemme hear it.

PAVLO: . . . Shit!

ARDELL: And what you think a all the "folks back home," sayin' you
a victim . . . you a animal . . . you a fool. . . .

PAVLO: They shit!

ARDELL: Yeh, Baby; now I know you. It all shit.

PAVLO: It all shit!

ARDELL: You my man again.

PAVLO: It shit.

ARDELL: Lemme hear it! My *main* man.

PAVLO: SHIT!

ARDELL: Main motherfuckin' man.

PAVLO: OH, SHIT!

ARDELL: GO!

PAVLO: SHIT!

ARDELL: GET IT! GET IT!

PAVLO: (*a howl into silence*) SHHHHHHHHHIIIIIIIIIITTTTTTT-
TTTTTTtttttttt!
(*And four men enter, carrying the aluminum box of a coffin,
while two other men go across the back of the stage doing the
drill, the marching and twirling rifles that were done at the end of*

Act One. They go now, however, in the opposite direction. The coffin is placed beside PAVLO.)

ARDELL: That right. How you feel? You feel all right? You gotta get that stuff outa you, man. You body know that and you body smart; you don't get that outa you, it back up on you, man, poison you.
(*The four men are placing PAVLO in the coffin. There is no precision in anything they do. All is casual, daily work.*)

PAVLO: But . . . I . . . I'm dead!
(*The men turn and leave.*)

ARDELL: Real soon; got wings as big as streets; got large, large wings. (*Slight pause.*) You want me to talk shit to you? Man, sure, we siftin' things over. We in a bar, man, back home, we got good soft chairs, beer in our hands, go-go girls all around; one of 'em got her eye on you, 'nother one thinkin' little bit on me. You believe what I'm sayin'. You *home*, Pavlo. (*Pause.*) Now . . . you c'mon and you be with me. . . . We gonna do a little singin'. You be with me. (*Sings*) Saw some stockin's . . . on the street . . .

PAVLO: (*faltering*) Saw some . . . stockin's . . . on . . . the street . . .
(*Slight pause.*)

ARDELL: . . . Wished I was . . . between those . . . feet . . .

PAVLO: Wished I was between those feet!
(*Slight pause.*)

ARDELL and PAVLO: (*together*) Once a week, I get to town. They see me comin', they jus' lay down. . . .

ARDELL: Sergeant, Sergeant, can't you see . . .

PAVLO: Sergeant, Sergeant, can't you see . . .

ARDELL: All this misery's killin' . . . . me . . .

Pavlo: All this misery's killin'—
  (*And* ARDELL *lets the coffin lid slam shut, cutting* PAVLO *off.*)

ARDELL: Ain't no matter what you do . . . Jody done it . . . all to
  you. . . .
  (*Slight pause.* ARDELL *is backing away.*)
  Lift your heads and lift 'em high . . . Pavlo Hummel . . . passin'
  by . . .
  (ARDELL *disappears upstage. The coffin stands in real light.*)

THE TOOTH
OF CRIME

Sam Shepard

THE TOOTH OF CRIME

Sam Shepard is considered by many critics to be the single most important playwright produced by the Off-Broadway theatre movement. While no other American playwright has won more than two Obies, Shepard has won the incredible number of ten—for *Chicago* (1966), *Icarus's Mother* (1966), *Red Cross* (1966), *La Turista* (1967), *Forensic and the Navigators* (1968), *Melodrama Play* (1968), *The Tooth of Crime* (1973), *Action* (1975), *Curse of the Starving Class* (1977), and *Buried Child* (1979).

The Tooth of Crime was first performed in London in July 1972. Its first American performance took place in November 1972 at the McCarter Theatre in Princeton, New Jersey (with Frank Langella in the starring role), and its Off-Broadway premiere was the Performance Group's controversial production in March 1973.

The focus of Shepard's play is on myth and language. The basic myth is that of the aging gunfighter who must fight one last duel—updated in *The Tooth of Crime* as two competing rock stars. The form of their duel is language—the two rock stars engage in a shoot-out of words. The American past, present, and future—our attitudes toward competition, aging, and death, and the myths we use to deal with them—are perfectly captured in Shepard's brilliant idioms and stunning stage imagery.

"Mr. Shepard has gathered his forces and produced a splendidly provocative play," wrote Clive Barnes in the New York *Times*. "The play is about change and renewal, past and present, and our sense of history and human continuity . . . The implications of the play, its depth and its layers, are almost tantalizing. Nothing is so obvious that it can be definitively analyzed—you can see as much as you like in the play, or as little."

John Lahr, in *The Village Voice*, wrote that "as literature, this is Shepard's best piece of sustained writing . . . Shepard's protean style gives him unusual and interesting perspectives which rarely get onto the American stage . . . The words have a logic of their own; they lure an audience deeper into Shepard's unique world, always confident of the intelligence behind them."

Many critics felt that the Performance Group's environmental production of *The Tooth of Crime* was inappropriate for a play with such an emphasis on language rather than conventional action. An environmental production, as championed by the Performance Group's Richard Schechner, treats the entire theatre as one space, with no formal separation between stage and audience—in this case, the playing area was filled with stairs, ramps, and various climbing structures. As the action moved from one section of the space to another, the audience simply followed the performers and sat or stood wherever they pleased.

In the words of theatre critic Michael Feingold, *The Tooth of Crime* has a "multi-faceted richness that is often dazzling . . . The play is an achievement, a solid point in a young writer's rich and complex artistic progress."

THE TOOTH OF CRIME was first performed Off-Broadway by the Performance Group in New York City in March 1973. The cast was as follows:

HOSS	*Spalding Gray*
BECKY LOU	*Joan MacIntosh*
STAR-MAN REFEREE }	*Elizabeth LeCompte*
GALACTIC JACK DOC }	*Stephen Borst*
CHEYENNE	*James Griffiths*
CROW	*Timothy Shelton*

The play was directed by Richard Schechner; the sets were designed by Jerry Rojo; the music was composed by Sam Shepard.

ACT ONE

Scene: A bare stage except for an evil-looking black chair with silver studs and a very high back, something like an Egyptian Pharaoh's throne but simple, centre stage. In the dark, heavy lurking Rock and Roll starts low and builds as the lights come up. The band should be hidden. The sound should be like 'Heroin' by the Velvet Underground. When the lights are up full, Hoss enters in black leather rocker gear with silver studs and black kid gloves. He holds a microphone. He should look like a mean Rip Torn but a little younger. He takes the stage and sings 'The Way Things Are'. The words of the song should be understood so the band has to back off on volume when he starts singing.

'The Way Things Are'
Hoss: You may think every picture you see is a true
              history
of the way things used to be or the way things are
While you're ridin' in your radio or walkin' through
the late late show ain't it a drag to know you just
              don't know
you just don't know
So here's another illusion to add to your confusion
Of the way things are

Everybody's doin' time for everybody else's crime
              and
I can't swim for the waves in the ocean
All the heroes is dyin' like flies they say it's a sign a'
the times

And everybody's walkin' asleep eyes open—eyes
                    open

So here's another sleep-walkin' dream
A livin' talkin' show of the way things seem

I used to believe in rhythm and blues
Always wore my blue suede shoes
Now everything I do goes down in doubt

But sometimes in the blackest night I can see a little
                    light
That's the only thing that keeps me rockin'—keeps
                    me rockin'

So here's another fantasy
About the way things seem to be to me.
(*He finishes the song and throws down the microphone and yells off stage.*)
Becky Lou!
(BECKY *comes on in black rock and roll gear. She's very tall and blonde. She holds two black satchels, one in each hand. They should look like old country-doctor bags.*)

BECKY: Ready just about.

HOSS: Let's have a look at the gear.
(BECKY *sets the bags down on the floor and opens them. She pulls out a black velvet piece of cloth and lays it carefully on the floor then she begins to take out pearl-handled revolvers, pistol, derringers and rifles with scopes, shotguns broken down. All the weapons should look really beautiful and clean. She sets them carefully on the velvet cloth. Hoss picks up the rifles and handles them like a pro, cocking them and looking down the barrel through the scope, checking out the chambers on the pistols and running his hands over them as though they were alive.*)
How's the Maserati?

BECKY: Clean. Greased like a bullet. Cheyenne took it up to 180 on the Ventura Freeway then backed her right down. Said she didn't bark once.

Hoss: Good. About time he stopped them quarter-mile orgasms. They were rippin' her up. Gotta let the gas flow in a machine like that. She's Italian. Likes a full-tilt feel.

Becky: Cheyenne's hungry for long distance now. Couldn't hold him back with nails. Got lead in his gas foot.

Hoss: These look nice and blue. Did the Jeweler check 'em out?

Becky: Yeah, Hoss. Everything's taken care of.

Hoss: Good. Now we can boogie.

Becky: What's the moon chart say?

Hoss: Don't ask me! I hired a fucking star-man. A gazer. What the fuck's he been doin' up there.

Becky: I don't know. Last I knew it was the next first quarter moon. That's when he said things'd be right.

Hoss: Get that fucker down here! I wanna see him. I gave him thirteen grand to get this chart in line. Tell him to get his ass down here!

Becky: O.K., O.K.
(*She exits, Hoss caresses the guns.*)

Hoss: That fuckin' Scorpion's gonna crawl if this gets turned around now. Now is right. I can feel it's right. I need the points! Can't they see that! I'm winning in three fucking States! I'm controlling more borders than any a' them punk Markers. The El Camino Boys. Bunch a' fuckin' punks. GET THAT FUCKER DOWN HERE!!!
(*Star-man enters with Becky. He's dressed in silver but shouldn't look like Star Trek, more contemporary silver.*)
O.K., slick face, what's the scoop. Can we move now?

Star-man: Pretty risky, Hoss.

Hoss: I knew it! I knew it! You fuckin' creep! Every time we get hot to trot you throw on the ice water. Whatsa matter now.

Star-man: Venus is entering Scorpio.

Hoss: I don't give a shit if it's entering Brigitte Bardot. I'm ready for a kill!

Star-man: You'll blow it.

Hoss: I'll blow it. What do you know. I've always moved on a sixth sense. I don't need you, meatball.

Becky: Hoss, you never went against the charts before.

Hoss: Fuck before. This time I feel it. I can smell blood. It's right. The time is right! I'm fallin' behind. Maybe you don't understand that.

Star-man: Not true, Hoss. The El Caminos are about six points off the pace. Mojo Root Force is the only one close enough to even worry about.

Hoss: Mojo? That fruit? What'd he knock over?

Star-man: Vegas, Hoss. He rolled the big one.

Hoss: Vegas! He can't take Vegas, that's my mark! That's against the code!

Star-man: He took it.

Hoss: I don't believe it.

Becky: We picked it up on the bleeper.

Hoss: When? How come I'm the last to find out?

Star-man: We thought it'd rattle you too much.

Hoss: When did it happen!

Star-man: This morning from what the teleprompters read.

Hoss: I'm gonna get that chump. I'm gonna have him. He can't do that. He knew Vegas was on my ticket. He's trying to shake me. He thinks I'll just jump borders and try suburban shots. Well he's fuckin' crazy. I'm gonna roll him good.

Becky: You can't go against the code, Hoss. Once a Marker strikes and sets up colors, that's his turf. You can't strike claimed turf. They'll throw you out of the game.

Hoss: *He* did it! He took my mark. It was on my ticket goddamnit!

Star-man: He can just claim his wave system blew and he didn't find out till too late.

Hoss: Well he's gonna find out now. I'll get a fleet together and wipe him out.

Becky: But, Hoss, you'll be forced to change class. You won't have solo rights no more. You'll be a gang man. A punk.

Hoss: I don't care. I want that fuckin' gold record and nobody's gonna stop me. Nobody!

Star-man: You gotta hold steady, Hoss. This is a tender time. The wrong move'll throw you back a year or more. You can't afford that now. The charts are moving too fast. Every week there's a new star. You don't wanna be a flybynight mug in the crowd. You want something durable, something lasting. How're you gonna cop an immortal shot if you give up soloing and go into a gang war. They'll rip you up in a night. Sure you'll have a few moments of global glow, maybe even an interplanetary flash. But it won't last, Hoss, it won't last.

Becky: He's right, Hoss.

Hoss: O.K., O.K. I'm just gettin' hungry that's all. I need a kill. I haven't had a kill for months now. You know what that's like. I gotta kill. It's my whole life. If I don't kill I get crazy. I start eating away at myself. It's not good. I was born to kill.

Star-man: Nobody knows that better than us, Hoss. But you gotta listen to management. That's what we're here for. To advise and direct. Without us you'd be just like a mad dog again. Can't you remember what that was like.

Hoss: Yeah, yeah! Go away now. Go on! I wanna be alone with Becky.

Star-man: O.K. Just try and take it easy. I know you were wired for a big kill but your time is coming. Don't forget that.

Hoss: Yeah, all right. Beat it!
   (Star-man *exits leaving* Hoss *alone with* Becky. *He looks around the stage dejected. He kicks at the guns and pulls off his gloves.*)
   I'm too old fashioned. That's it. Gotta kick out the scruples. Go against the code. That's what they used to do. The big ones. Dylan, Jagger, Townsend. All them cats broke codes. Time can't change that.

Becky: But they were playin' pussy, Hoss. They weren't killers . . . You're a killer, man. You're in the big time.

Hoss: So were they. My Pa told me what it was like. They were killers in their day too. Cold killers.

Becky: Come on. You're talkin' treason against the game. You could get the slammer for less than that.

Hoss: Fuck 'em. I know my power. I can go on Gypsy Kill and still gain status. There's a whole underground movement going on. There's a lot of Gypsy Markers comin' up.

Becky: Why do you wanna throw everything away. You were always suicidal like that. Right from the start.

Hoss: It's part of my nature.

Becky: That's what we saved you from, your nature. Maybe you forgot that. When we first landed you, you were a complete beast of nature. A sideways killer. Then we molded and shaped you and sharpened you down to perfection because we saw in you a true genius killer. A killer to end them all. A killer's killer.

Hoss: Aw fuck off. I don't believe that shit no more. That stuff is for schoolies. Sure I'm good. I might even be great but I ain't no genius, Genius is something outside the game. The game can't contain a true genius. It's too small. The next genius is gonna be a Gypsy Killer. I can feel it. I know it's goin' down right now. We don't have the whole picture. We're too successful . . . We're insulated from what's really happening by our own fame.

Becky: You're really trying to self-destruct aren't you? Whatsa matter, you can't take fame no more? You can't hold down the pressure circuits? Maybe you need a good lay or two.

Hoss: Your ass. I can handle the image like a fuckin' jockey. It's just that I don't trust the race no more. I dropped the blinkers.

Becky: You're not gettin' buck fever are ya'?

Hoss: Get outa' here!

Becky: Come on. Put it in fourth for a while, Hoss. Cruise it. You can afford to take it easy.

Hoss: GET THE FUCK OUTA' HERE!!!

Becky: O.K., O.K. I'm your friend. Remember?

Hoss: Yeah, sure.

Becky: I am. You're in a tough racket. The toughest. But now ain't the time to crack. You're knockin' at the door, Hoss. You gotta hold on. Once you get the gold then you can back off. But not now.

Hoss: I'm not backin' off. I'm just havin' a doubt dose.

Becky: Maybe I should call a D.J. One a' the big ones. Then you could sit down with him and he could lay the charts out right in front of you. Show you exactly where you stand.

Hoss: That's a good idea. Good. Go get one. Get Galactic Jack and his Railroad Track. Tell him to bring his latest charts. Go on!

Becky: O.K. I'll be back.
(*She exits.* Hoss *stalks around the stage building up his confidence.*)

Hoss: She's right! She's right goddamnit! I'm so fucking close. Knockin' at the door. I can't chicken out of it now. This is my last chance. I'm gettin' old. I can't do a Lee Marvin in the late sixties. I can't pull that number off. I've stomped too many heads. I'm past shitkicker class now. Past the rumble. I'm in the big time. Really big. It's now or never. Come on, Hoss, be a killer, man. Be a killer!
(*Music starts. He sings 'Cold Killer'.*)
   'Cold Killer'
   I'm a cold killer Mama—I got blood on my jeans
   I got a Scorpion star hangin' over me
   I got snakes in my pockets and a razor in my boot
   You better watch it don't get you—It's faster'n you
                    can shoot
   I got the fastest action in East L.A.
   I got the fastest action in San Berdoo
   And if you don't believe it lemme shoot it to you

   Now watch me slide into power glide—supercharged
                    down the line
   There ain't no way for you to hide from the killer's
                    eye
   My silver studs, my black kid gloves make you cry
                    inside
   But there ain't no way for you to hide from the
                    killer's eye

I'm a cold killer Mama—and I've earned my tattoo
I got a Pachooko cross hangin' over you
I got whiplash magic and a rattlesnake tongue
My John the Conqueroot says I'm the cold gun

Now watch me slide into power-glide supercharged
down the line
There ain't no way for you to hide from the killer's eye
My silver studs, my black kid gloves make you cry
inside
But there ain't no way for you to hide from the
killer's eye.

(*The song ends.* BECKY *enters with* GALACTIC JACK, *the disc jockey. He's white and dressed like a 42nd Street pimp, pink shirt, black tie, black patent leather shoes, white panama straw hat and a flash suit. He talks like Wolfman Jack and carries a bundle of huge charts.*)
Ah! The man. Galactic Jack and his Railroad Track.

GALACTIC JACK: That's me, Jim. Heavy duty and on the whim. Back flappin', side trackin', finger poppin', reelin' rockin' with the tips on the picks in the great killer race. All tricks, no sale, no avail. It's in the can and on the lam. Grease it, daddyo!
(*He holds out his hand palm up for* Hoss *to give him five.* Hoss *holds back.*)

Hoss: Back down, Jack. Just give it to me straight. Am I risin' or fallin'.

GALACTIC JACK: A shootin' star, baby, High flyin' and no jivin'. You is off to number nine.

Hoss: Show me what you got. Just lay it out on the floor.

BECKY: Shall I get ya'll some drinks?

Hoss: Yeah. Taquila Gold. What do you take, Jack?

GALACTIC JACK: Not me, baby. I'm runnin' reds all down the spine. Feelin' fine and mixin's a crime.

BECKY: Right.

(*She exits.* JACK *lays his chart on the floor.* Hoss *and* JACK *crouch down to get a close inspection.*)

GALACTIC JACK: O.K. Here's the stand on the national band. The game's clean now. Solo is the word. Gang war is takin' a back seat. The Low Riders are outa' the picture and you is in, Jim. In like a stone winner.

Hoss: Don't type it up, Jack. Just show me how it's movin'. I was ready to take Nevada clean and that meathead Mojo Root Force rolled Vegas.

GALACTIC JACK: Yeah I heard that. Supposed to be on your ticket too. Bad news.

Hoss: He can't get away with that can he?

GALACTIC JACK: I can't dope them sheets, Hoss. You'll have to consult a Ref for the rules or go straight to the Keepers.

Hoss: I can't go to the game Keepers. They'll ask for an itinerary and question past kills. I can't afford a penalty now. I need every point.

GALACTIC JACK: Well lookee here. There's movement all around but no numero uno. That's what they're backin' their chips on you for, boy. The bookies got you two to one.

Hoss: That close?

GALACTIC JACK: All of 'em runnin' it down to you. There's Little Willard from the East in his formula Lotus. Fast machine. Doin' O.K. with a stainless steel Baretta.

Hoss: Willard's solo now?

GALACTIC JACK: Yeah but no threat. Just a front runner. Lots a' early speed but can't go the distance. Here's one outa Tupalo called Studie Willcock. Drivin' a hot Merc, dual cams, Chrysler through and through. Fast but not deadly. He's offed four in a week and almost had Arkansas wrapped up but he's fadin' fast. You're it, Jim. You is the coldest on the circuit.

Hoss: What about this mark? (*pointing at the charts*)

GALACTIC JACK: Oh yeah, that's Grease Jam. Got a supercharged Mini Cooper. Takes the corners. Tried a hit on St. Paul and almost had Minnesota to its knees when he blew a head gasket. Some say he's even been offed by the El Caminos.

Hoss: Those guys are pressin' it pretty hard. They're gonna get blown off sooner or later.

GALACTIC JACK: No doubt. No need to pout. The course is clear. Maybe a few Gypsy Killers comin' into the picture but nothin' to fret your set.

Hoss: Gypsies? Where? I knew it. I got a feeling.

GALACTIC JACK: Just some side bets. They go anonymous 'cause a' the code. One slip and they is pissed. You can dig it. They's playin' with the king fire.

Hoss: But they got a following right? They're growing in the poles?

GALACTIC JACK: Hard to suss it yet, man. Some poles don't even mention their kills for fear of the Keepers comin' down on 'em. I could maybe sound some flies for ya'. See if I could whiff some sniff on that action.

Hoss: Yeah, do.

GALACTIC JACK: What's the keen to the Gypsy scene. These boys are losin' to the cruisin' baby.

Hoss: They've got time on their side. Can't you see that. The youth's goin' to 'em. The kids are flocking to Gypsy Kills. It's a market opening up, Jack. I got a feeling. I know they're on their way in and we're going out. We're gettin' old, Jack.

GALACTIC JACK: You just got the buggered blues, man. You been talkin' to the wrong visions. You gotta get a head set. Put yer ears on straight. Zoot yerself down, boy. These Gypsies is committin' suicide. We got the power. We got the game. If the Keepers whimsy it all they do is scratch 'em out. Simple. They're losers, man. The bookies don't even look past their left shoulder at a Gypsy mark. They won't last, man. Believe me.

HOSS: I don't know. There's power there. Full blown.

GALACTIC JACK: They don't know the ropes, man. Rules is out. They're into slaughter straight off. Not a clean kill in the bunch.

HOSS: But they got balls. They're on their own.

GALACTIC JACK: So are you. Solo's the payolo.

HOSS: But I'm inside and they're out. They could unseat us all.

GALACTIC JACK: Not a King. The crown sticks where it fits and right now it looks about your size.

HOSS: What if they turned the game against us. What if they started marking us!

GALACTIC JACK: That's revolution, man.

HOSS: You hit it.

GALACTIC JACK: Old time shuffle. Don't stand a chance at this dance.

HOSS: But that's how we started ain't it. We went up against the Dudes. Wiped 'em out.

GALACTIC JACK: The Dudes weren't pros, man. You gotta see where you stand. I do believe you is tastin' fear. Runnin' scared. These Gypsies is just muck-rakers. Second hand, one night stand. They ain't worth shit on shinola in your league. Dig yourself on the flip

side. You're number one with a bullet and you ain't even got the
needle in the groove.

Hoss: We'll see. Somethin's goin' down big out there. The shit's
gonna hit the fan before we can get to the bank.

Galactic Jack: Take a deep knee bend, Hoss. It's just the pre-vic-
tory shakes. Tomorrow you'll have the gold in your hand. The
bigee. Don't be shy, I tell no lie. Catch ya' on the re-bop. Say bye
and keep the slide greased down.

Hoss: Yeah. Thanks.
  (Jack *collects his charts and exits.* Hoss *paces and talks to himself.*)
  (*to himself*) Come on, come on. Confidence, man. Confidence.
  Don't go on the skids now. Keep it together. Tighten down. Talk
  it out. Quit jumpin' at shadows. They got you goose bumped and
  they ain't even present. Put yourself in their place. They got
  nothin'. You got it all. All the chips. Come on dice! Come on
  dice! That's it. Roll 'em sweet. The sweet machine. Candy in the
  gas tank. Floor it. Now you got the wheel. Take it. Take it!
  (Becky *enters with the drink.* Hoss *catches himself.*)

Becky: What happened to Jack?

Hoss: We ran the session.

Becky: Here's your drink.

Hoss: Thanks. Listen, Becky, is Cheyenne ready to roll?

Becky: Yeah. He's hot. Why?

Hoss: Maybe we could just do a cruise. No action. Just some scout-
ing. I'm really feelin' cooped up in here. This place is drivin' me
nuts.

Becky: Too dangerous, Hoss. We just got word that Eyes sussed
somebody's marked you.

Hoss: What! Marked *me*? Who?

Becky: One a' the Gypsies.

Hoss: It's all comin' down like I said. I must be top gun then.

Becky: That's it.

Hoss: They gotta be fools, man. A Gypsy's marked *me*?

Becky: That's the word from Eyes.

Hoss: Where is he?

Becky: Vegas.

Hoss: Vegas? Oh now I get it. Mojo. He's hired a Gypsy to off me clean. That's it. That fuckin' chicken shit. I'm gonna blast him good. Doesn't have the balls to come down to me. Gotta hire a Gypsy.

Becky: Might be just a renegade solo, Hoss. They're all lookin' to put you under. You're the main trigger. The word's out.

Hoss: Don't you get it? The Root Force is slipstreamin' my time. Takin' my marks and hirin' amateurs to rub me out. It's a gang shot. They're workin' doubles. I gotta team up now. It's down to that. I gotta get ahold a' Little Willard. Get him on the line.

Becky: Hoss, don't fly off, man. You're safe here.

Hoss: Safe! Safe and amputated from the neck down! I'm a Marker man, not a desk clerk. Get fucking Willard to the phone! And tell Cheyenne to come in here!
(Becky *exits*)
O.K. Now the picture brightens. I can play for high stakes now. I can draw to the straight, outside or in. I'm ready to take on any a' these flash heads. Vegas is mine, man. It belongs in my pocket. The West is mine. I could even take on the Keepers. That's it. I'll

live outside the fucking law altogether. Outside the whole shot. That's it. Why didn't I think a' that before!
(CHEYENNE *enters in green velvet with silver boots and racing gloves.*)

CHEYENNE: You want me, Hoss?

HOSS: Yeah! Yeah I want you! You're my main man.
(*He gives* CHEYENNE *a bear hug.*)
Listen, Cheyenne, we done a lotta' marks in our time. Right?

CHEYENNE: Yeah.

HOSS: Good clean kills. Honest kills. But now the times are changin'. The race is deadly. Mojo Root Force is movin' in on turf marks and tryin' to put me out with a Gypsy.

CHEYENNE: A Gypsy?

HOSS: Yeah.

CHEYENNE: They can't do that. It's against the code.

HOSS: Fuck the code. Nobody's playin' by the rules no more. We been suckers to the code for too long now. Now we move outside. You remember Little Willard?

CHEYENNE: East Coast. Drove a Galaxie. Into Remington over and unders.

HOSS: Yeah. He's changed his style now. Got himself a Lotus Formula 2 and a Baretta.

CHEYENNE: Sounds mean.

HOSS: He is man. And I trust him. He was right with me when we took off the Dudes. Becky's on the phone to him now. He's our man. Just him and us.

CHEYENNE: But Root Force has probably got Vegas locked up, Hoss. It's gonna be hard penetration.

Hoss: We rolled Phoenix didn't we?

CHEYENNE: Yeah.

Hoss: Tuscon?

CHEYENNE: Yeah.

Hoss: San Berdoo?

CHEYENNE: Yeah.

Hoss: So Vegas ain't no Fort Knox.

CHEYENNE: So it's back to the rumble?

Hoss: Temporary. Just temporary. We can't sit back and let the good times roll when the game's breakin' down.

CHEYENNE: I don't know. I love the game, Hoss. I ain't hot to go back to gang war.

Hoss: We got to now! Otherwise we're down the tubes.

CHEYENNE: What about the Keepers?

Hoss: Fuck them too. We'll take 'em all on.

CHEYENNE: The critics won't like it.

Hoss: The critics! They're outside, man. They don't know what's goin' on.

CHEYENNE: What about our reputation. We worked hard to get where we are. I'm not ready to throw that away. I want a taste a' that gold.

HOSS: I'm surrounded by ass holes! Can't you see what's happened to us. We ain't Markers no more. We ain't even Rockers. We're punk chumps cowering under the Keepers and the Refs and the critics and the public eye. We ain't free no more! Goddamnit! We ain't flyin' in the eye of contempt. We've become respectable and safe. Soft, mushy chewable ass lickers. What's happened to our killer heart. What's happened to our blind fucking courage! Cheyenne, we ain't got much time, man. We were warriors once.

CHEYENNE: That was a long time ago.

HOSS: Then you're backing down?

CHEYENNE: No. I'm just playin' the game.
(CHEYENNE *exits*)

HOSS: God! Goddamnit! This is gettin' weird now. Solo ain't the word for it. It's gettin' lonely as an ocean in here. My driver's gone against me and my time's runnin' thin. Little Willard's my last chance. Him and me. He's runnin' without a driver, so can I. The two of us. Just the two of us. That's enough against the Root Force. He's East Coast though. Maybe he don't know the Western ropes. He could learn it. We'll cruise the action. He'll pick up the streets. Cheyenne knows the West though. Born and raised like me. Backyard schoolin'. Goddamn! Why's he have to go soft now! Why now!
(BECKY *enters*)
You get Willard?

BECKY: No.

HOSS: How come! I need him bad. Keep tryin'!!

BECKY: He's dead, Hoss. Shot himself in the mouth.

HOSS: Who told you?

BECKY: His Rep. They just found him in New Haven slumped over an intersection. They say his car was still runnin'.

Hoss: Why'd he go and do that? He was in the top ten and risin'.

BECKY: Couldn't take it I guess. Too vulnerable. They found a pound of Meth in the back seat.

Hoss: Becky, I'm marked. What the fuck am I gonna do? I can't just sit here and wait for him to come.

BECKY: Least you'll know he's comin'. If you go out cruisin' he's liable to strike anywhere, any time. A Gypsy's got the jump on you that way.

Hoss: What if I busted into Vegas myself? Just me. They'd never expect somethin' like that. I could take off Mojo and split before they ever knew what happened.

BECKY: You're dealin' with a pack now, man. It ain't one against one no more.

Hoss: Well what am I gonna do!

BECKY: Wait him out. Meet him on a singles match and bounce him hard. Challenge him.

Hoss: What if he snipes me?

BECKY: We got the watch out. We'll give him the usher routine. Say that you've been expecting him. That'll challenge his pride. Then fight him with shivs.

Hoss: Shivs! I ain't used a blade for over ten years. I'm out of practice.

BECKY: Practise up. I'll get you a set and a dummy.

Hoss: O.K. And call in the Doc. I need a good shot.

BECKY: Good.
(*She exits.* Hoss *stalks the stage.*)

Hoss: Backed into a fucking box. I can't believe it. Things have changed that much. They don't even apprentice no more. Just mark for the big one. No respect no more. When I was that age I'd sell my leathers to get a crack at a good teacher. I would. And I had some a' the best. There's no sense of tradition in the game no more. There's no game. It's just back to how it was. Rolling night clubs, strip joints. Bustin' up poker games. Zip guns in the junk yard. Rock fights, dirt clods, bustin' windows. Vandals, juvies, West Side Story. Can't they see where they're goin'! Without a code it's just crime. No art involved. No technique, finesse. No sense of mastery. The touch is gone.
(BECKY *enters with* DOC *who is dressed in red.* BECKY *has two knives and a dummy which she sets up centre stage right.* Hoss *sits in his chair.* DOC *has a syringe and a vial of dope and a rubber surgical hose.* Hoss *rolls his sleeve up and* DOC *goes about shooting him up.*)
Oh, Doc, it's good to see ya'. I'm in need. I'm under the gun, Doc.

DOC: Yeah. Things are tough now. This'll cool you out.

Hoss: Good. Doc, what do you think about Gypsy Kills. Do you think it's ethical?

DOC: Haven't thought too much about it actually. I suppose it was bound to happen. Once I remember this early Gypsy. I guess you'd call him a Gypsy now but at the time he was just a hard luck fella name a' Doc Carter. Little got to be known of the man on account a' the fact that he was ridin' a certain William F. Cody's shirttail all through the West, and, for that matter, half around the planet. Anyhow, ole Doc came to be known as the 'Spirit Gun of the West' and a well-deserved title it was, too. That boy could shoot the hump off a buffalo on the backside of a nickel at a hundred paces. To this very day his saddle is settin' in some musty ole Wyoming museum decorated with a hundred silver coins. Each one shot through and through with his Colt .45. And all surroundin' this saddle is pictures tall as a man of this William F. Cody fella pallin' it up with the Indians. Ole Doc never got out from behind the shadow a' that Cody. But I suppose nowadays he'd just take over the whole show. Don't rightly know what made me think a' that. Just popped into my mind.

Hoss: Yeah. It's just funny finding myself on the other side.

Becky: It ain't revolution, man. This Gypsy's a hired trigger from Mojo. He ain't a martyr.

Hoss: But he works outside the code.

Becky: Fuck it. All you gotta worry about is gettin' him before he gets you.

Hoss: You were one of the ones who taught me the code. Now you can throw it away like that.

Becky: It's back down to survival, Hoss. Temporary suspension. That's all.

Hoss: I don't think so. I think the whole system's gettin' shot to shit. I think the code's going down the tubes. These are gonna be the last days of honor. I can see it comin'.

Doc: There. That oughta' do you for a while.

Hoss: Thanks, Doc.

Doc: If you need any crystal later just call me down.

Hoss: Thanks, man.
    (Doc *exits*)

Becky: You wanna try these out?
    (*She offers the knives to* Hoss. *He goes limp and relaxed in the chair.*)

Hoss: Not now. Just come and sit with me for a while.
    (Becky *sits at his feet. He strokes her hair.*)
    Becky?

Becky: Yeah?

Hoss: You remember the El Monte Legion Stadium?

Becky: Yeah.

Hoss: Ripple Wine?

Becky: Yeah.

Hoss: The Coasters?

Becky: (*she sings a snatch*) 'Take out the papers and the trash or you don't get no spendin' cash.'

Hoss: (*sings*) 'Just tell your hoodlum friend outside. You ain't got time to take a ride.'

Becky: 'Yackety yack.'

Hoss: 'Don't talk back.'
(*They laugh. Hoss stops himself.*)
Don't let me go too soft.

Becky: Why not. You've earned it.

Hoss: Earned it? I ain't earned nothin'. Everything just happened. Just fell like cards. I never made a choice.

Becky: But you're here now. A hero. All those losers out there barkin' at the moon.

Hoss: But where am I goin'? The future's just like the past.

Becky: You gotta believe, Hoss.

Hoss: In what?

Becky: Power. That's all there is. The power of the machine. The killer Machine. That's what you live and die for. That's what you wake up for. Every breath you take you breathe the power. You live the power. You are the power.

Hoss: Then why do I feel so weak!

Becky: The knife's gotta be pulled out before you can stab again. The gun's gotta be cocked. The energy's gotta be stored. You're just gettin' a trickle charge now. The ignition's gotta turn yet.

Hoss: Yeah. It's just hard to wait.

Becky: It's harder for movers. You're a mover, Hoss. Some people, all they do is wait.

Hoss: Maybe I should take a ramble.

Becky: Where to?

Hoss: Anywhere. Just to get out for a while.

Becky: You carry your gun wherever you go.

Hoss: Listen, maybe I should go on the lam.

Becky: Are you crazy?

Hoss: No, I'm serious. I'm gettin' too old for this. I need some peace.

Becky: Do you know what it's like out there, outside the game? You wouldn't recognize it.

Hoss: What about New York? Second Avenue.

Becky: What Second Avenue? There ain't no Second Avenue. They're all zoned out. You wouldn't stand a snowball's chance in hell of makin' it outside the game. You're too professional. It'd be like keepin' a wild animal as a pet then turnin' him back loose again. You couldn't cope, Hoss.

Hoss: I did it once. I was good on the streets. I was a true hustler.

Becky: The streets are controlled by the packs. They got it locked up. The packs are controlled by the gangs. The gangs and the Low Riders. They're controlled by cross syndicates. The next step is the Keepers.

Hoss: What about the country. Ain't there any farmers left, ranches, cowboys, open space? Nobody just livin' their life.

Becky: You ain't playin' with a full deck, Hoss. All that's gone. That's old time boogie. The only way to be an individual is in the game. You're it. You're on top. You're free.

Hoss: What free! How free! I'm tearin' myself inside out from this fuckin' sport. That's free? That's being alive? Fuck it. I just wanna have some fun. I wanna be a fuck off again. I don't wanna compete no more.

Becky: And what about the kill? You don't need that?

Hoss: I don't know. Maybe not. Maybe I could live without it.

Becky: You're talkin' loser now, baby.

Hoss: Maybe so. Maybe I am a loser. Maybe we're all fuckin' losers. I don't care no more.

Becky: What about the gold record. You don't need that?

Hoss: I don't know! I just wanna back off for a while. I can't think straight. I need a change. A vacation or something.

Becky: Maybe so. I heard about a place, an island where they don't play the game. Everybody's on downers all day.

Hoss: That sounds good. What about that. Maybe you could find out for me. All I need is a week or two. Just to rest and think things out.

BECKY: I'll see what I can do.

HOSS: Jesus. How'd I get like this?

BECKY: It'll pass.

HOSS: Sing me a song or somethin' would ya? Somethin' to cool me off.

BECKY: O.K.
  (*She sings*)
    'Becky's Song'
    Lemme take you for a ride down the road
    Lean back in the tuck and roll
    The radio's broken and I got no beer
    But I can ease your load

        Listen to the song that the V-8 sings
        Watch the rhythm of the line
        Isn't it some magic that the night-time brings
        Ain't the highway fine

    Tell me where ya' wanna go just take yer pick
    All I'm really doin' is cruisin'
    Take ya' down to Baton Rouge—New Orleans
    Pick us up a Louisiana trick

        Listen to the song that the V-8 sings
        Watch the rhythm of the line
        Isn't it some magic that the night-time brings
        Ain't the highway fine

    You could tell me stories of your yesterdays
    I could break out a few a' mine
    Roll down the window and kiss the wind
    Anyway ya' want to ease the time

        Listen to the song that the V-8 sings
        Watch the rhythm of the line
        Isn't it some magic that the night-time brings
        Ain't the highway fine
  (*The song ends and* CHEYENNE *enters.*)

CHEYENNE: Say, Hoss. We just got tapped that the Gypsy's made it through zone five. He's headed this way.

Hoss: Already? What's he drivin'?

CHEYENNE: You won't believe this. A '58 black Impala, fuel injected, bored and stroked, full blown Vet underneath.

HOSE: I'm gonna like this dude. O.K. let him through.

CHEYENNE: All the way?

Hoss: Yeah. Stop him at the mote and sound him on a shiv duel.

CHEYENNE: Shivs? You ain't in shape for blades, Hoss.

Hoss: I can handle it. Walk on.

CHEYENNE: O.K. (*he exits*)

BECKY: Good. He's finally comin'. This'll get ya' back on your feet, Hoss. Your waitin' time is over.

Hoss: Go tell the Doc I want some snow.

BECKY: You want the fit or snort?

Hoss: Snort. Hurry up.

BECKY: Right.
    (BECKY *exits. Hoss* picks up the knives and stalks the dummy. He *circles it and talks to the dummy and himself. As he talks he stabs the dummy with sudden violent lunges then backs away again. Blood pours from the dummy onto the floor.*)

Hoss: O.K. Gypsy King, where's your true heart. Let's get down now. Let's get down. You talk a good story. You got the true flash but where's yer heart. That's the whole secret. The heart of a Gypsy must be there!

(*He stabs at the heart of the dummy then backs off.*)
Maybe not. Maybe yer colder than that. Maybe in the neck.
Maybe it pumps from the neck down. Maybe there!
(*He stabs at the neck then backs off. Blood gushes out.*)
All right. All right. A secret's a secret. I can give you that much.
But it comes from this end too. I'm your mystery. Figure me. Run
me down to your experience. Go ahead. Make a move. Put me in
a place. An inch is fatal. Just an inch. The wrong move'll leave
you murdered. Come on. Lemme see it. Where's the action?
That's not good enough for the back lot even. Here's one!
(*He makes a quick move and stabs the dummy in the stomach.*)
Now I get it. There ain't no heart to a Gypsy. Just bone. Just
blind raging courage. Well that won't do you, boy. That won't
take you the full length. Yer up against a pro, kid. A true champion Marker. Yer outclassed before the bell rings. Now you've
stepped across the line, boy. No goin' back. Dead on yer feet. (*to
himself*) What am I gettin' so wired about? This kid is a punk. It
ain't even a contest. He's still ridin' in the fifties. Beach Boys
behind the eye balls. A blonde boy. A fair head. Gang bangs,
cheap wine and bonfires. I could take him in my sleep. I could. I
could—
(BECKY *enters with* DOC. DOC *has a large sheet of foil with
mounds of cocaine on it. He sets it down on the chair.*)

BECKY: How's it goin'?

HOSS: Something's lacking. I can't seem to get it up like the other
kills. My heart's not in it.

DOC: Have some a' this.
(*He holds out a rolled up hundred dollar bill.* HOSS *takes it and
goes to the coke.*)

HOSS: Yeah. Maybe that'll help.
(*He takes the bill and snorts the coke as he talks.*)
You know, I been thinkin'. What if the neutral field state failed
one time. Just once.

BECKY: Like this time for instance?

Hoss: Yeah. Like this time.

Becky: Then you're a gonner.

Doc: It shouldn't fail, Hoss. You've been trained.

Hoss: I know, but what if an emotional field came through stronger.

Becky: Like love or hate?

Hoss: Not that gross, not that simple. Something subtle like the sound of his voice or a gesture or his timing. Something like that could throw me off.

Becky: You're really worried about this Gypsy.

Hoss: Not worried. Intrigued. His style is copping my patterns. I can feel it already and he's not even here yet. He's got a presence. Maybe even star quality. His movements have an aura. Even his short. I mean nobody rides a '58 Impala to do battle with a star Marker.

Becky: He's just a fool.

Doc: You gotta stay disengaged, Hoss. The other way is fatal.

Hoss: Maybe not. Maybe there's an opening. A ground wire.

Becky: For what. He's come to knock you over, man.

Hoss: O.K. but I can play in his key. Find his tuning. Jam a little before the big kill. I don't have to off him soon's he walks in the door.

Doc: You'd be better off. He's probably got eyes to work that on you.

Hoss: I don't think so. He's got more class than that. I can feel him coming. We might even be in the same stream. He's got respect.

BECKY: Respect! He's a killer, man.

HOSS: So am I. There's another code in focus here. An outside code. Once I knew this cat in High School who was a Creole. His name was Moose. He was real light skinned and big, curly blond hair, blue eyes. He could pass easy as a jock. Good musician. Tough in football but kinda dumb. Dumb in that way—that people put you down for in High School. Dumb in class. He passed as white until his sister started hangin' around with the black chicks. Then the white kids figured it out. He was black to them even though he looked white. He was a nigger, a coon, a jungle bunny. A Rock Town boy from that day on. We ran together, Moose and me and another cat from Canada who dressed and wore his hair like Elvis. They put him down too because he was too smart. His name was Cruise and he got straight A's without readin' none a' the books. Slept in a garage with his aunt. Built himself a cot right over an old Studebaker. His mother was killed by his father who drove skidders for a lumber company up near Vancouver. Got drunk and busted her in the head with a tire iron. The three of us had a brotherhood, a trust. Something unspoken. Then one day it came to the test. I was sorta' ridin' between 'em. I'd shift my personality from one to the other but they dug me 'cause I'd go crazy drunk all the time. We all went out to Bob's Big Boy in Pasadena to cruise the chicks and this time we got spotted by some jocks from our High School. Our own High School. There were eight of 'em, all crew cut and hot for blood. This was the old days ya' know. So they started in on Cruise 'cause he was the skinniest. Smackin' him around and pushin' him into the car. We was right in the parking lot there. Moose told 'em to ease off but they kept it up. They were really out to choose Moose. He was their mark. They wanted him bad. Girls and dates started gathering around until we was right in the center of a huge crowd a' kids. Then I saw it. This was a class war. These were rich white kids from Arcadia who got T-birds and deuce coups for Xmas from Mommy and Daddy. All them cardigan sweaters and chicks with ponytails and pedal pushers and bubble hairdo's. Soon as I saw that I flipped out. I found my strength. I started kickin' shit, man. Hard and fast. Three of 'em went down screamin' and holdin' their balls. Moose and Cruise went right into action. It was like John

Wayne, Robert Mitchum and Kirk Douglas all in one movie. Those chumps must a' swung on us three times and that was all she wrote. We had all eight of 'em bleedin' and cryin' for Ma right there in the parking lot at Bob's Big Boy. I'll never forget that. The courage we had. The look in all them rich kids' faces. The way they stepped aside just like they did for 'Big John'. The three of us had a silent pride. We just walked strong, straight into that fuckin' burger palace and ordered three cherry cokes with lemon and a order a' fries.

DOC: Those were the old days.

HOSS: Yeah. Look at me now. Impotent. Can't strike a kill unless the charts are right. Stuck in my image. Stuck in a mansion. Waiting. Waiting for a kid who's probably just like me. Just like I was then. A young blood. And I gotta off him. I gotta roll him or he'll roll me. We're fightin' ourselves. Just like turnin' the blade on ourselves. Suicide, man. Maybe Little Willard was right. Blow your fuckin' brains out. The whole thing's a joke. Stick a gun in your fuckin' mouth and pull the trigger. That's what it's all about. That's what we're doin'. He's my brother and I gotta kill him. He's gotta kill me. Jimmy Dean was right. Drive the fuckin' Spider till it stings ya' to death. Crack up your soul! Jackson Pollock! Duane Allman! Break it open! Pull the trigger! Trigger me! Trigger you! Drive it off the cliff! It's all an open highway. Long and clean and deadly beautiful. Deadly and lonesome as a jukebox.

DOC: Come on, Becky, let's leave him alone.

HOSS: Yeah. Right. Alone. That's me. Alone. That's us. All fucking alone. All of us. So don't go off in your private rooms with pity in mind. Your day is comin'. The mark'll come down to you one way or the other.

BECKY: You better rest, Hoss.

HOSS: Ya' know, you'd be O.K., Becky, if you had a self. So would I. Something to fall back on in a moment of doubt or terror or even surprise. Nothin' surprises me no more. I'm ready to take it all on.

The whole shot. The big one. Look at the Doc. A slave. An educated slave. Look at me. A trained slave. We're all so pathetic it's downright pathetic. And confidence is just a hype to keep away the open-ended shakes. Ain't that the truth, Doc?

Doc: I don't know.

Hoss: Right. Right. 'I don't know' is exactly right. Now beat it, both of ya' before I rip your fuckin' teeth out a' yer heads!! GO ON BEAT IT!!!
(BECKY *and* Doc *exit.* Hoss *sits in his chair and stares out in front of him. He talks to himself sometimes shifting voices from his own into an older man's.*)
(*old*) All right, Hoss, this is me talkin'. Yer old Dad. Yer old fishin' buddy. We used to catch eels side by side down by the dump. The full moon lit up the stream and the junk. The rusty chrome flashin' across the marsh. The fireflies dancin' like a faraway city. They'd swallow the hook all the way down. You remember that? (*himself*) Yeah. Sure. (*old*) O.K. You're not so bad off. It's good to change. Good to feel your blood pump. (*himself*) But where to? Where am I going? (*old*) It don't matter. The road's what counts. Just look at the road. Don't worry about where it's goin'. (*himself*) I feel so trapped. So fucking unsure. Everything's a mystery. I had it all in the palm of my hand. The gold, the silver. I knew. I was sure. How could it slip away like that? (*old*) It'll come back. (*himself*) But I'm not a true Marker no more. Not really. They're all countin' on me. The bookies, the agents, the Keepers. I'm a fucking industry. I even affect the stocks and bonds. (*old*) You're just a man, Hoss. Just a man. (*himself*) Yeah, maybe you're right. I'm just a man.
(CHEYENNE *enters*)

CHEYENNE: Hoss. He's here.
(Hoss *stays seated, relaxed. He has an air of complete acceptance.*)

Hoss: Good. He's here. That's good. What's his name?

CHEYENNE: He calls himself Crow.

Hoss: Crow. That's a good name. Did you sound him on the duel?

Cheyenne: Yeah. He's game. He looks tougher than I thought, Hoss.

Hoss: Tough. Tough? (*he laughs*) Good. A tough Crow.

Cheyenne: What'll I tell him?

Hoss: Tell him I like his style. Tell him I'm very tired right now and I'm gonna cop some z's. He can take a swim, have a sauna and a massage, some drinks, watch a movie, have a girl, dope, whatever he wants. Tell him to relax. I'll see him when I come to.

Cheyenne: O.K. You all right, Hoss?

Hoss: Yeah. Just tired. Just a little tired.

Cheyenne: O.K.

Hoss: Thanks, man.

Cheyenne: Sure.
(Cheyenne *exits.* Hoss *stays seated looking out.*)

Hoss: Maybe the night'll roll in. A New Mexico night. All gold and red and blue. That would be nice. A long slow New Mexico night. Put that in your dream, Hoss, and sleep tight. Tomorrow you live or die.

END OF ACT ONE

ACT TWO

Scene: *The stage is the same. The lights come up on* Crow. *He looks just like Keith Richard. He wears highheeled green rock and roll boots, tight greasy blue jeans, a tight yellow t-shirt, a green velvet coat, a shark tooth earring, a silver swastika hanging from his neck and a black eye-patch covering the left eye. He holds a short piece of silver chain in his hand and twirls it constantly, tossing it from hand to hand. He chews a stick of gum with violent chomps. He exudes violent arrogance and cruises the stage with true contempt. Sometimes he stops to examine the guns on the floor, or check out the knives and the dummy. Finally he winds up sitting in Hoss's chair. A pause as he chews gum at the audience. Hoss enters dressed the same as in Act One.* Crow *doesn't move or behave any different than when he was alone. They just stare at each other for a while.*

Hoss: My sleuth tells me you're drivin' a '58 Impala with a Vet underneath.

Crow: Razor, Leathers. Very razor.

Hoss: Did you rest up?

Crow: Got the molar chomps. Eyes stitched. You can vision what's sittin'. Very razor to cop z's sussin' me to be on the far end of the spectrum.

Hoss: It wasn't strategy man. I was really tired. You steal a lotta' energy from a distance.

CROW: No shrewd from this end either. We both bow to bigger fields.

HOSS: You wanna drink or somethin'?

CROW: (*he laughs with a cackle*) Lush in sun time gotta smell of lettuce or turn of the century. Sure Leathers, squeeze on the grape vine one time.

HOSS: White or red?

CROW: Blood.

HOSS: Be right back.

CROW: No slaves in this crib?

HOSS: They're all in the pool watchin' a movie.

CROW: Very Greek.

HOSS: Yeah. Just relax, I'll be right back.
(Hoss *exits*. CROW *gets up and walks around thinking out loud*.)

CROW: Very razor. Polished. A gleam to the movements. Weighs out in the eighties from first to third. Keen on the left side even though he's born on the right. Maybe forced his hand to change. Butched some instincts down. Work them through his high range. Cut at the gait. Heel-toe action rhythms of New Orleans. Can't suss that particular. That's well covered. Meshing patterns. Easy mistake here. Suss the bounce.
(CROW *tries to copy* Hoss's *walk. He goes back and forth across the stage practising different styles until he gets the exact one. It's important that he gets inside the feeling of* Hoss's *walk and not just the outer form*.)
Too heavy on the toe. Maybe work the shoulders down. Here's a mode. Three-four cut time copped from Keith Moon. Early. Very early. Now. Where's that pattern. Gotta be in the 'Happy Jack' album. Right around there. Triplets. Six-eight. Here it comes. Bat-

tery. Double bass talk. Fresh Cream influence. Where's that?
Which track? Yeah. The old Skip James tune. Question there.
Right there. (*sings it*) 'I'm so glad, I'm so glad, I'm glad, I'm
glad, I'm glad.' Yeah. Ancient. Inborn. Has to be a surgery. Grind
down.
(*He hears* Hoss *coming and darts back to the chair and sits as
though he'd never moved.* Hoss *enters with a bottle of red wine
and two glasses. He hands one to* Crow *and then he pours himself
one and sets the bottle down.*)

Hoss: Ya know I had a feeling you were comin' this way. A sense. I
was onto a Gypsy pattern early yesterday. Even conjured going
that way myself.

Crow: Cold, Leathers. Very icy. Back seat nights. Tuck and roll pillow time. You got fur on the skin in this trunk.

Hoss: Yeah, yeah. I'm just gettin' bored I guess. I want out.

Crow: I pattern a conflict to that line. The animal says no. The
blood won't go the route. Re-do me right or wrong?

Hoss: Right I guess. Can't you back the language up, man. I'm too
old to follow the flash.

Crow: Choose an argot Leathers. Singles or LPs. 45, 78, 33⅓

Hoss: I musta' misfed my data somehow. I thought you were raw,
unschooled. Ya' know? I mean, maybe the training's changed
since my time. Look, I wanna just sound you for a while before
we get down to the cut. O.K.? You don't know how lonely it's
been. I can talk to Cheyenne but we mostly reminisce on old kills.
Ya' know. I don't get new information. I'm starving for new food.
Ya' know? That don't mean I won't be game to mark you when
the time comes. I don't sleep standin' up. Ya' know what I mean?
It's just that I wanna find out what's going on. None of us knows.
I'm surrounded by boobs who're still playin' in the sixties. That's
where I figured you were. Earlier. I figured you for Beach Boys in
fact.

CROW: That sand stayed on the beach with me. You can suss me in detail Leathers. What's your key?

HOSS: This is really weird, me learnin' from you. I mean I can't believe myself admitting it. Ya' know? I thought I could teach you somethin'. I thought you were playin' to the inside. Choosin' me off just to get in the door. I mean I know you must be Mojo's trigger, right?

CROW: De-rail Leathers. You're smokin' the track.

HOSS: Eyes traced a Nevada route. It don't matter. If you ain't from The Root Force you're on the Killin' floor Jack. Anyway you cut it you're a corpse. So let's lay that one on the rack for now. Let's just suspend and stretch it out.

CROW: We can breathe thin or thick. The air is your genius.

HOSS: Good. Now, first I wanna find out how the Gypsy Killers feature the stars. Like me. How do I come off. Are we playin' to a packed house like the Keepers all say?

CROW: (*he cackles*) Image shots are blown, man. No fuse to match the hole. Only power forces weigh the points in our match.

HOSS: You mean we're just ignored? Nobody's payin' attention?

CROW: We catch debris beams from your set. We scope it to our action then send it back to garbage game.

HOSS: Listen chump, a lotta' cats take this game serious. There's a lotta' good Markers in this league.

CROW: You chose ears against tongue Leathers. Not me, I can switch to suit. You wanna patter on my screen for a while?

HOSS: Sorry. It's just hard to take. If it's true. I don't believe we could be that cut off. How did it happen? We're playing in a vacuum? All these years. All the kills and no one's watching?

CROW: Watching takes a side seat. Outside. The Game hammered the outside.

HOSS: And now you hammer us with fucking indifference! This is incredible. It's just like I thought. The Outside is the Inside now.

CROW: (*he cackles*) Harrison, Beatle did that ancient. It cuts a thinner slice with us. Roles fall to birth blood. We're star marked and playing inter-galactic modes. Some travel past earthbound and score on Venus, Neptune, Mars.

HOSS: How do you get to fucking Neptune in a '58 Impala!

CROW: How did you get to earth in a Maserati?

HOSS: There! Why'd you slip just then? Why'd you suddenly talk like a person? You're into a wider scope than I thought. You're playin' my time Gypsy but it ain't gonna work. And get the fuck outa' my chair!!
(CROW *slides out of the chair and starts walking around, twirling his chain and chomping his gum.* HOSS *sits down. He sips his wine. Slowly through the dialogue* CROW *starts to get into* HOSS's *walk until he's doing it perfect.*)

CROW: Your tappets are knockin' rock-man. I sense an internal smokin' at the seams.

HOSS: Yeah, so this is how you play the game. A style match. I'm beginning to suss the mode. Very deadly but no show. Time is still down to the mark, kid. How's your feel for shivs anyway?

CROW: Breakdown lane. Side a' the road days.

HOSS: Yeah, well that's the way it's gonna be. I ain't used a blade myself for over ten years. I reckon it's even longer for you. Maybe never.
(HOSS *begins to switch into a kind of Cowboy-Western image.*)
I reckon you ain't never even seen a knife. A pup like you. Up in Utah we'd used yer kind fer skunk bait and throw away the skunk.

CROW: Throwin' to snake-eyes now Leathers.

HOSS: So you gambled your measly grub stake for a showdown with the champ. Ain't that pathetic. I said that before and I'll say it again. Pathetic.
(CROW *is getting nervous. He feels he's losing the match. He tries to force himself into the walk. He chews more desperately and twirls the chain faster.*)
You young guns comin' up outa' prairie stock and readin' dime novels over breakfast. Drippin' hot chocolate down yer zipper. Pathetic.

CROW: Time warps don't shift the purpose, just the style. You're clickin' door handles now. There'll be more paint on your side than mine.

HOSS: We'd drag you through the street fer a nickel. Naw. Wouldn't even waste the horse. Just break yer legs and leave ya' fer dog meat.

CROW: That's about all you'll get outa' second. Better shift it now Leathers.
(HOSS *shifts to 1920s gangster style.*)

HOSS: You mugs expect to horn in on our district and not have to pay da' price? Da' bosses don't sell out dat cheap to small-time racketeers. You gotta tow da' line punk or you'll wind up just like Mugsy.
(CROW *begins to feel more confident now that he's got* HOSS *to switch.*)

CROW: Good undertow. A riptide invisible moon shot. Very nice slide Leathers.
(HOSS *goes back to his own style.*)

HOSS: Don't give me that. I had you hurtin'. You were down on one knee Crow Bait. I saw you shakin'.

CROW: Fuel injected. Sometimes the skin deceives. Shows a power ripple. Misconstrued Leathers.
(CROW *is into* HOSS's *walk now and does it perfect.*)

HOSS: You were fish tailin' all over the track meathead! I had you tagged!

CROW: Posi-traction rear end. No pit stops the whole route. Maybe you got a warp in your mirror.

HOSS: There's no fuckin' warp. You were down!

CROW: Sounds like a bad condenser. Points and plugs.

HOSS: Suck ass! I had you clean! And stop walkin' like that! That's not the way you walk! That's the way I walk!
(CROW *stops still. They stare at each other for a second.* HOSS *rises slow.*)
All right. I can handle this action but we need a Ref. I ain't playin' unless we score.

CROW: It's your turf.

HOSS: Yeah, and it's stayin' that way. I'm gonna beat you Gypsy. I'm gonna whip you so bad you'll wish we *had* done the shivs. And then I'm gonna send you back with a mark on your forehead. Just a mark that won't never heal.

CROW: You're crossin' wires now Leathers. My send is to lay you cold. I'll play flat out to the myth but the blood runs when the time comes.

HOSS: We'll see. You're well padded Crow Bait but the layers'll peel like a skinned buck. I'm goin' to get a Ref now. You best use the time to work out. You ain't got your chops down. You're gonna need some sharpening up. When I get back it's head to head till one's dead.

(Hoss *exits. The band starts the music to* CROW's *song. He sings.*)

'Crow's Song'

CROW: What he doesn't know—the four winds blow
  Just the same for him as me
  We're clutchin' at the straw and no one knows the law
  That keeps us lost at sea

  But I believe in my mask—The man I made up is me
  And I believe in my dance—And my destiny

  I coulda' gone the route—of beggin' for my life
  Crawlin' on my hands and knees
  But there ain't no Gods or saviors who'll give you
                    flesh and blood
  It's time to squeeze the trigger

  But I believe in my mask—The man I made up is me
  And I believe in my dance—And my destiny

  The killer time—will leave us on the line
  Before the cards are dealt
  It's a blindman's bluff—without the stuff
  To reason or to tell

  But I believe in my mask—The man I made up is me
  And I believe in my dance—And my destiny

(*The song ends.* Hoss *enters with the* REFEREE. *He's dressed just like an N.B.A. ref with black pants, striped shirt, sneakers, a whistle, baseball cap and a huge score-board which he sets up down right. He draws a big 'H' on the top left side of the board and big 'C' on the other. He separates the letters with a line down the middle. As he goes about his business* Hoss *talks to* CROW.)

HOSS: I suppose you wouldn't know what's happened to my people? Becky. Cheyenne, Doc, Star-Man—they're all gone. So's my short.

CROW: Lotsa' force concentration in this spot Leathers. Could be they got bumped out to another sphere. They'll be back when the furnace cools.

Hoss: I don't fancy tap dancers Crow Bait. I like both feet on the ground. Nailed. Joe Frazier mode.

Crow: I vision you brought the rule, man.

Hoss: Yeah. He's gonna see that things stay clean. Points scored and lost on deviation from the neutral field state.

Crow: I'd say you already broke the mercury in round one.

Hoss: That don't count! We start when he's ready.

Crow: I can't cipher why you wanna play this course, Leathers. It's a long way from shivs.

Hoss: Just to prove I ain't outside.

Crow: To me or you?
(Hoss *considers for a second but shakes it off.*)

Hoss: I don't know how it is with you but for me it's like looking down a long pipe. All the time figurin' that to be the total picture. You take your eye away for a second and see you been gyped.

Crow: 'Gyped'—coming from 'Gypsy'.
(*Through all this the* Ref *puts himself through several yoga positions and regulated breathing exercises, cracks his knuckles, shakes his legs out like a track star and runs in place.*)

Hoss: I'm gonna have fun skinnin' you.

Crow: If narrow in the eye ball is your handicap then runnin' a gestalt match figures suicidal. Look, Leathers, may be best to run the blades and forget it.

Hoss: No! You ain't no better than me.

Crow: You smell loser, Leathers. This ain't your stompin' turf.

Hoss: We'll see.

Crow: It took me five seconds to suss your gait. I ran it down to Skip James via Ginger Baker. How long's it gonna take you to cop mine?

Hoss: I ain't a Warlock I'm a Marker.

Crow: So stick to steel. Pistols. How 'bout the ancient chicken? Masarati against the Chevy. That's fair.

Hoss: I see you turnin' me in. I ain't stupid. I'm stickin' with this route Gypsy and that's what you want so can the horseshit. There's no Marker on the planet can out-kill me with no kinda' weapon or machine. You'd die with the flag still in the air. That's straight on. But too easy. I'm tired of easy marks. I'm drawin' to the flush. I'm gonna leave you paralyzed alive. Amputated from the neck down.

Crow: Just like you.

Hoss: We'll see.
(Ref *wipes himself off with a towel and tests his whistle.*)

Ref: All right. Let's get the show on the road. We all know the rules. When the bell rings, come out swingin'. When it rings again go to your corners. No bear hugs, rabbit punches, body pins or holdin' on. If a man goes down we give him five and that's it. After that you can kick the shit out of him. Ready? Let's have it!
(*An off-stage bell rings. The band starts slow, low-keyed lead guitar and bass music, it should be a lurking evil sound like the 'Sister Morphine' cut on 'Sticky Fingers'. Hoss and Crow begin to move to the music, not really dancing but feeling the power in their movements through the music. They each pick up microphones. They begin their assaults just talking the words in rhythmic patterns, sometimes going with the music, sometimes counterpointing it. As the round progresses the music builds with drums and piano coming in, maybe a rhythm guitar too. Their voices*

build so that sometimes they sing the words or shout. The words remain as intelligible as possible like a sort of talking opera.)
Round 1

CROW: Pants down. The moon show. Ass out the window. Belt lash. Whip lash. Side slash to the kid with a lisp. The dumb kid. The loser. The runt. The mutt. The shame kid. Kid on his belly. Belly to the blacktop. Slide on the rooftop. Slide through the parkin' lot. Slide kid. Shame kid. Slide. Slide.

HOSS: Never catch me with beer in my hand. Never caught me with my pecker out. Never get caught. Never once. Never, never. Fast on the hoof. Fast on the roof. Fast through the still night. Faster than the headlight. Fast to the move.

CROW: Catch ya' outa' breath by the railroad track.

HOSS: Never got caught!

CROW: Catch ya' with yer pants down. Whip ya' with a belt. Whup ya' up one side and down to the other. Whup ya' all night long. Whup ya' to the train time. Leave ya' bleedin' and cryin'. Leave ya' cryin' for Ma. All through the night. All through the night long. Shame on the kid. Little dumb kid with a lisp in his mouth. Bleedin' up one side and down to the other.

HOSS: No! Moved to a hard town. Moved in the midnight.

CROW: Comin' in a wet dream. Pissin' on the pillow. Naked on a pillow. Naked in a bedroom. Naked in a bathroom. Beatin' meat to the face in a mirror. Beatin' it raw. Beatin' till the blood come. Pissin' blood on the floor. Hidin' dirty pictures. Hide 'em from his Ma. Hide 'em from his Pa. Hide 'em from the teacher.

HOSS: Never did happen! You got a high heel. Step to the lisp. Counter you, never me. Back steppin' Crow Bait. History don't cut it. History's in the pocket.

CROW: The marks show clean through. Look to the guard. That's where it hides. Lurkin' like a wet hawk. Scuffle mark. Belt mark. Tune to the rumble. The first to run. The shame kid. The first on his heel. Shame on the shame kid. Never live it down. Never show his true face. Last in line. Never face a showdown. Never meet a face-off. Never make a clean break. Long line a' losers.

(*All the other characters from Act One come on dressed in purple cheerleader outfits. Each has a pom-pom in one hand and a big card with the word 'Victory' printed on it. They do a silent routine, mouthing the word 'Victory' over and over and shaking their pom-poms. They move around the stage doing a shuffle step and stupid routines just like at the football games. CROW and HOSS keep up the battle concentrating on each other. The REF bobs in and out between them, watching their moves closely like a fight ref.*)

HOSS: Missed the whole era. Never touched the back seat.

CROW: Coughin' in the corner. Dyin' from pneumonia. Can't play after dinner. Lonely in a bedroom. Dyin' for attention. Starts to hit the small time. Knockin' over pay phones. Rollin' over Beethoven. Rockin' pneumonia. Beboppin' to the Fat Man. Drivin' to the small talk. Gotta make his big mark. Take a crack at the teacher. Find him in the can can. There he's doin' time time. Losin' like a wino. Got losin' on his mind. Got losin' all the time.

HOSS: You can't do that!

(*At some point the cheerleaders all come down stage in a line, turn their backs on the audience, take their pants down and bend over bare assed. When the bell rings marking the end of the round, they all turn around and show the reverse side of their cards which has the word 'Fight' in big letters. Then they all hobble off with their pants around their ankles giggling like school kids.*)

CROW: In the slammer he's a useless. But he does his schoolin'. Tries to keep a blind face. Storin' up his hate cells. Thinks he's got it comin'. Bangin' out the street signs. Tryin' to do his time time. Turns into a candy-cock just to get a reprieve. Lost in the long sleeve. Couldn't get a back up. So he takes his lock up. Calls it bitter medicine. Makes a sour face. Gotta pay his dues back. Fakin' like a guru. Finally gets his big chance and sucks the warden's dinger. Gotta be a good boy. Put away the stinger. Put away the gun boy. I'll take away your time. Just gimme some head boy. Just get down on your knees. Gimme some blow boy. I'll give ya' back the key. I'll give ya' back the key boy! Just get down on my thing boy! Just get down! Get on down! Get on down! Get down! Get down! Get down! Come on!

(*The bell rings. The music stops. The cheerleaders flash their cards and exit. REF goes to the score-board and without hesitation chalks up a big mark for CROW. CROW lies flat on his back and relaxes completely. He looks like he's dead. HOSS paces around nervous.*)

HOSS: What the fuck! What the fuck was that! (*to the* REF) You call that fair? You're chalkin' that round up to him! On what fucking grounds!

REF: Good clean body punches. Nice left jab. Straight from the shoulder. Had you rocked on your heels two or three times. No doubt about it.

HOSS: Are you kiddin' me! If flash and intensity is what you want I can give you plenty a' that. I thought we were shootin' honest pool. This kid's a fuckin' fish man. Nothin' but flash. No heart. Look at him. Wasted on his back and I'm still smokin'.

REF: (*looking at his watch*) Better get some rest. You got thirty seconds left.

HOSS: I don't need rest. I'm ready to rock. It's him that's stroked out on the fuckin' floor, not me. Look at him. How can you give him the round when he's in that kinda' shape.

REF: Good clean attack.

HOSS: Clean! You call that clean? He was pickin' at a past that ain't even there. Fantasy marks. Like a dog scratchin' on ice. I can play

that way if I was a liar. The reason I brought you into this match
was to keep everything above the table. How can you give points
to a liar.

REF: I don't. I give 'em to the winner.
(*The bell rings.* CROW *jumps to his feet. The band strikes a note.*
HOSS *steps in. He speaks to the band.*)

HOSS: All right look. Can the music. This ain't Broadway. Let's get
this down to the skinny.

REF: What's going on! Play the round!

HOSS: What'sa matter, Crow Bait? Afraid to do it naked? Drop the
echo stick and square me off.

CROW: You should be past roots on this scale, Leathers. Very ret-
rograde.

HOSS: Don't gimme that. I wanna strip this down to what's necessary.

CROW: (*laughing*) Necessity?

REF: This is against the code. Either play this round or it's no
match.

CROW: We'll walk this dance so long as sounds can push round
three. Certain muscles have gone green on me, Leathers. You can
cipher.
(*The bell rings again.* HOSS *and* CROW *put down their mikes
slowly and deliberately as though they both had knives and agreed
instead to wrestle.* REF *moves around them. The band remains
quiet.*)
Round Two

HOSS: (*talking like an ancient delta blues singer*) Chicago. Yeah,
well I hear about all that kinda 'lectric machine gun music. All
that kinda 'lectric shuffle, you dig? I hear you boys hook up in the
toilet and play to da mirror all tru the night.

CROW: (*nervously*) Yeah. Well, you know, twelve bars goes a long way.

HOSS: (*growing physically older*): It come down a long way. It come down by every damn black back street you can move sideways through. 'Fore that even it was snakin' thru rubber plants. It had Cheetahs movin' to its rhythm. You dig?

CROW: Yeah. Sure. It's a matter a' course.
(CROW *moves to get away from him as* HOSS *becomes a menacing ancient spirit. Like a voodoo man.*)

HOSS: Yo' 'yeah' is tryin' to shake a lie, boy. The radio's lost the jungle. You can't hear that space 'tween the radio and the jungle.

CROW: It's in my blood. I got genius.

HOSS: Fast fingers don't mean they hold magic. That's lost to you, dude. That's somethin' sunk on another continent and I don't mean Atlantis. You can dig where the true rhymes hold down. Yo' blood know that if nothin' else.

CROW: Blood. Well listen, I need some spray on my callouses now and then, but it's not about endurance.

HOSS: Ha! Yo lost dew claw. Extra weight. You ain't come inside the South. You ain't even opened the door. The brass band contain yo' world a million times over.

CROW: Electricity brought it home. Without juice you'd be long forgot.

HOSS: Who's doin' the rememberin'? The fields opened up red in Georgia, South Carolina. A moan lasted years back then. The grey and blue went down like a harvest and what was left?

CROW: That scale hung itself short.

HOSS: What was left was the clarinet, the bass drum, the trumpet. The fixin's for a salad. All hung gold and black in the pawnshop window. All them niggers with their hollers hangin' echoes from the fields. All the secret messages sent through a day a' blazin' work.

CROW: I can't do nothing about that. I'm in a different time.

HOSS: And what brought their heads up off the cement? Not no Abraham Lincoln. Not no Emancipation. Not no John Brown. It was the gold and black behind them windows. The music of somethin' inside that no boss man could touch.

CROW: I touch down here, Leathers. Bring it to now.

HOSS: You'd like a free ride on a black man's back.

CROW: I got no guilt to conjure! Fence me with the present.

HOSS: But you miss the origins, milk face. Little Brother Montegomery with the keyboard on his back. The turpentine circuit. Piano ringin' through the woods. Back then you get hung you couldn't play the blues. Back when the boogie wasn't named and every cat house had a professor. Hookers movin' to the ivory tinkle. Diplomats and sailors gettin' laid side by side to the blues. Gettin' laid so bad the U. S. Navy have to close down Storyville. That's how the move began. King Oliver got Chicago talkin' New Orleans. Ma Rainey, Blind Lemon Jefferson. They all come and got the gangsters hoppin'.

CROW: I'm a Rocker, not a hick!

HOSS: You could use a little cow flop on yer shoes, boy. Yo' music's in yo' head. You a blind minstrel with a phoney shuffle. You got a wound gapin' 'tween the chords and the pickin'. Chuck Berry can't even mend you up. You doin' a pantomime in the eye of a hurricane. Ain't even got the sense to signal for help. You lost the barrelhouse, you lost the honkey-tonk. You lost your feelings in a suburban country club the first time they ask you to play 'Risin' River Blues' for the debutante ball. You ripped your own self off

and now all you got is yo' poison to call yo' gift. You a punk chump with a sequin nose and you'll need more'n a Les Paul Gibson to bring you home.
(REF *blows his whistle.*)

REF: Hold it, hold it, hold it!
(Hoss *snaps back to himself.*)

Hoss: What's wrong?

REF: I don't know. Somethin's funny. Somethin's outa whack here. We'll call this one a draw.

Hoss: A draw!

REF: I can't make heads or tails outa this.

Hoss: I had him cut over both eyes!

REF: We leave it. Let's get on with round 3.

Hoss: Look at him! He's unconscious standin' up.

REF: Play the round!
(*The bell rings.* CROW *jumps into action, dancing like Muhammad Ali.* Hoss *moves flatfooted trying to avoid him.* CROW *is now on the offensive. The music starts again.*)
Round 3

CROW: So ya' wanna be a rocker. Study the moves. Jerry Lee Lewis. Buy some blue suede shoes. Move yer head like Rod Stewart. Put yer ass in a grind. Talkin' sock it to it, get the image in line. Get the image in line boy. The fantasy rhyme. It's all over the streets and you can't buy the time. You can't buy the bebop. You can't buy the slide. Got the fantasy blues and no place to hide.

Hoss: O.K. this time I stay solid. You ain't suckin' me into jive rhythms. I got my own. I got my patterns. Original. I'm my own man. Original. I stand solid. It's just a matter of time. I'll wear you to the bone.

CROW: Collectin' the South. Collectin' the blues. Flat busted in Chicago and payin' yer dues.

HOSS: Kick it out fish face! This time you bleed!
(REF *blows his whistle. The music stops.*)

REF: (*to* HOSS) No clinches. This ain't a wrestlin' match.

HOSS: I was countering.

REF: Just keep daylight between ya'. Let's go.
(*The music starts again.* CROW *goes back to the offense.*)

HOSS: (*to* REF) I was countering, man!

CROW: Ain't got his chops yet but listens to Hendricks. Ears in the stereo lappin' it up. Likes snortin' his horses too chicken to fix. Still gets a hard on but can't get it up.

HOSS: Backwards tactics! I call a foul!
(REF *blows his whistle again.*)

REF: No stalls. Keep it movin'. Keep it movin'.

HOSS: I call a foul. He can't shift in midstream.

REF: Let's go, let's go.

HOSS: He can't do that!
(REF *blows his whistle again. The music comes up.*)

CROW: Can't get it sideways walkin' the dog. Tries trainin' his voice to sound like a frog. Sound like a Dylan, sound like a Jagger, sound like an earthquake all over the Fender. Wearin' a shag now, looks like a fag now. Can't get it together with chicks in the mag. Can't get it together for all of his tryin'. Can't get it to-

gether for fear that he's dyin'. Fear that he's crackin' busted in two. Busted in three parts. Busted in four. Busted and dyin' and cryin' for more. Busted and bleedin' all over the floor. All bleedin' and wasted and tryin' to score.
(REF *blows his whistle.*)

HOSS: What the fuck's wrong now?

REF: I'm gonna have to call that a T.K.O.

HOSS: Are you fuckin' crazy?

REF: That's the way I see it. The match is over.

HOSS: I ain't even started to make my move yet!

REF: Sorry.
(HOSS *lets loose a blood-curdling animal scream and runs to one of the pistols on the floor, picks it up and fires, emptying the gun into the* REF. REF *falls dead.* HOSS *should be out of control then snap himself back. He just stands there paralyzed and shaking.*)

CROW: Now the Keepers'll be knockin' down your hickory, Leathers.

HOSS: Fuck 'em. Let 'em come. I'm a Gypsy now. Just like you.

CROW: Just like me?

HOSS: Yeah. Outside the game.

CROW: And into a bigger one. You think you can cope?

HOSS: With the Gypsies? Why not. You could teach me. I could pick it up fast.

CROW: You wanna be like me now?

HOSS: Not exactly. Just help me into the style. I'll develop my own image. I'm an original man. A one and only. I just need some help.

CROW: But I beat you cold. I don't owe you nothin'.

HOSS: All right. Look. I'll set you up with a new short and some threads in exchange for some lessons.

CROW: No throw Leathers.

HOSS: I'll give ya' all my weapons and throw in some dope. How's that?

CROW: Can't hack it.

HOSS: All right, what do you want? Anything. It's all yours.
    (CROW *pauses*)

CROW: O.K. This is what I want. All your turf from Phoenix to San Berdoo clear up to Napa Valley and back. The whole shot. That's what I want. (HOSS *pauses for a while, stunned. Then a smile of recognition comes over him.*)

HOSS: Now I get it. I should cut you in half right now. I shoulda' slit yer throat soon's you came through the door. You must be outa' yer fuckin' cake man! All my turf?! You know how long it's taken me to collect that ground. You know how many kills it's taken! I'm a fuckin' champion man. Not an amateur. All my turf! That's all I've got.

CROW: Yer throwin' away yer reputation, so why not give me yer turf. You got nothin' to lose. It won't do you no good once the Keepers suss this murder.

HOSS: I still got power. The turf is my power. Without that I'm nothin'. I can survive without the image, but a Marker without no turf is just out to lunch.

CROW: I thought you wanted to cop Gypsy style.

HOSS: I do but I need my turf!!

CROW: The Gypsies float their ground, man. Nobody sets up colors.

Hoss: *You* want it bad enough. What's a' matter with you. You movin' outa' Gypsy ranks?

Crow: Razor Leathers.

Hoss: Wait a minute. You tricked me. You wanna trade places with me? You had this planned right from the start.

Crow: Very razor. An even trade. I give you my style and I take your turf.

Hoss: That's easy for you and hard for me.

Crow: You got no choice.

Hoss: I could just move out like I am and keep everything. I could make it like that.

Crow: Try it.

Hoss: You got it all worked out don't ya, fish face? You run me through a few tricks, take everything I got and send me out to die like a chump. Well I ain't fallin' for it.

Cross: Then what're you gonna do?

Hoss: I'll think a' somethin'. What if we teamed up? Yeah! That's it! You, me and Cheyenne. We start a Gypsy pack.

Crow: I'm a solo man. So are you. We'd do each other in. Who'd be the leader?

Hoss: We don't need a leader. Cheyenne could be the leader.

Crow: Not on my time. Rip that one up, Leathers.

Hoss: How did this happen? This ain't the way it's supposed to happen. Why do you wanna be like me anyway. Look at me. Everything was going so good. I had everything at my finger-tips. Now I'm outa' control. I'm pulled and pushed around from one image to another. Nothin' takes a solid form. Nothin' sure and final. Where do I stand! Where the fuck do I stand!

CROW: Alone, Leathers.

HOSS: Yeah, well I guess I don't got your smarts. That's for sure. You played me just right. Sucked me right into it. There's nothin' to do but call ya'. All right. The turf's yours. The whole shot. Now show me how to be a man.

CROW: A man's too hard, Leathers. Too many doors to that room. A Gypsy's easy. Here, chew on some sap.
(*He hands* Hoss *a stick of gum.* Hoss *chews it in a defeated way.*)
Bite down. Chew beyond yourself. That's what ya' wanna shoot for. Beyond. Walk like ya' got knives on yer heels. Talk like a fire. The eyes are important. First you gotta learn yer eyes. Now look here. Look in my eyes. Straight out.
(Hoss *stands close to* CROW's *face and looks in his eyes.* CROW *stares back.*)
No! Yer lookin' in. Back at yourself. You gotta look out. Straight into me and out the back a' my head. Like my eyes were tunnels goin' straight through to daylight. That's better. More. Cut me in half. Get mean. There's too much pity, man. Too much empathy. That's not the target. Use yer eyes like a weapon. Not defensive. Offensive. Always on the offense. You gotta get this down. You can paralyze a mark with a good set of eyes.

HOSS: How's that?

CROW: Better. Get down to it. Too much searchin'. I got no answers. Go beyond confidence. Beyond loathing. Just kill with the eyes. That's it. That's better. Now. How do you feel?

HOSS: Paralyzed.

CROW: That'll change. The power'll shift to the other side. Feel it?

HOSS: No.

CROW: It'll come. Just hang in there. Feel it now?

Hoss: No. Can I blink now?

Crow: Yeah. Give 'em a rest.
(Hoss *blinks his eyes and moves away.*)
It'll come. You gotta practise like a musician. You don't learn all yer licks in one session. Now try out yer walk. Start movin' to a different drummer man. Ginger Baker's burned down. Get into Danny Richmond, Sonny Murray, Tony Williams. One a' them cats. More Jazz licks. Check out Mongo Santamaria, he might get yer heels burnin'. (Hoss *starts moving awkwardly around the stage.*)

Hoss: I never heard a' them guys.

Crow: O.K. pick one. Any one. Pick one ya' like.

Hoss: Capaldi.

Crow: Too clean man. Try out Ainsley Dunbar. Nice hot licks. Anyone that gets the knife goin'. You gotta slice blacktop man. Melt asphalt.

Hoss: Keith Moon.

Crow: Too much flash. Get off the cymbals. Stop flyin' around the kit. Get down to it. Get down.

Hoss: Buddy Miles.

Crow: Just loud, man. Blind strength but no touch.

Hoss: Let's go on to somethin' else.

Crow: O.K. Body moves. Do a few chick moves. Fluff up yer feathers. Side a' the head shots. Hand on the hip. Let the weight slide to one side. Straight leg and the opposite bent. Pull on yer basket.
(Hoss *tries to follow.* Crow *acts out all the gestures with a slick cool.*)
Spit out yer teeth. Ear pulls. Nose pulls. Pull out a booger. Slow

scratches from shoulder to belly. Hitch up yer shirt. Sex man. Tighten yer ass. Tighten one cheek and loosen the other. Play off yer thighs to yer calves. Get it all talkin' a language.

Hoss: Slow down! I ain't a fuckin' machine.

Crow: Yer gettin' it. Yer doin' O.K. It's comin'. Talk to yer blood. Get it together. Get it runnin' hot on the left side and cold on the right. Now split it. Now put it in halves. Get the top half churnin', the bottom relaxed. Control, Leathers. Ya' gotta learn control. Pull it together.

Hoss: I'm not prepared. I can't just plunge into this. I gotta have some preliminaries.

Crow: O.K. You're right. Tell ya' what. Sit down in the chair and relax. Just take it easy. Come on.

Hoss: Maybe I'm too old.

Crow: Come on, just sit yerself down.
(Hoss *sits in the chair.* Crow *paces around him.*)
We gotta break yer patterns down, Leathers. Too many bad habits. Re-program the tapes. Now just relax. Start breathin' deep and slow. Empty your head. Shift your attention to immediate sounds. The floor. The space around you. The sound of your heart. Keep away from fantasy. Shake off the image. No pictures just pure focus. How does it feel?

Hoss: I don't know. Different I guess.

Crow: Just ease down. Let everything go.
(Becky *comes on down left facing the audience. She wears a black wig and is dressed like Anna Karina in 'Alphaville'. She caresses herself as though her hands were a man's, feeling her tits, her thighs, her waist. Sometimes when one hand seems to take too much advantage she seizes it with the other hand and pushes it away.* Hoss *seems to turn into a little boy.*)

Hoss: You won't let nobody hurt me will ya'?

CROW: Nobody's gonna hurt ya'.

HOSS: Where have I been. All this time. No memory. I was never there.
(BECKY *talks straight out to the audience. But directs it at* Hoss.)

BECKY: I never knew you were that kind of a guy. I thought you were nice. A nice guy. I never thought you'd be like the others. Why do you do that? You know I'm not that kind of a girl. Come on. I just wanna talk. I wanna have a conversation. Tell me about yourself. Come on. Don't do that. Can't we just talk or something. All right, I wanna go then. Take me home. Come on. Let's go get a Coke. Come on. I mean it. Don't do that! Don't!
(*Her hands pull off her sweater. The wig comes off with it. She's wearing a stiff white bra underneath. She struggles against her hands then lets them go then struggles again.*)
Can't we go back. I'm going to be late. Can't we just kiss? No! Don't! Come on. I don't wanna do this. I'm not that kind of a girl. Look, just keep your hands off! I mean it. I don't like it. I just wanna talk. Tell me something nice.
(*Her hands rip off her bra and feel her tits.*)
Just talk to me. Tell me about your car. What kind of an engine has it got? Come on. Don't! Do you go racing a lot? Don't you take it down to the strip. No! Don't do that! Has it got overhead lifters. I really like those fat tires. They're really boss. Cut it out! No! Stop it! Don't!
(*Her hands unzip her skirt and tear it off. One hand tries to get inside her panties while the other hand fights it off.*)
I don't go all the way. I can't. I've never ever gone this far before. I don't wanna go all the way. I'm not that kind of a girl. I'll get pregnant. Stop it! All right, just get away from me! Get away! I'm getting out. Let me outa' the car! Let me out! Don't! Let go of me! Let go! (*she starts screaming*) Let me out! Let me out! Let me out! Let me out!
(*She picks up her clothes and runs off.*)

CROW: How is it now?

HOSS: I don't know. Trapped. Defeated. Shot down.

CROW: Just a wave. Time to scoop a Gypsy shot. Start with a clean screen. Are you blank now?

HOSS: I guess.

CROW: Good. Now vision him comin'. Walking towards you from a distance. Can't make out the face yet. Just feel his form. Get down his animal. Like a cat. Lethal and silent. Comin' from far off. Takin' his time. Pull him to ya'. Can you feel him?

HOSS: I think so. It's me. He's just like me only younger. More dangerous. Takes bigger chances. No doubt. No fear.

CROW: Keep him comin'. Pull him into ya'. Put on his gestures. Wear him like a suit a' clothes.

HOSS: Yeah. It *is* me. Just like I always wanted to be. (*The band starts playing the first two chords to 'Slips Away'.* CHEYENNE, STAR-MAN, DOC *and* GALACTIC JACK *come on dressed in white tuxedos with pink carnations in their lapels. They stand in a tight group and sing harmony notes to the music. They move in perfect choreographed movements like the old A capella bands. The music should build slowly with* Hoss's *voice until he stops talking and the* SINGERS *go right into the song.*)
Mean and tough and cool. Untouchable. A true killer. Don't take no shit from nobody. True to his heart. True to his voice. Everything's whole and unshakeable. His eyes cut through the jive. He knows his own fate. Beyond doubt. True courage in every move. Trusts every action to be what it is. Knows where he stands. Lives by a code. His own code. Knows something timeless. Unending trust in himself. No hesitation. Beyond pride or modesty. Speaks the truth without trying. Can't do anything false. Lived out his fantasies. Plunged into fear and come out the other side. Died a million deaths. Tortured and pampered. Holds no grudge. No blame. No guilt. Laughs with his whole being. Passed beyond tears. Beyond ache for the world. Pitiless. Indifferent and riding a state of grace. It ain't me! IT AIN'T ME! IT AIN'T ME!!
(*He collapses in a ball and holds himself tight. The* FOUR GUYS *sing.*)

'Slips Away'

FOUR GUYS: I saw my face in yours—I took you for
                                    myself
    I took you by mistake—for me
    I learned your walk and talk—I learned your mouth
    I learned the secrets in your eye

        But now I find the feelin' slips away
        What's with me night and day is gone

    Where you left off and I begin
    It took me time to break the line
    And on your own is tough enough
    Without the thread that we got broken

        But now I find the feelin' slips away
        What's with me night and day is gone

    If we could signify from far away
    Just close enough to get the touch
    You'd find your face in mine
    And all my faces tryin' to bring you back to me

        But now I find the feelin' slips away
        What's with me night and day is gone
        (*repeat chorus*)
    (*The song ends. The* FOUR GUYS *exit.*)

CROW: Hey, Leathers. Come on man it's time to cope. Get ready to
bop. The world's waitin'.
    (Hoss *doesn't move.*)
    Leathers, you gotta move out to it now. I taught ya' all I know.
    Now it's up to you. You got the power.
    (Hoss *rises holding the gun in his hand.*)

HOSS: In the palm a' my hand. I got the last say.

CROW: That's it. Get ready to roll. You're gonna knock 'em dead.

HOSS: Knock 'em dead.

CROW: Yeah. What about it.

Hoss: You know somethin' Crow? I really like you. I really have respect for you. You know who you are and you don't give a shit.

CROW: Thanks, Leathers.

Hoss: I just hope you never see yourself from the outside. Just a flash of what you're really like. A pitiful flash.

CROW: Like you?

Hoss: Like me.

CROW: No chance, Leathers. The image is my survival kit.

Hoss: Survival. Yeah. You'll last a long time Crow. A real long time. You're a master adapter. A visionary adapter.

CROW: Switch to suit, Leathers, and mark to kill.

Hoss: Tough as a blind man.

CROW: Tough enough to beat the champ.

Hoss: Yeah. You win all right. All this. Body and soul. All this invisible gold. All this collection of torture. It's all yours. You're the winner and I'm the loser. That's the way it stands. But I'm losin' big, Crow Bait. I'm losin' to the big power. All the way. I couldn't take my life in my hands while I was alive but now I can take it in death. I'm a born Marker Crow Bait. That's more than you'll ever be. Now stand back and watch some true style. The mark of a lifetime. A true gesture that won't never cheat on itself 'cause it's the last of its kind. It can't be taught or copied or stolen or sold. It's mine. An original. It's my life and my death in one clean shot.
(Hoss *turns his back to the audience. And puts the gun in his mouth. He raises one hand high in the air and pulls the trigger with the other. He falls in a heap. This gesture should not be in slow motion or use any jive theatrical gimmicks other than the ac-*

tor's own courage on stage. To save the actor's face from powder burns an off-stage gun should be fired at the right moment. CROW *stands silent for a while.*)

CROW: Perfect, Leathers. Perfect. A genius mark. I gotta hand it to ya'. It took ya' long enough but you slid right home. (*he calls off stage*) All right! Let's go!
(BECKY *and* CHEYENNE *enter, dressed like they were in Act One.*)
Becky, get some biceps to drag out these stiffs. Get the place lookin' a little decent. We're gonna have us a celebration.

BECKY: I had a feeling you'd take him. Was it hard?

CROW: Yeah. He was pretty tough. Went out in the old style. Clung right up to the drop.

BECKY: He was a good Marker man. One a' the great ones.

CROW: Not great enough.

BECKY: I guess not.
(*She exits.* CROW *talks to* CHEYENNE *who eyes him.*)

CROW: You eye me bitter wheel-boy. What's the skinny?

CHEYENNE: I guess you want me to drive for you now.

CROW: Maybe. I hear you're the top handler in the gold circuit.

CHEYENNE: You hear good.

CROW: I cipher you turnin' sour though. Suicidal like the master. I don't fashion goin' down to a Kami-Kazi collision just after I knock the top.

CHEYENNE: You're cuttin' me loose?

CROW: That's it.

CHEYENNE: You got big shoes to fill Gypsy. They'll be comin' for you next.

CROW: Naw. That's fer lames. I'm throwin' the shoes away. I'm runnin' flat out to a new course.

CHEYENNE: (*looking at* Hoss's *body*) He was knockin' at the door. He was right up there. He came the long route. Not like you. He earned his style. He was a Marker. A true Marker.

CROW: He was backed up by his own suction, man. Didn't answer to no name but loser. All that power goin' backwards. It's good he shut the oven. If he hadn't he'd be blowin' poison in non-directions. I did him a favor. Now the power shifts and sits till a bigger wind blows. Not in my life run but one to come. And all the ones after that. Changin' hands like a snake dance to heaven. This is my time Cowboy and I'm runnin' it up the middle. You best grab your ticket and leave the Maserati with the keys.

CHEYENNE: Sure.
(*He reaches in his pocket and pulls out the keys to the car.*)
Good luck.
(*He throws the keys at* CROW's *feet and exits.* CROW *smiles, bends down slowly and picks up the keys. He tosses them in his hand. The band starts the music.* CROW *sings 'Rollin' Down'.*

   'Rollin' Down'
CROW: Keep me rollin' down
    Keep me rollin' down
    Keep me in my state a' grace
    Just keep me rollin' down

    I've fooled the Devil's hand
    I've fooled the Ace of Spades
    I've called the bluff in God's own face
    Now keep me from my fate

    If I'm a fool then keep me blind
    I'd rather feel my way
    If I'm a tool for a bigger game
    You better get down—you better get down and pray

Just keep me rollin' down
Keep me rollin' down
Keep me in my state a' grace
Just keep me rollin' down.
(*The song ends. The lights go to black.*)

THE HOT L
BALTIMORE
Lanford Wilson

THE HOT L BALTIMORE

Of all of Lanford Wilson's plays, *The Hot L Baltimore* has certainly received the most honors: In its year-long run in New York City, it won not only the Obie Award for the best Off-Broadway play of 1973, but the New York Drama Critics Circle prize for best American play of 1973, the Outer Critics Circle award, and the John Gassner playwriting award.

The missing "e" in the marquee over the hotel (and in the play's title) gives us a clue to the major themes of *The Hot L Baltimore*. This is not to be about a Grand Hotel, with fabulous characters and a glamorous plot, but about a place of faded elegance and lost dreams, peopled with wandering souls and the small dramas of everyday life. Yet with unabashed sentiment, Wilson celebrates the simple virtues of kindness, respect, and hope. As one of his characters says, in Wilson's characteristically colloquial and poignant language: "I just think it's really chicken not to believe in anything!"

One of Wilson's innovations, later copied by other playwrights, was the device of overlapping dialogue. Two or three couples often talk simultaneously in the play, starting and stopping together, in an effect both musical and realistic. The set, designed by Ronald Radice, turned the stage, in the words of the New York *Times* drama critic, "into an authentically seedy hotel lobby, complete with buzzing switchboard, potted plants, and what appears to be a marble staircase—a reminder of the Baltimore's elegant past."

Clive Barnes wrote in the *Times*, "It is an easy play to love . . . Mr. Wilson is both funny and sad about today, and the combination is an unbeatable winner." Also writing in the New York *Times*, critic Mel Gussow said: "Lanford Wilson writes with understanding and sensitivity about unwanted people. His characters are locked in interior worlds, clinging to solitary, futile dreams—and stubborn about not being defeated . . . At the playwright's invitation we share lives that are both comic and wistful. This is a play to be savored and cherished."

Born in Missouri in 1937, Lanford Wilson came to New York City in his early twenties and immediately became an actor, director, and designer for the Caffe Cino and Cafe La Mama theatres, two of the most prolific and influential showcases of Off-Broadway talent in the early 1960s. In 1969, after having worked at several other Off-Broadway theatres, Wilson founded the Circle Repertory Company with director Marshall Mason, and over the next decade its productions won over a dozen Obies, a record unmatched by any other theatre.

Since 1963 Lanford Wilson has written at least one play a year—over thirty plays to date—and has received numerous awards, including the Vernon Rice Award in 1968, the National Institute of Arts and Letters Award in 1974, and a second Obie Award, for *The Mound Builders*, in 1975.

In addition to the Obie which was given to Lanford Wilson for *The Hot L Baltimore*, Marshall Mason won an Obie for his direction of the play and Mari Gorman won an Obie for her performance as Jackie.

THE HOT L BALTIMORE was first presented on February 4, 1973, at the Circle Theatre in New York City. Producers Kermit Bloomgarden and Roger Ailes transferred the Circle Theatre Company production to the Circle-in-the-Square Theatre, where it reopened on March 22, 1973, with the following cast:

BILL LEWIS	*Judd Hirsch*
GIRL	*Trish Hawkins*
MILLIE	*Helen Stenborg*
MRS. BELLOTTI	*Henrietta Bagley*
APRIL GREEN	*Conchata Ferrell*
MR. MORSE	*Rob Thirkield*
JACKIE	*Mari Gorman*
JAMIE	*Zane Lasky*
MR. KATZ	*Antony Tenuta*
SUZY	*Stephanie Gordon*
SUZY'S JOHN	*Burke Pearson*
PAUL GRANGER III	*Jonathan Hogan*
MRS. OXENHAM	*Louise Clay*
CAB DRIVER	*Peter Tripp*
DELIVERY BOY	*Marcial Gonzales*

The play was directed by Marshall Mason, with sets by Ronald Radice, costumes by Dina Costa, and sound by Charles London.

THE PEOPLE

MR. KATZ: The hotel manager. Thirty-five, balding a little but hiding it. Firm and wary and at times more than a little weary. Dark, in an inexpensive dark suit. A baritone

MRS. OXENHAM: The day desk clerk–phone operator. Forty-five and firm; quick-speaking with no commerce

BILL LEWIS: The night clerk. Thirty, large-featured, well-built in a beefy way, a handsome but not aggressive face. He covers his difficulty in communicating his feelings for the Girl with a kind of clumsy, friendly bluster. Baritone

PAUL GRANGER III: A student, twenty. Blond, angular, and taut. His tenor voice is constrained by anxiety, he speaks and moves sporadically. Clear, lightly tanned complexion

MRS. BELLOTTI: The mother of a former tenant, fifty-five. Round and thin-voiced; complains to get her way, she is a whining fighter. Neatly but not expensively dressed. A sigher

THE RESIDENTS

MR. MORSE: Seventy, craggy, with a high, cracking voice. Morse moves slowly, with great energy and a sense of outrage

MILLIE: A retired waitress, sixty-eight, with good carriage and a lovely voice. Elegance marred by an egocentric spiritualism

THE GIRL: A call girl, nineteen. Light, blonde, maddeningly curious; a romantic enthusiasm and a youthful ebullience, which is perhaps unconsciously exaggerated for its appeal in her trade

APRIL GREEN: A prostitute, over thirty. A large and soft pragmatist with a mellow alto laugh and a beautiful face

SUZY: A prostitute, thirty. She is hopelessly romantic and hard as nails. A mezzo

JACKIE: Twenty-four. Jeans, boots, her name written on the back of her denim jacket. Her manner, voice, and stance are those of a young stevedore. To her humiliation, she is, under the manner, both femininely vulnerable and pretty

JAMIE: Jackie's brother. Pale, small, and wiry. A little slow (one suspects browbeaten). Alert but not quick. Always listening to his sister. Nineteen

THE SCENE

Once there was a railroad and the neighborhood of the railroad ter-
minals bloomed (boomed) with gracious hotels.

The Hotel Baltimore, built in the late nineteenth century, remod-
eled during the Art Deco last stand of the railroads, is a five-story establishment intended to be an elegant and restful haven. Its history
has mirrored the rails' decline. The marble stairs and floors, the
carved wood paneling have aged as neglected ivory ages, into a dull
gold. The Hotel Baltimore is scheduled for demolition.

The theater, evanescent itself, and for all we do perhaps itself
disappearing here, seems the ideal place for the representation of the
impermanence of our architecture.

The lobby is represented by three areas that rise as the remains of
a building already largely demolished: the Front Desk, the lounge,
and the stairway.

Much of the action of the play is in the area behind the Front
Desk. It should be open to the audience so we can follow the routine of the staff. Above this inner sanctum is a Rivera-style mural
depicting the railroad's progress westward. Against the mural are
stacked dozens of record books, boxes of files and letters. A broken
TV is used as a table for paperbacks, a hotplate, and a radio. There
is a card table; folding chairs where the hookers congregate; the
usual switchboard (which should be practical); pigeonholes; and a
sweeping desk that faces the lounge.

The lounge: a sofa and three or four chairs, none original to the
hotel, are all re-covered in plastic fabric. There is a table large
enough to set up a checkerboard. From the lounge the marble stairway rises and curves, leading off to one side.

There could be an elevator with a barricade across the doors.

There is a door to a broom closet and the skeletal indication of the front door.

Over the center of the lobby is a non-working and almost unseen bronze chandelier that serves as the source of power, via two extension cords, for the tinny radio and the office hotplate.

About the radio: the play is designed to incorporate music popular during production. The music plays in the theater before the acts, and as the lights dim, the sound fades into the radio on stage. At the end of the acts the radio music builds again, moving into the house. The first and third acts should end with a positive song with an upbeat, a song that one has heard in passing a dozen times but never listened to closely.

The time is a recent Memorial Day.

ACT ONE

(PAUL GRANGER III *is asleep in a chair.* BILL *and* GIRL *are behind the desk; he is at the switchboard, she is sitting beside, watching the operation. Six lines are plugged into the board. A radio is just audible.*)

BILL: (*into the mouthpiece*) It's seven o'clock. (*He disconnects one line.*) It's seven o'clock. (*He disconnects another.*)

GIRL: How do you do that? You plug everybody in at once, then just keep ringing until everybody answers, huh?

BILL: It's seven o'clock. (*Starts to disconnect the line.*) I don't know; I ain't been out, I got no idea.

GIRL: (*impulsively into the phone*) Miserable. Terrible; it's raining and cold and—

BILL: (*Quickly disconnecting the line.*) Don't do that. I told you, you can't do that if you're gonna sit back here.

GIRL: I want to find out what you're doing all the time.

BILL: You see why I don't have time to talk in the morning— (*Into the phone*) It's seven o'clock.

GIRL: I just answer the—

BILL: You don't answer, you ask questions. (*Ringing.*) Come on.

GIRL: It helps me get awake.

BILL: It doesn't help me any when I'm trying to—

GIRL: —When you wake up, don't you like a pleasant little—

BILL: (*Into the phone.*) It's seven o'clock. Seven o'clock. (*Leaving the switchboard, turning off the radio.*) When I wake up, I get up.

GIRL: (*Taking up the call sheet.*) Six different people having to get up at seven o'clock. I'd hate it.
(BILL *looks at her disapprovingly, then notices something on the stairs.*)

BILL: Who's there? Who's up on the—

MILLIE: (*Overlapping*) Good morning, Billy; don't let me frighten you. (*She starts a slow descent into the light.*)

BILL: Morning, Millie.

MILLIE: (*To herself*) I don't know why it should tire me going down the stairs. I believe my body's metabolism can't get it through its head that I'm in retirement. You'd think after six months I'd be able to sleep past six-thirty; but I can't even manage to get back to sleep in the morning.

BILL: (*Overlapping from "head"—Ringing.*) Son of a bitch.

GIRL: Who's that? Maybe they didn't get in till late last night.

BILL: No, he's like that every morning. Same thing every morning. (*To* MILLIE—*who has reached the desk*) You see what they're doing to the Pioneer? I drive by.

GIRL: That was such a beautiful place! Why do they tear everything down?

MILLIE: (*She takes a morning paper and goes to the sofa.*) No, no, what would I care now?

BILL: They really built that old place; they're having a hell of a time getting it down.
(*Behind* GIRL'S *back*) That's not the only building going under the ball, you know.
(*Indicating this hotel.*)

MILLIE: So I hear. Well . . .

GIRL: (*Overlapping "well"*) Where do you live?

BILL: (*To* MILLIE) Don't you want to—

GIRL: Where do you live? You said you drive by the Pioneer.

BILL: Uptown; don't poke me.

GIRL: Who do you live with? Are you married?

BILL: Come on! (*Turning to the switchboard; disconnecting the last line.*) It's seven o'clock.

GIRL: What are you doing? He didn't answer.

BILL: I'm giving up on him. What's the matter, Millie, kinda hate to see it go?

MILLIE: No, I have no feelings about it either way. They couldn't afford the staff to keep it up any more. I long ago gave up being sentimental about losing propositions.

GIRL: Don't; I'm just going to get depressed. I really hate it that nobody cares about any— This used to be the most exclusive medium-sized hotel anywhere on the Eastern Seaboard line. This place was built—

BILL: How'd you suddenly get onto talking about—

GIRL: —in eighteen hundred and something.

BILL: What's this place got to do with the Pioneer?

GIRL: Oh, dummy. I can recognize a picture of my own hotel when it's on the front page of the newspaper.

BILL: Yeah, when was that?

GIRL: They used a picture from its grand opening.

MILLIE: I didn't realize it was this place, but I don't suppose I've looked at the building, really, in years.

GIRL: Oh, it looks just like it used to, only dirty.

BILL: (As MRS. BELLOTTI enters) That's some news, huh?

MRS. BELLOTTI: (At the desk, to BILL) Excuse me, is Mr. Katz in?

GIRL: He comes in at seven-thirty.

BILL: (To the GIRL) Just never— No, he comes in—ain't in yet.

MRS. BELLOTTI: I don't think I've talked to you; I'm Mrs. Bellotti. Horse Bellotti's mother. Mr. Katz is gonna give him another chance, ain't he? He ain't gonna kick him out, is he?
(As she starts to come right into the office, BILL jumps at her, leaving the board.)

BILL: Here, you can't come back here. Don't come back here. That gate ain't supposed to be left open.

MRS. BELLOTTI: (Overlapping) I can talk from here, this is fine; you'll talk to him, to Mr. Katz, won't you? You look like a nice young man. 'Cause I don't know what his daddy and me are going to do if he don't—

BILL: (Cutting in) —I don't know nothin' about it. I got nothin' to do with it.

GIRL: (*Answering the phone.*) Hotel Baltimore, good morning.

BILL: (*Returning to the chair, shooing her out.*) He'll do what he wants to about it. Come on.

GIRL: I'll connect you.

MRS. BELLOTTI: Only he can't kick him out. I don't want him coming back to some strange place somewhere else. Does he want more money? Is that what it is? Does he want more money? 'Cause Horse's bill is always paid full on the first of every week; he's never been a day late with it. Is that what he wants?

BILL: (*Ignoring her. He has replugged a line. Ringing.*) Damnit.

GIRL: You gonna try him again? (*Reaching.*) Let me ring him.

BILL: No! Come on—make us a—why don't you make us a cup of tea?

GIRL: Millie, you want a cup of tea?

MILLIE: (*Looking up from the paper.*) No, thank you, Martha.

GIRL: (*Wincing.*) Ohhh, it's not Martha any more; I hate it.

MILLIE: I thought you had decided to settle on Martha.

GIRL: No! I mean I did, but I hate it. Where's the mailman? It's after—

MILLIE: On Memorial—

GIRL: Oh, I can't bear days when there's no mail delivery. Weekdays. What's this stuff?

BILL: That's something for you to do; those go in the boxes.

GIRL: (*Taking up the stack of thirty-five envelopes.*) Terrific. Oh, no. You know what it is? It's our— Oh, that's horrible, I certainly am not. It's our things. Eviction notices. "Newgate Development and Management"—

MILLIE: Let me see.

GIRL: Oxenham can do it; she'll love it. Just tell me how long a notice they're giving us. (*Her attention now is on the pigeonholes.*) Can you imagine people not picking up their mail? How can they bear it? Two-twelve. Must be a salesman. (*Takes four or five letters from the box.*) Baltimore, Baltimore. Boring. Denver. Something Idaho.
(*To* BILL)
What does that say?

BILL: Don't take people's mail out of their—

GIRL: I'm gonna put it back—what does that say?

BILL: If you can't read it, I can't.

GIRL: (*Categorizing it.*) Some sloppy town in Idaho. Washington, D.C. I've been over every inch of Idaho twice. Sugar beets, potatoes, and cows. Denver is gorgeous. (*Going on—another box.*)

BILL: Don't mix those up.

GIRL: I'm not. Don't bother me. Annapolis—nowhere. Baltimore. New York, Baltimore. Here's one I don't know. Franklin, Louisiana. No idea. Millie, you ever heard of Franklin, Louisiana?

MILLIE: Down on the Gulf, I believe.

GIRL: In the heel or the toe? You know.

MILLIE: Well. The ball of the foot.

GIRL: Around Saint Martinville?

MILLIE: South of there; right on the Gulf.

GIRL: Right. (*Disposes of it.*) Swamp City. No wonder.
(*As* MRS. BELLOTTI *starts to move away, ignored*)
You come back at seven-thirty—quarter to eight, and he'll be here.

MRS. BELLOTTI: (*Immediately drawn back.*) Has he said anything? To you? 'Cause I don't think he really has it in for Horse. He just doesn't understand him. He shouldn't have gone in; really. And he's only been in for five months, so you know it wasn't anything bad; he's a nice boy. He's just different. He's been to a psychiatrist and he gave him a complete examination and he said there wasn't anything wrong with David mentally; he's just shy. I tell him— Horse . . . you should meet someone. He's too adult to live with us. He's thirty-six. He and his dad don't get along. I tell him he has to *try* to meet people—to meet a girl, and he says how would I do that? And I don't know what to tell him . . .

GIRL: (*As* BILL *disconnects the plug*) You giving up on him again?

BILL: He'll call down to Oxenham at ten o'clock, mad as the devil.

MRS. BELLOTTI: You think he'll let him stay?

BILL: Mr. Katz is in by eight o'clock, you come back then.

MRS. BELLOTTI: I just came by on my way to— I'm supposed to be home with Frank 'cause he's on morphine and God knows what condition he might be in. We're all the way out in— You think he'll be to work by eight o'clock? Is there a place where I can get a cup of coffee or something? Or I'll just sit here and wait till he comes in if he's going—

BILL: There's a place on the corner's got real good coffee.
(GIRL *punches him—it has notoriously bad coffee.*)

MRS. BELLOTTI: That's what I'll do; 'cause I can't afford to go all the way home and come back. And I can't talk to him on the phone 'cause he won't come to—(*Fades off and listens.*)

BILL: That Pioneer used to be a pretty slick place, did it?

MILLIE: (*Putting the notice in her purse.*) Oh, yes . . . thirty years ago or more, people found it a pleasant enough place to spend their money.

BILL: President Taft used to go there?

MILLIE: President Coolidge. The father of the "constructive economy"! I served him quite often. He always sat his party in my station.
(MRS. BELLOTTI *wanders off and out.*)

GIRL: Does she have a son that lives here?

BILL: I don't know *who* she was. You can't come back here if you don't close that gate.
(*To* MILLIE)
He a pretty good tipper, was he?

MILLIE: President Coolidge? Not at all.

BILL: No?

MILLIE: No tip at all. He didn't pay and he didn't tip. I think the pleasure was supposed to be mine.

BILL: You're a hard one, Millie.

MILLIE: (*Pleased.*) No, no . . . not really.

GIRL: Did it have ghosts? I mean it had been there so long . . . probably not, though, huh? In a restaurant?

MILLIE: Oh, yes. There were a number of *spirits*. One or two who never left the dining room. They were almost as much a fixture as I was. One particularly.

BILL: Didn't nobody sit on him?

MILLIE: Oh, *she* never sat. She was very shy; she just stood about, near the doorway. We often saw her when we were cleaning up.

GIRL: Who was she?

MILLIE: Someone who liked the restaurant, it would seem.

GIRL: Are there ghosts here? There are, aren't there?

MILLIE: They don't like to—

GIRL: I *knew* it! I *knew* it!

MILLIE: They don't like to be talked about; it would only upset them.

GIRL: Well, Lord knows I'm not going to upset them! Could you tell my fortune? Because I believe in— Oh! Listen!
(*In the beat of silence there is the echo of a train, not far off.*)
Oh, no! (*In a rage of disappointment.*) That's the Silver Star! Oh, damn! Doesn't that just make you want to *cry*? How can they do that!?

BILL: I think she's got the schedules and bells and whistles all memoriz—

GIRL: (*Angry.*) There's no schedule involved in it. I don't think they have schedules any more. Silver Star is due in at four-nineteen; she's more than three damn hours late. I get so mad at them for not running on time. I mean it's their own damn schedule, I don't know why they can't keep to it. They're just miserable. The service is so bad and hateful, and the porters and conductors, you just can't believe it isn't deliberate. I think they're being run by the airlines.
(*To* MILLIE)
Do you have stock in the railroads? Could you do something? Write somebody?

MILLIE: Oh, no; I don't have much stock. Certainly not in the railroads. I can't imagine anyone with any business sense just now—

GIRL: Where will they go?

MILLIE: Who?

GIRL: The ghosts? When they tear the hotel down? What'll happen to them?

MILLIE: Oh . . . they'll stay around for a while wondering what's become of everything. Then they'll wander off with people. They form attachments.

BILL: (*As the board lights up*) Now what does he want? (*Phone.*) Yeah? Front desk.

APRIL: (*Entering; from off.*) All right, all right, what's the story this time? Last week it was a plumber in the basement; two weeks before that he said the boiler was busted; the time before that, the coldest fuckin' day of the year, he's got some excuse so stupid I can't even remember it.

BILL: (*Phone.*) You put in a call for seven o'clock. It's seven o'clock. (*Disconnects.*) Whadda you want, April?

APRIL: (*Overlapping*) Seven o'clock? Who you tellin'—it's no goddamned seven o'clock—it's not been light more than—

GIRL: I told you two weeks ago; spring ahead fall back.

APRIL: What kind of monkey language is that supposed to—

BILL: —Don't you listen to the radio or read a—

APRIL: —The fuckin' daylight savings. (*Turning to go.*) Fall back on my ass; it's too scratchin' much. I don't know what anyone expects—

BILL: (*Overlapping*) It's been almost a month, April; you oughtta be used to it by now.

APRIL: (*Returning.*) Hey, come on, I gotta get to sleep—whatta you gonna do about the water?

BILL: What's wrong with it?

GIRL: It's cold.

APRIL: No. Last night it was cold. Tonight it's cold—and it's orange.

BILL: They're probably workin' on the pipes.

APRIL: Yeah, well, I'm gonna work on somebody's pipes. (*Hikes her leg up on his chair, looking and scratching.*) Things aren't wicked enough around here with—

BILL: (*Overlapping exchange*) —Come on, I'm not in your way, am I? What are you doing?—

APRIL: —I'm not bothering you—

BILL: —What have you got your leg up in the air—

APRIL: —You're not going to see anything—

BILL: (*Getting up.*) —What are you getting on me?—

APRIL: —Whadda you think, I'm lousy? (*Shaking her hair on him.*) Waaaaaaa!

BILL: Come on, whatta you doing? What the hell's wrong with you?

APRIL: (*Laughing.*) You really are an ass acher, you know it?

BILL: Whadda you want, April?

APRIL: Don't start with me. What I want, this hotel don't offer.

BILL: I'm trying to work here.

APRIL: What are you doing about the water?
(*He starts to speak.*)
Tell me you just work here.

BILL: (*Beat.*) What're you coming down here in your nightgown?

APRIL: What nightgown? This is a silk—Dacron kimono. This is a perfectly respectable garment. Whadda you think, I'm trying to turn you on? You're not my type.

BILL: I didn't know you had a type.

APRIL: (*Abstracted*) Yeah . . . well . . . I've got several types. Give me a cigarette. (*Helping herself; chuckling.*) A guy—yesterday— said, you sure smoke an awful lot—asked did I smoke in bed—I said . . . try me.
(*Laughs.*)

GIRL: That's dangerous. Smoking in bed.

BILL: (*Phone.*) Front desk. Yeah. Hold on. Hand me that book.

APRIL:
Morning, Millie.

GIRL:
What number?

MILLIE:
Good morning. I don't know whether to say good morning to you or good night.

BILL:
Two-eighteen. Just see if he's up on his bill.

GIRL: What does he pay—weekly?

BILL: Let me see it.

APRIL: Say good night to me and I'll curl up right here on the floor.

GIRL: He paid half and then the rest yesterday.

BILL: (*Into the phone*) Yeah. What was that number?
(*He writes it down—*GIRL *begins to dial before he is finished.*)
O.K.

APRIL: Thanks for the butt. Put a note in my hole I don't want to be rung till after four o'clock.

GIRL: Is that an eight or a zero?

BILL: Come on—three-eight-six-oh.

GIRL: (*To* APRIL) Don't forget to turn your clock up.

APRIL: I don't keep clocks. Clocks and dogs. My clock's outside my window on the front of the terminal. Says a quarter after five. Twenty-four hours a day. (*Laughing.*) I figger that's a good enough time for just about anything. (*Laughing.*) Guy came up to me last week—couldn't think of anything to say—said—"Uh, uh, excuse me, you don't happen to know what time it is, do you?" I said, Sure, it's a quarter after five. The son of a bitch was so surprised he looked at his goddamned watch. (*Laughs.*)

GIRL: (*Pause.*) What time was—

APRIL: I don't want to hear it. Whatever you're going to say. You're a real bring-down, you know it? I'd give a hundred bucks for her hair; I wouldn't turn a nickel for her brain.

GIRL: No, I got the joke, I just wondered what—

APRIL: Listen, don't listen to me. Kids now are a different breed. If I was sixteen I'd be just as— How old are you?

GIRL: Nineteen.

APRIL: Nineteen. Jesus. If I was nineteen and looked like that—

BILL: And know what you know now.

APRIL: Fuck what I know now. Give me the rest of it—I'll learn. You want to know the sad truth? If I looked like that I wouldn't have to know what I know now.

GIRL: Did you ever take a ride on a—

APRIL: What? On a what? (*Beat.*) Probably I did.

GIRL: Nothing. I don't want to know what you'd say.

APRIL: Yeah, well, I got that problem. Listen, I'm going to bed before I get bitter. (*Takes another cigarette.*) You tell Katz I'm after his balls if he ain't got hot water when I get up.

MR. MORSE: (*Overlapping a word or two—entering*) I have a complaint. Who's here? I have a complaint.

BILL: What's yours, Mr. Morse?

APRIL: Lay it on us, Mr. Morse.

GIRL: (*Simultaneous*) Morning, Mr. Morse.

MORSE: (*Simultaneous*) Listen to me.

BILL: Yeah.

MORSE: Listen to me!

BILL: I hear you.

MORSE: I'm going to hold the hotel responsible.

BILL: Why's that?

MORSE: Listen to my voice.

BILL: I hear you, Mr. Morse.

Morse: Listen to my voice. I can't afford to get a cold and I'm getting one.

Bill: That your complaint?
(April *laughs*.)

Morse: My window won't close. It's swelled tight and there is an inch crack that won't close all the way.

April: That's just advancing age, Mr. Morse.

Girl: You got the same complaint, huh?

April: I wouldn't go that far.

Jackie:
(*Entering, followed by* Jamie, *who goes immediately to the sofa and sits*.)
(To April.)
Listen, April, could I ask you a personal thing—one thing.

April:
I'm just trying to get to bed, lady.

Jackie:
Sure, right, that's cool.
(*To* Girl)
Bitch of a day, ain't it.
(*To* Bill)
Listen, Hal—er uh—Bill:
I pay my bill, right? I mean, you know the way I do things; like I haven't caused

Morse:
I put a towel into the crack and I wrapped up my chest and neck, and it still didn't help. And I—I am going to hold the hotel responsible, I got very little sleep.
You're responsible if something isn't done. Because there's *dampness* in my room. And if I'm taken to the hospital, I'm going to hold the hotel responsible for the bill!

any problems around here
—nothing like that—right?
That's not the way I op-
erate . . .

BILL: (*Overlapping*) Hold it, I can't hear you both at once. I'll
send someone up to close it for you, Mr. Morse. It just needs
some weight behind it.
(*To* JACKIE)
What is it now?

JACKIE: You're still not calling me Jackie. You know better than
that. I like everything out front. First name.

BILL: I can't remember everybody's name here.

JACKIE:
I been a friend here, right?
To you and these people.
We don't trespass on
people's feelings. Me and
my brother don't bother
anybody. I mean, we been
here what? Nearly a month:
you got the rent receipts
there. We been here, we
ain't complainers. That
ain't the way we live. We
don't have people up to our
rooms. (*As* BILL *is showing
no interest*) Second thought,
skip it, I'll wait for Katz.

MR. MORSE:
(*Slight retard.*)
That window should be
repaired. If it just needed
to be closed, I could close it
myself. I'm capable of
closing my own window.
You send a man up there
with hammer and nails and
tools. I'd do it myself if I
had the proper tools. And
I'm coming down with a
cold. With a severe cold.

APRIL: What's the matter, Mr. Morse, lose your tools?

MORSE: There's *dampness* in my *room*.

BILL: I'll send someone up to close it.

JACKIE: Sure ain't gettin' any warmer, is it? It's the East Coast. It's bad for your lungs to live this close to the ocean. It's bad for you.

MORSE: It's bad.

JACKIE: Your throat and chest.

GIRL: I didn't know that.

MORSE: And my health is on the point of breaking.

JACKIE: What's he got? You got a problem with your window? I'll shut it down for you. Give me your keys; it's no trouble.

BILL: No, no— (*He starts to get up as the phone buzzes.*)

JACKIE: People got to help one another, don't they?

MORSE: (*Taking out his keys.*) I'm coming down with a severe cold and I'm going to hold this hotel responsible. And my neck is getting stiff.

JACKIE:	BILL:
(*Taking the keys.*) I believe in helping each other where you can. It just needs somebody to put a few calories into it. It's no problem. (*She goes upstairs.*)	(*Phone.*) Front desk. Yeah. What's that? Nine, three? (*Writing.*) Is that in Baltimore? (*Starts to dial, notices* JACKIE.)

GIRL: Probably just needs a good push.

BILL: (*Phone.*) Hold it. (*Yelling after* JACKIE.) Come on! (*To phone*) Hold it. (*To Jackie*) You! What the hell's her name? Don't go up there. Hey! (*Sotto voce*) Son of a bitch. (*Back to phone.*) Yeah?

MORSE: You have no right to object if that young man wants to help me.

APRIL: Mr. Morse, you gotta throw away the mustard plaster and take something worthwhile to bed with you.
(*He mutters and heads to the lounge.*)
You want to volunteer, Lilac?

BILL: She's a little young for him, don't you think?

APRIL: That's all right; by the time he gets it up, she'll be old enough.

BILL: (*Phone.*) Four-three-oh-seven. Yeah. Been pretty quiet. No, she paid—

MORSE: There's somebody sleeping in my chair.

APRIL: They eat your porridge you're shit out of luck, ain't you, baby?

GIRL: He's waiting to see Mr. Katz.
(*To* APRIL.)
You want a cup of tea?

APRIL: Whatta you got? I'd kill for a chicken broth.

BILL: Come on! (*Turning to phone.*) Him too, the both 'em paid: receipts in the book. Naw. Naw, it's been pretty quiet. O.K.
(*Disconnects as* JAMIE *starts for the stairs.*)
Here! Where you going?

JAMIE: (*Freezing.*) I wasn't going any place.

BILL: You just stay down here till she comes back down here. Katz'll be in in a few minutes.

MORSE: Here. Boy. Where's our board?
(JAMIE *shrugs, hangdog; mumbles.*)
Either you want to play or you don't want to play.

JAMIE: I'll play.
  (*They look for the board.*)

GIRL: (*To* MORSE) Did you know they were going to tear down the—

MORSE: What?

GIRL: (*Louder.*) They're tearing down the hotel; they're gonna tear down this building.

MORSE: Good!

GIRL: Listen!

APRIL: What?
  (*A not too distant train bell.*)

GIRL: It's pullin' out.

APRIL: You got the ears of a bat.

GIRL: Holy—it's three hours late now; by the time it gets to Miami, it'll be six hours overdue again.

BILL: She knows what she's talking about; she's been on all of 'em.

APRIL: Trains give me a pain.

GIRL: I used to live right by a railroad track. I never waved to a single person who didn't wave back to me.

APRIL: The tracks I can take or leave.

GIRL: —If you saw something important to you neglected—like that. They've let the roadbeds go to hell. You have to close your eyes on a train. Or look out the window. That's still beautiful; some of it. In the country.

MORSE: APRIL:
  Where's the board? Bill?   The one time I remember
                                  taking—

BILL: What? Be quiet a minute. What?

MORSE: Somebody took the checkerboard.

BILL: I got it back here; you left it out. Nobody put it away last
  night.
  (*He hands it to the* GIRL, *who takes it to the lounge where* MR.
  MORSE *and* JAMIE *begin setting it up.*)

GIRL: Can I watch?
  (*Nothing.*)

MILLIE: When I was a girl I used to ride back and forth between
  Columbia and Baton Rouge on the Gulf Raider.

GIRL: I don't think I know that one.

MILLIE: Oh, it's not running any more, I'm sure. It was a wonderfully elegant coach. They had a shower . . . they had—

GIRL: They had a shower?

APRIL: On a train?

MILLIE: Oh, yes—I'd seen it a number of times. I decided once to
  take a shower before I retired. I walked the full length of the train
  in my bathrobe and slippers and shower cap, carrying a towel and
  my soap. Through the dining cars with everyone having dinner.
  I'm sure I'm the only person who ever took advantage of the
  shower. It was a marvelous train, very modern—Art Deco then—
  chrome and steel. Quite the thing.

GIRL: They used to keep on schedule, didn't they?

MILLIE: Well, I know the service was excellent; and one went from
  one wonderful terminal to another—

GIRL: —Only you should see them now—

MILLIE: —But the schedules? Oh . . . they (*Drifting away*) may have. Maybe not during the war when so many servicemen rode the trains; it seems they used to. It didn't matter so much if you came in a few hours late. I don't know. I've always thought of myself as a bit outside society; I never seem to understand what other people expect.

APRIL: I took a train once, and let me tell you I—

GIRL: —I don't want to hear it. Whatever you did. Whatever it was, I don't want to know.

APRIL: I was eight years old. What could I do?

GIRL: I don't care. Something. You probably got raped. I don't want to hear it.

APRIL: I most certainly did not get raped! I have never been raped! I'd say there was little likelihood of me *ever* getting raped.

MORSE: There's one missing. There's a red checker missing.
(*As* KATZ *enters, walking straight to the office*)
Somebody didn't put them back properly.

GIRL: Good morning.

KATZ: (*Taking off his coat.*) Morning. Who's the boy in the lobby?

BILL: Guy says he wants to see you.

KATZ: How long's he been there?

GIRL: Since about four.

BILL: Came in about four; said he'd wait.

MORSE: (*Coming to desk.*) There's a red checker missing from that box.

KATZ: —We've had complaints about your singing in the lobby again.

MORSE: (*Furious.*) Who? Who said anything? I have already complied with those complaints. I ought to do those exercises in my room but I moved to this lobby because people sleep during the day. Those exercises are important to my health. Prescribed by my physician and I—

KATZ: I'm just telling you—you create a scene.

MORSE: Who said it? I have a right to know who said it.

APRIL: Mr. Morse, for a seventy-year-old man with his voice going, you got a healthy set of pipes when you need 'em, ain't you?

MORSE: That singing is necessary to—

APRIL: Honey, I don't mind the singing; I just wish you'd learn the words to the song.

MORSE: —I have a right!—

APRIL: All right, Katz. Speaking of pipes—you know the hot water in this hotel?

KATZ: Yeah?

APRIL: Well, I hate to be the one to tell you, but I think it's coming down with hepatitis.

BILL: Damnit! Here, cover the board. I almost forgot that girl went up to Morse's room.

KATZ: What girl?

BILL: That girl with the brother. She—
(JACKIE *comes down before he can leave the desk area.*)
Don't go up to rooms here. Like that.

MORSE: Those exercises are important to my health.

JACKIE: His window was stuck. I helped him out. He ought to sleep with it open anyway; you can't talk to him about it.
(*To* KATZ)
Look at this here, now. I been waiting for you to get in. Did you see that Belair out there?

KATZ: I don't know, no.

JACKIE: Parked right in front of the door.

KATZ: I didn't see it.

JACKIE: Well, that's my wheels. I bought it two weeks ago. Paid cash. That's the way I like to do things—

JACKIE:	MORSE:
Only I can't put it on the road till I get plates. See, I was driving it, but a cop stopped me; 'cause the plates on it don't belong to it.	(*Yelling back hoarsely.*) People . . . are not . . . considerate . . . of other . . . people . . . is my complaint! (*Sits at checkerboard.*)

KATZ: Stopped for what?

JACKIE: For the plates. The plates was expired. Some pig. You're not listening to me—

KATZ: —What do you want? Say what you want. You and your brother both. You've always got angles—angles— I don't have the—
(*Shuts up as she rides over him.*)

JACKIE: (*Cued by "brother both"*) Could I have just three minutes of your time? That's all I'm asking, just three minutes of your time. See, the title's clear; it's clear and paid for cash. I got the inspection sticker—never mind what I had to go through—but I can't put it on the road without the plates and the thing is you got to get your insurance to get your plates. I didn't know anything about that 'cause I ain't had wheels in my name before.

KATZ: I don't know nothing about it; I don't drive a car.

JACKIE: (*Overlapping some*) That's what they told me. I just kept it out of the yard 'cause I told them I was getting the plates. And I went around—never mind where I had to go—what I have to have is Ten, Twenty, and Five. That's what they call it. Ten thousand for a single injury; twenty thousand for a multiple, and five for damages. Collision you don't have to have.

APRIL: I don't know why people have cars.

JACKIE: (*With a glance to her but no pause.*) —'Course every place has a different price: right there you know what kind of a racket they're running. Like the ones you've heard of are way-out-of-sight, off-the-wall clip joints. But the minimum I need for Ten, Twenty, and Five is $165; that's all it'd take to—

KATZ: I can't help you with it—

JACKIE: What with? With what? I'm not asking you for money. I'm not a borrower. I don't take a penny from nobody I don't know. I wouldn't have to pay the hundred, I'd just need sixty-five down and quarterly, if I hadn't got canned from the pet shop— Only I wasn't canned. I saw what was coming and walked out on them. The pansy manager was trying to get me fired so his little friend could have my job. I hit him with a birdcage and walked out on the bastard. He kept live snakes as pets, if you want to know the sort of person he was. Let them run loose in the shop at night.

GIRL: You hit him with a birdcage?

JACKIE: He was mincing down the aisle with this stack of birdcages, he made a crack I won't repeat; and I took one of 'em and slapped it alongside his head.

APRIL: I don't know why but I believe that.

JACKIE: He called me up, tried to tell me I owed him for a myna bird. There wasn't no goddamned myna bird in that cage. Where you going?—I'm trying to tell you something.

KATZ: I don't know what you're talking about. I'm working here. I got no time.

JACKIE: (As SUZY *and a client enter*) I'm telling you. If you'd stop interrupting. I need a friend. I'm in a bind. Straight out—that's the way I deal: I need a friend. That's what I'm saying; I need a pal.

KATZ: (To SUZY's JOHN, *who precedes her upstairs*) Here! Here! Where you going? Has he got a room?

SUZY: I hope you don't mean—

KATZ: —You! Hey, come down here!

SUZY: —What are you doing? Are you crazy? He's a friend of mine! We're going to have a little drink.
(KATZ *retires*.)
If you please. I'd appreciate it if you'd cool down. A little bit here.

SUZY'S JOHN: (*Whispered*.) Come on, Christ.

SUZY: I'm trying to clear up a misunderstanding, here.
(To KATZ)
I don't like to be prosecuted.

APRIL: You don't like what?

SUZY: (*Laughing with her*.) First thing you ever heard me say I didn't like, huh?
(*Laughs*.)
How about this crummy *weather*?

APRIL: (*Laughing.*) Those are the ugliest shoes I ever saw! (*Both laugh.*)

JACKIE: What's funny about them?

SUZY: She gave me those shoes—

SUZY AND APRIL: Last night! (*They laugh.*)

SUZY: You're three-nineteen.

JACKIE: We're tryin' to transact some business here.

SUZY: Ain't ya? Three-nineteen?

JACKIE: Yeah; me and my brother.

SUZY: I'm four-nineteen. I'm right over you.

SUZY's JOHN: (*A whisper.*) You're on the fourth goddamned floor of a walk-up?

SUZY: I hope I don't keep you awake.

SUZY's JOHN: Come on, would you?

JACKIE: You eat good food, you eat natural products, you don't have trouble sleeping.

SUZY: With the noise!

JACKIE: I never noticed no noise.

SUZY: Whadda you mean you never noticed no noise?

JACKIE: I never noticed no noise.

SUZY: (*Furious.*) Well, what the hell, are you deaf? (APRIL *laughs.*) What the hell are you laughing at?

SUZY'S JOHN: Come on, goddamnit. I ain't got all day. Get on with
  it.
  (*Touches her lightly.*)

SUZY: Just don't assault me, if you please.

SUZY'S JOHN: I said, I don't have all day. Come on, now, or forget it.

SUZY: (*To others*) Are you going to allow me to be assaulted?

SUZY'S JOHN: All right, then, forget it.

SUZY: I'm coming. Just don't rush me. These people are friends of
  mine. Learn to live at a leisurely pace. You live longer.

GIRL: Did you know they're tearing down the hotel?

SUZY: Tonight?

GIRL: We're all going to have to move before long. It's been sold.

SUZY: What do you mean, move?

KATZ:
  Go on up—not now; everybody does. They're tearing
  it down. You'll have to
  find another place.

SUZY:
  When? What is this? Who
  said? I don't move for nobody. To hell with it; find
  another place, where? I got
  eleven-foot ceilings in my
  room. Where am I going
  to find something like
  that?

KATZ: What do you care what your ceilings are?

APRIL: If you spent as much time looking at the ceilings as she does,
  you'd care what they looked like.

GIRL: I wonder what's gonna be where my room is? I mean, in that
  space of air? That space will still be up there where I lived. We

probably walk right under and right past the places where all kinds of things happened. A tepee or a log cabin might have stood right where I'm standing. Wonderful things might have happened right on this spot.

APRIL: Davy Crockett might have crapped on the stairs. Pocahontas might of got laid by—

SUZY: (*Overlapping*) You're horrible! You have no human soul! I thought that was a beautiful thought.

APRIL: People who get her space are gonna wonder why it's so hot.

SUZY: People who get yours are gonna wonder why it stinks. I hope they do tear it down; this place is disgusting!
(*Pushing the john ahead of her.*)
I suppose you'll use this as an excuse not to fix the elevator.
(*Exits.*)

APRIL: (*To* SUZY'S JOHN) Hey, keep your business out of her filthy mouth, up there!

KATZ: Every morning she's drunk and she acts up like that! (*Beat.*) People!
(*Pause.*)

JACKIE: So what I did was, I went to the bank. And they're willing to give me the money, even without the job, if I can get someone to co—

KATZ: (*Overlapping*) No! No! Can't do it. I'm not in the business. The hotel won't do it and I won't do it personally. Not even if I knew you, and I don't know you.

JACKIE: (*Simultaneously*) I'm not asking you for anything. It's not costing— I only want you to sign a paper. All I need is a signature. On a paper; your name on a paper.

KATZ: No. No. No.

JACKIE: (*Taking a pear from a paper sack, biting into it furiously.*) Your fuckin' name on a fuckin' piece of paper.

KATZ: Watch your voice.

JACKIE: Forget it. Skip it. I don't need it. Just come out and look at the car. Just see it—see if you—

KATZ: (*Re: a receipt—to* BILL) What is this? Who signed this?

JACKIE: You got a head harder than a bull's dick, you know that?

KATZ: Go on, don't hang around here with that talk.

JACKIE: We're not bothering nobody.
  (MRS. BELLOTTI *enters and crosses to desk.*)

KATZ: Eat outside.

JACKIE: Eat out, my ass! (*She goes to the lounge.*)

MRS. BELLOTTI: Excuse me, are you Mr. Katz? I expected an older man from your voice on the telephone. It must be wonderful to have a nice position like this at your age.
  (APRIL *hoots.*)
  Now, Mr. Katz, you're not gonna kick Horse out, are you? I got a letter from him and he said he was really gonna try hard this time. You're gonna give him one more chance, aren't you?

KATZ: No.

MRS. BELLOTTI: (*Contrite.*) What'd he do?

KATZ: He's crazy. He don't make sense. He don't talk sense. He's crazy.

MRS. BELLOTTI: It's the alcohol, that's what it is. I've told him but he gets out, and he gets so keyed up and nervous and anxious he takes a drink and he can't stop. People don't know what he's really like, like I do.

KATZ: He steals things.

MRS. BELLOTTI: You won't let him come—

KATZ: No. You gotta pick up his things. I told you before.

MRS. BELLOTTI: How can I do that? I'll have to take a little bit at a time. His daddy can't help, he had his leg took off; he can't get outta the house; he's on morphine.

KATZ: Take 'em like you got to take 'em, but take 'em.

MRS. BELLOTTI: What'd he do?

KATZ: He's crazy. Last time I let him come back he stole the telephone outta his room. Tried to sell it back to the hotel. Said there was no telephone in his room.

MRS. BELLOTTI: See. He didn't need the money either. He was making money clammin'. We bought him the rake—he saved eighty-five dollars and bought a boat, and then one day he sells the boat to a guy downtown for ten dollars. He said he wanted to sell something.
(*She wanders to the lounge by* JAMIE *and the* GIRL.)

GIRL: He won't let him come back?

MRS. BELLOTTI: (*Shakes her head.*) And my husband lost his leg. Did you know that?
(*Both* JAMIE *and* GIRL *shake their heads.*)
He always had trouble with it. He was a diabetic and he's had to watch what he eats for ten years. We thought he was going to be all right; then he got a craving.

JAMIE: Does he drink?

MRS. BELLOTTI: Oh, no, the doctor won't let him touch it.
(JAMIE *nods.*)
But last summer he got a craving for fruit. He ate fruit all summer and he got worse and worse and . . .

JAMIE: I thought fruit was healthy for you.

MRS. BELLOTTI: Not for a diabetic. With all that sugar.
(JAMIE *nods*.)
But he craved it. And he had to go to the hospital and they took
off his leg.

JAMIE: (*Simultaneous with her*) Took off his leg.

MRS. BELLOTTI: It was either that or—that was the alternative. And
he just got home from the hospital a month ago, and if he sees
Horse's things come into the house, I don't know what he'll do.
He already sent the neighbor girl I got watching him to the store
for apple juice. I came home and he'd drunk a gallon of it.

JAMIE: Our dad died of diabetes.

MRS. BELLOTTI: Isn't it a terrible thing?

JACKIE: Come here.
(JAMIE *goes to her*.)

MRS. BELLOTTI: I gotta get Horse's things.
(*After a beat she gets up with a sigh and goes to the desk.*)

JACKIE: What are you tellin' her?

JAMIE: She was telling me about her husband.

JACKIE: I heard what you said. You want me to leave you again? Is
that what you want?
(*He sulks*.)
You just mind your own business.
(*To* MILLIE)
He's a little mixed up.

MILLIE: I'm sure you'll straighten him out.

JACKIE: I hope that's a friendly remark.

JAMIE: She said her husband—

JACKIE: What have you been up to? Let me smell your breath.
(*He resists.*)
Let me smell your breath.
(*He does.*)
Are you tryin' to kill yourself with those cigarettes? Is that what you're doing? Where are they?

JAMIE: I just had one I found in the—

JACKIE: I don't want to know where you found it. Where's your angelica stick? I told you to suck on—

JAMIE: It doesn't work.

JACKIE: (*Getting another.*) That's because you're not sucking on it. You're not sucking it; you're chewing it. Suck it.
(*He resists.*)
Suck it.
(*As everyone turns*)
What the hell you looking at? Ain't you heard anybody say suck before?

MRS. BELLOTTI: (*Overlapping*) Could I have Horse's keys? To get his things?
(*She gets them.*)

GIRL: It really doesn't make any difference 'cause we all have to move anyway. They're tearing down the whole building, so we all have to move.

MRS. BELLOTTI: It's just so difficult to find a place that'll take him . . .

GIRL: I know.
(MRS. BELLOTTI *goes upstairs.*)

BILL: Whadda you know; you don't even know him.

KATZ: He's crazy.

GIRL: Well, anybody named Horse. By his own mother.

APRIL: Guy last week said I reminded him of his mother. (*Laughs.*) I— No, it's too dirty, I'm not gonna tell it.

BILL: I thought you were going to bed.

APRIL: (*Laughing.*) I kicked him out. I said—I wasn't entertaining no mother . . . (*Laughing.*) No, it's too dirty.

JACKIE: (*To* JAMIE) Now what's wrong with you?

BILL: (*To* GIRL) You been up the whole night, have you?

GIRL:	JACKIE:
I'm not sleepy any more; I think I had too much tea to sleep. (*Pause.*)	We'll get someone to sign it; you ain't worried about that, are you?

BILL: Don't worry about them; they ain't worth it. (*Pause.*)

GIRL:	JACKIE:
I'm not; I just don't like to see people need things is all. (*Pause.*)	We put the car on the road, we won't stop till we hit Utah.

BILL: Don't you think you better go to bed?

GIRL:	JACKIE:
I will before long; I don't sleep so much. (*Pause.*) You don't have to remind	What's wrong? We're gonna be all right. (*Pause.*) You don't have to think

me; I been up twenty-six
hours in a row.
(*Pause.*)
I just don't like to see
people . . . need things
is all.
(*Pause.*)

BILL:
Everybody needs somethin',
babe.

GIRL:
I just don't like to think
about it.

about it; I always come
through, don't I?
(*Pause.*)
We put the car on the road,
we won't stop till we hit
Utah.
(*Pause.*)
That's what you want, isn't
it?

JAMIE:
We're not going to Utah.

JACKIE: Whadda you mean?

JAMIE: We're not going.

BILL: Don't you want anything?

JACKIE: Don't talk so loud.

GIRL: Oh . . .

JAMIE: We're not going to Utah.

GIRL: I want everything.

JACKIE: Just shut up about it. I told you we'd go.

GIRL: For everybody.

JACKIE: They don't have to know our business.

GIRL: I want everyone to have everything. I really hate spring here.
Spring is the messiest thing I ever heard of. Dribble, dribble, dribble for three months straight. The radio said it'd be warm today:

it used to rain and then it'd be sunny. I mean, immediately. When I was a kid.

BILL: That was when you was a kid?

MR. MORSE: Your move.
(JAMIE *moves*; MR. MORSE *jumps him double.*)

GIRL: It almost never rained anyway. But when it did, just the next day all the cactus would bloom all over.

JACKIE: (*Almost a whisper.*) Miss? You know that loan shop? What time do they open, do you think? Would they be open by eight o'clock?

MILLIE: (*Quite loud.*) The pawnshop? I'd imagine a business like that, they would get an early start.

KATZ: (*Regarding the receipt.*) Whose name is that?

JACKIE: The bloodsuckers.

BILL: (*After a glance at the book.*) Martha? What'd you put here?

GIRL: Oh. That's "Lilac Lavender." Only I wasn't sure how to spell Lilac, so I kinda scrawled it. Whadda you think?
(*Both turn back without comment.*)

JAMIE: (*Getting up from the game as the long cry of a train whistle echoes through the lobby.*) I'm going to help that lady move her boy's stuff down.

BILL: Which one is that? Lilac?

GIRL: (*Moving to the lobby.*) That's a freighter. I don't think they even stop here.

MORSE: Here! Where are you going?

JAMIE: I'll come back; I'm not finished.

MORSE: You can't get up in the middle of the game. If you leave the game, I win.

JAMIE: (*From the stairs*) No, you don't.

MORSE: That's the way I play.

GIRL: (*Giving* PAUL *a gentle push.*) Hey, you said you wanted to see Mr. Katz?

PAUL: (*Stirring.*) Come on . . . (*Back asleep.*)

BILL: (*Phone.*) Four-three-oh-seven. Yeah. Martha?

GIRL: No joke, Bill, I really hate that name.

BILL: That's who she asked for. Don't take your calls down here.

GIRL: O.K., O.K. (*On phone.*) Hello; hi, Veda.

APRIL: (*Over*) You ever hear the one about the—

BILL: I don't want to hear it.

APRIL: What the hell kind of mood are you in?

BILL: I've had enough of your jokes for a morning.

KATZ: Don't sit back here; come on, there's a coffee shop on the corner.

GIRL: (*To* BILL) Gotta pencil?
    (*He gives her one.*)

APRIL: That's pretty good, honey, you get room service. I have to stand on the ever-loving corner.

BILL: Just knock it off.

APRIL: I wasn't talking to you, squirt.

BILL: Come on, get out—you aren't supposed to be behind here. This is private back here.

APRIL: You got a problem, don't take it out on me.

GIRL: Would you stop talking when I'm on the— I'll be there. (*Hangs up.*) That's pretty impolite!

BILL: You too, go on, get on out. You aren't supposed to be here.

GIRL: Mr. Katz said I could take calls here if I was down here instead of in my room.

BILL: Well, it's not my problem; I'm off.

MORSE: Where did he go to?

JACKIE: Just never mind.

APRIL: Where you gotta go?

GIRL: Not far; just up to the Haven Motel.

BILL: Far enough without any sleep.

GIRL: Would you stop being a daddy to me. You want to help, you can give me a lift.

BILL: I'm not giving you a lift; you can take a taxi; tell your john to pay for it.

GIRL: Thanks a lot.

BILL: It's not even eight o'clock in the morning; you're going out to turn a trick. You got to be out of your mind.

APRIL: When we gotta be out of here?

GIRL: You're really an ogre.

KATZ: One month, you gotta be out.

JACKIE: Whadda you mean, one month?

MILLIE: That's what's in the notice.

JACKIE: Let me see; where does it say that? You can't kick us out of here without a notice. Give me my mail. Did I get one?

MILLIE: (*Simultaneous*) I was going to tell you, but it was a little surprising. I thought you could wait and find out for yourself.

GIRL: One month? Where is Bill going to work?

BILL:
Just don't worry about me.

GIRL:
Yeah?

BILL:
Yeah. You don't worry about me working and I won't worry about you sleeping.

GIRL:
Did you know we were going to all be out in the street in that short a time and didn't tell me or anything?

BILL:
You're on the street now. Just because I know something doesn't mean I'm at liberty to tell it.

MORSE:
Good! Serve you all right!

JACKIE:
Maybe you don't care where you go; I happen to have specific plans.

MORSE:
Right. I don't care. What do I care where you go. I'll be glad to get rid of the lot of you.

JACKIE:
You dummy, you think you're going to stay here?

MORSE:
I don't intend to divulge my plans to anyone here. You aren't the only person with plans.

GIRL:

You knew! You knew we were going to have to go. You are really an ogre! You're terrible.

BILL:

I'll bet you don't even know what an ogre is.

GIRL:

I certainly do; I sleep with five or six every day.

BILL:

I don't want to hear about what you do.

GIRL:

Well, it certainly isn't any of your business. I don't understand you at all —

BILL:

—I don't care what you do with your life—

GIRL:

One minute you're friendly and nice and the next minute you're—

BILL:

—I just wish you were old enough or mature enough to know what you're throwing away. I personally don't care a dang what—

JACKIE:

(APRIL *and* KATZ *are cued in now.*)
To hell with it. I don't care. They can tear it down. I'm taking my brother and getting the hell out of here anyway.

MORSE:

Good. Nobody cares. We don't care!

JACKIE:

Tear it to hell!

MORSE:

Tear it to hell! RIP IT DOWN! (*He begins to unpack his barbells.*)

JACKIE:

I don't care if you tear it down this week. Because I don't intend to hang around here. That's not the way I am. I don't hang around where the damn building's coming down on my head. Fuck it. I got enough sense to get out when the gettin's good. This place would fall down in another six months anyway!
(SUZY's JOHN *comes down the stairs, walks directly through the lobby and out the front door.*)

GIRL:

—as bad as my own daddy. Worse. Because he at least didn't care what I did. He didn't even care if I was a hooker as long as I kept him in enough money to buy beer. That's why I left, only you're worse than he is.

BILL:

—you do with yourself or how many ogres you entertain in a day.

GIRL:

I'll bet you don't even know what an ogre is!

APRIL:

(*Cued above with* JACKIE's *"To hell with it."*)
If I'm expected to get out of here before my month's rent runs out, I know somebody who's going to get a fat refund on her bill.

KATZ:

Nobody is refunding anything. You stay through June. Nobody's paid past the month of June.

APRIL:

Don't expect to see my tail . . .
(SUZY, *off, begins to wail.*)
till the first of June, daddy. Just let me tell you right now. I don't care if the pipes bust and the place is flooded to the third floor.
(*She notices* SUZY *as she appears on the stairs.*)

SUZY: (*Off. Over* KATZ, APRIL, BILL, GIRL, JACKIE, *and* MR. MORSE. *Cued by* APRIL's *"Don't expect to see my tail . . ."*)
You bastard. What do you think you're doing. Come back here! YOU CHICKENSHIT!
(*She appears on the stairs wrapped in a towel and nothing else, wailing after the* JOHN. BILL *turns on the radio, furiously.*)

SUZY:

Come back here, you fuckin' masochist. He beat me! Why didn't you stop

KATZ:

Get upstairs. Get on, get out of the lobby. You can't come down here naked.

him? He locked the door on me! He pushed me out of my door and locked the door on me! Police! Why aren't you doing something? What do we pay you for, you yellow crud? Yellow crud!

APRIL:

What you doing with the towel, there, Suzy?
(*She laughs.*)

SUZY:

(*Each sentence makes* APRIL *laugh more.*)
What the hell are you laughing at? I'd like to see what you'd do. You shut up! You shut up! (*Slaps at her with the towel.*) You're disgusting! I'm calling the cops! I want to make a complaint! Against April Green! And against the management of this hotel! Scum!

PAUL:

(*Waking. Cued by "disgusting."*)
What the hell is this? What the hell is going on here? This isn't a hotel; this is a goddamned flophouse! This is a flophouse!

JACKIE:

What the hell are you doing?
(MR. MORSE *begins to march up and down swinging the barbells.* KATZ *catches sight of him now.*)

KATZ:

(*To* SUZY)
Suzy, get upstairs. I'm gonna call the cops on you. On all of you. They would as soon run your ass in again as look at you. Get up to your room. Go on or spend another night in the can; make your choice.

MORSE:

(*Singing.*)
O sole mio; O sole mio; O sole mio—
(*Over and over as he marches on.*)

JACKIE:

Get your ass back up those stairs. If my brother comes down and sees you like that, I'm going to take you apart. Who the hell do you think you are? I hope to hell they kick your ass out into the street!

KATZ:

Get up to your room;
what the hell is this? Don't
listen to April. Come on.
Get upstairs. April, you
shut up; I've had it with
you two.

SUZY:

You're right; that's exactly
what it is; it's a goddamned
flophouse. This is a flophouse!

JACKIE:

(*Over; cued by* PAUL.)
Right! This is a goddamned
flophouse. Exactly. A
fuckin' flophouse!

(JAMIE *carries a box down the stairs, dropping it when he sees the naked* SUZY. *Staring with his mouth open. The box contains hotel soap, towels, washcloths, etc., and things stolen from the neighborhood shops. Nearly everyone on stage laughs as* JAMIE *gapes at* SUZY *and the lights fade. The music soars over their laughter.* CURTAIN.)

ACT TWO

(*Music from the house fades into the radio.* MRS. OXENHAM *snaps it off.*

Natural tableau: In the lounge MILLIE *sits reading a newspaper.* MR. MORSE *and* JAMIE *study a checkerboard. At the desk,* MR. KATZ *looks at an open receipt book;* PAUL *leans on the counter, watching him.* MRS. OXENHAM *studies a stack of laundry lists. Afternoon.*

JAMIE, *without moving, studying the board, sucks on a stick of herb candy. This is the only thing happening. Rhythmically: suck—pause. Suck—pause. Suck—pause. Suck—pause. Suck—pause. Suck.*)

PAUL: (*Finally. Belligerently, which is his nature.*) Are you looking for it or are you doing something else?
(*Pause.* KATZ *writes something, frowns at book.* MRS. OXENHAM *turns a page.* JAMIE *sucks, moves.*)

MORSE: Huh!
(*He studies the board.*)
(MILLIE *looks up at them, smiles to herself, as she does most of the time, looks back to the paper.*)

PAUL: He left about a year ago, or a year and a half.

KATZ: I told you; he wasn't here. He was somewhere else.

PAUL: He was here. Is this the Hotel Baltimore? Is this 63 East Madison Street? Is this Baltimore? You have people who get mail here who don't live here?

KATZ: Ranger. No.

PAUL: Granger. G. Granger.

KATZ: No, nobody like that.

PAUL: Do you remember every—

KATZ: Ask Mrs. Oxenham; I don't know him.
(PAUL *looks at him. Takes in air, blows it out. Looks over toward* MRS. OXENHAM, *begins to move down the counter to her.* MR. MORSE *moves.*)

MRS. OXENHAM: (*Before he reaches her; suddenly busy.*) I don't remember him.

PAUL: (*Rapid exchange here.*) A little quiet guy; he'd be about sixty-eight or seventy; and he wears a little derby . . .

MRS. OXENHAM: (*Cutting in.*) No, if he was here I'd remember him.

PAUL: —Not "if." He was here—for two years; he wasn't a transient—

MRS. OXENHAM: —I don't know anything about it—

PAUL: —Well, do you keep records? You keep rent receipts? Do I have to tell you what to do?

MRS. OXENHAM: —I can't take time to go through two years of room receipts looking for someone who never lived here.

PAUL: You don't have to go through them, I'll go through them. You don't have to squat.

MRS. OXENHAM: You don't have to use that—

PAUL: —I'll go through them if you're paralyzed, lady—

MRS. OXENHAM: —We're not going to turn our records over to—

PAUL: —Listen, I been here twelve hours, all I been getting is a shell game here; you people think you're the C.I.A.

MRS. OXENHAM: We're not at your beck and call. We're doing you a favor.

PAUL: I don't see you doing diddle.
(*She glares at him, but in a minute, as a martyr, takes down a stack of record books.*)

MORSE: (*Immediately. As* JAMIE *moves*) You have to take your jumps.

JAMIE: I don't have to.

MRS. OXENHAM: What name was that?

PAUL: (*Beat.*) Granger. Paul Granger. G-r-a-n-g-e-r! (*Beat.*) P-a-u-l.

MRS. OXENHAM: Sit down; if it's in here, I'll call you. (*Beat.*) When was he here?

PAUL: It's been more than a year—like a year and a half.
(*He waits a moment as she begins looking. Then turns.*)

MRS. OXENHAM: (*To his back*) We're not a missing-persons bureau, you know.

PAUL: (*Sits in the lounge, disgusted. Looks around. Focuses on the checker game. Watches them a moment.*) You play chess?
(MORSE *and* JAMIE *turn to look at him, then back to the board.* PAUL *looks away.*)

MILLIE: I've been sitting here reprimanding myself for being so unobservant. I was realizing that there are very few people living here whom I would remember a year after they left. They come and go with such a turnover . . . and if he wasn't obtrusive . . .

PAUL: He wasn't.

MILLIE: I was at work by seven-thirty and usually not back before six; where was he employed, do you know?

PAUL: He wasn't. He was retired.
(MILLIE *goes back to her paper.* PAUL *sulks and lights a cigarette, looks over to* MRS. OXENHAM. *He becomes aware that* JAMIE *is looking at him.* JAMIE *is trying to frame a request for a cigarette.*)
Whatta you gawkin' at?
(JAMIE *snaps back to the game. Sucks.* MORSE *moves.* MILLIE *has glanced up and back down. The switchboard buzzes. The* GIRL *enters, sees a message in her mailbox, goes directly to the office.*)

MRS. OXENHAM: Four-three-oh-seven. We don't do that. I don't know anything about it. Who's calling?
(*To* KATZ)
It's another antique dealer about the fixtures.

KATZ: Give them the number.

MRS. OXENHAM: Call Newgate Development: RA 6–3700.
(*Disconnects.*)
(MRS. BELLOTTI *comes in. She tries to gesture, "I'm going upstairs to—" as* MR. KATZ *looks up and back down— She drops it and starts on up.*)

GIRL: (*Tosses message in wastebasket. To* KATZ) You know what I've decided, puddin'? They're not going to fix the water or the elevator or anything, are they? They're trying to force us to leave. Aren't they?

KATZ: You got a month's notice; that's the legal notice.

GIRL: Yeah, but you don't expect anyone to live here a month with conditions like that.

MRS. OXENHAM: We've got a man workin' on the boiler right now. I called him as soon as I came in.

MORSE: (*Overlapping, cued by "boiler." The exchange starts low and personal and builds.*) You can't move twice.

JAMIE: I'm not.

MORSE: You took your hand off it.

JAMIE: I did not.

MORSE: You moved your hand; take that back.

JAMIE: I did not!

MORSE: You did so, young man!

JAMIE: I was thinking.

MORSE: You're trying to cheat!

JAMIE: You're a liar!

(MORSE *takes* JAMIE's *checker from the board and throws it to the floor. Glares at him.* MILLIE *follows this exchange, looking from one to the other, just before the action.* PAUL *ignores it to the end or nearly [beat].* JAMIE *takes a checker of* MR. MORSE's *and throws it on the floor. They glare [beat].* MR. MORSE *takes a checker and throws it on the floor. Each further move is an affront. They glare.* JAMIE *getting hurt and belligerent;* MR. MORSE *angry and belligerent—* JAMIE *takes a checker and throws it to the floor [beat].* MR. MORSE *takes the candy stick from* JAMIE's *mouth and throws it to the floor [beat].* JAMIE *takes a pencil from* MR. MORSE's *pocket, breaks it in his hands, throws it on the floor.* MR. MORSE *stands.* JAMIE *stands.* MR. MORSE *takes up the board, spilling the checkers, and with difficulty tears it in two along the spine and throws it on the floor.* JAMIE *glares. Takes up the checker box, tears it in two, and throws it to the floor [beat].* MR. MORSE *overturns* JAMIE's *chair. Now they grapple, slapping weakly at each other and making incoherent noises and grunts, two very weak individuals trying to do injury to each other. Injury would be impossible. When they struggle,* MILLIE *stands to get away.*)

MR. KATZ: (*As* JAMIE *tears the box*) Here, that doesn't belong to you; stop it. Both of you; sit down and act right or you can't stay down here. Come on! Both of you!

GIRL: (*Overlapping*) Jamie. Shame on you. Come on, stop that, what are you doing; you two babies. Shame on you. Stop fighting. What are you doing?
(GIRL *reaches them as they separate.* MR. MORSE, *from humiliation, shuffles directly to the only door in sight.*)

KATZ: (*Also coming from behind the office.*) Where are you going? Here, you can't go in there—

GIRL: Mr. Morse, come back and apologize; don't go in—
(*To* KATZ)
Oh, he isn't going to hurt anything. My God!
(MORSE *closes door as she reaches him.*)

KATZ: —Get him out of there.

GIRL: Mr. Morse, you can't go in there, that's the broom closet. (*Knocks.*) Mr. Morse? You're sitting in there on the slop sink, aren't you? With all those smelly mops. Mr. Morse, Jamie's sorry.

JAMIE: (*To her, joining her as* KATZ *picks up checkers*) I am not!

GIRL: (*Grabbing him, putting her hand over his mouth. The contact of a girl confuses and amazes him as much as the situation.*) He's sorry.

MORSE: (*Offstage.*) No, he isn't.

GIRL: (*As* JAMIE *struggles to talk*) What?

MORSE: (*Offstage.*) He isn't sorry!

GIRL: You hurt him very badly.
(JAMIE *struggles to protest.*)

MORSE: (*Offstage. After a beat.*) Where?

GIRL: You blacked his eye.
(JAMIE *gasps at the scope of the lie.*)
(*To* JAMIE)
Come here. I want to show you something.
(*As she gets her purse*)

JAMIE: What?

GIRL: (*Digging in her purse, getting out the mascara.*) Something
fun.

JAMIE: What?
(GIRL *spits on the mascara.*)
No. No.

GIRL: Hold him, Mr. Katz.
(KATZ, *returning to the desk, gestures, "I want nothing to do with
any of you."*)
(*Hating it, protesting, struggling,* JAMIE *nevertheless lets her put
the darkening around his eye.*)

JAMIE: No, no, it's— Don't, come on! Don't mark me up.

GIRL: (*Over*) Mr. Morse, he's in pain! It's terrible; you ought to be
ashamed of yourself, Mr. Morse.

JAMIE: (*The second she releases him.*) Let me see.
(*She hands him the mirror.*)
(*Whining*)
No . . . He didn't do . . .
(MR. MORSE *opens the door.* GIRL *takes the mirror.* JAMIE *slaps
his hand over his eye.*)

GIRL: Go on—show him, Jamie. Show him what a brute he is. Show
him what an ogre he is.
(JAMIE *does, pouting as though it were real.*)

MORSE: Good. Good.
(JACKIE *enters*.)
(JAMIE *puts his hand back over his eye and goes to the lounge to pout*.)

JACKIE: (*Livid*.) Is anyone here driving a blue Plymouth? Does anyone in this hotel belong to a blue Plaza 1970—

KATZ: (*Overlapping*) What do I know, I don't know what kind— what are you coming in here; you're always upsetting people; accusing people.

JACKIE: (*Less excited*.) —I just want to know 'cause I got a scratch on my left front fender about two feet long. People have no respect for other people's property. You just got to learn that and live with it. Let me use your pen.
(SUZY, *with stoic bearing, walks down the stairs in her most conservative clothes. As* KATZ *glances up, her head raises slightly and she walks evenly on*.)
Is today a Jewish holiday? What's happening today? I been to three different pawnshops; they're every one closed.

MILLIE: I think it's Memorial Day.

GIRL: It's Memorial Day today.

JACKIE: The whole damn city's closed up like a nun; *something's* going on. Is the Post Office closed?

GIRL: Oh, sure.

MORSE: Where's the checkerboard?

KATZ: No more checkers. You get too excited.

JACKIE: What happened? What's wrong with your eye? Who put that goop on you?
(GIRL *is saying Shhhh!*)

JAMIE: He did.

JACKIE: All right, what's going on?

GIRL: Mr. Morse hit him.

MORSE: (*Overlapping some*) I hit him.

JACKIE: (*To* JAMIE) You starting fights with people now?
(*To* MORSE)
Why don't you pick on somebody your own size?

MORSE: That boy is a hellion, and I taught him a lesson.

GIRL: We were just kidding around.

JACKIE: (*Spitting on a handkerchief.*) Wipe that off your face.

GIRL: Shhhhhh!
(JAMIE *takes the handkerchief and sits.*)

MORSE: I hope you've all learned your lesson.

GIRL: You don't know your own strength, Mr. Morse. (*To* JACKIE)
It was just a joke.

JACKIE: Well, I don't want people joking with Jamie; he's not in
good health.

GIRL: We were just goofing.

JACKIE: (*Going to desk.*) Well, I don't want you goofing with him.
(PAUL *starts to get up.* MRS. OXENHAM *gives him a stony look and
opens the records.* GIRL *sees him.*)

GIRL: (*To* PAUL) You're still here; I thought you'd be gone. Did you
get a room?
(*Pause.*)

PAUL: I'm trying to get some information.

GIRL: Are you just in town?

PAUL: Yeah.

GIRL: Where from? (*Beat.*) How did you get here? Train? Hitch? Where's he from, Millie?

MILLIE: I'm sure if he wants you to know he'll tell you.

GIRL: Millie sees things, knows things, she sees ghosts and auras and things. And believes in things, like reincarnation and old Chinese religions like yoga—

MILLIE: I certainly do not. And yoga is something one practices, not something one believes in.

GIRL: Well, then you practice it.

MILLIE: I certainly don't practice yoga.

GIRL: Come on, you know what I mean—

MILLIE: I can't remember someone he'd like me to remember; I don't think he'll be much impressed.

GIRL: Who do you want?

PAUL: Are you one of the residents? How long have you been here?

GIRL: Lived here? Seven months. Before that I was everywhere; I'm from Arizona. Where are you from?
(PAUL *looks around.*)
I'll bet I've been there. I'll tell you the places I've been and you tell me if I name it. 'Cause when I left home I went every place, for almost six months. I didn't stop more than three days in any one—

PAUL: (*Getting up, going to the desk.*) Are you looking for it?

MRS. OXENHAM: When I find something I'll tell you.

GIRL: (*Whispered, to* MILLIE) Who's he looking for?

MILLIE: Ask him.

GIRL: Who're you looking for?

PAUL: My granddad. (*Sitting back down.*) You didn't know him. He probably left before you got here.

GIRL: Is he Mr. Morse? Mr. Morse, do you have grandchildren? (MR. MORSE *turns to go.*) You don't have to go.

KATZ: Stay out of that closet.

MORSE: (*Has actually swerved to the closet—now the stairs.*) I'm going to my room!

JAMIE: Good. Good riddance.

JACKIE: (*From the desk*) Just clam up over there.

KATZ: Come on, don't spread that stuff here.

JACKIE: I'm not bothering you. This is official.

KATZ: Go over there.

GIRL: Don't expect Mrs. Oxenham to help you. She's an ogre. She's not human. (*Distracted.*) Boy, this place. (*Looks around.*) I been up thirty-three hours. I'm not trying to find out your business, I just want to have a conversation. O.K., tell me if this is where you're from. Uh. Denver. Amarillo. Wichita. Oklahoma City. Salt Lake City. Fort Worth. Dallas. Houston. New Orleans. Mobile. Birmingham. Memphis. St. Louis—don't look down, I'm watch-

ing your eyes to see if you make a move when I say the right one. Kansas City. Omaha. Des Moines. San Francisco. Portland. Seattle. Spokane. Minneapolis. St. Paul. Milwaukee. Chicago. Indianapolis. Cincinnati. Columbus. Cleveland. Pittsburgh. Buffalo. Albany. Utica. Boston. New York. Providence. Atlanta. Tallahassee.
(PAUL *begins to smile.*)
Orlando. Tampa. Jacksonville. Daytona Beach. Palm Beach. Fort Myers. Fort—Fort Lauderdale! Fort Lauderdale!

PAUL: (*Smiling.*) No.

GIRL: Fort Myers.

PAUL: No.

GIRL: You smiled.

PAUL: I'm not from Fort Myers.

GIRL: Then where? St. Louis.

PAUL: No.

GIRL: 'Cause that's when you looked away.

PAUL: You haven't been to those places.

GIRL: I certainly have.

JAMIE: You've been to Salt Lake City?

GIRL: I been to every state in the Union. Some of them three times.

PAUL: That'd cost about—

GIRL: Yeah, I sold cookies. Come on, you're trying to distract me. Los Angeles.

PAUL: No.

GIRL: Bakersfield.

PAUL: No.

MILLIE: Louisville.
(*He looks at her—reaches for the paper; she hands it to him.*)

PAUL: Where is it?
(*He hands it back to her; she finds the item and returns the paper to PAUL.*)

GIRL: (*Overlapping the action. Amazed.*) Is that *right?* I would have *said* that.

JAMIE: Come on.

GIRL: (*To JAMIE*) I would. I've been there. I went from Knoxville to Chattanooga to Nashville to Evansville to Louisville to Cinci—
(*She notices something is wrong.*) What?
(*PAUL hands her the paper. She glances down, then up.*)
Your name's Paul? (*Back to the item.*) The third. What's St. Clemens?

PAUL: (*Pause.*) It's a work farm.

GIRL: What'd you get busted for?

PAUL: Selling grass.

GIRL: They give you two years—

PAUL: Shhh!

MILLIE: (*Whisper. At the same time.*) Now, not so—

GIRL: —for selling grass?

PAUL: You're supposed to drink sour-mash whiskey. You're not supposed to be selling grass. I was an example. They like their students drunk, they don't like them—

GIRL: You were in *school* and they gave you—

PAUL: Shh—come on.

GIRL: In college? (*Pause.*) I'm impressed. I didn't even make it past junior year in high school. I hated it.

PAUL: Don't let it bother you. It's just a way to keep the kids off the street.

MILLIE: It doesn't seem to be working, does it?

GIRL: (*As* PAUL *smiles at* MILLIE'S *joke and she smiles back*) Boy, I was terrible in high school. I failed every subject except geography. I was pretty good in history but I was a genius in geography. Naturally, I'd be good in something I couldn't possibly use. Actually, I do use it, though. Like when a john is shy or weird or something. I can ask him where he's from and get him talking. I don't think that's what Mrs. Whitmore had in mind when she taught us geography. (*Beat.*) You're looking for your granddad? Did he just disappear? While you were—"working"? Will they look for you?

PAUL: No. Do you mind?

GIRL: Did you just sneak off?

KATZ: (*To* JACKIE) What are you doing? What are you spreading that stuff around?

JACKIE: Come on, man, you're impossible; I'm not bothering you.

KATZ: You are. Bothering me. Go over there; get this stuff—

JACKIE: All right, come on. (*Gathering it up.*) I don't need a hassle. (*Moving.*) Man, I can't get my blood sugar up today. (*Sitting in lounge. Dumping her papers on the table: change-of-address cards, a copy of* Organic Gardening, *etc.*) I got about a dozen things to do here. I walked all over town this morning. We're getting out of here tomorrow.

JAMIE: Yeah?

JACKIE: I go to that insurance place; they give me a receipt for my money; I get that paper in my hand and we're gone.
(MRS. BELLOTTI *comes down the stairs, carrying a box, and exits.*)

GIRL: (*Almost a whisper. To* PAUL) She's taking out her son's clothes. She's got a husband with his leg off, and her son's been kicked out of here, and the father has sugar diabetes and hates the son anyway. God. I hear something like that and I just want to lock myself in the bathroom, order a sausage and anchovy pizza, and eat the entire thing. (*Pause.*) I occupied the bathtub on my floor once for three straight hours. You know those assorted boxes of bath salts with eight different scents? I put in one of each. I called the Pizza Shack—they'll deliver any time of the day or night anywhere in the city. I have their number on my wall about that big, like it was one of those numbers you call in case of emergency. I ordered a pizza. I filled up the tub and sat there for three solid hours. There wasn't a single bubble in the tub by the time I got out. It took me the rest of the day to unpucker. Of course . . . (*Raising her voice, using* JACKIE'S *magazine for a megaphone.*) . . . Now, that's out. There's no more hot water. They're trying to get rid of us.

JACKIE: Come on, don't mess with that. I mean, you can look at it but don't mislay it.

GIRL: What is it?

JACKIE: (*Continuing to fill out cards; tossing it off.*) That magazine you can't get on a newsstand. You have to order that magazine to come to your home. I gotta look up their offices 'cause I have to send them one of these change-of-address cards. You subscribe to it. You get one a month. It's fantastic. (*Pausing in her work a second.*) You know anything about growing rice?

GIRL: What?

JACKIE: Growing *rice?* It's a water plant, isn't it?

GIRL: I don't know.

JACKIE: 'Cause rice is nature's most perfect food. Because of the balance of its nutrients. That's what this country ought to be growin' instead of all that fuckin' wheat. You know those plants out past Fort McHenry? You know what they do?

GIRL: They're sugar plants, I thought.

JACKIE: Refining. Sugar refining. They take natural sugar and turn it into shit. And then they pollute the atmosphere doing it. You can't get people to care about the environment. Of their own planet. Did you see *Planet of the Apes?*

GIRL: No. I wanted to.

JACKIE: Well, they knew what was happening. (*Back to the magazine.*) You ought to read that. You know the great discoveries? Like the discovery of bacteria; and the discovery of uranium; the discovery of sulphur drugs? Like that?

GIRL: (*Serious, nodding.*) The discovery of penicillin . . .

JACKIE: Right. Well, the next major discovery—scientists are going to find this out, they're gonna be researching this. These people in this magazine already know it. (*Pause.*) Garlic.

MILLIE: What?

JACKIE: *Garlic.* It's biodegradable.
(MILLIE *and* PAUL *watch without expression; the* GIRL *listens seriously;* JAMIE *is aghast but excited.*)
You know DDT is out; DDT is killing us. You know that. (*Pause.*) Garlic juice. Has in it . . . (*Reaching for the magazine.*) . . . this is just one aspect; it has about four separate aspects . . .

(*Finding it.*) . . . it has in it three separate "All-i-um Sul-phates." Three separate killers. Bug killers. Which just happen to be the three separate strongest bug killers known to man.
(JAMIE *says with her,* "*known to man.*")
There's three different articles about garlic in this one issue.

GIRL: Is it all right to eat it? Because I've eaten it.

JACKIE: Sure, it's good for you. That's the amazing thing. But—for the insecticide, what you do is: you take—this is what we're going to do. We may be the first. On this scale. You take detergent suds, and the juice from Mexican hot peppers, and garlic juice. And you mix those together and it'll kill anything.

MILLIE: I'd think it would.

JACKIE: But it won't hurt the worms. The earthworms. That's what you want, because they're necessary to you.

GIRL: What are they for?

JAMIE: (*As* JACKIE *starts to speak*) Air.

JACKIE: A—a bunch of things. Different things. Where's your candy? (JAMIE *looks at* MR. KATZ.)
And . . . well, look at this. You probably never saw anything like this before. For real. (*She takes a paper from her purse—quite proud.*) That's a deed. A land deed. (*Hands it to the* GIRL.) That's for twenty acres. That's where our money went; that's a pretty good investment, considering. That's fifteen dollars an acre. We heard it advertised on the radio.

GIRL: That's fantastic. Where? (*She hands it to* PAUL.)

JACKIE: (*Looking over* PAUL's *shoulder.*) It's all in here—we have to find it—"Two miles—" It goes for miles—that's how big it is— "south of Pepin and six miles west of—"

GIRL: Carter. Sure. Utah.

JACKIE: We were driving down from Buffalo, we heard—

GIRL: Are you from Buffalo? I didn't know that.

JACKIE: We was headed down to Florida to work on the crops; we heard this offer— I said to hell with pickin' somebody else's tomatoes; we'll raise our own crops.

GIRL: (*Unsure.*) Sure . . .

JACKIE: We don't need no house. We're sleeping in a sleeping bag. If it rains, it gets nasty, we sleep in the car. We get sick of that, we move into a motel.

GIRL: How do you know there's a motel? If you've never been there?

JACKIE: Of course there's a motel; the country's gone to shit; there's always a motel.

GIRL: Don't you hate it? I spent the entire morning in a motel listening to some wheeler-dealer buying and selling most of the lumber south of the Mason Dix— (*Suddenly.*) Wait! Wait! Millie! Could I buy a railroad? Could I buy stock in a railroad? If I gave you six hundred dollars, could you go wherever it is and buy stock for me? Or could you take me there? And introduce me to your broker? Do you have a stockbroker?

MILLIE: No—I never had any interest in it; I only invested because there wasn't anything particular that I wanted. I wasn't interested in the stock—

GIRL: —You could go to the annual meetings; you could speak out—

MILLIE: —Oh, I don't know anything about it.

GIRL: You could tell them to shape up. Will you introduce me?

MILLIE: Surely; one day, if you're interested . . .

GIRL: Not one day. Not today because it's a holiday, but tomorrow.

MILLIE: Well, if you're still interested in it and you—

GIRL: —Come on, say yes.

MILLIE: If I feel like it, if you remind me.

GIRL: You don't live on this planet, Millie, you really don't.

MILLIE: No, I know, I never seemed to connect with the things—

GIRL: —I mean you're so sweet; a person just forgets completely how batty you are.

MILLIE: Fairly batty, I believe.

GIRL: Really, completely crackers sometimes.

MILLIE: —Well, not so bad as that, maybe—

GIRL: —But intelligent and all, you know—

MILLIE: —Oh, I was never completely stupid; just outside, I'm afraid, with no particular interest in peering in. When I realized that so much of people's preoccupation was in worldly houses, I realized that—

GIRL: I like that—worldly houses.

MILLIE: —that I was quite outside. I was one of fourteen, you know. I was the youngest of—

GIRL: Fourteen brothers and sisters?

MILLIE: Oh, I come from an enormous family; it wasn't at all unusual at the time; a huge old Victorian house outside Baton Rouge;

an amazing old house, really, with—when you ask about spirits— oh, well, you couldn't keep track of them all. Banging doors, throwing silverware, breaking windows. They were all over the house. There was a black maid—slave girl, I suppose, and a revolutionary soldier and his girl, and a Yankee carpetbagger, and a saucy little imp of a girl who sashayed about very mischievously. She'd been pushed out of a window and was furious about it. Storming through the upstairs, slamming windows shut all over the house. It was quite an active place.

GIRL: Oh, I love it.

MILLIE: And when my aunt died—a wonderful old lady. It had been her husband's house. I must have been only eight or nine. She died and her sisters and brothers—my father even—scrabbled over her silverware and clothes and jewelry. Even the pots and pans. One cook ran off with all the cooking vessels. None of the things meant anything to my aunt, of course; she hardly realized she had them. I remember my father, with a Georgian silver teapot in one hand and an epergne in the other, yelling, "If Ariadne were alive she'd be scandalized!" And I thought, no, she wouldn't, Daddy, she'd be very amused. At all of you.

GIRL: And you're like her.

MILLIE: Not really. I'm very silly; she was quite a marvelous lady. You couldn't be like that today.

GIRL: I think you are. You had a cook? Who ran away with the—

MILLIE: Oh, yes, for some reason she decided to take every kerosene lamp and taper in the house. My uncle had been very frugal about them, so I suppose she thought they were valuable. She ordered a wagon and loaded it full. She was so foolish, that poor woman. Completely mad, of course. A wonderful old battle-ax. Carrying off vast old zinc tubs—four feet across. God knows what use they had, and big old copper vats and pans, skillets, spoons, wooden spoons, even the slop jars. While everyone was upstairs squabbling over the linen. They came down for supper—we had an enormous old-fashioned wood stove in the kitchen; she had managed to dismantle half of that before she gave up. (*Chuckles.*) I still remember all of them sitting around in the dark eating bread and jelly sandwiches. There wasn't even a coffeepot!

PAUL: I don't get it.

MILLIE: (*Hand on his knee, embrace.*) Nor did I, Paul, I didn't get it at all. But I thought it was very amusing. (*Beat.*) Spirits are very peaceful, of course. They don't act up unless there's tension in a household. But oh, my! That night! Did they carry on! You've never heard such caterwauling!

GIRL: Oh! I want to see it! Spirits doing that! Don't you hope it's true! I mean scientifically true? I want them to come up with absolute scientific proof that there are spirits and ghosts and reincarnation. I want everyone to see them and talk to them. Something like that! Some miracle. Something huge! I want some *major miracle* in my lifetime!

JACKIE: Did you know the first two hours after you pick them, green beans lose twenty percent of their vitamin C?

GIRL: How much have they got?

JACKIE: A lot, but you shouldn't eat them. What you should eat is kale.

JAMIE: Kale.

JACKIE: It's a kind of lettuce. And lettuce has opium in it—if you know how to get it out.

JAMIE: (*With her*) . . . to get it out.

MRS. OXENHAM: (*As* MRS. BELLOTTI *comes in and goes upstairs*) Here's your party. Young man?

PAUL: (*Jumping up—going to the desk.*) Me?

MRS. OXENHAM: This isn't going to tell you anything. It's just a rent receipt.

PAUL: Is that your signature?

MRS. OXENHAM: I can't remember every person who pays rent here two years later.

PAUL: He was very quiet and neat. He wore a derby. He had a very soft voice and he was—shit, don't you ever look at people?

MRS. OXENHAM: That's all I can tell you, I told you it wouldn't do any good.

PAUL: Do you remember if he left a forwarding address?

MRS. OXENHAM: We don't accept forwarding addresses.

PAUL: Grayish hair and—

MRS. OXENHAM: That's all I know; I don't remember him.

PAUL: Would you remember it if he fell dead in the lobby? If he was found in his room—?

MRS. OXENHAM: That didn't happen.
(*Phone.*)
Front desk.
(*Writes down a number, looks in the book, and dials.*)

GIRL: He wore a derby?

PAUL: He was a workman. When he retired he wore a suit and a derby, because he wanted to look like he was retired . . .

GIRL: What is a derby? Really? (*Pause.*) Are you from a poor family?

PAUL: No.

GIRL: Oh. Were you close? To him?
(*Pause.*)

PAUL: He squinted a little . . .

GIRL: You were, weren't you? Close.

PAUL: He wanted to come live with Mom and Dad, and they wrote
him they didn't have room for him. They didn't want him.
(*To* MILLIE)
He sang songs . . . all the time . . . under his breath . . . My
sister . . .

GIRL: What? Your sister?

PAUL: She talked about him all the time . . . she told me about
. . . what he was . . . like—like what he was like.

GIRL: She told you? Didn't you—ever meet him?

PAUL: How could I meet him, I was always off in some goddamned
school.

GIRL: And you want—

PAUL: *I* want him! *I* have room for him!

GIRL: Well, don't take it out on me.

JACKIE: Where did he work?

PAUL: I called them. They started getting his pension checks back—
they don't know where he is . . .

JACKIE: You finished with that, I don't want to lose that.
(*Magazine*—GIRL *hands it to her.*)

GIRL: What did he do?

PAUL: He worked. Mother's family had about a billion dollars' worth of whiskey distilleries—that's why Dad married—Granddad kept right on working. They were all so damn high-society they wouldn't associate with anyone like—

GIRL: You don't talk to the person you're talking to. Did anybody ever tell you that? You talk to yourself. You don't look at people.

PAUL: (*Glowers at her. Finally*) He was an engineer.

GIRL: Oh, God; every boy in Phoenix Central High was "going into engineering"; that's all they ever talked about was their T squares and slide rules. I never did tell them I didn't know what engineering was; maybe you can tell me. What'd he do? Exactly?

PAUL: (*Glowers.*) He was—

GIRL: —Relax.

PAUL: Huh?

GIRL: Relax. You're all tense. You're just like a— You're all tense. (*Pause.*) What'd he do?
(*Pause.*)

PAUL: Who?

GIRL: Your granddad?

PAUL: He was an engineer. For the railroad. He drove the Baltimore and Ohio between—

GIRL: (*On "Ohio," standing, bursting into tears.*) NO! No! Oh! Oh! He drove a train! Oh, I want to meet him! I want to talk to him!

PAUL: Well, you find him; you think of a way and I'll let you talk to him.

THE EFFECT OF GAMMA RAYS ON
MAN-IN-THE-MOON MARIGOLDS

Beatrice (Obie-winner Sada Thompson) wants her daughter
Tillie (Pamela Payton-Wright) to look pretty for
the finals of the science contest.

THE BASIC TRAINING OF PAVLO HUMMEL
Corporal Ardsley (Albert Hall), a Greek chorus figure, speaks from bitter experience to the innocent recruit Pavlo Hummel (William Atherton).

THE TOOTH OF CRIME
Cheyenne (left, Jim Griffiths) warns Hoss (Spalding Gray) of Crow's imminent arrival for the shoot-out, as members of the audience watch in the background.

THE HOT L BALTIMORE
Jamie (Zane Lasky) and April (Conchatta Ferrell) find a moment to dance as their hotel-home crumbles around them.

AMERICAN BUFFALO
Obie-winner Mike Kellin as Teach (left) lectures Don and Bob on the finer points of petty crime.

BAD HABITS
Society's cure for an individual's "bad habits," according to playwright Terrence McNally, is to put him in a straitjacket.

GIRL: Somewhere! You don't know. How I feel! You can, too. If he was here, of course you can find him. Stay for Bill; I'll help you. Oxenham isn't any good, she wouldn't look for her own grand-father—and I don't even know the day people; the afternoon people are temporary and, anyway, I got to get some sleep and Bill comes on at twelve.

PAUL: I was here last night.

GIRL: Yes, but you didn't tell us what you were doing—dummy—why didn't you say something?

PAUL: I gotta be somewhere tomorrow.

GIRL: Come on, everyone's gotta be somewhere tomorrow; I want to meet him. Where was his run? Do you know? Did you know him at all?

JACKIE: Come on, don't jiggle the table.

MILLIE: I think—
(MR. MORSE *has been coming down the stairs— He works his mouth, waves his arms, but no words come out.* MILLIE *stands.* KATZ *goes to him.* MRS. OXENHAM *stands. The* GIRL *sees him.* JACKIE *does too. Finally, almost reaching the landing.*)

MORSE: Been-been-taken-everything-that-person. I been robbed. I been robbed.

KATZ: What?
(JACKIE *starts to leave.*)

MORSE: That person.

KATZ: Where you going? You were up there, weren't you?

JACKIE: I got things to attend to.

KATZ: You're not attending to no more business for a minute.

JAMIE: She didn't touch your things. She hasn't been near your things.

KATZ: You just keep out of it.

JACKIE: I helped him out with a problem he had. I don't know what you're talking about. You been picking on me ever since I came here. That's all you know, because you don't like the way I look or the way I dress or something! You don't like the way I live!

MORSE:
That's the person. Took my wife's things. That's all I have in this world.

JAMIE:
She didn't go up there.

KATZ:
All I'm saying is, give it back. Turn it over to him. And all of it and this minute. Everything you took. What's missing, Mr. Morse? What are you missing from your room?

MORSE: What?

KATZ: What's gone, what are you missing?

MORSE: My things! My wedding cuff links and my necklace that belonged to my wife! And my mother!

JACKIE: Yeah, well, I didn't take his fucking mother; he's crazy.

MORSE: And four rings; a gold ring and a sapphire ring and—I don't remember . . .

JACKIE: (*Overlapping from* "*sapphire*") I got things to do—you can search my car and you can search my room— I've got nothing to hide; we got business.

KATZ: (*Grabbing her.*) You're not leaving.

JACKIE: Why me? Why not somebody else? Let me go or I'll kill you, you son of a bitch—

KATZ: (*Struggling with her.*) Give me her purse—
(GIRL *shakes her head.*)
Give me her damn— (*Wrenching it away from her; dumping it on the floor.*) I been listening to you talking about pawnshops.

JACKIE: (*Flailing; but held back by one arm.*) No; get out of my personal things. That belongs to me—those things belong to me.
(As KATZ *finds a knotted silk man's sock at the bottom of her purse*)
That ain't his. Stop it!

MORSE: Give me that! Give me my things!!
(KATZ *hands it to him.*)

KATZ: That right there could get you ten years!

JACKIE: *I got dreams, goddamnit! What's he got?*
(KATZ *lets go of her.* MORSE *goes to the stairs.*)
(*She sags into a chair.*)
What's he got?

MORSE: (*Deeply shaken.*) I'm going to report this incident.

KATZ: You're going up to your room. You got your stuff—is that all of it?

JACKIE: (*Weakly*) You robbed me.

MORSE: I'm calling the police.

JAMIE: I'll beat you up!

KATZ: Your phone's out of order. It's your own damn fault to let people in your room.

MORSE: (*Going up and off; mumbling.*) I have my rights.

KATZ: You got no rights here.
(*To* JACKIE)
I want you and your brother both out of here tonight.

JACKIE: I'm paid up here till—

KATZ: I'll refund your rent money—out tonight, or I turn you in myself.

GIRL: Not from Mr. Morse. He doesn't have anything. He never hurt anybody.

JACKIE: You ripped off one of your scores, you told me so.

GIRL: He could afford it.

JACKIE: Just because you have protection. (*Returning pen.*) I don't want you thinking I'm taking your fuckin' ink pen. (*At desk.*)

GIRL: I wasn't going to tell you, but you got nothing.

JACKIE: I got what I need.

GIRL: That land you got won't grow nothing. I know that place. I may not know much but I know that—

JACKIE: What are you talking about? You're a liar—you don't know anything about it. That's farmland.

GIRL: —because I been there. On the Rio Grande Zephyr. It's nothing but a desert—a salt desert, it don't even grow cactus. Six miles west of Carter, two miles south of Pepin—it's desert for a hundred miles.

JACKIE: It's farmland! That's farmland! I got brochures. I got pictures.

GIRL: Even I know better than to buy land from the radio. You can't get farmland for that price nowhere. You ought to be ashamed of yourself, robbing Mr. Morse.

JACKIE: (*Snatching up the deed, putting it in her purse.*) I know what I'm doing for my brother and . . .

(*Goes about collecting her things— She knows instinctively that it is true.*) You may not know anything about growing . . . we know what we're doing. (*She blindly collects her papers, stuffing them into her bag.*)
(*Pause.*)

JAMIE: That's not fair . . .

JACKIE: Be still.

GIRL: Or maybe . . . maybe I'm wrong. Maybe I have it mixed up. I don't want to hurt anybody.

JACKIE: Ain't nobody been hurt by you or . . .

JAMIE: Anybody. (*He is about to burst into tears.*) You're—

JACKIE: (*Crying out.*) Shut up! (*Looks around, sits, falls into a chair.*) Boy . . . everything I try . . . (*Pause.*) I liked you, too. Well. We live and learn. (*Getting up, taking her purse and bag.*)

GIRL: Oh, Jesus.

JACKIE: Come on. We're gonna go eat.
(*JAMIE goes out.*)
We were getting out of here tomorrow, a few hours one way or the— (*The energy drains from her; her mind scattered, she stands blindly holding back tears.*)

GIRL: Jackie?
(*JACKIE starts and runs out, the GIRL runs after her.*)
Maybe it was a lie. I was just mad. I haven't had any sleep. Forget I said it. Please.
(*MRS. BELLOTTI immediately comes down the stairs and follows them out, carrying another box. MILLIE has moved to the shadows of the stairway. PAUL stands in the center of the lobby.*)

MILLIE: Your grandfather is alive, Paul.
(*The lights begin to fade. He looks for her, sees her.*)

PAUL: Where is he?

MILLIE: Oh, I have no idea. I don't know him. I never met him. I only know that he isn't dead.

PAUL: How do you know?

MILLIE: I don't know how I know. I never know how I know; I just know he isn't dead.
(MILLIE *and* PAUL *freeze. The lights are very dim.* KATZ *and* MRS. OXENHAM *prepare and leave.* BILL *enters and turns on the radio.* MILLIE *moves upstairs.* PAUL *stares after her as the music from the radio spreads to the house and the lights dim out.*)

ACT THREE

(*Midnight. On stage,* BILL *and* MR. MORSE. BILL *is at the switchboard.* MR. MORSE *sits in the lounge, not at ease.* BILL *opens a sack from a deli and takes out a sweet roll. He takes a sip of coffee from a paper container. He glances at a note left on the board, plugs in the board while still standing, glancing at the clock. Rings. Sips coffee.*)

BILL: It's twelve- (*Glance at clock.*) oh-six. You getting up? Good morning—Billy Jean, Lilac Lavender, Martha. No, no talk, come down if you want to gab.
(*As* APRIL *appears, descending the stairs, wearing a long diaphanous gown*)
April's down here.

APRIL: (*To herself*) Down, down, down . . .

BILL: No, I got work to do.
(*Disconnects, smiling at the phone. Then to* APRIL)
Look at you, done up fit to kill.

APRIL: That seems to be the consensus. Evening, Mr. Morse, baby.

BILL: One of those nights, huh?

APRIL: Bill, tonight wasn't even in the book. You see that john just walked out of here?

BILL: Didn't pay any attention to him.

APRIL: Just the least bit flaky.

BILL: Yeah? What's the problem?

APRIL: If my clientele represents a cross section of American manhood, the country's in trouble.

BILL: I'd think it would be.

APRIL: I don't need it from you this morning. I called Martha's pizza palace and ordered a pizza, that's how bad it is.

BILL: That bad, huh? You get to bed?

APRIL: (*She laughs.*) No, Bill, what can I tell you? It was one of those nights. The room got a workout. I turned fifteen on the floor, twenty in the tub, and fifteen across the top of the dresser. I'm not lying. Definitely flaky. Usually I can count on one in five getting a little experimental.

BILL: Not today, huh?

APRIL: Today we drew a full house. (*Laughs.*) Guy says, "What's that?" I say, "That's the tub, that's where I keep the alligator, better stay back: you ain't got nothing you can afford to lose." Says, "I'd kinda like to make it in the tub." I say, "Honey, look: you ever see one of these? It's a bed. It's kinda kinky but let me show you how it works." End up, we make it in—

BILL: (*Said with her*) In the tub.

APRIL: Right. Tell him all we got is cold water, it's gonna do you no good; nothing would do. (*Laughs.*) He gets in, sits down, I turn on the water and nearly scalded his balls off.

BILL: I got it fixed.

APRIL: Yeaaah! Spanking red from the butt down. Loved it. Stayed in for twenty minutes. Very groovy experience for him. If I knew he was coming, I'd have dug out the rubber duck.

BILL: Anything to get somebody to like you.

APRIL: Like me? Pay me. They know me from the wallpaper.
(*To* MR. MORSE)
Don't they, darlin'?

MR. MORSE: It's too hot.

APRIL: You noticed that, did you?

MR. MORSE: It's no good for my health. You got to have circulation of air. This hotel is overheated. They're trying to make us all sick.

APRIL: See that. There's always a logical explanation for everything.

GIRL: (*Entering in a terry robe and slippers.*) Morning, Bill. Morning, honey.

BILL: You get any sleep?

GIRL: Did I? I fainted. Besides, with Oxenham guarding the gates, there wasn't any point. She is absolutely no help at all. Where's Paul? That guy?

BILL: No messages.

GIRL: You seen him since you been on? That guy who fell asleep in the lobby last night.

BILL: Went out; left his bag.

GIRL: (*Shaking herself awake.*) Oh, golly! Brufff! Oh, it's getting warm. Cross your fingers. Maybe it's finally spring.

BILL: Supposed to get up to seventy today.

APRIL: Two more weeks and everything will stink.

GIRL: (*Taking a bit of his roll.*) Anyway, we got a project.

BILL: You do, huh? Come on, that's breakfast.

GIRL: Not *me*. We do. (*She goes to the files.*)

BILL: Don't pull that crap—what are you doing?

GIRL: Didn't your mother ever tell you; the first warm day you start the cleaning. (*Occupied with pulling out boxes of files.*)

BILL: (*Over*) No joke, that stuff's dirty. Wear some clothes when you come down here.

GIRL: Come on, I told Paul you'd help him or he would have given up, so you got to help too.

BILL: Oxenham will have your hide; you know that.

GIRL: I'll put them back. I figure there are all those boxes in the basement. I can go through those too.

BILL: What boxes?

GIRL: Don't you even explore your own place of business?

BILL: (*Buzzer rings.*) I just work here. There's rats down there; you can't go down—come on.
(*As she dumps a pile of boxes*)
What are you doing? What do you want with those?

GIRL: Answer your phone.

BILL: (*Into the phone.*) Hold it.

GIRL: That fellow who was here—

APRIL: Freak.

GIRL: That freak who was here is looking for his "long-lost grand-dad." Everyone has been about as helpful as a stick. And we're going to find some trace of the old man. Something to go on.

BILL: (*Phone.*) Yeah? (*Dials.*) Don't pull those things out here.

GIRL: Don't you like mysteries? Don't you want to help someone? Besides, you're going to anyway, because I volunteered you. The man may be lost; he may have amnesia; he was a trainman, Bill. He drove the B and O for twenty-six years. And he's in there.

BILL: (*Phone.*) They don't answer. (*Disconnects.*) I don't know where the hell you get your energy. How long did you sleep?

GIRL: Long. Six hours or more. April, where were you for the action? You missed the excitement.

APRIL: I saw plenty of action: you're right, I missed the excitement.

GIRL: Did you hear about the— Did you tell them, Mr. Morse?

APRIL: Mr. M. is none too spry tonight.

GIRL: Where are they? Jackie and Jamie? Did they leave?

BILL: Who's that?

APRIL: Flotsam and Jetsam?

BILL: Note here says three-nineteen's checking out. Car's not out front.

APRIL: Don't tell me that heap actually moves.

GIRL: It better move, they've been eighty-sixed.

BILL: (*Mock disappointment.*) Awww, that's too bad.

GIRL: I gotta have something. You want a cup of tea?

BILL: I could stand a cup of tea. There any water in there?

GIRL: Yeah, it's fine. April?

APRIL: Huh? Yeah, sure. What?

GIRL: Tea. Mr. Morse?

APRIL: Like a cup of tea, Mr. Morse?

MORSE: Too hot.

GIRL: This will take forever.

JAMIE: (*Entering.*) Has Jackie been here?

BILL: Don't know; I just got on.
  (*Sotto voce to* APRIL)
  Is he Flotsam or is he—

APRIL: He's a sweetie, aren't you, baby? We thought you were gone.
  Is who here?

JAMIE: Is Jackie back yet?

APRIL: Ain't seen—her. Where's she supposed to be?

JAMIE: (*Looking at the* GIRL.) She went to get gas for the car.

GIRL: Morning, Jamie. Are you speaking to me?
  (*Beat.*)

JAMIE: Morning.

GIRL: You look sleepy; you sleepy?
  (*He is—shakes his head no.*)
  What time did you get up?

JAMIE: Six.

APRIL: You had a nap?

GIRL: Six this morning?

JAMIE: Every morning.

APRIL: You helping her carry things down?

JAMIE: She took her stuff—I have to take my own, though. That's the way we do it.

GIRL: (*Back to files.*) This is going to be a snap.

APRIL: What time did she go out for gas?
(*Beat.*)

JAMIE: 'Bout six.

APRIL: This evening. Well, see, she's probably looking for natural gas.

JAMIE: No lead.

APRIL: (*To* BILL) No way.
(*Phone buzzes.*)

BILL: Four-three-oh-scven.

APRIL: (*To* JAMIE) Honey, I don't really think it's necessary to drag down a lot of things till she gets here.

JAMIE: (*He looks to the front door and hardly takes his eyes off it.*) This is it.

BILL: (*Holding receiver.*) Billy Jean? Billy Jean?

GIRL: "Billy Jean"? That's three weeks ago. I can't, I'm in the middle—ask who it is—he won't tell you.

APRIL: Here! (*Rushes to the phone.*) Hello, this is Miss Billy Jean's "girl"; she's in the tub; could I ask who's calling her, please? (*Pause.*) Umm hmmm. I'll tell her. It's Mr. Last-month-all-night-at-the-Statler-Hilton, madam, shall I toss him in?

GIRL: Oh, God. What do you call it when a guy has really terrible breath?

APRIL: Par for the run.

GIRL: Well, this guy has a terminal case of par for the run. (*Gives herself completely to phone.*) Hi. You're back. Of course I do, silly, Penthouse B.

APRIL: (*Poking* BILL.) Penthouse B.

GIRL: It's great to *talk* to you; only I'm freezing. I will not, you could get electrocuted.

BILL: For what?

APRIL: Talking on the phone in the tub.

GIRL: Well, that's a lot better, only I can't. Mom's in town; isn't it a drag? You did? Was that all you liked? That wasn't my fault if I got a little carried away. Listen, could I send over a great friend? (APRIL *laughs.*) O.K., then just call Veda. But you call me back when you're in town again, you hear? I won't promise anything; not with you. Bye, bye. (*Hangs up.*) Jesus. Can you imagine the drag? Dinner and eight hours in the feathers and he thinks he's Rockefella giving you fifty dollars.

BILL: I don't like you taking those calls down here.

GIRL: You gave it to me. (*Back to books.*) I mean, if a person is interested in making any money, the man ought to realize. The money's in turnover, not in lay there.

SUZY: (*Comes clicking down the stairs, carrying four small suitcases, setting them down. She is dressed in a skin-tight, very short pink suit.*) That's just the first load. Don't anybody get up. I got it arranged so I can do it all myself.

BILL: That's a pretty snappy outfit, Suzy.

SUZY: (*Going.*) Don't you just love it?
(*Gone.*)

APRIL: I kinda liked that pink jobby she had on last night. Would you look at that luggage? That girl has got to be the cheapest whore in town.

GIRL: I got it! I got one. See? (*Pokes* BILL.) I'll bet I haven't been here five minutes. Oxenham could have told him that; he didn't ask any leading questions.

BILL: What have you got?

GIRL: I know when he left. I got them renting his room out.
(*To other files.*)
Now what? I don't know what half of this stuff is. Letters. Terrific—

BILL: Come on.

GIRL: What if he wrote to change his address or send things? Or any of a thousand reasons. That's where you'd find a return address—

BILL: (*Overlap*) Put those rent books back in there—

GIRL: —When I'm finished. Why don't you let me cover the board and you go out and get us a hamburger before they close.

BILL: April ordered a pizza.

APRIL: Yeah, ought to be here any minute.

GIRL: Thank God; you're a sister of mercy. What's this? Wrong year. See, I know when he left. I only have to look at the one month or a little after. What's in the broom closet; there's dozens of boxes in there; they're probably years old, aren't they?

BILL: I haven't been in there.

JAMIE: Excuse me . . .

GIRL: (*Looks up—slows down some.*) Me? What, Jamie . . . ?

JAMIE: I don't know your name . . .

GIRL: I know—I'm working on it. What's wrong, honey?

JAMIE: Did you really go there? (*Pause.*) We heard that the Mormons was good farmers . . .

GIRL: I imagine they are. They've irrigated all the— Jamie, there aren't any Mormons *near* where your land is; there's nothing near there. I mean, I didn't get out, but it's just white sand—it's salt and soda, it looks like. Cactus can't even grow there.

JAMIE: If we brought water, we could . . .

GIRL: Jamie, you irrigate that land, you'd have twenty acres of Bromo-Seltzer.

SUZY: (*With two more pieces of unmatched luggage and a box tied with an extension cord.*) Listen, I'll be right back down. I got a surprise.

BILL: What's happening? Are you checking out?

SUZY: (*Dumps it.*) Yes, love; do up my bill. Take it out of—here— take it out of that. Don't anybody leave the lobby; you gotta promise me. (*She is gone.*)

APRIL: You gotta give it to her; the girl really knows what looks good on her.

GIRL: God, this is going to be depressing.

APRIL: What's that?

GIRL: No, I won't read them. God, they're depressing. All filed away. Nobody will ever answer them.

BILL: Just look at the envelope; you don't have to read them.

GIRL: I know, but I can't help it. Half of this is from the Welfare Department—from everywhere. I sat down over in the park and this perfectly normal-looking woman sat down. Well dressed, sixty years old—and she started talking to me . . . Jesus. It really gets me that a normal person never opens her mouth. It's only the crazies that'll talk to you.

APRIL: What's her story?

GIRL: Oh . . . she feeds dogs. Stray dogs. She goes around to all the butcher shops and for three hours every day she feeds the poor stray dogs—I mean, it's probably a good thing to do; but you got to be crazy even to do anything good. She says isn't it wonderful to be able to have something like that. Says she considers herself lucky because there's so many dogs in Baltimore.

APRIL: I consider myself *un*lucky because there's so many dogs in Baltimore.

GIRL: I think she was trying to convert me.

BILL: Come on, you're getting filthy there. Look at that.

APRIL: I always say if a lady—

GIRL: (*As* PAUL *enters*) Where have you been? Where'd you go?

PAUL: I went to eat.

GIRL: Did you bring anything back, I'm starving. April, where's that pizza? Never mind— Look; come here and look; my God, I'm not going to do this by myself.

PAUL: (*To the desk.*) What is it?

GIRL: Just follow this. Room two-oh-three—that's your granddad's receipt. That's for December 14—that's probably the one Oxenham showed you—they go back forever—but—look at this. December 21 I didn't find anything—nothing for his room at all. Then. December 28. J. Smith. Room two-oh-three. So he left between the fourteenth and the twenty-first of December. Probably on the twenty-first, when his week was up.

PAUL: Doesn't really matter . . .

GIRL: It's a fact. A first fact. If we're going to call like the Salvation Army or flophouses or hospitals, we've got a specific date. You can't expect them to look through six months of records. Also, I have a cop friend on the pussy posse, but I don't think I should go to them first thing—on account of your experience. We don't want them getting curious.

PAUL: That doesn't tell you anything.

GIRL: It certainly does! You came here knowing nothing, you've got to narrow it down.
(*The sound of a train.*)
Listen! Son of a bitch. What time is it?

BILL: (*Glances at clock.*) Twelve—[whatever]

GIRL: An hour and a half late. Jesus. And that's good. And they're conscientious. The engineers—it's not their fault; it's everyone else doesn't give a— Still, it's better than yesterday, they sailed through at five-thirty; they might as well just cancel the whole run; tell people to take the planes. I really have no use for airplanes; I'd be just as happy if every one fell into the sea like what's his name.

PAUL: Icarus.

GIRL: No, it was Gary Cooper or Cary Grant; I get them all mixed up. The Continental came through this afternoon on time—I sent the front office a telegram of congratulations—I honestly did.

Anyway, besides this, phone calls: they keep a record of every out-going call; we could find people in town he called. He must have known someone. Nobody's so shy they don't know someone. I don't care what kind of hat he wore.

SUZY: (*Flushed, coming down the stairs with two bottles of champagne and a shopping bag.*) All right, here it is. This is it; it's cold too; I've had it in the fridge all afternoon. Bill, open this up, we're having a toast. I called the cab already, kids, so we just got a minute, but that ain't cheating us out of a little party.

APRIL: Open it, Bill.

JAMIE: Are you going too?

SUZY: I sure am, honey. I don't need to have a place falling down around me before I take action. I got paper cups and everything. Mr. Morse, you're going to have a drink, honey, aren't you? It's nice and cold.

APRIL: He'll love it.

BILL: It's morning for me; I'm not on your schedule.

SUZY: That's the best time in the world to drink it; champagne doesn't have a time to drink it. Come on. I just wish we had some nuts. I didn't have time to think of everything.

JAMIE: I got some. In my bag.

SUZY: That's all right, honey, they're yours, we don't—
(*She is pouring.*)

JAMIE: No, I got lots of them. (*He takes two large jars from his bag.*)

SUZY: Don't anybody drink till we have a toast.

APRIL: Where the hell did you get those?

JAMIE: We always have them; we got a whole case of them.

APRIL: Jesus Christ, they're soy beans.

JAMIE: They're great for you. And they're good.

GIRL: I want something, if I'm going to be drinking champagne;
I've not had a bite.

SUZY: Hold your cup, honey. This is the real stuff.
(*Next is* PAUL.)
Take a cup.

PAUL: No, thanks, I'm not—
(*To* BILL)
I got a bag in—

SUZY: (*Overlapping*) Yes, come on; we may be a flophouse, but we
know class: see, I remember. Only nobody else, 'cause there ain't
that much; if anybody comes in, we're just drinking ginger ale.

BILL: (*Raising his glass.*) Uh . . . uh . . . To Suzy!

SUZY: (*Immensely pleased.*) No! Not to me! Come on, to this place!
To . . .

APRIL: To us!

ALL: To us!
(*They drink the toast and make appropriately enthusiastic re-
sponses.*)
This is the real stuff.

APRIL: These things are good.

GIRL: They are, they're great.

SUZY: You can't eat soy beans with champagne! Well, that's sweet,
honey—isn't he cute—where's the dy—his sister?

APRIL: She went for "gas." At six o'clock. This afternoon. She'll be right back.

SUZY: Oh. (*Beat.*) Hey, these are real good. What'd you say they was?

JAMIE: Barbecue-flavor soy beans. With sea salt and tomato powder.

APRIL: I think it's the sea salt that does it.

SUZY: O.K. One more round. There's plenty more. While it lasts. (*Pouring around.*) This is California champagne. This isn't that New York State stuff. One of my johns told me the difference. New York wines are made with a whole different kind of grape. It's all in the grape.

GIRL: I didn't know champagne was made out of grapes. I thought—

APRIL: What'd you think it was made out of, soy beans?

SUZY: (*Overlapping a bit*) Sure it is; California grapes are the same grapes they use in the French champagne. The Frenchies brought them over and planted them in California. In New York they got the wrong grape!

APRIL: Cheers, everybody.

SUZY: (*Overlapping*) I love champagne because you got to share it with people; sittin' around drinking champagne all by yourself without an event would be like jerkin' off.

APRIL: Well, we got a first-class event here.

GIRL: I'll tell you one thing I'm not going to do; I'm not going to move from here.

APRIL: I'm with you. We'll throw ourselves in front of the wrecking ball.

GIRL: Besides, I have a friend who knows law and I hate to blow it on the one month's notice, but it's three months'. And then we don't have to move.

PAUL: (*To* BILL) They all got friends into something.

GIRL: Baltimore used to be one of the most beautiful cities in America.

APRIL: Every city in America used to be one of the most beautiful cities in America.

GIRL: And this used to be a beautiful place. They got no business tearing it down. April and me and Mr. Morse and Millie. And Jamie.

SUZY: That's a delegation with balls.

GIRL: Where's Millie?

BILL: Millie went to bed. Said she was gonna try to sleep.

SUZY: She ought to be having some of this.

BILL: They might not get it torn down. They got a committee now to try to save it.

SUZY: Yeah, they also got antique people calling every ten minutes making bids on the door knobs. My money's on the vultures every time.

APRIL: This is fantastic stuff, Suzy. You're a dedicated woman.

GIRL: Who would we go to to make a protest?

SUZY: Only . . . (*With pride.*) . . . I got to tell you. I'm not moving into another hotel. I got an apartment. On the twelfth floor. It's got five rooms. There's a doorman; there's only one other girl sharing it with me.

APRIL: Wait; this is very familiar—

SUZY: —She's a sweetheart. She's read everything ever printed. Even newspapers.

APRIL: A wife-in-law.

SUZY: —Well, there's nothing in the arrangement that calls for that tone of voice. And I can have a pet if I want one. And I do. I've longed for a pet. I love animals.

APRIL: People who keep animals in the house are sick. Pets and pimps.

SUZY: I would be very good to an animal.

APRIL: I don't care, it's still sick.

SUZY: I have great love for animals.

GIRL: What kind of an animal?

SUZY: All kinds. All animals. Puppies and kittens and little calves and ponies, and all of them.

APRIL: And a cuddly little woolly black pimp.

SUZY: All non-human animals. And fish. I don't like tropical fish.

APRIL: My husband used to keep fish.

GIRL: I didn't know you were married.

APRIL: I didn't either.
  (*To* SUZY)
  Who is it?

BILL: What's a wife-in-law?

GIRL: (*Overlapping*) Come on, Bill, how long have you worked here?

APRIL: (*Overlapping*) Ask Suzy about wife-in-law arrangements. She's the authority—

SUZY: (*Overlapping*) It's nothing like that. She *asked me*; I'll be the wife, honey. I'm nobody's second fiddle. You don't have to worry about me. She's just there to keep house as far as we're concerned —she'll be the in-law. She can't turn two hundred a day.

APRIL: Who is he? Are you going back with Eddie?

SUZY: I certainly am not. Who do you think I am? I may have a soft spot in my heart but I don't want—

APRIL: (*Overlapping*) You got a soft spot in your head.

SUZY: —This man is not like that. Eddie was a pimp; this man is a man.

APRIL: Who's the boy friend this time?

SUZY: Not this time. This is my first *real friend*. Eddie was a pimp.

APRIL: You're telling me; a pimp fink.

SUZY: This man is a man!

APRIL: Yeah, what does he do?

SUZY: He does nothing! And he does it *gorgeously!*

BILL: How'd you get talked into another arrangement like that?

APRIL: They don't talk, they croon.

SUZY: Tell me you don't need someone; maybe you don't, but I do; I need love!

APRIL: All you have to say to a hooker is cottage small by the water-fall and they fold up.

SUZY: You know I don't appreciate that word.

APRIL: Whadda you call it?

SUZY: I am not a that-word; I am a friendly person and it gets me in trouble.

APRIL: —You're a professional trampoline.

SUZY: That is why I'm leaving! Derision! Derision! Because I'm at-tacked with derision every time I try to do something wonderful. Driven into the arms of a common pimp!
(APRIL *hoots.*)

GIRL: We're just thinking about you, Suzy.

APRIL: (*Overlapping*) You've been down this road.

BILL: (*Overlapping*) How's this one any better than Eddie?

SUZY: Just don't worry about it. Billy's never beat up one of his wives . . . ever!

APRIL: Jesus God, she's going with Billy Goldhole.

SUZY: That is not his name. And to call him by that name is to show your ignorance. And if you say he's beat up on anybody, I don't believe it.

CAB DRIVER:	APRIL:
(*Entering.*)	Go on, I don't want to have
Somebody here order a taxi?	anything to do with you.

SUZY: Yes. Here! This here. (*She starts to pick up some of the lug-gage.*)

CAB DRIVER: I'm not a moving van, lady. What is this?

SUZY: This stuff here; you can't take it quick enough.

CAB DRIVER:	SUZY:
I'm double-parked out there. I can't take all that. Where you going to? With this crap?	Don't sweat it, mister. I'm taking my share. I'll pay double the meter.

SUZY: I'm leaving this hole. Hole. Hole. Move it.

CAB DRIVER: I said I'm double-parked out there, lady. I'm not in the—

SUZY: You're double-parked. Tell me about it. The whole fuckin' country is double-parked. I hope they tear down the place with all (*Picking up almost all the luggage as she rants.*) you in it. Goody-two-shoes included. I'm just sorry I gave you a little party. You don't know enough to appreciate it.

CAB DRIVER: Come on, lady, shake it.

SUZY: Shove it.
  (*They exit.*)

GIRL: She's got to be the worst judge of character in Baltimore.

APRIL: She's gotta be the worst character in Baltimore.

BILL: She drew the cops here four times in one night once.

APRIL: Whadda you say, Mr. Morse? Unstable woman, huh?

MR. MORSE: (*Who has not been following; still holds his untasted cup.*) Very good. Thank you.

GIRL: I wonder if the apartment has eleven-foot ceilings.

APRIL: It's got an eleven-inch licorice lollipop is what it's got.

SUZY: (*Bursting back into the lobby, bawling. Super-emotional, hugs them in turn while speaking and is gone with the last word.*) I'm sorry. I know you love me. I can't leave like that. Mr. Morse. We been like a family, haven't we? My family. Baby. I'm not that horrible. I can't be mad. Bill. I'll always remember this.
(*Gone.*)
(*A few seconds of stupefied, gawking silence.*)

PAUL: I got a bag back there.

BILL: Yeah. (*Handing it to him.*)

GIRL: Hey. Paul. You're supposed to be doing this with me. You're supposed to be helping.

PAUL: No, that's O.K. You don't have to do that.

GIRL: Did you find him? While you were out?

PAUL: (*Overlapping*) Of course I didn't find him; he's gone. That doesn't tell you anything.

GIRL: Well, we knew he was gone; the thing we're trying to do is find him.

PAUL: He could be anywhere.

GIRL: He could be *some*where.

PAUL: It's not your problem. It was a bad idea. Thanks.

GIRL: You got room for him, I thought. Hey. *Talk*, for God's sake. You're worse than a dummy, at least they use sign language. What are you doing?

PAUL: I'm trying to go, do you mind?

GIRL: How can you be so interested in something—

PAUL: —Would you get off my back? What's your problem? I didn't ask for you to help me. I didn't ask you.

APRIL: She volunteered. You got some gripe, write to her; she collects stamps.

GIRL: Oh, I do not.

PAUL: Look, you're probably being very nice; but thanks, anyway, O.K.? Granddad isn't here. They don't know where he is. Nobody here knows where he is. It's all the same.

GIRL: Not yet; but I can find him. Nobody vanishes.

PAUL: It's just as well, probably. I got things to do.

GIRL: —It just isn't as easy as you thought. You been bitching Oxenham for being no help. Let us help.

PAUL: *I* wanted to find him. He'd move out of a place like this the first chance he got; he wasn't a derelict. You don't know him. (MILLIE *begins to come down the stairs.*)

GIRL: I said I wanted to know him.

APRIL: Hey, Millie.

MILLIE: (*Vaguely*) Oh . . . hello, then . . .

PAUL: (*Mumbled*) Well, I'm sorry . . .

BILL: Thought you were sleeping.
(*She raises a hand as if to say, That isn't important.*)

GIRL: Millie, tell him not to give up. Tell him we can find him or he's gonna just give up.

MILLIE: Oh, that's too bad.

APRIL: Ought to be easy enough to find. Ten-foot white-haired giant. Chops down cherry trees; doesn't lie about it.

GIRL: Come on, April; he was a trainman.

PAUL: Thanks, anyway, I'm sorry I got you involved. I'm not calling the Salvation— (*Begins to go.*)

GIRL: I *like* getting involved. Paul? You know what armor is? I had a scientologist tell me this. You're tied in knots all through your— Are you going to keep on looking for him?
(*Silence—*PAUL *glares at her.*)

APRIL: Knock once for yes and—

PAUL: It's not your business one way or the other, is it?
(*To them quietly*)
Thanks very much, anyway. Thanks for your interest.

GIRL: (*Over "thanks very"*) You don't care about him. What if he's in—
(*He goes.*)
—some home for the— You! Boy, you're a—

APRIL: Creep.

GIRL: Creep. Well, I don't know if he doesn't really care or if we scared him off.

BILL: You can't help people who don't want it.

GIRL: I think he probably has trouble making friends.

APRIL: I think he has trouble making water.
(*Pause. To* MILLIE)
Have a drink of Suzy's champagne. Help you sleep.

MILLIE: (*Taking a cup.*) Oh, I doubt that.

GIRL: Well, damn piss hell poot.

BILL: Just watch your language back here, O.K.?

APRIL: (*Pouring.*) Come on . . .

GIRL: (*Dialing the phone.*) No, it makes me . . .

APRIL: Bill?

BILL: Don't get me drunk here, now.

APRIL: Jamie? Come on. We won't tell her.
(JAMIE *comes to get the drink and goes back to the lounge.*)

GIRL: (*On the phone.*) Penthouse B. Is he in the dining room?
Well, tell him Billy Jean— No, don't bother; I couldn't bear it.
No message. (*Hangs up.*) I could just kill Paul Granger. That's
why nothing gets done; why everything falls down. Nobody's got
the conviction to act on their passions.

APRIL: Go kill him then.

GIRL: I mean, it's his idea to find him. I don't think it matters what
someone believes in. I just think it's really chicken not to believe
in anything!

BILL: (*Pouring another.*) Come on, join us.

GIRL: No, I'm going to take a bath while there's hot water. I'm just
filthy.

BILL: Come on, drink to Suzy.

GIRL: (*Taking the cup—to* MILLIE) Suzy left us.

MILLIE: Again?

APRIL: Exactly. God help her.

GIRL: (*Drinks.*) I hate that. You like that, Jamie?

JAMIE: It's O.K.

MILLIE: Well. I've got no business down here.

APRIL: Drinking champagne, huh?

GIRL: I'm going up too.
(*She starts upstairs;* BILL *starts to pick up the books. Preoccupied.*)
Don't you put those away; I'm not finished with those.
(BILL *looks off after her, aching.*)

APRIL: (*Snaps her fingers lightly at him. One. Two. Three. Four.*)
Hey. Hey.

BILL: Come on, April; knock it off. (*He sits at the switchboard.*)

APRIL: Bill, baby, you know what your trouble is? You've got Paul Grangeritis. You've not got the conviction of your passions.

JAMIE: April? What time is it?

APRIL: It's a quarter after—(*Looks at* BILL.)

BILL: (*A glance at the clock.*) Twelve-thirty. Nearly.

APRIL: She probably got stopped on account of the license.

BILL: (*Under his breath*) Sure she did.
(*To* MILLIE, *who is retiring*)
Millie, you want a wake-up call?

MILLIE: (*Almost laughing*) Oh—no point in—unless you just feel like talking. Good night, everyone.

MR. MORSE: Paul Granger is an old fool!

MILLIE: Did you know him, Mr. Morse? Oh, God . . . I felt one of us should . . . remember him.

MR. MORSE: He's an old fool.

APRIL: (*Turning on the radio.*) You tell 'em, baby.

BILL: Try to sleep this time.

MILLIE: (*Going off.*) Well, if it happens . . .

APRIL: (*To* JAMIE *as the song comes on the radio*) Come on, Jamie. Off your butt. Come on; dance with me. This may be your shining hour.

JAMIE: No, come on.

BILL: She's just teasing you.

APRIL: Hell I am.

JAMIE: I don't feel like it.

APRIL: You eaten anything today?
  (*He nods.*)
  What? Some health-nut crap?

JAMIE: Bacon and eggs and a hamburger.

APRIL: What kind of health food is that?

JAMIE: There's no health-food place close enough.

APRIL: Come on; you're so shy, if someone doesn't put a light under your tail, you're not going to have passions to need convictions for.
  (JAMIE *walks uncertainly to* APRIL.)
  (*A pizza* DELIVERY BOY *enters.*)

DELIVERY BOY: Somebody order a pizza here?

BILL: April?

APRIL: (*Without looking at him; taking the check.*) Take it up to the second-floor john.

BILL: Second floor, turn right. The door at the end of the hall. (DE-LIVERY BOY *goes.*)

JAMIE: I don't know how.

APRIL: Nobody knows how. What does it matter; the important thing is to *move*. Come on; all your blood's in your tail.

BILL: It's twelve-thirty; he's been up all day; he doesn't want to dance.

APRIL: Sure hc does.

JAMIE: Tell me how.

APRIL: Come on, they're gonna tear up the dance floor in a minute; the bulldozers are barking at the door. Turn it up, Bill, or I'll break your arm.
(*He turns it up a little.*)
Turn it up!
(*More.*)
(APRIL *and* JAMIE *latch arms, go one way, then back. She joins in singing with the radio, and as the lights fade and they turn back, circling the other way, he joins in as well.* BILL *stares off, then smiles at them.* MR. MORSE *sips the drink and watches on.*)

BAD HABITS
Terrence McNally

BAD HABITS

While the plays of Terrence McNally prove that Off-Broadway is not always solemn, they also prove that even the most hilarious comedies can also be deadly serious.

In the words of Arthur H. Ballet, currently the director of the theatre program of the National Endowment for the Arts, "McNally's niche in the pantheon of dramatists is rightly as a comic writer—never a buffoon grinding out cheap little jokes, but rather a most perceptive participant . . . His perception has become a simile which he uses again and again to probe and prod both sensitivities and sensibilities, to stab at shibboleths, to expose fears and pretenses."

Dunelawn, the second act of *Bad Habits*, originally opened Off-Off-Broadway; when McNally added *Ravenswood*, the first act, the complete play opened Off-Broadway at the Astor Place Theatre in February 1974. The reviews and audience response were so enthusiastic that the play moved to Broadway's Booth Theatre three months later.

Reviewing *Bad Habits* in the New York *Times*, Clive Barnes wrote: "Mr. McNally is an unusual American comic playwright . . . The lines that get the biggest laughs are never jokes as such, but simply summing up comments on situations."

Calling McNally "a major force and figure in American theatre," Arthur H. Ballet wrote that "as with any significant writer, McNally's plays are deceptive: they point in one direction but go in quite another. They are not what they seem to be, and in that mystery lies the potential of greatness. In that split between the laughing surface and the puzzling center rests theatrical excitement."

"*Bad Habits* moves with a velocity only slightly tardier than light," wrote Stefan Kanfer in *Time* magazine. "The wit and venom are rarely interrupted by anything but laughter."

The "bad habits" of the title refer to the characters' love of life, a gusto and affirmation that is threatened by the strait-laced advocates of perfectibility. Not so much comedies of manners as comedies of neuroses, the play shows that the quirks and idiosyncracies of the human personality, our "bad habits," are not aspects of our characters that must be eliminated but are the very qualities that make us human.

In addition to honoring McNally for his script, the Obie committee awarded a citation to Robert Drivas for his direction. *Bad Habits* also won the Dramatists Guild award for 1974, and in 1975 McNally was selected for a National Institute of Arts and Letters award. McNally is also the author of three Broadway triumphs—*And Things That Go Bump in the Night*, the *Noon* section of *Morning, Noon, and Night*, and *The Ritz*, which was later made into a movie.

BAD HABITS opened on February 4, 1974, at the Astor Place Theatre, and on May 5, 1974, at the Booth Theatre in New York City. The cast, in order of appearance, was as follows:

For RAVENSWOOD:

OTTO	*Henry Sutton*
APRIL PITT	*Cynthia Harris*
ROY PITT	*F. Murray Abraham*
JASON PEPPER, M.D.	*Paul Benedict*
DOLLY SCUPP	*Doris Roberts*
HIRAM SPANE	*Emory Bass*
FRANCIS TEAR	*J. Frank Lucas*
HARRY SCUPP	*Michael Lombard*

For DUNELAWN:

RUTH BENSON, R.N.	*Cynthia Harris*
BECKY HEDGES, R.N.	*Doris Roberts*
BRUNO	*Henry Sutton*
MR. PONCE	*Emory Bass*
DR. TOYNBEE	*J. Frank Lucas*
MR. BLUM	*F. Murray Abraham*
MR. YAMADORO	*Michael Lombard*
HUGH GUMBS	*Paul Benedict*

The play was produced by Adela Holzer and directed by Robert Drivas. Scenery and costumes were designed by Michael H. Yeargan and Lawrence King; lighting by Ken Billington.

RAVENSWOOD

Bright sunlight. Lush green foliage forms a wall Upstage. Heaven on earth. Stage Left is a table with Dom Perignon champagne, coffee service, orange juice, etc. Three chairs are at the table. A small rolling cart Upstage Left holds towels and suntan cream. Stage Right are two chairs and a small table, shaded by a beach umbrella. We hear lively baroque music. When the house lights are out, and before the stage lights come up, the music changes. Now it is "Wein, Du Stadt Meiner Traume" ("Vienna, City of My Dreams"). When the lights come up we see that the music is coming from the cassette recorder that Otto carries from a shoulder strap.

He enters down the aisle through the audience carrying a bouquet of flowers. As he carefully arranges them on the Stage Right table, we hear the offstage voices of April and Roy Pitt.

APRIL: (*offstage*) We're here!

ROY: (*offstage*) Hey, where is everybody? Does somebody wanna give us a hand with these things? (OTTO *exits behind the foliage wall, and returns carrying three large expensive pieces of luggage.* APRIL PITT, *carrying a makeup kit, and* ROY PITT, *with a tennis bag, follow him in.*)

APRIL: So this is Ravenswood! Nice. Very nice.

ROY: What do you mean nice? It's terrific! Look at that clay court, honey. Real clay. Can you stand it? (OTTO *starts off down the aisle with the luggage.*)

APRIL: That's Vuitton, Buddy.

OTTO: Ja, Fraulein.

APRIL: Just thought I'd mention it.

OTTO: Ja, Fraulein. (*He is gone.*)

APRIL: Jesus, Roy, it's the Gestapo. I just hope this Pepper fellow's all he's cracked up to be.

ROY: I told you: he's just gonna have us talk to each other.

APRIL: We talk to each other all the time. What's he gonna do?

ROY: Listen.

APRIL: Just listen? A hundred and forty-five clams a day and he just listens? I knew I should have checked this guy out first.

ROY: Look what he did for Sandy and Reg.

APRIL: Sandy and Reg are lesbians and they're not in show business. They run a pet shop in Montauk for Christ's sake!

ROY: But they're happy.

APRIL: Sure, they're in dyke heaven, those two. I'm talking about us, Roy.

ROY: So am I, April. You told the answering service where I'd be? I don't want to miss that call from the Coast. (*He starts off down the aisle. The lively baroque music is heard again very softly off right.*)

APRIL: I'm beginning not to like the smell of this whole setup. When's our first session? This Pepper character doesn't deliver, we're gonna blow this nickel joint and head straight for L.A. Right, Roy? (*But* ROY *is following* OTTO *and the luggage.*) I said easy with the Vuitton, schmuck! (*She follows them off. The stage is empty a beat. The music has gotten louder.* JASON PEPPER, M.D., *enters with* DOLLY SCUPP. *He is in an electric wheelchair with a blanket on his lap. The music is coming from a cassette recorder built into the chair. Also, the chair has an ashtray, a small shelf on the side [for holding a book later], a holder for a martini glass, and a ship's bell for calling* OTTO. DOLLY SCUPP *is carrying a shoulder-strap-type handbag, and a book. Her right foot is in an orthopedic foot covering.* DR. PEPPER *is drinking a martini and smoking a cigarette. He and* DOLLY *listen to the end of the music, then he turns off the cassette.*)

DR. PEPPER: Over there's our lake. A pond you might call it, but I like to think of it as a lake. After all, it's the only body of water for miles and miles. In the winter it's frozen over and quite covered with snow. And now look at it. Ah, the seasons, the seasons! I do love the seasons. What would we do without them? (*Thunder.* DR. PEPPER *puts both hands to his head and gingerly fingers his skull.*) Don't tell me that's not the music of the spheres. It's a day like this that makes you think the world is coming to an end. Only the real joke is, it's not going to rain. Oh don't get me wrong, I don't enjoy playing God or the weatherman, but I don't have this porous platinum plate in my head for nothing, either.

DOLLY: You look different on your book jacket.

DR. PEPPER: I know. Taller. May I? (DOLLY *gives him the book she has been carrying under her arm.*) MARRIAGE FOR THE FUN OF IT! Oh God, are people still reading this old thing?

DOLLY: Everybody who's still married.

DR. PEPPER: I thought I knew something in those days.

DOLLY: You're being modest.

DR. PEPPER: It's my only virtue.

DOLLY: That's one more than me.

DR. PEPPER: Harry didn't tell me you were coming.

DOLLY: He didn't know. I woke up this morning and said to myself, "I'm driving up to Ravenswood today." Don't ask me why. I just had this sudden urge to see you.

DR. PEPPER: It's a delightful surprise.

DOLLY: I hope so.

DR. PEPPER: Your absence has made Harry's rehabilitation somewhat more difficult, you understand. I prefer to treat couples who are having difficulties *as* couples.

DOLLY: There's nothing wrong with me, if that's what you're driving at.

DR. PEPPER: Should I be?

DOLLY: Is my husband getting any better, Dr. Pepper?

DR. PEPPER: It's Jason, Mrs. Scupp. Please, I insist on it. Until we're over that little hurdle we're nowhere. And you're right, it's high time we had a little chat. Coffee?

DOLLY: Thank you. (*She crosses to the table and helps herself.*)

DR. PEPPER: Cigarette?

DOLLY: No, thanks.

DR. PEPPER: It's a special tobacco, imported from Panama, that's been fertilized with hen feces. I don't think you'll find them at your A&P in Scarsdale.

DOLLY: I wouldn't think so.

DR. PEPPER: They have an extraordinarily . . . *pungent* taste.

DOLLY: I don't smoke.

DR. PEPPER: You're joking.

DOLLY: I gave them up years ago.

DR. PEPPER: During the big scare, huh? So many of you poor bastards did. Will it bother you if I . . . ? (*He is lighting his cigarette.*)

DOLLY: Not at all. My doctor insisted.

DR. PEPPER: And who might that be?

DOLLY: Dr. Fernald.

DR. PEPPER: Helmut Fernald up at Grassyview? I might've known
he'd jump on the bandwagon.

DOLLY: No, George Fernald in White Plains, the County Medical
Center.

DR. PEPPER: He wouldn't drive a white Buick station wagon, usually
there's a couple of dalmatians yapping around in the back, and be
married to one of the McIntyre sisters, would he?

DOLLY: I don't think so. Our Dr. Fernald's married to a Korean girl
and I'm pretty sure they have a dachshund. I don't know what he
drives. He's just our family doctor.

DR. PEPPER: Well that explains it. The curse of modern medicine,
that lot.

DOLLY: Dr. Fernald?

DR. PEPPER: Your friendly, neighborhood, family G.P. Now don't
get me started on *that*, Mrs. Scupp.

DOLLY: I thought the majority of doctors had stopped smoking, too.

DR. PEPPER: (*Exhaling.*) And doesn't that just sound like something the majority of doctors would do? Fortunately, there remain a few of us who refuse to be stampeded along with the common herd. I'm referring to men like Peabody Fowler of the Heltzel Foundation and Otis Strunk of the Merton Institute, of course. (DOLLY *shakes her head.*) Rand Baskerville out at Las Palmetas? Claude Kittredge up at Nag's Head?

DOLLY: I'm sorry, but I'm not familiar with them.

DR. PEPPER: Who is? I can't discuss colors with a blind person, Mrs. Scupp.

DOLLY: But surely, Doctor, you're not suggesting that smoking is good for you?

DR. PEPPER: Of course not.

DOLLY: I didn't think so.

DR. PEPPER: What I *am* suggesting is that *not* smoking is conceivably worse.

DOLLY: I don't follow.

DR. PEPPER: Do you want to talk turkey or not, Mrs. Scupp?

DOLLY: Of course I do! And please, call me Dolly.

DR. PEPPER: Hello, Dolly.

DOLLY: Hello.

DR. PEPPER: Well, hello, Dolly.

DOLLY: It's my curse.

DR. PEPPER: You think Dr. Pepper is easy? Now let's start at the beginning and I'll try to keep it in layman's terms.

DOLLY: Thank you.

DR. PEPPER: Everything in life is bad for you. The air, the sun, the force of gravity, butter, eggs, this cigarette . . .

DOLLY: That drink.

DR. PEPPER: That coffee! Canned tuna fish.

DOLLY: No.

DR. PEPPER: It's true! It's loaded with dolphin meat. There's an article on canned tuna fish in this month's *Food Facts* that will stand your hair on end.

DOLLY: I love tuna fish.

DR. PEPPER: Don't we all?

DOLLY: I don't care what they put in it.

DR. PEPPER: Neither do I. Right now, this very moment, as I speak these words, you're ten seconds closer to death than when I started. Eleven seconds, twelve seconds, thirteen. Have I made my point? Now, how would an ice-cold, extra-dry, straight-up Gordon's gin martini grab you? (*He rings the service bell.*)

DOLLY: I'm afraid it wouldn't.

DR. PEPPER: Ah, vodka is the lovely lady from Scardale's poison. (*He rings again.*)

DOLLY: I'm on the wagon.

DR. PEPPER: You don't smoke, you don't drink . . .

DOLLY: And it's Larchmont. And I would like to talk about my husband. (OTTO *appears from the aisle.*)

OTTO: Ze newlyweds have arrived.

DR. PEPPER: Ze newlyweds Pitt?

OTTO: Ja, Herr Doktor. I put zem in ze little honeymoon cabin.

DR. PEPPER: Good, Otto, good. Tell them we'll have our first session after lunch. Show them the lake, the stables, the tennis courts. The grand tour, Otto.

OTTO: I could give Mrs. Pitt a rubdown, maybe?

DR. PEPPER: No, Otto.

OTTO: Whirlpool?

DR. PEPPER: Nothing, Otto. Just the tour.

OTTO: (*Seeing that* DR. PEPPER's *glass is empty.*) Ze usual?

DR. PEPPER: Last call, Mrs. Scupp.

DOLLY: I'll have a Tab, maybe.

OTTO: Nein Tab.

DOLLY: Fresca?

OTTO: Nein Fresca.

DOLLY: Anything dietetic.

OTTO: Nichts dietetic, nichts!

DOLLY: Water, then.

OTTO: Wasser?

DR. PEPPER: Wasser fur das frau!

OTTO: Jawohl, Herr Doktor.

DR. PEPPER: (OTTO *has turned to go.*) Und Otto! Dry-lich! Dry-lich! Dry-lich fur ze martini! (OTTO *exits.*) It's an extraordinary race. Is Scupp German?

DOLLY: We don't know what it is.

DR. PEPPER: Then I can say it: I can't stand them. It was a German who incapacitated me.

DOLLY: The war?

DR. PEPPER: My wife. She pushed me down a short but lethal flight of stairs backstage at the Academy of Music in Philadelphia.

DOLLY: How horrible!

DR. PEPPER: It was the single most electrifying experience of my life.

DOLLY: But why would anyone do such a thing?

DR. PEPPER: In my wife's case it was self-defense.

DOLLY: You mean you tried to kill her?

DR. PEPPER: Symbolically. It's funny how no one ever asks why it was a flight of stairs backstage at the Academy of Music; you must admit, it's not your usual place for an attempted homicide. My wife was a lieder singer. She'd just given an all-Hugo Wolf recital. She asked me how I thought it went and I said, "Maybe the only thing in the world more boring than an all-Hugo Wolf recital is your singing of an all-Hugo Wolf recital." The remark just kind of popped out of me. And when it popped, she pushed and down

I went. Four short steps and here I am. Don't look so tragic, Mrs. Scupp. No Anita Wertmuller and her all-Hugo Wolf recital and no Ravenswood. We divorced, of course, and she remarried some California grape-grower. Otto used to accompany her. Now Otto accompanies me. Having been unhappy in marriage, hopefully I can help others to solve their marital difficulties. Look for the silver lining, yes?

DOLLY: You never remarried?

DR. PEPPER: What on earth for? The third and fourth toes of your left foot, wasn't it?

DOLLY: The second and third of the right.

DR. PEPPER: Accidents will happen.

DOLLY: Not with a remote-control power lawnmower, Doctor.

DR. PEPPER: Those things are devils.

DOLLY: Harry was sitting on the porch controlling it. I was sunbathing.

DR. PEPPER: He didn't go into the details.

DOLLY: Of course he didn't. That's why he's here.

DR. PEPPER: He said there'd been an accident and that was why you hadn't come here with him.

DOLLY: I wouldn't have come with him even if it hadn't happened. I'm sorry, but I can't afford to take any more chances with a man like that.

DR. PEPPER: That's what marriage is, Mrs. Scupp.

DOLLY: Not with a husband who tried to kill you, it isn't! Two toes, doctor.

DR. PEPPER: Two legs, Dolly. (*Thunder.* DR. PEPPER *feels his head again.*)

DOLLY: Is my husband getting any better yet, doctor?

DR. PEPPER: I think Harry's about ready to leave Ravenswood. (HIRAM SPANE *enters. He is in a long bathrobe, beach sandals, and wearing sunglasses. He goes to the table and pours champagne and orange juice into the same glass.*)

DOLLY: I hope you're right.

DR. PEPPER: He'll be along shortly. You can see for yourself. Good morning, Hiram!

HIRAM: Morning? I was hoping it was late afternoon. I haven't been up this early since I saw Mother off on the Graf Zepelin.

DR. PEPPER: I'm sure you never saw anyone off on the Graf Zepelin, Hiram.

HIRAM: Well it was something that moved and I was there to see her off! Now I remember. Of course! It was the *Andrea Doria*.

DOLLY: Did she go down with it?

HIRAM: Cornelia Margaret Spane, my mother, never went down with or on anything. I don't believe we've been introduced. Bitch.

DR. PEPPER: This is Mrs. Scupp, Hiram.

HIRAM: I don't care who she is.

DR. PEPPER: Harry's wife.

HIRAM: Well why didn't you say so? How do you do, Mrs. Scupp? I'm sorry, you're not a bitch. And I'm only a bitch when I've got a head on me like this one. I thought *I* mixed a wicked vodka stinger! What did your husband do? Study alchemy?

DOLLY: Harry? Drinking? My Harry? Harry Scupp?

HIRAM: I understand the A.A. has a warrant out for his arrest.

DOLLY: I don't think we're talking about the same man.

HIRAM: The way I feel this morning we're probably not.

DR. PEPPER: Why don't you take that dip now, Hiram?

HIRAM: Good idea, Jason. With any luck, maybe I'll drown. You like to swim, Mrs. Scupp?

DOLLY: I love to, but . . . (*She indicates her injured foot.*)

HIRAM: Come on, I believe in the buddy system: you start to drown, I'll save you. I start to drown, forget it.

DOLLY: I didn't bring a suit.

HIRAM: That never stopped anyone around this place. What do you think I've got on under here?

DOLLY: I blush to think.

HIRAM: You blush to think? I've got to live with it! If that goddamn snapping turtle doesn't attack me again, doctor, you can tell Otto I'll be joining you here shortly for my Bullshot. (*He goes down the aisle.*)

DR. PEPPER: Hiram Spane of the Newport Spanes. They own everything. (FRANCIS TEAR *enters. He is wearing a bathing cap, a bathrobe and rubber bathing shoes. He pours himself a glass of orange juice.*)

DOLLY: (*Still staring down the aisle.*) Is he a patient here?

DR. PEPPER: Hiram's been a patient here since I founded Ravenswood.

DOLLY: What's his problem?

DR. PEPPER: You're looking at him.

DOLLY: (*Finally seeing* FRANCIS.) Oh my God!

DR. PEPPER: Francis Tear of the Baltimore Tears. They made their fortune in plumbing. Good morning, Francis! You just missed each other.

FRANCIS: We're not speaking today.

DR. PEPPER: You and I?

FRANCIS: Hiram and me. He said something very cutting to me last night. Hurt me to the quick, he did. I don't think I'm ready to forgive him yet.

DR. PEPPER: Fine, fine, there's no point in rushing it.

FRANCIS: (*To* DOLLY.) Do you think I look like an embryo, madam?

DOLLY: Not at all.

FRANCIS: Thank you.

DR. PEPPER: This is Mrs. Scupp, Francis.

FRANCIS: Hello.

DR. PEPPER: Harry Scupp's wife.

FRANCIS: Well I didn't think it was his mother. I'm Francis Tear of the Baltimore Tears. We made our fortune in plumbing!

DOLLY: Yes, I know.

FRANCIS: Somebody had to do it.

DOLLY: I suppose so.

FRANCIS: What are you in?

DOLLY: I'm just a housewife.

FRANCIS: So's Hiram! He's also in distress. Psychic distress, Doctor!

DR. PEPPER: Not now, Francis, please. I like your new bathing slippers.

FRANCIS: Do you? Hiram's mother had them sent. Hiram's mother has everything sent.

DOLLY: How nice for you.

FRANCIS: You never met Hiram's mother. You don't think I look silly in these, Jason?

DR. PEPPER: Not at all. There may be fairies at the bottom of somebody's garden but there are very sharp rocks at the bottom of my lake.

FRANCIS: Do you, Mrs. Scupp?

DOLLY: They go with the cap.

FRANCIS: That's what I was hoping. I think it's important to look your best at all times. You never know. It must be Jewish, Scupp.

DOLLY: I was telling Jason, we don't know what it is.

FRANCIS: It's Jewish. It was a pleasure, Mrs. Scupp. (*He turns to go.*)

DOLLY: Likewise, Mr. Tear.

FRANCIS: Call me Francis. Everyone else does. Except Hiram. You should hear some of the things he calls me. (*Exiting down the aisle.*) Oh, no, Hiram! I get the raft today! You had it yesterday! And this doesn't mean I'm speaking to you yet! (*He is gone.*)

DR. PEPPER: Eighteen years they've been together.

DOLLY: Are they . . . ?

DR. PEPPER: I don't think so, but if they are, I'd like to be a fly on that wall. No, I think they're just old, old friends.

DOLLY: I didn't know you treated male couples at Ravenswood.

DR. PEPPER: A male couple is better than no couple at all. Love is where you find it.

DOLLY: That's true.

DR. PEPPER: Don't be blind, it's all around you, everywhere. (OTTO *returns with the martini and glass of water.*)

DOLLY: Thank you.

DR. PEPPER: Danke, Otto.

OTTO: Ze Fraulein would like a rubdown, maybe?

DOLLY: I don't think so.

OTTO: (*Shrugging.*) Okay. (*He takes an* Opera News *off of the towel cart, opens it, sits and reads.*)

DR. PEPPER: Cheers! You were saying?

DOLLY: Doctor . . . (*She fidgets.*)

DR. PEPPER: Don't mind Otto. It would take a lot more than your lawnmower to get his nose out of that magazine.

DOLLY: Why did Harry try to kill me?

DR. PEPPER: Do you still want to talk turkey, Mrs. Scupp?

DOLLY: About Harry? Of course I do.

DR. PEPPER: About you.

DOLLY: What is that supposed to mean?

DR. PEPPER: Does Labor Day weekend, 1963, the parking lot outside Benny's Clam Box in Rockport, Maine, do anything for you?

DOLLY: I don't know. Should it?

DR. PEPPER: Think hard.

DOLLY: Benny's Clam Box.

DR. PEPPER: Harry was packing up the trunk of the car and you put the car into reverse.

DOLLY: Oh, that! How did you know?

DR. PEPPER: We have very complete files on our guests here, Mrs. Scupp. Ravenswood is a far cry from the Westchester County Medical Center and your quack G.P. with his Korean war bride and poodle!

DOLLY: Dachshund!

DR. PEPPER: Sorry!

DOLLY: Leave it to Harry to tell you about a silly accident like that.

DR. PEPPER: He was in traction for two months.

DOLLY: I didn't see him back there. What are you driving at, Doctor?

DR. PEPPER: Eight months later you tried to run him over with a golf cart at the Westchester Country Club.

DOLLY: It was an accident. My foot got stuck on the accelerator.

DR. PEPPER: Nobody drives a golf cart on the putting green.

DOLLY: I do! I did. I still do.

DR. PEPPER: That time he was in traction for three months.

DOLLY: You're making mountains out of mole hills, Doctor. My foot got stuck. I had new golf shoes. What's your point?

DR. PEPPER: A year later he asked you if there was water in the swimming pool before diving in.

DOLLY: I thought he'd asked me should he wash our Puli.

DR. PEPPER: Your Puli didn't end up in White Plains Hospital with a broken leg. Let's talk about the incident at the archery tournament.

DOLLY: Let's not.

DR. PEPPER: It's quite a story.

DOLLY: *His* version.

DR. PEPPER: I'd love to hear yours.

DOLLY: I didn't tell him to change the target when he did.

DR. PEPPER: How about his forced high dive in Acapulco?

DOLLY: He *fell*.

DR. PEPPER: Nearly six hundred feet.

DOLLY: I didn't push him.

DR. PEPPER: And what about your safari to East Africa last winter?

DOLLY: He didn't tell you about that, too?

DR. PEPPER: Harry's just lucky he's not the one who's stuffed and mounted over your fireplace, Mrs. Scupp.

DOLLY: I was delirious. A touch of malaria, I remember. I mistook him for something else.

DR. PEPPER: An albino orangutan? No, you didn't.

DOLLY: I don't want to hear these things!

DR. PEPPER: You said you wanted to talk turkey, Mrs. Scupp. All right, here's the real turkey: you and your husband have been trying to kill one another since Labor Day weekend, 1963. Why? (A pause.)

DOLLY: Has he been neat, Doctor?

DR. PEPPER: Neat?

DOLLY: Neat.

DR. PEPPER: Oh, neat! A little over-fastidious when he got here, perhaps . . .

DOLLY: I'm talking about coasters, Doctor.

DR. PEPPER: Coasters?

DOLLY: Those things you put under glasses so they don't leave a ring.

DR. PEPPER: I can't stand them.

DOLLY: Neither can I.

DR. PEPPER: Always sticking to the bottom of your glass and then dropping off.

DOLLY: I loathe coasters.

DR. PEPPER: I loathe people who shove them at you.

DOLLY: Then you loathe Harry.

DR. PEPPER: I don't follow.

DOLLY: Harry is the king of coasters. He adores coasters. He lives coasters. He *is* coasters. He's even tried to crochet coasters. Doctor, he can be upstairs sound asleep and I can be downstairs in the den watching television late at night and he'll come in with a coaster for my glass. He wakes up at three a.m. worrying I'm making rings.

DR. PEPPER: I don't know how you put up with it.

DOLLY: I haven't Doctor, he goes into my closet and straightens my shoes.

DR. PEPPER: Usually they wear them.

DOLLY: I wish he would. I wish he *would* put them on. Maybe he'd break a leg. But no, he just straightens them. I bet you put your toilet paper on wrong, too.

DR. PEPPER: I beg your pardon?

DOLLY: Did you know you could put a roll of toilet paper on the dispenser wrong? I didn't 'til I married Harry. "Dolly! How many times do I have to tell you? The paper should roll *under* from the inside out, not *over* from the outside down."

DR. PEPPER: Over from the? . . .

DOLLY: I try, but I can't remember.

DR. PEPPER: Under from the? . . .

DOLLY: He won't let me have down pillows in the house. They crush, he says. We're into total foam rubber. I hate foam rubber.

DR. PEPPER: I'm allergic to it.

DOLLY: I'm up to my ass in it. Doctor, this is a man who goes around straightening license plates in a public parking lot.

DR. PEPPER: Now honestly, Mrs. Scupp . . .

DOLLY: If they're dirty, he wipes them!

DR. PEPPER: What about in bed?

DOLLY: In bed?

DR. PEPPER: I mean, what's he like in bed?

DOLLY: I don't remember.

DR. PEPPER: Surely, Mrs. Scupp . . .

DOLLY: I never noticed.

DR. PEPPER: Never?

DOLLY: Our wedding night was terrific. From then on, it's been down hill all the way. His hobby is tropical fish. I hate tropical fish, Doctor.

Dr. Pepper: You hate tropical fish?

DOLLY: Not all tropical fish. Harry's tropical fish. There's something about them. Maybe it's the fact he talks to them. Or the names he gives them. Eric, Tony, Pinky. There's one round, mean-looking one he calls Dolly. When they die he buries them in the backyard. We're the only house in Larchmont with a tropical fish cemetery in the backyard. I know this sounds crazy, Doctor, but I hate those fish. I resent them in my living room and I resent them under my lawn. I'm a mature, sensible and, I think, rather intelligent woman and I hate those fish. How do you hate a tropical fish? (*She stands.*) You know something else I hate? Stereo equipment. Harry's got woofers, weefers, tweeters, baffles, pre-amps. He puts gloves on when he plays those records. White gloves like your friend. (*She indicates* OTTO.) Don't get me started, Doctor. There's so many thing about Harry I hate. I hate his black Volvo station wagon with the snow tires on in August. He worries about early winters. He worries about everything. We're the only people in Larchmont with drought insurance. (*She is pacing.*) I know it's none of my business, but I hate the way he dresses. I hate his big, baggy boxer shorts. The only shoes he'll wear are those big clumpy cordovans. Even on the beach. But my favorite outfit is his "Genius At Work" barbecue apron he wears over the pink Bermuda shorts and black, knee-high Supphose. Oh, I'm married to a snappy dresser, Doctor! And try taking a trip with him. He reads road signs. Every road sign. Out loud. "Soft shoulders, Dolly." "Slippery when wet, Dolly." "Deer crossing, Dolly." "Kiwanis Club meeting at noon, Wednesday, Dolly." Who gives a good goddamn? He's not even a member of the Kiwanis Club! Who'd want him? A man who puts on an apron after a bridge party and vacuums up isn't exactly a load of laughs. Neither is a man who takes you to Arizona for your anniversary. You know what's in Arizona? The London Bridge! Don't get me wrong, Doctor. I love my husband. I just can't stand him. So don't make too much out of that incident with the lawnmower. That was just the straw that broke the camel's back!

DR. PEPPER: And a very attractive camel she is, too.

DOLLY: Thank you.

OTTO: (*Looking up from his magazine.*) Rubdown, Frau Scupp?

DR. PEPPER: Nichts! (*Turning to* DOLLY, *as* OTTO *resumes reading.*) Listen to me, Mrs. Scupp. I'm not famous for saving marriages. I'm not even certain I believe in them. I'm famous for successful marriages for people who want to be married. I think I can help you but you have to want me to help you. (HARRY *is heard calling, "Otto! Otto!" offstage.*) Harry's coming. I've done all I can for him. It's up to you, now.

DOLLY: I'm frightened.

DR. PEPPER: Given your track record, I think Harry is the one with cause for alarm. (HARRY *enters. He, too, is dressed for swimming. He carries a small cardboard box.*)

HARRY: Otto! Otto! Good morning, Jason.

DOLLY: Hello, Harry.

HARRY: (*Embracing* DOLLY.) Dolly . . . Doll. Doll! Doll, baby! Hey, this is terrific!

DOLLY: Harry, you're crushing me!

HARRY: I could eat you alive! You didn't tell me she was coming up.

DR. PEPPER: I didn't know.

HARRY: What a great surprise!

DOLLY: I'm beginning to wonder.

HARRY: What're you talking about? I've been up here so long even Eric and Frac down at the lake were starting to look good to me. So was Martin Borman over there. Good morning, Otto.

OTTO: Gut morgen, Herr Scupp. Ze usual?

HARRY: What time is it? It's early. I better stick with the Bloody Marys. Hot, Otto. Very, very hot. Lots of Tabasco and lots of the white stuff.

OTTO: Jawohl, Herr Scupp.

DOLLY: Harry!

HARRY: Otto makes a fantastic Bloody Mary. Takes the roof of your head off and leaves it there.

DR. PEPPER: Last call, Mrs. Scupp. (DOLLY *shakes her head.*) Bitte, Otto . . . (*He holds up his martini glass.* OTTO *nods and goes.*)

HARRY: You look wonderful. Doesn't she look wonderful, Jason?

DR. PEPPER: That's what I've been telling her.

DOLLY: I've lost a little weight.

HARRY: I can see that.

DOLLY: You haven't.

HARRY: It's that high-cholesterol diet they've got me on. You know, I never thought I'd get sick of Eggs Benedict and chocolate mousse!

DOLLY: You're meant to be on low-cholesterol.

HARRY: Talk to my doctor!

DR. PEPPER: Harry likes high-cholesterol. You'll excuse me for a few minutes, won't you? (DR. PEPPER *rolls offstage.* DOLLY *composes herself.*)

HARRY: How are the kids?

DOLLY: Oh, Harry, they're just fine.

HARRY: Yeah?

DOLLY: Yeah . . . fine.

HARRY: That's great . . . that's just great.

DOLLY: I've got your *Hi-Fi Stereo Review*'s and *Popular Aquarium*'s in the car.

HARRY: Thank you.

DOLLY: And the summer pajamas you wrote for.

HARRY: The blue cottons?

DOLLY: I thought you meant the yellow drip-drys.

HARRY: That's okay.

DOLLY: I'm sorry.

HARRY: Really, it doesn't matter.

DOLLY: It's a pleasant drive up here.

HARRY: I hope you saw those warning signs on that bypass outside of Inglenook.

DOLLY: Oh, I did. I thought of you when I read them.

HARRY: An average of thirteen and a half people get killed there every year.

DOLLY: I'll be extra careful on the way back.

HARRY: When are you leaving?

DOLLY: I don't know. It depends. What's in the box?

HARRY: Oh . . . Henry.

DOLLY: Henry?

HARRY: My angel fish.

DOLLY: What happened?

HARRY: Evelyn killed him.

DOLLY: Who's Evelyn?

HARRY: My blue beta.

DOLLY: That's awful.

HARRY: It's just a fish. (*He throws the box over the wall of foliage.*)

DOLLY: You always used to give them such nice burials.

HARRY: I guess I'm getting cynical in my old age. So what's new?

DOLLY: Nothing much.

HARRY: I guess you sold the lawnmower.

DOLLY: No. It's in the garage waiting for you.

HARRY: Thanks.

DOLLY: It's broken, of course.

HARRY: I wasn't really trying to get you with it.

DOLLY: Yes, you were, Harry. Why?

HARRY: (*Exploding.*) There were a million reasons! It was hot. The refrigerator needed defrosting. The car keys were upstairs when they should have been downstairs. The house was still a mess from your bridge party. You forgot to renew my subscription to *High Fidelity* and they'd sent you three warnings already.

DOLLY: *Hi-Fi Stereo Review!*

HARRY: You knew how much I was looking forward to that comparative analysis of Dolby-ized cassette decks with ferric oxide heads! There was a new water ring on the telephone stand. Things like that.

DOLLY: Did I have the toilet paper on right?

HARRY: As a matter of fact, you did. What happened?

DOLLY: I don't know. I lost my head!

HARRY: Only someone had been playing my stereo. There were fingerprints on my Christmas album.

DOLLY: Who would be playing a Christmas album in June?

HARRY: I didn't say *when* they were put there, I just said I found them.

DOLLY: What were *you* doing playing a Christmas album in June?

HARRY: I wasn't. I just happened to be doing my six-month record cleaning that day. They weren't your fingerprints.

DOLLY: Thank you.

HARRY: They weren't the kids', either.

DOLLY: Well, at least I had the toilet paper on right.

HARRY: I conceded that point.

DOLLY: Well?

HARRY: It was blue!

DOLLY: That's all they had!

HARRY: It was blue! Our bathroom is red! Everything is red! The sink, the tub, the tile, the towels, the shower curtain! You know I don't like a clash. I like everything to match!

DOLLY: That's all they had!

HARRY: You asked me why. I'm telling you why. There were permanent press sheets on the bed.

DOLLY: Cotton's scarce.

HARRY: I can't sleep on permanent press. They're too hot. They're like flame sheets. Things like that. Like I said, it was hot. There were a million reasons. Then, when I saw you staked out on the lawn in your bathing suit, I just kind of lost control with the mower. What was it with me?

DOLLY: The coasters.

HARRY: Even that time in Acapulco?

DOLLY: It was always the coasters.

HARRY: I wasn't going to mention it, but . . . (*He motions to* DOLLY's *glass. She picks it up from the table.*)

DOLLY. I'm sorry.

HARRY: It's okay! (*He takes the glass from her and puts it on the table without a coaster.*)

DOLLY: Dr. Pepper seems to think you're ready to go home.

HARRY: (*He takes out a cigarette.*) He's done wonders for me, Doll.

DOLLY: When did you take that up?

HARRY: A couple of months ago. You want one?

DOLLY: No, thank you.

HARRY: They're fertilized with chicken shit, honey.

DOLLY: I know. (OTTO *has returned with the Bloody Mary.*)

HARRY: Thanks, Otto.

OTTO: Rubdown, Herr Scupp?

HARRY: Not just now, Otto. Maybe later, hunh?

OTTO: Jawohl. (OTTO *exits.*)

DOLLY: You look terrible, Harry.

HARRY: I'm a little hungover.

DOLLY: From what?

HARRY: Margaritas. They're vicious, Dolly. Stay away from them.

DOLLY: What were you doing drinking margaritas?

HARRY: The Plungs.

DOLLY: Who?

HARRY: The Plungs.

DOLLY: What are the Plungs?

HARRY: Jeanine and Billy Plung. This young couple from Roanoke I got friendly with while they were up here. We had a little farewell party for them last night. Jeanine had me dancing the rhumba with her until nearly three.

DOLLY. You can't rhumba, Harry. You can't even foxtrot.

HARRY: Jeanine says I'm a natural.

DOLLY: I thought they were taking care of you up here.

HARRY: They are. I never felt better in my life.

DOLLY: Why would you start smoking at your age?

HARRY: I like to smoke.

DOLLY: That's not a good enough reason.

HARRY: I can't think of a better one.

DOLLY: Margaritas! And the rhumba, Harry! How old was this woman?

HARRY: Twenty-two, twenty-three.

DOLLY: Harry, what's gotten into you?

HARRY: I'm my old self again! It's me, Harry Scupp with the DeSoto roadster with the rumble seat and the good hooch and let's have a good time and "Beat Port Chester, Larchmont!" and Glen Island Casino and Dolly Veasey is my number one date. It's gonna be like the old times again, Doll.

DOLLY: We never had old times like that.

HARRY: It's never too late.

DOLLY: And what do you mean, "your old self"?

HARRY: I love you. I don't want to kill you anymore.

DOLLY: You never had a DeSoto roadster. We took the bus.

HARRY: I'm talking about life, Dolly. Joie de vivre. You want to see what I've been doing since I've been up here? Close your eyes. (DOLLY *won't*.) I'm not going to hit you. Go over there and close your eyes. (DOLLY *won't*.) I want to show you something. It's a surprise. (*She is still doubtful.*) Well, close your eyes! (DOLLY *closes her eyes, and immediately extends her hand in front of her as a feeler.* HARRY *takes something off the towel cart.*) It's incredible you should be here today. I just finished this last night. Okay, Doll, open.

DOLLY: What is it?

HARRY: An ashtray.

DOLLY: An ashtray?

HARRY: Isn't it pretty? I mean, did you know I had a sensitivity like that all bottled up inside me? I didn't.

DOLLY: You're sure it's an ashtray?

HARRY: It's a nude study of Jeanine.

DOLLY: Jeanine Plung?

HARRY: Isn't that pretty?

DOLLY: She's naked!

HARRY: Well, how else do you sculpt a nude? I did one of Billy Plung I'm thinking of turning into a lamp.

DOLLY: What you're suggesting, Harry, is that you were somewhat more than just friendly with these people.

HARRY: Oh, I was! You'd go crazy over them and vice-versa.

DOLLY: I wouldn't count on it.

HARRY: Now wait right there. There's something else I want to show you. Don't move. (*He runs off.*)

DOLLY: Doctor!

DR. PEPPER: (*Emerging, with* OTTO *following.*) What do you think of the change?

DOLLY: What have you done to him?

DR. PEPPER: He's called you "honey" several times at least.

DOLLY: "They're loaded with chicken shit, honey," is what he said. You mean Harry and these Plung people . . . ?

DR. PEPPER: Just Mrs. Plung.

DOLLY: Where was Mr. Plung while all this was going on?

DR. PEPPER: Rumor has it with Otto.

DOLLY: I wouldn't be surprised. And you just allowed all this to happen?

DR. PEPPER: There are no rules at Ravenswood, Mrs. Scupp.

DOLLY: Which means that you let my husband go off into the woods with that horrid Plung woman!

DR. PEPPER: How did you know she was horrid? That's one secret I thought I'd kept to myself. She's a dreadful woman. I don't know what your husband ever saw in her. He would've been better off with Otto.

DOLLY: I'm beginning to think you made my husband do all these horrible things.

DR. PEPPER: I've never made anyone do anything, Mrs. Scupp. That's the secret of my success here, such as it is. I allow everyone to do exactly as he pleases.

DOLLY: At your prices I'd hardly call that a bargain.

DR. PEPPER: You'd be surprised how few people know what it is they want.

DOLLY: I know what I want.

DR. PEPPER: Do you, Mrs. Scupp?

DOLLY: I thought I did until I saw Harry like this.

HARRY: (*From offstage.*) I'll bet you didn't know I was a frustrated song-and-dance man, did you, Doll? (HARRY *rushes back in. He has a ukulele and a tap board.*) Now you're really gonna get a kick out of this. You know how I always overdo things? That's because of my masculine insecurity coming out. I didn't even know I had masculine insecurity until Jason here got his hands on me. It turns out I've got a singing voice. And feet, too. Dolly, I got rhythm! Sit down. I want you to see this. (HARRY *hands* DR. PEPPER *the uke.* OTTO *produces a small foot-pedal drum and a set of cymbals from behind the towel cart. They launch into a lively, twenties-type popular song. It's obvious* HARRY's *been practicing. He's still pretty terrible, but he's having fun. He tap dances, too, and ends with a big finish.*)

DOLLY: Stop it! I can't stand seeing you like this.

HARRY: You can't stand seeing me like what?

DOLLY: Singing, dancing, smoking, drinking! Making ashtrays!

HARRY: I told you it was a new me. Wait'll they see this down at the country club! (*He launches back into the song. This time, his big finish is even bigger than before. Finally* DOLLY *hurls the ashtray across the stage, smashing it.*) You broke my ashtray.

DOLLY: I'm taking you home.

HARRY: You broke my ashtray.

DOLLY: I thought you came here to get better.

HARRY: You broke my ashtray! (*He is advancing on her.* DOLLY *is trying to get something out of her purse.*)

DR. PEPPER: Harry!

DOLLY: (*Producing an aerosol can and pointing it at* HARRY.) Harry!
(HIRAM *and* FRANCIS *are heard calling to* HARRY *from the lakeside.*
"*Harry! Harry!*")

HARRY: I promised Hiram and Francis I'd race them out to the raft.
They're like kids that way . . . they'll keep it up all morning until
I do. (*He runs down the aisle.* DOLLY *is trembling.*)

DR. PEPPER: What is that?

DOLLY: Mace!

DR. PEPPER: It's too bad my wife didn't carry one of those. Too bad
for me, that is.

DOLLY: You said he was better!

DR. PEPPER: You still don't see the change?

DOLLY: Not the change I wanted!

DR. PEPPER: Harry loved that piece of sculpture.

DOLLY: What have you done to him?

DR. PEPPER: No, Harry's done it to himself. Maybe it's your turn
now.

DOLLY: Maybe it isn't!

DR. PEPPER: Know what you want, Mrs. Scupp. That's the first step.

DOLLY: I want a good marriage.

DR. PEPPER: Then give me three months.

DOLLY: And I want to be happy.

DR. PEPPER: Make it three and a half.

DOLLY: That's not much, is it?

DR. PEPPER: Sometimes it's everything. Now: it's a beautiful summer's day, God's in his heaven and all's right with the world. Harry will be waiting for you down by the lake. I'd go to him if I were you.

DOLLY: I'm still a little frightened to be with him. With my foot like this, I can't go swimming. Maybe I could ask him to take me boating.

DR. PEPPER: I wouldn't push my luck. Try skimming stones, Mrs. Scupp.

DOLLY: It's Dolly. Please. Call me Dolly?

DR. PEPPER: Okay, Dolly.

DOLLY: It always happens.

DR. PEPPER: I know what you're going to say.

DOLLY: I always get a crush on doctors! (DOLLY *exits down the aisle.* DR. PEPPER *sits sipping his martini and smoking.* OTTO *starts his tape machine. We hear "Wein, Du Stadt Meiner Traume!"* OTTO *picks up* HARRY's *tap board, takes it to the towel table, and begins clearing the breakfast things.*)

DR. PEPPER: That's not at all what I thought she was going to say.

OTTO: Crush? Was ist crush?

DR. PEPPER: Mrs. Scupp thinks she likes me.

OTTO: Everyone likes Herr Doktor.

DR. PEPPER: That's because everyone thinks Herr Doktor likes them. You're playing your favorite song again, Otto.

OTTO: Ja. My mother used to sing this song.

DR. PEPPER: It's a beauty.

OTTO: My mother was a pig. Herr Doktor would like something?

DR. PEPPER: Herr Doktor just wants everyone to be happy. (*Just then a tennis ball bounces on stage.* ROY *and* APRIL PITT, *dressed for tennis and carrying their racquets, appear briefly down the aisle.*)

ROY: Hey, Mac, you want to send that back?

APRIL: What's the matter with you? Throw the ball back, you creep!

DR. PEPPER: Otto. (*He points to the ball.* OTTO *returns the ball to* ROY.)

APRIL: Thanks a lot.

ROY: Yeah, thanks loads. (*They disappear up the aisle.*)

DR. PEPPER: Das ists ze newly-weds Pitt?

OTTO: Ja.

DR. PEPPER: (*Holding out his empty glass.*) Bitte, Otto. (HIRAM *and* FRANCIS *are returning down the aisle. We hear* FRANCIS *yelling,* "*We beat you!*") Better make that three. Make that drei cocktails, Otto.

OTTO: Jawohl. (*He goes.*)

DR. PEPPER: Who won?

FRANCIS: (*Singing, skipping almost.*) Harry and me! Harry and me! Harry and me!

HIRAM: They ganged up on me as usual.

FRANCIS: We beat you! We beat you! Da da da we beat you!

HIRAM: Well, Harry beat you.

FRANCIS: And we both beat you!

HIRAM: I was worried about that turtle.

FRANCIS: Even with these on, I beat him. (*Indeed, water is sloshing out of his rubber bathing slippers.*) I beat you! I beat you!

HIRAM: I am going to beat you black and blue if you keep that up, Francis!

DR. PEPPER: Boys, boys!

FRANCIS: I'm still not speaking to you!

HIRAM: That's a blessing!

FRANCIS: But . . . (*Very softly.*) I beat you! I beat you!

DR. PEPPER: Hiram, did you tell Francis he looked like an embryo?

HIRAM: If I'd seen him in that bathing cap, I'd've said he looked like a prophylactic.

FRANCIS: Hiram is a poor sport! Hiram is a poor sport!

HIRAM: If there's anything more vulgar than swimming, it's a swimming race.

FRANCIS: It was his idea.

HIRAM: Does that sound like me, Jason?

FRANCIS: It was, too!

HIRAM: You see what I have to put up with?

FRANCIS: Last night after dinner you said, "Let's challenge Harry Scupp to a swimming race tomorrow."

HIRAM: Are you sure you can't do anything for him, Doctor?

FRANCIS: You did, you did!

HIRAM: I'd suggest a lobotomy but obviously he's already had one.

FRANCIS: I cross my heart, he did!

HIRAM: Several, from the look of it!

FRANCIS: (*Getting quite hysterical.*) He lies, Doctor, he lies! He did suggest a swimming race after dinner with Harry Scupp last night! He did! He did!

DR. PEPPER: Don't hold it back, Francis.

FRANCIS: (*A real tantrum now: feet and fists pounding the ground.*) Tell him! Tell him it was your idea, Hiram! Tell him, tell him, tell him, tell him, tell him, tell him, tell him, tell him! (*He is exhausting himself as* HIRAM *interrupts.*)

HIRAM: All right! So it *was* my idea. I don't like to lose. It's the Spane in me. A Baltimore Tear wouldn't understand that. (*Genuinely.*) Oh I'm sorry, Francis. (FRANCIS *sulks.*) Now get up. You know I can't stand to see you grovel like that.

FRANCIS: I'm not groveling, Hiram. I'm letting it all out for once. Right, Doctor?

DR. PEPPER: Just keep going. I think we might be getting somewhere.

FRANCIS: He always wants to compete with me. I can't help it if I always win. I don't even want to win. I just do. Backgammon, bridge, whist, Chinese checkers, Mah-jongg . . .

HIRAM: You never beat me at Mah-jongg.

FRANCIS: Yes, I did. That time in Morocco.

HIRAM: I don't count that.

FRANCIS: Why not?

HIRAM: I had dysentery.

FRANCIS: So did I!

HIRAM: I said I was sorry!

FRANCIS: I always win! At anything! Anagrams, Parcheesi, Scrabble, tennis . . .

HIRAM: That's table tennis, Francis!

FRANCIS: Well I win, don't I? Like I always do? I can't lose to him at anything! And he hates me for it! Oh he just hates me to death!

HIRAM: While you're down there crowing, Francis, why don't you tell the doctor the *real* story?

FRANCIS: What real story?

HIRAM: What real story!

FRANCIS: I don't know what you're talking about!

HIRAM: Why don't you tell him about Celine? (*A short pause.*) I didn't think so.

DR. PEPPER: Who is Celine?

HIRAM: A Welsh Corgi we had when we lived on 69th Street.

DR. PEPPER: It's a lovely little dog.

HIRAM: Francis killed her.

FRANCIS: It was an accident.

HIRAM: He threw her out of the window.

FRANCIS: I didn't throw her out the window. She jumped.

HIRAM: Of course she did!

FRANCIS: You weren't there. She jumped out!

HIRAM: Celine hadn't jumped *anywhere* since Mummy's car backed over her in New Hope three years before! You threw that dog!

FRANCIS: She'd been trying to catch this big fly in her mouth when suddenly she just sailed out the window right after it.

HIRAM: Do you really expect Dr. Pepper to believe that cock and bull story?

FRANCIS: It's true. It's true!

DR. PEPPER: What floor were you on?

FRANCIS: The fourteenth.

HIRAM: The fatal fourteenth.

FRANCIS: I didn't throw her.

HIRAM: Well who left that window open?

FRANCIS: You couldn't breathe that night.

HIRAM: And you were thinking of yourself first, as usual!

DR. PEPPER: No air-conditioning?

FRANCIS: This was years ago.

HIRAM: When dog-killers could still get away with something as simple as an open window. God knows what he'd come up with today.

DR. PEPPER: What a ghastly story.

HIRAM: Most crimes of passion are. Francis was jealous of her. Celine adored me, couldn't stand him. She used to pee in his closet out of spite. So he killed her.

FRANCIS: If you say that again I'm going to smack your face for you.

HIRAM: Say what? You dog murderer! (FRANCIS *flies at him.*)

FRANCIS: I am not a dog murderer! You take that back!

DR. PEPPER: Don't hold it back. (*They struggle. They do minor violence to each other.*)

FRANCIS: Take it back! Take it back, take it back, take it back, take it back, take it back . . . (DR. PEPPER, *watching from the sidelines, offers encouragement during the encounter.*)

DR. PEPPER: That's right, boys, let it out. Let it out. No holding back, now. That's right, that's right. Just let everything out now. (*During the struggle* OTTO *returns with the drinks. He looks to* DR. PEPPER, *who motions him to let the combatants be.* OTTO *shrugs, sits down with his magazine. Finally,* HIRAM *overwhelms* FRANCIS *and, pinning him down, lightly slaps his face and arm.*)

HIRAM: Have you lost your mind? Don't you ever lift a hand to me again as long as you live, do you hear me? Ever! Ever, ever, ever, ever, ever. (*One last little slap.*) Ever. (HIRAM *and* FRANCIS *collapse with exhaustion.*)

DR. PEPPER: All right now?

FRANCIS: I don't think Ravenswood is working out for us.

HIRAM: Of course Ravenswood isn't working out for us! Why should it?

DR. PEPPER: Did you ever think of getting another dog?

HIRAM: No more dogs. Celine was a terrible shedder.

FRANCIS: Another one would probably just pee in my closet, too.

HIRAM: Or maybe mine next time.

FRANCIS: No more dogs, Hiram? Promise?

HIRAM: The only reason we stay together is because no one else in the world would put up with us.

DR. PEPPER: If you can leave here having realized that much, I'll be satisfied.

HIRAM: *You'll* be satisfied?

DR. PEPPER: And so should you.

HIRAM: We are, I suppose. We are.

FRANCIS: You're the only real friend I've ever had, Hiram.

HIRAM: And I'm sure Dr. Pepper can see why. Help me up, will you? I think I twisted something. (FRANCIS *struggles to his feet, then helps* HIRAM *up.*)

FRANCIS: Are we dressing for lunch?

HIRAM: I don't know about the end of the Baltimore Tear line but the last remaining Newport Spane is. Otto, where's my Bullshot? (*As they move toward the drinks, another tennis ball bounds across the stage.* ROY *and* APRIL *are heard yelling from the back of the house.*)

ROY: (*Offstage.*) Ball!

APRIL: (*Offstage.*) Ball!

ROY: *Ball!*

APRIL: *Ball!*

HIRAM: Who are those dreadful people?

DR. PEPPER: The Pitts.

FRANCIS: Pitts? What kind of name is Pitts?

HIRAM: Appropriate! (*He gulps his Bullshot.*)

APRIL: Hey, you, Mac, you wanna throw that ball back for Christ's sake?

HIRAM: (*Speaking straight out in the direction of* APRIL's *voice.*) My name is not Mac, I'm not your ball boy, and why don't you try fucking yourself, madam! Come on, Francis. (*They exit.* DR. PEPPER *is alone with the tennis ball.*)

ROY: (*Running down the aisle.*) Hey, you can't talk to my wife like that! (*To* APRIL, *who is following him.*) Will you please go back there? We'll lose our place on the court.

APRIL: I'll get the court back! I want to see you handle something for once!

ROY: (*Leaping on stage.*) I told you I'm gonna flatten that S.O.B.! Keep the court! (APRIL *and* ROY, *still carrying their racquets, search around the stage.*) Where'd he go?

DR. PEPPER: Good morning.

ROY: We saw you talking to him!! Now where is he?

DR. PEPPER: Who?

Roy: That guy who insulted my wife!

Dr. pepper: Your wife?

April: What do I look like? His dog?

Dr. pepper: You must be Mr. and Mrs. Pitt.

Roy: Yeah, as a matter of fact, we *are*.

April: And they got some nice class of people up at this place!

Roy: (*Cautioning her.*) Honey! I think we've been recognized.

Dr. pepper: I'm afraid so.

Roy: Celebrity-time!

April: Oh, Christ!

Roy: (*Taking off his sunglasses and shaking* Dr. pepper's *hand.*) Hi, Roy Pitt. Nice to see you. We were hoping to be a little incognito up here! It's just as well. I think actors who wear big sunglasses are big phonies. This is my wife, April James.

April: Hi, April James. Nice to see you.

Dr. pepper: April James?

April: It's my professional name.

Roy: You see that, honey? Even with these things on he recognized us.

Dr. pepper: And what do *you* do, Mrs. Pitt?

April: What do you mean, "What do I do?" I'm an actress. Thanks a lot, buddy.

Roy: She's an actress.

APRIL: I don't even know you but I really needed that little ego boost.

ROY: Honey, of course he recognized me. My movie was on the Late Show last night. "Cold Fingers." He probably caught it.

APRIL: God knows you did.

ROY: It's the power of the medium! You know that kind of exposure.

APRIL: "Cold Fingers" should have *opened* on the Late Show.

ROY: Now don't start with me.

APRIL: Boy, I really needed that little zap.

ROY: He's a dummy.

APRIL: You must have seen me in something. How about "Journey Through Hell" for Christ's sake! You didn't see me in "Journey Through Hell"?

DR. PEPPER: Were you in that?

ROY: That was my beautiful April all right!

APRIL: You bet your sweet ass it was!

DR. PEPPER: That was a wonderful movie, Mrs. Pitt.

APRIL: You see that? Another zap?

ROY: April wasn't in the movie. She created the role off-Broadway . . . didn't get the film version!

APRIL: Boy, this is really my day!

ROY: She was brilliant in that part.

APRIL: I know. Too bad the play didn't support me.

DR. PEPPER: I enjoyed the film, too.

APRIL: I bet you did.

ROY: Hey. Try to cool it with her, will you?

APRIL: Try *Random Thoughts and Vaguer Notions*, why don't you?

ROY: That one was on Broadway. April was one of the stars.

DR. PEPPER: I wasn't able to catch it.

APRIL: It ran nearly eighty performances. You didn't exactly have to be a jackrabbit.

ROY: April!

APRIL: Before you zap me again, I didn't do the movie of that one, either.

ROY: You never read notices like she got for that one. Show 'em to him, honey.

APRIL: They're in the car. I break my balls trying to make that piece of garbage work and they sign some WASP starlet for the movie version thinking she's going to appeal to that goddamn Middle American drive-in audience.

ROY: I don't really think you can call Googie Gomez a WASP starlet.

APRIL: White bread! That's all she is, white bread!

ROY: (*Calling down the aisle.*) Hey, that court's taken, Buddy. We got it reserved.

APRIL: You heard him!

DR. PEPPER: I think that's the ground keeper.

ROY: That's okay, Mac! Sorry! Hang in there!

APRIL: Hi! April James! Nice to see you!

ROY: Hi! Roy Pitt! Nice to see you! Ssh! Sssh!

APRIL: What is it?

ROY: I thought I heard our phone.

APRIL: Way out here? What are you? The big ear?

ROY: You sure you told the service where I'd be?

APRIL: Of course I did. I might be getting a call, too, you know.

ROY: I'm expecting an important call from the coast. I'm not usually this tense.

APRIL: Hah!

ROY: This could be the big one, April.

APRIL: Almost anything would be bigger than "Cold Fingers." (OTTO *has appeared.*)

ROY: (*Starting to do push-ups.*) You got one hell of a thirsty star out here, waiter.

APRIL: Two thirsty stars.

OTTO: I am not a waiter. My name is Otto.

ROY: Hi, Otto. Roy Pitt, nice to see you.

APRIL: Hi, Otto. April James, nice to see you.

ROY: (*Now he is doing sit-ups.*) What are you having, honey?

APRIL: A screwdriver.

ROY: I'll have some Dom Perignon. The champagne.

APRIL: Roy!

ROY: It's included.

APRIL: Eighty-six the screwdriver. I'll have the same.

OTTO: The Fraulein would like a nice rubdown, maybe?

APRIL: From you?

ROY: Just bring the Dom Perignon, will you?

DR. PEPPER: Oh, and Otto! (*He holds up his glass.*)

OTTO: Jawohl. (*He goes.*)

APRIL: (*Sits, and looks at* DR. PEPPER's *wheelchair for the first time.*) I want to apologize for earlier when we yelled at you for the ball. We didn't realize you were . . . like that.

DR. PEPPER: Half the time I don't realize it myself.

APRIL: We do lots of benefits, you know.

ROY: April's been asked to do the Mental Health and Highway Safety Telethons two years straight.

APRIL: Easter Seals wanted me last month but they weren't paying expenses.

ROY: Nobody's blaming you, honey.

APRIL: I mean there's charity and then there's charity. I mean you gotta draw the line somewhere, right? What am I? Chopped liver?

ROY: Easter Seals wouldn't even send a limousine for her! Our agent told them they could take their telethon and shove it. (ROY *is opening up a sun reflector.*)

APRIL: What are you doing?

ROY: You don't mind if we don't play tennis for a while? I want to get some of the benefits.

APRIL: There's not enough sun for a tan.

ROY: That's what you think. It's a day like this you can really bake yourself. Just because the sky's grey doesn't mean those rays aren't coming through. Make love to me, soleil, make love to me.

APRIL: (*She is sitting near* DR. PEPPER. ROY *is sprawled out with his reflector under his chin. He just loves lying in the sun like this.*) What are you in for?

DR. PEPPER: The usual.

APRIL: A bad marriage, huh? That's too bad. You're probably wondering what we're doing here. I know on the surface it must look like we got a model marriage. But believe me, we got our little problems, too. Don't look so surprised. Roy's got an ego on him you could drive a Mack truck with. Show biz marriages ain't nothing to write home about. Half our friends are divorced and the other half are miserable. Naturally, they don't think we're going to make it. Think. They *hope.* But we're going to show them. Right, honey?

ROY: Right.

APRIL: Have you had a session with Dr. Pepper yet?

DR. PEPPER: Many. (*He picks up the book he took from* DOLLY *and opens it.*)

APRIL: Is he all he's cracked up to be?

DR. PEPPER: I think so, but of course I'm prejudiced. (*He smiles at* APRIL *and begins to read.*)

APRIL: He's gonna have his hands full with that one.

DR. PEPPER: (*Looking up.*) I'm sorry . . . ?

APRIL: Skip it. (DR. PEPPER *returns to his book.* APRIL *silently mouths an obscenity at him and turns her attention to* ROY.)

ROY: Honey! You're blocking my sun.

APRIL: You're just gonna lie there like that?

ROY: Unh-hunh.

APRIL: So where's my reflector?

ROY: I told you to pack it if you wanted it.

APRIL: I want it.

ROY: You said you didn't want to get any darker.

APRIL: I'm starting to fade.

ROY: No, you're not.

APRIL: It's practically all gone. Look at you. You're twice as dark!

ROY: It's not a contest, honey.

APRIL: I mean what's the point of getting a tan if you don't maintain it? Roy!

ROY: (*For* DR. PEPPER's *benefit, but without looking up from the reflector.*) Do you believe this? I was with my agents all day and I'm supposed to be worried about a goddamn reflector!

APRIL: Just give me a couple of minutes with it.

ROY: It's the best sun time now.

APRIL: You know I've got that audition Wednesday.

ROY: No. N.O. (APRIL *gives up, gets the tin of cocoa butter off the cart and begins applying it.*) April's up for another new musical. They were interested in us both, actually, but I've got these film commitments.

APRIL: Tentative film commitments.

ROY: You're getting hostile, honey.

APRIL: What's hostile is you not packing my reflector.

ROY: *I* was busy with my agents. *You* are getting hostile.

APRIL: I've got a career, too, you know.

ROY: (*Sitting up, he drops the reflector and motions for quiet.*) Ssshh!

APRIL: (*Grabbing the reflector.*) Hello? Yes, we're checking on the availability of Roy Pitt for an Alpo commercial!

ROY: Shut up, April! (*He listens, disappointed.*) Shit. (*Then he sees* APRIL.) Hold it. Stop it! (*He grabs the reflector and lies back.*)

APRIL: Roy!

ROY: After that? You've gotta be kidding! I wouldn't give you this reflector if you whistled "Swanee River" out of your ass.

APRIL: I can, too.

ROY: I know. I've heard you.

APRIL: Just lie there and turn into leather.

ROY: I will.

APRIL: There are other things in the world more important than your sun tan, you know.

ROY: Like yours?

APRIL: For openers.

ROY: Like your career?

APRIL: Yes, as a matter of fact.

ROY: Will you stop competing with me, April? That's one of the reasons we came here. I can't help it if I'm hotter than you right now.

APRIL: That could change, Roy. Remember "Star Is Born."

ROY: Well, until it does, love me for what I am: Roy Pitt, the man. But don't resent me for my career.

APRIL: I know, Roy.

ROY: I love you for what you are: April James, the best little actress in New York City.

APRIL: What do you mean, "best little actress"?

ROY: I'm trying to make a point, honey!

APRIL: As opposed to what? A dwarf?

ROY: If we're going to have a good marriage and, April, I want that more than anything . . . !

APRIL: More than you wanted the lead in "Lenny"?

ROY: I didn't want "Lenny."

APRIL: He would've crawled through broken glass for that part!

ROY: I didn't want "Lenny." Now goddamit, shut up!

APRIL: I can't talk to you when you get like that.

ROY: Get like what? You haven't laid off me since we got in the car.

APRIL: You know I'm upset.

ROY: We've all been fired from shows.

APRIL: Before they went into rehearsal? I'm thinking of slitting the *two* wrists this time, Roy!

ROY: Actually, Heather MacNamara isn't a bad choice for that part.

APRIL: She's the pits!

ROY: We're the Pitts! (*Breaking himself up, then . . .*) We liked her in "The Seagull."

APRIL: You liked her in "The Seagull." I'd like her in her coffin.

ROY: Obviously they're going ethnic with it.

APRIL: She isn't even ethnic. She's white bread. I'm ethnic. I want a hit, Roy. I need a hit. I'm going crazy for a hit. I mean, when's it my turn?

ROY: Honey, you're making a shadow.

APRIL: I'm sorry.

ROY: That's okay. Just stick with me, kid. We're headed straight for the top.

APRIL: Roy?

ROY: What, angel?

APRIL: Your toupee is slipping. (ROY *clutches at his hairpiece.*) Roy wears a piece.

ROY: It's no secret. I've never pretended. It's not like your nose job!

APRIL: Don't speak to me. Just lie there and turn into naugahyde like your mother!

ROY: Honey! I almost forgot. Your agent called! They're interviewing hostesses for Steak & Brew.

APRIL: Give him skin cancer, God, give him skin cancer, please!

DR. PEPPER: Excuse me, I know it's none of my business, but how long have you two been married?

APRIL: Three months.

ROY: And you were right the first time, it's none of your business.

APRIL: But we lived together a long time before we did.

ROY: Not long enough.

APRIL: Eight *centuries* it felt like!

ROY: Do you have to cry on the world's shoulder, April?

APRIL: I want us to work, Roy! I love you.

ROY: I know. I love you, too, April.

APRIL: You're the best.

ROY: *We're* the best.

APRIL: You really think this Pepper fellow can help us?

DR. PEPPER: I'm no miracle worker.

ROY: You?

DR. PEPPER: Hi, Jason Pepper. Nice to see you.

ROY: You're Dr. Pepper?

DR. PEPPER: Only to my worst enemies. Let's make it Jason, shall we?

APRIL: Oh Roy!

ROY: The least you could've done was told us!

APRIL: I'm so ashamed!

ROY: Talk about seeing people at their worst!

DR. PEPPER: I'm used to that.

ROY: Yeah, but you haven't heard the other side of the story.

DR. PEPPER: And I'm sure it's a good one, too.

APRIL: Roy, I could just die. (HIRAM *and* FRANCIS *enter. They wear striped blazers, ascots, and white summer flannels. They cross to the table and will begin playing cards.*)

HIRAM: You know what they say about white flannels, don't you, Jason? The devil's invention. Never out of the cleaners.

FRANCIS: I put mine on first, of course, and then he decided he was going to wear his!

HIRAM: Don't be ridiculous.

FRANCIS: We *look* ridiculous.

DR. PEPPER: I think you both look rather dashing.

HIRAM: Thank you, Jason.

FRANCIS: Monkey see, monkey do.

DR. PEPPER: This is Mr. and Mrs. Pitt.

ROY: And you owe my wife an apology.

HIRAM: I don't recall speaking to you, Mac.

ROY: Now, look, you . . .

APRIL: It doesn't matter.

ROY: To me it does. You're my wife!

APRIL: Not in front of . . . (*She motions toward* DR. PEPPER.) . . . please?

HIRAM: Hiram Spane of the Newport Spanes, Mrs. Pitt. I've got a foul temper and a vicious tongue. Someone yells "ball" at me and they start working overtime. And that's about as much of an apology as you're going to get out of me.

APRIL: Thank you.

HIRAM: This is Francis Tear of the Baltimore Tears.

APRIL: Hi. April James, nice to see you. This is my husband, Roy.

ROY: (*Pumping* FRANCIS' *hand.*) Hi, Roy Pitt. Nice to see you.

FRANCIS: Do you like to swim?

HIRAM: Francis!

FRANCIS: I just asked!

ROY: (*Gesturing for silence.*) Ssshh! Sshh! Sshh!

HIRAM: I beg your pardon?

ROY: Shut up! (*He listens, hears something.*) There it is! (*He and* APRIL *cross their fingers.*)

ROY & APRIL: (*In unison.*) Baby, baby, baby! (ROY *runs off.*)

HIRAM: Is your husband mentally deranged, Mrs. Pitt?

APRIL: He's been expecting that call.

HIRAM: That wasn't my question.

APRIL: He's an actor. It might be a job. Normal people wouldn't understand. (*She sits.*) How long have you two been married?

FRANCIS: We're not married, Mrs. Pitt.

APRIL: Oh!

HIRAM: Oh?

APRIL: How nice.

FRANCIS: That's what you think.

APRIL: We have lots of friends like that in the city.

HIRAM: Like what?

APRIL: Like you two. We're both in show business. We have to, practically.

HIRAM: Well, we're not in show business, Mrs. Pitt, and we certainly don't have to have friends like you.

APRIL: Did I say something wrong?

HIRAM: And I'm sure you're just getting started. Excuse me. (*He turns back to his card game.*)

APRIL: I was just trying to make small talk. I got better things to do than yak it up with a couple of aunties, you know!

HIRAM: I don't think normal therapy is going to work with that woman, Jason. Why don't you try euthanasia?

APRIL: Look, mouth!

DR. PEPPER: Children, children! (HARRY *appears down the aisle.*)

HARRY: Otto! Otto, pack my bags and put them in the car. Just leave something out for me to change into. It's the black Volvo station wagon, the one with snow tires. You can't miss it. And then how about a round for everyone?

OTTO: Jawohl, Herr Scupp. (*He goes.*)

HARRY: I'm leaving, Jason.

FRANCIS: Harry's leaving, Hiram!

HIRAM: I can see that, Francis.

DR. PEPPER: I haven't officially released you, Harry.

HARRY: I'll save you the trouble. I'm officially releasing myself. What were you planning on, Jason? Keeping me here 'til Doomsday?

DR. PEPPER: Where's Dolly?

HARRY: She's decided to stay. Try to help her, Jason.

DOLLY: (*Entering from the aisle.*) Harry! Harry!

DR. PEPPER: What happened down by the lake?

HARRY: What didn't happen, you mean.

DOLLY: It was like our honeymoon.

HARRY: Don't make it sound too dramatic, Dolly. We just decided that our marriage was better than no marriage at all. I do what I want and she does what she wants. It's called compromise, honey, and it's the secret of a good marriage. If I want to fool around with someone you're going to let me because that's what I want to do and you want what I want. And if you want to fool around you won't because I don't want you to and you don't want what I don't want.

DOLLY: That's called compromise?

HARRY: That's called marriage.

DR. PEPPER: That's called *your* marriage.

DOLLY: That's called divorce.

DR. PEPPER: Take it or leave it, Mrs. Scupp.

DOLLY: There's a choice? I think I'm doing the right thing, Jason.

HARRY: I think we're doing the right thing, Jason.

DOLLY: I hope so, Harry.

DR. PEPPER: Just so long as it makes you both happy. (DOLLY *reaches for* HARRY's *cigarette and takes a deep, satisfying drag.*) How is it?

DOLLY: Like honey. It's like someone just poured ten years of honey down my throat.

DR. PEPPER: This is Mrs. Pitt. She and her husband have just arrived. (ROY, *returning, steps right in.*)

Roy: Hi, Roy Pitt. Nice to see you. Hi, Roy Pitt. Nice to see you.

April: Hi, April James. Nice to see you. (*To* Roy.) Did you get it?

Roy: It looks good but nothing definite.

April: When would you leave?

Roy: We'll talk about it later. (*To* Francis.) Hi, Roy Pitt. Nice to see you.

Dolly: Wait a minute! Wait a minute! The Retarded Children Telethon, right? That's her, honey! The girl we were so crazy about. You sang . . . "Do, do, do."

April: That was for Leukemia, actually, the Leukemia Telethon.

Dolly: Oh, we think you're just terrific. You're headed straight for the top. I hope your line of work keeps you busy, Mr. Pitt. You're in for a lot of lonely days and nights.

April: Roy's an actor, too.

Dolly: Are you, dear? (*She turns to* Harry) You know something: I don't think we would've had so many problems if we'd had more in common.

April: Dr. Pepper's really helped you, then?

Dolly: Helped him. We'll see about me. (Harry *lets out a sudden, urgent scream.*)

Dr. pepper: How was it?

Harry: Fantastic.

Dolly: Is he going to be doing that often?

Dr. pepper: That depends on you.

DOLLY: If he pulls that in the middle of a board meeting he's going to be looking for a new job.

DR. PEPPER. You might try it yourself sometime.

DOLLY: Me? I'm as cool as a cucumber.

DR. PEPPER: What brought that one on, Harry?

HARRY: The truth?

DR. PEPPER: You're still at Ravenswood.

HARRY: I want to shtup Mrs. Pitt.

ROY: Hey!

HARRY: You see how her tennis outfit's all slit up the side? There's no tan line. You know how women who are tan all over drive me crazy, Jason.

ROY: What did you say?

APRIL: It's okay, Roy. He just said he *wanted* to shtup me. He didn't *do* it. (DOLLY *lets out a sudden, urgent scream.*)

DR. PEPPER: How do you feel?

DOLLY: Hoarse.

HARRY: You'll get used to it. (OTTO *has returned with a tray of champagne. He passes it around. Everyone takes one as* HARRY *turns to* HIRAM *and* FRANCIS.) I'm really gonna miss you two guys, you know. Take good care of her for me, will you?

HIRAM: When you come back for her, God knows we'll still be here. I think we're probably permanent.

FRANCIS: We're just lucky Hiram's mother can afford it.

HIRAM: You're just lucky Hiram's mother can afford it.

FRANCIS: Goodbye, Harry. I'll miss you.

DOLLY: No! No farewell toasts. I propose a welcome toast to the new arrivals.

HARRY: You can't drink to yourself.

DOLLY: All right! Here's to new marriage and the Pitts.

HARRY: Here's to our old one, honey.

HIRAM: Here's to friendship.

FRANCIS: Here's to Hiram.

HIRAM: Why thank you, Francis.

ROY: Here's to April James.

FRANCIS: April who, Hiram?

HIRAM: Some little RKO starlet, obviously.

APRIL: Here's to Hollywood and Mr. and Mrs. Roy Pitt.

DOLLY: Doctor?

DR. PEPPER: Here's to . . . all of you.

OTTO: Here's to Ravenswood. (*They drink. Then* HARRY *starts to sing "Auld Lang, Syne" and they all join in. Much applauding, hugging, and laughing.*) Lunch ist served. (*They break apart and start making their exits.*)

HARRY: Goodbye, Jason. And thank you. She's all yours now.

DOLLY: I'll walk you to the car.

HARRY: (*To* ROY.) Hey! Now I know where I've seen you! "Lenny"! You were in "Lenny"!

ROY: (*With a sudden, urgent scream.*) "Lenny"!!

HARRY: What did I say?

APRIL: Nothing. It's all right. Goodbye.

DOLLY: Come on, Harry.

HARRY: So long, Jason. (DOLLY *and* HARRY *are gone.*)

APRIL: He's a dummy. What does he know? You're Roy Pitt, the best actor in the business.

ROY: What am I? Chopped liver? I'll probably get that movie but it doesn't go for three months. (*They start off down the aisle.*)

APRIL: Listen, I wasn't going to mention this, but since you brought it up: you think there's anything in it for me?

ROY: A terrific part. They want a name but I'll mention you for it first thing.

APRIL: I'll test, but first-class, Roy. They're gonna have to fly me out there first-class. (*They are gone. There is more and more thunder.* DR. PEPPER *looks up at the sky.*)

FRANCIS: Hiram? (*He exits down the aisle.*)

HIRAM: Will somebody just look at these flannels? Soiled already! This time I'm sending your mother the bill. Old Bingo Money, that's all she is . . . (*He follows* FRANCIS *off.*)

FRANCIS: (*From the aisle.*) Do you think Mrs. Scupp would like to play badminton after lunch?

HIRAM: If she did, she wouldn't want to play with you. (DR. PEPPER *watches everyone exit as* OTTO *returns to wheel him in for lunch.*)

DR. PEPPER: Lasse!

OTTO: Herr Doktor does not want lunch today? (DR. PEPPER *shakes his head.*) Herr Doktor would like a martini? (DR. PEPPER *shakes his head.*) A little rubdown, maybe?

DR. PEPPER: Herr Doktor just wants everyone to be happy.

OTTO: Happy?

DR. PEPPER: Du bist happy, Otto?

OTTO: Was ist happy?

DR. PEPPER: A good question, Otto. (OTTO *goes.* DR. PEPPER *lifts his glass in a toast.*) So long, Harry. (*Thunder and lightning.* DR. PEPPER *feels his skull. The guests are heard singing in the distance.* DR. PEPPER *sings along with them to himself, very quietly and slowly. His voice trails off. The curtain falls.*)

END OF THE PLAY

DUNELAWN

*The setting is outdoors. The stage is bare except for a high wall run-
ning the length of the Upstage cyclorama. Also, there is a small
stone bench on the right and scraggly tree on the left.* NURSE BENSON
strides on. NURSE HEDGES *follows, pushing a medical cart.*

NURSE BENSON: Hello. Ruth Benson, R.N., here. At ease. Let's get
one thing perfectly straight before we begin. I am your friend. No
matter what happens, I am your friend. So is Nurse Hedges.
(NURSE HEDGES *smiles.*) But you know something? You are your
own best friend. Think that one over. I'll say the bell tolls. It tolls
for all of us. Welcome to Dunelawn. Shall we begin? (*She claps
her hands.*) Bruno! (BRUNO *wheels in* MR. PONCE *in a wheelchair.*
BRUNO *is a horror;* MR. PONCE *is a crabby old man.*) Good morning, Bruno. Put him over there. Facing the sun! That's right,
Bruno. Thank you, Bruno. Now go and get Mr. Blum.

BRUNO: (*Looking/leering/lusting at* NURSE HEDGES.) I'm supposed
to mow the lawn.

BENSON: After you've brought everyone out here you can do that.

BRUNO: (*Still leering at* NURSE HEDGES.) Dr. Toynbee says I'm supposed to mow.

BENSON: You can mow later, Bruno, mow all day.

BRUNO: (*Taking a swig of whiskey from his hip flask.*) Mow and
trim the hedges. All the hedges need trimming, Dr. Toynbee says.

(*Provocatively, to* HEDGES.) It's going to be a hot one. A real scorcher all right.

BENSON: Bruno!

BRUNO: I'm going, Benson, don't wet your pants. (*He turns to go, then turns back to* HEDGES.) Hey! (NURSE HEDGES *looks at him.*) Hubba hubba! (*He winks, leers, laughs, exits.*)

BENSON: Ugh! (*Then, clapping her hands.*) Well, Mr. Ponce! Good morning, Mr. Ponce! How are we feeling today?

MR. PONCE: What do you think?

BENSON: I think you're feeling one hundred per cent better, that's what I think!

MR. PONCE: Who asked you?

BENSON: Maybe you don't realize it, Mr. Ponce, but you are.

MR. PONCE: I want a drink.

BENSON: I didn't hear that.

PONCE: I want a drink!

BENSON: (*At a sound from* NURSE HEDGES.) What is it, Hedges? You'll have to speak up, dear.

NURSE HEDGES: Are we using serum?

BENSON: Yes, serum! Of course, serum! (*The two nurses busy themselves at the medical cart during the following.*)

PONCE: Liquor! Liquor! I want liquor!

BENSON: Honestly, Becky, I don't know what's gotten into you lately.

HEDGES: I'm sorry.

PONCE: I want a drink, somebody!

BENSON: You're sniveling again, Hedges.

HEDGES: I am?

PONCE: Will somebody please get me a good stiff drink?

BENSON: I'll cure you of that if it's the last thing I do.

HEDGES: I don't mean to snivel. I don't want to snivel. I just do it I guess.

PONCE: I need a drink. I must have a drink!

BENSON: Well we'll soon put a stop to that.

HEDGES: You're so good to me, Ruth!

BENSON: I know. Syringe, please.

PONCE: I don't want to stop! I like to drink! It's all a terrible mistake!

HEDGES: (*Admiringly, while* BENSON *prepares to administer the injection.*) No, I mean it. You're really interested in my welfare. I'm so used to women being catty and bitchy to one another, I can't believe I've found a friend who's deeply and truly concerned about me.

PONCE: How much do you want, Benson? How much cold, hard cash?

BENSON: It's called love, Becky.

HEDGES: I guess it is.

PONCE: Look at me, Benson, I'm making a cash offer.

BENSON: Good old-fashioned l-o-v-e.

HEDGES: Well I appreciate it.

PONCE: Where's Toynbee? Get me Toynbee!

BENSON: You're turning into a wonderful, warm, desirable woman, Hedges.

HEDGES: Thanks to you.

BENSON: Oh pooh! (MR. PONCE *sees that she is about to stick him with the needle. He begins to yell and babble. He begins to jump up and down in the wheelchair as if he were strapped to it. His blanket falls off. He is! Also, he's wearing a straitjacket.*)

PONCE: Goddamn it, I want a drink and I want it now! I want a drink! I won't calm down until I get a drink! (*He's making quite a racket and carrying on like a wild caged beast.* BENSON *stays in control.* HEDGES *panics.*)

BENSON: Mr. Ponce! I'm not going to give you this injection as long as you keep that up. You're just wasting your time.

HEDGES: Do you want me to get help?

BENSON: I didn't hear that, Hedges.

HEDGES: I'm sorry.

BENSON: And don't start sniveling again.

HEDGES: So good to me!

BENSON: I'll have to report this to Dr. Toynbee, Mr. Ponce. I'm sorry, but my hands are tied. (DR. TOYNBEE *strolls on. He has sad, benign eyes and a smile to match.* MR. PONCE *immediately quiets down at the sight of him and hangs his head in shame.)* Good morning, Dr. Toynbee.

HEDGES: *(Almost a little curtsey.)* Good morning, Dr. Toynbee. (DR. TOYNBEE *smiles, nods and looks at* MR. PONCE.)

BENSON: Doctor, I think Mr. Ponce wants to leave Dunelawn.

PONCE: No!

BENSON: I don't think he deserves to be here. I'd say he's abused that privilege. (BENSON *unfastens the straps that hold* PONCE *to the wheelchair.)*

PONCE: I'm sorry. I don't know what came over me.

BENSON: Get up.

PONCE: It was a temporary relapse, Doctor. I'm so ashamed, believe me, it won't happen again.

BENSON: *(Letting him out of the straitjacket.)* There's a long line of decent, honorable people waiting to get in here, Mr. Ponce. A very long line. And I think you'd better step right to the end of it. Well go ahead, you're free to leave now.

PONCE: I can't look at you, Dr. Toynbee, I'm so ashamed.

BENSON: No one asked you to come here and no one's keeping you.

PONCE: Don't look at me like that, Dr. Toynbee!

BENSON: He said he wanted a drink. He demanded one, in fact. He even tried to bribe me, Doctor. (TOYNBEE, *his eyes never off* PONCE, *sadly shakes his head.)* Naturally I refused. So did Nurse Hedges.

HEDGES: *(Almost curtseying again.)* Yes, yes I did, Dr. Toynbee.

BENSON: Fortunately he revealed his true colors before I was able to administer the syringe. I'll have Bruno pack your things at once, Mr. Ponce. You'll find your statement in the check-out office. You won't be charged for today, of course. Now should they call your wife and family to come and get you or would you prefer the limousine service?

PONCE: Benson, wait, please!

BENSON: Dr. Toynbee is a very busy man, Mr. Ponce. Your wife and family or the limousine?

PONCE: I'm not leaving. I won't let you throw me out like this. You're sending me straight back to the gin mills if you kick me out of here. I'm not ready to leave yet. I'm not strong enough.

BENSON: Dr. Toynbee's heard all this, Mr. Ponce.

PONCE: (*Putting the straitjacket back on.*) Look, look, see how much I want to stay?

BENSON: Take that off, Mr. Ponce.

PONCE: (*To* HEDGES.) Fasten me up, fasten me up!

HEDGES: Dr. Toynbee?

PONCE: The straps, the straps, just fasten the straps.

HEDGES: (*Moved.*) Poor Mr. Ponce.

BENSON: I wouldn't do that, Hedges.

HEDGES: Dr. Toynbee? (TOYNBEE, *slowly, sadly, benignly, nods his head.* HEDGES *buckles* MR. PONCE *up in the straitjacket.*)

PONCE: Thank you, Doctor, thank you! (*He would like to thank* DR. TOYNBEE, *but now, of course, there is no way to do it.*) I'll be good, I'll be better! You'll see, you'll see! This will never happen again. Come on, Benson, you heard the doctor!

BENSON: Surely, Doctor, you're not going to . . . ? (*Again* TOYNBEE *nods his head.*) That man is a saint.

PONCE: God bless him.

BENSON: Dr. Toynbee is a saint.

PONCE: I am so grateful and so happy.

BENSON: A saint!

PONCE: I could kiss his hand for this. (*He tries to, and can't.*)

BENSON: Should I proceed with the injection, Doctor? (DR. TOYNBEE *smiles and nods.*) Hedges. (HEDGES *helps her prepare another syringe as* DR. TOYNBEE *moves to* MR. PONCE *and stands directly behind him. He looks down at him, puts one hand on each shoulder and fixes him with a sad and solemn stare.*)

PONCE: I can't bear it when you look at me like that. You're so good, Doctor, so good! I know how rotten I am. But someday I'll be able to look you in the eye. I'll make you proud of me. I'll make me proud of me. I don't want to be me anymore. (DR. TOYNBEE *smiles and bends down to* MR. PONCE's *ear. When he does finally speak, it is totally unintelligible gibberish.*) You're so right, Doctor! Everything you say is so right! (TOYNBEE *turns to go.*) God bless you.

BENSON: Thank you, Dr. Toynbee!

HEDGES: Thank you, Dr. Toynbee!

BENSON: Goodbye, Dr. Toynbee!

HEDGES: Goodbye, Dr. Toynbee! (TOYNBEE *acknowledges them with a wave of the hand and strolls off.*) What a wonderful man he is.

BENSON: That man is a saint.

HEDGES: And so good.

BENSON: Why can't we all be like him?

HEDGES: How do you mean?

BENSON: Perfect.

PONCE: Please, Benson, hurry up.

HEDGES: I think you're perfect, Ruth.

BENSON: You're sweet.

HEDGES: You are.

BENSON: Not really. And certainly not like Dr. Toynbee.

PONCE: Come on, Benson, before I get another attack.

BENSON: Do you realize he has absolutely no faults? Absolutely none.

HEDGES: No wonder he seems so good.

BENSON: He's perfect, Becky. I don't see why I can't get you to understand that. He has no place left to go.

PONCE: My hands, Benson, they're starting to shake!

BENSON: Dr. Toynbee wasn't born perfect. He worked on it and there he is.

HEDGES: You make it sound so easy.

BENSON: Take it from me, Becky, it isn't.

HEDGES: You're telling me.

BENSON: You're making wonderful progress.

PONCE: Oh my God, I'm starting to hallucinate.

HEDGES: Any progress I'm making is entirely thanks to you, I hope you know.

PONCE: A jeroboam of Bombay Gin!

HEDGES: I don't want to be perfect, Ruth, I know I never could be. Not like you.

BENSON: Oh pooh, Becky, just pooh!

PONCE: I'm salivating, Benson. Have you no mercy?

BENSON: Hang on there, Mr. Ponce, just hang on there another second.

PONCE: I'm going fast. I . . . I . . . I want a drink. I want a drink! *I want a drink!!!* (BENSON *sticks him with the needle.*) I . . . I . . .

BENSON: Now what did you just say you wanted, Mr. Ponce?

PONCE: (*A beatific smile spreading across his face.*) I don't want anything!

BENSON: Let's fix your chair now, so you get the sun.

PONCE: Yes, that would be nice, miss. Thank you, thank you.

BENSON: (*As she makes* PONCE *more comfortable.*) I pity your type, Mr. Ponce. Two martinis before dinner, wine with, a cordial after, and a couple of scotch on the rocks night caps. Social drinking, you call it. Rummies, I say, every last one of you.

PONCE: (*A long, contented sigh.*) Aaaaaaaaaaah!

BENSON: All right now?

PONCE: I don't want anything. Any bad thing.

BENSON: Good for you.

PONCE: I'm going to make it, Benson. I'm going to be all right. (*His head falls over.*)

BENSON: Of course you are. And if you want anything, I'll be right over . . . (*She takes his head and points it towards the medical cart.*) . . . there.

PONCE: No, miss, I don't want a thing. (BENSON *tiptoes over to* HEDGES.)

BENSON: Whew!

HEDGES: I admire you so much!

BENSON: Becky Hedges!

HEDGES: You can help me to get rid of my faults until you're blue in the face, but I'll never be the beauty you are.

BENSON: You're an adorable person, Becky.

HEDGES: I'm not talking about adorable. I'm talking about beauty. No one ever told Elizabeth Taylor she was adorable.

BENSON: Do I have to say it? Beauty is skin deep. Besides, Elizabeth has a lot of faults.

HEDGES: You're changing the subject. Ruth, look at me.

BENSON: Yes?

HEDGES: Now tell me this is a beautiful woman you see.

BENSON: What are you driving at, Becky?

HEDGES: Nothing. I just wish I were beautiful like you. And I don't want you to just *say* I am.

BENSON: I wouldn't do that to you.

HEDGES: Thank you.

BENSON: I said you were adorable.

HEDGES: And I said you were beautiful.

BENSON: It's out of my hands.

HEDGES: It's out of mine, too.

BENSON: You're sniveling again.

HEDGES: I know.

BENSON: (*She pulls* HEDGES *over to the bench and sits her down.*) Becky, listen to me. You think I'm beautiful. Thank you. I can accept a compliment. I know I'm beautiful. I can't lie to myself anymore. But what good did it do me as far as Hugh Gumbs was concerned?

HEDGES: Such a beautiful name!

BENSON: There you go again, Becky.

HEDGES: I didn't snivel that time.

BENSON: You made a stupid, flattering, self-serving, Minnie Mouse remark, which is much worse. Hugh Gumbs is not a beautiful name and you know it.

HEDGES: I'm sorry. I'll be good. I'll be better. Finish your story.

BENSON: I don't even remember where I was.

HEDGES: You were talking about your beauty and how little good it did you as far as Hugh Gumbs was concerned.

BENSON: That man wouldn't even look at me. Looks had nothing to do with it. I know that now. Ask Hugh Gumbs! And I know I'm more beautiful than that hussy he abandoned me for. In my heart of hearts, I know that Mildred Canby is not a beautiful woman.

HEDGES: Mildred who?

BENSON: Mildred Canby.

HEDGES: What a horrible name, too.

BENSON: Attractive, yes. Beautiful, no. Now what Hugh Gumbs wanted in a woman, what every man wants in any woman, is something deeper than beauty. He wants character. He wants the traditional virtues. He wants womanly warmth.

HEDGES: You can say that again.

BENSON: Believe me, Hugh Gumbs is a very unhappy man right now. How could he not be? Mildred Canby had even less character and more faults than I did. And less beauty, too. I knew that marriage wouldn't last. (*She takes out her compact.*)

HEDGES: Don't cry, Ruth.

BENSON: Me? Cry? Why should I cry?

HEDGES: Because you lost Hugh?

BENSON: I'm grateful to him! He broke my heart, I don't deny it, but if it hadn't been for Hugh I would never have been forced into the soul-searching and self-reevaluation that ended up with the 118-pound, trim-figured woman you say is so beautiful standing in front of you. No, when I think back on Ruth Benson then and compare her to Ruth Benson now, I thank my lucky stars for Hugh.

HEDGES: (*As* BENSON *continues to gaze at herself in the compact mirror.*) You're so wise, Ruth.

BENSON: Am I?

HEDGES: Wise about love.

BENSON: I wonder.

HEDGES: You are.

BENSON: We'll see.

HEDGES: I'm not.

BENSON: (*Still distracted.*) Hmmmmmmmm?

HEDGES: Wise about love. I'm downright dumb about it. If I weren't, I'd be married to Tim Taylor right this very minute. What I wouldn't give for another chance at him!

BENSON: (*Regaining herself.*) Buck up, Hedges.

HEDGES: Oh I will, Ruth. I'm just feeling a little sorry for myself. I don't know why. If you want to know the truth, I haven't thought of Tim Taylor one way or the other for a long time.

BENSON: I should hope not. A man who smokes is a very bad emotional risk.

HEDGES: Tim didn't smoke.

BENSON: But he drank. It's the same thing. Rummies, every last one of them.

HEDGES: Did Hugh Gumbs drink?

BENSON: Among other things.

HEDGES: It must have been awful for you.

BENSON: It was heck. Sheer unadulterated heck.

HEDGES: That sounds funny.

BENSON: Believe me, it wasn't.

HEDGES: No, what you just said. About it being heck. I'm still used to people saying the other.

BENSON: It won't seem funny after a while. You'll see. (DR. TOYNBEE *strolls across the stage, smiling benignly, reading a book.*) Good morning, Dr. Toynbee!

HEDGES: Good morning, Dr. Toynbee! (*To* BENSON.) That man is so good, Ruth!

BENSON: I worship the ground he walks on.

HEDGES: Oh me, too, me, too! I'd give anything to be just like him.

BENSON: Goodbye, Dr. Toynbee! And thank you!

HEDGES: Goodbye, Dr. Toynbee! And thank you! (DR. TOYNBEE *exits down the aisle, waving.*) Ruth?

BENSON: What?

HEDGES: I know it's none of my business, but I've seen that look in your eyes whenever Dr. Toynbee passes.

BENSON: What look?

HEDGES: You know.

BENSON: The only look, as you put it, in my eyes when Dr. Toynbee passes is one of sheer and utter respect. Certainly not the look you're so grossly alluding to. You're out of line, don't you think. Hedges? You're certainly in extremely bad taste.

HEDGES: You're not sweet on the good doctor?

BENSON: Dr. Toynbee is above that.

HEDGES: I know but are you? (BENSON *slaps her.*) Is any woman? (BENSON *slaps her again and they fall into each other's arms crying.*) I'm sorry, Ruth, I didn't mean to hurt you. You've been so good to me! I'm such a different person since I've been with you! I don't even know who I am anymore and I say these silly, dreadful, awful things! I don't recognize myself in the mirror in the morning. I've changed so much it scares me.

BENSON: You haven't changed. You've improved, refined, what was already there. I always had this figure, don't you see? Even when I weighed all that weight, I still had this figure.

HEDGES: Even when you were up to 230?

BENSON: I was never 230.

HEDGES: You told me you were . . .

BENSON: I was never 230! Now shut up and listen, will you?

HEDGES: I'm sorry, Ruth.

BENSON: I didn't change anything. Mr. Ponce over there isn't changing. He's only emerging, with our help and Dr. Toynbee's, into what he really and truly was in the first place: a non-drinker.

PONCE: A rum swizzle!

BENSON: People are born without any faults, they simply fall into bad habits along life's way. Nobody's trying to *change* anybody, Becky. It's the real them coming out, that's all.

HEDGES: The real them!

BENSON: Look, face it, you've got big thighs, that's the real you. Now I've got nice thighs, as it turns out, but I didn't always know that.

HEDGES: I don't think I can get any thinner.

BENSON: I'm not talking about diets. I'm talking about the real you and your G.D. big thighs!

HEDGES: That's exactly what Tim Taylor didn't like about me. And now that I'm getting thinner they look even bigger. I *know!* I'm sniveling again! I don't know what to do about them, Ruth! (*She is desperately hitting her thighs.*)

BENSON: Wear longer skirts!

HEDGES: Now you really are cross with me!

BENSON: You can be so dense sometimes. I mean really, Hedges, I'm talking about a whole other thing and you start sniveling about diets. You can diet all you want and you're still going to end up with big thighs. That's not the point.

HEDGES: What is it, then?

BENSON: Oh there's no point in talking to you about it!

HEDGES: I'm sorry.

BENSON: And stop that horrible sniveling!

HEDGES: I'm never going to get any better. I have just as many bad habits as when I came here. We just keep pretending I'm improving when the real truth is, I'm getting worse! (*She races to the medical cart and hysterically prepares one of the syringes.*)

BENSON: What are you doing?

HEDGES: Why shouldn't I? I'm no better than any one of them and I'm supposed to work here!

BENSON: Give me that! (*They struggle.*)

HEDGES: Let me do it, Ruth!

BENSON: Have you lost your mind?

HEDGES: I wish I was dead! (BENSON *topples* HEDGES, *who falls in a heap, and takes away the syringe. Almost without realizing, she reaches inside her blouse and takes a package of cigarettes out of her bosom, puts one in her mouth and strikes a match.* HEDGES *raises her head at the sound.*) Ruth!

BENSON: (*Realizing what she has done.*) Oh my God. I wasn't thinking!

HEDGES: You of all people!

BENSON: I wasn't going to smoke one!

HEDGES: It's a full pack.

BENSON: It's a courtesy pack. In case I run into someone. They're not mine. I've given it up. I swear to God I have. You've got to believe me.

HEDGES: I don't know what to think.

BENSON: Becky, please!

HEDGES: If you say so, Ruth. (BRUNO *enters pushing* MR. BLUM *in a wheelchair.*)

BENSON: It took you long enough!

BRUNO: I suppose it did. Where do you want her?

BENSON: (*Pointedly.*) Him. I want *him* over there. Facing the sun, next to Mr. Ponce. That's where I want *him*, Bruno. And then when you've put him there, I want you to bring out Mr. Yamadoro. And I want you to do it quickly this time.

BRUNO: I told you I was supposed to mow.

BENSON: We know, Bruno.

BRUNO: Mow and trim me some hedges. Hey! (*He gives* HEDGES *his hubba hubba leer.*)

BENSON: You're a beast, Bruno.

BRUNO: (*To* HEDGES.) You got a light, baby?

HEDGES: No!

BRUNO: You, dog face?

BENSON: You know I don't. Matches and all other smoking paraphernalia are strictly forbidden here.

BRUNO: (*Taking out a hip flask.*) Yeah?

BENSON: So is alcohol.

BRUNO: No shit. (BRUNO *downs a swig.*)

BENSON: The only reason Dr. Toynbee allows them to you is to set an example to the guests here. A bad example. On a human self-improvement ten scale, you rate about a minus fifty. You're a walking, sub-human nightmare, Bruno.

BRUNO: (*For* HEDGES' *benefit.*) Sure is a hot one coming on. A real scorcher.

BENSON: Must you, Bruno?

BRUNO: Must I what?

BENSON: Stand there like that?

BRUNO: (*To* HEDGES.) Now she don't like the way I stand.

BENSON: It's deliberately provocative.

BRUNO: What is that supposed to mean?

BENSON: Only you're about as provocative to a woman as a can full of worms. Now either get Mr. Yamadoro out here or I'll report you to Dr. Toynbee.

BRUNO: I'm going, Benson. Hold your bowels. (*He doesn't move. He is trying to think.*) What you said about a can full of worms . . . I got desires. That's all I know, I got desires and I like to do 'em. (*He goes.* HEDGES *curiously starts to follow.* BENSON *claps her hands, and* HEDGES *joins her.*)

BENSON: Good morning, Mr. Blum! How are we feeling today? Doesn't that sun feel good on you? And that delicious breeze from the ocean! And listen to those birds chirp! It's a day like this that makes you wish summer lasted all year! (*As she chatters away, she is preparing a syringe for* MR. BLUM.) When I was a little girl, we spent our summers in Vermont and my brothers and I used to go swimming in a little pond!

MR. BLUM: Your cap, Benson. (*It's a gently desperate plea.*)

BENSON: Hmmmmmm?

BLUM: Please. Just let me wear your cap. I won't hurt it. I'll just sit here and wear it. I won't say a word.

BENSON: Mr. Blum, I thought you were improving!

BLUM: I am, Benson, I swear to God I am! I just want to wear your cap for a little while. What's wrong with that? It doesn't mean anything. It's just a cap. I mean it's not like I asked to wear your skirt or your shoes or your stockings or anything! I'm all over that. A man could wear a cap like yours without it meaning anything.

BENSON: Does Dr. Toynbee know this?

BLUM: Are you crazy? Of course not!

BENSON: I'll have to tell him.

BLUM: It's not what you're thinking!

BENSON: We were all so proud of the progress you were making!

BLUM: As well you should be! I'm proud, too! Benson, I haven't been in full drag in six weeks! You know what I was like when Martha brought me here. You've seen how I've changed. You couldn't force me at gunpoint to put your shoes on.

BENSON: (*Immediately suspicious.*) My shoes?

BLUM: *Yes, your shoes!* Don't torment me like this! Your cap, Benson, it's all I'm asking for. Stop me before I want more.

BENSON: It's out of the question, Mr. Blum.

BLUM: I want that cap! I need that cap! I'm begging you for that cap!

BENSON: Forget the cap! The cap is out!

BLUM: Five minutes, Benson, have a heart!

BENSON: Five minutes with the cap and next it will be the shoes and then the skirt and you'll be right back where you started. I know your kind, Mr. Blum.

BLUM: (*Bitterly.*) Do you, Benson?

BENSON: Give them a cap and they want your panty hose!

BLUM: What of it?

BENSON: You're here to change, not get worse! Think of your wife!

BLUM: What of her? I can't wear a size eight!

BENSON: Then think of your daughters.

BLUM: They're goddamn pygmies, too! I'm surrounded by stunted women.

BENSON: Do you know what they call people like you?

BLUM: Fashionable!

BENSON: You're a man, Mr. Blum, you were meant to dress like one!

BLUM: You're not God, Benson, don't you tell me how to dress!

BENSON: (*Holding back the syringe from him.*) I don't have to take that from you, Blum!

BLUM: What do you know about it?

BENSON: If you persist in defying me . . . !

BLUM: What does any woman know about it?

BENSON: Not only will I withhold this syringe . . . !

BLUM: Garter belts, Benson.

BENSON: I will fill out a report . . . !

BLUM: Merry widows!

BENSON: And give it to Dr. Toynbee!

BLUM: Black net stockings! Red garters, strapless tops! Sequins!

BENSON: All right for you, Blum, all right for you! (*She starts out.*)

BLUM: Picture hats! That's right, Benson, you heard me, picture hats! (DR. TOYNBEE *strolls on.*)

BENSON: Good morning, Dr. Toynbee.

HEDGES: Good morning, Dr. Toynbee! (DR. TOYNBEE *smiles and nods.*)

BENSON: I want you to see something, Doctor.

BLUM: (*Head bowed, suddenly mortified.*) Please, Benson, don't. (BENSON *begins to take off her cap.* BLUM *watches in growing terror.* TOYNBEE *looks at* BLUM *with such a great sadness.*) Benson, don't do this to me, not in front of him. Please. I beg of you. I'll change. I swear I'll change!

BENSON: He asked to wear my cap, Doctor. I think he should wear it. (*She puts the hat on his head.* BLUM *writhes and twists in his straitjacket in the wheelchair as if he were on fire.*)

BLUM: No! No! Take it off! Take it off! (*As* BLUM *writhes and screams,* TOYNBEE *takes out his handkerchief and dabs at his eyes. Even* HEDGES *cries.*)

BENSON: You've made Dr. Toynbee cry, Mr. Blum. I just hope you're pleased with yourself.

HEDGES: I can't watch, Ruth.

BENSON: (*Shielding her.*) It's all right, Becky, it's going to be all right.

HEDGES: To see the poor doctor cry!

BENSON: Sshh, sshh! Dr. Toynbee's here now. Everything will be all right. (DR. TOYNBEE *slowly dries his eyes, puts away the handkerchief, and goes to* BLUM.) Look Becky! (TOYNBEE *takes the cap off* BLUM. *At once,* BLUM *is silent and hangs his head.* TOYNBEE *stands looking down at him.*) That man is a saint. (TOYNBEE *hands the cap back to* BENSON, *then turns and talks to* BLUM. *Again we can't understand his gibberish.*) Dr. Toynbee has that rare spiritual quality that when he just looks at you with those clear grey eyes of his you suddenly feel so ashamed of yourself you could just vomit.

HEDGES: Such a good man! (*Now* BLUM *is the one who is crying.* TOYNBEE *asks for the syringe with a gesture.* BENSON *gives it to him and he injects* BLUM. BENSON *wheels* BLUM *next to* PONCE, *who is beginning to stir restlessly.*)

PONCE: (*Very slurred.*) Bartender! I'll have a perfect Rob Roy on the rocks. I want a little service here, bartender!

BENSON: Doctor . . . ? (TOYNBEE *smiles benignly and nods his head. He motions to* HEDGES *that she should administer the shot.*)

HEDGES: Me, Doctor . . . ? (TOYNBEE *smiles at her and nods his head.* HEDGES *approaches* PONCE *with a syringe.*)

PONCE: Make it a double Dewar's on the rocks and hold the ice. (HEDGES *looks to* TOYNBEE *for encouragement. He smiles and nods his head. She injects* PONCE.) Ouch!

BENSON: (*Sharply.*) Hedges!

PONCE: Goddamn mosquitos!

HEDGES: He moved! (TOYNBEE *prevents* BENSON *from helping* HEDGES *out with a benign "Let her do it" gesture.* HEDGES *administers the syringe with no little difficulty.* PONCE *smiles blissfully.*) I did it, Ruth!

BENSON: We saw you, Hedges.

HEDGES: I really did it, all by myself! Doctor? (TOYNBEE *smiles and nods and begins to stroll off.*)

BENSON: Thank you, Dr. Toynbee!

HEDGES: Thank you, Dr. Toynbee!

BENSON: Goodbye, Dr. Toynbee!

HEDGES: Goodbye, Dr. Toynbee! (*Spinning herself around.*) Oh, Ruth, Ruth, Ruth!

BENSON: Calm down, Hedges, it was only an injection.

HEDGES: (*Still spinning.*) He's so tremendously, terrifically and terribly good!

BENSON: You're not telling me anything about him I already didn't know. Now give a hand here, will you?

HEDGES: And you know something else? I'm a little sweet on the good doctor myself! (*She is still spinning and singing and dancing when* BENSON *slaps her.*)

BENSON: Snap off of it, Hedges!

HEDGES: I'm sorry. You were right to do that. I'm not even worthy to mention his name. Who am I to think Dr. Toynbee even knows I'm alive? I'm dirt, Ruth. Next to him, I'm dirt.

BENSON: Well . . .

HEDGES: Don't deny it. I know what I am. I've got big thighs and I'm dirt.

BENSON: You're too rough on yourself, Hedges.

HEDGES: I have to be if I'm ever going to get rid of my faults and be like you!

BENSON: I won't say "Don't aim too high, Becky" . . . how could I? But I will say "Don't aim too high too soon."

HEDGES: (*Hugging her.*) Why are you so good to me? Everyone at Dunelawn is so good to me!

BENSON: Because we all love you and want to see you reach your full potential.

HEDGES: Zero defects.

BENSON: That's right, Becky, zero defects. No faults, no failings, no fantasy. It's a beautiful goal.

HEDGES: It sounds religious when you say it. With me it just sounds hopeless.

BENSON: Mark my word, Rebecca Hedges, R.N., the day you become perfect will be the most important day in your life.

HEDGES: It will?

BENSON: Mark my words. (BRUNO *wheels in* MR. YAMADORO *in a wheelchair. He, too, is straitjacketed and fastened down.*)

BRUNO: Okay, Benson, that's the Webster Hall lot. Where do you want him?

BENSON: Over there, Bruno.

BRUNO: Hey! (HEDGES *looks at him.*) Hubba hubba!

BENSON: Thank you, Bruno. You can go now.

BRUNO: Who says I was talking to you?

BENSON: Aren't you supposed to mow now?

BRUNO: Maybe.

HEDGES: Mow and trim some hedges.

BENSON: Don't talk to that man.

BRUNO: That's right, pussycat. Mow and trim me some hedges.

BENSON: Then do it, Bruno.

BRUNO: Don't burst your bladder, Benson, I'm going. And don't think I ain't forgot that can of worms, horse-face.

BENSON: Bruno!

BRUNO: Stick around, kid. (HEDGES *looks at him. He winks, leers.*) Yes sir, a good hot day to trim me some hedges. (*He saunters off.*)

HEDGES: The way he keeps saying that gives me the creeps. You'd think he meant me. (*She shudders.*) Jeepers creepers!

BENSON: Good morning, Mr. Yamadoro.

HEDGES: Ruth!

BENSON: What?

HEDGES: (*Referring to her charts.*) That's not Mr. Yamadoro . . . ! (BENSON *pushes her away from* MR. YAMADORO, *furious.*) But it's not. It's Mr. Luparelli. Vincenzo Luparelli, Ithaca, New York. It says so right here.

BENSON: He likes to be called Mr. Yamadoro. That's the reason he's here.

HEDGES: I'm sorry. I forgot.

BENSON: You forget everything! (*She turns back to* MR. YAMADORO.) Good morning. Mr. Yamadoro, how are we feeling today? Any improvement?

MR. YAMADORO: Much better, thank you, Nurse.

BENSON: What about your urges?

YAMADORO: You mean . . . ? (*He lowers his eyes, blushes.*) . . . I can't say it.

BENSON: Yes or no? (YAMADORO *shakes his head "No."*) Isn't that wonderful! Did you hear that, Becky? Mr. Yamadoro feels he's improving!

HEDGES: (*In all innocence.*) That's what they all say.

BENSON: Watch your step, Hedges.

HEDGES: Well, how come none of them ever seems to get any better? (BENSON *slaps her and takes her aside.*)

BENSON: Don't ever say that again!

HEDGES: But they don't. (BENSON *slaps her again.*)

BENSON: Don't ever even think it! (*She is shaking* HEDGES.) Dr. Toynbee knows what he's doing. It's not his fault if his patients don't.

HEDGES: I'm sorry. I just never looked at it like that.

BENSON: Well maybe it's high time you did.

HEDGES: (*Still being shaken.*) Now you're really, really cross with me!

BENSON: A word against Dr. Toynbee and what he's trying to do here is a slap in my face!

YAMADORO: Slap! (*He giggles.*)

BENSON: Now look what you've done. You've excited him. (*Indeed,* YAMADORO *has been vibrating with pleasure ever since this outbreak of violence of theirs.* BENSON *goes to him,* HEDGES *following.*) Now calm down, Mr. Yamadoro.

YAMADORO: You hit her. You hit her. Good for you, Benson, good for you!

BENSON: I didn't hit her, Mr. Yamadoro.

YAMADORO: You slap her then.

BENSON: No one slapped anyone.

YAMADORO: (*Calming down.*) They didn't?

BENSON: Did they, Nurse Hedges?

HEDGES: Oh no.

BENSON: What you saw may have looked like a slap but it wasn't.

HEDGES: Why would anyone want to slap me, Mr. Yamadoro?

BENSON: Sshh! You'll provoke him again!

YAMADORO: Impossible! It was nothing, nothing at all. A momentary relapse. My urges all are gone, my desires now like water.

BENSON: Pain, Mr. Yamadoro? You're not thinking about pain?

HEDGES: Now *you* are, Ruth!

BENSON: I have to find out!

YAMADORO: Pain? There is no such thing.

BENSON: But in your fantasies? Come on, you can tell Benson.

YAMADORO. I'm over all that.

BENSON: Are you? Imagine, imagine Mr. Yamadoro, a beautiful, voluptuous woman . . . blonde, why not? . . . and she is at your mercy.

HEDGES: Ruth!

BENSON: I know what I'm doing!

YAMADORO: So far nothing.

BENSON: She looks at you, the tears streaming down her cheeks, the drug you've given her has begun to wear off, she's your prisoner and she can't escape. She sees your glowing slit eyes fixed on her fingernails. You want to pull them off, don't you, Mr. Yamadoro? One by one! (*Aside to* HEDGES.) The fingernails, that's what they go for, these Jap sadists.

YAMADORO: (*Non-plussed.*) Continue.

BENSON: (*More and more graphically.*) Aaaaaiiiiieeeeeeee! She screams. Aaaaaaiiiieeeeee! Again and again! But you are implacable. Your cruelty knows no bounds. Your lust is insatiable. (*Angry aside to* HEDGES.) Don't just stand there, Hedges, help me out!

Hedges: Aaaaaaiiiiieeeeee!

BENSON: But the room is sound-proofed and her bonds hold fast. Every exquisite torment the Oriental mind has devised you visit upon her helpless, quivering, palpable flesh.

HEDGES: Aaaaaaiiiiieeeeee!

BENSON: There is no mercy, God is dead, and Satan reigns triumphant!

HEDGES: Aaaaaaiiiiieeeeee!

BENSON: (*Savagely.*) Well, Mr. Yamadoro?

YAMADORO: (*Quietly.*) I feel a strange calmness over me. All human desires and passions spent. I desire nothing of the flesh.

BENSON: (*Triumphantly.*) You see?

HEDGES: He really does seem better.

YAMADORO: I really am, missy.

BENSON: Of course he is. (*They start to prepare a syringe.*)

YAMADORO: Dr. Toynbee is a saint.

BENSON: Back to work, Hedges.

YAMADORO: (*To* PONCE *and* BLUM.) Don't tell Benson, but I just had an orgasm. (*He giggles.*)

BENSON: Can you manage this one yourself, too?

HEDGES: I think so.

BENSON: Good girl.

HEDGES: Thanks to you. (HEDGES *moves in close to inject* YAMADORO. *He tries to bite her. She screams.*) Mr. Yamadoro, I thought we were over all that!

YAMADORO: It's never over! (*He is violent in the chair.*)

BENSON: Give me that. (*She takes the syringe, grabs him in an armlock, and injects him.*) This'll hold him.

YAMADORO: (*A long moan.*) Mamma Mia! (BENSON *and* HEDGES *begin readjusting the wheelchairs. All three patients smile out at us seraphically.*)

BENSON: Look at them. Like babies now. It's a beautiful sight.

HEDGES: Everyone should take Dr. Toynbee's serum. Then the whole world would be perfect. No wars, no greed, no sex. No nothing. (BRUNO *enters with a letter from the office.*)

BENSON: Mr. Ponce, Mr. Blum and Mr. Yamadoro are going to be all right, Becky. It's only the Brunos of this world that are hopeless.

BRUNO: Hey, you in the white dress with the bird's legs!

HEDGES: I feel good just looking at them like this.

BRUNO: You want this, tight ass? (*He shows the letter.*)

BENSON: You're looking at the future, Becky.

HEDGES: In our lifetime?

BENSON: (*Sadly shaking her head.*) I'm afraid we're just the pioneers.

BRUNO: Hey, ugly-puss, I'm supposed to give you this.

HEDGES: A perfect world with perfect people.

BENSON: Someone has to do it.

BRUNO: There's a new patient, dog-face!

BENSON: Well, why didn't you just say so?

BRUNO: I did! (BENSON *takes the papers from him, starts reading them over.* BRUNO *exits, but not before a little "Hey!" and a few silent leers towards* HEDGES.)

BENSON: Becky!

HEDGES: What is it, Ruth?

BENSON: I've been given another chance. Read this. I'm the luckiest woman alive. He's here. He's at Dunelawn. I've got him where I want him at last! Oh God!

HEDGES: Is it the same Hugh Gumbs?

BENSON: Do you know how many years I've waited for this moment? Hugh Gumbs wants to be a new person and I'll be the one helping him to mold his new self.

HEDGES: If I were you, I mean if this was Tim Taylor being admitted to Dunelawn, I wouldn't be standing here talking about it. I'd fly to him.

BENSON: But . . . (*Indicating the patients.*)

HEDGES: Go on. I can take care of everything.

BENSON: You're a doll.

HEDGES: Now it's my turn: oh pooh!

BENSON: What am I waiting for? Wish me luck!

HEDGES: Luck! (*They kiss.* BENSON *dashes off.* PONCE, BLUM *and* YAMADORO *are smiling.* HEDGES *goes to the cart, gets a book, and crosses to the bench. Reading:*) "A CRITIQUE OF PURE REASON" by Immanuel Kant. (BRUNO *sticks his head up over the wall and whistles softly.*) "To Becky, with all my love, Ruth Benson, R.N." So good to me! (BRUNO *whistles again.* HEDGES *finally sees him.*) Please, Bruno, I'm trying to concentrate. It's difficult material.

BRUNO: I thought we'd never ditch horse-face.

HEDGES: We?

BRUNO: It's just you and me now, Hedges.

HEDGES: I don't know what you're talking about.

BRUNO: I seen you.

HEDGES: Seen me what?

BRUNO: Looking at me.

HEDGES: I never looked at you.

BRUNO: I'm provocative. You heard Benson.

HEDGES: Provocative as a can full of worms is what she said.

BRUNO: (*Climbing down from the wall and approaching her.*) Only it ain't what she meant, is it now?

HEDGES: I'm not speaking to you, Bruno.

BRUNO: Benson looks at me, too.

HEDGES: Don't be ridiculous.

BRUNO: I seen her.

HEDGES: Ruth Benson wouldn't look at you if you were the last man on earth.

BRUNO: Around this place, that's exactly what I am. What do you say, Hedges?

HEDGES: You mean . . . ?

BRUNO: I got a waterbed.

HEDGES: I don't care what you got. You're supposed to be mowing!

BRUNO: I'm done mowing.

HEDGES: Then trim some hedges! No, I didn't mean that. Stay back, Bruno. Don't come near me. I'll call Dr. Toynbee.

BRUNO: Toynbee looks at me, too.

HEDGES: Mr. Ponce! Mr. Ponce!

BRUNO: They all look at me.

HEDGES: (*Freeing* MR. PONCE *from his chair and jacket.*) You've got to help me, Mr. Ponce. He won't leave me alone. I'm frightened. I'll get you a case of liquor if you help me!

BRUNO: (*Exposing himself.*) Hubba, hubba, Hedges. (HEDGES *screams and frees* MR. BLUM.)

HEDGES: Mr. Blum, I'll let you wear my cap or anything you want of mine if you'll just listen to me a minute. You don't understand.

BRUNO: (*Exposing himself again.*) Twenty-three skiddo! (HEDGES *screams again, turns to* YAMADORO *and releases him, too.*)

HEDGES: Mr. Yamadoro, you've got to help me! You're the only one left. I'll let you hit me, if you'll just get up now.

YAMADORO: A strange inner peace has subdued the fires of my soul.

HEDGES: Oh shut up, you dumb Jap!

BRUNO: Your place or mine, toots? Let's go, sugar!

HEDGES: Help! Help! Help! (*She runs off.* BRUNO *goes after her.*)

PONCE: We're free.

BLUM: I know.

YAMADORO: Yes, yes, yes, yes, yes.

PONCE: I don't want to leave, though.

BLUM: (*Draping the sleeve of his straitjacket around him like a boa.*) Neither do I.

YAMADORO: Celestial harmonies ring in my ears.

BLUM: What does that mean?

YAMADORO: I don't know.

PONCE: I once drank twelve extra-dry Gordon's gin martinis in the Monkey Bar at the Hotel Elysee.

BLUM: You should have seen me at the Beaux Arts Ball that time I took first prize. I went as Anouk Aimée.

YAMADORO: Exquisite woman.

BLUM: Yes, yes.

PONCE: Never heard of her.

YAMADORO: Wonderful fingernails. (HEDGES *runs across, pursued by* BRUNO.)

HEDGES: Bruno the gardener is going to rape me and the three of you just sit there! Doesn't anybody care?

BRUNO: Hubba, hubba, Hedges! (*They are gone.*)

PONCE: I was so rotten when I was out there and over the wall.

BLUM: I could never find a pair of white heels that fit.

YAMADORO: Did I ever tell you gentlemen about Monique?

PONCE: I used to love to drink on Saturday. There's something about a Saturday.

BLUM: Do either of you realize what a really good dresser Nina Foch was?

YAMADORO: Monique was from Trenton. A lovely girl. (HEDGES *enters upstage and tiptoes down to the house.* BRUNO *suddenly appears from behind the hedge.*)

BRUNO: Hubba, hubba, Hedges! (HEDGES *screams as they run out down the aisle. From the back of the house, we hear a "Help!," then the ripping of cloth.*)

PONCE: It's nice here.

BLUM: Peaceful.

YAMADORO: I desire nothing now.

PONCE: Dr. Toynbee's serum.

BLUM: That man is a saint.

YAMADORO: Dunelawn is heaven on earth.

PONCE: I am so happy right now.

BLUM: We all are, Mr. Ponce.

YAMADORO: Life is beautiful.

PONCE: I can't stop smiling.

BLUM: And the sun smiles on us.

YAMADORO: And we smile back at it. (*He starts to sing, very softly —a World War I type campaign song is suggested.* BLUM *joins him. It becomes a duet in close harmony.* PONCE *just looks at them. When they finish, he speaks.*)

PONCE: I hate that song. (HEDGES *appears House Left.*)

HEDGES: What is it exactly that you want from me, Bruno? (BRUNO, *appearing House Right, responds.*)

BRUNO: Hubba, hubba, Hedges!

HEDGES: You'll regret this, Bruno, believe me, you won't be happy! (HEDGES *screams, and they both disappear.*)

PONCE: We really could leave now, you know.

BLUM: We'd just go back to what we were.

PONCE: You think so?

BLUM: I know.

YAMADORO: Oh, Monique! (*The three of them are really smiling now.*)

PONCE: A gin fizz with real New Orleans sloe gin. Disgusting.

BLUM: Fredericks of Hollywood. Revolting.

YAMADORO: Nina Foch spread-eagled. Hideous. (*This time it is* PONCE *who starts singing the song. The others join him for a short reprise as they each try to banish their private demon. They are just finishing when* BENSON *wheels in* HUGH GUMBS, *still wearing his bedraggled street clothes.*)

HUGH GUMBS: Aaaaaaaaaaaaaaa!

BENSON: Mr. Gumbs, please!

HUGH: Aaaaa!

BENSON: You must try to control yourself.

HUGH: Aaaaaaaaaaaa!

BENSON: You're disturbing the others!

HUGH: Aaaaaaaaaaaa!

BENSON: It's obvious you're in great distress, Mr. Gumbs, but surely . . .

HUGH: I'm desperate, Nurse. You name it and I've got it, done it or used it.

BENSON: As soon as I've gone over your forms . . .

HUGH: Couldn't I just have my injection first?

BENSON: In a moment, Mr. Gumbs.

HUGH: I don't know if I can hold out.

BENSON: (*Keeping her head down, looking at her charts.*) Smoking. Three packs a day.

HUGH: That's right, Nurse.

BENSON: That's a lot, Mr. Gumbs.

HUGH: I'm not even being honest with you. It's closer to five.

BENSON: Five packs?

HUGH: Six, seven, I don't know! Some nights I set my alarm and wake up at fifteen minute intervals and have a cigarette.

BENSON: Why?

HUGH: Why? Because that's how much I like to smoke! What kind of a question is that? Why? Why do people do anything? Because they like it! They like it!

BENSON: Even when it's bad for them?

HUGH: Yes! That's exactly why I'm here! I'm a liar. I'm a klepto-maniac. I chase women. I bite my nails. You've got to help me!

BENSON: Thank God, Hugh, thank God!

HUGH: What?

BENSON: (*Back to the forms.*) A terrible drinking problem.

HUGH: The worst.

BENSON: How much exactly?

HUGH: Bloody Mary's at breakfast, martinis before lunch . . .

BENSON: How many?

HUGH: Two, and three before dinner.

BENSON: Wine with your meals?

HUGH: No.

BENSON: Well that's something.

HUGH: Aquavit. And three or four cherry heerings after dinner and hot saki nightcaps; that's in the winter.

BENSON: In the summer?

HUGH: Cold saki.

BENSON: It sounds like you still have your drinking problem all right.

HUGH: Still?

BENSON: I mean in the summer, too. (*Aside.*) Oh, Hugh, Hugh, you're breaking my heart!

HUGH: Aaaaaaaaaaaaa!

BENSON: I want to help you, Mr. Gumbs!

HUGH: Then do it! Can't we do all this after the injection?

BENSON: I'm afraid not.

HUGH: (*Indicating the others.*) Look at them! How cured they seem!

BENSON: You will be, too, Hugh. Excuse me, I meant Mr. Gumbs.

HUGH: That's the first thing I'd like to change about me. My name. How could any woman love a Hugh Gumbs?

BENSON: You mustn't torment yourself like that!

HUGH: I can't help it. I meet a woman and it's fine about the drinking, fine about the smoking, it's even fine about the . . . never mind . . . but when I tell them my name, it's all over. Ask yourself, nurse, would you want to go through life as Mrs. Hugh Gumbs?

BENSON: Surely there was one woman, somewhere in your life, who didn't mind your name?

HUGH: One, just one.

BENSON: You see?

HUGH: My mother, for Christ's sake! Please, can't I have my first injection?

BENSON: We're nearly done. A moment ago you said when you met a woman it was "even fine about the . . ." What's your "about the," Mr. Gumbs?

HUGH: I can't tell you.

BENSON: I must have it.

HUGH: Believe me, you don't want it.

BENSON: Your worst habit, Mr. Gumbs, I've got to have it.

HUGH: What are you going to do with it? (TOYNBEE *enters, smiling as usual.*)

BENSON: This is Hugh Gumbs, Dr. Toynbee, a new patient. He won't tell me what his worst habit is. (DR. TOYNBEE *goes to* HUGH *and stands, looking down at him with his hands on his shoulders, then bends and mumbles his unintelligible gibberish.* HUGH *bows his head, deeply ashamed, then motions* DR. TOYNBEE *to lean forward while he whispers his worst habit into his ear, with much pantomiming.* DR. TOYNBEE *straightens up, clearly appalled at what he has just heard, and leaves without even looking at* BENSON.) In addition to all that, what really brings you to Dunelawn?

HUGH: I've told you.

BENSON: I thought perhaps there might be a somewhat more personal reason. I only meant perhaps someone else is responsible for your coming here.

HUGH: Like who?

BENSON: A woman.

HUGH: You're telling me! Say, and you're going to think I'm crazy, did you ever work for an answering service?

BENSON: No.

HUGH: Your voice sounds so familiar.

BENSON: I know.

HUGH: There was this real battle-axe on my service about five years ago. For a minute, you sounded just like her. Where was I?

BENSON: A woman.

HUGH: Oh yeah, a woman. Yes, there is one.

BENSON: Tell me about her.

HUGH: (*With a sigh.*) She was very beautiful, very feminine, very desirable. Everything a man could want. Intelligent, decisive, yet strangely yielding.

BENSON: (*Almost a murmur.*) Yet strangely yielding!

HUGH: She's probably the finest woman alive on the face of this earth.

BENSON: Her name, Mr. Gumbs?

HUGH: Char-burger! Did you ever work part-time in Char-burger on East 63rd Street!

BENSON: I'm afraid not.

HUGH: You sound so familiar and I never forget a voice. Eleven o'clock news weather girl, maybe?

BENSON: No. Her name, Mr. Gumbs?

HUGH: (*A tormented memory.*) Mildred Canby! Can I have my injection now?

BENSON: What about Ruth Benson?

HUGH: Ruth Benson?

BENSON: I believe that's the name on your biography here.

HUGH: I don't remember telling anyone anything about Ruth Benson.

BENSON: You were delirious when they brought you in.

HUGH: I was?

BENSON: You were raving about a Ruth Benson. That's all you said. Ruth Benson. Ruth Benson. Over and over again.

HUGH: What do you know?

BENSON: She must have been very important to you.

HUGH: Not particularly.

BENSON: I'll be the judge of that. Tell me about her.

HUGH: The main thing I could tell you about Ruth Benson is that she was fat. About 280, I'd say.

BENSON: I'm sure she was never 280, Mr. Gumbs.

HUGH: You never saw Ruth Benson.

BENSON: 230 maybe, but not 280!

HUGH: The point is she was fat, right? I mean she was circus fat.

BENSON: I know the type. Go on, Mr. Gumbs.

HUGH: What else about her? I think Ruth Benson is the only person, man, woman or child, I ever asked to take a bath. She used to smoke six packs a day, minimum. Cigarillos. Nicotine stains right up to her elbows! I don't guess she ever drew a sober breath. My main image of her is passed out on the floor like a big rancid mountain. And talk about being a slob! She had dust balls under her bed the size of watermelons. She didn't just have roaches in her kitchen. She raised them. It was like a goddamn stud farm in there. You'd light the oven and there'd be a flash-fire from all the grease.

BENSON: It sounds like Ruth Benson was a woman with a lot of bad habits.

HUGH: She was an out and out pig.

BENSON: I can't help noticing a special glow that comes into your voice every time you mention her name.

HUGH: We had a lot in common, Ruthie and I. I'll never forget the night we each caught the other at precisely the same instant picking their nose. God, she was gross.

BENSON: There's that glow again.

HUGH: Just thinking of her with all those fingers up there and I have to smile. You're bringing back a lot of bad memories, Nurse. I haven't thought of Ruth Benson and her soiled sheets in a long time. Your voice sounds so familiar. (BENSON *is making a big show of raising her skirt to fix a stocking.*) You have beautiful legs, Nurse.

BENSON: Familiar voice, unfamiliar legs.

HUGH: The legs look like some movie star, the voice still sounds like that answering service.

BENSON: (*Straightening up.*) Don't you know who I am yet, Hugh? No, don't say anything until I've finished. I'm not going to turn around until you tell me that you want me to turn around. I'm glad you don't recognize me. There's no reason that you should. I did it all for you, Hugh. Hugh Gumbs. Like your name, it wasn't easy. But I didn't mind the suffering, the self-humiliation, the incredible self-discipline. I wanted to torture myself into becoming someone a man like you could love and I have. Let me finish! I'm brutally honest with myself. That's not enough, I know, but it's a beginning. When I look in a mirror now I can say yes, yes, I like that person. I'm not smug, Hugh, I just know my own worth. For five years I've made myself thoroughly miserable so that today I could make you happy and I did it all for love. (*A pause.*) Now yes or no, Hugh, do you want me to turn around? (*A pause.*)

HUGH: Who are you?

BENSON: (*Turning to him, ecstatic.*) It's me. Ruth.

HUGH: Ruth?

BENSON: Ruth Benson.

HUGH: Fat Ruth Benson?

BENSON: Yes, yes!

HUGH: You don't look like Ruth.

BENSON: (*She is so happy.*) I know, I know!

HUGH: You don't sound like her, either.

BENSON: Voice lessons, darling.

HUGH: You don't even smell like Ruth.

BENSON: Zest, Dial, Dove, Lava!

HUGH: You have such beautiful legs.

BENSON: I worked for them.

HUGH: Your teeth.

BENSON: All caps.

HUGH: And your . . . (*He indicates her breasts.*)

BENSON: Exercises.

HUGH: Your big hairy mole.

BENSON: Cosmetic surgery.

HUGH: It's really you?

BENSON: It's really me. The real me and it's all for you, Hugh, I did it all for you.

HUGH: You did?

BENSON: And now that I've found you again I'm not going to let you go this time.

HUGH: You didn't let me go the last time. I let you go.

BENSON: It doesn't matter. The point is you won't want to let me go this time. Oh Hugh, I'm going to make you very, very happy. You're the luckiest man alive.

HUGH: (*Shaking his head.*) No, Ruth, no.

BENSON: What's wrong?

HUGH: It would never work, Ruth.

BENSON: Of course it will work. It has to work.

HUGH: I couldn't do it to you.

BENSON: Yes, you can. You can do anything you want to me, don't you see?

HUGH: Ruth, I've committed myself to Dunelawn, I've gotten so bad.

BENSON: Do you love me?

HUGH: Love you?

BENSON: Be blunt with me, Hugh.

HUGH: I don't even recognize you, you're so terrific looking.

BENSON: Forget the way I look now and ask yourself: do you love me?

HUGH: You're so far above me now.

BENSON: From down there, do you love me?

HUGH: I didn't love you when you were fat and rotten. I can't love you now that you're beautiful and perfect and have such terrific legs.

BENSON: I'm not perfect.

HUGH: Well nearly.

BENSON: Nearly's not enough. Nearly's never enough. I still have my faults, too, darling.

HUGH: Like what? Name one.

BENSON: I can't off the top of my head but I'm sure I do somewhere.

HUGH: You see, it's hopeless. You're the sky above and I'm the mud below. Maybe someday I'll be worthy of you but right now I want to forget all about you and try to improve myself, too, and maybe, just maybe, you'll still be up there in the stratosphere, all shiny like an angel, when I poke my head up through the clouds.

BENSON: That was poetic, Hugh.

HUGH: And what does someone like me do with an angel?

BENSON: Love her.

HUGH: From a very great distance.

BENSON: Where are you going?

HUGH: I don't know.

BENSON: I'm coming with you.

HUGH: Angels fly. I've got to crawl first.

BENSON: I'm not an angel. Forget the angel.

HUGH: You're an angel!

BENSON: I'm not an angel!

HUGH: You're an angel!

BENSON: I'm not an angel!

HUGH: No, you're an angel, Ruth!

BENSON: I'm not an angel! It's the goddamn white uniform!

HUGH: You're an angel. I can't even ask you for a cigarette.

BENSON: Yes. Yes you can. Take the whole pack. I'll light it for you. You want a drink, darling, I'll get you a drink. Bruno! Go ahead, bite your nails. Do anything you want. I love you. (*She puts her fingers in her nose.*) It can be just like old times together!

HUGH: Start that up again and I'll crack your jaw open! (*He pulls her hand away.* BENSON *dissolves in tears.*) Oh, Ruthie, Ruthie! Don't you see how I'd drag you down? Trying to please me you'd only degrade yourself. Please, let's not talk about it anymore. Just give me the injection.

BENSON: Then you don't love me?

HUGH: I can't love you right now, you're just too darn good for me.

BENSON: (*Fixing him with a new glance, all heavy-lidded and seductive.*) You think? (*She starts coming for him. She kisses him. A very long kiss.* HUGH *hardly responds.*)

HUGH: Can I please have that injection now?

BENSON: (*Her last resort.*) All right, Hugh, and remember, you asked for it.

HUGH: (*Indicating the others.*) I just want to be like them.

BENSON: You will, Hugh, you will. (HEDGES *and* BRUNO *enter.* HEDGES' *uniform is askew. She looks worn-out and dazed.*)

HEDGES: Ruth! Ruth! Ruth!

BENSON: Becky!

HEDGES: I'm turning in my cap, Ruth.

BENSON: Becky, what's wrong?

BRUNO: Hubba, hubba, Benson.

BENSON: What has he done to you?

HEDGES: Bruno and I are going to be married.

BENSON: What?

BRUNO: You heard her, mutt-face.

BENSON: What happened, Becky?

HEDGES: I'm in love, Ruth!

BENSON: What has that beast done to you?

HEDGES: Bruno's been saving up for a trailer. We're moving to Fort Lauderdale. Bruno's mommy has a pizza stand down there. This is goodbye, Ruth.

BENSON: (*Slaps her.*) Snap out of it, Hedges.

HEDGES: (*Finally, at long last and it's about time: snapping out of it and slapping her back.*) You snap out of it! That's all you do is slap people. (*She slaps her again.*) Only now you'll have to find someone else to slap!

YAMADORO. (*He is vaguely interested.*) Slap! (*Instead of doing anything,* HUGH *just sits there and pulls his coat over his head.*)

BENSON: All the time I've invested in you.

HEDGES: Are you ready, Bruno?

BENSON: You must be crazy.

HEDGES: I'm *happy!*

BENSON: I thought you cared about improving yourself.

HEDGES: Bruno likes me the way I am.

BENSON: He's a beast.

HEDGES: And I've got goddamn big thighs! Nobody's perfect!

BENSON: What about Dunelawn?

HEDGES: I won't miss it.

BENSON: What about Dr. Toynbee?

HEDGES: That man is a saint.

BENSON: Then why would you leave him?

HEDGES: He gives me the creeps.

BENSON: Zero defects, Becky?

HEDGES: (*Glowing.*) That's Bruno.

BRUNO: (*Triumphant.*) Hubba, hubba, Benson!

BENSON: Don't even speak to me!

BRUNO: Let's go, sugar.

HEDGES: (*She turns to* PONCE, BLUM *and* YAMADORO.) If any of you had any sense, you'd come with us. There's enough room in Bruno's microbus for everyone. (*She fastens her cap on* MR. BLUM's *head, then turns to* HUGH.)

BENSON: Just go, you . . . you pizza waitress!

HEDGES: Are you Hugh Gumbs?

HUGH: Yes, yes I am.

HEDGES: Are you in for it!

BRUNO: Hubba, hubba, dog-face!

HEDGES: Hubba, hubba, Ruth! (*They are gone.*)

BENSON: You'll regret this, Hedges, you'll regret this for the rest of your life! (*She turns to* HUGH.) Oh, Hugh, you see how terrible other people are! Thank God for Dunelawn and Dr. Toynbee. I'll get your injection right away. (HUGH *gets out of his wheelchair.*) Where are you going?

HUGH: I can't stay here with you, Ruth. I'm not even worthy of Dunelawn. Maybe I'll come back to you one day, a better and worthier man. If not, I know you'll find someone good enough for you.

BENSON: It's a rotten world out there. It'll destroy you.

HUGH: It already has. (*He starts to go.*)

BENSON: (*Concealing the syringe.*) One last kiss. (*They kiss.* BENSON *has the syringe in her hand, poised to inject him.* DR. TOYNBEE *enters.* BENSON *is mortified.*) Dr. Toynbee! I'm so ashamed. I . . . Mr. Gumbs was just leaving.

HUGH: That woman is perfect! (*He goes up the aisle.*)

BENSON: I don't know what happened, Dr. Toynbee. I left them with Nurse Hedges and she's gone off to Florida to open a pizza stand with Bruno and the love of my life is gone again and I'm having a nervous breakdown because I don't understand people anymore. It's so good here. You're so good. Why would anyone want to leave Dunelawn when all we're trying to do is help them to be perfect? (BENSON *is shattered. She is holding on to* DR. TOYNBEE *for support. He puts his arm around her and takes her to the wheelchair left empty by* HUGH GUMBS.) You're so good, Dr. Toynbee. It's the end of summer. (DR. TOYNBEE *goes to the cart to get a syringe.*) I won't cry. I refuse to cry. It's you and Dunelawn I'm thinking of. Not myself. The world is filled with men like Hugh Gumbs. But someone somewhere is the man for me. Zero defects. No faults, no failings, no fantasies. Where is he, Dr. Toynbee? (*She looks up into* DR. TOYNBEE's *eyes as he injects her. A wonderful smile lights up her face.*) Oh yes! (DR. TOYNBEE *gets a straitjacket hidden behind the wheelchair and carefully puts* BENSON's *arms through it. Meanwhile,* BLUM *begins to sing again, very softly, the same World War I campaign song.* PONCE, YAMADORO, *and even* BENSON *join him. They are all smiling blissfully. In the distance, we hear even more voices beginning to sing.* DR. TOYNBEE *smiles benignly at his three male patients. Then down at* NURSE BENSON. *Then up at us. He takes a step forward and starts to address us in his unintelligible gibberish, as a few leaves fall from the scraggly tree. The lights fade.*)

END OF THE PLAY

AMERICAN BUFFALO
David Mamet

AMERICAN BUFFALO

The myth of the struggling young playwright arriving in the big city with little more than a handful of tattered scripts clutched in his hands and almost overnight winning recognition as a major new talent in the theatre was not a myth in the case of David Mamet. Three of his plays were produced Off-Broadway in 1976—*Duck Variations, Sexual Perversity in Chicago,* and *American Buffalo*—the latter two winning him an Obie Award as the best new playwright of the year.

What particularly impressed the judges, in addition to Mamet's marvelous ear for dialogue, was the twenty-eight-year-old writer's wide range of subject matter—from metaphysical reflections on death, to sexual farce, to an exploration of the relationship between money and violence in American culture. Indeed, *The Village Voice* called Mamet "the most promising American playwright to have emerged in the 1970s."

American Buffalo won its award after appearing only three weekends, in February 1976, at Off-Broadway's St. Clement's church basement theatre. Largely as a result of the Obie, which brought the play to a producer's attention, *American Buffalo* was restaged on Broadway the next year, with Robert Duvall and John Savage in the cast, and won virtually unanimous praise from the critics.

Mel Gussow, reviewing the Off-Broadway production in the New York *Times,* wrote: "David Mamet has a feeling for the contradictions that make up everyday conversation . . . His dialogue is not simply overheard, but it has the glow of reality."

Critic Julius Novick, reviewing the play in *The Village Voice*, wrote that Mamet "has not tried to make poetry out of the way people talk; he has made music instead . . . Mamet is already perhaps the most exquisite verbal stylist among American playwrights."

As these quotes indicate, the immediate appeal of Mamet's plays lies in their wonderful sense of language. As Mamet himself has said: "I became fascinated by the way the language we use, its rhythm, actually determines the way we behave, more than the other way around."

American Buffalo is partly about the relationship between language and behavior, about the poetry of obscenity, but it is also about loyalty and responsibility and betrayal, about the relationship between money and business and violence. The central action of the play revolves around three petty thieves who are planning to burglarize a valuable coin collection.

"What I was trying to say in *American Buffalo*," Mamet has said, "is that once you step back from the moral responsibility you've undertaken, you're lost. We have to take responsibility. Theatre is a place of recognition, it's an ethical exercise, it's where we show ethical interchange. I'm interested in what Tolstoy said—that we should treat human beings with love and respect and never hurt them. I hope *American Buffalo* shows that, by showing what happens when you fail to act that way."

Four more Mamet plays have been staged Off-Broadway since 1976—*The Water-Engine, A Life in the Theatre, The Woods,* and *Reunion*—and there can be little doubt that his voice will be one of the most important in American theatre in the years ahead.

AMERICAN BUFFALO was first performed in New York City on January 23, 1976, at St. Clements Theatre, with the following cast:

DONNY DUBROW	*Michael Egan*
BOBBY	*J. T. Walsh*
TEACH	*Mike Kellin*

The production was directed by Gregory Mosher; set by Akira Yoshimura; lighting by Gary Porto.

CHARACTERS

DONNY DUBROW, a man in his late forties. The owner of Don's Resale Shop.

WALTER COLE, called TEACHER, a friend and associate of DONNY.

BOBBY, DONNY's gopher.

THE SCENE

Don's Resale Shop. A junkshop.

THE TIME

One Friday. Act One takes place in the morning; Act Two starts around 11:00 that night.

ACT ONE

Don's Resale Shop. Morning. DONNY *and* BOBBY *are sitting.*

DON: So? (*Pause.*) So what, Bob? (*Pause.*)

BOB: I'm sorry, Donny. (*Pause.*)

DON: Alright.

BOB: I'm sorry, Donny. (*Pause.*)

DON: Yeah.

BOB: Maybe he's still in there.

DON: If you think that, Bob, how come you're here?

BOB: I came in. (*Pause.*)

DON: You don't come in, Bob. You don't come in until you do a thing.

BOB: He didn't come out.

DON: What do I care, Bob, if he came out or not? You're sposed to watch the guy, you watch him. Am I wrong?

BOB: I just went to the back.

DON: Why? (*Pause.*) Why did you do that?

BOB: 'Cause he wasn't coming out the front.

DON: Well, Bob, I'm sorry, but this isn't good enough. If you want to do business . . . if we got a business deal it isn't good enough. I want you to remember this.

BOB: I do.

DON: Yeah, *now* . . . but later, what? (*Pause.*) Just one thing, Bob. Action counts. (*Pause.*) Action talks and bullshit walks.

BOB: I only went around to see if he's coming out the back.

DON: No, don't go fuck yourself around with these excuses. (*Pause.*)

BOB: I'm sorry.

DON: Don't tell me that you're sorry. I'm not mad at you.

BOB: You're not?

DON: (*Pause.*) Let's clean up here. (BOB *starts to clean up the debris around the poker table.*) The only thing I'm trying to teach you something here.

BOB: Okay.

DON: Now lookit Fletcher.

BOB: Fletch?

DON: Now Fletcher is a standup guy.

BOB: Yeah.

DON: I don't *give* a shit. He is a fellow stands for something—

BOB: Yeah.

DON: You take him and you put him down in some strange town with just a nickel in his pocket, and by nightfall he'll have that town by the balls. This is not talk Bob, this is action. (*Pause.*)

BOB: He's a real good cardplayer.

DON: You're Fucking A he is, Bob, and this is what I'm getting at. Skill. Skill and talent and the balls to arrive at your own *conclusions*. The fucker won four hundred bucks last night.

BOB: Yeah?

DON: *Oh* yeah.

BOB: And who was playing?

DON: *Me* . . .

BOB: Uh huh . . .

DON: And *Teach* . . .

BOB: How'd Teach do?

DON: Not too good.

BOB: No, huh?

DON: No. . . . and Earl was here . . .

BOB: Uh huh . . .

DON: And Fletcher.

BOB: *How'd* he do?

DON: He won four hundred bucks.

BOB: And who else won?

DON: Ruthie, she won.

BOB: She won, huh?

DON: Yeah.

BOB: She does okay.

DON: *Oh* yeah . . .

BOB: She's an okay cardplayer.

DON: Yes, she is.

BOB: I like her.

DON: Fuck, I like her, too. There's nothing wrong in that.

BOB: No.

DON: I mean she treats you right.

BOB: Uh huh. How'd she do?

DON: She did okay. (*Pause.*)

BOB: You win?

DON: I did alright.

BOB: Yeah?

DON: Yeah. I did okay. Not like *Fletch* . . .

BOB: No, huh?

DON: I mean, Fletcher, he plays *cards*.

BOB: He's real sharp.

DON: You're goddam right he is.

BOB: I know it.

DON: Was he born that way?

BOB: Huh?

DON: I'm saying was he born that way or do you think he had to learn it?

BOB: Learn it.

DON: Goddam right he did, and don't forget it. Everything, Bobby: it's going to happen to you, it's *not* going to happen to you, the important thing is can you *deal* with it, and can you *learn* from it. (*Pause.*) And this is why I'm telling you to stand up. It's no different with you than with anyone else. Everything that I or Fletcher know we picked up on the street. That's all business is . . . common sense, experience, and talent.

BOB: Like when he jewed Ruthie out that pigiron.

DON: What pigiron?

BOB: That he got off her that time.

DON: When was this?

BOB: On the back of her truck.

DON: That wasn't, I don't think, her pigiron.

BOB: No?

DON: That was *his* pigiron, Bob.

Bob: Yeah?

Don: Yeah. He bought if off her. (*Pause.*)

Bob: Well, she was real mad at him.

Don: She was.

Bob: Yup.

Don: She was mad at him?

Bob: Yeah. That he stole her pigiron.

Don: He didn't steal it, Bob.

Bob: No?

Don: No.

Bob: She was *mad* at him . . .

Don: Well, that very well may be, Bob, but the fact remains that it was *business*. That's what business *is*.

Bob: What?

Don: People taking *care* of themselves. Huh?

Bob: No.

Don: 'Cause there's business and there's friendship, Bobby . . . there are many things, and when you walk around you *hear* a lot of things, and what you got to do is keep clear who your friends are, and who treated you like what. Or else the rest is garbage, Bob, because I want to tell you something.

Bob: Okay.

DON: Things are not always what they seem to be.

BOB: I know. (*Pause.*)

DON: There's a lotsa people on this street, Bob, they want this and they want that. Do anything to get it. You don't have *friends* this life . . . You want some breakfast?

BOB: I'm not hungry. (*Pause.*)

DON: *Never* skip breakfast, Bob.

BOB: Why?

DON: Breakfast . . . Is the most important meal of the day.

BOB: I'm not hungry.

DON: It makes no earthly difference in the world. You know how much nutriative benefits they got in coffee? Zero. Not one thing. The stuff eats *you* up. You can't live on coffee, Bobby. And I've told you this before. You cannot live on cigarettes. You may feel *good*, you may feel *fine*, but something's getting overworked, and you are going to pay for it. Now: What do you see me eat when I come in here every day?

BOB: Coffee.

DON: Come on, Bob, don't fuck with me. I *drink* a little coffee . . . but what do I *eat*?

BOB: Yoghurt.

DON: Why?

BOB: Because it's good for you.

DON: You're goddam right. And it wouldn't kill you to take a vitamin.

BOB: They're too expensive.

DON: Don't worry about it. You should just take 'em.

BOB: I can't afford 'em.

DON: Don't worry about it.

BOB: You'll buy some for me?

DON: Do you need 'em?

BOB: Yeah.

DON: Well, then, I'll get you some. What do you *think?*

BOB: Thanks, Donny.

DON: It's for your own good. Don't thank *me* . . .

BOB: Okay.

DON: I just can't use you in here like a zombie.

BOB: I just went around the back.

DON: I don't care. Do you see? Do you see what I'm getting at? (*Pause.*)

BOB: Yeah. (*Pause.*)

DON: Well, we'll see.

BOB: I'm sorry, Donny.

DON: Well, we'll see. (TEACHER *appears in the doorway and enters the store.*) Good morning.

BOB: Morning, Teach. (TEACHER *walks around the store a bit in silence.*)

TEACH: Fuckin' Ruthie, fuckin' Ruthie, fuckin' Ruthie, fuckin' Ruthie, fuckin' Ruthie.

DON: What?

TEACH: Fuckin' *Ruthie* . . .

DON: . . . yeah?

TEACH: I come in to The Riverside to get a cup of *coffee*, right? I sit down at the table Grace and Ruthie.

DON: Yeah.

TEACH: I'm gonna order just a cup of coffee.

DON: Right.

TEACH: So Grace and Ruthie's having breakfast, and they're done. *Plates* . . . *crusts* of stuff all over . . . So we'll shoot the shit.

DON: Yeah.

TEACH: Talk about the *game* . . .

DON: . . . yeah.

TEACH: . . . *so* on. Down I sit. "Hi, hi." I take a piece of toast off Grace's plate . . .

DON: . . . uh huh . . .

TEACH: . . . and she goes "Help Yourself." Help myself. I should help myself to half a piece of toast it's four slices for a quarter. I should have a nickel every time we're over at the game, I pop for coffee . . . cigarettes . . . a *sweetroll*, never say word. "Bobby, see who wants what." Huh? A fucking *roast-beef* sandwich. (*To* BOBBY.) Am I right? (*To* DONNY.) Ahh, shit. We're sitting down, how many times do I pick up the check? But—No!—because I never go and make a big *thing* out of it—it's no big thing—and flaunt like "This one's on me" like some bust-out asshole, but I naturally assume that I'm with friends, and don't forget who's who when someone gets *behind* a half a yard or needs some help with—huh?—some fucking rent, or drops enormous piles of money at the track, or someone's *sick* or something . . .

DON: (*To* BOB.) This is what I'm talking about.

TEACH: Only—and I tell you this, Don. Only, and I'm not, I don't think, casting anything on anyone: from the mouth of a Southern bulldyke asshole ingrate of a vicious nowhere cunt can this trash come. (*To* BOB.) And I take nothing back, and I know you're close with them.

BOB: With Grace and Ruthie?

TEACH: Yes.

BOB: I like 'em.

TEACH: I have always treated everybody more than fair, and never gone around complaining. Is this true, Don?

DON: Yup.

TEACH: Someone is *against* me, that's their problem . . . I can look out for myself, and I don't got to fuck around behind somebody's back, I don't like the way they're treating me. Or pray some brick *safe* falls and hits them on the head, they're walking down the street. But to have that shithead turn, in one breath, every fucking sweetroll that I ever ate with them into GROUND GLASS—I'm wondering were they eating it and thinking "This guy's an idiot to blow a fucking *quarter* on his friends" . . . this hurts me, Don. This hurts me in a way I don't know what the fuck to do. (*Pause.*)

DON: You're probably just upset.

TEACH: You're fuckin A I'm upset. I am *very* upset, Don.

DON: They got their problems, too, Teach.

TEACH: *I* would like to have their problems.

DON: All I'm saying, nothing *personal* . . . they were probably, uh, *talking* about something.

TEACH: Then let them talk about it, then. No, I am sorry, Don, I cannot brush this off. They treat me like an asshole, they *are* an asshole. (*Pause.*) The only way to teach these people is to kill them. (*Pause.*)

DON: You want some coffee?

TEACH: I'm not hungry.

DON: Come on, I'm sending Bobby to The Riverside.

TEACH: Fuckin' joint . . .

DON: Yeah.

TEACH: They harbor *assholes* in there . . .

DON: Yeah. Come on, Teach, what do you want? Bob?

BOB: Yeah?

DON: (*To* TEACH.) Come on, he's going anyway. (*To* BOB, *handing him a bill.*) Get me a Boston, and go for the yoghurt.

BOB: What kind?

DON: You know, plain, and, if they don't got it, uh, something else. And get something for yourself.

BOB: What?

DON: Whatever you want. But get something to *eat*, and whatever you want to drink, and get Teacher a coffee.

BOB: Boston, Teach?

TEACH: No?

BOB: What?

TEACH: Black.

BOB: Right.

DON: And something for yourself to eat. (*To* TEACH.) He doesn't want to eat.

TEACH: (*To* BOB.) You got to eat. And this is what I'm saying at the Riverside. (*Pause.*)

BOB: Black coffee.

DON: And get something for yourself to eat. (*To* TEACH.) What do you want to eat? An English muffin. (*To* BOB.) Get Teach an English muffin.

TEACH: I don't want an English muffin.

DON: Get him an English muffin, and make sure they give you jelly.

TEACH: I don't want an English muffin.

DON: What do you want?

TEACH: I don't want anything.

BOB: Come on, Teach, eat something. (*Pause.*)

DON: You'll feel better you eat something, Teach. (*Pause.*)

TEACH: (*To* BOB.) Tell 'em to give you an order of Bacon, real dry, real crisp.

BOB: Okay.

TEACH: And tell the broad if it's for me she'll give you more.

BOB: Okay.

DON: Anything else you want?

TEACH: No.

DON: A cantaloupe?

TEACH: I never eat cantaloupe.

DON: No?

TEACH: It gives me the runs.

DON: Yeah?

TEACH: And tell him he shouldn't say anything to Ruthie.

DON: He wouldn't.

TEACH: No? No, you're right. I'm sorry, Bob.

BOB: It's okay.

TEACH: I'm upset.

BOB: It's okay, Teach. (*Pause.*)

TEACH: Thank you.

BOB: You're welcome. (BOB *starts to exit.*)

DON: And the plain if they got it.

BOB: I will. (*Exits.*)

DON: He wouldn't say anything.

TEACH: What the fuck do *I* care . . . (*Pause.*) Cunt. (*Pause.*) There is not one loyal bone in that bitch's body.

DON: How'd you finally do last night?

TEACH: This has nothing to do with that.

DON: No, I know. I'm just saying . . . for *talk* . . .

TEACH: Last night? You were here, Don. (*Pause.*) How'd *you* do?

DON: Not well.

TEACH: Mmm.

DON: The only one won any money, Fletch and Ruthie.

TEACH: (*Pause.*) Cunt had to win two hundred dollars.

DON: She's a good cardplayer.

TEACH: She is *not* a good cardplayer, Don. She is a mooch and she is a locksmith and she plays like a woman. (*Pause.*) *Fletcher's* a cardplayer, I'll give him that. But *Ruthie* . . . I mean, *you* see how she fucking plays . . .

DON: Yeah.

TEACH: And always with that cunt on her shoulder.

DON: Grace?

TEACH: Yes.

DON: Grace is her partner.

TEACH: Then let her *be* her partner, then. You see what I'm talking about? Everyone, they're sitting at the table and then Grace is going to walk around . . . fetch an *ashtray* . . . go for *coffee* . . .

this . . . and everybody's all they aren't going to hide their cards, and they're going to make a show how they don't hunch *over*, and like that. I don't give a shit. I say the broad's her fucking partner, and she walks in back of me I'm going to hide my hand.

DON: Yeah.

TEACH: And I say anybody doesn't's out of their mind. (*Pause*.) We're talking about money for chrissake, huh? We're talking about cards. Friendship is friendship, and a wonderful thing, and I am all for it. I have never said different, and you know me on this point. Okay. But let's just keep it *separate* huh, let's just keep the two apart, and maybe we can deal with each other like some human beings. (*Pause*.) This is all I'm saying, Don. I know you got a soft-spot in your heart for Ruthie . . .

DON: . . . yeah?

TEACH: I know you like the broad and Grace and, Bob, I know he likes 'em, too.

DON: He likes 'em.

TEACH: And I like 'em too. I know, I know. I'm not averse to this. I'm not averse to sitting down. I know we *will* sit down. These things happen, I'm not saying that they don't . . . and yeah, yeah, yeah, I know I lost a bundle at the game and blah blah blah. (*Pause*.) But all I ever ask—and I would say this to her face—is only she remembers who is who and not to go around with *her* or Gracie either with this attitude. "The Past is Past, and this is Now, and so Fuck You." You see?

DON: Yes. (*Long pause*.)

TEACH: So what's new?

DON: Nothing.

TEACH: Same old shit, huh?

DON: Yup.

TEACH: You seen my hat?

DON: No. Did you leave it here?

TEACH: Yeah. (*Pause.*)

DON: You ask them over at the Riv?

TEACH: I left it here. (*Pause.*)

DON: Well, you left it here, it's here.

TEACH: You seen it?

DON: No. (*Pause.*)

TEACH: Fletch been in?

DON: No.

TEACH: Prolly drop in one or so, huh?

DON: Yeah. You know. You never know with Fletcher.

TEACH: No.

DON: He might drop in the *morning* . . .

TEACH. Yeah.

DON: And then he might, he's gone for ten or fifteen days you never know he's gone.

TEACH: Yeah.

DON: Why?

TEACH: I want to talk to him.

DON: (*Pause.*) Ruth would know.

TEACH: You sure you didn't *see* my hat?

DON: I didn't see it. No. (*Pause.*) Ruthie might know.

TEACH: Vicious dyke.

DON: Look in the john.

TEACH: It isn't in the john. I wouldn't leave it there.

DON: Do you got something up with Fletch?

TEACH: No. Just I have to talk to him.

DON: He'll probably show up.

TEACH: Oh yeah . . . (*Pause. Indicating objects on the counter.*)
What're *these*?

DON: Those?

TEACH: Yeah.

DON: They're from 1933.

TEACH: From the thing?

DON: Yeah. (*Pause.*)

TEACH: Nice.

DON: They had a whole market in 'em. Just like anything. They license out the shit and everybody makes it.

TEACH: Yeah? I knew that.

Don: Just like now. They had *combs*, and *brushes* . . . you know, brushes with the thing on 'em . . .

Teach: Yeah. I know. They had . . . uh . . . what? Clothing too, huh?

Don: I think. Sure. Everything. And they're guys they just collect the stuff.

Teach: They got that much of it around?

Don: *Shit* yes. It's not that long ago. The thing, it ran two years, and they had (*I* don't know) all kinds of people every year they're buying everything that they can lay their hands on that they're going to take it back to Buffalo to give it, you know, to their Aunt, and it mounts up.

Teach: What does it go for?

Don: The compact?

Teach: Yeah.

Don: Aah . . . *You* want it?

Teach: No.

Don: Oh. I'm just asking. I mean, *you* want it . . .

Teach: No. I mean somebody walks *in* here . . .

Don: Oh. Somebody walks *in* here . . . This shit's fashionable . . .

Teach: I don't doubt it.

Don: . . . and they're gonna have to go like fifteen bucks.

Teach: You're fulla shit.

DON: My word of honor.

TEACH: No shit.

DON: Everything like that.

TEACH: A bunch of fucking thieves.

DON: Yeah. Everything.

TEACH: (*Snorts.*) What a bunch of crap, huh?

DON: *Oh* yeah.

TEACH: Every goddam thing.

DON: Yes.

TEACH: If I kept the stuff that I threw *out* . . .

DON: . . . yes.

TEACH: I would be a wealthy man today. I would be cruising on some European Yacht.

DON: Uh huh.

TEACH: Shit my father used to keep in his *desk* drawer.

DON: My Father, too.

TEACH: The *basement* . . .

DON: Uh huh.

TEACH: Fuckin' toys in the back*yard*, for chrissake . . .

DON: Don't even talk about it.

TEACH: It's . . . I don't know. (*Pause.*) You want to play some gin?

DON: Maybe later.

TEACH: Okay. (*Pause.*) I dunno. (*Pause.*) Fucking *day* . . . (*Pause.*) Fucking *weather* . . . (*Pause.*)

DON: You think it's going to rain?

TEACH: Yeah. I do. Later.

DON: Yeah?

TEACH: Well, *look* at it. (BOBBY *appears carrying a paper bag with coffee and foodstuffs in it.*) Bobby, Bobby, Bobby, Bobby, Bobby.

BOB: Ruthie isn't mad at you.

TEACH: She isn't?

BOB: No.

TEACH: How do you know?

BOB: I found out.

TEACH: How?

BOB: I talked to her.

TEACH: You talked to her.

BOB: Yes.

TEACH: I asked you you weren't going to.

BOB: Well, she asked me.

TEACH: What?

BOB: That were you over here.

TEACH: What did you tell her?

BOB: You were here.

TEACH: Oh. (*Looks at* DON.)

DON: What did you say to her, Bob?

BOB: Just Teach was here.

DON: And is she coming over here?

BOB: I don't think so. They had the plain.

DON: (*To* TEACH.) So? This is alright. (*To* BOB.) Alright, Bob. (*Looks at* TEACH.)

TEACH: That's alright, Bob. (*To self.*) Everything's alright to some-one . . . (DON *takes bag and distributes contents to appropriate recipients. To* DON.) You shouldn't eat that shit.

DON: Why?

TEACH: It's just I have a feeling about healthfoods.

DON: It's not healthfoods, Teach. It's only yoghurt.

TEACH: That's not healthfoods?

DON: No. They've had it forever.

TEACH: Yoghurt?

DON: Yeah. They used to joke about it on *My Little Margie.* (*To* BOB.) Way before your time.

TEACH: Yeah?

DON: Yeah.

TEACH: What the fuck. A little bit can't hurt you.

DON: It's *good* for you.

TEACH: Okay, okay. Each one to his own opinion. (*Pause. To* BOB.) Was Fletcher over there?

BOB: No.

DON: Where's my coffee?

BOB: It's not there?

DON: No. (*Pause.*)

BOB: I told 'em specially to put it in.

DON: Where *is* it?

BOB: They forgot it. (*Pause.*) I'll go back and get it.

DON: Would you mind?

BOB: No. (*Pause.*)

DON: You gonna get it?

BOB: Yeah. (*Pause.*)

DON: What, Bob?

BOB: Can I talk to you? (*Pause.* DON *goes to* BOB.)

DON: What is it?

BOB: I saw him.

DON: Who?

BOB: The guy.

DON: You saw the guy?

BOB: Yes.

DON: That I'm talking about?

BOB: Yes.

DON: Just now?

BOB: Yeah. He's going somewhere.

DON: He is.

BOB: Yeah. He's puttin' a suitcase in the car.

DON: The guy, or both of 'em?

BOB: Just him.

DON: He got in the car he drove off??

BOB: He's coming down the stairs . . .

DON: Yeah.

BOB: And he's got the suitcase . . . (DON *nods*.) He gets in the car . . .

DON: Uh huh . . .

BOB: He drives away.

DON: So where is she?

BOB: He's goin' to pick her up.

DON: What was he wearing?

BOB: Stuff. Traveling clothes.

DON: Okay. (*Pause.*) Now you're talking. You see what I mean?

BOB: Yeah.

DON: Alright.

BOB: And he had a coat too.

DON: Now you're talking.

BOB: Like a raincoat.

DON: Yeah. (*Pause.*) Good. (*Pause.*)

BOB: Yeah, he's gone.

DON: Bob, go get me that coffee, do you mind?

BOB: No.

DON: What did you get yourself to eat?

BOB: I didn't get anything.

DON: Well, get me my coffee, and get yourself something to eat, okay?

BOB: Okay. Good. (*Exits. Pause.*)

DON: How's your bacon?

TEACH: Aaaahh, they always fuck it up.

DON: Yeah.

TEACH: This time they fucked it up too burnt.

DON: Mmmm.

TEACH: You got to be breathing on their neck.

DON: Mmmm.

TEACH: Like a lot of things.

DON: Uh huh.

TEACH: *Any* business . . .

DON: Yeah.

TEACH: You want it run right, *be* there.

DON: Yeah.

TEACH: Just like you.

DON: What?

TEACH: Like the shop.

DON: Well, no one's going to run it, I'm not here. (*Pause.*)

TEACH: No. (*Pause.*) You have to be here.

DON: Yeah.

TEACH: It's a one-man show.

DON: Uh huh. (*Pause.*)

TEACH: So what is this thing with the kid? (*Pause.*) I mean, is it anything, uh . . .

DON: It's nothing . . . *you* know . . .

TEACH: Yeah. (*Pause.*) It's *what* . . . ?

DON: You know, it's just some *guy* we spotted.

TEACH: Yeah. Some *guy*.

DON: Yeah.

TEACH: Some guy . . .

DON: Yeah. (*Pause.*) What time is it?

TEACH: Noon.

DON: Noon. Fuck.

TEACH: What? (*Pause.*)

DON: You parked outside?

TEACH: Yeah.

DON: Are you okay on the meter?

TEACH: Yeah. The broad came by already. (*Pause.*)

DON: Good. (*Pause.*)

TEACH: Oh, yeah, she came by.

DON: Good.

TEACH: You want to tell me what this thing is?

DON: (*Pause.*) The thing?

TEACH: Yeah. (*Pause.*) What is it?

DON: Nothing.

TEACH: No? What is it, jewelry?

DON: No. It's nothing.

TEACH: Oh.

DON: You know?

TEACH: Yeah. (*Pause.*) Yeah. No. I don't know. (*Pause.*) Who am I, a *police*man . . . I'm making conversation, huh?

DON: Yeah.

TEACH: Huh? (*Pause.*) 'Cause you know I'm just asking for talk.

DON: (*Moves phone to slider.*) Yeah. I know. Yeah, okay.

TEACH: And I can live without this.

DON: (*Reach for phone.*) Yeah. I know. Hold on, I'll tell you.

TEACH: Tell me if you *want* to, Don.

DON: I want to, Teach.

TEACH: Yeah?

DON: Yeah. (*Pause.*)

TEACH: Well, I'd fucking *hope* so. Am I wrong?

DON: No. No. You're right.

TEACH: I *hope* so.

DON: No, hold on; I gotta make this call. (*Dialing.*)

TEACH: Well, alright. So what is it, jewelry?

DON: No.

TEACH: What?

DON: Coins.

TEACH: Coins.

DON: Yeah. Hold on. (DON *hunts for a card, dials telephone. Into phone.*) Hello? This is Donny Dubrow. We were talking the other day. Lookit, sir, if I could get ahold of some of that stuff you were interested in, would you be interested in some of it? (*Pause.*) Those *things* . . . *Old*, yeah. (*Pause.*) Various pieces of various types. (*Pause.*) Tonight. Sometime late. Are they *what* . . . !!?? Yes, but I don't see what kind of a question is that—at the prices we're talking about . . . (*Pause.*) No, hey, no, I understand *you* . . . (*Pause.*) Sometime late. (*Pause.*) One hundred percent. (*Pause.*) I feel the same. Alright. Goodbye. (*Hangs up.*) Fucking asshole.

TEACH: Guys like that, I like to fuck their wives.

DON: I don't blame you.

TEACH: Fucking *jerk* . . .

DON: I swear to God . . .

TEACH: The guy's a collector?

DON: Who?

TEACH: The phone guy.

Don: Yeah.

Teach: And the other guy?

Don: We spotted?

Teach: Yeah.

Don: Him, too.

Teach: So you hit him for his coins.

Don: Yeah.

Teach: —And you got a buyer in the phone guy.

Don: Asshole.

Teach: The thing is you're not sitting with the shit.

Don: No.

Teach: The guy's an asshole or he's not, what do you care? It's business. (*Pause.*)

Don: You're right.

Teach: The guy with the suitcase, he's the mark.

Don: Yeah.

Teach: How'd you find him?

Don: In here.

Teach: Came in here, huh?

Don: Yeah.

TEACH: No shit. (*Pause.*)

DON: He comes in here one day, like a week ago.

TEACH: For what?

DON: Just browsing. So he's looking in the case, he comes up and with this *buffalohead* nickel . . .

TEACH: Yeah . . .

DON: From nine*teen*-something. I don't know. I didn't even know it's there . . .

TEACH: Uh huh . . .

DON: . . . and he goes, "how much would that be?"

TEACH: Uh huh . . .

DON: So I'm about to go "two bits," jerk that I am, but something tells me to shut up, so I go "you tell me."

TEACH: Always good business.

DON: *Oh* yeah.

TEACH: How wrong can you go?

DON: That's what I mean, so then he thinks a minute, and he tells me he'll just *shop* a bit.

TEACH: Uh huh . . .

DON: And so he's *shopping* . . . What?

TEACH: Some cops.

DON: Where?

TEACH: At the corner.

DON: What are they doing?

TEACH: Cruising. (*Pause.*)

DON: They turn the corner?

TEACH. (*Waits.*) Yeah. (*Pause.*)

DON: . . . And so he's shopping. And he's picking up a beat-up *mirror* . . . an old *kid's* toy . . . a *shaving* mug . . .

TEACH: . . . right . . .

DON: Maybe five, six things, comes to eight bucks. I get 'em and I put 'em in a box and then he tells me he'll go fifty dollars for the nickel.

TEACH: No.

DON: Yeah. So I tell him—get this—"not a chance."

TEACH: Took balls.

DON: Well, what-the-fuck . . .

TEACH: No, I mean it.

DON: I took a chance.

TEACH: You're goddam right. (*Pause.* DON *shrugs.*)

DON: So I say "not a chance," he tells me eighty is his highest offer.

TEACH: I knew it.

DON: Wait. So I go "ninety-five."

TEACH: Uh huh.

DON: We settle down on ninety, *takes* the nickel, leaves the box of shit.

TEACH: He pay for it?

DON: The box of shit?

TEACH: Yeah.

DON: No. (*Pause.*)

TEACH: And so what was the nickel?

DON: *I* don't know . . . some rarity.

TEACH: Ninety dollars for a nickel.

DON: Are you kidding, Teach? I bet it's worth five *times* that.

TEACH: Yeah, huh?

DON: Are you kidding me, the guy is going to come in here, he plunks down ninety bucks like nothing. *Shit* yeah. (*Pause.*)

TEACH: Well, what the fuck, it didn't cost you anything.

DON: That's not the point. The next day back he comes and he goes through the whole bit again. He looks at *this*, he looks at *that*, it's a nice *day* . . .

TEACH: Yeah . . .

DON: And he tells me he's the guy was in here yesterday and bought the buffalo off me and do I maybe have some other articles of interest.

TEACH: Yeah.

DON: And so I tell him "not offhand." He says that could I get in touch with him, I get some in, so I say "sure," he leaves his card, I'm sposed to call him anything crops up.

TEACH: Uh huh.

DON: He comes in here like I'm his fucking doorman.

TEACH: Mmmm.

DON: He takes me off my coin and will I call him if I find another one.

TEACH: Yeah.

DON: Doing me this favor by just coming in my shop.

TEACH: Yeah. (*Pause.*) Some people never change.

DON: Like he has done me this big favor by just coming in my shop.

TEACH: Uh huh. You're going to get him now.

DON: You know I am. So Bob, we kept a lookout on his place, and that's the shot.

TEACH: And who's the chick?

DON: What chick?

TEACH: You're asking Bob about.

DON: Oh yeah. The guy, he's married. I mean—*I* don't know. We *think* he's married. They got two names on the bell . . . Anyway, he's living with this chick, *you* know . . .

TEACH: What the hell.

DON: . . . and you should see this chick.

TEACH: Yeah, huh?

DON: She is a knockout. I mean, she is *real* nice lookin', Teach.

TEACH: Fuck *him* . . .

DON: The other day, last Friday like a week ago Bob runs in, lugs me out to look at 'em, they're going out on bicycles. The ass on this broad, un-be-fucking-lievable in these bicycling shorts sticking up in the air with these short handlebars.

TEACH: Fuckin' *fruits* . . . (*Pause.*)

DON: So that's it. We keep an eye on 'em. They both work. . . . Yesterday he rode his bicycle to work.

TEACH: He didn't.

DON: Yeah.

TEACH: (*Snorts.*) With the three-piece suit, huh?

DON: I didn't see 'em. Bobby saw 'em. (*Pause.*) And that's the shot. Earl gets me in touch the phone guy, he's this coin collector, and that's it.

TEACH: It fell in your lap.

DON: Yeah.

TEACH: You're going in tonight.

DON: It looks that way.

TEACH: And who's going in? (*Pause.*)

DON: Bobby. (*Pause.*) He's a good kid, Teach.

TEACH: He's a great kid, Don. You know how I feel about the kid. (*Pause.*) I *like* him.

DON: He's doing good.

TEACH: I can see that. (*Pause.*) But I gotta say something here.

DON: What?

TEACH: Only this—and I don't think I'm *getting* at anything—

DON: What?

TEACH: (*Pause.*) Don't send the kid in.

DON: I shouldn't send Bobby in?

TEACH: No. Now, just wait a second. Let's siddown on this. What are we saying here? Loyalty. (*Pause.*) You know how I am on this. This is great. This is admirable.

DON: What?

TEACH: This loyalty. This is swell. It turns my heart the things that you do for the kid.

DON: What do I do for him, Walt?

TEACH: Things. Things, you know what I mean.

DON: No. I don't do anything for him.

TEACH: In your mind you don't but the things, I'm saying, that you actually go *do* for him. This is fantastic. All I mean, a guy can be too loyal, Don. Don't be dense on this. What are we saying here? Business. I mean, the guy's got you're taking his high-speed blender and a Magnavox, you send the kid in. You're talking about a real *job* . . . they don't come in right away and know they been *had*. . . . You're talking maybe a safe, certainly a good lock or two, and you need a guy's looking for valuable shit, he's not going to mess with the stainless steel silverware, huh, or some digital *clock*. (*Pause.*) We both know what we're saying here. We both know we're talking about some job needs more than the kid's gonna skin pop go in there with a *crowbar* . . .

DON: I don't want you mentioning that.

TEACH: It slipped out.

DON: You know how I feel on that.

TEACH: Yes. And I'm sorry, Don. I admire that. All that I'm saying don't confuse business with pleasure.

DON: But I don't want that talk, only, Teach. (*Pause.*) You understand?

TEACH: I more than understand, and I apologize. (*Pause.*) I'm sorry.

DON: That's the only thing.

TEACH: Alright. But I tell you. I'm glad I said it.

DON: Why?

TEACH: Cause it's best for these things to be out in the open.

DON: But I don't want it in the open.

TEACH: Which is why I apologized. (*Pause.*)

DON: You know the fucking kid's clean. He's trying hard, he's working hard, and you leave him alone.

TEACH: Oh yeah, he's trying *real* hard.

DON: And he's no dummy, Teach.

TEACH: Far from it. All I'm saying, the job is beyond him. Where's the shame in this? This is not jacks, we get up to go home we give everything back. Huh? You want this fucked up? (*Pause.*) All that I'm saying, there's the least *chance* something might fuck up, you'd get the law down, you would take the shot, and couldn't find the coins *whatever*: if you see the least chance, you cannot afford to take that chance! Don? *I* want to go in there and gut this motherfucker. Don? Where is the shame in this? You take care of him, *fine*. Now this is loyalty. But Bobby's got his own best interests too. And you cannot afford—and simply as a *business* proposition—you cannot afford to take the chance. (*Pause.* TEACH *picks up a strange object.*) What is this?

DON: That?

TEACH: Yes.

DON: It's a thing that they stick in dead pigs keep their legs apart all the blood runs out. (TEACH *nods. Pause.*)

TEACH: Mmmm. (*Pause.*)

DON: I set it up with him.

TEACH: "You set it up with him" . . . You set it up and then you told him. (*Long pause.*)

DON: I gave Earl ten percent.

TEACH: Yeah? For what?

DON: The connection.

TEACH: So ten off the top: forty-five, forty-five. (*Pause.*)

DON: And Bobby?

TEACH: A hundred. A hundred fifty . . . we hit big . . . *whatever*.

DON: And *you* what?

TEACH: The *shot*. I go, I go *in* . . . I bring the stuff *back*—or wherever . . . (*Pause.*)

DON: And what do I do?

TEACH: You mind the Fort. (*Pause.*)

DON: Here?

TEACH: Well, yeah . . . this is the Fort. (*Pause.*)

DON: You know, this is real classical money we're talking about.

TEACH: I know it. You think I'm going to fuck with Chump Change? (*Pause.*) So tell me.

DON: Well, hold on a second. I mean, we're still talking.

TEACH: I'm sorry. I thought we were done talking.

DON: No.

TEACH: Well, then, let's talk some more. You want to bargain? You want to mess with the points?

DON: No. I just want to think for a second.

TEACH: Well, you think, but here's a helpful hint. Fifty percent of some money is better than ninety percent of some broken *toaster* that you're gonna have, you send the kid in. Which is providing he don't trip the alarm in the *first* place. . . . Don? You don't even know what the *thing* is on this. Where he lives. They got alarms? What *kind* of alarms? What kind of *this* . . . ? And what if—god forbid—the *guy* walks in? Somebody's nervous, whacks him with a tablelamp—you wanna get touchy—and you can take your ninety dollars from the nickel shove it up your *ass*—the good it did you—and you wanna know *why?* And I'm not *saying* anything . . . because you didn't take the time to go first-class. (BOBBY *re-enters with a bag.*) Hi. Bob.

BOB: Hi, Teach. (*Pause.*)

DON: You get yourself something to eat?

BOB: I got a piece of pie and a Pepsi. (BOB *and* DON *extract food-stuffs and eat.*)

DON: Did they charge you again for the coffee?

BOB: For your coffee?

DON: Yes.

BOB: They charged me this time. I don't know if they charged me last time, Donny.

DON: It's okay. (*Pause.*)

TEACH: (*To* BOB.) How is it out there?

BOB: It's okay.

TEACH: Is it going to rain?

BOB: Today?

TEACH: Yeah.

BOB: I don't know. (*Pause.*)

TEACH: Well, what do you think?

BOB: It might.

TEACH: You think so, huh?

DON: Teach . . .

TEACH: What? I'm not saying anything.

BOB: What?

TEACH: I don't think I'm saying anything here. (*Pause.*)

BOB: It *might* rain. (*Pause.*) I think *later*.

TEACH: How's your pie?

BOB: Real good. (TEACH *holds up the dead pigs leg spreader.*)

TEACH: You know what this is? (*Pause.*)

BOB: Yeah.

TEACH: What is it?

BOB: I know what it is.

TEACH: What?

BOB: I know. (*Pause.*)

TEACH: Huh?

BOB: What?

TEACH: Things are what they are.

DON: Teach . . .

TEACH: What?

DON: We'll do this later.

BOB: I got to ask you something.

TEACH: Sure, that makes a difference.

DON: We'll just do it later.

TEACH: Sure.

BOB: Uh, Don?

DON: What? (*Pause.*)

BOB: I got to talk to you.

DON: Yeah? What?

BOB: I'm wondering on the thing that maybe I could have a little bit up front. (*Pause.*)

DON: Do you *need* it?

BOB: I don't *need* it . . .

DON: How much?

BOB: I was thinking that maybe you might let me have like fifty or something. (*Pause.*) To sort of *have* . . .

TEACH: You got any cuff links?

DON: Look in the case. (*To* BOB.) What do you need it for?

BOB: Nothing.

DON: Bob . . .

BOB: You can trust me.

DON: It's not a question of that. It's not a question I go around trusting you, Bob . . .

BOB: What's the question?

TEACH: Procedure.

DON: Hold on, Teach.

BOB: I got him all spotted. (*Pause.*)

TEACH: Who?

BOB: Some guy.

TEACH: Yeah?

BOB: Yeah.

TEACH: Where's he live?

BOB: Around.

TEACH: Where? Near here?

BOB: No.

TEACH: No?

BOB: He lives like on Lake Shore Drive.

TEACH: He does.

BOB: Yeah.

TEACH: (*Pause.*) What have you got, a job cased?

BOB: I just went for coffee.

TEACH: But you didn't *get* the coffee. (*Pause.*) Now, did you?

BOB: No.

TEACH: Why?

DON: Hold on, Teach. Bob . . .

BOB: What?

DON: You know what?

BOB: No.

DON: I was thinking, you know, we might hold off on this thing. (*Pause.*)

BOB: You wanna hold *off* on it?

DON: I was thinking that we might.

BOB: Oh.

DON: And, on the money, I'll give you . . . forty, you owe me twenty, and, for now, keep twenty for spotting the guy. (*Pause.*) Okay?

BOB: Yeah. (*Pause.*) You don't want me to do the job?

DON: That's what I *told* you. What am I telling you?

BOB: I'm not going to do it.

DON: Not *now*. We aren't going to do it now.

BOB: We'll do it later on?

DON: (*Shrugs.*) But I'm giving you twenty just for spotting the guy.

BOB: I need fifty, Donny.

DON: Well, I'm giving you forty.

BOB: You said you were giving me twenty.

DON: No, Bob, I did not. I said I was giving you forty, of *which* you were going to owe me twenty. (*Pause.*) And you go *keep* twenty.

BOB: I got to give back twenty.

DON: That's the deal.

BOB: When?

DON: Soon. When you got it. (*Pause.*)

BOB: If I don't *get* it soon?

DON: Well, what do you call "soon"?

BOB: I don't know.

DON: Could you get it in a . . . day, or a couple of days or so?

BOB: Maybe. I don't *think* so. Could you let me have fifty?

DON: And you'll give me back thirty?

BOB: I could just give back the twenty.

DON: That's not the deal.

BOB: We could *make* it the deal. (*Pause.*) Donny? We could *make* it the deal. Huh?

DON: Bob, lookit. Here it is: I give you fifty, next week you pay me back twenty-five. (*Pause.*) You get to keep twenty-five, you pay me back twenty-five.

BOB: And what about the thing?

DON: Forget about it.

BOB: You tell me when you want me to do it.

DON: I don't know *that* I want you to do it. At this point. (*Pause.*) You know what I mean? (*Pause.*)

BOB: No.

DON: I mean, I'm *giving* you twenty-five, and I'm saying forget the thing.

BOB: Forget it for me.

DON: Yes.

BOB: Oh. (*Pause.*) Okay. Okay.

DON: You see what I'm talking about?

BOB: Yes.

DON: Like it never happened.

BOB: I know.

DON: So you see what I'm saying.

BOB: Yes. (*Pause.*) I'm gonna go. (*Pause.*) I'll see you later. (*Pause, looks at* DON.)

DON: Oh. (*Reaches in pocket and hands bills to* BOB. *To* TEACH.) You got two fives?

TEACH: No.

DON: (*To* BOB) I got to give you . . . thirty, you owe me back thirty.

BOB: You said you were giving me fifty.

DON: I'm sorry, I'm sorry, Bob, you're absolutely right. (*Gives* BOB *remainder of money. Pause.*)

BOB: Thank you. (*Pause.*) I'll see you later, huh, Teach?

TEACH: I'll see you later, Bobby.

BOB: I'll see you, Donny.

DON: I'll see you later, Bob.

BOB: I'll come back later.

DON: Okay. (BOB *starts to exit.*)

TEACH: *See* you. (*Pause.* BOB *is gone.*) You're only doing the right thing by him, Don. (*Pause.*) Believe me. (*Pause.*) It's best for everybody. (*Pause.*) What's done is done. (*Pause.*) So let's get started. On the thing. Tell me everything.

DON: Like what?

TEACH: . . . the *guy* . . . where does he *live* . . .

DON: Around the corner.

TEACH: Okay, and he's gone for the weekend.

DON: We don't know.

TEACH: Of course we know. Bob saw him coming out the door. The kid's not going to lie to you.

DON: Well, Bob just saw him coming *out* . . .

TEACH: He had a suitcase, Don, he wasn't going to the A&P . . . He's going for the weekend . . . (*Pause.*) Don, can you cooperate? Can we get started? Do you want to tell me something about coins? (*Pause.*)

DON: What about 'em?

TEACH: A crashcourse. What to look for. What to take. What to *not* take . . . this they can trace—that isn't *worth* nothing . . .

(*Pause.*) What looks like what but it's more *valuable* . . . *so*
on . . .

DON: First off, I want that nickel back.

TEACH: Donny . . .

DON: No, I know, it's only a fuckin' nickel . . . I mean big deal,
huh? But what I'm saying is I only want it back.

TEACH: You're going to get it back. I'm going in there for his coins,
what am I going to take 'em all except your nickel? Wake up.
Don, let's plan this out. The *spirit* of the thing? (*Pause.*) Let's not
be loose on this. People are *loose*, people pay the price . . .

DON: You're right.

TEACH: And I like you like a brother, Don. So let's wake up on this.
(*Pause.*) Alright? A man walks in here, well-dressed . . . With a
briefcase?

DON: No.

TEACH: Alright. . . . comes into a junkshop looking for coins.
(*Pause.*) He spots a valuable nickel hidden in a pile of shit. He
farts around he picks up this, he farts around he picks up that.

DON: He wants the nickel.

TEACH: No shit. He goes to check out, he goes ninety on the nick.

DON: He would of gone five times that.

TEACH: Look, don't kick yourself. Alright, we got a guy knows coins.
Where does he keep his coin collection?

DON: Hidden.

TEACH: The man hides his coin collection, we're probably looking the guy has a *study* . . . I mean, he's not the kind of guy to keep it in the *basement* . . .

DON: No.

TEACH: So we're looking for a study.

DON: A den.

TEACH: And we're looking, for, he hasn't got a *safe* . . .

DON: Yeah . . . ?

TEACH: . . . he's probably going to keep 'em . . . where? (*Pause.*)

DON: I don't know. His desk drawer.

TEACH: You open the middle the rest of 'em pop out?

DON: Yeah.

TEACH: Maybe. Which brings up a point.

DON: What?

TEACH: As we're moving the stuff tonight, we can go in like Gang-busters, huh? We don't care we wreck the joint up. So what else? We *take* it, or leave it?

DON: . . . well . . .

TEACH: I'm not talking *cash*, all I mean, what other stuff do we take . . . for our *trouble* . . . (*Pause.*)

DON: I don't know.

TEACH: It's hard to make up rules about this stuff.

DON: You'll be in there under lots of pressure.

TEACH: Not so much.

DON: Come on, a little, anyway.

TEACH: That's only natural.

DON: Yeah.

TEACH: It would be unnatural I wasn't tense. A guy who isn't tense, I don't want him on my side.

DON: No.

TEACH: You know *why?*

DON: Yeah.

TEACH: Okay, then. It's good to talk this stuff out.

DON: Yeah.

TEACH: You *have* to talk it out. Bad feelings, misunderstandings happen on a job. You can't get away from 'em, you have to deal with 'em. You want to quiz me on some coins? You want to show some coins to me? *list* prices . . . the bluebook . . . ?

DON: You want to see the book?

TEACH: Sure. (DON *hands large coinbook to* TEACHER.)

DON: I just picked it up last week.

TEACH: Uh hum.

DON: All the values aren't *current* . . .

TEACH: Uh huh . . .

DON: *Silver* . . .

TEACH: (*Looking at book.*) Uh huh . . .

DON: What's a *rarity* . . .

TEACH: Well, that's got to be fairly steady, huh?

DON: I'm saying against what *isn't.*

TEACH: Oh.

DON: But the book gives you a general idea.

TEACH: You've been looking at it?

DON: Yeah.

TEACH: You got to have a feeling for your subject.

DON: The book can give you that.

TEACH: This is what I'm *saying* to you. One thing. Makes all the difference in the world.

DON: What?

TEACH: Knowing what the fuck you're talking about. And it's so rare, Don. *So* rare. What do you think a 1929 S. Lincolnhead penny with the wheat on the back is worth? (DON *starts to speak.*) Ah! Ah! Ah! Ah! Ah! We got to know what *condition* we're talking about.

DON: (*Pause.*) Okay. What condition?

TEACH: *Any* of 'em. You tell me.

DON: Well, pick one.

TEACH: Okay, I'm going to pick an easy one. Excellent condition 1929 S.

DON: It's worth . . . *about* 36 dollars.

TEACH: No.

DON: More?

TEACH: Well, guess.

DON: Just tell me is it more or less.

TEACH: What do you think?

DON: More.

TEACH: No.

DON: Okay, it's worth, I gotta say . . . eighteen-sixty.

TEACH: No.

DON: Then I give up.

TEACH: Twenty fucking cents.

DON: You're fulla shit.

TEACH: My mother's grave.

DON: Give me that fucking book. (*Business.*) Go beat that.

TEACH: This is what I'm saying, Don, you got to know what you're talking about.

DON: You wanna take the book?

TEACH: Naaa, *fuck* the book. What am I going to do, leaf through the book for hours on end? The important thing is to have the *idea* . . .

DON: Yeah.

TEACH: What was the other one?

DON: What other one?

TEACH: He stole off you.

DON: What do you mean what was it?

TEACH: The *date*, so on.

DON: How the fuck do *I* know?

TEACH: (*Pause.*) When you looked it up.

DON: How are you getting in the house?

TEACH: The house?

DON: Yeah.

TEACH: Aah, you go in through a *window* they left open, something.

DON: Yeah.

TEACH: There's always something.

DON: Yeah. What else, if not the window.

TEACH: How the fuck do *I* know? (*Pause.*) If not the window, something else.

DON: What?

TEACH: We'll see when we get there.

DON: Okay, all I'm asking, what it *might* be.

TEACH: Hey, you didn't warn us we were going to have a *quiz* . . .

DON: It's just a question.

TEACH: I know it. (*Pause.*)

DON: What is the answer?

TEACH: We're seeing when we get there.

DON: Oh. You can't answer me, Teach?

TEACH: You have your job, I have my job, Don. I am not here to smother you in theory. Think about it.

DON: I am thinking about it. I'd like you to answer my question.

TEACH: Don't push me, Don. Don't front off with me here. I am not other people.

DON: And just what does that mean?

TEACH: Just that nobody's perfect.

DON: They aren't.

TEACH: No. (*Pause.*)

DON: I'm going to have Fletch come with us.

TEACH: Fletch.

DON: Yes.

TEACH: You're having him *come* with us.

DON: Yes.

TEACH: Now you're kidding me.

DON: No.

TEACH: No? Then why do you say this?

DON: With Fletch.

TEACH: Yes.

DON: I want some depth.

TEACH: You want depth on the team.

DON: Yes, I do.

TEACH: So you bring in Fletch.

DON: Yes.

TEACH: Cause I don't play your games with you.

DON: We just might need him.

TEACH: We won't.

DON: We might, Teach.

TEACH: We don't need him, Don. We do not need this guy. (DON *picks up phone.*) What? Are you *calling* him? (DON *nods.*)

DON: It's busy. (*Hangs up.*)

TEACH: He's probably talking on the phone.

DON: Yeah. He probably is.

TEACH: We don't need this guy, Don. We don't need him. I see your point here, I do. So you're thinking I'm out there alone, and you're worried I'll rattle, so you ask me how I go in. I understand. I see this, I do. I could go in the second floor, climb up a drainpipe, I could *this* . . . (DON *dials phone again.*) He's talking, he's talking, for chrissake, give him a minute, huh? (DON *hangs up phone.*) I am hurt, Don.

DON: I'm sorry, Teach.

TEACH: I'm not hurt for me.

DON: Who are you hurt for?

TEACH: Think about it.

DON: We can use somebody watch our rear.

TEACH: You keep your numbers down you don't *have* a rear. You know what has rears? Armies.

DON: I'm just saying, something goes *wrong* . . .

TEACH: Wrong, wrong, you make your own right and wrong. Hey Biiig fucking deal. The shot is yours, no one's disputing that. We're talking business, let's *talk* business: you think it's good business call Fletch in? To help us.

DON: Yes.

TEACH: Well then okay. (*Pause.*) Are you sure?

DON: Yeah.

TEACH: Alright, if you're *sure* . . .

DON: I'm sure, Teach.

TEACH: Then, alright, then. That's all I worry about. (*Pause.*) And you're probably right, we could use three of us on the job.

DON: Yeah.

TEACH: Somebody watch for the *cops* . . . work out a *signal* . . .

DON: Yeah.

TEACH: Safety in numbers.

DON: Yeah.

TEACH: Three-men jobs.

DON: Yeah.

TEACH: You, me, Fletcher.

DON: Yeah.

TEACH: A division of labor. (*Pause.*) Security. Muscle. Intelligence. Huh?

DON: Yeah.

TEACH: This means, what, a traditional split. Am I right? We got ten off the top goes to Earl, and the rest, three-way split. Huh? That's what we got? Huh?

DON: Yeah.

TEACH: Well, that's what's right. (*Pause.*) Alright. Lay the shot out for me.

DON: For tonight?

TEACH: Yes.

DON: Okay. (*Pause.*) I stay here on the phone . . .

TEACH: . . . yeah . . .

DON: . . . for Fletcher . . .

TEACH: Yeah.

DON: We meet, ten-thirty, 'leven, back here.

TEACH: Back here, the three . . .

DON: Yeah. And go in. (*Pause.*) Huh?

TEACH: Yeah. Where?

DON: Around the corner.

TEACH: Yeah. (*Pause.*) Are you mad at me?

DON: No.

TEACH: Do you want to play gin?

DON: Naaa.

TEACH: Then I guess I'll go home, take a nap, and rest up. Come back here tonight and we'll take off this fucking fruit's coins.

DON: Right.

TEACH: I feel like I'm trying to stay *up* to death . . .

DON: You ain't been to sleep since the game?

TEACH: *Shit* no—then that dyke cocksucker . . .

DON: So go take a nap. You trying to kill yourself?

TEACH: You're right, and you do what you think is right, Don.

DON: I got to, Teach.

TEACH: You got to trust your instincts, right or wrong.

DON: I got to.

TEACH: I know it. I know you do. (*Pause.*) Anybody wants to get in touch with me, I'm over the Hotel.

DON: Okay.

TEACH: I'm not the *Hotel*, I stepped out for coffee, I'll be back one minute.

DON: Okay.

TEACH: And I'll see you around Eleven.

DON: O'*Clock*.

TEACH: *Here*.

DON: Right.

TEACH: And don't worry about anything.

DON: I won't.

TEACH: I don't want to hear you're worrying about a goddamned thing.

DON: You won't, Teach.

TEACH: You're sure you want Fletch coming with us?

DON: Yes.

TEACH: Alright then so long as you're sure.

DON: I'm sure, Teach.

TEACH: Then I'm going to see you tonight.

DON: Goddam right you are.

TEACH: I am seeing you later.

DON: I know.

TEACH: Goodbye.

DON: Goodbye.

TEACH: I want to make one thing plain before I go, Don. I am not mad at you.

DON: I know.

TEACH: Alright, then.

DON: You have a good nap.

TEACH: I will. (TEACH *exits*.)

DON: Fuckin business . . .

(*Lights dim to black.*)

END OF ACT ONE

ACT TWO

Donny's Resale Shop. 11:15 that evening. The shop is darkened.
DONNY *is alone. He is holding the telephone to his ear.*

DON: Great. (*Hangs up phone.*) Great great great great great.
(*Pause.*) Cocksucking fuckhead . . . (*Pause.*) This is greatness.
(BOBBY *appears in the door to the shop.*) What are you doing
here?

BOB: I *came* here.

DON: For what?

BOB: I got to talk to you.

DON: Why?

BOB: Business.

DON: Yeah?

BOB: I need some money.

DON: What for?

BOB: Nothing. I can pay for it.

DON: For what?

BOB: This guy, I found a coin.

DON: A coin?

BOB: A Buffalohead.

DON: Nickel?

BOB: Yeah. You want it? (*Pause.*)

DON: What are you doing here, Bob?

BOB: I need money. (DON *picks up phone and dials. He lets it ring as he talks to* BOB.) You want it?

DON: What?

BOB: My buffalo.

DON: Lemme look at it. (*Pause.*) I got to look at it to know do I want it.

BOB: You don't know if you want it?

DON: I probably *want* it . . . what I'm saying, if it's *worth* anything.

BOB: It's a Buffalo it's worth something.

DON: The question is but what. It's just like everything else, Bob. Like every other fucking thing. (*Pause. He hangs up phone.*) Were you at the Riv?

BOB: Before.

DON: Is Fletch over there?

BOB: No.

DON: Teach?

BOB: No. Ruth and Gracie was there for a minute.

DON: What the fuck does that mean? (*Pause.*)

BOB: Nothing. (*Pause.*) Only they were there. (*Pause.*) I didn't *mean* anything . . . my nickel . . . I can tell you what it is. (*Pause.*) I can tell you what it is.

DON: What? What *date* it is? That don't mean shit.

BOB: No?

DON: Come *on*, Bobby? What's important in a coin . . .

BOB: . . . yeah?

DON: What *condition* it's in . . .

BOB: Great.

DON: . . . if you can—I don't know . . . count the hair on the Indian, something. You got to look it up.

BOB: In the book?

DON: Yes.

BOB: Okay. And then you know.

DON: Well, no. What I'm saying, the book is like you use it like an *indicator*—I mean, right off with *silver* prices . . . so on . . . (DON *hangs up phone.*) Shit.

BOB: What?

DON: What do you want for the coin?

BOB: What it's worth only.

DON: Okay, we'll look it up.

BOB: But you still don't know.

DON: But you got an idea, Bob. You got an idea you can *deviate* from. (*Pause.*)

BOB: The other guy went ninety bucks.

DON: He was a fuckin' sucker, Bob. (*Pause.*) Am I a sucker? Bob, I'm busy here. You see?

BOB: Some coins are worth that.

DON: Oddities, Bob. Freak oddities of nature. What are we talking about here? The silver? The silver's maybe three times face. You want fifteen cents for it?

BOB: No.

DON: So, okay. So what do you want for it?

BOB: What it's worth.

DON: Let me see it.

BOB: Why?

DON: To look in the goddam . . . Forget it. Forget it. *Don't* let me see it.

BOB: But the book don't *mean* shit.

DON: The book gives us *ideas*, Bob. The book gives us a basis for *comparison*. Look, we're human beings. We can *talk*, we can negotiate, we can *this* . . . you need some money? What do you need? (*Pause.*)

BOB: I *came* here . . . (*Pause.*)

DON: What do you need, Bob? (*Pause.*)

BOB: How come you're in here so late?

DON: We're gonna play cards.

BOB: Who?

DON: Teach and me and Fletcher. (TEACHER *enters the store.*)

DON: What time is it?

TEACH: Fuck is *he* doing here?

DON: What fucking time is it?

TEACH: Where's Fletcher? (*Pause.*) Where's Fletcher?

BOB: Hi, Teach.

TEACH: (*To* DON) What is he doing here?

BOB: I came in.

DON: Do you know what time it is?

TEACH: What? I'm late?

DON: Damn right you're late.

TEACH: I'm fucked up since my watch broke.

DON: Your watch broke?

TEACH: I just told you that.

DON: When did your watch break?

TEACH: The fuck do *I* know?

DON: Well, you look at it. You want to know your watch broke, all you got to do is look at it. (*Pause.*)

TEACH: I don't have it.

DON: Why not?

TEACH: I took it off when it broke. What do you *want* here?

DON: You're going around without a watch.

TEACH: Yes. I am, Donny. What am I, you're my *keeper* all a sudden?

DON: I'm paying you to do a thing, Teach, I expect to know where you are when.

TEACH: Donny. You aren't paying me to do a thing. We are doing something together. I know we are. My watch broke, that is my concern. The *thing* is your and my concern. And the concern of Fletcher. You want to find a reason we should jump all over each other all of a sudden like we work in a *bloodbank*, fine. But it's not good business. (*Pause.*) And so who knows what time it is off-hand? Jerks on the radio? The phone broad? (*Pause.*) Now, I understand nerves.

DON: There's no fuckin' nerves involved in this, Teach.

TEACH: No, huh?

DON: No.

TEACH: Well, great. That's great, then. So what are we talking about? A little lateness? Some excusable fucking lateness? And a couple of guys they're understandably a bit excited? (*Pause.*)

DON: I don't like it.

TEACH: Then *don't* like it, then. Let's do this. Let's everybody get a writ. I got a case. You got a case. Bobby—I don't know what the fuck *he's* doing here . . .

Don: Leave him alone.

Teach: Now I'm picking on him.

Don: Leave him alone.

Teach: What's he doing here?

Don: He came in.

Bob: I found a nickel.

Teach: Hey, that's fantastic.

Bob: You want to see it?

Teach: Yes, please let me see it. (Bob *hands nickel, wrapped in cloth, to* Teach.)

Bob: I like 'em because of the art on it.

Teach: Uh huh.

Bob: Because it *looks* like something.

Teach: (*To* Don) Is this worth anything?

Bob: We don't know yet.

Teach: Oh.

Bob: We're going to look it up.

Teach: Oh, what? Tonight?

Bob: I think so. (Don *hangs up phone.*)

DON: Fuck.

TEACH: So where is he?

DON: How the fuck do I know?

TEACH: He said he'd be here?

DON: Yes, he did, Teach.

BOB: Fletcher?

TEACH: So where is he, then? And what's *he* doing here?

DON: Leave him alone. He'll leave.

TEACH: He's going to leave, huh?

DON: Yes.

TEACH: You're sure it isn't like the bowling league, Fletch doesn't show up, we just suit up Bobby, give him a shot, and *he* goes in? (*Pause.*) Aaah, fuck. I'm sorry. I spoke in anger. I'm sorry, I'm sorry. Everybody can make mistakes around here but me. I'm sorry, Bob, I'm very sorry.

BOB: That's okay, Teach.

TEACH: All I meant to say, we'd give you a fuckin' suit, like in football . . . (*Pause.*) and you'd—You know, like, whatever . . . and *you'd* go in. (*Pause. To* DON.) So what do you want me to do? Dress up and lick him all over? I said I was sorry, what's going on here. Huh? In the *first* place. I come in, I'm *late* . . . *he's* here . . . (*Pause.*)

DON: Bobby, I'll see you tomorrow, okay? (*Picks phone up and dials.*)

BOB: I need some money.

TEACH: (*Digging in pockets.*) What do you need?

BOB: I want to sell the *buffalo* nickel.

TEACH: I'll buy it myself.

BOB: We don't know what it's worth.

TEACH: What do you want for it?

BOB: Fifty dollars.

TEACH: You're outta your fuckin' mind. (*Pause.*) Look. Here's a fin. Get lost. Okay? (*Pause.*)

BOB: It's worth more than that.

TEACH: How the fuck do you know that?

BOB: I think it is. (*Pause.*)

TEACH: Okay. You keep the fin like a loan. You *keep* the fuckin' nickel, and we'll call it a loan. Now go on. (*Hands nickel back to* BOB.)

DON: (*He hangs up phone.*) Fuck.

BOB: I need more.

TEACH: (*To* DON.) Give the kid a couple of bucks.

DON: What?

TEACH: Give him some money.

DON: What for?

TEACH: The nickel. (*Pause.*)

BOB: We can look in the book tomorrow.

DON: (*To* TEACH.) You bought the nickel?

TEACH: Don't worry about it. Give him some money. Get him out of here.

DON: How much?

TEACH: What? *I* don't care . . .

DON: (*To* BOB.) How much . . . (*To* TEACH.) What the fuck am I giving him money for?

TEACH: Just give it to him.

DON: What? Ten? (*Pause. Digs in pocket, hands bill to* BOB.) How is that, Bob? (*Pause. Hands additional bill to* BOB.) Okay?

BOB: We'll look it up.

DON: Okay. Huh? We'll see you tomorrow.

BOB: And we'll look it up.

DON: Yes.

BOB: (*To* TEACH.) You should talk to Ruthie.

TEACH: Oh, I should, huh?

BOB: Yes.

TEACH: Why?

BOB: Because. (*Pause.*)

TEACH: I'll see you tomorrow, Bobby.

BOB: Goodbye, Teach.

TEACH: Goodbye.

DON: Goodbye, Bob.

BOB: Goodbye. (*Pause.* BOB *exits.*)

DON: Fuckin *kid* . . .

TEACH: So where is Fletcher?

DON: Don't worry. He'll be here.

TEACH: The question is but when. Maybe his watch broke.

DON: Maybe it just did, Teach. Maybe his actual watch broke.

TEACH: And maybe mine didn't, you're saying? You wanna bet? You wanna place a little fucking wager on it? How much money you got in your pockets? I bet you all the money in your pockets against all the money in my pockets, I walk out that door right now, I come back with a broken watch. (*Pause.*)

DON: Calm down.

TEACH: I am calm. I'm just upset.

DON: I know.

TEACH: So where is he when I'm here?

DON: Don't worry about it.

TEACH: So who's going to worry about it then?

DON: Shit.

TEACH: This should go to prove you something.

DON: It doesn't prove anything. The guy's just late.

TEACH: Oh. And I wasn't?

DON: You were late, too.

TEACH: You're fuckin' A I was, and I got bawled out for it.

DON: He's late for a reason.

TEACH: I don't accept it.

DON: That's your privilege.

TEACH: And what was Bob doing here?

DON: He told you. He wanted to sell me the nickel.

TEACH: That's why he came here?

DON: Yes.

TEACH: To sell you the Buffalo?

DON: Yes.

TEACH: Where did he get it?

DON: I think from some guy.

TEACH: Who? (*Pause.*)

DON: I don't know. (*Pause.*)

TEACH: Where's Fletcher?

DON: I don't know. He'll show up. (DON *picks up phone and dials.*)

TEACH: He'll show up.

DON: Yes.

TEACH: He's not here now.

DON: No.

TEACH: You scout the guy's house?

DON: The guy? No.

TEACH: Well, let's do that, then. He's not home. Hang up. (DON *hangs up phone.*)

DON: You wanna scout his house.

TEACH: Yeah.

DON: Why? Bob already saw him when he went off with the suit-case.

TEACH: Just to be sure, huh?

DON: Yeah. Okay.

TEACH: You bet. Now we call him up.

DON: We call the guy up.

TEACH: Yeah. (*Pause.*)

DON: Good idea. (*Picks up phone. Hunts guy's number. Dials. To himself.*) We can do this.

TEACH: This is planning . . . This is preparation. If he answers . . . (DON *shhhhs* TEACH.) I'm telling you what to do if he answers.

DON: What?

TEACH: Hang up. (DON *starts to hang up phone.*) No. *Don't* hang up. Hang up now. Hang up *now!* (DON *hangs up phone.*) Now look: if he *answers* . . .

DON: . . . yeah?

TEACH: Don't arouse his fucking suspicions.

DON: Alright.

TEACH: And the odds are he's not there, so when he answers just say you're calling for a wrong fucking *number,* something. Be simple. (*Pause.*) Give me the phone. (DON *hands* TEACH *the phone.*) Gimme the card. (DON *hands* TEACH *card.*) This is his number? 221-7834?

DON: Yeah. (TEACH *snorts.*)

TEACH: Alright. I dial, I'm calling for somebody named "June" and we go interchange on number. (*Pause.*) We're gonna say like, "Is this 221-7834?"

DON: . . . yeah?

TEACH: And they go, "No." I mean "-7843." It *is* -7834. So we go, very simply, "Is this 221-7843?" and they go "No," and right away the guy is home, we still haven't blown the shot.

DON: Okay. (TEACH *picks up phone and dials.*)

TEACH: (*Into phone.*) Hi. Yeah. I'm calling . . . uh . . . is June there? (*Pause.*) Well, is this 221-7843? (*Pause.*) It is? Well, look I must of got the number wrong. I'm sorry. (*Hangs up phone.*) This is bizarre. Read me that number.

DON: 221-7834.

TEACH: Right. (*Dials phone. Listens.*) Nobody home. See, this is a careful operation . . . check and re-check! (*Hangs up.*) You wanna try it?

DON: No.

TEACH: I don't mind that you're careful, Don. This doesn't piss me off. What gets me mad, when you get loose.

DON: What do you mean?

TEACH: You know what I mean.

DON: No, I don't.

TEACH: Yes you do. I come in here. The Kid's here.

DON: He doesn't know anything.

TEACH: He doesn't.

DON: No.

TEACH: What was he here for, then?

DON: Sell me the Buffalo.

TEACH: Sell it tonight.

DON: Yeah.

TEACH: A valuable nickel.

DON: We don't know. (*Pause.*)

TEACH: Where is Fletch?

DON: I don't know. (*Picks up phone and dials.*)

TEACH: He's not home. He's not home, Don. He's out.

DON: (*Into phone.*) Hello?

TEACH: He's in?

DON: This is Donny Dubrow.

TEACH: The Riv?

DON: I'm looking for Fletcher. (*Pause.*) Okay. Thank you. (*Hangs up.*)

TEACH: Cocksucker should be horsewhipped with a horsewhip.

DON: He'll show up.

TEACH: Fucking Riverside, too. Thirty-seven cents for take-out coffee . . .

DON: Yeah. (*Picks up phone.*)

TEACH: A lot of nerve you come in there for sixteen years. This is not free enterprise.

DON: No.

TEACH: You know what is free enterprise?

DON: No. What?

TEACH: The freedom . . .

DON: . . . yeah?

TEACH: Of the *Individual* . . .

DON: . . . yeah?

TEACH: To Embark on Any Fucking Course that he sees fit.

DON: Uh huh . . .

TEACH: In order to secure his honest chance to make a profit. Am I so out of line on this?

DON: No.

TEACH: Does this make me a Commie?

DON: No.

TEACH: The country's *founded* on this, Don. You know this.

DON: (*Hanging up phone.*) Did you get a chance to take a nap?

TEACH: Nap nap nap nap nap. Big deal.

DON: (*Pause.*) Yeah.

TEACH: Without this we're just savage shitheads in the wilderness.

DON: Yeah.

TEACH: Sitting around some vicious campfire. That's why *Ruthie* burns me up.

DON: Yeah.

TEACH: Nowhere dyke. . . . And take those fuckers in the concentration camps. You think they went in there by *choice?*

DON: No.

TEACH: They were *dragged* in there, Don . . .

DON: . . . yeah.

TEACH: Kicking and screaming. *Gimme* that fucking phone. (*Grabs phone. TEACH dials phone. Hangs up.*) He's not home. I say *fuck* the cocksucker.

Don: He'll show up.

Teach: You believe that?

Don: Yes.

Teach: Then you are full of shit.

Don: Don't tell me that, Teach. Don't tell me I'm full of shit.

Teach: I'm sorry. You want me to hold your hand? This is how you keep score. I mean, *we're* all here . . .

Don: Just, I don't want that talk.

Teach: Don . . . I talk straight to you 'cause I respect you. It's kickass or kissass, Don, and I'd be lying if I told you any different.

Don: And what makes you such an authority on life all of a sudden.

Teach: My life, Jim. And the way I've lived it. (*Pause.*)

Don: Now what does that mean, Teach?

Teach: What does that mean?

Don: Yes.

Teach: What does that *mean*?

Don: Yes.

Teach: Nothing. Not a thing. All that I'm telling you, the shot is yours. It's one night only. Too many guys know. All I'm saying. Take your shot.

Don: Who knows?

Teach: You and me.

DON: Yeah.

TEACH: Bob and Fletcher. Earl, the phone guy, Grace and Ruthie, maybe.

DON: Grace and Ruth don't know.

TEACH: Who *knows* they know or not, all that I'm telling you, a fact stands by itself. Don't go fuck yourself over with appearances. It's not always so clear what's going on. Like Fletcher that time and the pigiron.

DON: What was the shot on that?

TEACH: He stole some pigiron off Ruth.

DON: I *heard* that . . .

TEACH: That's a fact. A fact stands by itself. And we must face the facts and act on them. You better wake up, Don, right now, or things are going to fall around your *head,* and you are going to turn around to find he's took the joint off by himself.

DON: He would not do that.

TEACH: He would. He is an animal.

DON: He don't have the address.

TEACH: He doesn't know it.

DON: No.

TEACH: Now, that is wise. Then let us go and take what's ours.

DON: We have a deal with the man.

TEACH: With Fletcher.

DON: Yes.

TEACH: We had a deal with Bobby.

DON: What does that mean?

TEACH: Nothing.

DON: It don't.

TEACH: No.

DON: What did you mean by that?

TEACH: I didn't mean a thing.

DON: You didn't.

TEACH: No.

DON: You're full of shit, Teach.

TEACH: I am.

DON: Yes.

TEACH: Because I got the balls to face some facts? (*Pause.*) You scare me sometimes, Don.

DON: Oh, yeah?

TEACH: Yes. I don't want to go around with you here, things go down, we'll settle when we're done. We have a job to do here. Huh? Forget it. Let's go, come on.

DON: We're waiting for him.

TEACH: Fletcher.

DON: Yes.

TEACH: Why?

DON: Many reasons.

TEACH: Tell me one. You give me one good reason, why we're sitting here, and I'll sit down and never say a word. One reason. One. Go on. I'm listening.

DON: He knows how to get in. (*Pause.*)

TEACH: Good night, Don. (*Starts to go for door.*)

DON: Where are you going?

TEACH: Home.

DON: You're going home.

TEACH: Yes.

DON: Why?

TEACH: You're fucking with me. It's alright.

DON: Hold on. You tell me how I'm fucking with you.

TEACH: Come *on*, Don.

DON: You asked me the one reason.

TEACH: You make yourself ridiculous.

DON: Yeah?

TEACH: Yeah.

DON: Then answer it.

TEACH: What is the question?

DON: Fletch knows how to get in.

TEACH: "Get in." That's your reason?

DON: Yes. (*Pause.*)

TEACH: What the fuck they *live* in, Fort *Knox?* "Get in" (*Snorts.*)
You break in a *window,* worse comes to worse you kick the fucking
backdoor in. What do you think this is, the Middle Ages?

DON: What about he's got a safe?

TEACH: Biiiig fucking deal.

DON: How is that?

TEACH: You want to know about a safe?

DON: Yes.

TEACH: What you do, a *safe* . . . you find the combination.

DON: Where he wrote it down.

TEACH: Yes.

DON: What if he didn't write it down?

TEACH: He wrote it down. He's *gotta* write it down. What happens
he forgets it?

DON: What happens he doesn't forget it?

TEACH: He's gotta forget it, Don. Human Nature. The point being,
even he *doesn't* forget it, *why* does he not forget it?

DON: Why?

TEACH: 'Cause he's got it *wrote down*. (*Pause.*) That's why he *writes* it down. (*Pause.*) Huh? Not because he's some fucking turkey can't even remember the combination to his own *safe* . . . but only in the event that (god forbid) he somehow *forgets* it . . . he's got it wrote down. (*Pause.*) This is common sense. (*Pause.*) What's the good keep the stuff in the safe, every time he wants to get at it he's got to write away to the manufacturer?

DON: Where does he write it?

TEACH: What difference? *Here* . . . We go in, I find the combination fifteen minutes, tops. (*Pause.*) There are only just so many places it could be. Man is a creature of habits. Man does not change his habits overnight. This is not like him. And if he does, he has a very good reason. Look, Don: You want to remember something—you write it down. Where do you put it? (*Pause.*)

DON: In my wallet. (*Pause.*)

TEACH: Exactly! (*Pause.*) Okay?

DON: What if he didn't write it down?

TEACH: He wrote it down.

DON: I know he did. But just, I'm saying, from *another* instance. Some madeup guy from my imagination.

TEACH: You're saying in the instance of some guy . . .

DON: Some *other* guy . . .

TEACH: . . . he didn't write it down? (*Pause.*)

DON: Yes.

TEACH: Well, this is another thing. (*Pause.*) You see what I'm saying?

DON: Yeah.

TEACH: It's another matter. The guy, he's got the shit in the safe, he didn't write it *down* . . . (*Pause.*) Don . . . ?

DON: Yes?

TEACH: How do you know he didn't write it down?

DON: I'm, you know, making it up. (*Pause.*)

TEACH: Well, then, this is not based on *fact*. (*Pause.*) You see what I'm saying? I can sit here and tell you *this*, I can tell you *that*, I can tell you any fucking thing you care to mention, but what is the point? You aren't telling me he didn't write it down. All that you're saying, you can't *find* it. Which is only natural, as you don't know where to look. All I'm asking for a little trust here.

DON: I don't know.

TEACH: Then you know what? Fuck you. All day long. Grace and Ruthie Christ. What am I standing here convincing you? What am I doing demeaning myself standing here pleading with you to protect your best interests? I can't believe this, Don. Somebody told me I'd do this for you . . . For *anybody*—I'd call him a liar. I'm coming in here to efface myself. I am not Fletch, Don, no, and you should thank god and fall *down* I'm not. You're coming in here all the time that "He's so good at cards . . ." The man is a cheat, Don. He *cheats* at cards, Fletcher, the guy that you're waiting for.

DON: He cheats.

TEACH: Fucking A right, he does.

DON: Where do you get this? (*Pause.*) You're full of shit, Walt. You're saying Fletch cheats at cards. (*Pause.*) You've seen him. You've *seen* him he cheats. (*Pause.*) You're *telling* me this?

TEACH: The whatchamacallit is always the last to know.

DON: Come on, Walt, I mean, forget with the job and all.

TEACH: You live in a world of your own, Don.

DON: Fletch cheats at cards.

TEACH: Yes.

DON: I don't believe you.

TEACH: Ah. You can't take the truth.

DON: No. I am sorry. I play in this fucking game.

TEACH: And you don't know what goes on.

DON: I leave Fletcher alone in my *store* . . . He could take me off any time, day and night. What are you telling me, Walt? This is nothing but poison, I don't want to hear it. (*Pause. Cross to desk and sit.*)

TEACH: And that is what you say.

DON: Yes. It is. (*Pause.*)

TEACH: Think back, Donny. Last night. On one hand. You lost two hundred bucks. (*Pause.*) You got the straight, you stand pat. I go down before the draw.

DON: Yeah.

TEACH: He's got what?

DON: A flush.

TEACH: That is correct. How many did he take?

DON: (*Pause.*) What?

TEACH: How many did he take? (*Pause.*)

DON: One?

TEACH: No. Two, Don. He took two. (*Pause.*)

DON: Yeah. He took two on that hand.

TEACH: He takes two on your standing pat, you kicked him thirty
bucks? He draws two, comes out with a *flush?*

DON: (*Pause.*) Yeah?

TEACH: And spills his fucking Fresca?

DON: Yeah?

TEACH: Oh. You remember that?

DON: (*Pause.*) Yeah.

TEACH: And we look down.

DON: Yeah.

TEACH: When we look back he has come up with a king-high flush.
(*Pause.*) After he has drawed two. (*Pause.*) You're better than
that, Don. You *knew* you had him beat, and you were right.
(*Pause.*)

DON: It could happen.

TEACH: Donny . . .

DON: Yeah?

TEACH: He laid down five red cards. A heart flush to the king.
(*Pause.*)

DON: Yeah?

TEACH: I swear to God as I am standing here that when I threw my hand in when you raised me out, that I folded the king of hearts. (*Pause.*)

DON: You never called him out.

TEACH: No.

DON: How come.

TEACH: He don't got the address the guy?

DON: I told you he didn't. (*Pause.*) He's cheating, you couldn't say anything?

TEACH: It's not my responsibility, to cause bloodshed. I am not your keeper. You want to face facts, okay.

DON: I can't believe this, Teach.

TEACH: Friendship is marvellous.

DON: You couldn't say a word?

TEACH: I tell you now.

DON: He was cheating, you couldn't say anything?

TEACH: Don. Don, I see you're put out, you find out this guy is a cheat . . .

DON: According to you.

TEACH: According to me, yes. I am the person it's usually according *to* when I'm talking. Have you noticed this? And I'm not crazed about it you're coming out I would lie to you on this. *Fuck* this. On anything. Wake up, Jim. I'm not the cheat. I know you're not mad at me, who are you mad at? Who fucked you up here, Don? Who's not here? Who?

DON: Ruth knows he cheats?

TEACH: Who is the bitch in league with?

DON: Him?

TEACH: Oh, yes, Don. Oh yes. (*Pause.*) You know how much money they've taken out of that game?

DON: Yeah?

TEACH: Well, I could be wrong.

DON: Don't fuck with me here, Teach.

TEACH: I don't fuck with my friends, Don. I don't fuck with my business associates. I am a businessman, I am here to do business. I am here to face facts. Will you open your *eyes*. The kid comes in here, he has got a certain coin, it's like the one *you* used to have. The guy you brought in doesn't show, we don't know where *he* is. (*Pause.*) Something comes down, some guy gets his house took off. Fletcher, he's not showing up. Alright. Let's say I don't know why. Let's say *you* don't know why. But I know that we're both better off. We are better off, Don. What time is it?

DON: It's midnight.

TEACH: (*Pause.*) I'm going out there now. I'll need the address. (*Produces and starts to load revolver.*)

DON: What's that?

TEACH: What?

DON: That.

TEACH: This "gun"?

DON: Yes.

TEACH: What does it look like?

DON: A gun.

TEACH: It is a gun.

DON: (*Rise cross in Center.*) I don't like it.

TEACH: Don't look at it.

DON: I'm serious.

TEACH: So am I.

DON: We don't need a gun, Teach.

TEACH: I pray that we don't, Don.

DON: We don't, tell me why we need a gun.

TEACH: It's not a question do we *need* it . . . *Need* . . . Only that it makes me comfortable, okay? It helps me to relax. So, God Forbid, something inevitable occurs and the choice is—And I'm *saying* "god forbid"—it's either him or us.

DON: Who?

TEACH: The guy. I'm saying God forbid the *guy*—or somebody—comes in, he's got a knife . . . a cleaver from one of those magnetic *boards* . . . ?

DON: Yeah?

TEACH: . . . with the two *strips* . . . ?

DON: Yeah?

TEACH: And *whack*, and somebody is bleeding to death. This is all.

Merely as a deterrent. (*Pause.*) All the preparation in the world does not mean *shit,* the path of some crazed lunatic sees you as an invasion of his personal domain. Guys go nuts, Don, *you* know this. Public *officials* . . . *Axe* murderers . . . all I'm saying, look out for your own.

DON: I don't like the gun.

TEACH: It's a personal thing, Don. A personal thing of mine. A silly, personal thing. I just like to have it along. Is this so unreasonable?

DON: I don't want it.

TEACH: I'm not going without it.

DON: Why do you want it?

TEACH: Protection of me and my partner. Protection, deterrence. We're only going around the fucking *corner* for chrissake . . .

DON: I don't want it with.

TEACH: I can't step down on this, Don. I got to have it with. The light of things as they are.

DON: Why?

TEACH: Because of the way *things* are. (*Looks out window.*) Hold on a second.

DON: Fletcher?

TEACH: Cops.

DON: What are they doing?

TEACH: Cruising. (*Pause.*)

DON: They turn the corner?

TEACH: Hold on. (*Pause.*) Yes. They have the right idea. Armed to the hilt. Sticks, mace, knives . . . who knows *what* the fuck they got. They have the right idea. Social customs break down, next thing *everybody's* lying in the gutter. (A *knocking is heard at the door.*)

TEACH: Get down. Dowse the light.

DON: Lemme see who it is . . .

TEACH: Don't answer it.

BOBBY: (*From behind door.*) Donny?

TEACH: Great.

DON: It's Bobby.

TEACH: I know.

BOBBY: Donny? (*Pause.*)

TEACH: Don't let him in.

DON: He knows we're in here.

TEACH: So let him go away, then.

BOBBY: I got to talk to you. (DON *looks at* TEACH.)

DON: (*To* BOB.) What is it?

BOB: I can't come in?

TEACH: Get him outta here. (*Pause.*)

DON: Bob . . .

BOB: Yeah?

DON: We're busy here.

BOB: I got to talk to you. (DON *looks at* TEACH.)

TEACH: Is he alone?

DON: I think.

TEACH: (*Pause.*) Hold on. (TEACH *opens door and pulls* BOBBY *in.*) What, Bob? What do you want? You know we got work to do here, we don't need you to do it, so what are you doing here and what do you want?

BOB: To talk to Don.

TEACH: Well, Don does not want to talk to you.

BOB: I *got* to talk to him.

TEACH: You do not have to do anything, Bob. You do not have to do anything that we tell you that you have to do. (Sic)

BOB: I got to talk to Donny. (*To* DON.) Can I talk to you? (*Pause. To* DON.) I came here . . .

DON: . . . yeah?

BOB: . . . the Riverside?

DON: Yeah?

BOB: Grace and Ruthie . . . he's in the Hospital. Fletch. (*Pause.*) I only wanted to, like, *come* here. I know you guys are only playing *cards* this . . . now. I didn't want to disturb you like *up*, but they just I found out he was in the Hospital and I came over here to . . . tell you. (*Pause.*)

TEACH: With what?

BOB: He got mugged.

TEACH: You're so full of shit.

BOB: I think some Mexicans. (TEACH *snorts.*) He did. He's in the Hospital.

TEACH: You see this, Don?

DON: He's mugged?

BOB: Yeah, Grace, they just got back. They broke his jaw.

TEACH: They broke his jaw.

BOB: Yeah. Broke.

TEACH: And now he's in the Hospital. Grace and Ruthie just got back. You thought that you'd come over.

BOB: Yeah.

TEACH: Well, how about this, Don. Here Fletch is in Masonic Hospital a needle in his arm, huh. How about this.

DON: How bad is he?

BOB: They broke his jaw.

DON: What else?

BOB: I don't know.

TEACH: Would you believe this if I told you this this afternoon?

DON: When did it happen, Bob?

BOB: Like before.

DON: Before, huh?

BOB: Yeah.

TEACH: How about this, Don.

BOB: We're going to see him tomorrow.

DON: When?

BOB: I don't know. In the morning.

DON: They got hours in the morning?

BOB: I guess so.

TEACH: Hey, thanks for coming here. You did real good in coming here.

BOB: Yeah?

TEACH: (*To* DON.) He did real good in coming here, huh, Donny? (*To* BOB.) We really owe you something.

BOB: What for?

TEACH: Coming here.

BOB: What?

TEACH: Something.

BOB: Like what?

DON: He don't know. He's saying that he thinks we owe you something, but right now he can't think what it is.

BOB: Thanks, Teach.

TEACH: It's okay, Bob. (*Pause.* BOB *starts to exit.*) Stick around.

BOB: Okay. For a minute.

TEACH: What? You're busy?

BOB: I got, like, some things to do.

TEACH: Whaddaya got, a "date"?

BOB: No.

TEACH: What, then?

BOB: Business. (*Pause.*)

DON: Where did they take him, Bob? (*Pause.*)

BOB: Uh, Masonic.

DON: I don't think that they got hours start til after lunch.

BOB: Then we'll go then. I'm gonna go now.

TEACH: Hold on a second, Bob. I feel we should take care of you for coming here.

BOB: That's okay. I'll see you guys.

DON: Come here a minute, Bobby.

BOB: What, Donny?

DON: What's going on here?

BOB: Here?

DON: Yes. (*Pause.*)

BOB: Nothing.

DON: I'm saying what's happening, Bob?

BOB: I don't know.

DON: Where did you get that nickel from?

BOB: What nickel?

DON: You know what nickel, Bob, the nickel I'm talking about.

BOB: I got it off a guy.

DON: What guy?

BOB: I met downtown.

TEACH: What was he wearing?

BOB: Things. (*Pause.*)

DON: How'd you get it off him, Bob?

BOB: We kinda talked. (*Pause.*)

DON: You know what, you look funny, Bob.

BOB: I'm late.

DON: It's after midnight, Bob. What are you late for?

BOB: Nothing.

DON: (*Very sadly.*) Jesus. Are you fucking with me here?

BOB: No.

DON: Bobby.

BOB: I'm not fucking with you, Donny. (*Pause.*)

DON: Where's Fletcher? (*Pause.*)

BOB: Masonic. (DON *goes to telephone and dials information.*)

DON: (*Into phone.*) For Masonic Hospital, please.

BOB: . . . I *think* . . .

DON: (*To* BOB.) What?

BOB: He might not be Masonic.

DON: (*To phone.*) Thank you. (*Hangs up phone. To* BOB.) Now, *what?*

BOB: He might not *be* there . . .

DON: You said he was there.

BOB: Yeah, I just, like, I *said* it. I really don't remember what they said, Ruthie.

TEACH: Ruthie.

BOB: . . . so I just . . . *said* Masonic.

DON: Why?

BOB: I thought of it. (*Pause.*)

DON: Uh huh. (*To phone.*) Yes. I'm looking for a guy was just admitted. Fletcher Post. (*Pause.*) Just a short time ago. (*Pause.*) Thank you. (*Pause. To* BOB *and* TEACH.) She's looking for it. (*To phone.*) No?

BOB: I told you . . .

DON: You're sure? (*Pause.*) Thank you. (*Hangs up phone. To* BOB.) He's not there.

BOB: I told you.

TEACH: What did I tell you, Don?

DON: Where is he?

BOB: Somewhere else.

DON: This makes me nuts . . . Bobby . . .

BOB: Yeah? (*Pause.*) They broke his jaw.

DON: Who?

BOB: Some spics. I don't know. (TEACH *snorts.*) They did.

DON: Who?

TEACH: Yeah.

DON: Who is this "They," Bob, that you're talking about?

TEACH: Bob . . .

BOB: . . . yeah?

TEACH: Who are these people you're talking about?

BOB: They broke his jaw.

TEACH: They took it in them all of a sudden they broke his jaw.

BOB: They didn't care it was him.

TEACH: No?

BOB: No, Teach.

TEACH: So who is it takes him out by accident. Huh? Grace and
    Ruthie?

BOB: They wouldn't do that.

TEACH: I'm not saying they would.

BOB: (*To* DON.) What is he saying, Donny?

TEACH: Bob, Bob, Bob . . . what am I saying . . . (*Pause.*)

DON: Where's Fletch, Bobby?

BOB: Hospital.

TEACH: Aside from that.

BOB: All I know, that's the only place he is, Teach.

TEACH: Now don't get smart with me, Bob, don't get smart with me, you young fuck, we've been sweating blood all day on this and I don't want your smart mouth on it—fuck around with Grace and Ruthie, and you come in here . . . so all we want some answers. Do you understand? (*Pause.*) I told you "Do you understand this."

DON: You better answer him.

BOB: I understand.

TEACH: Then let's make *this* clear: Loyalty does not mean *shit* a situation like this; I don't know what you and them are up to, and I do not *care*, but only you come clean with us.

BOB: He might of been a different hospital.

TEACH: Which one?

BOB: *Any* of 'em.

DON: So why'd you say "Masonic"?

BOB: I just thought of it.

TEACH: Okay. Okay. . . . Bob?

BOB: . . . yes?

TEACH: I want for you to tell us here and now—and for your own protection—what is going *on*, what is set *up* . . . where *Fletcher* is . . . and everything you know.

DON: (*Sotto Voce.*) I can't believe this.

BOB: I don't know anything.

TEACH: You don't, huh?

BOB: No.

DON: Tell him what you know, Bob.

BOB: I don't know it, Donny. Grace and Ruthie . . . (TEACH *grabs a nearby object and hits* BOB *viciously on the side of the head.*)

TEACH: Grace and Ruthie up your ass, you shithead; you don't fuck with us, *I'll* kick your fucking head in. I don't give a shit . . . (*Pause.*) You *twerp* . . . (*A pause near the end of which* BOB *starts whimpering.*) I don't give a shit. Come in here with your fucking stories . . . (*Pause.*) Imaginary people in the hospital . . . (BOB *starts to cry.*) That don't mean shit to me, you fruit.

BOB: Donny . . .

DON: You brought it on yourself.

TEACH: Sending us out there . . . who the fuck knows what . . .

BOB: He's in the hospital.

DON: Which hospital?

BOB: I don't know.

TEACH: Well, then, you better make one up, and quick.

DON: Bob . . .

TEACH: Don't back down on this, Don. Don't back down on me, here.

DON: Bob . . .

BOB: . . . yeah?

DON: You got to see our point here.

BOB: (*Whimpering.*) Yeah, I do.

DON: Now, we don't want to hit you . . .

TEACH: No.

BOB: I know you don't.

TEACH: No.

DON: But you come in here . . .

BOB: . . . yeah . . .

DON: . . . the only one who knows the score . . .

BOB: Yeah . . . My ear is bleeding. It's coming out my ear. Oh, fuck, I'm real scared.

DON: Shit.

BOB: I don't feel good.

TEACH: Fuckin' kid poops out on us . . .

BOB: Don . . .

TEACH: Now what are we going to do with this?

DON: You know, we didn't want to do this to you, Bob.

BOB: I know . . .

DON: We didn't want to do this. (*Phone rings.*)

TEACH: Great.

DON: (*To phone.*) What? What the fuck do *you* want?

TEACH: It's the guy?

DON: It's Ruthie. (*To phone.*) Oh yeah, we heard about that, Ruth.

TEACH: *She's* got a lot of nerve . . .

DON: (*To phone.*) From Bobby. Yeah. We'll *all* go. (*Pause.*) I thought he was at Masonic? Bobby. Well, okay, that's where we'll go then, Ruthie, we aren't going to go and see him at some hospital he isn't even *at* . . . (*Pause.*) Bobby's not here. I will. Okay. I will. Around Eleven. Okay. (*Hangs up.*)

TEACH: (*To* BOB.) And you owe me twenty bucks.

DON: (*Dialing.*) For Columbus Hospital, please.

TEACH: Fuckin' medical costs . . .

DON: Thank you.

TEACH: And I'm never ever sick at sea.

DON: Yes. For Fletcher Post, please, he was just admitted? (*Pause.*) No. I only want to know is he alright, and when we go to see him. (*Pause.*) Thank you.

TEACH: What?

DON: She's looking. (*To phone.*) Yes? Yeah. Thank you very much. Yes. You've been very kind. (*Hangs up phone.*)

TEACH: What is he, *in* there?

DON: Yeah.

TEACH: And they won't let us talk to him?

DON: His jaw is broke.

BOB: I feel funny.

TEACH: Your *ear* hurts.

DON: Bob, it hurts, Bob?

TEACH: I never felt quite right on this.

DON: Go tilt your head the other way.

TEACH: I mean, we're fucked up here. We have not blown the shot, but we're fucked up.

DON: We are going to take you to the hospital.

TEACH: Yeah, yeah, we'll take you to the hospital, you'll get some *care*, this isn't a big deal.

DON: Bob, you fell downstairs, you hurt your ear.

TEACH: He understands?

DON: You understand? We're going to take you to the hospital, you fell downstairs.

TEACH: (*At door.*) This fucking rain.

DON: You give 'em your right name, Bob, and you know what you can tell 'em. (*Reaches in pocket, thrusts money at* BOB.) You hold on to this, Bob. Anything you want inside the hospital.

BOB: I don't want to go to the hospital.

TEACH: You're going to the hospital, and that's the end of it.

BOB: I don't want to.

DON: You got to, Bob.

BOB: Why?

TEACH: You're fucked-up, that's why.

BOB: I'm gonna do the job.

DON: We aren't going to do the job tonight, Bob.

TEACH: You got a hat or something keep my head dry?

DON: No.

BOB: I get to do the job.

TEACH: You shut up. You are going in the hospital.

DON: We aren't going to do the job tonight.

BOB: We do it sometime else.

DON: Yeah.

TEACH: He ain't going to do no job.

DON: Shut up.

TEACH: Just say he isn't going to do no job.

DON: It's done now.

TEACH: What?

DON: I'm saying, this is over.

TEACH: No, it's not, Don. It is not. He does no job.

DON: You leave the fucking kid alone.

TEACH: You want kids, you go have them. *I'm* not your wife. *This* doesn't mean a thing to me. *I'm* in this. And it *isn't* over. This is for me, and this is my question: (*Pause.*) Where did you get that coin?

BOB: What?

TEACH: Where'd you get that fucking nickel, if it all comes out now. (*Pause.*) He comes in here, a fifty dollars for a nickel, where'd you get it?

BOB: Take me to the hospital. (*Pause.*)

TEACH: Where did you get that nickel? I want you to watch this. (*Pause.*)

BOB: I bought it.

TEACH: Mother Fucking Junkies.

DON: Shut up.

TEACH: What are you saying that you bought that coin?

BOB: Yeah.

TEACH: Where?

BOB: A coinstore. (*Pause.*)

TEACH: You bought it in a coinstore.

BOB: Yeah. (*Pause.*)

TEACH: Why?

DON: Go get your car.

TEACH: What did you pay for it? (*Pause.*) What did you pay for it?

BOB: Fifty dollars.

TEACH: You buy a coin for fifty dollars you come back here. (*Pause.*) Why?

DON: Go get your fucking car.

TEACH: Why would you do a thing like that?

BOB: I don't know.

TEACH: Why would you go do a thing like that?

BOB: For Donny. (*Pause.*)

TEACH: You people make my flesh crawl.

DON: Bob, we're going to take you out of here.

TEACH: I can not take this anymore.

DON: Can you walk?

BOB: No.

DON: Go and get your car.

TEACH: I am not your nigger. I am not your wife.

DON: I'm through with you today.

TEACH: You are.

DON: Yes.

TEACH: Why? (*Pause.*)

DON: You have lamed this up real good.

TEACH: I did.

DON: Real good.

TEACH: I lamed it up.

BOB: He hit me.

DON: I know, Bob.

TEACH: Yes, I hit him. For his own good. For the good of all.

DON: Get out of here.

TEACH: "Get out of here"? And now you throw me out like *trash*? I'm doing this for *you*. What do I have to wreck this joint *apart*? He told you that he bought it in a *coinstore*.

DON: I don't care.

TEACH: You don't *care*? I cannot believe this. You *believe* him?

DON: I don't *care*. I don't *care* anymore.

TEACH: You *fake*. You fucking *fake*. You fuck your friends. You *have* no friends. No *wonder* that you fuck this kid around.

DON: You shut your mouth.

TEACH: You seek your friends with *junkies*. You're a joke on this street, you and him.

DON: Get out.

TEACH: I do not go out, no.

BOB: I eat shit.

DON: You get out of here.

TEACH: I am not going anywhere. I have a piece of this.

DON: You have a piece of *shit*, you fucking lame. (*Advancing on him.*)

TEACH: This from a man who has to buy his friends.

DON: *I'll* tell you friends, *I'll* give you friends . . . (*Still advancing.*)

BOB: Oh, fuck . . .

DON: The stinking deals you come in here . . .

TEACH: You stay away from me . . .

DON: You stiff this one, you stiff that one . . . you come in here you stick this poison in me . . . (*Hitting him.*)

TEACH: Oh, Christ . . .

BOB: I eat shit.

TEACH: Oh, my God, I live with madmen.

DON: All these years . . .

BOB: A cause I missed him.

DON: (*Advancing again.*) All these fucking years . . .

TEACH: You're going to hit me.

BOB: Donny . . .

DON: You make life of garbage.

BOB: Donny!

TEACH: Oh, my God.

BOB: I missed him.

DON: (*Stopping*.) What?

BOB: I got to tell you what a fuck I am.

DON: What?

BOB: I missed him.

DON: Who?

BOB: The guy.

DON: What guy?

BOB: The guy this morning.

DON: What guy?

BOB: With the suitcase.

DON: (*Pause*.) You missed him?

BOB: I eat shit.

DON: What are you saying that you lied to me?

BOB: I eat shit.

TEACH: What is he saying? (*Pause*.)

DON: You're saying that you lied?

TEACH: What is he saying?

DON: You're saying you didn't see him with the suitcase?

TEACH: This kid is hysterical.

DON: You didn't see him?

TEACH: He's saying that he didn't see him?

DON: When he left this morning.

TEACH: He's saying that he lied?

BOB: I'm going to throw up.

TEACH: He's saying he didn't see the guy? (*Pause.*) When he came out. I was in here. *Then* you saw him. When he had the suitcase. (*Pause.*) Then. (*Pause.*) You saw him *then.* (*Pause.* BOB *shakes his head no.*) My Whole Cocksucking Life. (TEACH *picks up the dead pig sticker and starts trashing the junkstore.*) The Whole Entire World. There Is No Law. There Is No Right And Wrong. The World Is Lies. There Is No Friendship. Every Fucking Thing. (*Pause.*) Every God Forsaken Thing.

DON: Calm down, Walt.

TEACH: We all live like the cavemen. (DON, *during the speech, tries to subdue* TEACH, *and finally does.*)

DON: Siddown. (*A pause.* TEACH *sits still.*)

TEACH: I went on a limb for you. (*Pause.*) You don't know what I go through. I put my dick on the choppingblock. (*Pause.*) I hock my fucking watch . . . (*Pause.*) I go out there. I'm out there everyday. (*Pause.*) There is nothing out there. (*Pause.*) I fuck myself. (*Pause.*)

DON: Are you alright?

TEACH: What?

DON: Are you alright?

TEACH: How the fuck do I know.

DON: You tire me out, Walt.

TEACH: What?

DON: I need a rest.

TEACH: This fucking day.

DON: (*Pause.*) My shop's fucked up.

TEACH: I know.

DON: It's all fucked up. (*Pause.*) You fucked my shop up.

TEACH: Are you mad at me?

DON: What?

TEACH: Are you mad at me? (*Pause.*)

DON: Come on.

TEACH: Are you?

DON: Go and get your car. Bob?

TEACH: (*Pause.*) Tell me are you mad at me.

DON: No.

TEACH: You aren't?

DON: No. (*Pause.*)

TEACH: Good.

DON: You go and get your car.

TEACH: You got a hat?

DON: No.

TEACH: Do you have a piece of paper?

DON: Bob . . . ? (TEACH *walks to counter, takes a piece of news-paper and starts making himself a paper hat.*)

TEACH: He's alright?

DON: Bob . . . ?

TEACH: Is he alright?

DON: Bob . . . ?

BOB: (*Waking up.*) What?

DON: Come on. We're taking you the hospital. (TEACH *puts on paper hat, and looks at self in window.*)

TEACH: I look like a sissy.

DON: Go and get your car. (*Pause.*)

TEACH: Can you get him to the door?

DON: Yeah. (*Pause.*)

TEACH: I'm going to get my car.

DON: You gonna honk?

TEACH: Yeah.

DON: Good.

TEACH: I'll honk the horn. (*Pause.*)

DON: Good. (*Pause.*)

TEACH: This fucking day, huh?

DON: Yeah.

TEACH: I know it. You should clean this place up.

DON: Yeah. (*Pause.*)

TEACH: Good. (*Exits.*)

DON: Bob.

BOB: What?

DON: Get up. (*Pause.*) Bob. I'm sorry.

BOB: What?

DON: I'm sorry.

BOB: I fucked up.

DON: No. You did real good.

BOB: No.

DON: Yeah. You did real good. (*Pause.*)

BOB: Thank you.

DON: That's alright. (*Pause.*)

BOB: I'm sorry, Donny.

DON: That's alright.

(LIGHTS DIM)

END

OBIE
AWARD
WINNERS

BEST NEW PLAY

1956: *Absalom* by Lionel Abel
1957: *A House Remembered* by Louis A. Lippa
1958: *Endgame* by Samuel Beckett
1959: *The Quare Fellow* by Brendan Behan
1960: *The Connection* by Jack Gelber
1961: *The Blacks* by Jean Genet
1962: *Who'll Save the Plowboy?* by Frank D. Gilroy
1964: *Play* by Samuel Beckett, and *Dutchman* by LeRoi Jones
1965: *The Old Glory* by Robert Lowell
1966: *The Journey of the Fifth Horse* by Ronald Ribman
1970: *The Effect of Gamma Rays on Man-in-the-Moon Marigolds* by Paul Zindel, and *Approaching Simone* by Megan Terry
1971: *House of Blue Leaves* by John Guare
1973: *The Hot L Baltimore* by Lanford Wilson, and *The River Niger* by Joseph A. Walker
1974: *Short Eyes* by Miguel Pinero
1975: *The First Breeze of Summer* by Leslie Lee
1976: *Sexual Perversity in Chicago* and especially *American Buffalo* by David Mamet
1977: *Curse of the Starving Class* by Sam Shepard
1978: *Shaggy Dog Animation* by Lee Breuer
1979: *Josephine* by Michael McClure (adaptation of the Franz Kafka short story)

BEST FOREIGN PLAY

1960: *The Balcony* by Jean Genet
1962: *Happy Days* by Samuel Beckett

1968: *The Memorandum* by Vaclav Havel
1970: *What the Butler Saw* by Joe Orton
1974: *The Contractor* by David Storey

BEST MUSICAL

1956: *Three Penny Opera* by Bertolt Brecht & Kurt Weill, adapted
      by Marc Blitzstein
1959: *A Party with Betty Comden & Adolph Green*
1962: *Fly Blackbird* by C. Jackson, James Hatch, & Jerome Eskow
1968: *In Circles* by Gertrude Stein & Al Carmines
1970: *The Last Sweet Days of Isaac* by Gretchen Cryer & Nancy
      Ford, and *The Me Nobody Knows* by Robert Livingston,
      Gary William Friedman & Will Holt

BEST PRODUCTION

1956: *Uncle Vanya* Fourth Street Theatre
1957: *Exiles* Renata Theatre
1959: *Ivanov* (Daniel Hineck and Harlan Quist)
1960: *The Connection* Living Theatre
1961: *Hedda Gabler* Fourth Street Theatre
1963: *Six Characters in Search of an Author* Martinique Theatre;
      and *The Boys from Syracuse* (musical) Theatre Four
1964: *The Brig* Living Theatre; and *What Happened* (musical)
      Judson Poets Theatre
1965: *The Cradle Will Rock* (musical) Theatre Four
1972: *The Mutation Show* Open Theatre
1976: *Rhoda in Potatoland* Richard Foreman

DISTINGUISHED PLAYS

1958: *The Brothers Karamazov* by Boris Tumarin & Jack Sydow
      (best adaptation); *The Crucible* by Arthur Miller, directed

by Word Baker (best revival); *Comic Strip* by George Panetta (best comedy); *Guest of the Nation* by Neil McKenzie (best one-act play)

1959: *Diversions* by Steven Vinaver (best revue)

1960: *Krapp's Last Tape* by Samuel Beckett, *The Prodigal* by Jack Richardson, and *The Zoo Story* by Edward Albee

1961: *The Premise* produced and directed by Theodore Flicker (best Off-Off-Broadway production)

1964: *Home Movies* by Rosalyn Drexler, and *Funny House of a Negro* by Adrienne Kennedy

1965: *Promenade* and *The Successful Life of Three* by Maria Irene Fornes

1966: *Good Day* by Emmanuel Peluso, and *Chicago, Icarus's Mother* and *Red Cross* by Sam Shepard

1967: *Futz* by Rochelle Owens, and *La Turista* by Sam Shepard

1968: *Muzeeka* by John Guare, *The Indian Wants the Bronx* by Israel Horovitz, and *Melodrama Play* and *Forensic and the Navigators* by Sam Shepard

1970: *The Deer Kill* by Murray Mednick, and *The Increased Difficulty of Concentration* by Vaclav Havel

1971: *The Fabulous Miss Marie* and *In New England Winter* by Ed Bullins, and *The Basic Training of Pavlo Hummel* by David Rabe

1973: *The Tooth of Crime* by Sam Shepard, *Big Foot* by Ronald Tavel, and *What If I Had Turned Up Heads?* by J. E. Gaines

1974: *Bad Habits* by Terrence McNally, *When You Comin' Back, Red Ryder?* by Mark Medoff, and *The Great MacDaddy* by Paul Carter Harrison

1975: *The Taking of Miss Janie* by Ed Bullins, *The Mound Builders* by Lanford Wilson, *Our Late Night* by Wallace Shawn, and *Action* by Sam Shepard

1977: *G. R. Point* by David Berry, *Fefu and Her Friends* by Maria Irene Fornes, *Domino Courts* by William Hauptman, *Gemini* and *The Transfiguration of Benno Blimpie* by Albert Innaurato, and *Ashes* by David Rudkin

1979: *The Writer's Opera* by Rosalyn Drexler, *Nasty Rumors and Final Remarks* by Susan Miller, *Vienna Notes* by Richard Nelson, *The Elephant Man* by Bernard Pomerance, and *Buried Child* by Sam Shepard

DISTINGUISHED FOREIGN PLAY

1967: *Eh?* by Henry Livings
1971: *Boesman and Lena* by Athol Fugard, *AC/DC* by Heathcote Williams, and *Dream on Monkey Mountain* by Derek Walcott
1973: *Not I* by Samuel Beckett, and *Kasper* by Peter Handke

DISTINGUISHED PRODUCTION

1971: *The Trial of the Catonsville Nine*
1977: *The Club, For Colored Girls Who Have Considered Suicide When the Rainbow Is Enuf,* and *Dressed like an Egg*

BEST PERFORMANCE

1964: Gloria Foster in *In White America*
1965: Roscoe Lee Browne, Frank Langella and Lester Rawlins in *The Old Glory*
1970: Sada Thompson in *The Effect of Gamma Rays on Man-in-the-Moon Marigolds*

BEST ACTRESS

1956: Julie Bovasso in *The Maids*
1957: Colleen Dewhurst in *The Taming of the Shrew, The Eagle Has Two Heads,* and *Camille*
1958: Anne Meacham in *Garden District*
1959: Kathleen Maguire in *The Time of the Cuckoo*
1960: Eileen Brennan in *Little Mary Sunshine*

1961: Anne Meacham in *Hedda Gabler*
1962: Barbara Harris in *Oh Dad, Poor Dad, Momma's Hung You in the Closet and I'm Feelin' So Sad*
1963: Colleen Dewhurst in *Desire Under the Elms*
1966: Jane White in *Coriolanus* and *Love's Labour's Lost*
1968: Billie Dixon in *The Beard*
1971: Ruby Dee in *Boesman and Lena*

BEST ACTOR

1956: Jason Robards, Jr. in *The Iceman Cometh*, and George Voskovec in *Uncle Vanya*
1957: William Smithers in *The Sea Gull*
1958: George C. Scott in *Richard III, As You Like It,* and *Children of Darkness*
1959: Alfred Ryder in *I Rise In Flame, Cried the Phoenix*
1960: Warren Finnerty in *The Connection*
1961: Khigh Dhiegh in *In the Jungle of Cities*
1962: James Earl Jones in *Clandestine on the Morning Line, The Apple,* and *Moon on a Rainbow Shawl*
1963: George C. Scott in *Desire Under the Elms*
1966: Dustin Hoffman in *The Journey of the Fifth Horse*
1967: Seth Allen in *Futz*
1968: Al Pacino in *The Indian Wants the Bronx*
1971: Jack McGowran in *Beckett*

DISTINGUISHED PERFORMANCES

1956: Alan Ansara, Roberts Blossom, Shirlee Emmons, Gerald Hiken, Peggy McKay, Addison Powell, Frances Sternhagen, Nancy Wickwire
1957: Thayer David, Jutta Wolf, Michael Kanc, Marguerite Lenert, Arthur Malet, Betty Miller
1958: Jack Cannon, Leonardo Cimino, Robert Geiringer, Tammy Grimes, Michael Higgins, Grania O'Malley, Nydia Westman

1959: Anne Fielding, Rosina Fernhoff, Zero Mostel, Lester Rawlins, Harold Scott, Nancy Wickwire

1960: William Daniels, Donald Davis, Patricia Falkenhain, Vincent Gardenia, John Heffernan, Jack Livingston, Elisa Loti, Nancy Marchand

1961: Godfrey Cambridge, James Coco, Joan Hackett, Gerry Jedd, Surya Kumari, Lester Rawlins

1962: Sudie Bond, Vinnette Carroll, Clayton Corzatte, Geoff Garland, Rosemary Harris, Gerald O'Laughlin, Paul Robeling, Ruth White

1963: Jacqueline Brooks, Joseph Chaikin, Olympia Dukakis, Anne Jackson, Michael O'Sullivan, James Patterson, Madeline Sherwood, Eli Wallach

1964: Philip Burns, Joyce Ebert, Lee Grant, David Hurst, Taylor Mead, Estelle Parsons, Diana Sands, Marian Seldes, Jack Warden, Ronald Weyland

1965: Brian Bedford, Roberts Blossom, Joseph Chaikin, Margaret De Priest, Dean Dittman, Robert Duvall, James Earl Jones, Rosemary Harris, Frances Sternhagen, Sada Thompson

1966: Clarice Blackburn, Marie-Claire Charba, Gloria Foster, Sharon Gans, Frank Langella, Michael Lipton, Kevin O'Connor, Jess Osuna, Florence Tarlow, Douglas Turner

1967: Tom Aldredge, Robert Bonnard, Alvin Epstein, Neil Flanagan, Bette Henritze, Stacy Keach, Terry Kaiser, Eddie McCarty, Robert Salvio, Rip Torn

1968: John Cazale, James Coco, Jean David, Cliff Gorman, Mari Gorman, Moses Gunn, Peggy Pope, Roy Scheider

1970: Beeson Carroll, Vincent Gardenia, Harold Gould, Anthony Holland, Lee Kissman, Ron Leibman, Rue McClanahan, Roberta Maxwell, Pamela Payton-Wright, Austin Pendleton, Fredericka Weber

1971: Susan Batson, Margaret Braidwood, Hector Elizondo, Donald Ewer, Sonny Jim, Stacy Keach, Harris Laskawy, Joan MacIntosh, William Schallert, James Woods

1972: Salome Bey, Maurice Blanc, Alex Bradford, Marilyn Chris, Ron Faber, Jean Hepple, Danny Sewall, Marilyn Sokol, Kathleen Widdoes, Elizabeth Wilson, Ed Zang

1973: Hume Cronyn, Mari Gorman, James Hilbrant, Stacy Keach, Christopher Lloyd, Charles Ludlam, Lola Pashalinski, Alice

Playten, Roxie Roker, Jessica Tandy, Douglas Turner Ward, Sam Waterston

1974: Barbara Barrie, Joseph Buloff, Kevin Conway, Conchata Ferrell, Loretta Greene, Barbara Montgomery, Zipora Spaizman, Elizabeth Sturges

1975: Reyno, Moses Gunn, Dick Latessa, Kevin McCarthy, Stephen D. Newman, Christopher Walken, Ian Trigger, Cara Duff-McCormick, Priscilla Smith, Tanya Berezin, Tovah Feldshuh

1976: Robert Christian, Pamela Payton-Wright, Priscilla Smith, David Warrilow, June Gable, Sammy Williams, Priscilla Lopez, Joyce Aaron, Mike Kellin, Roberts Blossom, Crystal Field, Tony LoBianco, T. Miratti, Kate Manheim

1977: Danny Aiello, Martin Balsam, Lucinda Childs, James Coco, Anne DeSalvo, John Heard, Jo Henderson, William Hurt, Joseph Maher, Roberta Maxwell, Brian Murray, Lola Pashalinski, Marian Seldes, Margaret Wright

1978: Richard Bauer, Nell Carter, Alma Cuervo, Swoozie Kurtz, Kaiulani Lee, Bruce Myers, Lee S. Wilkof

1979: Mary Alice, Philip Anglim, Joseph Buloff, Constance Cummings, Fred Gwynne, Judd Hirsch, Marcell Rosenblatt, Meryl Streep, Elizabeth Wilson

BEST DIRECTOR

1956: Jose Quintero, *The Iceman Cometh*

1957: Gene Frankel, *Volpone*

1958: Stuart Vaughn, *New York Shakespeare Festival*

1959: William Ball, *Ivanov* (foreign play), and Jack Ragotzy, Arthur Laurents cycle (American plays)

1960: Gene Frankel, *Machinal*

1961: Gerald A. Freedman, *The Taming of the Shrew*

1962: John Wulp, *Red Eye of Love*

1963: Alan Schneider, Pinter plays

1964: Judith Malina, *The Brig*

1965: Ulu Grosbard, *A View from the Bridge*

1967: Tom O'Horgan, *Futz*

1968: Michael Schultz, *Song for the Lusitanian Bogey*

DISTINGUISHED DIRECTION

1964: Lawrence Kornfeld
1966: Remy Charlip, Jacques Levy
1968: John Hancock, Rip Torn
1970: Alan Arkin, Melvin Bernhardt, Maxine Klein, Gilbert Moses
1971: John Berry, Jeff Bleckner, Gordon Davidson, John Hirsch, Larry Kornfeld
1972: Wilford Leach & John Braswell, Mel Shapiro, Michael Smith, Tom Sydorick
1973: Jack Gelber, William E. Lathan, Marshall W. Mason
1974: Marvin Felix Camillo, Robert Drivas, David Licht, John Pasquin, Harold Prince
1975: Lawrence Kornfeld, Marshall W. Mason, Gilbert Moses
1976: Marshall W. Mason, JoAnne Akalaitis
1977: Melvin Bernhardt, Gordon Davidson
1978: Robert Allan Ackerman, Thomas Bullard, Elizabeth Swados
1979: Maria Irene Fornes, Jack Hofsiss

DISTINGUISHED SETS, LIGHTING, OR COSTUMES

1956: Klaus Holm, Alvin Colt
1959: David Hays, Will Steven Armstrong, Nikola Cernovich
1960: David Hays
1962: Norris Houghton
1964: Julian Beck
1965: Willa Kim
1966: Lindsey Decker, Ed Wittstein
1967: John Dodd
1968: Robert La Vigne
1971: John Scheffler
1972: Video Free America (visual effects)
1974: Theoni Aldredge, Holmes Easley, Christopher Thomas

1975: Robert U. Taylor, John Lee Beatty
1976: Donald Brooks
1978: Garland Wright & John Arnone, Robert Yodice
1979: Theatre X, Jennifer Tipton

MUSIC

1959: David Amram
1961: Teiji Ito
1964: Al Carmines
1972: Micki Grant, Elizabeth Swados
1974: Bill Elliott
1976: Philip Glass

FOR DISTINGUISHED ACHIEVEMENT
IN 1969

The Living Theatre, *Frankenstein*; Jeff Weiss, *The International Wrestling Match*; Julie Bovasso, *Gloria and Esperanza*; Judith Malina & Julian Beck, *Antigone*; Israel Horovitz, *The Honest-to-Goodness Schnozzola*; Jules Feiffer, *Little Murders*; Ronald Tavel, *The Boy on the Straight-Back Chair*; Nathan George and Ron O'Neal, *No Place To Be Somebody*; Arlene Rothlein, *The Poor Little Match Girl*; Theatre Genesis, sustained excellence; The Open Theatre, *The Serpent*; Om Theatre, *Riot*; The Performance Group, *Dionysus in '69*

SPECIAL CITATIONS AND AWARDS

1956: The Phoenix Theatre, The Shakespearean Workshop
      Theatre, The Tempo Playhouse
1957: Paul Shyre
1958: The Phoenix Theatre, The Theatre Club, Lucille Lortel

1959: Hal Holbrook

1960: Brooks Atkinson

1961: Bernard Frechtman

1962: Ellis Rabb, *The Hostage*

1963: Jean Erdman, *The Second City*

1964: Judson Memorial Church

1965: The Paper Bag Players, Caffe Cino and Cafe La Mama

1966: Joseph H. Dunn, H. M. Koutoukas, Peter Schumann, Theatre for Ideas, Theatre in the Streets

1967: La Mama Troupe, The Open Theatre, Tom Sankey, The Second Story Players, Jeff Weiss

1968: The Fortune Society, The Negro Ensemble Company, San Francisco Mime Troupe, El Teatro Campesino

1970: Chelsea Theatre Center, Gardner Compton & Emile Ardolino, *Elephant Steps*, Andre Gregory, The Ridiculous Theatrical Company, Theatre of the Ridiculous

1971: *Orlando Furioso*, Kirk Kirksey

1972: Charles Stanley, Meredith Monk, Theatre of Latin America, Free the Army

1973: Richard Foreman, San Francisco Mime Troupe, City Center Acting Company, Workshop of the Player's Art

1974: The Bread and Puppet Theatre, The Brooklyn Academy of Music, CSC Repertory Company, Robert Wilson

1975: Andrei Serban for *Trilogy*, The Royal Shakespeare Company for *Summerfolk*, Charles Ludlam for *Professor Bedlam's Punch and Judy Show*, The Henry Street Settlement, Charles Pierce, Mabou Mines

1976: Ralph Lee, Morton Lichter & Gordon Rogoff, Santo Loquasto, Meredith Monk, Edward Bond, Neil Flanagan, *Chile! Chile!*, the Creators of A *Chorus Line*

1977: Barbara Garson, Manhattan Theatre Club, New York Street Theatre Caravan, Theatre for the New City, Philip Glass, Ping Chong, the Creators of *Nightclub Cantata*, Charles Ludlam, Carole Oditz, Douglas Schmidt and Burl Hass, Henry Millman & Edward M. Greenberg

1978: *Ain't Misbehavin'*, Eric Bentley, Joseph Dunn & Ira Koljonen, James Lapine, Jerry Mayer, Stuart Sherman, Squat, Winston Tong

1979: Gordon Chater, Richard Wherett, and Steve J. Spears for *The Elocution of Benjamin*; JoAnne Akalaitis, Ellen

McElduff, and David Warrilow for *Southern Exposure*; Tadeusz Kantor for *The Dead Class*; The Negro Ensemble Company for sustained excellence of ensemble acting; The French Department of NYU for its Samuel Beckett Festival

SUSTAINED ACHIEVEMENT

1975: Judith Malina and Julian Beck, Ted Mann and the Circle in The Square, Joseph Papp, Ellen Stewart, *The Fantasticks*
1977: Joseph Chaikin
1978: The Bread & Puppet Theatre
1979: Al Carmines